COMBAT AND COMMAND

The Story of an Airman in Two World Wars

by

Marshal of the Royal Air Force

Lord Douglas of Kirtleside

G.C.B., M.C., D.F.C.

with

Robert Wright

Simon and Schuster / New York

To Winston Churchill

WITH ADMIRATION AND AFFECTION

ACKNOWLEDGMENTS

In all the work that has been done on this book it was inevitable that I should have to call upon many people—some of whom are very old friends—for various kinds of information; and it is a pleasure for me to be able to express my gratitude for the readiness of the response that was shown by all. Many of them are named in the course of the story.

While the views that I have expressed and the opinions that I hold are mine, and therefore entirely personal, I should particularly like to offer my thanks to Mr. L. A. Jackets and the members of his staff of the Air Historical Branch of the Ministry of Defence, and to Miss R. E. B. Coombs, the librarian of the Imperial War Museum, for their patience and help in all the research work that had to be done.

A bibliography, even if confined only to books which have a bearing on the flying that was done in the two World Wars, would be a very long one. I shall have to limit myself to naming only those from which I have quoted. Wherever possible I have obtained permission to do that, and I am indebted to the authors and publishers concerned; but in some cases it has not been possible to locate the owners of the copyright. The list is as follows:

YEARS OF COMBAT
Harold H. Balfour, *An Airman Marches,* Hutchinson. Maurice Baring, *R.F.C. H.Q. 1914–1918,* Bell. Edmund Blunden, *War Poets 1914–1918,* Longmans and The British Council. Lewis Broad, *Winston Churchill,* Hawthorn Books. Ewan Butler and Gordon Young, *Marshal Without*

Glory, Hodder and Stoughton. Sir C. E. Callwell, *Field-Marshal Sir Henry Wilson*, Cassell. Sir Winston Churchill, *The World Crisis*, Charles Scribner's Sons. C. R. M. F. Cruttwell, *A History of the Great War*, Oxford University Press. Sir James E. Edmonds, *History of the Great War: France and Belgium, March–April, 1918*, Macmillan (permission of the Controller of Her Majesty's Stationery Office). Sir James E. Edmonds, *A Short History of World War I*, Oxford University Press. Cyril Falls, *The First World War*, Putnam's and Coward-McCann. Sir John French, 1st Earl of Ypres, *1914*, Constable. Charles H. Gibbs-Smith, *The Aeroplane: An Historical Survey*, Her Majesty's Stationery Office. C. G. Grey, *A History of the Air Ministry*, W. W. Norton & Co. Earl Haig, *The Private Papers of Douglas Haig 1914–1919* (edited by Robert Blake), Eyre and Spottiswoode. Franz Immelmann, *Immelmann: The Eagle of Lille*, John Hamilton. Ira Jones, *King of Air Fighters*, Ivor Nicholson and Watson. R. H. Kiernan, *Captain Albert Ball*, John Hamilton. Cecil Lewis, *Sagittarius Rising*, Harcourt, Brace & World. B. H. Liddell Hart, *A History of the World War 1914–1918*, Little, Brown and Co. Earl Lloyd-George, *War Memoirs of David Lloyd George*, Little Brown and Co. (permission of The Beaverbrook Foundations). J. B. McCudden, *Five Years in the Royal Flying Corps*, the Aeroplane and General Publishing Company. R. H. Mottram, *Journey to the Western Front*, Bell. Sir Walter Raleigh and H. A. Jones, *The War in the Air*, Oxford University Press (permission of the Controller of Her Majesty's Stationery Office). Manfred von Richthofen, *The Red Air Fighter*, the Aeroplane and General Publishing Company. Siegfried Sassoon, *Collected Poems*, The Viking Press. H. St. G. Saunders, *Per Ardua*, Oxford University Press. D. C. Somvervell, *A History of Tonbridge School*, Faber and Faber. C. H. Sorley, *Poems*, Cambridge University Press. Elliott White Springs, *War Birds: The Diary of an Aviator*, John Hamilton (permission of Mrs. Frances Springs). L. A. Strange, *Recollections of an Airman*, John Hamilton. Sir Frederick Sykes, *From Many Angles*, George G. Harrap. Barbara Tuchman, *The Guns of August*, The Macmillan Co. Johannes Werner, *Knight of Germany*, John Hamilton. Leon Wolff, *In Flanders Fields*, The Viking Press.

YEARS OF COMMAND

General H. H. Arnold, *Global Mission*, Harper & Row. Michael Balfour and John Mair, *Four-Power Control in Germany and Austria 1945–1946*, Oxford University Press. The Earl of Birkenhead, *The Professor and the Prime Minister*, Houghton Mifflin Co. Andrew Boyle, *Trenchard*, W. W. Norton & Co. General Lewis Brereton, *The Brereton Diaries*, William Morrow & Co. Sir Arthur Bryant, *The Alanbrooke Diaries*, Doubleday & Co. Alan Bullock, *Hitler, A Study in Tyranny*, Harper & Row. *The New Cambridge Modern History*, Vol. XII, *Era of Violence*, Cambridge University Press. Lord Casey, *Personal Experience: 1939–1946*, David McKay Co. Sir Winston Churchill, *The Second World War*, Houghton Mifflin Co. General Lucius D. Clay, *Decision in Germany*, Doubleday & Co. Basil Collier, *The Defence of the United Kingdom*, Her Majesty's Stationery Office. R. W. Cooper, *The Nuremberg Trial*, Penguin. Noel Coward, *Middle East Diary*, Doubleday & Co. Lord Cunningham, *A Sailor's Odyssey*, E. P. Dutton & Co. F. S. V. Donnison, *Civil Affairs and Military Government North-West Europe, 1944–1946*, Her Majesty's Stationery Office. John Ehrman, *Grand Strategy*, Vol. V, Her Majesty's Stationery Office. General Dwight D. Eisenhower, *Crusade in Europe*, Doubleday & Co. Cyril Falls, *The Second*

World War, Methuen. J. F. C. Fuller, *The Second World War,* Duell, Sloan & Pearce. Adolf Galland, *The First and the Last,* Ballantine Books. Philip Guedalla, *Middle East 1940–1942,* Hodder and Stoughton. Sir Arthur Harris, *Bomber Offensive,* The Macmillan Co. Hastings L. Ismay, *The Memoirs of General Lord Ismay,* The Viking Press. Sir Philip Joubert de la Ferte, *The Third Service,* Thames and Hudson. J. E. Johnson, *Wing Leader,* Ballantine Books. The Earl of Kilmuir, *Political Adventure,* Weidenfeld and Nicholson. Sir Ivone Kirkpatrick, *The Inner Circle,* The Macmillan Co. Eric Maguire, *Dieppe,* Jonathan Cape. Field-Marshal Viscount Montgomery, *Memoirs,* World. Robert Murphy, *Diplomat Among Warriors,* Doubleday & Co. General Sir Frederick Pile, *Ack-Ack,* Harrap. Lord Pakenham, *Born to Believe,* Jonathan Cape. Denis Richards and Hilary St. George Saunders, *Royal Air Force 1939–1945,* Her Majesty's Stationery Office. S. W. Roskill, *White Ensign, The British Navy at War,* © 1960 by U.S. Naval Institute, Annapolis, Maryland. Robert E. Sherwood, *Roosevelt and Hopkins,* Harper & Row. Sir John Slessor, *The Central Blue,* Frederick A. Praeger, Inc. Joseph W. Stilwell, *The Stilwell Papers,* Macfadden-Bartell Corp. *Trial of German Major War Criminals. Proceedings of the Military Tribunal at Nuremberg,* Her Majesty's Stationery Office. Sir Robert Watson-Watt, *Three Steps to Victory,* Odhams. Sir Charles Webster and Noble Frankland, *The Strategic Air Offensive Against Germany 1939–1945,* Her Majesty's Stationery Office. Chester Wilmot, *The Struggle for Europe,* Harper & Row. Field-Marshal Lord Wilson, *Eight Years Overseas,* Hutchinson. Leon Wolff, *Low Level Mission,* Doubleday & Co. Sir Peter Wykeham, *Fighter Command,* McClelland.

Contents

8 CONTENTS

24.	From Defense to Offense	442
25.	Swings and Roundabouts	460
26.	The Spice of Variety	483
27.	The Broadening Fronts	506
28.	Increasing Pressures	527
29.	A World Apart	548
30.	The Mounting Fury	567
31.	"One of the sharpest pangs"	581
32.	At Low Ebb	603
33.	A Test of Patience	620
34.	On Guard	638
35.	Constant Endeavor	655
36.	Realignments	673
37.	The Shapes to Come	694
38.	The Changing World	714
39.	A Matter of Conscience	736
40.	Impasse	756
	Index	773

Preface

I T HAS BEEN remarked upon by many people that those of us who have spent our lives in aviation make much of that element of chance which is called luck. That is understandable enough, for we who have been professional airmen from the early days of flying have spent a great deal of our time doing our best to keep under control the inescapable law that what goes up must come down. Today that control is firm enough. But it was not always so, and a large part of our way of thought has been conditioned by much of what happened in the beginning, when we were young and flying was still an adventure.

There has never been any doubt in my own mind about the way the vagaries of fortune have influenced the course of my life. Luck has been on my side. It was there even in the very beginning, in that I was born at a time that has enabled me to live through an intensely interesting, if perplexing, period: an age that has been extraordinarily vivid and complex and ever-changing.

The lives of those of the generation to which I belong have all been greatly affected by the two world wars that have bedeviled us in the first half of this century, and I am of an age that gave me the full opportunity to participate actively in both of them. During the four years of the First World War—in which so many of my contemporaries were killed—I was a fighter pilot in the Royal Flying Corps; and for seven years during and after the Second World War I was a Commander-in-Chief in the Royal Air Force. After leaving the Service, I spent fifteen years as chairman of one of the world's foremost civil airlines. Over a period of fifty years, I have been able to play a part that has not been inconsequential in the development of both military and civil aviation.

In the early days, we lived in a time of comparative innocence. After the end of the first war, we discovered that the emerging world was far from a simple one, and that it was by no means innocent. By the time the second war was over, and all innocence as we of the older generation had known it had died, there came

9

for me a period—almost an interlude—when I was in a position of some considerable authority, with responsibilities that went far beyond those which would normally fall to the lot of a professional airman. I was Commander-in-Chief and Military Governor of the British Zone of Occupied Germany during the critical years of 1946 and 1947. This assignment put me directly in the path of what had been sown in the wind; and I was to be one of those who experienced at first hand the beginning of the whirlwind that was to exact such a heavy toll.

One of the broader views of life which seems, for some inexplicable reason, to be accepted with ready assurance by so many people of our times is that it is easy to be wise after the event. From all that I have known in my life, and all my years of experience of both combat and command, I believe that the ability to be wise after the event is not at all easy, and that it is as precious an attribute as it is a surprisingly rare one. No amount of hindsight has enabled us to exercise the control over the course that, today, we seem to have to follow. All too often luck appears to play havoc with wisdom.

These are the influences that have in some ways dominated the telling, in as balanced a manner as one man's idiosyncrasies will allow, the story of my own experiences. For the sake of perspective, I have stressed the background of the times during which these experiences took place.

1 / Scottish Heritage

IF THERE IS one trait which appears to dominate the character of so many of those who bear the name of Douglas it is a fairly robust individualism. My father, Robert Langton Douglas, certainly lived up to that tradition: he was a man of quite extraordinary character. At the time of my birth in Oxford on December 23, 1893, he was in holy orders, a priest ordained in the Church of England; but such bonds could never hold a man of his temperament. By the time of his death in Italy in 1951, at the age of eighty-seven, he had become a Roman Catholic, an American citizen, an established historian, and a respected art critic specializing in the paintings of the Italian Renaissance.

Because of the vigor that was always so much a part of his nature, my father was also very fond of women. Although in the long run that quirk, if such it can be called, cost him dearly, it was no more than a taste that has been indulged in by many wise men. In the course of his long, full and creative life—creative in more senses than one—he was married three times, and he was the father of eighteen children. Eight of these children were, to my certain knowledge, illegitimate. It will possibly come as a disappointment to some when I reveal that I am one of my father's legitimate sons.

My father himself showed no particular interest in the history of his family, but one of his sisters was fond of holding forth on the subject. In my childhood I did not pay much attention to what she had to say, but when I was elevated to a peerage and there came the need for me to matriculate a coat-of-arms, I was compelled to give the matter some thought. I then found that there was a colorful and vigorous story attached to the history of the name of Douglas even though the name, which comes from the Gaelic *dubh glas,* means nothing more than "dark water." What appealed to me most in that story was that the Douglases were men given to leading rather than to being led.

One of the historians speaks of the name of Douglas as that of

11

"a Scottish noble family" which wielded at times a power that was both great and dangerous; and there can be little doubt that the stalwarts of the family, with its two branches, the Black and the Red Douglas, have for centuries been worthy representatives of the fighting spirit of the Scot. It is recorded that Sir William Douglas —the first Lord of Douglas—died while a prisoner of the English in the Tower of London in the year 1298. There is an even earlier historical reference to a William of Douglas, and that Christian name, along with Robert and Archibald, appear repeatedly in the long history of the family. My own first Christian name is William, but I have always been known by my second name, Sholto; and throughout my life as an airman I have always been referred to by that name—more often than not, I am glad to say, without any reference to my rank or even to my surname.

My own direct lineage started in the sixteenth century with another Sir William Douglas who became the first Earl of Queensberry. It was one of his descendants who drew up the code of laws—the Queensberry rules—for the governing of boxing, a so-called sport which I have always regarded as being a particularly revolting one. As a result of a land grant from King Charles the Second my ancestors lived in the West Indies for about a hundred and fifty years during the seventeenth and eighteenth centuries. They had estates in Jamaica which my great-grandfather inherited while he was still a child; but by the time that he had grown up he found that those who supposedly had been watching over his interests had swindled him out of almost everything. There were numerous lawsuits, but they were all to no avail; and by the time my grandfather, Robert Douglas, inherited what was left, he was forced to the conclusion that there was no point in a quest that had become futile. In any case, his interests were in other matters.

Because of reduced circumstances, my grandfather was sent to Trinity College, Dublin, rather than to either Oxford or Cambridge (which his parents would have preferred). After he got his degree, he became a clergyman in the Church of England. He was vicar of a parish in Sheffield, then rector of Bredgar, in Kent; and finally he was rector of Odell, in Bedfordshire. A well-known country parson and a leading British Israelite, he was well into his eighties when he died in 1910.

Some years before the turn of the century my father won an honors degree in modern history at New College, Oxford. He started to follow in his father's footsteps in the Church, only to abandon it all in favor of the extraordinary career as historian and critic that he was eventually to make for himself. My father had the mind of a scholar, and he was a fine conversationalist with a considerable turn of wit. He was also vivacious in temperament, and he possessed a great and natural charm. It was that vivacity, coupled with the charm, which led him all too easily into the sexual indulgences over which he seemed to have so little control. But for all that, my father was an industrious worker, and throughout his long life he was always an enthusiast. He was also, in his own way, ambitious: he wanted to build up a reputation as an art expert, and he wanted to make money in order to support his large family. He succeeded in both those aims, and I always admired him for the name that he made for himself in a highly specialized and very competitive field. In some important aspects of his life he was self-made: and in that, he set me a good example.

There were occasions in the early years when my father, for all the hard work, found himself financially on his beam-ends; but he persisted with his work, and he was only a little over thirty years of age when he began to make a name for himself as an art critic and an expert on Italian painting. By the beginning of this century he was voicing opinions which aroused considerable controversy, particularly with Bernard Berenson. His duels with Berenson were responsible, at least in part, for making him known. The two critics were well acquainted, but more as authoritative rivals in the art world than as friends.

After intense study and diligent research (which characterized all his work), my father became convinced, in the years of the 'nineties, that there were in existence fine specimens of the paintings of a long neglected Italian artist of the Renaissance: a Sienese painter of the mid-fifteenth century named Stefano di Giovanni Sassetta. Following an invitation to examine a painting which was at that time credited to Fra Angelico, my father claimed that it was not the work of Fra Angelico and that it was by Sassetta. An old and loyal friend of my father's, the art critic and collector Edward Fowles, once the head of the Duveen galleries in New York, stated only a short time ago: "The first mention in modern times of the existence of Sassetta as an important master in the Sienese School of painting is in Langton Douglas' book on *Fra Angelico,* published in the year 1900. Therein, on page 179, he mentions that in the Palazzo Saracini there is an Adoration of the Magi, a late work of Sassetta, long attributed to Fra Angelico himself."

For all his erudition, Bernard Berenson had made no mention of Sassetta in his book entitled *Central Italian Painters of the Renais-*

sance, which was published in 1897. My father mentioned the
omission in a long and detailed examination of the work of
Sassetta in an article in the *Burlington Magazine* of May, 1903,
and he finished with the statement: "It is time that 'poor Maestro
Stefano' received such meed as posterity can give, even though it
be but barren reward of posthumous praise." He scarcely expected
that Berenson would be "quick to jump on the bandwagon," as
Edward Fowles has put it.

A few months after the publication of my father's claims for the
recognition of Sassetta, Bernard Berenson had two articles published in the *Burlington Magazine* entitled "A Sienese Painter of
the Franciscan Legend." In these he discussed at great length the
work of Sassetta, completely ignoring, in a way that Edward
Fowles has described as "really outrageous," my father's earlier
study. Even the editor of the magazine felt compelled to add a note
to one item that Berenson discussed, stating that "it is only just to
mention that the first to publish its attribution to Sassetta was Mr.
Langton Douglas."

In the following month my father had published in the *Burlington Magazine* another article to which he gave the title "A Note on
Recent Criticism of the Art of Sassetta," and in that he demolished
so effectively many of the views expressed by Bernard Berenson
that not only was there nothing more that could be said but
Berenson had to withdraw two of his earlier books and replace
them with later, corrected editions. "Berenson did not reply,"
Edward Fowles has said; "he really could not." The great reputation as an art critic that Berenson rightly acquired during his long
lifetime is secure; but all too often it happens that when a man
becomes a legend in his own lifetime he is sometimes credited with
more than he is entitled to. Probably this explains why the well-
known art critic Sir Kenneth Clark, in the course of a television
interview some time ago, credited Berenson with "discovering"
Sassetta.

The stern necessity of having to provide for his many offspring
gave me plenty of opportunities to pull my father's leg about the
size of his large family, but although he accepted my teasing in a
good enough spirit he never at any time treated lightly his many
responsibilities. He always accepted and acknowledged his numerous children with a serious and considerate attention. He even
saw to it that his illegitimate children got off, in some ways, to a
better start in life than his legitimate ones—which offers in itself a
comment on his attitude—and there is no doubt that his interest in

women led him to be more generous toward his daughters than he was to his sons.

A touching indication of the solicitude that my father felt for all his children was revealed to us just before the outbreak of the Second World War in 1939. He had at that time a house in London, in Montagu Place, and he gave a cocktail party there for all his children and their children. I was by then his eldest surviving child, forty-five years of age and an Air Vice-Marshal in the Royal Air Force. The youngest of his children there was my half-sister Claire, then aged about seven, who was born of his third marriage. (My father was nearly seventy years of age when Claire was born—she is now married to J. D. Salinger, the well-known American writer and author of *The Catcher in the Rye.*) At that party it was quite obvious that he was delighted to have all of us around him.

Despite his fondness for us, and his generosity in doing all that he could to get us off to a good start in life, my father had no specific ambitions for his children. He saw to it that we were all well educated, but he did not try to influence us regarding the manner in which we should live our lives. In my own case, there was practically no influence at all. He provided us with a good education, and then he left us to fend for ourselves, although there was some indulgence toward his daughters. He was always pleased with any successes that we were able to achieve; but the provocative aspect of his humor almost compelled him to treat us as equals rather than to regard us merely as his children. He was right, I think, in adopting that attitude because it made us stand on our own feet.

Having inherited from my father quite a fair share of his independence of character, I suppose it was natural that my mother and I should not have been able to get along very well together. She was a good mother to me and to my brothers, and she devoted the whole of her life to caring for us and bringing us up, and I should not like to give the impression that I am in any way an ungrateful son. But it was an unhappy fact that temperamentally my mother and I did not hit it off particularly well; and she was always inclined to be overcritical of my work and my goals in life.

How it came about that my mother and father—he was a young curate working in London when they met—were ever attracted to each other enough to marry I do not know. My mother's maiden name was Margaret Jane Cannon, and she came from a family whose background was as different from my father's as it is possible to imagine. Her father was a printer who worked in London, where she was born; and her mother came from Glasgow. It was possibly the shrewd, practical soundness of my mother's character that led her to exert such great efforts on our behalf—efforts which went such a long way to offset the effects of my father's upsetting, even if attractive, weakness.

It has been said that I inherited my sense of humor from my father; but I am not the one to judge that. I know quite well that my humor, whatever it may be, is at times misunderstood, and this is something I regret. It has developed, I am inclined to believe, from an acute self-consciousness from which I have always suffered. What the psychiatrists would say about that I cannot pretend to know; but I do think that the breakup in my parents' marriage while I was still very young contributed to this wretched shyness. I am only too aware that whereas a provocative sense of humor can produce exhilarating discussion and comment, it can also, when betrayed by self-consciousness, lead much too often to misunderstandings. It is fortunate for me that this shyness has been limited largely to my social life: my work has never been handicapped by it. But I understand, without people having known it, why the comment has been made that I have succeeded in spite of myself.

At the time of my birth, my parents were living in Oxford; and my father was a secretary of the Church of England Temperance Society. He was also a curate and an assistant chaplain of Merton College. I was the second child, the first, a boy, having died in early childhood. There were two more boys after me, first Robert and then Archibald—named in the tradition of the Douglas family—and there was a span of only two years and eight months covering the births of the three of us. The last of the five children born of my father's first marriage was a girl, but she also died while she was still a baby. My mother had her full share of sadness in these early deaths of two of her children, not to mention the other troubles caused her by my father. At the end of her life I was her only child still alive. Our family relationship in our childhood was a perfectly normal one, and I was very attached to my two brothers, being particularly fond of Archie.

While we were still very young, my father found that writing and the study of history had become much more to his liking than the affairs of the church, although he was by no means a don. In the middle 1890's, while I was still an infant, we went with him to live in Italy, where he was for a while British Chaplain in Siena and

Perugia. My father took full advantage of this opportunity to study Italian history and the paintings and other works of art of the Renaissance. This was just before the intensive and critical study of Renaissance paintings and artists that began about the turn of the century. I was then very young, and I can remember nothing much of our stay in Italy, although my mother used to say that I learned to speak Italian faster than I did English. It was during this time in Siena that my father made his first discoveries about Sassetta, and he became so stimulated by his inquiries and studies that he decided then to follow the path of the historian rather than that of the clergyman.

After we returned to England in 1898, my father published an edition of Sir Geoffrey Fenton's *Tragicall Discourses,* a sixteenth-century translation that he had edited of stories from the French and Latin. He also began lecturing on Italian art under the Oxford University extension scheme. In 1900 he published his well-known book on Fra Angelico; but by that time he had taken what he thought would be a step forward in his career. He had accepted an appointment as professor of medieval history and dean of the Faculty of Arts at Adelaide University and had gone off to Australia. After he left, my mother and my brothers and I went to live with her parents in Tooting, in south London.

Free from the restraining influence of a wife and children, my poor father, with that susceptibility of his which knew all too little curbing, met and fell madly in love with an Australian girl not long after his arrival in Adelaide. This drove him to take the cruel step of asking my mother for a divorce. Such an event in those days of sixty years ago, particularly in the life of a clergyman, was of far greater consequence than it would be today. It was a callous, if not brutal, thing to do to my mother; but she divorced him, and that led to his having, in its formal phrasing, "to execute a deed of relinquishment under the provisions of the Clergy Disabilities Act," which was just another way of saying that he somewhat hurriedly left the Church. It also left him free to marry his Australian.

After the breakup of my parents' marriage—I was then seven years of age—there was very little money that my father could spare for us, and for a good many years after that we led a decidedly impecunious existence. Having to provide for two wives and three children presented my father with a serious problem, and at first he was hard pressed to make both ends meet; but he was determined that his interest in history should pay for his way of life. He went back to Italy and spent more time there, living and working again in Siena, one of the ancient cities of the Etruscans and a center of medieval Italian art.

In 1902 my father published his most important work: *A History of Siena.* It quickly became, and is to this day, one of the standard textbooks on this subject, in the Italian edition as well as in the English. The latter part of the book deals with the history of Sienese painting, and this was the springboard for his future specialty. This all came about at a most opportune time because Italian art of the Renaissance was then being "discovered," as the fatuous expression goes, and the paintings of that period became objects of the keenest interest to wealthy collectors, just as later they were to fall over each other to acquire the paintings of the French Impressionists and Post-Impressionists.

Spurred on by his interest and by his deep understanding and knowledge of the subject, my father also wrote, in addition to the important articles in the *Burlington Magazine,* many other critical studies. In speaking of what he accomplished during this period, the *Times* stated (on his death in 1951): "Perhaps his most permanent contribution to the study of art was the great work he did, in the early years of this century, in largely rewriting Crowe and Cavalcaselle's *History of Painting in Italy.*" This was an important work in four volumes, the last of which was published in 1909. By then, having established his reputation as an art critic, he was well on the road to building up a business as an art dealer.

But successful though my father was becoming in his professional life, his marital status was again in jeopardy, although this time it was not of his doing. After presenting him with three children, his second wife proceeded to give him some of his own medicine. She ran off with a Frenchman, leaving him to write the last word to his Australian idyl by divorcing her.

During my father's struggles to establish himself in his work, my mother and my two brothers and I, of necessity, lived a quiet and very simple life in a house in Balham, in south London. It was all that my mother could afford, and even then she had to stretch to the limit the small allowance that she received from my father. In its way our impecuniosity was an advantage because it did lead my brothers and me to a studious way of life. When I was about seven or eight, I wrote a letter to my father which he kept and which was returned to me after his death. When I read it, just over fifty years after having written it, I could not help feeling a little sad about the slightly pathetic note that it sounded. Apparently it had not been explained to me that my father had left our home for good because I wrote, in a childish hand, that "we often think of you as sleeping whilst we are having our dinner," which was a reference to his sojourn in Australia. And in referring to his book on Fra Angelico I added: "We all like the nice book you have written."

While we were living in Balham my brothers and I attended St. Mary's School, which was nearby. It is now a London County Council elementary school, but at that time it was one of those known generally as Church schools. Each week I used to take with me the ninepence which my mother gave me to pay for my tuition; and I am sure that this early contact with all types of children provided me with an invaluable foundation for a working knowledge of people. During those years in south London my brothers and I joined the other children at play on Tooting Bec Common, and there we made our first attempts at cricket and football; and, encouraged by our mother, we started singing in the choir of St. John's Church.

Of all the memories of my early childhood, it was perhaps the night of May 18, 1900, that made a particularly deep impression. It was the night the news came that Mafeking had been relieved after the seven long months of siege by the Boers in the war in South Africa. My brothers and I were not at all sure what the excitement was all about, and we sat up in bed and listened in awe to the shouts and the cries from the crowds giving vent to an outburst of general rejoicing as they surged about in Balham High Road.

At the turn of the century all the buses and the trams running through Balham were still drawn by horses, and whenever we used them there was always a scuffle among my friends, in which I was never left out, for the front seats on top next to the driver. It was while we were at St. Mary's school that the trams running along Balham High Road were electrified, and we schoolchildren were all lined up on the pavement on the occasion of the opening of the new service. On board the first tram there was the Prince of Wales, who later became King George the Fifth, and it was our task to cheer and to sing in our shrill little voices a song that we had learned for the occasion: "God Bless the Prince of Wales."

The elementary education that I received at St. Mary's School in Balham was a sound one, and when I left it at the age of about eleven and went on to Emmanuel School, in Wandsworth, I found that I could easily hold my own with the other boys of my own age in everything but Latin, a subject which was new to me. But I was at Emmanuel School only a year when my father, who was by then beginning to meet with some success in his work, suggested to my mother that an effort should be made to send us to a public school. The expense of educating all his children was a matter that he had to consider very carefully, and it was finally decided that my mother should move to Tonbridge because a large number of the boys enrolled at Tonbridge School—about a third of them in my time—were day boys. There were also reduced fees for those who lived within ten miles of Tonbridge Old Parish Church. So my mother found a suitable house in Tonbridge, and in 1905 she took us to live there. She continued to live in the vicinity until the time of her death fifty-three years later, seven years after the death of my father.

For a while my brothers and I attended, as day boys, a preparatory school in Tonbridge. There is an indication of the progress that I was making in a letter that I wrote to my father in November, 1905, at the age of twelve. I reported that I had "only read three of Scott's novels." I was also able to tell him that I was in the school first eleven. A year later I was writing to him to say that "we have been getting on very well at school. I took two prizes and Archie three," and that I was by then "head boy of the school."

When the time came for me to go to Tonbridge School I reported to my father that "I hope you will be pleased to hear that I have done very well in the entrance exam, and am in all probability going straight into the Middle Fifth, which is a record. I was examined by Mr. Lowry himself in Greek and Latin, and he said that I have a good chance for a scholarship." By then I had also developed the usual schoolboy interest in photography—which was later to be of assistance to me in a way I least expected—and I spoke in another letter of "sending you three examples with love from Bob and Archie." But a few months later, in a letter that I wrote to my grandfather, I had to report that I was "rather disappointed at failing to get a scholarship."

I had been at Tonbridge for only a short time when it began to dawn on me that my home life was different from that of most of the other boys. Perhaps it was then I first became aware of the inherent self-consciousness which has always bothered me. I was to learn, while I was still very young, that this self-consciousness, no matter how much I struggled to control it, could lead me into the most awkward traps, and that in my efforts to correct the mistakes there came an over-compensation which only led to further difficulties. It was hard going having to be always on one's guard.

More than fifty years have passed since I was at school at Tonbridge, and when I look back, it seems to me that it was quite a civilized place. There was a lively interest in music, and we had many concerts and singing competitions; also we were greatly encouraged in all our reading. For all the views so widely held on the value of sending boys to boarding school, I think that there were certain advantages in being a day boy. For one thing, I had more time to myself, and I would work in the evenings at home in any way that I wished without having to sit in "prep" as the boarders had to between certain fixed hours. Since I was ambitious and hoped to win a university scholarship, I often stayed up until long after it would have been "lights out" had I been a boarder.

As a result of the good impression I had made in my examination for entrance to Tonbridge I was placed straight away in the Middle Fifth on the classical side. That, as I proudly told my father, was quite high up for a boy of fourteen, particularly since the classical side at Tonbridge at that time was a very good one. I had already made up my mind that I wanted to go up to Oxford— mainly because it was my father's university—but I knew that the only way of getting there would be through an exhibition or a scholarship. That induced in me from the start a definite purpose in working hard at classics. I made good progress, and by the time I was sixteen I was in the Upper Sixth.

We learned to work hard at Tonbridge, and I am particularly indebted to two of the school's most famous masters for what they taught me. One of these was the headmaster, Charles Lowry; and the other was Walter Maxwell Gordon, the head of the classical side. Gordon was a most impressive man in appearance, tall and massive in build. One of the school historians has said of him: "His portrait bust would have passed for that of a Roman Emperor." He was a truly wonderful schoolmaster. He was also my housemaster, and he took a keen personal interest in me and my work.

Under the guidance of Walter Gordon it was not just a simple matter of his imparting to us the routine, set knowledge that we were expected to acquire: he made us learn to take an interest in life itself. In the mornings, for instance, before we started our lessons, he would read out to us items from the *Times,* or he would talk to us for a quarter of an hour or so about some question of topical interest.

Over forty years after I was at school at Tonbridge (a few years after the end of the Second World War), I ran into Walter Gordon one evening in Dublin. By chance I went to the Abbey Theatre, which was always a favorite haunt of mine, and there I saw Gordon (who was an Ulsterman) among the crowd of people in the lobby. I made myself known to him, and the next morning we had breakfast together. He remembered me well, and I was amused by the way in which he commented, with the broad grin known so well to all his pupils, that I was the only one of his boys ever to earn a peerage. I did not see him again, and later I heard that he had died a short time after our meeting.

Our headmaster, Charles Lowry, was an Old Etonian who had been an assistant master at Eton and then headmaster at Sedbergh before he became headmaster at Tonbridge, where he reigned for fifteen years, including the years of the First World War. He was of a different vintage than Walter Gordon. Older and possibly finer, and not as robust, he was just as full of character. The deaths in the Great War of so many of those whom he had known during his years at Eton, Sedbergh and Tonbridge imposed upon him a very heavy strain. D. C. Somervell, in his *History of Tonbridge School,* says that Charles Lowry "had the most important of all gifts for headmastership; he was, by nature and without conscious effort, the kind of man that the ordinary boy believes he can understand, and feels impelled to admire, venerate and love. There was something about him, a kind of nobility, that was of more than common stature."

My life during those years at school at Tonbridge was rather uneventful, but it was a fairly happy one. I worked hard and, I believe, conscientiously. Although I had no outstanding natural aptitude for classics, I was ambitious and I did quite well. I also did well at games: in my last year I got into the first fifteen and I was in the rowing four. I should have liked to be good at cricket, in which I have always taken a great interest, but I was not, so I took up rowing instead. In the usual way I made many friends, but the one who was closest, and whose friendship lasted, was a boy of my own age named Gordon Alchin. He was a brilliant scholar and eventually he became a county court judge. Alchin and I started at Tonbridge at the same time, and we moved up in the school together until we were both in the Sixth Form. We were also in the same house, the head of which was one of three brothers by the name of Nott-Bower. (He retired only a few years ago after becoming Sir John Nott-Bower, Commissioner of the Metropolitan Police.)

There was only one aspect of public school life in the days of my youth to which I really took exception, and that was corporal punishment. When I became a prefect I firmly declined to have anything to do with it. I felt then, as I do now, that corporal punishment brutalizes those who administer it, and that it stirs up in the person upon whom it is inflicted too strong a feeling of resentment.

I was beaten only once during the years that I spent at Tonbridge, and I still resent it. The punishment did me no good whatsoever, and I hated the indignity of the whole performance, although I must admit that my resentment was heightened by my feeling that I was being punished unjustly. The circumstances themselves were trivial enough. The house Officers' Training Corps squad was being drilled on one of the playing fields, and the N.C.O. in charge of us, a prefect from another house, was useless at giving orders. Somehow or other he had got us marching line abreast straight toward a hedge at the side of the field. He became thoroughly muddled, and he either forgot or could not get out the one word of command that would halt us. My companions stopped of their own accord when they got to the hedge and merely stood there waiting for further orders; but I felt that I should continue to do as I was told, so I went straight on, forcing my way through the hedge and marching on across the next field. No order had been given to halt, and it was clearly my duty to press on regardless of all difficulties. To my annoyance that was labeled impertinence, and I was soundly thrashed for it.

A far pleasanter side of our lives during those early years was the use we made of our holidays. In the spring of 1912, when I was just over eighteen years of age, Gordon Alchin and I spent three weeks wandering around Italy. Although this was actually my second visit to that country, it was the first of which I have any definite memory. The idea for the trip came from my father. He thought it would help us in our classical studies, and he carefully worked out an itinerary and provided us with introductions which would enable us to make the most of visits to Florence, Rome, Naples, Paestum and Venice. During the three weeks that Alchin and I spent on our tour we went everywhere we could, and we saw many of the art galleries and classical ruins, and several times we went to the opera.

That tour of Italy gave me a taste for the country that has endured, and nowadays I go there at least two or three times a year—although I wince at the thought of how expensive everything has become compared with what travel abroad cost in my youth. Before we left England my father gave me twenty pounds to cover all my expenses. During the three weeks that we were away I managed to spend twenty-two pounds, borrowing, at the end, the extra two pounds from Gordon Alchin. The second-class train fares for each of us for the entire trip came to just over seven pounds, and our accommodations, food, drink and all our other expenses amounted to about fifteen pounds each over the entire three weeks.

Part of our summer holiday of 1912 we spent at our annual O.T.C. Camp at Farnborough, and it was there that I saw an airplane for the first time. The Tonbridge School O.T.C. along with the O.T.C.'s from twenty or thirty other schools was encamped under canvas on the rising ground at Farnborough Aerodrome, which is today the site for the stands and exhibits at the famous annual air show. Below us the airfield was much the same as it is today, except that it was much smaller and there were no concrete runways; and the Royal Aircraft Factory, as the Royal Aircraft Establishment was known in those days, was already there, across the other side of the field from our camp.

I spent most of my spare time at Farnborough watching from a distance the flying that was going on and the aircraft that were being tested. I suppose those aircraft must have been B.E.1's and B.E.2's, which were among the first to be built there. We learned that one of the test pilots who was flying them was a young man by the name of Geoffrey de Havilland, and it was also said, to my great interest, that he was even then doing a great deal of the actual designing of the airplanes. Within a very short time I became fascinated with this new business of flying, and I spent every moment I could spare watching it and wondering if there was not some way in which I could indulge in what appeared to be such a marvelous sport. But I was still a schoolboy, and I felt in my heart that the chance of my ever flying was very remote. I did not even know that the Royal Flying Corps had been founded only a few weeks before.

In that year of 1912, when I was eighteen, I was bracketed top of the Upper Sixth at Tonbridge, and I was awarded a Leaving Exhibition, valued at seventy-five pounds. This was of great importance to me because of my ambition to go up to Oxford. Later in the year I went to the university, and I sat for two separate scholarship examinations, one for Magdalen and the other for a group including New College—which had been my father's college—Exeter and Corpus Christi. I did not do as well in these examinations as I should have, mainly, I think, because I was overanxious and nervous, and rather shy in the unfamiliar and awe-inspiring atmosphere of the university. To my great disappointment none of the colleges saw fit to award me a scholarship.

This failure of mine was also a disappointment to Walter

Gordon, who had thought that I was certain to get a classical scholarship. I returned to Tonbridge thoroughly disheartened. But fortunately for me, the examiner of the Upper Sixth at the end of the following Michaelmas term was Mr. E. C. Marchant, who was a classical fellow at Lincoln College, Oxford, and sub-rector of the College. He took such a favorable view of my work in that examination that I was offered an exhibition at Lincoln College valued at thirty pounds a year. Marchant was a charming man with a pretty turn of wit, and he later became my tutor.

With this prize and my leaving exhibition, and some help from my father, I was able to realize my ambition, and I went up to Oxford in the autumn of 1913. Gordon Alchin had won a good scholarship at Brasenose and he started reading law, but I had not made up my mind about what I was going to do. Lincoln at that time was the only college at Oxford at which the age limit for sitting for the scholarship examination was twenty instead of the usual nineteen, so I sat for the examination again in 1913 as an undergraduate. The rector of Lincoln College was Dr. W. W. Merry, a well-known Greek scholar, and as luck would have it I managed to turn out a pretty good set of Greek verse. This apparently made such a good impression on Merry that I "converted my try" and I was awarded a classical scholarship worth sixty pounds a year. But I was not to enjoy the benefit of it because it did not become effective until October, 1914, and by then I was engaged in pursuits that were less academic.

Although I was born in Oxford, I have no early memories of it as a child, and it was not until the autumn of 1913, when I came to know well the university and the town, that I learned to appreciate the subtlety of its appeal. I was to spend only a year there, but it came to exert a strong influence in my life, and I have always enjoyed a feeling of warmth, almost as if it were home, for the town and the university.

When I first went up to Oxford I had no idea at all about what I was going to do with my life, but in those days few of us did at that stage in our education. If I had any immediate objective at all it was to get a good class in Hon. Mods. and then in Greats. Oxford of that time still belonged to an old world, and there was no indication that very shortly afterward that world was to collapse and almost disappear. Few of us gave any serious thought to whether it was a world that was altogether desirable. We were there to learn about a way of life that had evolved over a long period of time, and how we were to fit into that life. There were, of course, those whose object in being at the university was to work, but not everyone had an intense and compulsive drive to become highly educated; and although the growth of scientific studies and the movement toward specialization in all studies were under way they had not yet made any great impact.

Odd though it may sound now, most of the undergraduates at Oxford in my time were there because it was thought to be socially desirable, and for many, sport was a great deal more important than what was described as "mere scholarship." Most of the parents of the undergraduates thought that the years spent at the University would teach their sons to be men of the world and enable them to mix well with other people. Many undergraduates worked quite happily for a pass degree and no more, and I cannot help feeling that they gained more in the long run from what Oxford has to offer than do the students in these days of specialization and high-pressure cramming.

The life that we were able to lead in our colleges was unquestionably a pleasant one. There were plenty of social activities; we read a great deal and we talked even more, and it was at this time that I first became interested in the Labour movement. My reading then, as now, covered a wide field, and it included some of the Fabian pamphlets. I also attended some of the meetings organized by the Fabian Society. But my interest in socialism really came more from a personal conviction than from any academic or intellectual interest. It was bred of an innate sense of a need for justice in the relationships between human beings. This conviction had started developing in my mind long before I went up to Oxford.

While I was young I had never been aware of what I was later to recognize with some distaste as a consciousness of class. That was due mainly to the sound common-sense way in which my mother saw to it that my brothers and I were brought up, and to the broadening experience of my early school days in Balham. But at Tonbridge, for all the generous breadth of the attitude there, and later in a more pronounced way at Oxford, I was made aware that this class consciousness certainly did exist, and I was forced to realize that for reasons that were blatantly unjust, opportunities for all men were by no means equal. That came to me as a very disturbing discovery. I found that I had an instinctive and very strong aversion to any form of snobbery, and from that time on I always felt compelled to do all that I could to try to understand the position of the underdog. It was that which led to my becoming a confirmed Socialist.

Such was the life that I led during my one year at Oxford that I did practically no work at all, although I knew that I would have to make up for that in the long vacation of 1914. My time was given over largely to sport, and I used to turn out for practically everything. Lincoln was a very small college in those days, with not more than sixty or seventy undergraduates, and one had a good opportunity of representing it in almost any of the inter-college games. I played rugger, soccer and a little hockey, and I stroked the College Torpid and rowed two in the eight in my first year. My weight then was about eleven and a half stone, and I was down for the trial eights for the university crew the following year; but that was for a race that the fates decided should be replaced by a much sterner one. As a freshman I played in the rugger trials at Oxford as a wing forward, and I even got as far as the final trial, but I was a bit on the light side for a university forward.

There was another feature of our lives as undergraduates at Oxford before the First World War that was almost entirely different from what is permitted today, and it was not without its own humor. We were not allowed to have anything whatsoever to do with women; we were forbidden to meet them even in the town. Whenever I wanted to spend a few hours with my girl friend of the moment I had to take the train from Oxford and go as far afield as the Thames at Pangbourne in order to be free from the restrictions that were imposed upon us. On one of my visits to Oxford a short time ago I saw a card on the notice board at the entrance to Lincoln which stated that any ladies visiting the undergraduates in their rooms had to be out of those rooms by ten-thirty at night. What an enviable emancipation! Such a radical change from the strict regulations of my day must at least save the undergraduates quite a bit in train fares.

That year which I spent so happily at Oxford just before the outbreak of the First World War marked the end of an era. At the beginning of the year the mood in Britain was still tranquil enough, and for all the stirrings of the earthquake beneath the outwardly placid surface in Europe it appeared to most of us that life would continue, at least in Britain, in the same more or less even temper.

There were a few foreign observers who thought that we had our heads buried in the sand, but we paid very little attention to them. One of those who viewed with alarm the gathering storm was Colonel E. M. House, the famous personal envoy of the President of the United States. He made a special journey to study the state of affairs in Europe, and what he had to say over fifty years ago echoes strongly in our ears today. "The situation is extraordinary," he reported to President Wilson. "It is militarism run stark mad. Unless someone acting for you can bring about a different understanding there is some day to be an awful cataclysm. There is too much hatred, too many jealousies. The whole of Germany is charged with electricity. It only needs a spark to set the whole thing off." In an obscure corner of the Balkans the flint and the tinder that were to provide that spark were already clutched in the hands of a group of young assassins.

The social season in London during the year 1914 was a particularly brilliant one, helped by the splendid weather of the spring and the summer. I had formed an early taste for the theater which, that year, was alive and interesting; and one of the new plays that I saw was Shaw's *Pygmalion,* which was running at His Majesty's with Mrs. Patrick Campbell and Sir Herbert Tree. I went to see it with my mother and my brothers, and I thought, perhaps a little unchivalrously, that Mrs. Campbell was a bit old for the part of Eliza.

Oxford had stimulated in me an even greater interest in reading, and the flood of new books contained many exciting prospects. There were giants at work, and not the least of them was H. G. Wells. Ever preoccupied with foreshadowing the shape of things to come, he published that year—the year, it must be remembered, was 1914—what was described as "an imaginative work" entitled *The World Set Free.* In it Wells spoke about a bomb which made use of the forces that could be released in the smashing of the atom.

June was a magnificent month. At Henley the Americans, with a crew from Harvard University, won for the first time the final of the Grand. And then, on June 28, there appeared in the newspapers a report of yet another incident in the tiresome Balkans: the heir to the throne of Austria-Hungary and his wife had been brutally assassinated in a far-off town in Bosnia by the name of Sarajevo.

When I read in the newspaper the reports of that incident I also noticed that there were some vague murmurings that it might lead to a war. But that, I thought, was all a little silly. International affairs in those days were rather locked away in a world of their own, the world of secret diplomacy. They were left to the care of the experts, and since we did not have then what has since become known as "mass communication," there was no reason why any of us who were not in that secret world should have had any inkling of what we would have to face in the very near future.

2 / "...as to a dance"

WHEN I LOOK BACK over the years to the late summer and the autumn of 1914, and I think about the way in which the peace and the orderliness of our lives were shattered by what was to become the most dreadful war that man has ever waged, I find it a little touching to recall that I went into action mounted on a horse with a sword dangling at my saddlebow. My views then about war were quite unrealistic and far from serious. A poem by Maurice Baring entitled "Per Ardua, 1914–1918" contains a delightful line about the first squadrons of the Royal Flying Corps setting out for France "as gaily as to a dance." That strikes just the note on which so many of us went off to the war.

That first war produced an extraordinary wealth of what came to be called "soldier poets." They were young men who spoke in the most articulate way of what they felt and what they saw as soldiers. "Deeper utterance than men ordinarily need or permit themselves to attempt," as Edmund Blunden has put it. We thought then in terms of "chivalrous obligation, the things that matter more than death," to quote again from Blunden. Rupert Brooke wrote of our mood, which then contained no shred of disenchantment; but he was to die before he could know anything of the discoveries that were to be made by Siegfried Sassoon and Robert Graves and Wilfred Owen and many other poets and writers who were to serve as fighting soldiers, not as mere on-lookers or observers.

So far as I was concerned, I imagined, as did so many others, that the war might be an interesting experience and even rather fun, and I was almost afraid it would all be over before I would be given a chance to get into it. There was a generally optimistic view that it would all be over by Christmas, but that was not at all to my liking. To those of my generation, the concept of war, fed as we were on the legends of heroism, was one of great adventure, the rewards for which were either magnificent glory or a clean death.

We who were in our late teens and our early twenties in 1914

29

did not know that war could produce a depth of misery to which even death would be preferable; and we did not know then anything about the horror that was to be inflicted upon what came to be so well known as the Western Front. The names of the Somme and Ypres were merely those of a river in northern France and an ancient town in Belgium. Writing quite recently about what we felt at that time, the historian Cyril Falls has expressed his own feelings in the statement: "The modern intellectual is inclined to look with impatience upon the ardor with which they went to war. Looking back, the intensity—and I dare add the purity—of that spirit still moves me deeply." I find myself moved in the same fashion.

When I went up to Oxford in October, 1913, I continued with my training in the O.T.C. and I joined the signals section of the infantry. But for a new interest, I would have stayed in the infantry, and that might have meant that my life would have taken an entirely different course. The new interest was a desire to learn to ride a horse. Since that desire was only a mild one it is even possible that I would not have done anything about it if I had not been influenced by a charming young New Zealander named Denis O'Rorke, who was a freshman with me at Lincoln.

A keen horseman, O'Rorke had joined the artillery unit of the O.T.C. I happened to remark to him one day that I thought I would rather like to learn to ride, and he immediately suggested that I transfer from the infantry to the artillery. He and his brother, who was also in the artillery section, brought some pressure to bear—it was not particularly easy to make such a change—and I was able to transfer to the gunners. In that way I learned to ride, and occasionally I was even able to borrow a horse, which suited my pocket because I was always pretty hard up. By the summer of 1914 I had become a driver in the artillery O.T.C., all my drill being on the well-known eighteen-pounder.

So far as our knowledge of world affairs during those last days of the peace was concerned, we undergraduates were not exactly well informed, but that was not entirely our fault. One quite reputable newspaper, for instance, even went so far as to talk aout "a grim conspiracy to get us into the war" and counseled neutrality. It was not until a few days before the war actually broke out that the English newspapers began to present the news with any appreciation of the gravity of a situation that had been brought about by secret diplomacy and secret obligations. There was also still in most people's minds a preoccupation with the question of Home

Rule for Ireland. But in any case general interest centered more on a prize fight that was to take place in London for the world heavy-weight title in which our own Gunboat Smith would be facing a very young Frenchman by the name of Georges Carpentier. That did not mean a great deal to me then, but now, over fifty years later, I have come to know Carpentier quite well through meetings with him in his pleasant bar just off the Champs Élysées and quite close to the offices of British European Airways in Paris.

When it finally became obvious that war was almost certain—even if it was very much against the wish of a great many people, including the majority of the Members of Parliament—I was staying with Gordon Alchin. When he had gone up with me to Oxford he had also become a member of the artillery unit of the O.T.C. Alchin's people had a house in Hastings, and while we were there one of our lighter pursuits was a particularly beautiful creature, Violet by name, who possessed a long, thick blond pigtail. When we were not keeping her company, Alchin and I spent our time reading all that we could lay hands on in the way of news about the threatened war.

And then it came, and from eleven o'clock at night on August 4, 1914, we were at war with Germany. All that day we had known weather that was recorded as some of the loveliest of the year. At the mention of patriotism we all felt an instant quickening of the pulse. It was a proud time, and before the word patriotism came to acquire the stigma that now unhappily gives too many people cause to look the other way. They lost a great deal when they lost that pride in themselves.

Gordon Alchin and I knew no hesitation about deciding, as soon as war was declared, just what we were going to do. We were not alone in that: practically everyone up at Oxford volunteered for service. On a visit that I made to Lincoln College in 1915 I found only one of those of my year still there, and that was because he had been found medically unfit. Later, even he managed finally to get into the Army. I am one of the very few of my year at Lincoln who survived, and whenever I have occasion to attend any gatherings in Oxford—I am now an Honorary Fellow of the College—there is a most noticeable gap caused by the absence of those of my generation who were killed in the First World War.

It was only to be expected that Gordon Alchin and I should apply for commissions in the artillery, because that was the arm for which we were best qualified. We were summoned for inter-views, which we passed, and we were then sent on for medical examinations. To my surprise and horror, not to say utter disgust, I was told by the medical officer that I had failed because, it was alleged, I had flat feet. I was very indignant; it was the first time that such an absurd finding had been made, and I quickly pointed out to the examining officer that I was a good runner, that I played class rugger, and that I had always walked quite long distances for pleasure. Moreover, I said, I could not see what flat feet had to do with it when I was going into the artillery.

The arguments that I advanced seemed to put an entirely different complexion on the medical aspect of my case. Flat feet, it appeared, did not matter in the mounted arm, and I was promptly passed as fit for active service. I have often wondered how long this alleged condition would have kept me out of the Army if I had not argued with that medical officer, and what a difference being turned down would have made. But I passed the examination, and that was what mattered. On August 15, 1914, eleven days after the outbreak of war, Gordon Alchin and I received our commissions in the artillery.

With my commission I received a notice from the War Office instructing me to report to the gunnery school at Shoeburyness. I went through a short artillery course there, and then I was posted to the Royal Field Artillery depot at Newcastle. Already there was an acute shortage of gunner subalterns, largely because under peacetime conditions there had been no ammunition columns. When the war broke out these had had to be formed as quickly as possible, and every spare gunner subaltern was promptly posted off to an ammunition column and then to France.

On my arrival at Newcastle I found that there were in the depot no regular gunner officers. The commanding officer was a survival from the Boer War of fourteen years before who had been brought out of retirement; and the adjutant, although a competent man, was a regular who had also been in retirement for some years. We who had learned our drill at the University O.T.C.'s were the only ones who were at all competent to handle the eighteen-pounders which we were apparently going to use, so that almost immediately we found ourselves, subalterns through we were, instructing not only the gunners but also the other officers at the depot, including the C.O.

The landing in France in 1914 of that gallant band of the original British Expeditionary Force was completed by the middle of August. Almost immediately they went into action, alongside the French Army, trying to stem the tide of the hordes of the advancing German Army. The enemy was working in accordance

with its vaunted and unscrupulous Schlieffen plan: unscrupulous in
that it was founded on the deliberate violation of Belgian neutrality. Only a week after their arrival in France the "Old Con-
temptibles" of our splendid little regular army of the B.E.F. had to
endure a difficult retreat from Mons. It was a maneuver that
turned out to be a miraculous escape. The scale of our effort was
small compared to that of the French, but again I find in the views
expressed by Cyril Falls the words that most fittingly express what
we all felt and have continued to feel about the quality of the men
who made up our army of that time: ". . . the world of those
years witnessed the upsurge of an enthusiasm for ideals, of determination and bravery in face of death and suffering, of generosity of
spirit, which may not reappear on so wide a scale. There was
something sublime in the endurance of these men."

The nature of the fighting in Belgium and France during those
first weeks of the war was along traditional lines, open and fluid,
with pitched battles fought and won and lost to the accompani-
ment of movement—in our case backward—over quite large
areas. And then the nature of the waging of the war changed, and
that pattern of the opening stages was not to reappear until some
twenty-five years later. Early in September the Allied retreat in
France before the invading Germans was slowed down, and there
came the Battle of the Marne. The stand there brought about
conditions that pointed to the shape of things to come, and it led to
our own armies stopping the retreat and standing and offering
resistance. The British Expeditionary Force took root in the open,
rolling country of Picardy and the heavy soil of Flanders.

My own information about what was happening came only from
the newspapers, and along with everybody else I was rejoicing in
what we were being told about our victories and the scale of our
effort. As was to happen too often, we were misled. Why, one
cannot help asking now, must there have been so much public
misinformation? The answer reveals only too clearly the attitude of
officialdom in those days toward the release of information to the
public. Those who were fully informed were a mere handful, and
they kept the news to themselves. There was no such thing as
public relations because officialdom thought it best that the public
should remain in stupefied ignorance. The Press was not altogether
to blame for the unreliability of the news.

The Battle of the Marne, which halted the acute threat of the
German spearhead in the direction of Paris, lasted through the
second week of September, and in a sense it was the first great

turning point of the war. A few of the most advanced of the patrols of the invading German Army were only about ten miles from the city. In the studies that I was to make later in my career I came to know enough about the way in which this battle was fought and about all the results that were achieved; but my actual memory of that time delights more in what we heard about the fantastic exploits of the taxi drivers of Paris. In the emergency faced by the French Army six hundred taxis were pressed into service to transport reinforcements to the front. Packed tight with soldiers and their equipment and their rations, the taxis twice made the journey from the city out across the forty-odd miles of the countryside to the war, delivering their passengers at the scene of the fighting on the Marne. It was an exploit that has been fittingly described by the American historian Barbara Tuchman as "the last crusade of the old world."

The achievements of the Allies during that critical week were the result of a masterly advantage being taken of the mistakes made by the enemy and they brought us, in halting the Germans, our first tangible success. They also put an end to the German hope for a quick victory. Immediately afterward there came the four-day Battle of the Aisne; and this was the beginning of the long years that so many men spent lurking in so many different kinds of holes in the ground. The methods of waging war changed; the artillery, with its insatiable appetite for ammunition, and the trenches with their evil frills of barbed wire became the main features of what was to be known as the Western Front.

While I was still fretting about not being able to get out to France before the war ended, there came, early in October, signs of more active employment. I was posted from the depot in Newcastle to the Ammunition Column of the 5th Brigade, Royal Horse Artillery. This was part of the 8th Division then forming up at Hursley Park, near Winchester. Quite by chance I had found my way into the company of the elite of the gunners; and to my delight I learned that we were due to make an early move to France. The commanding officer of the Ammunition Column was a retired gunner major, and the only other subaltern besides myself was a young man from London University, in whose O.T.C. he had received his training.

Although my relationship with my C.O. became, in a very short time, somewhat strained, there was one other association that started at Hursley Park that was to bring to me some unexpectedly happy moments. I was provided with a fine young charger named Tommy, and of him I became quite inordinately proud. For his sake as well as my own, I tried hard to put up a good show; that meant, by R.H.A. standards, that I had to aim at the impossible task of doing more than my best.

The 5th Brigade, Royal Horse Artillery, was made up largely of units that prior to the war had been serving overseas, and we were equipped with thirteen-pounders. Two famous specimens of this gun are today on exhibition in the Imperial War Museum in London, one of them being the very first British gun to open fire on the Western Front. Designed for lightness so that it could fight with the cavalry, it had been brought into service in the Army in 1903. It was to see a tremendous amount of service, without any change in design, throughout the whole of the First World War; and it was put to a great variety of uses, even to being mounted on lorries and used as a mobile antiaircraft gun. The shell was three inches in diameter and weighed in the shrapnel variety twelve and a half pounds; and the maximum range was nearly five miles. The overall weight of the gun and its carriage was just under one ton.

For two reasons I shall never forget the excitement of our departure for France in the early days of November, 1914. First of all, I felt that I was very lucky in being able to get into the show so quickly; secondly, I was proud of the fact that we were a decidedly smart outfit. It was also true, of course, that we knew nothing whatsoever about war.

By the time we arrived at the Front there had already ended the "race to the sea" that had come about through the effort on the part of the Germans to outflank the Allies to the north and so to get to the Channel ports. The more the Germans had extended their lines in that race over northeastern France and Belgium, the more we did the same thing, and the Front now stretched northward up past Bapaume and Arras and Béthune on to Ypres in Belgium, and then off to the northwest to the Channel. Each side had been trying to turn the flank of the other, but neither had been able to gain an advantage, and the time had come for them to settle down to a brutish slugging match that was to sway backward and forward for a long time to come; the width of the area of the opposing lines as they snaked their way across France seldom was more than a few miles.

The British Army was moved north, occupying the line between Béthune and Ypres, and in the middle of October the First Battle of Ypres got under way. The 8th Division went into the line just south of the Belgian frontier, in the neighborhood of Armentières.

The 5th Brigade, Royal Horse Artillery, was to support the newly established front at Laventie, which was a short distance south of the River Lys. Our strength consisted of three batteries of six guns in each; and our ammunition was entirely of shrapnel. Although that ammunition was effective enough in fighting in the open, it was quite useless against trenches. There was also a great shortage even of that, and very soon after we arrived in the line we had only four guns out of each battery in action, and, incredible though it sounds, those guns were each rationed to firing a paltry four rounds per day. We were not a very formidable threat to the enemy.

But for all that, we endeavored to wage war in a way that we thought was the correct one. We were a smart and efficient outfit with some two hundred men, mostly regulars, to each battery, and two hundred fine horses. But I could not help thinking to myself that it was such a terrible waste of manpower and effort because, for all our thorough training and smartness, we seemed to be able to produce practically nothing that was lethal to the enemy. A great deal of time was spent polishing the metal pieces of the harness, the guns were all in spick-and-span condition, halters were pipe-clayed, and we were in every respect a sight to behold. But when we got down to fighting it was only too obvious that the batteries of the French seventy-fives working alongside us were achieving results which were much more effective.

The first sight we had of those French gunners caused in us feelings of the strongest disapproval. Their horses were ungroomed and draped with dilapidated and unpolished harness, and to our astonishment they rode around with large bundles of straw and hay for fodder tied in haphazard fashion on the tops of the guns. The men themselves, cigarettes dangling from their lips, slouched in their saddles and rode in a fashion that, by the standards of the Royal Horse Artillery, was disgracefully slipshod. But as soon as we saw them in action alongside our own batteries, we realized that for all our spit and polish they were playing a far more important part in the war. We might be smarter—an R.H.A. battery going into action was a fine, dashing sight—but they had better guns and better ammunition, and since they were excellent gunners their fire was much more accurate and effective than ours.

Our guns were positioned in revetted pits just behind the lines between Estaires, on the River Lys, and Laventie, and it was the job of the Ammunition Column to keep the supply of shells going up to them from the dump in the rear. With the officer in charge leading the way, two or three wagons were enough (owing to the shortage of ammunition) to make the journey each day at dusk, when there was still enough light to be able to see where we were going but not enough for us to be observed by the enemy. It was usually dark by the time we got up to the gun emplacements. It was the rule that all rations and supplies and reliefs should go up under cover of darkness, and there was far more general activity by night than by day. The broad light of day was reserved for the actual fighting, which was becoming a gruesome business with far more slaughter than had been expected.

Although I was spared having to live in the trenches, there is a curious reflection on our activities in a letter I wrote to my father after I had been in France only a few weeks. "Would you mind getting for me a small automatic pistol with ammunition?" I asked. "The revolver you bought me worked exceedingly well, but it is too bulky to produce easily and to carry about with comfort in my pocket. Quite a number of officers near here have been shot at night by snipers and it is not quite safe to stroll about at night without some means of self-defense, for instance when I am turning out the guard." By the standards of today it was an odd state of affairs that an officer at the front should have to write home for a revolver—in those days such items had to be provided by the officer himself—and even odder that those at home could purchase so easily such weapons and ammunition.

Once we were at the Front any prospects of the war being over by Christmas were soon forgotten, and we had to settle down to making the best we could of that first winter in France. The glorious weather of the summer became a rueful memory, and only shortly after our arrival we had to endure almost constant rain which turned the soft ground of the flat countryside into vast areas of mud of a particularly clinging and messy variety.

"The weather is bitter," I wrote to my father late in December, "one day a hard frost, the next a deluge of rain or snow. The men are over their knees in water in the trenches largely owing to the fact that the Germans are deliberately trying to swamp us by damming the river and ditches." I asked if he would send me four pair of gum boots which I could distribute to my N.C.O.'s, "who would appreciate them highly."

I cannot remember now what security restrictions there were regarding the writing of letters at that time. If there were any, they must have been strangely ineffective, judging from the letters that I was able to write to my father. If I had voiced my opinions in such a way during the Second World War I would probably have been court-martialed. Of the activity at the Front just before the end of

1914, for instance, I wrote: "The British troops are not advancing an inch, although we have made one or two attacks. The French are not progressing far. These damnable newspapers make mountains out of molehills: we occasionally do manage to get forward a few yards, and of course next day we have in the headlines GREAT ADVANCE IN FRANCE. All bunkum." And then I went on to state: "The German artillery seems pretty dominant just now, possibly through our shortage of ammunition."

That I should be exchanging these views so freely with my father was largely because of an extraordinary step that he had taken. By the summer of 1914 he was doing quite well in his profession of art historian and critic and in the canny dealing in paintings which, given the necessary astuteness, can be so profitable. But that was not enough for a man of his temperament. Dyeing his hair and giving his age as forty—he was ten years older than that—he enlisted as a private in the Army Service Corps. By the time I got to France my father was serving on Salisbury Plain, which he found bitterly cold and wet. Being a practical man, as well as a romantic, he had his tailor in London line the tunic of his private's uniform with fur—muskrat if I remember right—to keep out the worst of the cold. He was longing to get into the war in some active way. In sympathizing with him about that, I finished one letter to him that winter with the comment, "I hope to see you here soon." Knowing him as I did, I was not altogether surprised when eventually he wangled his way out to France.

The beastliness of the weather continued, and since all our horses were out in the open they were very soon squelching around up to their knees in mud. I became particularly depressed over the miserable conditions that these poor animals had to endure. Those that we had in the Ammunition Column were not of the same standard as those with the batteries, which had brought their horses with them from Egypt; but even these were soft after having been in a semitropical climate for a long time. Horses were of paramount importance to the Army, and since mechanization was still a thing of the future, we relied on them for a wide variety of work. The British Expeditionary Force alone was using over sixty thousand horses.

On our part of the Front, from La Bassée to Messines, activity on both sides was fairly restrained; but not so many miles to the north of us there had been raging that First Battle of Ypres. It was probably the most vicious battle that had taken place up to that time. Each of the belligerents was trying to turn the other's northern flank, and the Germans confidently expected to be able to smash through the numerically inferior British and Belgian forces and thrust their way to the Channel ports of Calais and Ostend, then down to the south in a sweeping movement behind the armies of the Allies.

But instead of the success that the Germans hoped for, there had been a head-splitting collision. Only a few miles to the north, the east and south of the old Flemish town of Ypres, in a large semicircle around it, the main fighting on the Western Front took place. Constant and repeated hand-to-hand clashes of the utmost ferocity were fought in October and November as our Army made a stand against the German onslaught, and out of it there came the immortal Ypres Salient.

Although this salient around Ypres was to become embarrassing to us in the years that lay ahead—it was apparently held only for prestige, so that we could say that Ypres was never abandoned—it was nevertheless to provide in the course of those years as moving a chapter as any that has ever been recorded in the history of our country. The Germans very nearly achieved their objective of turning our flank in that winter of 1914–15, but they could not go on enduring the terrible losses that were inflicted upon them. One stage alone of that First Battle of Ypres is known in their military history as "The Massacre of the Innocents at Ypres."

By the end of November the fighting died down, and both sides sought cover in the sodden ground. All over the Salient there came to be attached to the Belgian names of the various farms and small villages the new names that our people had given them—names such as Mouse Trap Farm, Cheddar Villa, Polygon Wood, Sanctuary Wood, Hill 60 and a host of others never to be forgotten. Six or seven miles from Ypres, to the northeast, a village on a ridge held by the Germans provided them with a view over the whole of the Salient. Its name was Passchendaele, and the story of that village was to be written vividly into history. For the next four years our men were to look out across those few miles of a tormented, pulverized countryside—I came to see a lot of what happened to it—and up the slopes to that one point; and well might "passion" be a part of its name.

When it became apparent during the winter of 1914–15 that this war was going to last quite a long time, there also increased in intensity the squabbling that had already been going on in high places. I was only a very young and junior officer in the first war, and I knew nothing at first hand about all this squabbling, although later in the war the rows that went on were of such an intensity that echoes were heard even at the Front.

That there should be differences between us and the French was only to be expected. Their whole philosophy of the way war should be waged was based on a fanatical and disastrous doctrine of always ruthlessly attacking: a mystique that was quite alien to our way of thinking. In the study of the war that I had to make when I became a professional I came to understand what a dreadful effect that philosophy had on the whole future of France. That study also revealed to me more fully the ugliness of the bickering and the backbiting indulged in so freely by men of stature who should have known better. This study of the first war conditioned my views in a way that was of distinct value to me in the second war. I have always borne in mind, not without feelings of some anger, that the clashes during the years of 1914–18 between the men who were our leaders were largely the result of personal ambitions, and were indulged in well behind the Front on which so many faithfully fought and died.

The commander-in-chief of the British Expeditionary Force for the first fifteen months of the war was Field Marshal Sir John French. During that time I was a very junior officer in the B.E.F., and the C.-in-C. was an Olympian figure, as exalted in rank as I was lowly. My interest in him now would possibly be no more than academic but for the hand of chance which, forty-seven years later, linked our names. After the Second World War I was promoted to the rank of Marshal of the Royal Air Force, which in itself is the equivalent of that of a field marshal, and I was made a Knight Grand Cross of the Order of the Bath. In 1961 my banner was hung in the impressive Chapel of the Order in Westminster Abbey, the Henry VII Chapel, just off which is the lovely little Chapel of the Battle of Britain. When I went to the Abbey I found that the Chapel stall that had become mine, one of the ancient stalls that stand beneath the banners, had been occupied, with one intervening holder, by Field Marshal the Earl of Ypres (Sir John French). The plaques of our crests and our names are alongside each other in the stall.

One of the corps commanders under Sir John French at the start of the war was Lieutenant-General Sir Douglas Haig. Four months later Haig took command of one of the two armies into which the expanding British Expeditionary Force was divided, and the division in which I was serving came under him. The evidence about the questionable way in which French conducted himself is conclusive; but around Haig controversy has never ceased to rage, and even with the passing of the years this subject does not seem to have lost any of its power to stir up old arguments.

The war on the Western Front, which was less than a hundred miles from what we knew as home, had already become a war of attrition. It was waged in incessant rain and freezing cold across a narrow strip of countryside that was being torn to shreds. Because of the trenches and barbed wire, there developed an urgent requirement for a change in our ammunition. What we needed was high explosive in place of shrapnel, and one day I ventured to express that opinion to my commanding officer.

Having been casehardened in the traditions of the Royal Horse Artillery, my C.O. looked upon all subalterns, and in particular his own, as utter nonentities. But I was fresh from Oxford, where the undergraduate has always regarded talking as an important part of his way of life and freedom of speech as an essential. I was accustomed to telling people what I thought. My C.O. apparently had his thoughts also, and one of them must have been that I was a self-opinionated young upstart. He became very annoyed with me for having the temerity to air my views about the ammunition I thought we should have; from that time on there was a pronounced coolness in our relationship.

Curbing my impulse to go on criticizing and having to conform to the irritating pattern of the mute R.H.A. subaltern were restraints that I began to find oppressive. But a totally unexpected relief was at hand in the shape of an order that appeared one day inviting gunner subalterns to volunteer for duty as observers with the Royal Flying Corps. The main part of the work being done by the R.F.C. at that time was spotting and ranging for the artillery, and apparently it was thought that we gunners would make the best observers.

In 1912 after I had first seen airplanes being tested at Farnborough (a few weeks after the formation of the Royal Flying Corps) I had often thought about the adventure that was to be found in flying, and I had read about the use that had been made of planes in the war that broke out a few months later in the Balkans. But even by 1914, it was still for me a most intriguing discovery to find that airplanes were being used over the Western Front.

When I got to France and up to the Front I began to see more of the aircraft of the R.F.C. They flew from fields quite near our ammunition dump, and I used to watch them as they went out over the lines and were shot at by the enemy antiaircraft gunners. It all seemed to me to be very exciting. In a way I think that I sensed then what Walter Raleigh was later to express so admirably when he wrote: "Those who were privileged to watch the performance of our flying men in the war know that there is developed in them a temper not less remarkable and not less worthy of cultivation—the temper of the air. War in the air demands a quickness of thought and nerve greater than is exacted by any other kind of war. It is a deadly and gallant tournament."

At the time I received the notice about the Flying Corps, my work in the Ammunition Column could never have been described as a tournament. It had settled down into a dull routine of hauling our meager supplies of shells up to the batteries and then returning to the back areas; and even if a few shells were flung at us now and again as we were going up or returning, it was not a particularly exciting business. Apart from that, my day was occupied with looking after the horses—and too many of them, poor brutes, were dying from exposure. There was little that I could do to help them, although I did try to build up some sort of hard standing for them out of rubble; but it was all a pretty hopeless effort, and I was finding that the life of a gunner subaltern was becoming a pretty depressing business.

The possibility that was now presented of being able to fly had in it the greatest fascination, and as I watched those who were lucky enough to be doing it that fascination soon became something akin to a passion. What with the tyranny of my commanding officer and the mud and the misery of the animals, and the discomfort of being literally stuck on the ground, I came to feel that aviation—even if I was only an observer—was the life for me. I put in an application for a transfer to the Royal Flying Corps, and since the only good feature about my relationship with my C.O. was his readiness to see the back of me, I doubt if any such application was ever approved quicker than that one.

By then I had been in France just under two months, and in a surprisingly short time I received orders to report for duty with No. 2 Squadron, Royal Flying Corps, which was operating from a field near Merville, alongside the River Lys about three or four miles from Estaires.

On Christmas Eve, a German aircraft dropped a small bomb which exploded without doing any damage in a garden in Dover: the first time England was ever subjected to a raid from the air. A few hours after that, on Boxing Day, 1914, three days after my twenty-first birthday, I mounted my treasured charger Tommy and in company with my groom I rode across the flat, highly cultivated country which surrounds the River Lys and reported for duty at the airfield near Merville.

My orders were for an attachment to the R.F.C. for three weeks, to see if I liked it and if they liked me sufficiently for the change to be made a permanent one—that is, for the duration of the war. I cannot believe that there are many Air Force officers, certainly not of the most senior rank, who can say that they first reported at a squadron headquarters for duty mounted on a charger and accompanied by a groom. I sent my groom back with Tommy to my old unit; that was the last that I was ever to see of either of them.

The only adverse criticism that I received from anybody on the step I had taken in joining the Royal Flying Corps came from my mother. In a letter to me she wrote: "You must be mad."

3 / Air Observer

JUST OVER fifty years have passed since the Royal Flying Corps was formed in the spring of 1912. Of all that has since been written on the early development of flying, and about the growth of the Air Force in particular, I have found of greatest interest the superb introduction which the distinguished writer Sir Walter Raleigh contributed to *The War in the Air,* the account of the work done by the air forces of the Commonwealth in the First World War. It was published in 1922, almost immediately after the end of that war; and in speaking of the emergence of flying Raleigh said: "When a nation is fighting for its life, money and energy are expended without check, and it may be doubted whether in the whole history of mankind any art in its infant stage has been so magnificently supported and advanced by war as the art of flying was supported and advanced by the greatest war of all."

I was able to make my start in flying at a time when it was still in its infancy—the Royal Flying Corps had been in existence only just over two and a half years—and at a stage when experiments were being made with the blending of the art and the science under the great stimulation of that war. Until shortly before the war, the general feeling on the part of the crusty Service diehards had been that these wretched airplanes could not possibly be of any use to the armed forces. For one thing, the noise frightened the horses. But despite that, the Army had been forced to explore the possibilities of aviation, and there was formed in the spring of 1911, after some early experiments at an airfield at Larkhall, on Salisbury Plain, a unit that was known as the Air Battalion of the Royal Engineers. This was made up of two companies: No. 1, working with airships and balloons; and No. 2, flying airplanes. When the Royal Flying Corps was established a year later these two companies, still filling the same roles, became No. 1 and No. 2 Squadrons, R.F.C. (the latter was formed at Farnborough only a few weeks before I first went there as a schoolboy).

When the war broke out in 1914, the Royal Flying Corps consisted of four squadrons made up of just over sixty airplanes; but it was ready to proceed immediately overseas. The Royal Naval Air Service had a strength of thirty-nine airplanes, fifty-two seaplanes, and seven airships. We were lucky to have had that many aircraft, because up to that time the Government had shown an astonishing reluctance to provide the money needed for any developments in flying. It was only through the enthusiasm of a small band of individualists—many of whom were civilians who learned to fly at their own expense—that we had any appreciable air service upon which the Army could rely.

"The Germans, who as a people fall easy victims to agreeable sentiment, indulged extravagant hopes from war in the air," Walter Raleigh commented. "The English, who are less excitable, were comparatively slow as a nation to appreciate the importance of the new invention." A comment was even made in one official report that up to the end of the year 1911 "we stood to gain nothing by forcing a means of warfare which tended to reduce the value of our insular position and the protection of our sea-power."

This lack of vision apparently caused the authorities to overlook altogether the fact that with the first flight across the Channel from France to England—made by the Frenchman Louis Blériot in the year 1909—our so-called insularity had come to an end. On the other hand, foresight was possibly obscured by the unshakable belief that prevailed in the minds of all Englishmen that our defense rested in the strength of our formidable Royal Navy.

But the freely expressed aims and ambitions that constituted the German menace finally did make an impact on the official mind; and some effort was directed in the months immediately preceding the outbreak of war in 1914 to redress the balance in this new and entirely unexplored field of air power. The impetus that the war gave to this effort is revealed in the way in which the air services expanded. By the time that it ended with the Armistice in 1918, the Royal Air Force on the Western Front alone consisted of 99 squadrons, and the total number of airplanes and seaplanes in the Service was 22,647. Moreover, they were aircraft of far greater power and efficiency than the machines of 1914. In 1918 the R.A.F. could justly claim that it had become "the largest and the strongest of the air forces in the world."

By the time the Royal Flying Corps set off for France, in the middle of August, 1914, No. 2 Squadron had already left the nest at Farnborough (the first to do so). It was flying from a new airdrome at Montrose, in Scotland. The squadron flew south, and on the morning of August 13 one of its airplanes was the first British aircraft ever to land in France on the business of war. A B.E.2b piloted by Lieutenant H. D. Harvey-Kelly took off from Dover, flew across the Channel, and at twenty minutes past eight landed in a field near Amiens.

The sole purpose of the Royal Flying Corps at that time was reconnaissance, with the pilots and the observers working as the eyes of the Army. The first aerial reconnaissance ever performed by the R.F.C.— made on August 19, 1914—was flown by Captain P. B. Joubert de la Ferté, of No. 3 Squadron, and Lieutenant G. W. Mapplebeck, of No. 4 Squadron. The latter was killed a year or so later; the former, a prewar regular officer in the Royal Field Artillery who had transferred to the R.F.C. in 1913, became well known in the Second World War as an air chief marshal and commander-in-chief of Coastal Command.

During the first weeks in France, the squadrons of the R.F.C. were constantly on the move. There was an almost daily change of airfields during the retreat from Mons and the fluid state of the fighting after that. Later, with the establishing of a Front and the drawing up of opposing lines of trenches, the squadrons were able to settle down to finding the most suitable positions behind that Front from which to operate. Commenting on those first days in France and the constant moves that were made, Philip Joubert has said: "The extraordinary part was the contrasts that one experienced from day to day, one night sleeping under a hedge in a thunderstorm; the next in a comfortable private house; the third in the most modern type of hotel with every luxury and convenience."

Right from the beginning it was apparent that, in addition to the war itself, there was another serious hazard in the flying our pilots were going to have to do in France. The prevailing winds blew from the west, and they were to be a severe handicap to us throughout the war. Although they made it easy enough for us to fly over to the enemy, they all too often made it difficult for us, in our low-powered aircraft, to get back. This was of importance even in those early days, because there had already occurred the first indications of what lay ahead: incidents had occurred that were to lead to actual fighting in the air.

One of the early birds in the Royal Flying Corps was a man named Louis Strange. He had learned to fly as a civilian before the war, and in the course of time he was to make quite a name for himself as a pilot in both world wars. Strange gave a lot of thought to fighting in the air, and he was one of the first to mount in his aircraft a primitive Henri Farman, a Lewis machine gun which his observer could use, with some difficulty, for attack as well as defense. Ten days after their arrival in France the R.F.C. were subjected to the indignity—described by Strange as "wild excitement"—of watching the first German airplane ever to fly over a British airfield. Two of our machines took off in an attempt to engage the enemy with hand grenades and bombs; and Strange and his observer followed them in the aircraft fitted with the Lewis gun. But they could get no higher than 3,500 feet, and the German went on flying unmolested at about 5,000 feet. When Strange landed he was given instructions to discard the Lewis gun and the mounting that he had devised, and his observer was told that from then on he would have to make do with a rifle.

"I was bitterly disappointed," Strange has said, "and I was ready to back my opinion to any money that before long all aircraft on both sides would carry machine guns." Fortunately this belief in the future of the machine gun in the air was shared by other pilots and observers, even if authority was inclined at first to frown upon it. In spite of orders they persisted in their efforts to find the most effective way of mounting guns in an aircraft.

Toward the end of that first November of the war, Strange became involved in an affair which Walter Raleigh offered in the official history as an illustration of "how the air work of the Germans may sometimes have been impeded by a certain defect of sympathy in the German officer class." It was the odd custom in the German air force—a custom which, I believe, was still observed in the second war—for the observers to be in command of the aircraft, and quite often these observers were officers and the pilots were noncommissioned officers.

Just after the First Battle of Ypres, Louis Strange and his observer, using that Lewis gun of theirs, shot down a German two-seater. Strange landed and went to examine the crashed enemy aircraft. He found that although the machine had about twenty bullet holes it was otherwise undamaged. He then listened with astonishment to the story, told him by some soldiers, of what had happened after the aircraft landed. The observer was an officer in the Prussian Guards, and he had thought at first that his pilot, a noncommissioned officer, was wounded. But when he found, after they were safely on the ground, that the pilot was quite uninjured and had merely lost his nerve, he flew into a rage, broke away from his captors, knocked the pilot down, and began kicking him savagely.

"If ever a collection of incidents shall be made, under the title

'How the War was Lost and Won,' to illustrate the causes of things," Walter Raleigh commented, "this little drama will deserve a place in it."

There was never any lack of ingenuity among the pilots of those early days, and one stunt that was tried out I had good reason to remember during the time I served as a commander-in-chief of Fighter Command in the Second World War. In the retreat from Mons, one of the pilots of No. 3 Squadron conceived the idea of dangling a hand grenade from a long piece of cable in front of an enemy aircraft, trying to get it to explode when the grenade became entangled in the propeller of the other machine. It was an idea that smacked all too strongly of the flavor that I came to know later of some of the schemes put forward in all seriousness during the second war by Professor Lindemann with the backing of Winston Churchill.

Heavy demands were soon made on the ingenuity of the designers and the engineers at home because, for all the early opposition to the use of machine guns in the air, it did not take long for those at R.F.C. Headquarters in France to realize that they needed machines that could fight as well as fly. The Germans were pressing hard on the heels of their foresight in building up their air arm before the war, whereas we in England still had no airplane engine industry worth mentioning, and only a handful of people who understood airplane design. There was a desperate need for an aircraft industry which could be rapidly developed and expanded by mass production.

This was a challenge of the kind that is only too familiar to the British. That we are so slow in getting off the mark is a fault we have always recognized. But although we seem to do so little about correcting that fault, we are a curiously formidable people once we are challenged. We are also lucky in always being blessed with a select few who possess highly original minds. Under the spur of necessity, there was developed in Britain not so very long after the war broke out an effective and powerful aircraft industry, as well as a great plan for training men for the air service: pilots, observers, mechanics of all kinds, and men of the many and varied trades called for in the new Service.

Very soon after joining the Royal Flying Corps, I discovered that there were many others who had felt as I had about the possibility of the war being over before we would have a chance to take a good crack at the enemy. It was even recorded that members of the squadron to which I was reporting for duty had locked and sealed the doors in their quarters at Montrose (Scotland), with notices attached stating that nothing was to be touched until they returned.

After the rigid discipline that I had known in the Royal Horse Artillery, the free and easy way in which things were done in the R.F.C. was very much to my liking. Although most of the pilots were regular Army officers—there were a few former civilians belonging to the R.F.C. Special Reserve—they were all men of a different breed from those I had become accustomed to since joining the artillery. I was now in the company of individualists, some of whom, I was soon to find, could even be regarded eccentric if not downright crazy. All that, in itself, held for me a distinct attraction. It also appeared that few of them had any great opinion of the Army and its way of life. Many of them had been serving in the squadron for some time—since well before the outbreak of war—and all the aircraft with which the squadron was equipped were of quite early vintage. Of the three flights in the squadron, two were equipped with B.E.2a's and B.E.2b's, and one with the R.E.5.

In his autobiography, *R.F.C., H.Q., 1914–1918,* Maurice Baring recorded that on February 5, 1915, he spent a night with No. 2 Squadron. He mentioned one of the songs that we sang in which there was the line: "It's a long way to 8000." What Baring did not mention was the point of that song, which was an oblique reference to the indifferent climbing powers of our aircraft of those days. Our engines, all said and done, were of only seventy horsepower, and it took us a long time to get up to a reasonable height—more often than not over an hour of hard climbing—and with some of the more sorely tried of our airplanes we could not get there at all.

We always tried to get as high as we could before crossing the lines in order to limit the effectiveness of "archie," as we all derisively called the enemy antiaircraft fire. Baring recorded in his diary as early as a month after the outbreak of war that the pilots in No. 5 Squadron called the antiaircraft gun (there seemed to be only one which gave them trouble in those days) "Archibald." I have always understood that they had adopted the name from a popular song, the key line of which was "Archibald . . . certainly not!" In the first war the word "archie" was used as freely and was as full of meaning as "flak" in the second war.

"We had a good deal of music after dinner," Maurice Baring wrote of that visit, "and the pilots sang." One of the most amusing

of my first impressions of life in the mess in the Royal Flying
Corps was of this cheerful readiness to gather around and give
voice to songs about flying. It was another of the aspects of the
laying down of the tradition, and our songs became an interesting
and often amusing expression of our way of life.

The most famous of all the Flying Corps songs was "The Bold
Aviator," sometimes known as "The Dying Airman," and it is a
perfect example of the humor that was developing in the Flying
Corps. It was also the oldest of our songs, having come into
existence with the forming of the R.F.C. I came to know it first
during our lighter moments in the No. 2 Squadron mess at Merville. Throughout the first war it was sung by all ranks on every
occasion.

There are several versions of the song, but the one that I
remember best started off with:

> *The Young Aviator lay dying,*
> *And as in the hangar he lay, he lay,*
> *To the mechanics who round him were standing*
> *These last parting words he did say:*

And then would come the famous chorus which even now has the
power to evoke the warmest memories of those early days of my
life in France with the Royal Flying Corps. Vigorously we would
bawl:

> *Take the cylinders out of my kidneys*
> *The connecting rod out of my brain, my brain,*
> *From the small of my back take the camshaft,*
> *And assemble the engine again.*

No account of the activities of the Flying Corps during the First
World War would be complete without some mention from time to
time of Maurice Baring. He had become a distinguished writer and
journalist long before the war broke out; and in the most casual
and delightful way he found himself in uniform and sent out right
at the very beginning as a staff officer and A.D.C. to General Sir
David Henderson, who first commanded the R.F.C. in France. A
plumpish, bald-headed, middle-aged man of the intellectual type
that one would never have associated with any of the fighting
services, and certainly not with the air service, Baring had an
endearing manner all his own, and through that and his under-

standing of us he was to become one of the great characters of the
R.F.C.

The aircraft used by the flight in No. 2 Squadron in which I was
to serve were the B.E.2a and B.E.2b. Originally designed and built
as early as 1911, they evolved from a great deal of experimental
work and were the first of the practical machines supplied to the
Royal Flying Corps. The initials B.E. were a memorial to the first
man to fly the English Channel, standing for Blériot Experimental.
This two-seater biplane became the most famous of all the early
aircraft designed by the Royal Aircraft Factory at Farnborough.

As far back as August, 1912, Geoffrey de Havilland, who had
had a big hand in the design of the B.E., created a British record
by flying one to the unheard-of height of just over 10,500 feet,
taking an hour and twenty minutes to do it. His passenger on that
occasion was Major Frederick Sykes, later to become a Chief of
the Air Staff. In describing the flight in his book *From Many
Angles,* published in 1942, Sykes pays an agreeable tribute, even
truer today than when it was written, to the man who was his pilot
on that flight thirty years before. "It is difficult to estimate the debt
which British aviation owes to Captain Geoffrey de Havilland," he
wrote. "From early days until now he has never ceased his successful efforts for aeronautical progress. He is the most modest and
likeable of men, and . . . he deserves all the success which he
has achieved."

One of the pilots in No. 2 Squadron when I joined it at the end
of 1914 was Geoffrey de Havilland's brother, Hereward. He had
been a test pilot at Farnborough before the war; and after a lifetime spent in aviation he retired only a few years ago from the De
Havilland Aircraft Company. Of our three Flight Commanders, one
was R. B. (Barry) Martyn, formerly of the Wiltshire Regiment.
Martyn was a small, lively man, always laughing and treating everything as a great joke. Thirty years later, in the Second World War,
he served as a controller at an airfield in Coastal Command during
the time that I was commander-in-chief. But the outstanding pilot
in the squadron was undoubtedly H. D. Harvey-Kelly. With fair
hair topping a rubicund complexion, he was one of the most
likeable of men, and he was already famous for his great sense of
humor and his lighthearted approach toward everything he ever
did. Even in the zestful company of the Flying Corps he was a
noted individualist.

Of all those pioneers in flying who contributed to the rugged
strength of the squadron, the man who made the strongest impres-

sion on me, and who was to exert a great influence in my life, was Wilfrid Freeman. He was a slim, dark, handsome man with an attractively quizzical expression on his face, very intelligent and with a nicely cynical turn of humor. I quickly formed a great liking for him, and he was to become one of my closest friends right up until the time of his death. A regular soldier who had started his career in the Manchester Regiment, Freeman learned to fly in 1912 at his own expense at a flying school in France. He had then volunteered for service with the Royal Flying Corps. It was not until many years later that I learned that he had loathed the life in the Army; but I can say from my own knowledge of him that he found his niche in the Royal Air Force. Eventually he became one of our most distinguished air chief marshals.

There is on record an account—described as "a notable adventure"—of the way in which Wilfrid Freeman and another of the pilots of No. 2 Squadron very nearly put "paid" to their careers less than a month after their arrival in France. It was one of the first of the exploits in which so many of the air crews of the Air Force, in both world wars, were later forced to indulge. During a reconnaissance flight together in the same airplane their machine developed trouble in the tail unit, and they had to land in a small field surrounded by enemy troops. Although the aircraft was badly broken in the landing they clambered safely out of the wreckage and dashed off into the woods.

After staying in hiding in the trees until it was dark, our two heroes sneaked stealthily by night through the scattered Germans —there were then no established lines—swam a river, dried out their clothes in a farmhouse, and then continued on their way across country. By the time they eventually got safely back to the squadron, after an absence of over two days, they were feeling rather pleased with themselves; but their self-esteem was quickly deflated when they were sharply reminded by their commanding officer that pilots were not to fly together in the same aircraft unless they were ordered to do so. If that escapade had occurred only a few weeks later, when the front lines had become established and impenetrable, they probably would have wound up as prisoners-of-war.

One of the reasons why the Royal Air Force has always offered encouragement to a certain quality of individuality is to be found in the attraction that flying had in those early days for men whose outlook on life was tinged with an exceptional independence. By the time I joined the R.F.C. it was already commanded by men who, while still being in the Army, had purposely sought the freedom of the air. In the R.F.C. they found themselves, as well as a way of life.

No. 2 Squadron was in one of the three wings that comprised the Royal Flying Corps, and our wing commander was Lieutenant-Colonel H. M. Trenchard, formerly of the Royal Scots Fusiliers. A tall, gaunt man with a thatch of unruly hair and a largish tooth-brush mustache, he was already forty-one years of age when he learned to fly—only two or three years before; and he was that great man who was to become the first Marshal of the Royal Air Force and the first Viscount Trenchard. The lieutenant-colonels commanding the other wings were C. J. Burke, formerly of the Irish Regiment and known popularly as "Pregnant Percy," and H. R. M. Brooke-Popham, who had been in the Oxfordshire and Buckinghamshire Light Infantry. Burke was later killed in the front lines after he had insisted upon serving again for a while with the Infantry. Brooke-Popham eventually became very well known as an air chief marshal.

There were others already in the R.F.C. who were also to become in time famous leaders. In the beginning it was only a small branch of the Army, and nearly all those who were in it were known to one another. A flight commander in what was known as "the wireless squadron"—the name itself contained a curious prophecy of what lay ahead for him—was a captain who had started his career in the Royal Garrison Artillery. Eventually he became an air chief marshal who won everlasting fame as the commander-in-chief of Fighter Command during the Battle of Britain in 1940. It was that great achievement which led to his becoming the first Lord Dowding of Bentley Priory, his title so appropriately created from the name of the place which is still the headquarters of Fighter Command. In command of one of the new squadrons of the R.F.C. being formed at home was a Major Newall who had been in the Army in India, where he had first come to know Dowding. He became Chief of the Air Staff at the beginning of the Second World War, a Marshal of the Royal Air Force, and the first Lord Newall.

These were some of the men who paved the way, and others of an adventurous bent followed them. Of the men my own age who later joined the R.F.C. and became well-known senior officers in the Service, Arthur Harris was a bugler with the 1st Rhodesian Regiment, serving during those first months of the war in German West Africa. He eventually became Marshal of the Royal Air Force Sir Arthur Harris, of Bomber Command fame. Arthur

Tedder had done well at Cambridge University—of which he is now Chancellor—and he was serving in the Colonial Civil Service in Fiji when war broke out. Tedder tried without success to join the Australian Army, so he returned to England and was commissioned in the Dorsetshire Regiment. At the end of the Second World War he also became a Chief of the Air Staff and a Marshal of the Royal Air Force: the first Lord Tedder.

Only a little older than I am, the famous "Peter" Portal was up at Oxford as an undergraduate at Christ Church at the same time I was at Lincoln. In 1914 he had been so eager to get into the thick of things that he had not waited for a commission. On the outbreak of war he had joined the Royal Engineers in the ranks; although he knew nothing about motorcycles, which he was to ride, he was sent out to France almost immediately as a dispatch rider. During that first winter he was commissioned while serving in France, and he became a signals officer in the R.E's. In 1915 he transferred to the R.F.C. as an observer. He learned to fly, and he soon became one of the finest reconnaissance pilots and squadron commanders on the Western Front. During the Second World War he was our distinguished Chief of the Air Staff and one of the greatest of our war leaders: a Marshal of the Royal Air Force and the first Viscount Portal.

There were others who were on their way to the war from various parts of the Empire. Keith Park was on a troop ship from New Zealand. He was to serve in the field artillery at Gallipoli as an N.C.O., and he was commissioned while still there and sent to France. Despite the serious wounds he received while fighting as a gunner on the Somme, he learned to fly and eventually became a very well-known pilot in France. Later he shared with Dowding the honors of the Battle of Britain, and today he is known as Air Chief Marshal Sir Keith Park.

The airfield we used on the outskirts of the village of Merville was nothing more than a large grass field about four hundred yards across. It was situated in the dull, flat countryside between the River Lys, which it bordered, and the Forest of Nieppe, both of which were to become well-known landmarks for airmen. Several small canvas hangars, each large enough to house one aircraft, stood along one side of the field; but they seemed to have a habit of blowing down whenever there was a high wind. Our squadron headquarters was in a farmhouse on another side of the field, with rooms allotted to each of the three flights. During the day we used that accommodation as a place to sit and wait for instructions and have our lunch; and at night we returned to the squadron mess and billets in the village.

The work of the squadron during that first winter of the war was to assist the 4th Corps of the First Army, which was commanded by General Sir Douglas Haig and entrenched on the part of the Front that stretched south from Armentières to Festubert. It was a flat and rather drab and uninteresting part of the country, with the hillier parts of Messines Ridge and the Ypres Salient to the north, and the innumerable mounds of the tippings from the coal mines of the area around Loos and Lens to the south. Although there were already indications of the fighting that was taking place, the countryside had not yet been clawed into the state of mangled desolation that it was to become only a few months later. Our task was to observe and photograph through daily reconnaissance the whole of the area behind the German lines facing us and as far east as Lille. We were also constantly at work helping to direct the fire of the heavy batteries of the 4th Corps by watching from the air and signaling back the results.

For some odd reason there was only a very sketchy definition of the roll of observer at the time I joined the R.F.C., and we were given extraordinarily little training in the work that we were to do. Efforts had been made before the war to decide on some way of training observers, but up until shortly before I joined the squadron there was no definite assignment of any particular personnel to observing duties. The work had been carried out either by the actual pilot of the machine or by another pilot sent along as a passenger, or even on occasion by any one of the noncommissioned officers who could be spared from his other work. An instance of this occurred a few days after the arrival of the R.F.C. in France. It fell to the lot of the disciplinary sergeant-major of No. 2 Squadron, D. S. Jillings by name, to go off on patrol as an observer. He and his pilot ran into heavy rifle and machine-gun fire from the ground, and Jillings was wounded in the buttock, thus achieving the dubious honor of being the first British airman to be wounded in the air. "This casualty seemed to bring the German armies nearer than a dozen unmolested reconnaissance could have done," the official historian recorded. In the second war Jillings was to serve as a wing commander on my staff during the time I was at Fighter Command.

It was because of the haphazard way in which men of all ranks and trades were being used as observers that more definite plans for this work were formulated and a request was sent out for gunner subalterns to act as observers. But even then, all our training had to be done right on the job with the squadrons. For our work with the artillery, there had just been introduced a system of signaling between the ground and the aircraft with an electric lamp similar to the one which later became so well known as the Aldis lamp. Wireless had been brought into use in aircraft on the Front during the Battle of the Aisne, nearly four months before; but that was work for the more knowledgeable specialists. Since I was to be a straightforward observer, with the main job of spotting for the artillery, the first thing I had to do was to learn to signal in Morse code with the electric lamp.

My classroom at the airfield was a large barn alongside the farmhouse, and in this I sat on a pile of straw, gassed by the stench from the usual farmyard midden just outside, and freezing from the cold. In a letter to my father I made a crisp reference to the weather we were having at that time. "It is abominable," I wrote. "Most days clouds cover the skies which not only make observing impossible but also send down rain and snow until our landing ground is flooded and it is almost impossible to bring a machine safely to earth."

There were also occasions when the high winds stopped all flying because such was the speed of our aircraft—sixty to seventy miles an hour—that when we tried to fly into the teeth of the wind we found ourselves standing still. During a particularly bad storm one night the R.F.C., with few enough airplanes as it was, had thirty machines wrecked, sixteen of them beyond repair, and No. 3 Squadron was completely out of action for several days.

I sat in that barn for what seemed to be days on end learning the Morse code and the use of the lamp; then one day my commanding officer casually told me that I was to go off with Barry Martyn as his observer. We made a reconnaissance flight over the front lines in the direction of Lille. It was actually the first time that I had ever flown in an airplane, and I had practically no idea at all where we were from the time that we took off until the time that we landed. Not being able to recognize the features on the ground—I had never even seen what the ground looked like from the air before—meant that so far as my contribution to the reconnaissance was concerned I was worthless.

By the time we landed back at Merville I felt that I had made a complete hash of things. But Barry Martyn, in his kindly way, came to my rescue, and he filled in the reconnaissance report for me and saved me from complete disgrace. All that really came out of that flight is the claim I can make that the first time that I ever flew in an airplane was as an observer on an operational war patrol under pretty heavy antiaircraft fire. It was at least a quick introduction to the work that I was to do, and from that time on I did a great deal of flying. I was able to teach myself how to read a map from the air and how to find my way around, and so, largely through trial and error, I became more proficient as an observer.

Our two-seater B.E.2a's and b's were sturdy biplanes. Even though they were primitive enough, they at least had the promise of the shape that airplanes were to take in the very near future. The pilot sat in the back seat and the observer in the front, which was an inconvenient and clumsy arrangement and the wrong way around, and we would fly over the batteries with which we were to work at a height of between three and four thousand feet. Calling them up by signaling with the lamp, which was always a struggle for the observer because he had to manipulate a cumbersome contraption in the full blast from the propeller, we would let them know we were ready to go to work, and we would continue signaling to them the results from the shells which they were flinging over, with any corrections that were needed. We would fly backward and forward between the batteries and the targets, and the whole business was really quite effective so long as we had reasonably good visibility.

I had not been with the squadron very long before it became known through casual gossip that in my schooldays I had been interested in photography. Such was the way things were done in those early days that I promptly found myself appointed the squadron specialist. "My slight knowledge of photography has proved of immense use," I wrote to my father. "Today I got several snapshots of German trenches on our front from a height of five thousand feet." It sounds quaint now to refer to that kind of photography as taking "snapshots," and I know that it will cause the later photographic reconnaissance experts to smile a little wryly; but it does at least indicate to what extent we were pioneers in this field.

In the official history there is a reference to these early efforts of ours in photography which states: "Wing Commander W. S. Douglas, then an observer in No. 2 Squadron, tells how he was appointed air photographer to his unit because he had had a camera as a boy. He cut a rectangular hole in the bottom of his cockpit in a B.E.2a, and his practice, when the area to be photographed nearly filled the aperture, was to push his camera through the hole and take his snapshot. 'This procedure,' he says, 'was not too easy in the cramped space available, especially as the weather was cold and bulky flying kit a necessity. Each plate had to be changed by hand, and I spoilt many plates by clumsy handling with frozen fingers. A proportion of the photographs, however, were successful.' "

This performance invariably led to my becoming nearly frozen because the draught that came up through the hole in the floor was intensely cold and it completely numbed my hands and feet. But in spite of that I did manage to get quite a good coverage of the trench system on our corps front; and it was through this particular work that I first came into personal contact with our wing commander, Lieutenant-Colonel Trenchard. Because of the tone of his voice he was already known by the nickname of "Boom."

The photographic officer in No. 3 Squadron, the one next in the line to the south of us, was another observer by the name of C. C. Darley. He was a great enthusiast in his work, and he had been able to get some good photographs. Whenever Trenchard visited our squadron he would pull out of his pocket a bunch of Darley's photographs which he would show to me with encomiums, apparently believing that he was inciting me to better efforts. But Darley and I discovered, in talking with each other, that Trenchard used to do the same thing the other way around on his visits to No. 3 Squadron, showing Darley my best efforts, and we agreed that the old boy was only wasting his time.

I was soon flying almost every day and sometimes twice a day, and in a letter to my father I commented: "At present we see very few German machines: I expect they are reserving themselves for the spring, especially as the English pilots are, owing to the climate in which they are trained, more skillful than any other nation in battling against these gusty winds that we are getting now."

Actual fighting between aircraft in the air at the beginning of 1915 was still a rare event. Only slight importance was attached to air fighting at that time because one's chance of ever shooting down a German machine was very slight. This meant that the personal danger to the pilots and observers in an aerial combat was equally small. The German antiaircraft fire loomed much larger in our thoughts as a danger than any threat that might come from the airplanes of the enemy.

Our armament in the air was largely a matter of personal choice, and it consisted of either a Colt automatic or a cavalry carbine. But even the weight of these weapons proved at times to be a nuisance. In the official history there is an account that I put on record of the first time I ever came across a German machine at close quarters in the air. I was flying that day with Harvey-Kelly, and the story of what happened then and immediately afterward reads now, over fifty years later, as a human and personal story rather than a scientific report. In it I stated:

"Both the pilot and myself were completely unarmed. Our machine had not been climbing well, and as I was considered somewhat heavy for an observer, Harvey-Kelly told me to leave behind all unnecessary gear. I therefore left behind my carbine and ammunition. We were taking photographs of the trench system to the north of Neuve Chapelle when I suddenly espied a German two-seater about a hundred yards away and just below us. The German observer did not appear to be shooting at us. There was nothing to be done. We waved a hand to the enemy and proceeded with our task. The enemy did likewise. At the time this did not appear to me in any way ridiculous—there is a bond of sympathy between all who fly, even between enemies. But afterwards just for safety's sake I always carried a carbine with me in the air. In the ensuing two or three months I had an occasional shot at a German machine. But these encounters can hardly be dignified with the name of 'fights.' If we saw an enemy machine nearby, we would fly over towards it, and fire at it some half-dozen rounds. We scarcely expected to shoot the enemy down; but it was a pleasant break in the monotony of reconnaissance and artillery observation. I remember being surprised one day to hear that an observer of another squadron (his name, Lascelles, sticks in my memory to this day, though I never met him), had shot down a German machine in our lines with a rifle."

The first time I began to appreciate the potentialities of air fighting was when we started experimenting, as those in the other squadrons were doing, with the mounting of a Lewis gun at the back of the observer's seat. This gave the observer a limited opportunity to fire backward, over the pilot's head. The aircraft with which this was done was the new B.E.2c, which was the first of the B.E.s to have control through ailerons instead of through the warping of the wings. It also had a new type of engine, of ninety horsepower.

I was very eager to try my hand with that gun, and for my first patrol with it in the new aircraft I went off with my flight commander on a photographic reconnaissance. We ran into a German two-seater, and my pilot slipped into a convenient position for me to open fire. Facing backward, I started blazing away over the top of his head. It is amusing now to recall that one had to be ahead of one's target and flying away from it before one could fire back at it; but at the time I was far from amused. In my eagerness I must have opened fire too soon and at much too great a range because the enemy merely turned away quite unharmed and went about his business. I was very disappointed and even somewhat surprised at my lack of success. But that was not to be wondered at because I knew very little about the mechanism of the Lewis gun and I had only the haziest of ideas about the deflection needed to allow for the relative speeds and positions of the two aircraft. That in itself was an aspect of fighting in the air which had not yet been developed or taught.

By this time I was writing to my father to say: "I enjoy flying immensely, and I hope to get taken on as a permanent observer." Although my attachment to the R.F.C. in the first place had been for a period of three weeks, even after nearly six weeks I was explaining in another letter to my father that "I hope to be wearing the forage cap soon." That was a reference to the cap worn in the R.F.C. which we all considered to be a very smart piece of headgear. "It is not absolutely settled yet whether I stay on here as an observer or not," I added. "My application has gone through to G.H.Q., but has stuck there for a time." Shortly after that I was informed that my application had been approved, and so my transfer to the Royal Flying Corps was completed.

Activity on our part of the Western Front had been fairly quiet after the First Battle of Ypres had died down with the onset of winter; but with the approach of the spring of 1915 there came, early in March, a renewal in the more intensive fighting. The First Army attacked on our part of the line at Neuve Chapelle, a small, dull village that was scarcely more than a cluster of a few houses. Three weeks later the Second Army, to the north of us, launched an attack on a huge artificial mound that had been built up years before through the dumping of vast quantities of earth from a railway cutting nearby. This great mound was in the southern part of the Ypres Salient, and it was to become well known as Hill 60. Then, in the third week of April, there came the Second Battle of Ypres. This time the Germans attacked, and for the first time in the war they made use of poison gas.

The struggle in the Ypres Salient was still going on when another offensive was launched by us on our part of the Front with the battles known as Aubers Ridge and Festubert—which were really continuations of the attack on Neuve Chapelle. We flew a great deal in both these battles, but so far as I could see from the air, not a great deal was achieved. The war merely seemed to sink deeper into the ground.

While two of the flights of our squadron were engaged in reconnaissance and photography the third flight specialized in working
with wireless, which, although primitive in its design, was capable
of some quite remarkable results. Wilfrid Freeman was the second
in command of this flight, and while the Battle of Neuve Chapelle
was going on he asked me one day if I would like to go with him
on a reconnaissance over the front line. I jumped at the chance.
That was the first occasion on which Freeman and I worked
together, and it was the beginning of our long friendship. For the
part that he played as a pilot during that battle Freeman received
one of the first of the Military Crosses awarded to members of the
Royal Flying Corps.

Our work flying over the Front at Neuve Chapelle enabled us to
take yet another important step forward. From the photographs
that we were able to get with cameras specially designed for us—at
the instigation of a group of enthusiastic specialists, one of whom
was our wing photographic officer, who was later to become Lord
Brabazon of Tara—were made the first maps of the enemy trench
systems. These were used in the battle, and it was the first time that
a British army was able to go into action with what was described
as "a picture of the enemy's hidden defenses."

Most of the flying that I did during that battle was with
Hereward de Havilland, observing the results of the artillery
barrages "in which," to quote from Maurice Baring, "more shells
were fired than during the whole of the South African War." On
one occasion de Havilland and I were quite happily at work out
over the enemy lines watching with satisfaction the result of our
barrage when suddenly he throttled back the engine. In the silence
that followed we could both hear a series of curious rumbling
noises which neither of us could understand at first. Suddenly it
dawned upon us that these noises were being caused by the shells,
our own shells, as they hurtled past us, too rapidly to be seen, on
their way to their targets. We were obviously sitting right in their
path, so we wasted no time in getting out of that area.

When we spoke to some of the others about what we had
experienced, we learned that quite a number of our aircraft and
crews were being hit by the shells of our own barrages—a threat to
our safety that we had not counted on. It only added to the ever-
present hazard from the archie of the enemy guns, about which I
wrote to my father at this time saying: "The flying is very pleasant,
except for the anti-aircraft guns, which sometimes get too close to

be pleasant. They are rather trying as one feels so terribly obvious in midair, so very easy to hit."

In addition to spotting for the artillery and photographic reconnaissance we were also attempting to develop further our efforts, rudimentary though they were, at bombing from the air; and in the course of this work one of our pilots performed a feat that, because I was closely and personally connected with it, stamped itself indelibly on my mind. It could so easily have led to my own death, and I still wonder about what a close shave I had, and how I was stopped from doing something that I badly wanted to do by the reaching out of the curious hand of chance.

By late April we were receiving more and more detailed orders to bomb targets behind the enemy lines. I was flying quite a lot by then with a pilot by the name of W. B. Rhodes-Moorhouse. A small, slight, sandy-haired man of extraordinary vitality, he was one of the pioneers of flying in England, and he had already been a pilot for two years before he qualified for his certificate as early as 1911. He was a member of the Royal Flying Corps Special Reserve.

During the afternoon of April 26 the squadron received instructions to bomb Courtrai, which was well behind the German lines, in order to disrupt the movement of enemy troops to the area of the Ypres Salient. Rhodes-Moorhouse was detailed to the task, and he realized that with his B.E.2a he would just be able to carry a bomb of one hundred pounds. A load as heavy as that meant dispensing with the observer. I begged him to take me with him and we had quite an argument about it, but he firmly refused on the grounds that he simply would not be able to manage with my extra weight on board.

Instructed to use his own discretion about the height from which he should bomb, Rhodes-Moorhouse made sure of his attack on the railway line west of the station at Courtrai by flying at a height of only three hundred feet. He was subjected to very heavy rifle and machine-gun fire, particularly, in the case of the latter, from the belfry of the church in Courtrai, which was almost at the level at which he was flying; and immediately after successfully bombing his objective he was hit in the abdomen, and then again in the thigh and in one hand. He managed to fly the thirty-five miles back to our airfield, never at any time more than a few hundred feet from the ground. He landed, and when we helped him out of his aircraft and saw the full extent of his wounds we were amazed that the poor chap had ever managed to get back. I also noticed that half a dozen bullet holes had appeared in the observer's seat: it was quite obvious that I would not have survived if I had been with him.

Before he was taken to the hospital Rhodes-Moorhouse insisted on making a full report on the flight and on the results he had achieved. He died the next day, and the memory of his funeral is a particularly sad one for he was a most likeable and gallant man. Just before he died he had read to him a message from the Commander-in-Chief which stated: "But for the pressure of urgent work, the Field-Marshal Commanding-in-Chief would have visited 2nd Lieut. Moorhouse himself to express his admiration of his courage and the way in which he carried out his duties yesterday." Following that came the announcement that he had been awarded the Victoria Cross. It was the first to be won by an airman.

Although born in England, Rhodes-Moorhouse had strong family ties with New Zealand, and the view was expressed recently by Linda Rhodes-Moorhouse, his widow, that his "courage and endurance" were possibly the result of an infusion of the blood of the vigorous fighters of that country. There might be something in that because in addition to the honor of sharing in that first V.C. of the air, New Zealand also produced the only man to win the Victoria Cross twice in the Second World War.

When Linda Rhodes-Moorhouse spoke in that way about the character of her husband, she was linking it with that of their son, who was born in 1914. He was named William after his father, and he learned to fly while he was still very young, and he became a pilot in the Auxiliary Air Force. He was killed, shortly after winning a Distinguished Flying Cross, while fighting in the Battle of Britain.

There was a definite, if unintentional, understatement in the manner in which I had expressed myself to my father about my liking for flying. I had made up my mind very quickly after I started flying as an observer that I wanted to be more than a mere passenger. As soon as I was sure I was firmly transplanted and a member of the R.F.C. I made application for training as a pilot.

The commanding officer of our squadron at that time was Major Tom Webb-Bowen. A regular Army officer, formerly in the Bedfordshire Regiment, Webb-Bowen was one of the original pilots of the Royal Flying Corps when it was first formed. Tall and always immaculately turned out, he was already thirty-five years of age by the time he took over command of the squadron. Later he became a well-known senior officer in the R.A.F., although he did earn for himself at one time a reputation for being a martinet. We were to come in contact with each other quite often during the course of the next twenty-five years; and when the second war broke out, he came out of retirement and for a time was on my staff at the Headquarters of Fighter Command.

Applications from observers for training as pilots were readily accepted in those early days because the demand for pilots in the rapidly expanding air service was becoming a matter of some urgency. By the last week in May the ten-day Battle of Festubert had come to an end, and activity on our part of the Front began to quiet down a little. I was then informed by Webb-Bowen that my request had been approved. To my immense delight I was at last to become a pilot.

4 / Fledgling

ALL OF THE countless thousands of those who have ever gone through the business of learning to fly know what an anxious groping into the unknown it is when one comes to take the first steps. That was probably even more the case in the early days of the Royal Flying Corps than it is today because so much less was known then about flying instruction. But I was lucky, and it was not as severe an ordeal for me as it was for those who were starting off from scratch. I already had the valuable experience that I had gained through flying as an observer with a squadron at the Front. And for my initial instruction, instead of going home to be trained I had to make only a fairly short cross-country journey from Merville to a place named Le Crotoy, on the French coast at the mouth of the River Somme, near which the R.F.C. had a small flying school for observers who were already on active service in France.

There were four or five instructors at this school, with about the same number of airplanes, all of which were Caudrons. These somewhat weird and primitive French machines were biplanes with bottom longerons that acted as skids which ran along the ground and provided the main connection between the cumbersome arrangement of the four landing wheels and the tail assembly. The engine was the famous Gnôme, a rotary of eighty horsepower; and the fuselage was a chunky affair bunched in between a fairly enormous and fanciful top main plane and a much smaller lower plane. I often wondered what would have happened if, without knowing it, we had ever damaged one of these longerons as they slid along the ground. The tail unit would certainly have come off as soon as we tried to get into the air.

For all its cumbersome appearance I grew to like flying the Caudron, even if it did have the gliding angle of a brick. I discovered that the best way to go about landing was to point the nose down at a steep angle and to aim about twenty yards short of the place on the airdrome where I wanted to come to a stop.

65

Holding the aircraft in the dive until I was about fifty feet off the ground and then pulling the stick smartly back into my stomach would sit the machine down quite comfortably, and it would come to a halt after a very short run.

I started my initial instruction at Le Crotoy on May 26, 1915, five months to the day after I had first reported for duty with the R.F.C. My instructor was Lieutenant T. L. S. Holbrow, another of those who had transferred to the air service from the Royal Engineers. He had served as a pilot with No. 2 Squadron from the days before the war, and had been a member of that select band that had first arrived in France with the R.F.C. in the middle of the previous August. Holbrow was a most conscientious man in his work, and always went to a great deal of trouble to make sure that I understood everything that he was telling me.

During my first week of training I had four hours and twenty minutes of dual instruction with Holbrow in the course of thirteen flights, six of which were on one day. On June 2 I was allowed to make my first solo flight, which lasted ten minutes. I then did ten minutes more, flying with Holbrow, and that was followed by a test lasting an hour. That much dual instruction was quite a lot, even exceptional, for those days, and I can only assume that either I must have been rather slow to learn or that Holbrow was really being unusually careful about my training.

In that last hour I had to do a figure eight in the air and make several landings on a certain spot marked out on the airfield. I did it all quite satisfactorily, and in the afternoon I received the Aviator's Certificate of the Royal Aero Club, the one given to me being number 1301. At that time this international certificate was required of all pilots before they could be accepted by the Royal Flying Corps. In the wording of the certificate there is a statement that the issuing body is recognized as "the sporting authority in the British Empire" granted this right. That phrasing was a relic of the prewar days, and it could scarcely be said of our intentions, by the time I received my certificate, that they were sporting.

With that much achieved in the short space of only seven days I was then sent back to England to complete my training. Several new flying training schools had been organized, and the one to which I was sent was on the airfield at Shoreham, on the coast of Sussex, which is still in use. Experienced pilots who had been at the Front for some time were being sent back to serve as instructors at these new schools in England. Wilfrid Freeman was one of them, and when I got to Shoreham I found to my delight that he was to finish off my training.

Under the shrewd guidance that was typical of the influence that Wilfrid Freeman came to exert in my life I went through a course of dual and solo flying on the Maurice Farman Shorthorn, which was such a famous workhorse of the training schools in the early days of the Royal Flying Corps. It was another of the French machines upon which we were so dependent in the days before our own aircraft industry had got into its stride. Already antediluvian, it was a large, clumsy biplane with the engine and the propeller at the back of the two-seater cockpit—a pusher as opposed to a tractor—but it performed valiant service in the training of pilots at the beginning of the First World War.

Throughout my Service life spells of being overseas always gave me cause to look forward with the greatest eagerness to getting back to England. During the first war it was for periods of leave from the Front, and even in those days it was more than a matter of merely having a rest from the fighting. I was beginning to experience the feeling that I was always to know whenever I had to go abroad for more than a period of a few weeks: a longing to get home that had in it a definite tinge of homesickness. I have always enjoyed traveling abroad, but I do not like to be away for very long. Being in France during the war was of intense interest, but at the back of my mind there was always the pleasant prospect of returning to England, and in the whole course of the first war it did not even enter my mind that I might, for instance, make a visit to Paris. I have always liked London and all that it has to offer: a way of life that I have found congenial. So whenever my turn for leave came around I always returned like a homing pigeon to London.

Another aspect of being able to get back to England at reasonable intervals that was important to me was that it gave me a chance to look around and to bring myself up to date on what had been happening. Anyone who has ever served either on the ground or as air crew in a fighting squadron—and one cannot possibly know what the Air Force is all about until one has served with a squadron—knows that the life is so absorbing that there is no time or inclination left for any outside interests. That was even truer during the first war than it was during the second, because nearly all of us were overseas. In France we lived in a tight little world of our own. It was a world that was exciting, always interesting, and at times very dangerous; and our lives revolved around the squadron and our flying. That does not mean to say that we were not informed in a general way about what was going on: I think that we were pretty well informed when one remembers how limited the means of communication were in those days. But life in a front line squadron was lived at such a pitch that there was little time left for anything more than thoughts about the patrol just completed and the preparations for the next one.

Earlier in the year, while still in France, I had written to my father: "I hear that the last of the regular troops are out here, so that I expect that Kitchener's army will begin to arrive soon. I wonder what they are like!" Why I should have put in that exclamation mark I cannot remember. I was one of the few civilians among so many professionals, and perhaps I had already absorbed some of the natural skepticism of the professional soldier about the value of the amateurs. If that was the reason, then I was quite wrong. The volunteers who were making their appearance were of splendid stuff; and what was of great importance was that under the forceful drive that Kitchener exerted in his recruiting campaigns they were coming forward.

To those of my generation there are some names from the days of our early manhood that will always ring sharply in our memory; and if one is to appreciate the history of those times, and the impact that its unfolding made upon us over fifty years ago, one must know something about the men who bore those names. Some of them were giants, but they were all human.

Towering above everybody in public esteem was Lord Kitchener. He was already sixty-four years of age when the war broke out, and after a lifetime of great service in the Army he had been created an earl and made a field marshal. His name carried with it tremendous prestige, and when he was made Secretary of State for War he was able to assume a position of very great power. But all too soon it became apparent to the politicians that Kitchener had no time whatsoever for his fellow cabinet ministers, and it is even recorded that he found repugnant the necessity to have to reveal military secrets to those "with whom he was barely acquainted."

On the other hand, and for all his stiffness, Kitchener was a man of foresight, and he became so interested in developing the new air service that he pressed as a matter of the utmost importance for a rapid expansion. In the early months of 1915 a very ambitious program was put up to him for this expansion of the Royal Flying Corps. It called for at least fifty service squadrons and all that would be needed in training and manufacturing to support them. Kitchener sent the plan straight back—"without an hour's delay," it is recorded—to those whose job it was to implement it, making only one comment: a scribbled note reading, "Double this. K."

In trying to understand what happened behind the scenes during the years of 1914–18 and how one should view it, I agree with the military historian Liddell Hart, who has said: ". . . my pursuit of the truth has not been interrupted by recourse to the pot of hypocritical varnish that is miscalled 'good taste.' " As a people we are altogether too prone, when challenged to speak of any truth that may not be exactly to our liking, to start mumbling and muttering about matters of taste. We had heard a little out in France about what had been happening in other places, but it was not until I got back to England that I was able to take in something of the broader picture. It was a depressing enough one.

In his introduction to *The Private Papers of Douglas Haig, 1914–1918,* first published as recently as 1953, the Oxford historian Robert Blake offers this comment: "The history of the First World War is full of the difficulties created by the mistrust and suspicion which befogged the relations of the soldiers and the politicians." One of the most heated of all the quarrels that disturbed the scene in the spring of 1915 was over the shortage of the supply of ammunition. This was something of which I did have firsthand knowledge through my own experiences as a gunner in the front line only six months before. Also, after I joined the Flying Corps, I had continued to hear news from friends of mine in the artillery. It was something that I have never ceased to feel angry about, and there can be no controversy about it because what happened came to be only too well documented. The sordid intrigue that had gone on in practically all quarters was called a crisis. It would have been much better named a scandal.

If there was one man who should have been in a position to know all about the acute shortage of munitions that we were having to endure that man was Lord Kitchener, even though he and the Commander-in-Chief in France were at loggerheads. But Kitchener was reporting to the Prime Minister in the middle of April that he had been assured by Sir John French that "with the present supply of ammunition he will have as much as his troops will be able to use on the next forward movement." Why Kitchener should have stressed this is not clear, because French held no such views about the quantity of the ammunition that he had available. "After all my public and private appeals, I lost any hope that I had entertained of receiving help from the Government as then constituted," French wrote in his book *1914,* which was published immediately after the end of the war, and which has been so vigorously attacked by historians for its unfortunate distortions.

In this book, on the same page as that quotation, there is recorded the Commander-in-Chief's reactions at the Battle of Aubers Ridge in the second week in May, a battle in which I participated as an observer in the R.F.C., and which was nothing but a calamity. "I clearly saw the great inequality of the artillery duels," French stated, "and, as attack after attack failed, I could see that the absence of sufficient artillery support was doubling and trebling our losses in men. I determined on taking the most drastic measures to destroy the apathy of a government which had brought the Empire to the brink of disaster. A friend was standing by my side on the tower, and to him I poured out my doubts and fears and announced my determination. He warned me that the politicians would never forgive the action I proposed, and that it meant certain recall from the command in France. But my decision was made, and I immediately started for my headquarters, fully determined on my future course of action."

After some crafty planning there appeared in the *Times* on May 14 an article that was based on information deliberately provided for it by Sir John French and written by Colonel Charles Repington, the controversial military correspondent. It was alleged that the effectiveness of our army in France was being severely handicapped through a shortage of munitions, particularly high explosive shells. When I read that article in the *Times* I felt, as all of us did out in France, that at last the truth was seeing the light of day. It produced, in Robert Blake's words, "a political sensation of the first magnitude," and there was a mighty stirring up of a hornet's nest. On the one hand, French was treating Repington as a guest and feeding him the most confidential information while, on the other hand, Haig was refusing to see the correspondent and giving his staff instructions that they were not to speak to any correspondents. The intrigue was matched only by the tortuous game that was being played in Whitehall. The press had a field day, and because of my own personal interest in the origin of it, all the astonishing charges and countercharges that were made have remained in my mind as a memory of a particularly sordid affair.

There was one other event of wide public interest in that month of May, 1915, that was to affect greatly the fortunes of my father. On the seventh, only a week before the publication of the Repington article, the Germans sank off the coast of Ireland the great transatlantic passenger liner *Lusitania*. It was a move, albeit a pretty stupid one, in the stiffening up of their submarine blockade of Great Britain.

The *Lusitania* was one of the largest and most up-to-date passenger ships afloat, and it was operated by the Cunard Line on the important run between Great Britain and the United States. On her way from New York to Southampton she was torpedoed without warning by a German submarine, and 1,198 people were drowned, including about 100 Americans. This action by the Germans shocked the whole world, and it aroused in the people of the United States feelings of the deepest indignation.

Among those who were drowned when the *Lusitania* went down was Sir Hugh Lane, the Director of the National Gallery of Ireland and a famous figure in the world of art. His name is known today for the way in which it has come to be linked with the distressing squabble over the ownership of his valuable collection of pictures. Just over a year after Lane's death my father was appointed to take his place in Dublin as Director of the National Gallery.

I spent only just over two weeks under instruction at the airdrome at Shoreham, and during that time I did a little over six hours of flying on Maurice Farman Shorthorns. All of it was in brief flights learning, under Wilfrid Freeman's eagle eye, the finer points of handling an aircraft. On July 1, I was posted as a pilot for still further training to No. 14 Squadron. This was a new squadron that had been formed in February, and it was stationed on the heath at Hounslow. They were getting it ready to go overseas, and there was in it the usual mixed bag of aircraft—Maurice Farman Shorthorns and Longhorns and Caudrons—but it was intended that we should be re-equipped with the lastest B.E.2c's before we went overseas, and we started getting the first of these machines toward the end of July.

Only a week after arriving at Hounslow I experienced the first of the many crashes, some of them serious and some of them trivial, that came inevitably to punctuate the whole of my career in the Air Force, even during the time when I was an air chief marshal in the second war. I took off one day from Hounslow for a practice flight in a Maurice Farman, but I was only about a hundred feet off the ground when the engine started cutting. Losing power, I found myself heading straight for some trees, and to avoid smashing into them I made a quick and very rough landing in an orchard, carefully steering my aircraft between two of the fruit trees. But there was not enough room. Both pairs of wings were neatly chopped off, and I went gently rolling on in the cockpit with the undercarriage and center section intact. "Smashed machine," my logbook states, "engine intact." Of far more importance to me, I was also intact.

I did as much flying as I could, and took the opportunity of getting in as much time as possible on the B.E.2c, but there were other activities in which some of us rather overindulged. We could not fly all the time, and since we were a rather wild lot of young- sters, and much too close to London for our own good, we managed in the usual way to get into quite a lot of what was looked upon as trouble. Eventually it had to come to a head. None of us could afford cars of our own, and one evening several of us commandeered the squadron ambulance and drove it up from Hounslow for a night out at the Piccadilly Hotel, which was then one of our favorite haunts. We parked the ambulance in front of the hotel in Piccadilly and left it there until we were ready to go back to Hounslow in the early hours of the morning. By then the provost marshal's boys were after us. That was the last straw, and our wing commander moved us out of the reach of temptation by ordering the squadron down to Gosport, where he had his head- quarters. There, he felt, he could keep a closer eye on our be- havior.

Late in July, just before going to Gosport, I was sent to the Central Flying School at Upavon for my final test as a pilot. This famous airfield on the Upavon Downs of Salisbury Plain was one of the first of those established by the R.F.C., and it is still in use. I passed that final test in a way that led to an entry in my logbook which reads: "Passed exam at C.F.S. (80%). Allowed to put up wings." One of the proudest moments that I have ever known in my life was when I changed the half-wing of the observer—which was awarded only after one had flown on operations over the front lines, and which I had been wearing since it had come into use a short time before—for the wings of a pilot of the Royal Flying Corps. Flying as a pilot I had to my credit by that time a total, including dual, of just over twenty-five hours.

My stay with No. 14 Squadron at Gosport was fortunately only a very short one, and it was brought to an end through my getting into trouble that was not of the London variety. I was doing some practice flying in a Caudron one day when the engine failed. Forced to land short of the airfield, I came down in a field of cabbages and promptly turned over, finishing up on my back. "Lost engine and smashed machine," my logbook states.

Our commanding officer, Major G. E. Todd, was another of the early pilots of the R.F.C. who had transferred to the air service

from the Welsh Regiment; he had been one of the flight commanders in No. 2 Squadron when it had first gone out to France.
He was not exactly impressed with what I had done, and when he
was told a few days later to select some of his pilots to send out to
France as replacements I was one of those whom he appeared to
be quite glad to get rid of. Although he did not know it, I was
delighted with what he thought was a form of punishment, because
I had learned that No. 14 Squadron was under orders to proceed to
the Middle East. My heart was set on getting back to France.

By the time that I received my orders I had done a total,
including dual, of thirty-two hours and fifteen minutes' flying as a
pilot, which was rather above the average for pilots before they
were sent out to the Front. Since I also had all the invaluable
experience that I had gained during the five months that I had
spent in France as an observer, I could claim by then that I was
quite experienced in the air. But from the flying that I had already
done at the Front I had learned the lesson that actual time in the air
was all important, and that every additional hour would be of great
benefit when my time came for active service. So when I was told
that I could take a week's leave before proceeding overseas I asked
if, instead, I could spend the week with the squadron in order to
get some more hours in the air. I do not know what my commanding officer thought about one of his younger officers forgoing the
possibility of a further joust with the delights that were to be found
in London. He gave no indication of his feelings about that or
about the possibility of my doing further damage to his precious
aircraft. He merely agreed to my staying on.

In the week that followed I was able to add nearly eight hours to
my flying time, and when I finally returned to France as a pilot I
had a total of forty hours and five minutes to my credit. In the
summer of 1915 the average pilot going to the Front could not
have had much more than twenty hours of flying all told, and I
knew of some who were sent to France with as little as fourteen
hours in their logbooks. I can only describe that as sheer murder:
no pilot should ever have been sent overseas so grossly short of
training. It was a state of affairs about which, as the years passed
and as it continued to be the rule, I came to feel very strongly, and
I did not hesitate to voice my criticism of it.

Whatever else they may have been short of at the Front they
were at least enjoying a splendid period of fine weather when I
arrived back in France as a pilot on August 18, 1915. Flying was a
sheer delight. After a short stay at the airdrome at St-Omer, which

was a rather untidy jumble of canvas hangars and sheds around
the airfield making up the depot—and in so many ways the
home—of the Royal Flying Corps in France in the First World
War, I was posted to No. 8 Squadron. They had arrived in France
in April, and they were working from an airfield near Marieux,
halfway between Amiens and Arras. The squadron was under the
command of a Scot by the name of Major A. C. H. MacLean. He
was fiery and efficient, and he was a good C.O. I immediately liked
MacLean, and I was to learn a great deal from him about flying
and the handling of a squadron.

We were in the wing commanded by one of aviation's great
characters, Lieutenant-Colonel W. S. Brancker. A distinguished
officer who had had a great deal to do with the planning of the
Royal Flying Corps, he was a lively and likable man whose appearance was notable for the manner in which he wore a monocle.
It was always glued firmly in place, and it remained there even
when he climbed out of a crash. Later he became one of the
pioneers in the new sphere of civil aviation, and I was to come to
know him well both during and after the war. Formerly in the
Royal Artillery, Sefton Brancker had served in the Boer War in
South Africa, and as early as 1910 he had learned to fly in the first
airplanes ever to appear in India.

But for all his ability as an administrator, Sefton Brancker was
not a good pilot, and that in itself provided, through an incident
that occurred later in the war, a good indication of the character of
the man. He had become a major-general, and flying around by
himself on a tour of inspection he made a very bad landing at one
of the airfields. Because of all the flying gear that he was wearing
there was no way in which his rank could be known, and when he
taxied in he was roundly ticked off by a junior instructor for his
atrocious landing and ordered to take off and try again. Brancker
quietly did as he was told, and not until he was down again and
out of his aircraft did he reveal his rank by taking off his flying
coat. Such was the nature of the man that he did it all without any
comment.

It was to Sefton Brancker, while he was serving at the War
Office, that Kitchener had given his perceptive order for an increase in the size of the Air Force, and he and Boom Trenchard
were the two men largely responsible for that expansion. By the
summer of 1915 the Flying Corps on the Western Front had
reached a strength of twelve squadrons, with 161 airplanes; and in
place of Sir David Henderson, who had returned to the War Office,

we had Trenchard, now a brigadier-general, in command of the R.F.C. in France.

After the First World War it was the custom for many of those who had served in France to make journeys that were almost in the nature of pilgrimages back to the places that they had known on the Western Front. Although I never felt any particular desire to return to the scene of my early exploits, an occasion did arise in the spring of 1959 for me to go back there, and what I found was of greater interest than I expected. Robert Wright, an old friend of mine who had been on my personal staff in the Royal Air Force during the Second World War, had expressed to me many times his interest in the first war, and he had worked out a plan for a tour that he wanted to make of the old battlefields. That aroused my curiosity about what there was still to be seen there, and together we visited the countryside covered by the old Western Front.

While I did the driving Wright acted as navigator, and we spent several days searching for the actual fields from which I had flown during the years between 1914 and 1918, and we were surprisingly lucky. Merville gave us no trouble at all, and I found that it was just as it had been forty-four years before: a very large, flat field that was again under cultivation. We spent a couple of days roaming around the northern part of the old Front, and then we drove south.

Picardy is much pleasanter country than that nearer the Belgian border. We stayed one night in Arras, and the next morning we started off to look for Marieux. Turning off the main road between Arras and Doullens we drove for a little while across lovely, rolling country, using the secondary roads, and again without any trouble I was able to locate the old, rough country road, scarcely more than a track, that wound its way from the small, quiet valley up through a forest and finally out on to some open fields. These fields were also under cultivation, and the only sign of any human activity was an old man working with a horse and plow. I stood there for a while looking out over the fields. Behind me were the trees in which we used to have our tents and our hangars, and it did not seem possible that forty-four years had passed since I had last been there.

It was a gentle and peaceful scene that I looked at that morning in 1959. But it had not always been so. When I reported there in the summer of 1915 it was a busy airfield with canvas hangars in a row in front of the wooden huts in the trees of the forest which stood along two sides of it. No. 8 Squadron was equipped mainly with B.E.2c's, and with that steady aircraft, the first to have real stability, we were on an equal footing with the German Air Force, for the threat from their Fokker had not yet made itself felt. But although our aircraft were now stable enough they were still very slow and they took a lot of urging. After a rather laborious climb taking up the best part of an hour, one could climb to just over 6,000 feet, although on one occasion I did manage to get a B.E.2c up to 11,000 feet. That was during a long reconnaissance of two hours and forty-five minutes' duration over the area occupied by the Germans, bounded by St-Quentin, Le Cateau and Cambrai.

The squadrons of the Royal Flying Corps had not yet started to specialize. Some of them had not even got to the stage where they were equipped with only the one type of aircraft, often having on their strengths quite a mixed bag of different types. A few weeks after my arrival in No. 8 Squadron, however, it was using only B.E.2c's.

With my posting to this squadron I knew that, in a way, my luck had been quite good, for I had not missed any important actions during the time that I had been away from the Front. Things had been fairly quiet on our part of the line since the Battle of Festubert during May, the war having boiled over on the Eastern Front, with the Germans and the Austrians pounding hard at the Russians. There had also been plenty of action on the Front on the Isonzo, in northern Italy, with the Austrians driving hard against our Italian allies. And in the eastern Mediterranean our efforts to force the Dardanelles had been dragging themselves out with no appreciable gains.

On the quieter Western Front, we in the Flying Corps continued to do something of everything: reconnaissance, artillery observations, photography, and bombing. We were nearly all equipped by this time with wireless sets, which were operated by the observers and which usually worked fairly well. But the observer still sat in the front seat. During the time that I had been in England all the aircraft had come to be equipped with machine guns, which the observers continued to fire backward over the tail, and now that I was a pilot it was my turn to know what it was like to have a Lewis gun yammering away only a few inches above my head.

In the flying that we did from Marieux we were working in cooperation with the 7th Corps. This was on the left flank of the newly formed Third Army of the British Expeditionary Force which had only just taken over from the French a section of the Front astride the Somme. By the middle of September we knew from what we could see from the air and hear from the general gossip that something was brewing, and there was a strong rumor of a big offensive. There had been a static condition in the war for some months because the more or less exhausted armies of both sides had sunk down into the ever-expanding systems of trenches. It was said of the rumored offensive—later to become known as the Battle of Loos, named after the coal-mining center to the north of us—that it would be the breakthrough. Everybody seemed to be very confident that it would meet with success, and it was not until long afterward that we, the small fry, were to learn that our own high command was of quite a different temper, and that they embarked on the venture only because the French insisted upon it.

The attack on the British part of the Front was to be made by the First Army, under the command of Sir Douglas Haig. He was very much against it, arguing that our supply of heavy artillery and the shells needed were still far from sufficient to warrant the launching of a major attack; and in this view he was supported by Sir William Robertson, the Chief of Staff of the British Expeditionary Force. Even the corps commander, Henry Rawlinson, upon whose shoulders the main brunt of the attack would have to be carried, disagreed with the feasibility of making it, and before it was even launched he stated: "It will cost us dearly, and we shall not get very far."

But the French generals were possessed of an unquenchable optimism based on that myth of the value of violently aggressive and brutal action. They were all in favor of a massive attack to be launched by them to the south, in Champagne, with British support in an attack to the north, in Artois; and their arguments and persuasion overcame the reluctance of the British leaders to embark upon an offensive in which they did not believe. Kitchener ruled that the B.E.F. must do its utmost to help the French Army, even though he was also ready to admit that we might suffer very heavy losses. This call to support France and the urgent need to help our Russian allies, against whom the Germans were winning impressive successes, sounded a note that was to become only too familiar twenty-five years later.

On September 21 the comparative quiet on the part of the Front to the north of us was suddenly shattered, and for four days there was an artillery bombardment of the enemy's front line. The weather had broken, and flying was becoming more difficult; but during that heavy shelling we were kept busy bombing the railway lines between Douai and Valenciennes in order to hinder the efforts that the Germans were making to bring up reinforcements.

On September 23 I made two longish patrols over the enemy
territory opposite the point from which our attack was to be
launched. Of the first, my logbook records: "B.E.2c 2047. Time
in the air two hours ten minutes; height 7000 feet; bombed railway
Douai-Valenciennes. Dropped one 100-lb. bomb and six 20-lb.
bombs on a junction near Valenciennes. Three 20-lb. bombs hit
rails square on northern line 100 yards from junction. Bombing
height 2000 feet."

The second entry for that day reads: "B.E.2c 2047. Time in
the air two hours and forty minutes. Bombing Douai-Valenciennes
railway line; spotted train at Wallers station; dropped 100-lb.
bomb on rails ten yards in front of train. Rails torn up and engine
destroyed. Also dropped ten incendiary bombs which missed.
Bombing height 400 feet." Thinking about that now, so many
years later, I feel that my youthful optimism must have led me
astray in claiming that the engine was destroyed. It would not have
been possible, even close as I did plant that bomb, for one of only
112 pounds to destroy a French railway engine. I undoubtedly
damaged it and put it out of action, but no more than that. It was
through firsthand experience such as this that I was able to assess
with a shrewder eye than was possibly suspected the highly colored
claims that my pilots sometimes put in during the Second World
War. I knew what it was to make those attacks, and I also knew
how, in the heat of a successful action, one was inclined to over-
estimate the results.

On both the flights that I made that day my observer was
Gordon Alchin, my friend from our time together at school and at
Oxford. He had also transferred from the artillery to the R.F.C.,
and he had come to No. 8 Squadron as an observer only shortly
before this occasion on which we were able to go into action
together. As I came in on the second flight to bomb the train,
Alchin and I saw a French peasant standing on the top of a
haystack just alongside the railway lines. He was jumping up and
down and he threw his hat in the air and was obviously cheering us
on, even though he was quite close to the spot where our bomb
fell.

On the day that the Battle of Loos was launched—the 25th of
September and a day of quite unpleasant weather—we were
instructed to bomb the railway between Douai and Valenciennes
again. I did not have an observer with me on that flight, and my
logbook states: "Dropped 20-lb. bombs on bridge over the canal
which fell into the water and detonated ten yards from bridge.
Dropped three 20-lb. bombs on railway near Wallers, one rail

destroyed. Dropped 100-lb. bomb on iron bridge carrying light rail over main line. Hit brick support, light rail destroyed, and brickwork scattered over main line. Height 130 feet. Much rifle fire. Lost my way returning under clouds at 400 feet. Found Cambrai: chased by a Hun. Archie at 2800: crossed line 2000 feet. 12 to 15 hits on machine."

One of the other aircraft with me on that patrol was shot down, and the pilot and observer, who had done some flying with me, were lost. This particular flight is also mentioned in the official history, and it was by far the most dashing effort that I had made up to that time, because not only did I come in very low to do my bombing but I was also subjected to heavy enemy fire.

I was helped a great deal on that flight by another pilot from the squadron who was later to become an old and trusted friend—in the second war he was still supporting me at Fighter Command as my air officer in charge of administration. His name was H. R. Nicholl, and he flew close to me the whole time, looking after my tail as well as doing his own bombing. Although on the old side for a pilot in those days—he was thirty-three years of age and to us that made him quite an old gentleman—and despite his quiet and unobtrusive manner, "Daddy" Nicholl, as he later became known with affection in the R.A.F., was just as determined and as forceful in his flying as any of those who were in their very early twenties. A sturdy, reliable and very likable man with a good but quiet sense of humor and an attractive, slightly quizzical smile, he had wangled his way into the Royal Flying Corps through the good offices of Sir David Henderson, to whom he was related, and he had learned to fly only a few months before.

The Hun who chased me that day gave me a nasty fright because it was the first time that I had a fairly close view of the latest of the German single-seater fighters: the dreaded Fokker monoplane. It was not to be the last. The Royal Flying Corps was about to face a time during which we who were pilots were going to learn many lessons, and most of those lessons were to be learned the hard way. One of them was that we could indulge in low flying with much greater safety than we had thought possible; and we learned that through the necessity of having to return at times as quickly as we could from bombing at low altitude.

There is one entry in my logbook at this time about one of my bombing raids on a "munitions store south of Péronne" that carries with it an additional note about the nature of some of our contacts with the enemy in the air. After recording that I dropped my bombs, "but missed with all," the note reads: "Saw Fokker

mono just below me. Lewis gun jammed. Fired six shots with
revolver. Chased back over lines." I like the idea of blazing away
at the Hun with a revolver, but I can only think now that I must
have been in a surprisingly audacious mood. Those Fokkers were
not to be treated that lightly.

The weather continued to deteriorate, and on one occasion I ran
into a heavy rainstorm near Valenciennes, with thick, low cloud. I
climbed up into the cloud with the intention of finding my way
back by compass, only to discover that the compass was spinning
because I had very foolishly allowed it to run short of liquid. There
was nothing I could do but come down again and fly under the
cloud and try to map-read my way back. As the cloud was down to
nearly a thousand feet I rather expected, since I was well over
enemy territory, to be shot down from the ground. The Germans
fired at me, and they went on doing it all the way back to the lines;
but when I landed safely at Marieux I found that my airplane had
been hit only a couple of times. Other pilots were having the same
experience, and it was in this way that we learned that the danger
in flying low over enemy antiaircraft and machine-gun fire was not
as great as we had thought.

The Battle of Loos was fought over the flat, dull, open country
between La Bassée Canal and the mining area around Lens, all of
it some miles to the north of our airfield. When it began, we who
had no way of knowing what had been going on behind the scenes
had got ourselves worked up to the belief that success was in the
air. Our unfounded optimism was in for a rude shock. The French
attack in the south was a failure; and on our own Front, there was
an astonishing lack of organization in bringing up the reserves so
desperately needed after an initial success had been gained in
penetrating the German forward positions. Our advancing troops
were left with no support, and the Germans were able to close the
gaps and beat off our wilting attacks.

The main reason for our failure at Loos was the extraordinary
oversight in not providing, right from the beginning, for the reserves that would be needed. For some unaccountable reason these
reserves were kept too far back, and just when they were needed to
consolidate the gains that our troops had made they were not
available. Our attack degenerated and crumpled; and all along the
line, from north to south, both sides suffered fearful casualties.
Those of the British and the French came to a total of a quarter of
a million; and the German figure was quoted as just over two
hundred thousand. In case there should still persist the belief that

generals die in bed, three of the British divisional commanders, all major-generals, were killed.

The Battle of Loos had been called the "unwanted battle." It lasted fourteen days, and it came to a close on October 8. In describing what happened, the official historian has made the final comment that it "had not improved the general situation in any way and had brought nothing but useless slaughter of infantry." Immediately after it was over, there was the usual uproar about who was to blame. There can be no doubt that there was a strange lack of foresight on the part of our Commander-in-Chief. From the very start, French had been unable to give any satisfactory assurances about the disposition of the reserves, and he had not provided any even after the battle started. For that he has since been accused of having "lost the battle in the first few hours."

With all the arguments boiling up there soon developed a brisk quarrel between the Commander-in-Chief and his First Army commander. "If there had been even one division in reserve close up we could have marched right through," Douglas Haig is reported to have commented; and in a letter to Kitchener a few days after the battle started he wrote: "We were in a position to make this the turning point of the war. . . ."

In his appreciation of Douglas Haig, the historian Robert Blake has said that Haig "had long doubted French's abilities as a commander, but from considerations of friendship and loyalty he had hitherto kept his views to himself." But that is not exactly true of Haig. It is well known that he had been expressing criticism of French long before this. Opinion in almost all quarters, including those at home, over the way in which the reserves for the initial stages of the battle had been handled soon became so heated that very sharp questions came to be asked. The tenseness of the situation was not helped in any way when it was revealed that Sir John French had even, for some inexplicable reason, misdated in his dispatch the time when he did make available to Haig the reserves that should have been transferred to him so much earlier.

As a result of the failure at Loos and the quarreling that followed it, Sir John French was relieved of his command, and in his place we got as our Commander-in-Chief the inflexible Sir Douglas Haig. Then fifty-four years of age, Haig was to continue as the British C.-in-C. for the rest of the war. Earlier in the year, during the time that I had spent as an observer with No. 2 Squadron, I had on several occasions seen him as he went about his business. Haig's headquarters in Merville was not far from our squadron mess. In our eyes he was, of course, a very important person, for

we were only small fry, most of us no more than second lieutenants. Always very smartly turned out—a hallmark for which he
was famous—Haig nevertheless struck me at the time as being of a
reasonably benevolent mien even if he was a famous general.

But that was in the days before benevolence became suspect,
and before Siegfried Sassoon had learned to speak for all those who
came to know the full force of the misery that was peculiar to the
First World War. Sassoon would not have written then as he wrote
later in his short poem "The General," which ends with the
devastating lines:

> "He's a cheery old card," grunted Harry to Jack
> As they slogged up to Arras with rifle and pack.
> .   .   .   .   .
> But he did for them both by his plan of attack.

5 / A Joyous Scrap!

WHEN MY FATHER took the step of enlisting in the Army for service as a private shortly after the outbreak of war it was a move on his part that caused not a little astonishment in the minds of most of his friends; but he did not stay long in the ranks. Being an individualist was a fine thing, and it was natural for him to select a difficult path to follow; but having done that and made the gesture he then proceeded very sensibly to organize his affairs so that he could continue to enjoy, as much as possible, the comforts of the life to which he had become accustomed. But even then, and despite all the responsibilities that the increasing size of his family brought to him—not to mention those of the work that he was doing—he did manage after he was commissioned in the Army Service Corps to wangle his way overseas. While I was with No. 8 Squadron at the Front he arrived for duty at the large Army base at Boulogne, where he served during part of 1915 and 1916; and on several occasions when I passed through on my way to or from England I was taken by him for a decent meal at one of the better restaurants.

By the autumn of 1915 my mother could reflect upon the not altogether happy thought that her entire family was in the Army, for my two brothers had by then also joined up. Archie was the brainiest of the three of us, and he had done exceptionally well at Tonbridge. Following the Foundation Scholarship that he had won on first going there, he had been elected to the Judd Scholarship in the following year, and so, even at the age of fourteen, he was off to a flying start. In 1914 and 1915 he won the school prizes for Latin Lyrics and Divinity, and then he gained an open Classical Scholarship at Trinity College, Oxford. In his last term at school he was a cadet officer in the O.T.C., and instead of going up to Oxford in the autumn of 1915 he chose to follow, purposely I felt, in my footsteps. He was commissioned in the artillery that summer, and in November, 1915, he was in France, first in an ammunition column and then with a battery.

My other brother, Bobbie, who was between Archie and me in age, also did quite well at Tonbridge. He was not as brilliant as Archie, and he rather surprised Walter Gordon by winning a Classical Scholarship at Christ's College, Cambridge. Bobbie was by nature solid and easygoing, and although his record in games at Tonbridge had not been particularly distinguished he did get his Third XV colors for rugby, and he was a good cross-country runner, which gives some indication of his temperament: steady, plodding, and very reliable. Instead of going up to Cambridge, however, he joined the Royal West Kent Regiment in October, 1914, and almost immediately after that he was sent out to India.

With the ending of the Battle of Loos, the heavy fighting that had been taking place on the ground on our part of the Front quieted down, and for the rest of the second winter of the war both sides stood on guard. That did not mean that we in the R.F.C. were allowed to enjoy any slackening off in our work. During the weeks that followed we did a great deal of flying, and that resulted in an ever-increasing number of encounters with the dreaded Fokker monoplanes. It was possibly the period of my most intensive flying as a combat pilot because I had no other duties to occupy my thoughts. During this time we were engaged upon an extraordinary variety of tasks, and all the time we were having to fight off the vigorous attacks that the enemy were making upon us in the air, and many of the patrols that I made were quite hectic ones. From just a few of the entries in my logbook it can be seen that we were jacks-of-all-trades.

October 23rd. Distant reconnaissance to Béthune, Cambrai, Le Cateau and Epéhy. Low clouds at Cambrai. Did remainder of reconnaissance at 1500 feet. Shot up badly from St. Vaast. Saw a couple of Fokkers who did not attack, probably because they did not see me owing to clouds.

November 24th. Bombing Achiet-le-Grand. 100 lb. and three 20 lb. bombs fell on line just north of station. Three 20 lb. bombs fell on huts to N.E. of same.

Same date. 14 photos of trenches Serre-Beaumont-Adinfer Wood.

November 26th. Attempted wireless. Clouds 2700. Dropped four 20 lb. bombs on Gommecourt Wood.

November 30th. Bombing stores at Miraumont. Very strong west wind. Dropped bombs. 100 lb. bomb fell on stores, 6 20 lb. bombs missed. Hell from archie all the way home against the wind. Crossed trenches 2000 feet.

December 5th. Wireless show near Bois du Biez. Landed in dark.

December 10th. Attempted photography but too cloudy. Reconnaissance to Martinpuich to map light railway. Met Albatros 300 feet above us and gave chase and gave him half a drum. He turned back towards Bapaume. We followed and met a Fokker 500 feet below us. He dived without fighting.

December 11th. Photography around Bois d'Adinfer. Saw a two tailed Hun aeroplane and gave chase. Just failed to catch him.

December 12th. Bombed aerodrome at Hervilly in a covey. 3 20 lb. bombs and some incendiaries fell on aerodrome. Then attacked by Fokker monoplanes. Saw another B.E.2c from No. 13 Squadron being attacked so went to help him. Fokker left him and came for me. I manœuvered for ten minutes, dodging bursts. Finally got in a couple of bursts with tracer bullets and he dived for the earth. Saw another Fokker who did not attack.

Several times in these brief descriptions of the patrols there is mentioned those prevailing westerly winds that were of so much advantage to the Germans. After bombing Hervilly airdrome on one occasion I got lost because of low clouds over Péronne. "Beat back against strong wind," my logbook states, "and found myself just south of Arras and landed at French aerodrome." Those westerly winds were always a disadvantage, and having to work our way back against them only added to the wear and tear of flying our slow and relatively cumbersome aircraft over enemy territory.

Although the pressure of circumstance had compelled our people to become more air-minded, it was not until we were well into the second year of the war that the aircraft industry in Britain reached a state of effectiveness that made us more or less independent of the French factories. The French had been more than adequately prepared well before we came to appreciate what was needed; and by the outbreak of war they possessed a fine air service, and they had well-established factories capable of turning out enough engines, airframes and spare parts to supply their own service and ours as well. Fortunately, they helped out the R.F.C. willingly enough, and that enabled our own industry at home to develop and expand. But it was not until 1916 that we were in a position to start producing our own new aircraft in any quantity and give thought to developing types that were more suited to the changing conditions of the war in the air.

There were those in the Royal Flying Corps and the French air service who saw clearly enough by the late summer of 1915 that a big change would have to be made in the way we were operating, and that specialization would have to come about in the very near future. We had some aircraft in use which were designed for fighting purposes, but they were largely experimental, and the R.F.C. had not yet progressed much beyond the two-seater general-purpose airplane, the most effective of which was still the B.E.2c.

The Germans were the first in the field with the pure fighter, or the scout, as it was called at that time, and I learned at first hand all about that when they introduced the Fokker monoplane in the summer of 1915. For some months during the autumn and the winter that followed the Fokker enabled the Germans to hold a large measure of control of the air, and their fighter pilots exacted from us a very heavy toll.

Hard on the heels of that supremacy in the air, and before it was even really established, the Germans started indulging in the most astonishing adulation of their fighter pilots, and it was then that we began to hear more and more about men like Oswald Boelcke and Max Immelmann. These were the first two great German heroes of the air, and their names are now written splendidly into flying history. It was not until later in the war that our people came to understand the value of some form of hero worship and to give more attention to the names of our outstandingly successful pilots; but we never at any time reached the hysteria indulged in by the Germans.

Long after the war there was revealed in the books that came to be written about Boelcke and Immelmann the extraordinary lengths to which this adulation was allowed to go. They were both very good and courageous pilots, as I found in my own contacts with them in the air. That I freely admit. Undoubtedly they were also pioneers in the creation of the role of the fighter pilot. But when I came to read the books about them it was a little sad to find a note that was somewhat arrogant, particularly in the letters that they wrote when they had the whip hand. They both appeared to think that in the winter of 1915 the German Air Force had swept us completely out of the skies, and that we never dared to venture over their lines. For all their superiority, that simply was not true, as I know from my own experience, and as I have shown in quoting from my own logbook. We were always over enemy territory, and it was only because we were over there that they were able to hit us so hard.

In the beginning, the Fokker appeared only alone or in company with one other machine. My impression of it when I first saw this monoplane from the air—it was very difficult to see at any distance—was that it appeared to be a tiny, thin black line in the

sky with a blob in the middle of it. At first the German pilots did
not seem to be able to handle their new mount with any great
degree of confidence; and a report came to us through Intelligence
that the machine was a difficult one to fly. During the Battle of
Loos I ran across one of them not far from their airdrome near
Douai, and fortunately I had an observer with me. The Fokker
dived on us twice from the rear and on each occasion I turned in
under it, my observer getting in a burst or two with his machine
gun. After the second dive the Fokker turned away and disappeared into the haze.

In the beginning we were not greatly impressed by this new
German fighting machine; but during October and November the
Fokker began to appear in increasing numbers, and the German
pilots seemed to acquire a greater dexterity in handling it. They
had not yet learned to fly in formation, but two or three of their
pilots began to work together in a loose sort of combination. After
that we began to have our losses, all of which made us do some
very hard thinking. We spent a lot of time discussing among
ourselves the problems with which we were now faced, which
meant, in fact, that we were being forced by circumstance to work
out the basic principles of the tactics of fighting in the air. It was
an aspect of war that was entirely new.

The first question that had to be answered was one that was
very hotly debated. What action should be taken when one was
attacked by an enemy aircraft, such as the Fokker, capable of a
superior performance? Should one turn in under the attacker and
so try to dodge his fire? Or should one continue to fly straight on
so as to give one's observer a steady chance to get in a good shot?
The most gallant pilot we had in No. 8 Squadron held firmly to the
view that the correct course was to fly straight on, but I disagreed
with him. In a very short time we came to learn in the hard school
of experience that the best maneuver was to turn in to the attack.
That knowledge and our realization that we could go in for low
flying with much greater safety than we had thought possible were
the two very important discoveries we made in those early days of
learning in a hard school.

Cyril Falls has said of the airmen of the first war: "The young
men of the air forces, national and racial characteristics apart,
resembled each other closely." I am sure he is right about that.
Although I had no way of appreciating it at the time, I was to
discover long after the war that there was much I would have
found to my liking in the characters of Oswald Boelcke and Max

Immelmann, had I been able to meet them under circumstances more congenial than those of our brisk encounters in the air. One of those encounters was to become a highlight of my experiences during the first war, and it was to lead to my taking a keen interest in knowing more about the lives of these two men.

Oswald Boelcke was the second of the three sons of a schoolmaster. He was a Prussian, born in Saxony, and he has been described as having fair hair, sincere blue eyes and a "frank, open disposition . . . the best athlete in the gymnasium . . . a born leader." He decided upon a military career while he was still quite young, and from school—where, it was said, he "was by no means a model classical scholar"—he went into the Army early in 1911. He was then twenty-one years of age. From the outset Boelcke liked the Army, but he was not altogether happy about his work as an officer in signals; and when he saw airplanes being flown for the first time he commented in a letter to his parents that "flying is a fine game."

On numerous occasions in the letters that Boelcke wrote he referred to the enjoyment he found in dancing, in which he indulged with enthusiasm. I can understand that because it was at about the time that he and I met—under circumstances that were far removed from the ballroom floor—that I was also beginning to enjoy dancing. Later I became enthusiastic about it, not only for the sheer enjoyment of it—"dancing is a sport now," Boelcke once said—but also because being a reasonably good dancer afforded one the best opportunity, in the face of brisk competition, of getting to know the prettiest girls.

Two years after joining the Army, and after his brother Wilhelm had already been trained as an observer, Oswald Boelcke was taught to fly. It was then that he came to appreciate one of the first lessons that all military airmen have had to understand and to endure: the need for patience. "If only there was not so much endless, aimless standing about and waiting!" he commented.

Awarded his certificate as a pilot on August 15, 1914, only eleven days after we went to war with Germany, Boelcke was sent immediately to the Front. He joined his brother's squadron and was paired with him to make up a team of pilot and observer. They were to continue to fly together for quite a long time, and in the curious way in which the Germans operated, the brother, the observer, was the captain of the aircraft. It was a state of affairs which Boelcke apparently regarded as a perfectly natural one. "I hardly worried my head about the locality of the flight, the observations or the results of the reconnaissance," he wrote in a letter.

"Wilhelm did all that, and I seldom had anything to say about it."

But Oswald Boelcke's inclinations were more, in the words of his biographer Johannes Werner, "for honourable, open combat"; and when the aircraft designer Anthony Fokker found a way of firing a machine gun through the propeller of his new monoplane in 1915, Boelcke quickly grasped the possibilities that were offered for aggressive, independent action. He was the first pilot to fly the new Fokker single-seater as a fighting machine. That was as early as May, 1915. He then set about looking for enemy airplanes so that, through actual experience, he could evolve ways of shooting them down. His success cost us dearly, and he became the first of the German pilots to be entrusted with the command of a unit of fighters.

The name that Oswald Boelcke made for himself has always been associated with that of Max Immelmann if only because they worked so closely together, but the character of Boelcke makes a greater appeal to the imagination. Immelmann was born in Dresden, in Saxony, and he was just over five months older than Boelcke. His father was the owner of a cardboard factory, and he had a sister and a brother; but his father died while they were all quite young. From the beginning Immelmann showed, in his brother's words, "a studious disposition and a love for anything technical," although it was clear that his study was not to be with books. He was essentially a practical man, and everything had to be done with his hands, and he learned from actual manipulation how everything worked. After the usual schooling he, too, entered the Army, but although, as explained by his brother, "he would like to be a soldier . . . he has no desire for an officer's career because he does not wish to be bound by the stiff etiquette of a particular caste."

Max Immelmann shared with Boelcke a liking for mountain climbing, and he was also an excellent gymnast and acrobat. He joined the Army, in the engineers, at almost exactly the same time that Boelcke did, although they were then quite unknown to each other. Just over a year later he resigned in order to study engineering. Immelmann was also very keen on dancing.

When the war broke out, Max Immelmann applied for training as a pilot. But since he was in the reserve he was summoned back to the engineers. "Service here is idiotically dull, dull," he stated in a letter. "It is a disgusting idea to be on garrison duty during the war." In November his application for a transfer to the air service was approved, and early in February, 1915, he passed his tests.

After a few weeks as a pilot in France on artillery observation he was sent to join a newly formed unit near Douai, opposite our part of the Front. It was there that he first met Oswald Boelcke, who had been posted to the same unit. "It soon transpired that we suit one another very well," Immelmann wrote in a letter in which he described a trip that he and Boelcke and another pilot made into Douai. "None of us smokes, and we practically never touch alcohol, but we are very fond of cakes."

Immelmann watched and listened to the designer Anthony Fokker as the latter gave Oswald Boelcke his initial instruction on the handling of the new Fokker scout monoplane; and Boelcke, in turn, gave Immelmann his first instruction in flying this aircraft. Boelcke was speaking of combats in the air at this time as "a glorious business'; but it was Immelmann who was the first to shoot down one of our aircraft while flying a Fokker, accomplishing it only three days after Boelcke had taught him to fly the plane. "He had never flown against the enemy in a Fokker and had never fired his guns before," Boelcke wrote, "and then he had the luck to catch a defenseless biplane over our airdrome, because the Englishman had left his observer at home to save weight for his bombs." That in itself is admission enough that we were over their lines and not, as they were too often given to saying, staying behind the safety of our own.

In a book that Franz Immelmann wrote after the war about his famous brother, he spoke of this particular combat, and he made the statement: "We may class his initial victory as the first one achieved by a pilot fulfilling the functions of a fighting scout." Three weeks later Boelcke scored his first victory in a Fokker; and from then on the competition between them became intense. Quite often they flew together, and while we who were flying over that part of the Front saw them at work and felt the weight of their attacks, the German people were regaled with glowing accounts of their victories. Both men were showered with all the decorations and honors that their country had to offer, and late in October, 1915, Immelmann was writing to his mother to say: "It is incredible how much I am honored. I simply cannot describe it. My mail has swollen vastly since I have become a famous man." By the following April he was recording the fact that among the honors that had been heaped upon him there were no less than six orders of knighthood.

That first success of Immelmann's with a Fokker was at the beginning of August, 1915, and it occurred just over two weeks before I arrived back at the Front. During the weeks that followed, we saw develop the maneuver that came to be written into flying history as the "Immelmann turn." When the Fokker first came into use the German pilot would dive on his prey, in some cases almost vertically, then fire, and continue his dive until he was out of range of any return fire that might come from the aircraft that he had attacked. Immelmann evolved a different way of doing things. He did not dive away. After making his attack, to quote the official description, "the airplane rears up as if to loop, turns sideways over the vertical, and then comes out in the opposite direction." This enabled Immelmann to make another quick attack, and the result of the maneuver, "in which height is gained at the same time as direction is changed," filled us with a somewhat reluctant admiration.

From the time of the Battle of Loos onward, the Fokkers in the hands of pilots such as Boelcke and Immelmann began to cause us a great deal of concern. The high command of the Royal Flying Corps on the Western Front had realized quite early that there would have to be a change in the way our aircraft were being used, and by late in July, 1915, Brooke-Popham, one of the three wing commanders of the R.F.C., had summed it up in an official letter. "The German aeroplanes are becoming far more active," he stated, "and are making a regular habit of attacking our machines when on reconnaissance, and we are having to fight for all our information." With the appearance of pilots as able as Boelcke and Immelmann this became even more apparent, and there began to emerge an appreciation of the very real importance of fighting in the air.

Both Britain and France had been given a chance before the war to engage the services of a young Dutch aircraft designer named Anthony Fokker, but they had turned him down. It cost them dearly in so many ways. Fokker had been at work developing a monoplane as far back as 1912; and with German support he had continued to improve his design to such an extent that quite early in the war the Germans ordered this aircraft built in some quantity. It was a mid-wing monoplane of a very simple and clean-cut design and with a good performance, although it did have a tendency, when handled too roughly, to break up in the air.

The feature about the Fokker monoplane that was to give us such an initial fright, and later to cause us such heavy casualties, was the way in which the pilot could fire his machine gun directly through the propeller. This enabled the German pilots to fly around and, for the first time in military flying, shoot at us in the perfectly normal way, by aiming their aircraft at us. The only answer that we could make was with the Lewis gun fired by our observers over the tails of our aircraft. Some of us even went so far as to have two Lewis guns in tandem fitted on the mounting in the observer's cockpit of the B.E.2c.

But the Germans were not the only ones who were producing frightening tricks. There was one small one that I had a hand in, although it only lasted for a day. We had delivered to us at Marieux at the end of the Battle of Loos the prototype of what was known as the B.E.9, an aircraft which we promptly named the "Pulpit." It was a B.E.2c with an extension built out in front of the propeller which provided the observer with a fine, if lonely, seat from which he could shoot forward instead of backward. He had the propeller whirling around on a ball-race right behind his head, and that and the engine were between him and the pilot.

The Pulpit was rather an ungainly-looking affair, and it certainly frightened some of our people; but our reaction was nothing to compare with the Huns' when I flew it for what was possibly the only time that it was ever used on operations over the lines. On October 26 I took it on a "patrol and reconnaissance" lasting an hour and twenty minutes. At the first sight of this weird contraption the Huns appeared to become terror-stricken, and they promptly fled. But nothing worthwhile could be developed from the Pulpit. It was too slow. I said of it in my logbook that it was "rather sluggish, but very stable." A few weeks later I flew it back to St-Omer and we heard nothing more about it.

A couple of days after our Christmas celebrations, three German aircraft flew over our airfield at Marieux and dumped a load of bombs on us just after I had returned from a photographic reconnaissance. That stung us, even if it was only a little of the medicine that we had been giving them. The following day Gordon Alchin was badly injured in a crash on the airfield, and a busted nose and some broken bones led to his being sent home. On the whole I had managed to avoid getting into too much trouble, but on the very next day, December 29, I was subjected in the space of a little over half an hour to what was just about the most hair-raising experience that came my way in the First World War. It was also one that wound up in the pages of the history books.

Next to Gordon Alchin, the man who had become my closest friend in the squadron at this time was a pleasant and charming young Scot named David Glen, a son of a minister of the Kirk. He was a notably courageous young pilot. On December 29, he and I,

both of us flying B.E.2c's, were ordered to do an extensive reconnaissance as far as Cambrai and St-Quentin. Glen was to act as my
escort. The entry that I made about that flight in my logbook after
I got back reads:

December 29th. Observer Lieut. Child. 2 hours 45 minutes. Height
6,500 feet. Reconnaissance to Cambrai and St-Quentin. Archie very
good near Cambrai. Then met six Huns. Glen, my escort, was shot
down, followed by two of the Huns. I was then set upon by the remainder. Child, my observer, downed one Hun. We fought the remaining three for half an hour. Petrol began to get low and engine sump
was hit. So, relying on the stability near the ground of the B.E.2c as
against Fokker, came down in steep spiral to 10 feet above the ground.
Came back from Cambrai to Arras just over the trees. Huns shot like
mad. Child turned Lewis gun on to one lot of Huns by a farmhouse.
Saw several small convoys and a staff officer on horseback. Fokkers left
us a mile from the lines. Climbed to 800 feet and dived over the
trenches. Engine failed and landed among French heavy batteries just
south of Arras. About 100 holes in machine. Engine sump pierced 1½
inches from bottom.

The whole experience was very unpleasant and there were
frightening moments; the bare details by no means tell the whole
story. Other people must also have thought it was quite an
adventure because just over a week after it happened I read a long
and detailed account of it in the *Times* of January 6, 1916.
Naturally, no names were given. Under an impressive and pointed
heading—A RISKY AIR DIVE. BRITISH PILOT'S FINE EXPLOIT. SIX
MACHINES TO TWO—there was given "an account of an air combat" that had been circulated as a supplement to an unnumbered
Corps Summary. Some of the fanciful phrasing in this official
account, which was obviously written by an Army Intelligence
Officer who was not very familiar with the Flying Corps, reads
somewhat quaintly, and parts of it have twists of humor that must
surely have been quite unintentional.

"The Fokker is a monoplane, expressly built and contrived for
fighting and for pursuit of the enemy," it stated, "to which duties
its activities are by strict order confined, and for which it is
specially adapted on account of its high speed." In referring to the
way in which the machine gun was used the statement spoke of
"the correct aim of the gun being ensured by manipulation of the
whole machine, just as the correct aim of a torpedo from a submarine is contrived by manipulation of the boat itself."

The report of the fight then went on to explain that "its pilot decided that escape could only be sought by a very risky dive to within 20 ft. of the ground—risky in that it necessitated a descent by very steep spirals at a speed of quite 100 miles an hour, with little room to recover. Only very delicate and confident handling could ensure the success of this manœuver, which only the absence of other means of escape could justify." There was no delicacy about what I did with the B.E.2c on that particular occasion: I was tearing around for all I was worth, intent only on getting away from those Fokkers, and I was much too scared ever to be aware of the confidence with which I was so pleasantly credited.

"Skimming along just above the ground, as skims a grouse under a hawk, our machine, hard pressed, turned westward for home," the account read. "The fight continued . . . the German machines giving up the chase when about a mile from the German lines. Our airplane being unable to rise higher than 800 feet owing to the engine having been hit in the fight, pilot and observer were subjected to very heavy rifle, machine-gun and field artillery fire, which the machine fortunately survived, although its planes and spars were damaged, and more than one of its stays nearly severed."

In referring to our "stays" I imagine that the nonflying intelligence officer meant the flying wires that were used to brace the wings of our biplanes. In the B.E.2c the most important of these were duplicated so that even if one was hit, the wings would still hang together. When we were flying we noticed no particular strain on the struts and the various wires which held together and supported the upper and lower wings, but they were of the utmost importance, and a few lucky shots by one's opponent could cause them to collapse.

Passengers in modern transport aircraft—particularly those designed by Sir George Edwards (the outstanding example of which is the Viscount used so extensively by British European Airways)—will have noticed that the tips of the single wing are flexible, and that in flight there is a noticeable movement. Our biplanes of forty-odd years ago were absolutely rigid in structure, and in some respects, the wings were braced in too stiff a way. When an excessive strain was imposed upon them, as there was, for instance, in the heat of a battle, there was no margin for flexibility, and the wings could be, and sometimes were, broken off.

In flight we could quite often see the fabric with which the wings were covered rippling from the effect of the air flowing over it. Bad maintenance and lack of proper doping of the fabric to keep it tight would allow it to become slack, and then it could be ripped off, particularly if one had to go into a fast dive. Since we had no parachutes, we were all too well aware that these faults could easily develop, and there was ever present in our minds the need to keep an eye on our actual flying and so preserve our aircraft.

In the last paragraph of the report there was the accurate comment that "the anxieties of the position had for long been greatly increased by the knowledge that only sufficient petrol remained in the tank to bring the machine just within the friendly lines if a direct course was pursued, so that to be driven in any degree out of that course would have been fatal." It finished with the statement that "the chances of ever reaching home had seemed remote, but an expiring effort landed the machine just within the French lines south-east of Arras." By the time we did get safely down on the good earth, I think that James Child, poor chap, must have thought that he had expired.

When we finally got back to the squadron at Marieux and our story and other reports that had come in were considered, the general opinion was that James Child and I must have been through a pretty terrifying experience, and that we were very lucky to be alive. All squadron records of both world wars are preserved at the Air Ministry in London, and quite recently there was produced for me from the records of No. 8 Squadron the official account written immediately after Child and I had made our report.

"The reconnaissance machine [Douglas's] was then attacked from behind by a Fokker," it reads. "Fire was opened and a tracer bullet hit the enemy aircraft which nose-dived and was still going down when three others attacked. At this moment one Lewis gun jammed and the other had a series of stoppages. The unequal fight continued for fifteen to twenty minutes and then Douglas spiralled down to twenty feet from the ground, followed by the Fokker to 1,000 feet. When the B.E. started flying westwards at only fifteen feet from the ground one enemy aircraft dived but retired to 1,000 feet on meeting hot fire from Child [Douglas's observer]. Eventually, two enemy aircraft gave up the chase but returned on seeing Douglas climbing to attack the third machine. The B.E. could get no higher than 800 feet as the engine was failing. All three Fokkers followed almost to the lines but made no further attacks."

These reports were not the last that I was to know of the adventure of that day. Some time later I learned in a roundabout way that the two Fokker pilots who had jumped me and who had led me such a hell of a dance were, in fact, none other than the famous Oswald Boelcke and Max Immelmann. One of them as an adversary would have been more than enough; but to have both of them wading into me at the same time could be considered, in its odd way, a signal honor even if it was also a terrifying one.

About a year or so later a book about Boelcke was published in Germany, a copy of which fell into the hands of Wilfrid Freeman. He had a translation made, and he sent me the extract giving an account of the fight that Boelcke and Immelmann had had with me on December 29, 1915. Many years later I found an English edition of this book which bore the title *Knight of Germany*. It was written by Johannes Werner, and in it Boelcke's diary is quoted for an account of how he and Immelmann had a scrap with a British pilot who, in Boelcke's words, "was ready for a tussle." He then went on to say:

That was a fine fight. I had to deal with a tough fellow, who defended himself stoutly. But I forced him on to the defensive at once. Then he tried to escape me by turns, etc., and made an effort to get at me on my weak side. He did not succeed, but the only success I scored was forcing his machine even further down—we began at 2,000 metres, and in a short time I fought him down to less than one thousand. Finally he could defend himself no longer, because I had mortally wounded his observer. It was now a comparatively easy job to shoot the fellow down, but when we got to eight hundred metres I ran out of ammunition because I had previously used some of it on two others. That was his salvation. We now circled round each other, but neither could do the other any harm. Finally Immelmann came to my aid, and the fight began all over again. I kept on attacking merrily, so as to confuse the Englishman. We managed to force him down to one hundred metres and waited for him to land, but he went on flying about like a madman all over the place, with the pair of us behind him. I tried to cut off his further progress by flying at him, etc.; then my engine gave out, and I had to land. I could just see my opponent disappearing behind the next row of trees and thought he would land there; I was delighted and, arming myself with a Verey pistol—I had no other weapon at hand— I rode across on horseback to take the fellow prisoner. But he had flown on. I made enquiries everywhere and rang up—no definite news obtainable. Then in the evening there came a report that the Englishman actually flew over the trenches at a height of one hundred metres and got home. Smart of the fellow; he won't have many imitators! Immelmann could not go on shooting at him because his gun jammed. That was no victory, but a joyous scrap.

I was extremely lucky to get away with my escape from two such formidable opponents. I had had a fair amount of experience by then in low flying behind the German lines, particularly during the bombing attacks that we had carried out in the Battle of Loos, and I had already come to the conclusion that if I was ever forced down by any Fokkers, the best way of escaping from them would be to come down very low and try to get back at tree-top height. Boelcke and Immelmann left me little choice but to put this into practice because of the favorite method of attack by the Fokker pilots: a steep dive down on to their target.

In the attacks that our opponents made on my homeward flight, I was too low down for Immelmann to indulge in any of his fancy maneuvers; at one point I dodged around a wood in a hair-raising lefthand turn below the level of the trees. That must certainly have put off whichever of the two Fokkers was attacking me at that moment. James Child behaved very gallantly all through the fight, and he managed to get in some good bursts at the enemy as they came diving down on our tail.

Oswald Boelcke was led into believing that he had killed my observer because Child, who was facing backward and firing over my head, became so physically sick from the violent way I had to toss our aircraft about that he finally fell over and threw up all over me. This made things more than a little awkward because his vomit came all over my helmet and goggles, temporarily blinding me. I had to fly the rest of the way back without goggles because I had neither the time nor the opportunity to clean them.

In his diary Boelcke records that Immelmann shot down the other British aircraft just before he joined in the attack on me. This was the aircraft flown by David Glen. It was Glen who had held to the theory that the right thing to do if attacked by Fokkers was to fly straight on and to rely on one's observer to shoot down the enemy. His observer was a very good gunner who had shot down one Fokker a week or two before this episode. This maneuver was undoubtedly a brave one, but I did not feel brave enough to follow it, and I had argued with Glen all along that the right thing to do was to fly in such a way that one would throw off the aim of the enemy fighter. I was convinced that in a dual between a Fokker firing through the propeller and an observer in a B.E.2c with a rather wobbly Lewis gun shooting back over the tail, the former was far more likely to win.

So keen was the interest shown by his friends in the squadron in what had happened in that scrap that one of them, quite wrongly I felt, could not resist telling me in the strictest confidence that a recommendation had been put forward that I should be awarded the Victoria Cross. That was assessing far too highly the value of the part I had played, and the recommendation was turned down,

quite rightly in my opinion, by Tom Webb-Bowen, my former
C.O. in No. 2 Squadron, who had become our wing commander.
The V.C. is an award for unselfish bravery, and for saving the lives
of others; and in my case, I heard, it was thought that I had been
saving my own skin. That, I consider, is a fair enough comment on
the whole affair.

In recalling what happened that day I do remember, curiously
enough, that in the heat of combat I had no particular sensation of
fear, although I was undoubtedly scared. I have always found that
fear is much worse in anticipation than it is in reality. I was
thoroughly frightened as Glen and I flew steadily toward Cambrai
with half a dozen enemy fighters dancing about in the sky just in
front of us, and it called for quite an effort on my part to keep on
with the reconnaissance.

Being frightened was a sensation that I came to know with
increasing frequency as the fighting in the air became more intensive, and I used to get just as windy as the other pilots and
observers when we set off and climbed on our way to our offensive
patrols. But in the heat of a fight I was too busy to go on being
frightened. When an enemy fighter attacked me and tried to get on
my tail I found that, more often than not, I got extremely annoyed,
particularly when I knew that he had actually opened fire at me.
My first reaction was to think to myself: "The bastard . . . what
the devil does he think he's doing?" And then, when a fuller realization of what was going on had roused my ire, my thought would
become: "My God . . . he's trying to kill me! I'd better bloody
well kill him first."

It was anger, if nothing else, that appeared to drive out the fear.
But there was perhaps more to it than that, for in driving out fear
that anger protected me from harm by stimulating me to avoid getting into harm's way. In all the flying that I did during the first war
the nearest that I came to being wounded in combat was to receive,
one day during my time at Marieux, a trivial graze from a bullet
across one of my wrists. There again, luck was on my side, for so
many of my friends who were both better pilots and braver men
than I were killed.

During the first eighteen months of the war, the British Expeditionary Force played a comparatively small though important part
in the great struggle that went on in France. We had helped in that
struggle, and we had paid dearly, and France, whose losses had
been nothing short of shattering, would hardly have survived
without our help. But the numerical strength of the B.E.F., even

after eighteen months, amounted to only about a sixth of the total numbers of the Allies on the Western Front; and although we were fighting on a vitally important part of that Front, the stretch of the line held by us was a small part of its overall length.

That the Germans had gained, for the time being, the upper hand in the air was a fact that none of us could deny, and we watched those Fokkers with a very wary eye. But the historians have recorded that we still went about our work of reconnaissance and bombing, and I should feel flattered, I suppose, that Boelcke referred in such terms of praise to my part in the scrap that I had with him over their territory. It was almost the only occasion upon which he did offer such praise of one of his enemies. On the other hand, it would appear, from all the accounts that have come to us, that both Boelcke and Immelmann showed a pleasant courtesy and consideration toward those of our pilots and observers who lived after being shot down by them.

By the new year of 1916, both Boelcke and Immelmann were being fêted by the Emperor, kings and the whole of the German nation. "This was the period when not only the whole army but all the civilians at home followed the competition in victories between Boelcke and Immelmann with joyous excitement," Johannes Werner has written. In the middle of January, 1916, even though they had only eight victories each to their credit, they were both awarded the order Pour le Mérite, which was roughly the German equivalent of the Victoria Cross. They were the first German airmen to receive this highly prized decoration.

On the very day in January, 1916, when the whole German nation was rejoicing over the announcement of these latest awards to their foremost pilots, there was issued from the headquarters of the Royal Flying Corps an order which, in the words of the official historian, "brought about, at a stroke, one of the drastic changes in the air war—formation flying, and crystallised the effects of the whole Fokker dominance." This order laid down "as a hard and fast rule that a machine proceeding on reconnaissance must be escorted by at least three other fighting machines . . . in close formation. Flying in close formation must be practised by all pilots."

The tactics of formation flying had not yet been evolved, and fighting in formation was still very much the subject of speculation. But important steps forward were taken in this field through the use of the new types of aircraft which were being delivered to the R.F.C. As a result of the urgent requests from the Front for a more efficient fighter to combat the Fokker, the R.F.C. began to

receive from our own factories the F.E.2b and the D.H.2; and the
French were supplying the redoubtable Nieuport Scout.

All these new aircraft were biplanes. The British models—both
of which were designed originally by Geoffrey de Havilland—were
pushers, with the engines and the propellers at the back of the
cockpits. The F.E.2b was a two-seater with a particularly spacious cockpit which enabled the observer, who occupied the front
seat, to move about quite freely and to enjoy a wide field of fire to
the front. The D.H.2 was a single-seater pusher. The Nieuport was
an effective and attractive tractor of simple lines, a single-seater
with a Lewis gun mounted on the top wing and firing over the
propeller. It was by far the best of the fighters by the spring of
1916, and it was to perform magnificently after it came into
service just before the start of the Battle of the Somme.

I was fortunate in not having to face the last few weeks of the
Fokker scourge. Almost immediately after my encounter with
Boelcke and Immelmann, I was sent back to England to become a
flight commander, with promotion to the rank of captain. With
that I came to know again what a curious experience it was to
emerge from the confined world of the Front into the larger world
at home. Or was it the other way round? The world at home was
less exciting, but it had become a strangely perplexing one. So
much seemed to be happening for which there was no apparent
reason, and if one was possessed of an inquiring mind it was
difficult to get answers that made sense.

But if I felt perplexed, how much more puzzled were our
leaders. Winston Churchill had reached the state where, as he put
it, "I was out of harmony with the views which were prevailing and
to which the Prime Minister had at last submitted. I was also
distressed at the methods of indecision arising from conflicting
opinions which at this time pervaded and paralysed the conduct of
the war."

With the knowledge that he "knew too much and felt too keenly
to be able to accept Cabinet responsibility for what I believed to be
a wholly erroneous conception of war," Churchill offered his
resignation from the Government in the middle of November,
1915. This eager forty-one-year-old went straight out to France to
serve for a time with the Grenadier Guards near Laventie on a
refresher course in actual soldiering. A few weeks later Douglas
Haig was recording in his diary: "Winston Churchill has been
doing duty in the trenches, and the C.O. of the Battalion . . .
speaks highly of his keenness."

Within a short period that redoubtable fighter, who had given up soldiering fifteen years before, completed the extraordinary journey all the way from being a cabinet minister of considerable standing and experience to serving as a lieutenant-colonel in command of the 6th Royal Scots Fusiliers in the front-line trenches on the Western Front. The second in command of that battalion was a young Scot by the name of Archibald Sinclair. He was the man who was to serve Churchill and the country so well as Secretary of State for Air in the Second World War—in which capacity I came to know him very well—and who is today known as Viscount Thurso.

In the humbler and far more dangerous life which he led as an officer at the Front, Winston Churchill found that, to quote him again, "the conviction came into my mind with absolute assurance that the simple soldiers and their regimental officers, armed with their cause, would by their virtues in the end retrieve the mistakes and ignorances of Staffs and Cabinets, of Admirals, Generals and politicians—including, no doubt, many of my own." No matter what may be said about him for the way in which he behaved at times when he later became our great war leader, I am quite sure that Churchill never lost sight of that conviction.

From the manner in which he conducted himself during the times that his battalion was in the line, it was clear that Winston Churchill was out to wage war. In his biography of Churchill, Lewis Broad describes the way in which, at night, Churchill "would order his men to put up bursts of rifle and machine-gun fire until the enemy in alarm replied. Then he would telephone to the artillery demanding support, and more than once the nocturnal 'hate' of the 6th Royal Scots Fusiliers led to a general flare up in the sector." That sector was only a few miles from where I had served as a gunner over a year before; and it was a good thing he was not there then and calling for artillery support, because the shortage of our supplies of ammunition would very quickly have brought to a halt his attempts to stoke up the war.

By the time this almost private war of Churchill's was being waged around Ploegsteert, just to the north of Armentières, I was already back in England. On January 1, 1916, my name appeared among those listed as having been mentioned in dispatches; and from the *Gazette* for January 14 I learned that James Child and I had both been awarded the Military Cross.

6 / Disillusion

IN THE MINDS of the men of my generation the year 1916 stands for only one thing: the battles that were waged on the Somme during the summer and the autumn. In those battles there died the last shreds of the blithe spirit with which we had set off to the war nearly two years before, and in its place came the beginning of the disillusionment that was to enter into the hearts and the minds of so many of my generation. The war had become a bitter test of endurance. The battles that were waged no longer lasted just a few days: they stretched out, in some cases, over periods of weeks, and they were all fought in highly congested areas and under the most gruesome conditions.

Those who were endeavoring to write—or felt compelled to write—about what they were experiencing were already sensing the change that had taken place, and, in the words of Edmund Blunden, "madness seemed totally to rule the hour." Charles Hamilton Sorley, a Scotsman who was only twenty years of age when he was killed in the Battle of Loos, had already sounded the note of what was to follow when he wrote:

> *When you see millions of the mouthless dead*
> *Across your dreams in pale battalions go,*
> *Say not soft things as other men have said,*
> *That you'll remember. For you need not so.*

The American poet Alan Seeger, who had joined the French Foreign Legion and was killed in the summer of 1916 on the French Front at Verdun, had already written his poem beginning with the well-known line: "I have a rendezvous with death."

It was in that year of 1916 that the world which we had been brought up to believe in finally seemed to fly to pieces, and the bare mention to us of the Somme will never fail to give us cause to ponder for a moment and to recall, each in his own way, what it meant to us. In my own case, I was again one of the lucky ones: I spent only a short time there during the actual battles that were fought through the summer and the autumn.

Ever since Roman times—largely because it is one of the natural lines of defense for Paris—that particular stretch of country in northeastern France that lies between the River Somme and its tributary the Ancre has been the scene of many struggles and battles. Edward III was there on his way to Crécy, and Henry V crossed the river on his way to Agincourt. The rolling stretches of uplands and shallow valleys of that part of Picardy, which is not unlike Salisbury Plain, were to provide for us, as with the Ypres Salient, names that have lived in our history. High Wood, Thiepval, Trones Wood, Martinpuich, Fricourt, Delville Wood, Ginchy, Combles, and many others join those of the Salient. But in comparison with the confined area of the Ypres Salient, the Somme provided open and comparatively unobstructed country over which there was the possibility of a wide range of action. Such was the nature of the country of the Somme that quite often the chalk lying under much of the region provided just what was needed for strong defensive excavations. (The Germans made good use of that.) Both sides dug extensive trench systems, which could be seen from the air as endless tangles of spidery white lines. It was a countryside that I knew well from having flown over it a great deal during my time as a pilot in No. 8 Squadron during the previous autumn and winter; and I came to know it all even better in the flying that I was to do over it two years after that.

When I got back to England at the beginning of the new year I was given a week's leave, and after that I was posted as a flight commander to No. 18 Reserve Training Squadron at the airdrome at Montrose, in Scotland. This was one of the first of the airfields used by the Royal Flying Corps, No. 2 Squadron having arrived there from Farnborough in February, 1913. Equipped with B.E.2c's, some Curtis trainers and a few Martynside Scouts (although given the name of "scouts" they were never successfully employed as such), our job in the reserve squadron was to give pilots their final training before they went overseas. We were under the command of Euan Rabagliati—known fondly in the Air Force as "Ragbags"—who had been in the Yorkshire Light Infantry before transferring to the Royal Flying Corps before the war; and he was another of those stalwarts who had gone out to the Front, as a pilot in No. 5 Squadron, when the R.F.C. had first proceeded to France. A small, slim, lively character, "Ragbags" had a sharp mind and an even sharper tongue. We came to know each other well during the time that I spent at Montrose, and it was the beginning of a long friendship.

By the beginning of 1916, the Royal Flying Corps had evolved under the stress of trial and error, and through the shrewd guidance of Boom Trenchard, into the shape that it was to take for the rest of the war. The duties that we were required to perform were more clearly defined, and they fell into two categories: artillery observation, photography and reconnaissance on the immediate fronts of each of the corps; and long-range reconnaissance, bombing and fighting in the air for each of the armies. The R.F.C. was formed into brigades, each of which contained wings, and in these were grouped the squadrons.

Under this new arrangement the fighters were to support the air offensive that was so strongly believed in by Trenchard right from the very beginning. The fighters formed separate units, and their task was to operate apart from, but in support of, those engaged in the work of reconnaissance and bombing. This soon led to a closer cooperation between the fighters and the attacking infantry in the line; and with that and the escorting of the reconnaissance and other aircraft there evolved the more definite role that the fighters were to play. It was a role that was to develop in the immediate future even more than we expected, with increasing attention being given to the weapons with which we were equipped. "The old days of taking snap shots at the enemy . . . were over and done," Hilary St. George Saunders wrote of this period in his history of the Air Force published under the title *Per Ardua*. "Now the Vickers or the Lewis gun was as indispensable a part of the aeroplane as was its engine."

The pilots sent to us at Montrose had already completed their elementary flying training, and my work during the first five months of 1916 was the supervision of instruction in flying the more advanced types of aircraft. I gave my pupils a high proportion of their dual instruction myself. It was dull work after operational flying in France. My only exciting experience during that time occurred one afternoon while I was leading a formation of my pupils on a flight up to Aberdeen. One of them was forced to land in a field alongside the Glasgow-Aberdeen railway line. I went down to see if I could find out what had happened, and I flew low across the field, about ten feet off the ground. In what was to follow I had good reason to be thankful that the Martynside Scout I had chosen to fly that day was a solidly built aircraft, even if it was rather chunky and not a success as a fighter.

After crossing most of the field I suddenly saw that I was heading straight into twenty or thirty telegraph wires which were strung alongside the railway line. It was too late to be able to zoom over them, there was not enough room to get underneath, and I was forced to fly slap into them. They acted as a net, which caught the aircraft, pulled it up all standing, and then dropped it down on its back on the railway lines. It was very careless and indeed foolish of me not to have kept a sharper lookout, but I had been concentrating on trying to see what had happened to my pupil and his aircraft. Fortunately I came out unscathed, which is a good indication of how, with the much slower and lighter aircraft of those days, we could get away with crashes that in faster and weightier machines would have been fatal. To the annoyance of the railway authorities that crash held up the trains between Glasgow and Aberdeen for several hours.

While I was out in France, I had on occasion landed back at Marieux as it was getting dark, but I could not claim that I had any real experience of flying at night. At Montrose I purposely tried my hand at more elaborate night flying, and early in February I flew for a while after nightfall in a B.E.2c, completing what was then quite a venture by landing with the help of flares. "Easier than expected. Could see sea and lights, but not wood or roads," I recorded in my logbook.

All this helped to round out my general experience, and by March I was doing a great deal of flying as an instructor, quite often making six or seven flights a day in B.E.2c's and Avro 504K's. The latter was superlatively light and easy to handle, and it was the most successful training aircraft we had during those early years. After my first flight in it I wrote: "Liked it immensely: only just scraped in landing." Later that month I went down to Farnborough to do some flying with an R.E.7—one of the "reconnaissance experimental" aircraft designed and built there—and to test with it a new bombsight that had been devised. My only memory of this aircraft is that it was a heavy lump of a thing.

Early in April my brother Archie came to stay with me for a few days at Montrose while on leave from his battery in France. I took him for his first flight in an airplane: about thirty minutes in a B.E.2c. He promptly made up his mind that flying was also the life for him, and he took a step further in following in my footsteps by applying for a transfer to the R.F.C. He remained with his battery in France until June, and was then attached to the Flying Corps as an observer.

While my brother was making these plans for his own future I had a quite unexpected stroke of luck. By then I had been a flight commander in the Reserve Squadron for four months, but I had not had any experience as a flight commander in an operational squadron. Instead of remaining as a flight commander, however, I took two steps forward when, toward the end of May, I was sent to Stirling to start forming an entirely new squadron. This was to be No. 43, and I started it with a nucleus of mechanics provided by the reserve squadron with which I had been serving, and a bunch of raw pilots straight from elementary training school. My orders were to get the squadron up to a standard that would be sufficiently operational for us to be able to proceed to France toward the end of the year. I was then twenty-two years of age, and this was my first taste of having a command that was entirely my own.

The months of 1916 that I was able to spend in Scotland—the first time that I ever actually lived there—were very happy ones for me. The history of the country of my family's origin had always appealed to me, and I found a great deal of pleasure in being in Stirling, the gateway to the Highlands. Our airdrome at Stirling was a grass field on Raploch, an open space just under the castle hill which has now been developed as a housing estate. I did quite a lot of flying from there over different parts of Scotland, and I also continued to give a good deal of instruction to my new pilots, making good use of the airfield below the castle which was said to have been an ancient tilting ground.

There were no proper buildings on our new airfield, except for a farmhouse which had been commandeered and in which I lived with my senior officers. The rest of those who joined us lived in tents—although I did manage to get a couple of wooden hangars erected for our aircraft—and we enjoyed a fine open-air and carefree life. For our training we had Avro 504K's and B.E.2c's and a few Armstrong-Whitworths of a type that rather resembled the B.E.2c. We spent the whole of the summer at Stirling, and at the end of August we moved south to Netheravon, in Wiltshire. It was intended that we should be re-equipped with the Sopwith 1½ Strutter and sent as quickly as possible to France. More pilots were provided, and by the end of September I had the great fun of recording in orders that Gordon Alchin—who had learned to fly during the summer—was on the strength of my squadron.

The way in which the Fokker monoplane had gained the upper hand on the Western Front earlier in the year had led to a demand that our engineers and designers follow up on this idea of firing a machine gun through a propeller. Suggestions for such a gear had been made by some engineers in England before the war. Nothing had come of that, but under pressure from the R.F.C. in France the designers produced early in 1916 the first of the famous Sopwith 1½ Strutters. With that, there was provided one answer to the Fokker monoplane.

A two-seater biplane of quite a fair streamlining in its design, the 1½ Strutter had the pilot sitting in the front seat for the first time, right up behind a Clerget engine of one hundred horsepower. He had a good view ahead and downward, and also for the first time the pilot had a fixed Vickers machine gun in front of him which he could fire through the propeller. The observer sat in the back seat—which was a much more sensible place for him to be—with a Lewis gun on a quite effective mounting which he could swivel around in almost any direction. The 1½ Strutter had a speed of one hundred miles an hour, and it could climb to ten thousand feet in under eighteen minutes—great improvements over the performance of the B.E.2c.

The open cockpits of the aircraft we flew in the First World War provided us with much more fresh air than the air crews had in later years. We got none of the stink of cordite, for instance, that filled the enclosed cockpits of some of the aircraft of the second war because even though our guns were right up under or over our noses the slip stream rapidly blew everything away. On the other hand, the rotary engines of our early aircraft threw out a fine spray of the castor oil that was used for lubrication. This caused a strong and rather unpleasant smell, and the burnt oil from the exhausts quite often blackened the faces of the pilots.

The Sopwith 1½ Strutter had been designed for use by the Royal Naval Air Service and as a replacement for the B.E.2c, and the first deliveries of this new aircraft had gone to the Navy. By the early summer of 1916, just prior to the offensive planned to take place on the Somme, it was realized that the Royal Flying Corps was very seriously short of aircraft, and Trenchard made an urgent plea that we be brought up to the strength that had been planned and which would be needed if we were to give the Army full cooperation. The Admiralty generously handed over the new aircraft that they had just received, and the R.F.C. was able to put them to very good use in the increasing activity in the air over the Western Front.

By the time that the combined British and French offensive on the Somme was launched in the summer of 1916—one of the objectives of which was to try to relieve the pressure of the

German attacks on the French to the south, at Verdun—Trenchard had already become recognized (in fact as well as in appointment) as the great natural leader of the Royal Flying Corps in the field. Those of us who knew him during the years of the first war also came to know that he contributed more than any other single man to the laying of the foundations upon which the Royal Air Force was built. It is inevitable that there should be arguments about some of Trenchard's ideas—I, for one, have never agreed with everything that he did—but he was unquestionably just the leader we needed at that time.

The war in the air was bringing about developments that called for constant changes as well as expansion, and the rivalry to meet the conditions under the pressures exerted was intense. It was a constant struggle to get better and faster aircraft into the hands of the pilots, and that struggle had a great effect on morale. One of the secrets of Trenchard's success was the way in which he fully appreciated the importance of that fact.

A few weeks before the start of the Somme offensive we read in the newspapers about an argument over the defects in our equipment. Maurice Baring described it as "one of the periodical air agitations," and he credited it to the politicians. "It is no use making an agitation for obtaining in a few days' time what it takes a year or more to make," he stated in his diary, adding that such agitation could only result in "danger of spread of alarm and despondency among the younger personnel of the R.F.C." But Baring knew better than anybody else that Trenchard was the man who could best handle this; and handle it he did.

Since the Western Front was one continuous line from the Channel to the Swiss border, the only way we could conduct any offensive action was by hurling an attack at the enemy that would be overwhelming in sheer weight, thus smashing a way through the opposition. This, in turn, called for a strategic offensive on the part of the Flying Corps that meant carrying the battle in the air well over enemy territory. We had to get at the German Air Force before they even had a chance to approach the lines and interfere with our direct cooperation with our own Army.

This role of being on the offensive was to become an increasingly important one for the Flying Corps, and it was pressed for by Trenchard in a manner that eventually gave rise to a great deal of criticism. In an important paper prepared by Trenchard during the battles on the Somme he discussed the future policy in the air, and he stated that "an aeroplane is an offensive and not a defensive weapon." Stressing his belief that "the moral effect produced by a hostile aeroplane . . . is out of all proportion to the damage which it can inflict," Trenchard spoke of "a policy of relentless and incessant offensive" while at the same time admitting that "it would still be impossible to prevent hostile machines from crossing the lines if they were determined to do so, simply because the sky is too large to defend . . . and because the aeroplane is fighting in three dimensions."

While having to admit that there was a great deal in what Trenchard said, I took particular note of the relentlessness of his offensive policy. There were many lessons learned on the Somme. In addition to the more exact definition of the part the fighters were to play, there were also developed during that summer of 1916 other very important features in the use that could be made of aircraft. The first was a greatly improved system of even closer cooperation between the Flying Corps and the gunners, with artillery observation aircraft playing a vital part in the battles. Both sides came to appreciate that, and the Germans later admitted that our work in this area was far superior to theirs. The second outstanding feature was the great strides made in air photography. Photographic interpretation became a more exact business, and it yielded a rich harvest. Bombing also became much more highly organized, with the introduction of the first serious attempts at night bombing.

Although I spent only a short time on the Somme toward the end of the campaign, the fighting and the flying done there during that summer were of the greatest interest to all of us, at the Front and away from it. A particularly vivid description of the opening of the offensive as seen from the air on Saturday, July 1, 1916, is the account given by Cecil Lewis in his book *Sagittarius Rising*. Although not published until many years after the war, this book is the best that I have read by an Englishman on actual flying in the First World War. Lewis was an eighteen-year-old pilot in No. 3 Squadron. They were flying French Morane single-and-two-seater aircraft, and they were engaged in artillery observation, photography and contact patrols. The commanding officer of the squadron was my former pilot, the inimitable Harvey-Kelly. In July, 1916, he was a major with a D.S.O. to his credit.

One of the flight commanders in No. 3 Squadron at that time was Captain C. F. A. (Peter) Portal. After transferring from the Royal Engineers to the R.F.C. in May, 1915, Portal had joined No. 3 Squadron as an observer—at the same time that I was going off to learn to fly. He had also flown, as I had, as an observer with

Harvey-Kelly—who had gone from No. 2 to No. 3 Squadron—before returning to England later in the year to be trained as a pilot. He had come back to the Front as one of the original members of No. 60 Squadron, which was to make a name for itself as one of the foremost of the fighter squadrons. Almost immediately after his arrival back in France, Portal had been sent to No. 3 Squadron to take the place of one of the flight commanders who had been killed. He was a pilot with the squadron through all the battles that took place on the Somme.

There is in Cecil Lewis's book a fine description of the countryside of the Somme seen from the air just before the battles started; in contrast to that, there is a very telling description of what it was like seen from the ground after the fighting had been going on for some time. He speaks of "a desolation, unimaginable from the air . . . diseased, pocked, rancid, stinking of death . . .": a sight that the official historian described as "a gigantic monotonous wound." There is something in what an American writer said recently when he compared the lot of those who fought on the ground with those who fought in the air: we in the air did at least smell better.

It was the intention, when No. 43 Squadron was first formed, that we should become a long-range strategical reconnaissance squadron—long-range, that is, for those days. For this we would need aircraft with which we could fight as well as observe. The Sopwith 1½ Strutter was the first two-seater developed since the outbreak of war that was suitable for such a purpose. By the time that we began to receive the 1½ Strutter, it had already proved its effectiveness at the Front. With that heartening news and the promising crews I had trained, I began to feel that I had under my command the makings of a good squadron. It was then decided that I should gain some personal experience at the Front in the use of the 1½ Strutter. I had just been promoted to the rank of major, and I went out to France to spend a little time with No. 70 Squadron, the first squadron to be equipped with this aircraft. They were flying from the airdrome at Fienvillers, a few miles to the west of the airfield at Marieux; and I was again in the area of the Somme over which I had done so much flying a year before with No. 8 Squadron.

Across the other side of the front line, at about the same time that I returned to France in October, 1916, a German pilot was reporting for duty whose experiences in the air service had run along lines that were curiously parallel to my own. His name was

Hermann Goering. Born in Bavaria on January 12, 1893, Goering
was one of his father's ten children by two wives. The father had
served in the Prussian Army, and eventually he became a senior
civil servant in the German Consular Service. "The Germany into
which young Hermann had been born was an exciting vigorous
place," it has been recorded in one biography of Goering. "The
nation, newly united, had begun to feel its strength."

In his childhood, Hermann Goering was described as a "turbulent, unbridled character." He grew up in the mountains around
Salzburg, in southern Germany, rather spoiled by a wealthy Jewish
bachelor who took a great interest in the Goering family. Although
he always preferred to think of himself as a Bavarian, Goering was
by birth and instinct a Prussian.

The features for which Hermann Goering distinguished himself
at school were his lack of interest in work, his arrogance, and his
delight in the bullying that came instinctively to him. One of his
teachers said of him: "He is a born revolutionary." And a school
report commented: "This boy always likes to have his own way."
It was natural for such a young Prussian that he should go into the
army. He had done surprisingly well as a cadet, and in March,
1912, just after he became nineteen years of age, he received his
commission and joined an infantry regiment.

But the German army soon discovered that in Hermann Goering
they had on their hands a young man possessed of an intolerable
bumptiousness; and because of his unbridled spirit, Goering found
garrison life in the army in peacetime unpleasantly restricting. A
very good shot, and with a marked preference for outdoor life,
Goering also did quite a lot of mountain climbing. When the war
broke out in 1914 he was at a place on the Western Frontier which
saw some of the first of the fighting, and he quickly revealed that
he possessed outstanding initiative and courage. But during that
first winter, Goering developed rheumatism in both legs of such
severity that it put him into hospital and threatened to end his
career as a soldier. He was saved from such a fate—unfortunately,
some will say—by his best friend in his regiment, a slightly older
man by the name of Bruno Loerzer, who was to remain one of
Goering's closest friends in all that lay ahead.

Another of those who had transferred from the infantry to the
newly formed air service just before the outbreak of war, Bruno
Loerzer was learning to fly at a training school not far from the
hospital in which Hermann Goering was railing against his fate.
Loerzer suggested to Goering that he apply for a transfer to the air
service. Goering did so; after some difficulties his application was

approved, and he became Loerzer's observer. It was said of Goering that he was a sound, reliable observer, and particularly good at photography. He flew with Loerzer over the Front opposite the French at Verdun; and in a very short time he received the Iron Cross, First Class, which was then a much scarcer decoration than it became later in the war.

By February, 1915, Hermann Goering was doing exactly the same kind of work that I was from across the other side of the lines: observing for the artillery, photographing, and making use of the earliest of the wireless sets. During the summer he learned to fly, and he returned to the Front as a pilot in the autumn of that year. But Goering's luck was not as reliable as mine. He was a good but rather rash and impetuous pilot, and he was severely wounded while flying, receiving a shot in the hip. After this incident he spent some months in the hospital. Late in 1916, he returned to the Front to a squadron under the command of his old friend Bruno Loerzer. From that time on Goering began to make a name for himself as one of the foremost of the German fighter pilots.

The squadron to which I reported at Fienvillers was on the airfield close by a village in which Trenchard had the Advanced Headquarters of the Royal Flying Corps; also on that airdrome was the headquarters of the Ninth Wing. No. 70 Squadron was in this wing, which had been commanded during the early Somme battles by "Stuffy" Dowding, then a lieutenant-colonel, but was in the hands of Cyril Newall by the time I got there.

Most of those who served in the R.F.C. have various mementos of the time that they spent in France and on the other fronts. I still have my flying jacket, which has a bullet hole in the sleeve. A memento that Dowding cherishes is the joy-stick of a B.E.2c that he was flying one day over the Somme. In one scrap he got into, a bullet grazed his hand and made a clean hole just under it in the metal joy-stick. There was other damage to his aircraft, and the close shave that Dowding had then was almost identical with one I experienced while I was flying with No. 8 Squadron. These are small enough incidents compared with what many ran into, but putting them on record now will possibly appeal to the humor of the fighter pilots that Dowding and I had under our command during the first three years of the Second World War. We may have been in their eyes the commanders-in-chief, and as such possibly appeared to be rather remote and austere figures; but we also had had our moments, including those of fright.

The work being done by the pilots and observers of No. 70 Squadron was in long-range reconnaissance, photography and offensive patrols; and they had already acquired a great and well-deserved reputation for gallantry in the face of the heaviest casualties suffered by any squadron on the Front at that time. It was out of his anxiety over the severity of those losses that there developed in Dowding's mind the intense feelings that he came to have about casualties; and that, in part, was the cause of the rift between him and Trenchard that perplexed so many of us and was not explained until many years later.

Strangely enough, and something that is unusual for me, my memory of the short period that I spent at the Front on this occasion is rather vague. This is due, I think, to my distress over the news, which arrived just as I was about to leave for France, that my brother Archie had been reported missing. My mother was very upset, and I went to see her before I left England. She begged me to do all that I could on the spot to try and find out what had happened to Archie. He had transferred from the artillery to the R.F.C. in June, and he had become an observer in No. 42 Squadron, arriving in France in August. Equipped with B.E.'s, they were flying from Bailleul, just to the north of the airdrome at Merville (from which I had first flown as an observer eighteen months before). They were engaged, as we had been, on artillery observation and the bombing of targets well behind the enemy lines.

After reporting to No. 70 Squadron, I went on to Bailleul, which was to the north of us, and I had a talk with the commanding officer of No. 42 Squadron. He told me that Archie and his pilot—a young man named V. F. H. Hugill, who had been at school at Tonbridge with us—had almost certainly been killed, because their aircraft was seen to disintegrate in the air over the German lines. At the time, he could not tell me whether the plane had been hit by German antiaircraft fire or by one of our own shells. It had happened in the same area where Hereward de Havilland and I had listened with apprehension during our flying in the spring of the year before to the rumbling of our shells as they passed us on their way to the enemy. We had to wait until March of the following year before we received through the Red Cross in Geneva confirmation of the deaths of my brother and young Hugill. The report forwarded from Berlin stated that they had been buried together by the Germans in one of their cemeteries at Copinghem, a small village just to the west of Lille.

It was not until a few months ago—so many years later—that I finally learned the actual details of the way Archie was killed. They were contained in a letter written to Hugill's father by another pilot who saw what happened. A bombing raid by our aircraft was in progress, and Hugill and my brother had been instructed to locate and attack the German antiaircraft guns. The eyewitness was flying at five thousand feet, and he met Hugill and Archie, who were flying about two thousand feet above him. He followed them about five hundred yards behind as they set off for the German lines.

It was late afternoon of the day upon which Archie's transfer to the Royal Flying Corps was gazetted, and very shortly after he crossed the lines, the German antiaircraft guns opened up and fifteen to twenty shells were seen to burst around his aircraft. It went into a steep dive which quickly became a vertical one, and when it was about five hundred feet from the ground it was seen to break up in the air. The aircraft struck a house just behind the German front-line trenches, but there was no fire. The eyewitness was of the opinion that the pilot must have been hit by the enemy antiaircraft fire and that he must have fallen forward over the controls, so holding down the nose of his aircraft.

All my life I have been conscious of how much I have missed the warmth of the relationship that Archie and I had enjoyed. For brothers we were unusually close to each other: I was very fond of him, and I think he was equally fond of me. Just over twenty years of age when he was killed, Archie was the apple of our mother's eye; and his death was all the more unhappy for me because of her grief. When I got back to England and told her about what had happened, she blamed me for it; and with the understandable illogicality of a distressed mother, she said, "It is all your fault. If you had not joined the R.F.C. Archie would be alive today."

In time Archie came to be buried in one of the Commonwealth War Graves Cemeteries near Bois Grenier, which is to the south of Armentières and quite near the place where I had first seen action as a gunner. On the tour of the Western Front that I made in 1959, I spent a night in Armentières. The next morning I drove by various side roads across the flat, highly cultivated country to try to find my brother's grave, which I had never seen.

It was a clean and pleasant spring morning. I had a little difficulty in finding Ration Farm Cemetery. It is out in the country a short distance from Bois Grenier, and it is only a small cemetery compared with the many large ones maintained so well in this part of France and Belgium by the War Graves Commission. I found that it was attractively laid out and carefully tended. The first hasty burials had been made there as early as November, 1914, when it was in the area over which the fighting was taking place; and during most of the war it was just over a thousand yards behind the front line, standing at the beginning of a communication trench that led up to it. Archie's grave is in good company, for it lies surrounded by the graves of men who came from many other parts of what we used to know in those days as the Empire.

During the short time that I spent with No. 70 Squadron at Fienvillers, I did several patrols with them over the lines, but I did not participate in any particularly strenuous operational flying—although there occurred about this time some of the fiercest fighting in the air of all the battles on the Somme. The weather had broken, and it was at times quite awful. But I was too upset over my brother's death to be able to give full attention to the actual flying. However, the history of No. 43 Squadron records that when I returned to Netheravon I was "greatly inspired and full of optimism about the future of the squadron."

One of the harshest lessons that we all had to learn was to push personal feelings and emotions caused by casualties into the back of our minds, and even, if possible, to forget them. I had work to do, and there were important developments in flying to which I had to pay attention. In a paper that I wrote during my time at the R.A.F. Staff College some years after the war I expressed my views about what happened in the air during the closing stages of the battles on the Somme. The most important feature of this period, so far as the R.F.C. was concerned, was that we held at that time a decisive superiority over the enemy. During those battles we were supplied with better aircraft, and we attained and maintained that superiority through our policy of keeping up the pressure of the offensive patrols that Trenchard called for, and for which he was severely criticized. Formation flying by a wedge of five or six machines was recognized by now as the basis of air tactics; and there were already in existence a few squadrons that were specializing in air-to-air fighting. The French had produced the Nieuport and the Spad, both single-seater fighters, biplanes of a good design; we had, in addition to the D.H.2 and the F.E.8, both of which were good single-seater fighters, the Sopwith 1½ Strutter. Thus, during the summer, the supremacy of the Fokker monoplane came to an end. But by the autumn—even before the end of the battles on the Somme—there were signs enough that the Germans were about to reverse the order again. They had new fighters making their appearance at the Front which were surpassing ours in performance, and the Germans were showing no less interest than we were in the formation of separate units of these specialized fighters.

One German writer has called attention to the fact that not one of the "first fifteen" Fokker pilots at the beginning of 1916 survived beyond the end of that year. My famous adversaries Oswald Boelcke and Max Immelmann were both killed. At the time of his death, a few days before the start of the Somme offensive, Immelmann had to his credit fifteen of our aircraft destroyed, which was a small total in the lists of the top-scorers of the first war. But he was one of the pioneers, and the others learned from his discoveries. In a fight on June 18 between four Fokkers and seven of our aircraft over the area between Lens and Lille, his machine was seen to break up in the air. He fell some six thousand feet locked in the wreckage of the forward part of the broken Fokker. The German view about what happened was reflected in the statement made by Boelcke that Immelmann "lost his life by a silly chance. All that is written in the papers about a fight in the air, etc., is rot. A bit of his propeller flew off; the jarring tore the bracing wires connecting up with the fuselage, and then that broke away."

The British version of the circumstances of Immelmann's death is quite different; our official historian claims that he was shot down by one of the aircraft that he was attacking: an F.E.2b of No. 25 Squadron. The pilot of this aircraft was Second Lieutenant G. R. McCubbin, and he had as his observer Corporal J. H. Walker. Immelmann came to be known by his people as "The Eagle of Lille," and he was given a military funeral of pomp and honor—"the ceremony was most impressive," Oswald Boelcke reported. He was buried in Dresden.

On the day after I returned to England, Oswald Boelcke took off in one of the latest of the German fighters, an Albatros. His unit had just been re-equipped with this new biplane; in the months ahead it became possibly the best and most effectively armed of all the fighters on the Front. Boelcke had been flying up to seven patrols a day. On that last one he and his companions got into a scrap with two of our fighters, D.H.2's of No. 24 Squadron. The fight took place over Flers, which was where we had first used our tanks—one of our new inventions—only six weeks before. In their combined efforts to shoot down our aircraft, Boelcke and one of his pilots collided—"only just the faintest touch," the other pilot later reported—and the tip of one of the wings of Boelcke's aircraft was torn off. He fell out of the sky out of control, crashed, and was killed.

Such was the spirit of the air forces in those days that our people prepared a laurel wreath which they dropped by parachute over the German lines. It bore the inscription: "To the memory of Captain Boelcke, our brave and chivalrous foe. From the British Royal Flying Corps." As with Max Immelmann (and in such contrast to the way we did things), Oswald Boelcke was given an impressive funeral, with a service in the cathedral in Cambrai. He was buried in the cemetery in Dessau, his home town in Saxony.

One of the German pilots flying with Oswald Boelcke on that last flight was a comparatively unknown young man named Manfred von Richthofen. Within a very short time he was to emerge as one of the most formidable killers of all the fighter pilots of the First World War. The eldest son of a well-to-do country family which had produced conscientious—the word is his—if unspectacular soldiers, Richthofen was born in Breslau, in Silesia, in that part of Germany which we know as Prussia. He was just a few months older than Hermann Goering, and in appearance he was all that we associated with the Prussian: clean-cut features, close-cropped hair, bold eyes, a handsome man in a hard, instinctively arrogant way. It was said of him that he was very fond of and good at shooting game birds and wild fowl, and that he was a shrewd hunter with a keen eye and the patience that was necessary to become good at this sport. Richthofen was destined from the beginning for the Army, and when he was twenty years of age he was commissioned in the Uhlans, the scouting cavalry considered the most dashing branch of the service.

As soon as war broke out, Manfred von Richthofen went with his unit to the Russian Front in Poland, where the Uhlans and the Cossacks met in slight clashes; but after only a very short time there, they were transferred to the Western Front. "I had no idea about the activity of our flying men," he stated in describing his activities in Belgium and France during the first few weeks of the war. "At any rate, I got tremendously excited whenever I saw an aviator. Of course I had not the slightest idea whether it was a German or an enemy. I had at that time not even the knowledge that the German machines were marked with crosses and the enemy machines with circles. The consequence was that every aeroplane we saw was fired upon." He need not have worried about that because our troops were only too inclined to do exactly the same thing.

By the autumn of 1914, Richthofen was commenting, "I am a restless spirit"; and that restlessness made the drabness of the trench warfare of that winter more than he could bear. In May, 1915, he transferred to the air service as an observer. (When one looks back over the records one cannot help being struck by the extraordinary number of us who got our start in flying that way.) "Now came my most beautiful time," Richthofen recorded. He was sent to a squadron on the Russian front "as quite a juvenile observer [who] had not the slightest idea of anything." In August, 1915, he was transferred back to the Western Front. Shortly after that there occurred an incident recorded in his autobiography—a scarce little book that was published in England in 1918—which is worth mentioning for its historical interest.

As an observer on a routine flight, Richthofen set off one day "to delight the English with our bombs." Of what happened then, he said: "Unfortunately my large machine, which was very well qualified for carrying bombs, had the stupid peculiarity that one could scarcely see the effect of a bombthrow, for the machine came after the throw between one's eye and the object, and covered it completely with its planes. This always made me wild, because one does not like to be deprived of one's amusement. If one hears a bang down below and one sees the delightful greyish-whitish cloud of the explosion in the neighbourhood of the object aimed at one is always very pleased. Therefore I waved to friend Zeumer that he should turn a little to one side. While waving to him I forgot that the infamous object on which I was travelling, my applebarge, had two air-screws which turned to the right and left of my observer-seat. I meant to show him where approximately the bomb had hit, and, bang! my finger was caught!"

A valuable comment was made about three years later on this account of Richthofen's curious, if slight, accident by C. G. Grey, who later became a well-known writer on aviation. He said: "From this disposition of the air-screws, and from the date of the occurrence, one assumes that this was one of the very earliest twin-engined Gothas, or A.E.G.'s, of the tractor type which the R.F.C. nicknamed 'Wong-wong' because of the curious noise made by the engines or air-screws when they ran out of step." This comment must be one of the earliest published references to the noise made by the engines of German aircraft, a noise that was to become only too distressingly familiar to our people at home in both world wars.

Early in October, 1915, while still an observer, Richthofen met Oswald Boelcke, whom he described as "a young and insignificant-looking lieutenant" even though he was filled with admiration for what Boelcke was achieving. Later that month Richthofen was taught to fly by the pilot with whom he had been working as an observer. He took his examination in Berlin, and on Christmas Day, 1915, he became a qualified pilot. A few weeks later Richthofen returned to France, and he flew as a pilot in two-seaters on the Front at Verdun, against the French; but just before the start of our offensive on the Somme, he was sent back to the Russian Front. While serving there he again met Boelcke, who was on a tour of inspection. Boelcke was forming the important fighter unit that he was to command on the Somme, and he selected Richthofen as one of his pilots. That was to be the turning point in Richthofen's career as an airman. On September 17—at the height of the battles on the Somme—he shot down the first of the many aircraft of the Royal Flying Corps that he was eventually to include in his score.

When one takes into consideration that on that day in September, 1916, Richthofen was flying a new type of aircraft—one of the latest versions of the single-seater Albatros—which he had received only the day before, his achievement in downing one of our F.E.2b's of No. 11 Squadron flown by an experienced pilot and observer was remarkable. Within two months Richthofen was claiming his eleventh victim. In this case it was the first of our more successful fighter pilots: Major L. G. Hawker, the commanding officer of No. 24 Squadron. I met Hawker a few times out in France. He was a prewar pilot who had transferred to the R.F.C. from the Royal Engineers. A shy, retiring man, absolutely dedicated to his work, he had already won a Victoria Cross for being the first of our pilots to shoot down three enemy aircraft in one day, and a D.S.O. for his exploits as a lone wolf on a hazardous bombing raid.

"During my whole life I have not found a happier hunting ground than in the course of the Somme Battle," Richthofen wrote a short time afterward.

It must have seemed to all our people that, right from the beginning of that summer of 1916, they were subjected to one unpleasant shock after another, all repercussions from the blows that were exchanged on land and at sea—and to a very much lesser degree in the air—by the armed forces. At the end of May came the Battle of Jutland, which was the only great naval battle of the First World War, and the last naval battle of any consequence in which the air played practically no part. Two great fleets—the Grand

Fleet of Britain and the German High Seas Fleet—were engaged in the North Sea under the command of no less than twenty-five admirals alone, and although the result was a draw, to the great disappointment of many, it did at least keep the German fleet pretty well bottled up in harbor for the rest of the war.

A week later, on June 6, hard on the heels of Jutland came the shattering news that Field Marshal Lord Kitchener had been lost, presumed drowned, when H.M.S. *Hampshire,* the warship on which he was traveling on a military mission to Russia, was sunk after hitting a German mine off the Orkneys. Although the Secretary of State for War had lost a great deal of his hold over the politicians, Kitchener was still, in the eyes of the public, a very great figure, and his contribution to our effort in the war had been immense.

Three weeks later, on July 1, the first of the battles on the Somme was launched. "It is a truism that the war of 1914–1918 revolutionized all ideas of time, in a military sense, and especially in the duration of its battles," Liddell Hart has written. The Somme was the outstanding example of that. On the first day we suffered the heaviest losses for any single day in the whole of the war; and from that time on it may truthfully be said that we, the British, took on the main burden of the war on the Western Front. The new armies that we had in the field—Kitchener's armies made up of volunteers and amateurs—proved themselves in the most magnificent way. But the fighting on the Somme went on for months, and the best of the men we had to offer paid for the glory they won, paid for it over and over again with the most dreadful casualties.

Figures alone can never tell the story of the way a whole generation of men was crippled. On that first day alone, our casualties on the Somme numbered fifty-seven thousand, of which twenty thousand men were killed or died of wounds. That slaughter went on until the Battle of the Somme ended in the mud of the winter. To those concerned it cost, all told, over one million casualties, with three hundred thousand British, French and German dead. What was achieved? Although historians have tried, none has really been able to say. Nor did our leaders seem to learn any lessons from the holocaust—how often that word can be used in speaking about the First World War—because the slaughter still went on under the names of other battles. It was that which made our military leaders in the Second World War, most of whom had served as young men in the earlier war, so determined to find the right answers to stalemate and attrition.

Whenever I allow my mind to summon up thoughts of the Somme memories are always recalled for me of the songs that we all sang in the first war, and they are memories that never fail to bring a lump into my throat. "Roses of Picardy" is more than a pleasantly sentimental song to those of my generation: it evokes a poignant memory of the sight of columns of disheveled troops, at times very muddy and torn, as they marched back from the trenches. "It's a Long Way to Tipperary" and "Pack Up Your Troubles in Your Old Kit Bag" were the favorites of the troops as they marched to and from desolation, and so far as I am concerned they will always be the marching songs of that particularly intense period. "If You Were the Only Girl in the World" ran like wildfire through the fancy of the men in France, and it stirred our youthful sentiments in a way that was then very moving and even now possesses a nostalgia that cannot be shared with anyone because it is so essentially a purely personal one.

It is the memory of those songs and the other songs we sang in the Flying Corps that seems to bring most strongly to my mind thoughts about my association with the men with whom I flew. They were men of every type, and their temperaments were of an astonishing variety. Some of them were beginning then to make names for themselves in the eyes of the public as well as those of their fellow airmen. The excessive adulation of their flying heroes that was indulged in by the Germans was something that the Royal Flying Corps was spared, and that was due mainly, I think, to the humor and the better sense of proportion of our own people. But it could not be altogether avoided, and during the battles on the Somme the names of our own aces began to appear in the limelight. There were pilots before that time who had met wth conspicuous success, but when the fighter—the lone-wolf scout—came into his own, he filled the role of the hero in the eyes of the public. All said and done, hero worship is an age-old response from those who stand and watch, and it is a natural and healthy enough response so long as it does not get out of hand. It is infinitely healthier than the revolting "anti-hero" school of thought that is now affected by so many.

The first of the great British fighter aces was Albert Ball, and his name flashed through the history of the first war with the intensity of a meteor. I knew Ball, but I could never say that I knew him well because, although he was a pleasant enough young man whom we all liked, he did not make any particular impression while he was on the ground. It was not until he got into the air that he came into his own, and then it was an entirely different matter. Ball was an extremely gallant pilot who did the most extraordinary things, the supreme individualist; and he became all this at a very early age. He was not quite eighteen years old when the war broke out. After some months in the Sherwood Foresters—he came from Nottingham—he learned to fly in the summer of 1915 and was seconded to the Royal Flying Corps at the end of January, 1916.

A few weeks before the start of the Somme offensive, Albert Ball started flying the new single-seater Nieuport Scout, and it immediately became apparent that he was ideally suited by temperament to the work of the fighter. But all his fighting was to be as a lone wolf: he was not interested in working with formations of aircraft. Ball would dash madly into the middle of any number of enemy aircraft, shoot down a couple of them, and then, knowing just when to pull out, charge off, more often than not having received quite a peppering himself. He celebrated his twentieth birthday during the battles on the Somme, and he performed the most astonishing feats, shooting down a host of Germans and making the most miraculous escapes. The history of this period is filled with accounts of his exploits. He was the outstanding member of No. 60 Squadron, and by the end of the year he had made a name for himself as our most adventurous fighter pilot.

The other outstandingly successful fighter pilot who was to appear at this time, second only to Ball, was James McCudden. I came to know him very well, and to admire him greatly both as a man and as a pilot. McCudden was a year older than Albert Ball and he came from a very different background. He adopted on his own initiative tactics that were entirely different from those practiced by the impetuous Ball. McCudden was a thoughtful tactician, and he was the originator of the formation fighter tactics which later became the rule—the flight sticking together and never allowing itself to be broken up.

During the months between July 1 and November 18, 1916—the day on which our offensive on the Somme came to a halt in a snowstorm—the Royal Flying Corps suffered heavy casualties: 308 pilots and 199 observers were listed as killed, wounded or missing. These casualties had severe repercussions on the training program at home, and we were stretched to the limit to make good the losses. But out of that campaign came the unanimous conclusion that air power had established its position in the scheme of things. Much lay ahead in the constant ebb and flow of the fortunes of war, but this greater understanding of the importance of the air made each side all the more determined to gain control of it. We were all launched upon a third dimension.

"The air flows over both land and sea; more than either land or sea it is the place of vision, and of speed and freedom of movement," Walter Raleigh wrote of the development of the air forces during 1916. "What we of this generation are witnessing is a process whereby the air shall come into its own. It will become the great highway for the traffic of peace; and in war, which cannot be abolished while man has interests that are dearer to him than his own comfort and safety, the forces of the air will be, not a late-found timid auxiliary to the forces of the land and of the sea, but their overseer and their director."

That statement appears in the first volume of *The War in the Air,* published in the year 1921. I read it shortly after the book came out; and now, well over forty years later, I cannot help but wonder at and be impressed by its astonishing prescience.

We who were intimately involved in actual warfare were concerned with a reality that was steadily becoming more pressing and very much grimmer, and in facing it, our attitude toward the waging of war was forced to change. If ever there was a clear indication of the nature of that change in the minds of those who were fighting in France, it is surely to be found in Siegfried Sassoon's poem "Base Details," which was written in 1917. There are lines in that poem that have sounded for me, ever since I first read them, a note of grim understanding; and they were to come to my mind often enough when I became a staff officer with large staffs under my own command. They also gave me a firm reminder, even if it was a wickedly cynical one, of the role that one has to play, particularly in the first three lines:

> *If I were fierce, and bald and short of breath,*
> *I'd live with scarlet Majors at the Base,*
> *And speed glum heroes up the line to death.*

But the sour note of cynicism that had stabbed its way into our understanding—it could never be said that it crept in: the violence that our men had known on the Somme was much too real for that—was not sweetened in any way by what was happening at home. Much has been said about the way our government changed at the end of 1916, with the fall of Herbert Asquith and the tortuous maneuver executed by Lloyd George in the last few steps of his final climb to power. It has been asked if the events on the political scene in December, 1916, did not mark the great turning point in the fortunes of this country. Just as what happened on the Somme cost us too dearly in the lives of the best of our manhood, so did the political machinations in London immediately afterward inflict upon us a wound that has never healed. I believe that is proved all too clearly in everything that has happened since then.

Ten years after the war, in 1928, a book by Lord Beaverbrook was published entitled *Politicians and the War 1914–1916*. This book has since come to be accepted by historians and biographers as one of value if one wishes to gain a complete picture of what went on during those years. I read the book when it first came out, and from it I gained one firm impression; a re-reading of it quite recently greatly strengthened that impression. This may have been partly the result of my own experiences of high command in the Second World War.

A great deal is said in Lord Beaverbrook's book about the patriotism of the politicians, and how that patriotism compelled them to behave in the way that they did, subjecting themselves to tensions that were tortuous and at times so difficult to understand. From my reading of the book I could not avoid coming to the conclusion that above all else these men were animated more by ambitions both extraordinary and largely personal.

Throughout his book there is constantly reiterated by Lord Beaverbrook the theme that the reason these politicians struggled so desperately for office was that they desired ardently to serve their country. No doubt their motives were mixed, and doubtless they did wish, in their own fashion, to serve their country; but after reading what Beaverbrook had to say—all of it written in a vein so characteristic of him—I was left with questions that were begging for answers. What about the fighting of the war itself? Were any thoughts ever given to those who were actually doing it? When, in the welter of all this political intrigue, did these politicians ever do any actual work? Or was the work solely the achievement of office and positions of power? To those of us who have been less anxious about achieving political power, this book presents an astonishing story.

But the outcome of the political struggle in December, 1916, and the coming to power of Lloyd George as Prime Minister, was to mark the beginning of an even sorrier story. It presented one of the worst aspects of the First World War, and it showed clearly how there was developing the full violence of the clash between the politicians and the generals. In February, 1917, this led to one of the most trying experiences to which a military commander can be subjected: his relegation in the interests of political expediency, entirely without his knowledge, to a position inferior to that which he has been holding and, at the same time, under a commander of another nation. I speak with feeling about that, and with some degree of sympathy for Douglas Haig, because I was to have to endure the threat of just such an experience, in a much smaller way, in the Second World War.

Early in 1917 the British and French politicians and military leaders met in a top-level conference at Calais. General Sir William Robertson, Chief of the Imperial General Staff, and Sir Douglas Haig, C.-in-C. of the British Expeditionary Force and recently promoted to the rank of field marshal, were presented with the agreed plans for future military operations before they had even been acquainted with what had been proposed. Quite unknown to them, and unknown even to the Secretary of State for War, Lloyd George had arranged in an astonishingly underhand fashion that Haig and his command of the British Army in France should come under the direction of Robert Nivelle, a French general junior to Haig. This deal was revealed in a callous fashion to Robertson and Haig at the conference at Calais, and it is small wonder that they felt they had been double-crossed by Lloyd George. It was a lesson to Haig that was sharp enough for him never again to trust Lloyd George, and bitter enough for him to suspect every move made by the Prime Minister from that time on. Cyril Falls has described the whole affair as "one of the most unsavoury episodes in British political-military relations."

7 / First Command

SHORTLY AFTER I returned from France in October, 1916, to my own squadron in England, I was dealt a very severe blow. Because of the heavy losses that the Royal Flying Corps had suffered in pilots and observers during the battles on the Somme, reinforcements were having to be rushed out to the squadrons in France as well as to the new squadrons that were on the verge of going to the front. At one fell swoop I was robbed of all my pilots and observers, including my three flight commanders. I had gone to such pains to train them, and I had become quite proud of them and of what I had achieved; but it was something that had to happen, and that was to go on happening, and I had to reconcile myself to it. Many young squadron commanders in the second war came to know the same thing, and it was something that, because of my own experiences in the earlier war, I hated having to do to them.

Although I was thus denuded of all my carefully trained air crews, raw replacements and some experienced pilots were quickly provided for me, and I then had to embark upon more training. Early in December, 1916, we were moved from Netheravon to Northolt, and then our new aircraft began to arrive, and by early in January of the new year we were fully equipped with our Sopwith 1½ Strutters. I soon discovered that I was particularly fortunate in having men of the caliber of those who were sent to join me at Northolt, and they and that well-known airdrome provided for me at that time the start of an interest that has lasted for many years. That was over forty-five years ago, and for many years I had only to turn around in my chair in my office at the headquarters of British European Airways at Ruislip and look out of the window and I could see across to the same airfield at Northolt, and even the actual hangar that housed our aircraft in 1917. For a time we made use of it in B.E.A. as a garage for some of our motor transport.

An even closer link with those days of 1917, and a far more personal one, is the well-known political figure Harold Balfour,

126

then a captain, who came to join me in No. 43 Squadron as one of my flight commanders. During the second war, Balfour was Under-Secretary of State for Air. Today, an old friend of long standing, he is better known as Lord Balfour of Inchrye. He is a member of the board of British European Airways.

Life in the Royal Flying Corps—as in the Royal Air Force—provided a way for expressing so clearly the aspect of the spirit of man that we have come to call the heroic. For all that mere fashion may dictate, the heroic will always be one of the attributes which most serves to make men of us rather than cringing puppets, and whenever I think of that spirit there comes to my mind the way in which Harold Balfour went about his flying when he first served under my command. He was then only twenty years of age, tall, slim and very alert. Well above the average in intelligence, he was a highly-strung youngster who was clearly feeling the strain of the great amount of active service and operational flying that he had done. Because of that his courage and what he achieved are all the more admirable, and he was a good example of the splendor of the spirit of the Royal Flying Corps.

There is no reason why I should not speak of this side of Harold Balfour's character because he has revealed it clearly enough, although quite unintentionally, in his book *An Airman Marches,* which was published over thirty years ago. A gay and at times an amusing book, it reflects so well the character of Balfour himself. But there is also revealed in it the underlying strength of purpose that he later came to show in his political career. It is also a very good self-portrait of a fighter pilot of the First World War.

Right from the outset there is revealed in Balfour's book a character trait of his early years which he describes as ". . . a rebellion against law, order and discipline as laid down by my elders and alleged betters." While still only sixteen years of age, he joined the Army shortly after the war broke out, and by the time of his seventeenth birthday he was already a second lieutenant in the King's Royal Rifle Corps and serving with his battalion in France. Balfour learned to fly at his own expense at Hendon in the middle of 1915—he had taken an interest in flying since childhood—and after transferring to the Royal Flying Corps he was back in France with the very good company assembled in No. 60 Squadron.

"I was hating the war," Harold Balfour wrote later, "and frightened of contest, mainly through being too young for the job we had to face and so unable to master and control my nerves." I knew that Balfour disliked intensely the whole business of war, but he was always a gallant fighter. His experiences while serving with

No. 60 Squadron in France had troubled him, and he has written about his lack of confidence; but by the time that he joined me in No. 43 Squadron he had regained that confidence, and he was anxious to have yet another go at active service.

It was of the greatest interest to me to find that another of the officers whom I had serving under me at Northolt matched well that spirit of Balfour's. He was a remarkable character, greatly admired throughout the Royal Flying Corps, by the name of Jack Scott. Considerably older than the average run of fighter pilots—being by then in his middle thirties—Scott was a successful barrister before the war, being associated with Lord Birkenhead. He was also an old friend of Winston Churchill's, with whom he had done some prewar flying.

Always cheerful and imperturbable, and charming in his manner toward everybody, Jack Scott was, for all his spirit, rather a ham-fisted pilot. He had had a very bad crash earlier in the war, breaking both his legs, and he could walk only with the help of sticks; but disabilities were not allowed to stand in his way. He brought pressure to bear and got himself sent to my squadron as a flight commander. Whenever the time came for him to fly he had to be lifted into and out of his aircraft. We all came to form such a warm admiration for him and the way in which he did things.

At first I felt rather awkward about giving orders to this thirty-five-year-old who was obviously a man of the world. I felt that such orders coming from a whippersnapper of only twenty-three years of age might be resented; but Jack Scott was to teach me a very good lesson both in the balance of maturity and the handling of men. Such was his charm and good humor that neither of us ever knew in our relationship anything approaching a difficult moment, and even though, up to that time, Scott had not done any operational flying at the Front, he very soon proved that he was a splendid leader of men.

In every squadron, as in every other unit in the Army, there was one man who could, through the way in which he conducted himself, make or break its efficiency. That man was the adjutant or, as he was known in those early days of the Royal Flying Corps, the recording officer. He could be, if he chose and if he had it in him, of great help—as a father confessor to the members of the squadron as well as a staunch and loyal supporter of the commanding officer. Again I was lucky in the man whom I had as my adjutant in No. 43 Squadron.

While I was in the process of forming the squadron at Stirling, I came to know the adjutant of the Depot of the Argyll and Suther-

land Highlanders, which occupied the Castle. His name was Tom
Purdey, and he was a member of the world-famous family of
gunsmiths. Purdey took a liking to the Flying Corps, and when he
applied for a transfer I managed to get him posted to me as my
squadron recording officer. He was an ebullient, notably cheerful
character, who, although non-flying, became universally popular
and almost as well known in the R.F.C. as Maurice Baring. He
could play the piano well, and his short, plump figure, almost
always wearing a kilt, was a welcome sight around the airfields and
in the squadron mess. He watched over our lives on the ground
with an exceptionally shrewd understanding.

It seemed to me, in my impatience to get the squadron to France
and into the thick of things, that far too much time was being
consumed at Northolt in equipping us with all that we needed and
in bringing the squadron up to scratch as a fighting unit. On top of
that, time and time again I was robbed of aircraft and crews. By
the new year of 1917 we were already three months behind in the
plan that had been laid down for us. But shortly after the middle
of January we were at long last sent on our way to France. Harold
Balfour and Tom Purdey went first, by sea, taking over the ground
personnel, transport and stores; and the aircraft of the squadron
set off from Northolt on January 17.

From the very outset we seemed to run into nothing but trouble.
Harold Balfour's deputy flight commander, who was leading B
Flight, the first of the flights to set off, stalled and crashed on take-
off in full sight of the whole squadron. He and his mechanic were
both killed, together with Balfour's small dog, which was being
carried in a bag in the rear cockpit of the aircraft. It was a disturbing enough start, but I did my best to keep the rest of the squadron
from becoming too discouraged, and I saw them all safely on their
way, waiting until the end before I took off myself.

From that bad start we seemed to run into continuous trouble.
No sooner were we in the air than the weather broke, and Jack
Scott had to lead his flight down the Thames so low that they were
flying below the top floor windows as they passed what was then
Adastral House, the headquarters of the Royal Flying Corps, on
the Embankment near Blackfriars Bridge. We had to land at
Lympne in Kent, and we spent the night there before we could
cross the Channel the next day. After reporting to St.-Omer we
were sent on to the airfield at Treizennes, near Aire, in the flat,
colorless country to the northwest of Béthune, only a few miles
from Merville.

Unfortunately we aircrew got to Treizennes long before the ground party arrived, and we spent two extremely uncomfortable days waiting for them to show up. That winter of 1916–17 was a brutal one, and it was bitterly cold at Treizennes. The ground was snow-covered—the first six weeks of the new year was a period of hard frost—and we had to camp out in bare, empty huts with only our flying kits to keep us warm. Never in my life have I been so cold as I was during the first forty-eight hours of my longed-for return to France.

Our miserable introduction to life at Treizennes was made just bearable by the kindness of the other squadron—No. 40—with which we were to share the airfield. They had been there for some time, and the squadron was under the command of Robert Loraine. A handsome and very well-known actor of middle age, Loraine was also a first-rate airman. His squadron was equipped then with F.E.8's, but soon after our arrival they got Nieuport Scouts. One of his flight commanders was the son of Lady Gregory, the famous Irish dramatist whom I was to meet in Dublin some months later.

The whole atmosphere of the airdrome at Treizennes was dominated by the character of Robert Loraine, and I readily agree with Harold Balfour's comment that "his organization was stage-managed with a masterly touch." I came to know Loraine very well both as an airman and, through going to the theater and enjoying his work, as an actor. The memory of his exuberant character that Harold Balfour and I share with an amusement that time has not dimmed is of the night on which he played a role that, while not on the stage, was typical of his attitude toward life.

A fire broke out in one of the hangars in which there were four of No. 40's aircraft, and it quickly raged through the petrol tanks and the wood and the canvas wings of the aircraft. There was nothing that any of us could do, and we just stood around and watched the blaze. But suddenly, reflected in the light from the fire, there appeared in front of us the arresting figure of Loraine. It was as if he had stepped out from the wings to take up his position in front of the footlights. This was the occasion for the star to play his part, and play it he did. Unbuttoning his trousers and aiming in the direction of the fire, he performed almost with contempt, and certainly with defiance, what Harold Balfour described as "a perfectly natural function." I could never have attempted to offer leadership with the touches of sheer flamboyance that Loraine displayed, but there was never any question about the devotion that his style inspired in those under his command.

There was one other man under whom we came to serve at that time who was also to provide me with a lesson in this matter of leadership. We were in the 1st Brigade of the Royal Flying Corps, which was commanded by Gordon Shephard, a brigadier who, for all his exalted rank, was only about thirty years of age. One of the earliest of the pilots in the Flying Corps, he was somewhat vacuous in appearance, with a receding chin and afflicted with a slight lisp—physically a colorless personality. But that was the only thing about him that was lacking in color.

Although Gordon Shephard was not a good pilot, his mind was of a brilliance that would undoubtedly have led to his becoming in time one of the great leaders in the Air Force; but that poor flying of his brought about his death in an accident before the end of the war, and so his name came to play only a minor role in the history of flying. In fact, it has come to be much better known for the part that he is said to have played in the creation of the novel *The Riddle of the Sands,* by Erskine Childers, who used him, young though he must have been, as a model for Carruthers, the hero of that well-known story. Described as "a record of secret service," the book was first published in 1903, and it deals in a curiously prophetic way with the discovery of a plot for a German invasion of England.

At the time when No. 43 Squadron had first been formed, some eight months before, the Sopwith 1½ Strutter offered a good answer to the threat from the existing German fighters, which had been superior to our own. It was then an excellent aircraft. But such was the speed of development that the 1½ Strutter was already outclassed by the time that we arrived in France. For a while during the battles on the Somme we had enjoyed superiority in the air, and then the Germans had regained the upper hand. We found that our precious aircraft were much too slow when pitted against the new Albatros and Halberstadt Scouts which the Germans had brought into use. These new German fighters were both single-seater biplanes of an advanced design, and they had more powerful engines than we had, and a much better rate of climb. In the hands of the German pilots, who were by no means lacking in the skill to take advantage of the upper hand that they had gained, they became a very real menace.

The way in which the affairs of the R.F.C. were conducted early in 1917 was dominated to a very large extent by the quality of our morale—something that must always be considered in any undertaking involving the temper of young men blessed with enthusiasm.

While I fully understood the reasons for the obsolescence of our aircraft—a result of the drive to increase as rapidly as possible the number of R.F.C. squadrons on active service in France—I nevertheless felt that it was wrong to expand regardless of the cost. It was a situation that was similar to one which I had to face nearly twenty years later when I became one of the commanders-in-chief in the Royal Air Force in the Second World War.

One fault that we found in our Sopwiths in the rough and tumble at the Front was that they were rather fragile aircraft. There had been too many cases in which, when roughly or clumsily handled, they had broken up in the air, and we had such a case in No. 43 Squadron only shortly after we arrived in France. But I knew that the aircraft itself was really strong enough to perform any maneuver, provided that it was handled with reasonable delicacy and lightness, so one day shortly after we arrived at Treizennes I took up one of our aircraft to demonstrate to my pilots just what could be done with it. In the back seat I had as passenger Tom Purdey, my adjutant, and thinking that thirteen might be the right number, psychologically, for such a display, I performed thirteen consecutive loops.

Everything about my demonstration went off very well until I landed, and then I found that I had not warned Purdey about what I was going to do, and that he had not been strapped in. Throughout the whole of the thirteen loops he had been hanging onto the fixtures in the interior of the cockpit, and grim death had been staring him in the face. He could all too easily have fallen out, and I was very angry with myself for such thoughtlessness on my part, although Purdey, after his first fright, took it all in good spirit. My pilots, I need hardly say, were delighted with what they thought was an enormous joke.

Though unintentional, this was just the sort of antic that I knew it was up to me to watch with the greatest of care. In addition to Jack Scott I had another pilot in the squadron, by the name of Major A. S. W. Dore, who was an older and more mature man, and between them they could very easily have written me off as being young and irresponsible. The reason for Dore's rank was that he was a major in a territorial battalion of the Worcestershire Regiment. He became so interested in the R.F.C. that he learned to fly, and he joined my squadron, still with the rank of major, as one of my ordinary flying officers.

A gallant pilot as well as a good one, Dore did very well with us, and when Jack Scott left to take command of No. 60 Squadron I gave Dore his flight. Eventually Wilfrid Freeman gave him command of the squadron when I had to give it up. Dore will be remembered by many of those who served in the Royal Auxiliary Air Force for the part he played in the formation at Hendon in 1930 of No. 604 Squadron, which came, under the command of John Cunningham, to be one of the foremost of my night fighter squadrons in Fighter Command in the Second World War.

As the commanding officer of a squadron at the Front, I found that what with all the other work that I had on my hands I was able to do much less operational flying than the rest of my flying officers and the flight commanders. I always tried to do as much as possible because I believed that it was good for squadron morale that the C.O. should also be in the thick of things. But there was a great deal of administrative work that I had to attend to, the first of this kind of work on active service that I experienced, and much as I disliked it at the time, it was to form an invaluable foundation for my work in the future.

Our arrival in France in the middle of that appalling freeze-up of the winter of 1916–17 made an immediate demand on any resourcefulness that I might have as a commanding officer because we were all of us—officers and airmen, and even the engines of our aircraft—frozen stiff. I had to find some way of getting around that and of at least thawing out the engines and getting everybody more comfortable, so I embarked upon a program of wangling and wire-pulling to get additional supplies from the local units of the Royal Army Service Corps and the Royal Engineers.

Requests for more supplies through official channels produced some results, but eventually I had to take the law into my own hands. Under the cover of darkness we conducted—much to the delight of those who participated in it—a large-scale raid upon the nearest dump of the Royal Engineers. From that we were able to gather enough timber and building materials to improve upon our meager accommodation. But even then it was a constant struggle to get enough fuel to burn in order to keep just barely warm.

No sooner were we settled in at Treizennes and well embarked upon active operational flying than we started having unexpectedly heavy casualties. On the heels of that there came to us an almost constant stream of replacements: new aircraft, new pilots and new observers. The Sopwith 1½ Strutter was not a particularly easy aircraft to maintain, and there were quite a number of modifications that we had to make before the new machines could be used. So the ground crews as well as the air crews were kept working at full pressure. All that added to the load of the administrative work for me.

The insufficient training of the pilots, and the almost complete lack of any training for the observers, meant that I also had to organize within the squadron a pretty thoroughgoing training school to try to bring the air crews up to some sort of operational standard. In an effort to achieve this I did a great deal of the flying instruction myself, because I did not think it would be at all fair to burden the hard-pressed operational pilots with this additional chore. On the other hand, these heavy demands on my time did relieve me from having to take a major part in the operational flying, which was not of a particularly inspiring nature.

Every night there would be brought to me a sealed envelope containing orders from Wing Headquarters, then under the command of Wilfrid Freeman, for our operations for the next day. Tough though some of those orders were, the fact that they came from Wilfrid Freeman meant that I was able to accept them with confidence. They would usually arrive when we were about halfway through dinner, and I would read them out and then give instructions about how they were to be executed. "Somehow food lost its attraction and spirits sank for an appreciable time after we knew the contents of that envelope," Harold Balfour has commented.

Just before dawn of the next day, the pilots and the observers who were to do the early patrols would be standing by their machines ready to take off as soon as it was light enough. On one of these patrols, a reconnaissance made not long after we arrived in France, we saw from the air and photographed indications that the enemy were preparing to retire from the salient which had been formed after the battles on the Somme in the long line between Arras and Noyon to the south. We found that the enemy were purposely withdrawing to very strongly fortified lines that they had prepared running from Lens to St.-Quentin. To these new lines our people gave the name of the Hindenburg Line.

The Germans had a name for that new front line which became much more familiar to us during the early months of the Second World War. They called it the Siegfried Line. Although in 1939 we boasted all too readily about hanging out our washing on the Siegfried Line, no such thoughts occupied our minds in 1917. Grim experience had already taught us to be much more realistic than that; and even grimmer experiences in the immediate future were to face the British Army in our efforts to breach one of the toughest defense lines ever built. The Germans successfully accomplished their carefully planned withdrawal during the latter part of February, and they were followed by the British Army having to work its way in slow time across an area that had been deliberately devasted by the retreating enemy.

Although we had made definite progress in exploring the methods of air fighting during those first two years of the war, we were still particularly conscious of the inferior performance of our aircraft in comparison with those of the enemy. We had no defense in armor, no self-sealing petrol tanks, and no parachutes. They were developments that were to come much later. We had to rely more on our wits and our skill in flying, and on the slowly evolving tactics of combat in the air. In all our minds, try as we did to make light of it, the fear that was constantly with us was of fire in the air. We could all too easily be set alight, and one of the most unpleasant experiences that we knew in the first war was to have to watch the helplessness of a friend going down in flames.

On one patrol early in 1917 I was flying in formation with my squadron when we were suddenly attacked by some Huns. After the first flurry was over I glanced across at the next aircraft beside me in our formation, and I saw that the observer, poor devil, was standing up in the back seat agitatedly trying to call to the attention of his pilot a glint of flame that was just starting to appear along the side of their aircraft. A moment later there was a violent explosion and the whole aircraft disintegrated. Such a sight was all too common in our flying of those days, and so far as I was concerned it was one of the most horrible that one could witness.

Our Sopwith 1½ Strutters suffered from the serious disadvantage of all the aircraft which were at that time powered with rotary engines—their performance fell off very rapidly when flying above ten thousand feet. Since the Germans already had in use their new single-seater fighters we were in trouble from the start. It seemed only such a short time before that we had managed to gain the upper hand over the Fokker monoplane; but here were the Germans yet again forging ahead of us.

Our work as a squadron was on the active front occupied by the First Army, and its purpose was the carrying out of reconnaissance, photography and offensive patrols over the lines between Armentières and Arras. The main object of our offensive patrols was to protect the aircraft of other squadrons which were at work on artillery observation; they were carried out by flights of five or six machines flying in close formation. But the superior performance of the enemy fighters did not give us much opportunity to launch any really effective attacks. After some hair-raising experiences, we found that, if we were to engage the enemy on anything approaching equal terms, it was necessary for us to fly underneath his formations so as to lure him into attacking us; and then we would trust to the good shooting of our observers to pick off the Huns as they came diving down to the attack.

It was solely because of the poor performance of our aircraft at height that we had to work in this way, but it was a miserable enough attempt at going on to the offensive. It was also bad for morale, and out of this experience I learned a lesson that was to stay with me for the rest of my Service career. That lesson was that in a fighting machine performance is of supreme importance. "Performance means the initiative—the most valuable moral and practical asset in any form of war," I wrote in the official paper that I was called upon to prepare after the war.

The German superiority in the air that we had to face during the early weeks of 1917 compelled us to take a very sharp look at the way in which we were going about our work. I came to feel that we would have to improve still further our formation flying, and that it was vitally necessary that we should discover how we could fight as a formation. Such tactics had been evolving, but now we were going to have to fly in formation with barely the length of a machine between the aircraft. That sounds simple enough today when we have become accustomed to the precision of the astonishing aerobatics that can be performed by our high-powered jets, but some fifty years ago we were exploring this new way of doing things with aircraft that were primitive and low-powered. Furthermore, I believed that we would have to increase the size of our formations from one flight to two or even three flights in order to cope with the formations of German fighters—they were obviously thinking as we were—which were beginning to appear over the Front in the neighborhood of Arras. It was also quite clear that it was imperative that we should improve the standard of our shooting.

The debut of No. 43 Squadron on the Western Front provided all of us with shocks and frights, and within a week Jack Scott, for one, landed back at Treizennes with his aircraft, as Harold Balfour described it, "riddled from end to end." His instrument panel and his gun sight were shot away, and yet Scott had miraculously escaped without even a scratch.

With the odds so much against us, we quickly discovered that our offensive patrols, made chiefly with the object of protecting the artillery observation aircraft, were going to call for fighting all the way. More often than not, even as we crossed the front lines to start our patrols which were to take place several miles over the enemy territory, we could see the German fighters getting into the most advantageous position from which to leap on us. Within all too short a time we were in the thick of things, with the Germans being just as offensively minded as we thought we were.

"From afar off we could watch these gaily painted Albatroses gambolling around each other and about the sky," Harold Balfour has said of those patrols. "They would be over Lens, looping, rolling and spinning, just like puppies with each other; but directly we got near our objective away they would swoop into the sun only to wait for the propitious moment in which to come headlong down on the top of our formation."

There was still so much that we had to discover in the hard school of experience. It had become vitally necessary that we should learn as quickly as possible, because it was a matter of either learning or being killed. We found, for instance, that a very effective way of coping with the superiority of the German fighters in their attacks upon us was for our formation to go into a tight circle, each of us close on the tail of the aircraft in front. While maintaining this circle we would gradually work our way back across the lines. If any of the German fighters tried to come down on our formation from above he would receive the full blast of the fire from the observers of all our aircraft. Although this meant that we were really going from the offensive to the defensive, it did force the enemy to keep his distance. On the other hand, we had to maintain that formation because the moment anybody fell out of it the German pilots would swoop on him and shoot him to pieces.

Our casualties during February and March were far too heavy, and scarcely a day went by without somebody being killed or wounded or going missing. But there was worse to come. When Douglas Haig and William Robertson were presented at the Calais Conference in February, 1917, with the plans for the future and asked to knuckle under to the proposal that the British Army should come under the command of the French, they both thought seriously about offering their resignations. In the face of that, Lloyd George was forced to compromise, but Haig had to agree to the staging of yet another offensive by us with which he was not in sympathy. Haig wanted to attack in Flanders, to the north, and so try to clear the Channel ports of the German occupation that was enabling the enemy to use those ports for the intensification of their extensive submarine campaign. But the French High Command had planned a big offensive at Verdun, to the south, and they called upon Haig to support their effort with an attack on the part of our line stretching to the north and the south of Arras. Such an attack was of direct concern to my squadron.

All through the winter that came after the battles on the Somme, the weather was quite frightful, but we kept up our pressure on the enemy; and then, on April 9, there was launched, on a front of some fourteen miles in length, the Battle of Arras. The most remarkable feature of the terrain on this part of the Front was Vimy Ridge, which stands two or three miles to the north of Arras. Our role was to be one of reconnaissance and photography. With the battle launched on Easter Monday, conditions for flying were far from pleasant at the outset, with strong southwesterly squalls and rain and sleet and at times even snow showers hampering our work.

On the afternoon of the first day of the battle, I went off on patrol in company with another aircraft from my squadron, and as soon as we got over the lines in front of Arras we spotted a German two-seater flying well above us. We promptly pulled up our noses and started after it, climbing as hard as we could go. The chase took us some miles inside Hun land before the enemy archie opened up, and almost immediately they scored a hit on my engine, which began to fail. I was forced to give up the chase and to turn back toward our lines, and I started looking for a suitable place to make a forced landing.

With all too little height in hand I just managed to get safely back over our own lines; but I could not get back far enough to reach one of our airfields, and I had to come down on what looked like a very rough piece of ground. It turned out that the roughness was the result of its being crisscrossed with the remains of an old system of trenches. At the last moment a small, open space appeared, and I hurriedly plonked my aircraft down on this in a pancake landing. Fortunately the undercarriage held up and I did not actually crash, but so narrow was the margin that when we came to a stop, my propeller was hanging over the lip of an old, abandoned trench. There was not even enough clear space for me to take off when the engine was replaced, and the aircraft had to be dismantled and taken back to Treizennes by road.

By the early spring we were running into the worst period, so far as casualties were concerned, that we were to experience in the whole of the First World War. During the month of March the Royal Flying Corps had lost 120 aircraft shot down, 59 of which fell in our lines and 61 in the German lines. During the next month, that month of April, 1917, I had in my own squadron alone over 100 per cent casualties. That does not mean that every pilot and observer in the squadron was shot down during the month—I still had at the end of it six or seven of the original crews—but reinforcements sent out to replace casualties were all too often shot down very soon, at times in a matter of only a few days, after their arrival at the Front. The official strength of my squadron was 32 pilots and observers, and during that month we had 35 casualties.

By then I had already lost the help of the redoubtable Jack Scott. He had taken over command of No. 60 Squadron, with which he went on to perform valiantly, not the least of his success being in the fostering of new young pilots, Billy Bishop among them, who were to become famous fighters. But I was lucky in being able to keep with me Harold Balfour, and I had to lean all the more heavily on him. Balfour and Tom Purdey, each in his own way, gave me splendid support, and Balfour remained with the squadron until toward the end of April, when he also got into trouble. I have always felt that the description in his book of what happened to him is both a splendid account of the flying of that time and a moving description of what he, such a high-strung youngster, went through in the fierce fighting that was taking place in the air.

On the tour that I made of the Western Front in the early spring of 1959, I spent an afternoon looking around Vimy Ridge. Almost exactly forty-two years had passed since Harold Balfour and I had flown over it. A huge Canadian memorial now surmounts the heights of the Ridge, and as I stood looking around there came to my mind thoughts about what had happened there when I was a young man. I recalled what a close shave Balfour had had at this place during the last stages of the Battle of Arras. I was at that moment facing east, looking out over the sharp drop from the crest of the Ridge down to the flat plain that stretches away toward Douai. It was over that plain that Balfour had got into difficulties in much the same way that I had only a very short time before.

The battle for Vimy Ridge had started in a snowstorm on a Sunday morning. "I was flying low over the lines that day, and this infantry battle was one of the most awe-inspiring and majestic sights that I ever saw during the war," Balfour wrote. "I flew down Vimy Ridge from north to south well below the level of the clouds a mile and a half the German side of the front line." The prevailing westerly winds caused Balfour to drift too far to the east, and since he was so low down he was constantly fired at from the ground.

Eventually his engine was hit and put out of commission, and all that he could do was try and glide back toward our lines, still being shot at all the time by the enemy.

As happened with so many of us, despite all the arguments that were put up in favor of it, Balfour was not strapped in, and it was probably that which saved his life, as it did mine a little later. He just managed to reach the top of Vimy Ridge, skimmed over it with a bare margin of only a few feet to spare, and then crashed slap on the edge of a mine crater. He was flung out of his machine a split second before the engine was rammed back into his seat—which would have pulverized him if he had been strapped in—and he landed head first in the mud.

Some Canadians—to whom Vimy Ridge means as much as Gallipoli does to the Australians—rushed from a dugout nearby and dragged Balfour and his injured observer to safety; and the Germans promptly sent over a few shells and completely demolished what was left of the aircraft. Although outwardly undamaged, Balfour was very badly shaken. He was severely concussed and he started throwing up. This crash, on top of the strain of all the strenuous flying that he had been doing, reduced him, he recalls, to a state of "crying to myself with fright and self-pity." It was a state that any man who makes a claim to honesty would be only too ready to acknowledge.

8 / Too Many Casualties

T HE BATTLE OF ARRAS in 1917, with the heavy casualties it cost the Royal Flying Corps, provided me with the most anxious period I was to know during the whole of my life in the Air Force. During the two years that I spent as Commander-in-Chief of Fighter Command in the Second World War, I was called upon to wage an offensive fighter campaign against the Luftwaffe that reminded me only too vividly of what had happened to us in the early spring of 1917. Our casualties had been much worse in the first war, but in 1941–42 I could not expect the young fighter pilots under my command to know much about that.

The severity of our losses early in 1917 was not entirely due to the superiority of the German fighters. Because of the continued demand for an increase in the numerical strength of the Royal Flying Corps, new pilots were still being sent to the Front with far from adequate training, even with insufficient hours of bare experience in the air. As one of the squadron commanders who had to accept these raw replacements, I came to feel very strongly about what I considered was a shortsighted policy, and I have been given no reason to change that view.

I am quite aware that Boom Trenchard admitted, as early as the beginning of 1916, that the pilots coming out to the Front were insufficiently trained, also that his complaint did lead to a great improvement in the system of training at home. But his insistence at the same time that there should be a rapid formation of more and more squadrons for service at the Front went a long way toward undermining that improved system. That magnificent eagerness of Trenchard's to use the air for offense led him, quite inadvertently, to make greater demands on the new pilots than were justified.

In the spring of 1917 the squadrons of the Royal Flying Corps outnumbered those of the German Air Force by about two to one; but numbers alone did not spell superiority. I have always felt that we would have been much better off if we had had fewer squadrons and had manned them with pilots who were better trained and who had greater experience; and quite a few of us who served on the Western Front and who were later to become senior commanders in the Royal Air Force felt the same way about Trenchard's policy of driving so hard almost regardless of cost.

I also came to believe that Trenchard was wrong in his opposition to fighter escorts for bombers. He believed that the bombers ought to be able to fight their way through on their own, but time and time again we found that the bombers suffered tremendous casualties when they ran into a strong force of enemy fighters. That conflict of views persisted even after the First World War, and it was to provide a lesson that we had to relearn in the early days of the second war. Even as late as 1942 the Americans, after they joined us in the second war, followed Trenchard's line of thought and at first made very light of the idea that bombers needed fighter escorts; but they quickly learned what was to be a very savage lesson; and all the daylight raids that they made from this country after their heavy losses in the beginning were escorted by long-range fighters.

But in those early months of 1917 all our views were conditioned by a situation developing rapidly in favor of the enemy. Even though Trenchard was opposed, in principle, to fighter escorts, quite a number of the bombing raids were escorted by fighters. This was probably done at the instigation of the brigade and wing commanders, who were more closely in touch with actual operations, and not with the approval of the General Officer Commanding.

When I recall what happened to those who were on active service in the First World War and I think about what so many had to endure, particularly in the trenches, it is inevitable that the intensity of my feelings should arouse in my mind, as it does in the minds of many others, a strong inclination to criticize. It is all too easy today, because of the intensity of the emotions that one can still feel, to fall into the habit of looking for some excuse to cavil at the decisions of the great men who were our leaders. This deliberate denigration is a fashion that has run riot in recent years in a manner which I think is deplorable; and I have not the slightest wish to become querulous about the splendid work that Boom Trenchard did and the magnificent influence that he exerted in France during the years of the First World War.

In always thinking of him as "Boom," and in always referring to him by that name rather than as Hugh Trenchard, there is a measure of the deep affection that I always had for that great man. I could no more speak of him as Hugh Trenchard than I could refer to "Stuffy" Dowding as Hugh Dowding: to me and to the others of my generation who have enjoyed the friendship of and felt a regard for these men, they are "Boom" and "Stuffy." Indeed, it would be stuffy of me to refer to them in any other way.

I have at times disagreed with certain views that Trenchard held; but despite that I have never had anything but the warmest admiration for our first great Air Commander. He was unquestionably a great man, but, as was only to be expected, he was not infallible. He made his share of mistakes, perhaps even more than his share. It was my good fortune that back in those early days I was one of those whom he took under his wing and in whom he placed his trust; and in time it came about that he was, perhaps above all others, the one man who set me on the path to what I, in turn, was able to achieve.

During those early months of 1917 I came to see quite a lot of Boom, and he made a great and lasting impression upon me. I had known him slightly from the time he had been my wing commander two years before, and while I was commanding No. 43 Squadron and he was General Officer Commanding the Royal Flying Corps in France, he often came to visit us at Treizennes, particularly during the period of our heaviest casualties. Although it was partly as a result of his aggressive policy in the air that we were having those shocking losses, it must not be thought that he was unaware of or indifferent to what was happening to us. Trenchard was very deeply concerned, although this did not change his opinion about what should be done. That some of us came to feel he was wrong in some of his ideas is another matter altogether.

The effect that Trenchard's visits had on the morale of the squadrons was almost magical. He was a tall man of a commanding presence which was coupled with a personality that was extraordinarily inspiring. And yet that personality in itself, or perhaps I should say the quality of it, is difficult to analyze. He was far from being what could be called articulate, and on paper he was almost chaotic. When he spoke, it was nearly always in a manner that was strangely disjointed, and sometimes it appeared that what he did manage to say was quite off the point. Perhaps it was the spirit and the great humanity of the man that counted, for those qualities shone through all the awkwardness. He had the unique ability of being able to raise the morale of those with whom

he came in contact in a manner out of all proportion to the visible
or audible manifestations of his spirit.

Whenever Trenchard visited a squadron he was almost invariably accompanied by Maurice Baring, and the relationship between these two men who were so entirely different from each
other never ceased to intrigue us. There was something about it
that was so heartwarming. They were both great characters, and
they undoubtedly had the deepest respect for each other: one a big,
gruff man of enormous drive and dedication; the other a gentle and
charming human being. Perhaps it was because they were both
such kindly men that they were able to work so well together.

Although I had first met Maurice Baring when he visited us
during my time with No. 2 Squadron, nearly two years before, it
was not until I arrived back in France with No. 43 Squadron that I
came to know him at all well; and then I was able to appreciate
more fully the interesting character of the man. He was the very
last man one would have expected ever to make any impact on the
Flying Corps; his delicate touch and sensitive imagination, one
would have thought, would be entirely out of place among the
somewhat brash youngsters of the squadrons. But this distinguished writer, who had started a career in the Foreign Office and
had then become an authority on Russia after living there for
several years, fitted perfectly into the role that he was to play as
A.D.C. to Trenchard and as the first and model personal assistant
to a C.-in-C. in the Royal Air Force.

Whenever we heard that Trenchard was going to pay us a visit,
it was always our hope that Maurice Baring would be with him
because Baring had a way all his own of getting things done. He
was not a soldier and he was not an airman; but he was a man with
a rare charm and gay humor. Essentially an individualist (which,
perhaps, was the reason why he was such a success in his work in
the R.F.C.), he made friends easily, and he quickly established
contact with the junior officers; and while Trenchard would be
making official inspections of the squadrons, Baring used to get
around and mix with and sound out the younger officers. With an
intuitive sense of balance, he would then brief Trenchard on his
own discoveries. This enabled Trenchard, in turn, to produce in
conversations with us odd bits of valuable information.

It was out of these visits to the squadrons that there came the
famous remark of Boom Trenchard's. He would talk to us and
listen to what we had to say, and then he would turn to the man
beside him, and in his gruff and kindly voice he would say: "Make
a note of that, Baring." It caught on, and in our lighter moments

we all used to imitate Trenchard behind his back and toss that remark of his to each other. One has only to re-read Baring's book, *R.F.C. H.Q., 1914–1918* (first published in 1920), to know how much this man of letters understood us and our problems— including some highly technical ones—while at the same time retaining his own interests.

It is possibly thought by those who have come after us and look upon us now as old fogies that the boisterous antics often indulged in at Air Force parties are of their own youthful invention. If that is so, they should have known some of the parties that at times blew up in the early days of the Royal Flying Corps. One of the star performers at those parties was Maurice Baring; and one of his turns was to balance a glass of port on his bald head and lie down flat on the floor and get up again, keeping the glass in position and without spilling a drop. This trick of Baring's came to be almost a part of the ceremony of any of the more or less formal R.A.F. dinners that Baring later came to attend; and on very special occasions he was known to perform his little trick with a bottle of champagne instead of the port, at the same time proceeding to undress while keeping the bottle balanced on his head.

If Maurice Baring ever considered that Boom had been a little too severe or harsh with some squadron or individual during an inspection, he would take it upon himself to soften up his master through one of what he called "Field Punishments for the General." The first of these would be inflicted as they drove away in Trenchard's car from the airfield. Baring would lean forward in his seat and look out of the window and up into the sky as if he were watching an airplane.

"What is it, Baring?" Trenchard would demand, his curiosity aroused by Baring's almost openmouthed interest. "What is it? What's happening up there?"

"Oh, nothing," Baring would reply. "I was only watching some birds."

Then Trenchard would know that, in the eyes of those whom he had just visited, he had behaved badly, and that Baring was telling him as much. And if Trenchard found that his pipe was mislaid— Field Punishment No. 2—he knew again that somewhere or other he had put his foot in it.

After the war was over Maurice Baring continued to be a friend to all of us who made our careers in the Royal Air Force. He returned to his own work and became a very well-known author. (For all my liking of the man himself, I have never been able to enjoy his novels. There is fine writing in them, but his characters never seemed to come alive for me, possibly because his stories were about people who lived in a way that was outside my own experience.)

Baring, like Trenchard, lived through the Second World War, dying in December, 1945; but the last ten years of his life were spent in the grip of a distressing paralysis. Perhaps the most touching indication of the value of Baring's contribution to the Royal Flying Corps is the way Trenchard himself quoted the comment made by the famous French leader General Foch: "There never was a staff officer in any country, in any nation, in any century, like Major Maurice Baring. He was the most unselfish man I have ever met or am likely to meet."

In the opening stages of the Battle of Arras we met with some success. But so far as the R.F.C. was concerned, the bad weather prevented all that had been hoped for from air reconnaissance. The German reserves were not fully observed and reported, and after only a couple of days, and in the fashion that was becoming all too familiar, the fighting on the ground came to a halt.

A week later there was launched to the south of us an offensive that the French Commander, the ill-fated General Nivelle, had prophesied would be a day of glory for France. It turned into an appalling disaster, partly because the Germans had documents in their hands revealing the plans for the French attack. For all the hopes and the courage of the French Army, they were soundly beaten and broken. Another reason for the French failure was an astonishing order given to the French air service. Just before the launching of Nivelle's offensive, between four and five hundred pilots were sent from the Front to Le Bourget to pick up new aircraft. So vague were their instructions—described by one historian as "inconceivable folly"—that the pilots took their time about returning, and many of them were not back at the Front until the second day of the attack.

Disappointment and disillusionment and further shocking losses, coming on top of reports of the revolution in Russia and rumors of strange goings-on in their own government, all but brought the French to their knees. It was then, in the spring of 1917, that there occurred an unhappy series of mutinies among the troops. Although not quite as violent as some alarmists have made them out to be—there were worse acts of treachery on the home front— these mutinies were nevertheless serious enough to shake to the core the whole of the French Army, and to leave scars upon it that are felt to this day. Had the Germans known more fully about those mutinies—they knew a little—or the extent to which they were threatening to spread, and had they acted promptly on the information that they did receive, it could have won them the war.

The disastrous failure of the French campaign meant that the British, in the north, had to keep up the pressure in order to draw the Germans away from our seriosly weakened allies. So Haig had to continue with his offensive around Arras much longer than he had anticipated. That led, in turn, to the R.F.C. being worked more strenuously in our efforts to cooperate with the Army, and we were dealt blows that were a great deal more severe than could ever be revealed in the mere figures of the total number of casualties, bad enough though these figures were. There were enough personal losses among those of us at the Front to make us all know, in the privacy of our own thoughts, the shock that comes with the harsh repetition of sudden death.

At the beginning of the month of April, the R.F.C. lost in the short space of five days 75 aircraft and 105 pilots and observers: 19 killed, 13 wounded, and 73 missing. There were also many more flying accidents during that brief period than was usual: 56 airplanes were wrecked. Even the official historian later felt compelled to comment: "These heavy losses by accidents were due in part to insufficiency of training which had been speeded up to the danger point. . . ." The threat of that danger point had been haunting me for some time, and now it was with us. But there was one ray of light, for it was during that week that the United States of America entered the war against Germany.

On April 5 the new Bristol Fighter, on which such high hopes were pinned, made its first operational appearance at the Front. It promised in every way to be an excellent aircraft, and it did become, in time, one of the mainstays of the Service. A two-seater biplane with plenty of power, it was rugged and tough, and it was very pleasing to the eye; but it got off to a terrible start. On that very first patrol, six Bristol Fighters of the newly equipped No. 48 Squadron, led by Captain W. Leefe Robinson, ran foul of Richthofen near Douai, and the Germans promptly shot down four of them and severely damaged a fifth. Of the four shot down one was Leefe Robinson. Two of the four were destroyed by Richthofen himself.

One of the dashing, good-looking characters of the Royal Flying Corps, Leefe Robinson was already well known to all of us and to the people at home as the most successful of the pilots who had so vigorously attacked the Zeppelins which had appeared on night bombing raids over England during the previous summer. Leefe Robinson had destroyed one of them in the most spectacular fashion, for which he received the Victoria Cross. After crashing in his Bristol Fighter (his engine was hit and put out of commission in the scrap with Richthofen), he spent the rest of the war as a prisoner, an experience which left him in such poor health that he fell an easy prey to influenza and died only a few weeks after the end of the war.

During the Battle of Arras the Ninth Headquarters Wing was still under the command of Cyril Newall. The squadrons of that wing were to the south of us, and No. 70, the squadron with which I had flown for a short time on the Somme some months before, was by then under the command of Arthur Tedder. Another of the squadrons, No. 19, was commanded by Harvey-Kelly. From time to time I used to see both men. Tedder was the quietly observant man that he has always been, not an easy man to get to know, with a strong, but sometimes perverse, sense of humor. Harvey-Kelly was always a delight, and his irrepressible good humor was the finest tonic that one could ask for.

By the end of April the weather began to improve, and with that, the fighting in the air became even more intense. Harvey-Kelly's squadron had been re-equipped with Spads, good French single-seater fighters, sturdy in construction and formidable in appearance, which had come into use at the time of the battles on the Somme. They had been on order for the Royal Navy, but the Admiralty had again come to the help of the expanding R.F.C. by giving them to us.

On April 26 I lost Harold Balfour as a result of his crash on Vimy Ridge, and three days after that came the worst possible news about Harvey-Kelly. During the course of a routine morning patrol with two other aircraft from his squadron he spotted a fair-sized formation of Richthofen's fighters. Harvey-Kelly had the advantage of height, and, not in the least daunted by the greater numbers of the enemy, he led his three Spads swooping, in the vigorous manner that was so typical of him, onto Richthofen's formation. There was a short and vicious engagement, and all three British pilots were shot down. Badly wounded, Harvey-Kelly was taken a prisoner, and a few days later we learned that he had died from his wounds.

On that day Manfred von Richthofen, in company with his brother Lothar, excelled himself; he was credited with having shot down five of our aircraft during the patrols he made during the morning and the afternoon. On the morning of the next day the

Germans introduced, for the first time over the front lines, a big change in their tactics. They flew in a massed fighting formation, combining in one group many more fighters than had been the custom up to that time. This was the first appearance of what we promptly named "Richthofen's Circus," a name that was to stick for the rest of the war to this large formation, which varied in size as the occasion demanded.

In the relentless cut and thrust of the war in the air, which, if not as brutal and as horrifying as the war on the ground, was nevertheless deadly enough, the Germans were quite as alert as we were to the necessity of developing as rapidly as possible the most suitable tactics for the new forms of fighting. The day of the lone wolf, who had no thought other than to seek out and destroy by himself, had already passed; and in the great change in the character of the air fighting that was coming about, the Germans not only beat us to it during those early months of 1917 in the introduction of better fighters: they also made more rapid advances in the use of massed fighting formations.

The early months of 1917 have been described as the golden period for Manfred von Richthofen. As the commander of one of these big formations equipped with the new Halberstadt and Albatros single-seater fighters, he came to the top; and by the end of April he had the very impressive score to his credit of fifty-six allied aircraft shot down.

During the whole of the time I spent in command of No. 43 Squadron in France, we had repeated struggles in the air with Richthofen, at first with his smaller unit, and then with his Circus. In a well-known photograph of the room in Richthofen's home which was kept as a museum containing all the trophies of his fighting there can be clearly seen, on one wall among the various identification numbers cut from the wreckage of the aircraft he shot down, the first (A/1108) of those of my own squadron that he destroyed. Before I left the squadron, shortly afterward, Richthofen had destroyed two more of my squadron's aircraft.

Just as we were benefiting from the leadership of our master fighters in the air, so did the Germans make the most of what there was to learn from their own outstanding pilots. But being a great fighter was not enough—and it was those who were tacticians as well who were contributing the most. Richthofen had proved himself as a pilot while serving under Oswald Boelcke, and when he, in turn, became the outstandingly successful German fighter pilot, he explored still further the best way of fighting in the air. He

taught his pilots to operate in the way that he wanted, which was
simply to guard his tail and protect him from attack while he
concentrated on shooting down our aircraft. I am not cavilling at
that. I think he was quite right to work in that fashion, and to
some extent I later came to adopt the same tactics with my own
squadron, giving our star the chance to inflict the heaviest damage.
Richthofen's methods enabled him to put up a tremendous score,
the size of which undoubtedly enhanced the morale of his own and
all the other German squadrons on the Western Front.

The weather being what it was during February and March,
flying on both sides of the lines had been somewhat restricted, but
during April Richthofen worked up to the fastest rate of scoring of
the entire time that he spent on the Western Front. He did not
escape altogether undamaged, and on one occasion in March he
had a close shave when his fuel tanks were punctured in an attack
by a British aircraft. With petrol pouring out and leaving a trail of
vapor behind his aircraft, he was lucky enough to be able to make
a forced landing without catching fire.

By then the all-red aircraft flown by Manfred von Richthofen—
red was the color adopted by him for all his own personal
machines—was a very familiar sight over our part of the Front;
but he was not the only German pilot whose name as well as
presence was becoming very well known to us. Because of the way
the Germans publicized their heroes, we came to know quite a lot
about our other opponents. One of them was Richthofen's young
brother, Lothar, who flew with him in the same unit and later in
the famous Circus. And a close friend of Richthofen's, who was
second only to him in the destruction that they were inflicting upon
us at that time, was a young man by the name of Werner Voss.

Voss, known to all of us as a particularly gallant opponent, was
born in Krefeld, in the Rhineland. He joined the Army and then
transferred to the air service a year after the outbreak of war. As
with so many of us on both sides, he had served first as an observer, but by May, 1916, he was a qualified pilot, flying with
Boelcke. Late in 1916 he started his scoring, and by the time we
ran up against him in the spring of the following year he had
already become known as a formidable fighter. He also had been
awarded the Pour le Mérite. Richthofen had had to learn through
hard experience all the skill that he came to display as a pilot; but
Voss was acknowledged to be the greatest natural pilot in the
German Air Force. (For that reason Voss had much in common
with our own Albert Ball.) But it was this natural skill as a fighter

that hampered him in developing as a leader. He seemed to prefer to go it alone.

The average age of Richthofen's flight commanders at this time was given as twenty-five and that of his pilots as twenty-one. If anything, it would appear that they were slightly older than we were; but it had become quite clear to both sides by that third summer of the war that fighting in the air was a young man's game. The Germans were also discovering that a great many of their young men were being killed, and they were becoming just as worried as we were about casualties. On the Front to the south of us at this time there was a German squadron facing the French in which, over a period of a very short time, the only pilot to survive was a twenty-one-year-old named Ernst Udet. Although he was eventually to become one of the greatest of the German fighter pilots, second only to Richthofen in the number of our aircraft that he shot down, Udet got off to a very slow start. In fact, he was lucky even to survive that start. Of all those against whom I flew in the First World War and who later rose to high rank in the Luftwaffe in the second war, Udet was the only one I ever met and got to know personally. That was to happen during the interwar years. I found him friendly and pleasant and, small though he was in stature, a man of great and forceful character.

Perhaps the most curious feature about Ernst Udet was the success that he achieved in spite of what at times appeared to be an extraordinary hesitancy in making up his mind about what he should do—although in the end the step that he took in sheer despair was decisive enough. He came from Munich, and he was eighteen years of age and a keen motorcyclist when the war broke out. For a while he served on the Western Front as a volunteer messenger, postman and traffic orderly. But right from the beginning of the war, Ernst Udet's imagination was fired by the promise of the adventure that was to be found in flying. His first application to join the air service was rejected, but with help from his father he learned to fly at his own expense, and after that he was accepted for the air service. He was flying as an N.C.O. pilot on the Western Front without any success in 1915; but at the end of the year he appeared to shoot down an enemy aircraft, a French Caudron. It was an indecisive encounter apparently because of Udet's marked reluctance to open fire.

Months later Ernst Udet was still showing this reluctance to engage his enemies in action, although he was a good enough pilot; but in March, 1916, he decisively destroyed his first opponent. From that time on he became more aggressive in his flying, and by

the spring of 1917 he was on his way to piling up the impressive
score that he eventually had to his credit.

After it became quite clear that the French attack in the south
had failed, Douglas Haig went ahead with his plans for the campaign in Flanders he had wanted all along; but in the meantime he
had to keep up the pressure on our part of the Front. What
happened then, over three weeks after the start of the Battle of
Arras, when our exhausted troops had to go on to the attack again,
was only too obvious to us because we in the Royal Flying Corps
were still trying through observation from the air to keep the Army
informed. During the first week of May we failed in our attacks on
our Front, and it was then that we faced one of our darkest periods
of the war.

On May 3, 1917, it is recorded, the squadron under my command "made history." At a quarter to four in the morning, our
infantry attacked the Hindenburg Line along a front of sixteen
miles, the most formidable section of which was around Bulle-
court, ten or twelve miles to the southeast of Arras. They broke
through in many places, but their success was only short-lived
because the enemy threw in quick counterattacks. Only two days
before, we had received orders that were specially designed for
such an event, and which, new in conception, were known as
counterattack patrols. We were instructed to fly these patrols from
dawn to darkness low down behind the captured positions, and we
were to concentrate on reporting immediately on the enemy preparations for counterattacks. "During the 3rd of May, however,
bombardment and counter-bombardment, attack and counterattack, made chaos of the battlefield, and the air observers could
seldom give definite information," the official history states.
"There was an exception in the morning when observers of No. 43
Squadron reported enemy troops massing in the trenches. . . ."

As soon as we put in this report, I was given instructions that
my squadron should make very low-level machine-gun and bomb
attacks on the enemy positions. We did this during the morning
and the afternoon of that day and the next. We flew at heights
varying from fifty to three hundred feet, shooting up and bombing
scattered parties of the enemy troops, trench positions and transport. We had already tried our hands at this new type of air
fighting during the month before around Vimy Ridge; but our
operations in what became known as the Third Battle of the
Scarpe, to quote again from the official history, "can be said to
have definitely established this novel development in the employment of aeroplanes directly to assist the troops on the ground,

operating in fact as 'tanks of the air.' " On one occasion I came down very low and started shooting at a row of German heads that had appeared along the top of a parapet. They shook me a little by answering back, and I could distinctly hear the popping of small arms fire flashing past my ears.

Our success appeared to be due mainly to the enemy's being so startled by the audacity of our attack and bombardment that they could not bring themselves to throw any very heavy fire at us. The Sopwith 1½ Strutter came into its own in this work, its performance and maneuverability near the ground being good; the chief danger that we had to face was from our own artillery barrage. When we shut off our engines for a moment we could clearly hear our own shells rumbling past our ears with a noise that sounded like a succession of trains passing through a tunnel. But we suffered no casualties from this new work, and that boosted enormously the morale of my pilots and observers. The results that we achieved brought congratulations from both the wing and the brigade commanders.

In my own thoughts about the early days of our Air Force, there are two features that I have always found of particular interest. The first is the way in which it sprang into existence over such a very short period of time; and the second is the diversity of background of the men who were to become most successful during that brief but intense beginning. Of all the outstandingly successful fighter pilots, only James McCudden could be described as a military professional, although Billy Bishop had made a start toward becoming a professional soldier before the war broke out. The others came from the widest possible sources, and those different backgrounds were to provide the new service with a healthy and vigorous start in life.

Billy Bishop was born in Ontario, Canada, and he was trained at the Canadian Royal Military Academy. On the outbreak of war he went to France with the Canadian Army; but in 1915 he transferred to the Royal Flying Corps. He served for several months at the Front as an observer before returning to England to learn to fly. He was back in France as a pilot in No. 60 Squadron in March, 1917, and his rise to fame was very rapid, with a huge score of enemy aircraft destroyed. I knew Bishop fairly well, and from time to time I saw quite a lot of him; but there was something about him that left one feeling that he preferred to live as he fought: in a rather brittle, hard world of his own. He has been described as a lone wolf, but I do not think that any of us came to know him or to understand his motives well enough to be sure about that. He was certainly not a lone wolf in the sense that we applied that description to Albert Ball. With the passing of the years Billy Bishop mellowed in a noticeable way, and when I met him again in the Second World War—he was then an air marshal in the Royal Canadian Air Force—he seemed to have become more likeable and companionable.

In the middle of April, just over two weeks after the Bristol Fighters first appeared in France, there was introduced on the Western Front a new aircraft that was to become one of our greatest fighters: the famous S.E.5. Many of us felt that it was the best fighter produced by Britain in the First World War. It was certainly one of the most beautiful little airplanes ever built, although it is only fair to admit that the warmth of my feeling for the S.E.5 is possibly due to the great amount of flying I did in it.

The first squadron to be equipped with the S.E.5 was No. 56, and in time this squadron became one of the foremost in the history of the Air Force. Formed in June, 1916, and at first on home defense with an assortment of various kinds of old aircraft, it was reorganized and equipped with the S.E.5 at the beginning of April, 1917. The pilots selected for the reorganized squadron became as great a band of enthusiasts and skilled fighters as was ever gathered together in one unit, and the group included several good friends of mine. Albert Ball was one of the flight commanders, and on April 22, 1917, he led the first patrol ever flown by the S.E.5 on the Western Front. It was to mark the beginning of our return to more equal terms with the enemy in the air.

This splendid little airplane was a biplane which, while of noticeable grace in design, was of unusually rugged construction. It was powered with a good Hispano-Suiza engine, and it was the first to be equipped with the new Constantinesco gear for firing a fixed Vickers machine gun through the propeller. Although at first this gear gave quite a lot of trouble, it eventually became the most successful in use in British aircraft. There was also a Lewis gun mounted on the top wing which fired over the propeller. We who were flying the older, outclassed, far slower and clumsier machines viewed with the greatest envy the arrival in France of No. 56 Squadron with their new S.E.5's.

Flying history was about to be written with the appearance of this new fighter over the Western Front. One of the best descriptions of the fine quality of this wonderful little airplane and what a pleasure it was to fly is to be found in Cecil Lewis's book *Sagittarius Rising*. In 1917 Lewis was still only eighteen years of age, but he was already immensely experienced in fighting at the Front, and he was one of those in Albert Ball's flight in No. 56 Squadron. Of one of his first flights in an S.E.5 he wrote: "The wing-tips of the planes, ten feet away, suddenly caught my eye, and for a second the amazing adventure of flight overwhelmed me. Nothing between me and oblivion but a pair of light linen-covered wings and the roar of a 200-horse-power engine! There was the fabric, bellying slightly in the suction above the plane, the streamlined wires, taut and quivering, holding the wing structure together, the three-ply body, the array of instruments, and the slight tremor of the whole aeroplane. It was a triumph of human intelligence and skill—almost a miracle. I felt a desire to touch these things, to convince myself of their reality. On the ground they seemed strong and actual enough, but here, suspended on an apparent nothing, it was hard to believe that flying was not a fantastic dream out of which I should presently awake."

By the beginning of May the name of Albert Ball was something to conjure with. In the short space of just over a year, this modest and gentle young man—he was still only twenty years old when he was killed—became a legend in the R.F.C. for his displays of sheer audacity. He was probably the most aggressive fighter pilot that the Air Force has ever had, and there can be little doubt that he must have gladdened enormously the heart of Boom Trenchard. Flying with extraordinary daring, Ball would tackle, singlehanded, any size of enemy formation; he would dash into the middle, throwing it into confusion, and shoot down one or two planes. Then he would make a brisk getaway before the others had time to recover from his attack. He did not seem to mind what odds he took on, and since he was a first-rate pilot and a very good shot, he had destroyed, by the spring of 1917, over forty German aircraft.

Such was the freedom of action allowed Albert Ball in his flying that he had for his own use with No. 56 Squadron both an S.E.5 and a Nieuport, with which he had scored so many of his earlier successes. The squadron was flying from the airdrome at Vert Galand, a well-known airfield of those days, about six miles from Doullens on the road to Amiens, and very close to the airfield at Marieux.

Toward the end of the first week in May, Ball had a violent battle in his S.E.5 with two Albatros single-seaters. He shot one of them down, and in making one of the head-on attacks he favored, he was very nearly rammed by the other. He shot that one down also, but not before return fire from the German had hit his engine.

The effects of this savage fight disturbed Ball so much that for a while after he landed back at Vert Galand he could not even talk coherently about what had happened to him.

So often the fact that most of us were very young came to our aid in those moments of extreme tension and fright, and it is on record that only a few hours later, Ball had recovered sufficiently to be able to write home: "When I am happy I dig in the garden and sing. I don't get much time off but what I get is enjoyed. Oh, won't it be nice when all this beastly killing is over and we can just enjoy ourselves and not hurt anyone. I hate this game, but it is the only thing one must do just now."

In another letter to his father, written a few hours later, he asked for some plants for his small garden, the care of which, in his moments off duty, provided him with a great deal of pleasure; and of the close shave that he had just had he wrote: "Oh, it was a good fight, and the Huns were fine sports. One tried to ram me after he was hit, and only missed by inches. I am indeed looked after by God, but oh, I do get tired of always living to kill, and am really beginning to feel like a murderer."

That was the last letter to his father that Ball was to write. The next day he was flying in his Nieuport, his S.E.5 being out of commission. He was on his own when he saw and attacked with his usual gusto four single-seater German fighters. He shot one of them down—the last of his many victories—and then, out of ammunition, he hurriedly made off for his own airdrome.

On May 7, only fifteen days after his reappearance over the Front, Albert Ball flew again in his S.E.5, leading an evening patrol of sixteen fighters: six Spads of No. 19 Squadron (which had just lost Harvey-Kelly) and ten S.E.5's of No. 56 Squadron. It was a dull evening with heavy clouds and rain, and the task of the fighters was to patrol the area of Douai and Cambrai from six-thirty in the evening until dusk, and to try to force some action with the German fighters. But the poor visibility caused the formation to split up. Nevertheless, they found what they were seeking, and one flight ran slap into the younger Richthofen and his formation—Manfred von Richthofen was on leave and had handed over command of his unit to his brother—and the fight was on.

Because of the bad weather there was no great mass engagement: it was more a matter of skirmishes in and out of cloud. But there were some of our foremost and most experienced fighter pilots engaged in those skirmishes, which were fast and deadly, and their names are all well recorded in Air Force history: names such as Ball, Knaggs, Meintjes, Hoidge, Maxwell, Lewis, Crowe, and Rhys-Davids. Among the Germans they were facing, all flying in Albatros single-seaters, there were also pilots of the highest order: Lothar von Richthofen, Allmenröder, and Wolff, all holders of the Pour le Mérite.

The fighting became scattered over a fairly wide area, and as the light began to fade with the approach of night, individual aircraft from both sides broke away and made for home. To add to the difficulty of seeing anything in the failing light, it had also started to rain. Albert Ball was still searching for the enemy, and he got behind and attacked a red Albatros scout flying near Loos. He was still firing at it when the two aircraft disappeared into a bank of cloud. Ball was not seen again, and there has never been a completely satisfactory explanation of the manner in which he met his death.

The Germans put out a report that Albert Ball was shot down by Lothar von Richthofen, but the German pilot himself was never able to confirm that. Richthofen had been wounded earlier in the engagement, and he had his hands full getting back to his own airdrome. It was possible that the Albatros Ball was attacking as they both went into cloud was Richthofen's. From all the evidence that was later examined with the greatest of care, it was found that Ball crashed and was killed at eight-thirty in the evening near the village of Annoeullin, well over the German front line, some ten or twelve miles to the east of La Bassée. His body was recovered from the complete wreckage of his S.E.5 by some French civilians, and the Germans saw to his burial. They did not tell us about that until some three weeks later, merely claiming at first that Ball had been shot down by the younger von Richthofen; but after the war the official decision was that Ball was shot down by German fire from the ground.

As recently as the summer of 1962, Albert Ball's sister stated that the family had received confirmation that he was brought down by antiaircraft fire, and that his body was interred with military honors in the German war cemetery at Annoeullin. His grave and the white marble cross that was erected after the war by Ball's father can still be seen there. They stand in the prominent position accorded the grave in the first place by the Germans in their desire to honor a gallant enemy.

Before his death Ball had already been awarded the D.S.O. with two bars and a Military Cross; and to these decorations there was added a posthumous Victoria Cross. His total number of victories in the air is recorded as forty-three. During the course of the war there were pilots who amassed higher scores, but none did better than Ball, and his coolness in always being prepared to take on any odds came at just the time when his particular style was most needed. He was perhaps the finest example that the Air Force has ever had of the truly great fighter pilot as an individualist.

The other squadron that was flying with us from Treizennes, No. 40, had also been well in the thick of the fighting. In March they were re-equipped with Nieuport Scouts, the French single-seater fighters, in place of the outdated F.E.8's in which they had been taking quite a thrashing. They also had a large turnover in pilots, and early in April, just in time to take part in the Battle of Arras, Edward Mannock, or "Mick" Mannock as he was generally known, joined them for his first tour of operational flying at the Front. Although he got off to a slow start, in the course of the next year Mannock was to carve out of the battles in the air a name for himself as one of our greatest—some say *the* greatest—of our fighter pilots.

My attention was first drawn to Mick Mannock one afternoon shortly after his arrival at Treizennes, in a fashion that was somewhat spectacular. I was standing with some of my pilots by one of our squadron hangars, and we were watching one of the Nieuports of No. 40 Squadron swooping down on a ground target used for practice firing on the range near the airdrome. I noticed that the pilot—who was Mannock, although I did not know that at the time—appeared to be diving the Nieuport rather more steeply and fiercely than was usual. As he started to pull out of the dive, the lower plane of his aircraft, which was narrower and shorter than the top plane, buckled and fell away. By all the laws that govern such events, that Nieuport should have gone plummeting to the ground; but Mannock, fully aware of what had happened, coolly throttled back his engine and managed, by first-rate flying and supported only by his top plane, to glide gently down into a field alongside our own airfield. He turned over on his back in landing, but he was unhurt. Inexperienced though he was, Mannock showed in that one incident that he was certainly made of the right stuff.

Although I did not know him as well as I came to know Jimmy McCudden, I did hear enough about Mick Mannock's story to realize that he was another of those men of exceptional character who contributed so much to the history of the early days of fighting in the air. Not only was he considerably older than the rest of us, but he was also almost blind in one eye, and he had managed in some mysterious fashion to fiddle his way through his medical examination for pilot without that defect being spotted. The manner in which he had got past so many obstacles and into the

Royal Flying Corps testified to the indomitable spirit of the man.

When the war broke out in 1914, Mannock was working for a telephone company in Turkey. He was interned for a while, and then, in a move that will delight those who have a taste for the oddities of history, the Turks allowed him to be repatriated because of his age and what was considered a generally poor state of health and eyesight. It was a mistake for which the enemy were to pay very dearly. On his return to England as a rejected crock, Mannock joined the Royal Army Medical Corps; and a short time after that he was commissioned in the Royal Engineers.

By then Mannock had developed, for some unaccountable reason, a powerful hatred for the Germans. That in itself was more unusual among those in the Flying Corps than might be imagined, because most of us had no great feeling of animosity: the Germans were the enemy that we had to cope with, but hatred of them, in an emotional sense, was a rare thing. Mannock became deeply impressed with the way in which Albert Ball had come to blaze his name across the skies of France, and he transferred to the Royal Flying Corps in August, 1916, finally arriving out on the Western Front eight months later.

Mick Mannock was the son of a soldier, born in Brighton; but although possessed of a lively Irish temperament, which he got from his mother, he was a lonely man. The rugged, forthright quality about his character—he was nearly ten years older than most of us—must have come from the background of his family life. It had not been an easy one because his father (who became a corporal in the Army) deserted his family while Mannock was still a child.

Tall, slim and dark, almost saturnine, Mick Mannock walked in a somewhat ungainly fashion. But for all that, what immediately impressed one was his vitality, which was so well expressed in his eyes. They were clear and of a piercing blueness. He spoke clearly and decisively, and I noticed on the occasions when I visited the No. 40 Squadron Mess as a guest that he was an excellent after-dinner speaker. There were also occasions when he expressed himself with a vehemence that was a little startling.

It was that vehemence of Mick Mannock's, and his forthrightness of expression, that left us in no doubt about the intensity of the patriotism that drove him on. And yet, because of the slowness of his start, there was at first a doubt in the minds of those with whom he flew about his ability and even his desire to fight. Being an older, more articulate, and more experienced man of the world, Mannock did not hesitate to voice his opinions, even if he had not yet proved himself. His self-assurance, while not being in the least arrogant, was resented by some of those who thought, because they happened to be scoring, that they knew better.

On May 9, 1917, Mick Mannock wrote up his diary for the past few days. It is of value to quote from it now because it gives in full an interesting account of his activities, and at the same time it shows that the pilots of the other squadron flying with us from Treizennes were having just as rough a time of it as we were in No. 43 Squadron.

"Lots of exciting news to tell," he wrote. "Went over the lines from north of Arras to five miles behind the German trenches at a height of less than fifteen feet, attacking Hun balloons. That was on the 7th—a Monday. Six of us—Captain Nixon (missing), Hall, Scudamore, Redler, Parry, and myself. All except the Captain (only been with us two days—the new Flight Commander referred to in my last note) returned safely but with machines almost shot to pieces. Hall crashed on home aerodrome, as did Scudamore; Parry crashed just our side of the lines, at the Canadian H.Q. Redler landed at Savy, but returned here later and damaged his machine on landing. I was the only one to return properly to the aerodrome, and made a perfect landing. We all got our objectives. My fuselage had bullet holes in it, one very near my head, and the wings were more or less riddled. I don't want to go through such an experience again. On the 7th also, I went to Omer to fetch a machine. Early the same morning (before the balloon 'Strafes') I had a scrap with a Hun—together with Captains Keen and Rastus. No luck though, although we put the 'wind up' him. I was immediately attacked by several 'red devils,' but managed to shake them off. I got separated from the others, and went scouting on my own. Keen returned and reported that he thought I went down, whereas there was much hand shaking upon my reappearance."

That first score of Mick Mannock's was made on the same day that Albert Ball was killed. And on that day, while Mannock was away on patrol and before he got back to our airdrome at Treizennes, I let myself in for one of the worst crashes that I ever experienced. The squadron was ordered to carry out an offensive patrol, and I detailed one of my flight commanders to lead it. I watched the squadron as they took off by flights and formed up; but just as they were disappearing into the distance I noticed that the leader's engine had apparently failed and that he was making a forced landing in a plowed field. This left the others without a competent leader because the deputy leader was a comparatively inexperienced pilot. Without somebody knowledgeable in charge they could easily have got into trouble, so I decided to get off in a hurry and take command. My own aircraft was standing in front of the hangars, and I yelled to a young Canadian observer, Lieutenant J. L. Dickson, who had only come to us the day before, to join me. He grabbed a Lewis gun and clambered into the back seat of my aircraft. I started up and took off, all in a violent hurry. I did not even wait to do up my safety belt.

As I tore off across the field I did not notice what I was later told was a large white horse at work with a plow in the adjoining field right in my line of take-off. I held the nose of my aircraft down so as to be able to zoom up after my squadron, but just as I was clear of the ground I hit the unfortunate plow horse slap on its backside with my under-carriage, and we crashed beyond it, upside down, in the plowed field. It was fortunate for me that I was thrown clear, through not having done up my safety harness, because the engine was slammed back into the pilot's seat. I shudder to think what would have happened to me if I had been strapped in. My poor observer was also thrown clear, landing on his head in the plow; and he was promptly taken off to the hospital.

When they collected me it was found that I was concussed, that my nose was bent across my face, and that I had received a hard bash in one eye, which was already swelling. I flatly refused to go to the hospital, and I spent the next twenty-four hours in bed in my hut, in considerable pain. Then Wilfrid Freeman came to see me, and apparently I babbled such nonsense to him that he immediately ordered that I should be whisked off to the hospital without any further delay. Later he told me about the nonsense I had talked—it was the sort of thing that appealed to his sense of humor. Such were the effects of concussion and the vanity of youth that in my prattling I seemed to be obsessed with the fear that my face was disfigured for life and that my girl friends would not want to have anything more to do with me. So off to the nearest hospital I went, and from there in a hospital train to Boulogne, and thence by boat to England, all of which marked the end, and a somewhat inglorious end at that, to my service with No. 43 Squadron.

It was a kind gesture on the part of whoever wrote the history of the squadron to record of my mishap that "the Squadron Commander was reluctantly compelled to relinquish his command." The only footnote worth adding to that is to place on record that in about a month my face was back to normal, and that, to my relief, I noticed no falling off in the ardor of my girl friends. In what I can only describe as an overeagerness to keep the record straight, Tom Purdey had me credited officially with a wound stripe.

9 / Fighters

THE SEVERE BEATING that I took in the crash at the airfield at Treizennes led to my spending a month in the hospital in London, after which I was given some leave. I spent part of the time in Dublin with my father on a visit that provided me with the rare opportunity of coming to know something of the cultural life of Ireland. My father had been given special leave from the Army and had by then taken up his appointment as director of the National Gallery of Ireland, so for a little while I was also able to enjoy a life that was vastly different from what was going on at the Front.

Apart from the brief rebellion by some disaffected Boers in South Africa in 1914, the only revolt that occurred throughout the British Empire during the years of the Great War was the unhappy Irish uprising of Easter, 1916. Great numbers of Irishmen of all political hues had joined up in the British forces right from the outbreak of war, and there was a strong and gallant Irish element in the Royal Flying Corps. But the split between the North and the South was a deep one, and the agitators among the latter continued to keep up a ruthless pressure for Home Rule.

On Easter Monday, 1916, had come open rebellion, and it had taken the British completely by surprise. For a week Dublin was paralyzed by street fighting, after which the rebels were suppressed in a way that led only to a simmering hatred and distrust of the British. While I had no sympathy with armed rebellion, I neverthe-less felt that the Irish should have been given the Home Rule that they wanted with such a deep emotion and fervor at a much earlier date than they eventually got it. We did ourselves a great deal of harm by acting in the way we did—my many Irish friends have never ceased to remind me of that. But during the first visit that I made to Dublin, only a year after the troubles, the tension had eased a little—although it was to flare up again later on—and at no time was I given any reason to feel ill at ease.

My father had taken over as director of the National Gallery of Ireland after the death of Sir Hugh Lane in the sinking of the

162

Lusitania. One of the unhappier aspects of that appointment was
that he became directly involved in the stupid dispute over Lane's
valuable collection of pictures, a dispute that for years caused too
much friction in Anglo-Irish relations. In his will, Lane had
originally left all these pictures (valued now at about £1,000,000)
to the city of Dublin; but when he found that the Irish were not
going to build a special modern gallery he suddenly changed his
will, and instead he left the pictures to the National Gallery in
London, where he lived. Our slowness in exhibiting these pictures
caused Lane to change his mind yet again, and he added a codicil
to the will reversing everything and leaving the collection again to
Dublin. Lane failed to have the codicil witnessed, and under
British law it was not valid. There was great indignation in Dublin
when the British insisted on sticking to the letter of the law and on
keeping the pictures; and that led to the dispute that lasted for well
over forty years and has only recently been settled with the
decision that the pictures be divided into two groups, each one to
be exhibited alternately in London and in Dublin.

I could never quite understand just why my father was made
director of the National Gallery of Ireland—he held the appointment for seven years—although he was by then an acknowledged
expert at judging the value and the authenticity of pictures. He was
undoubtedly a good administrator, but he had not the slightest
drop of Irish blood in his veins; the only very vague connection
with Ireland that he could claim was through his father's having
taken his degree at Trinity College, Dublin.

It was pleasant for me to be able to visit Dublin and to see my
father again because, in his usual way, he both charmed and
amused me. His assistant director at the time was James Stephens,
the poet and novelist, of whom I came to see quite a lot. Stephens
was a very likeable man who, born of poor parents, had grown up
in the slums of Dublin, and he had more or less educated himself.
It had been a very hard struggle for him until the publication of his
book *The Crock of Gold,* in 1912, after which he became recognized; and he was then able to develop his talents with more ease.
A tiny man, Stephens was an active Sinn Feiner, and he worked
hard for that cause; but the name that he made for himself was in
the world of letters and not as an agitator.

Under the terms of his contract, my father was required to
spend three months of each year in Dublin. On my leave during
the summer of 1917 I stayed with him at the Shelbourne Hotel.
Through his work he moved freely in the intellectual and artistic

circles of Dublin, and since it was a time in the life of the Irish capital of vigorous literary and artistic endeavor—one could almost say that what was going on in Dublin during that period was an artistic inspiration to all Britain—it was of the greatest interest to me. The Abbey Theatre was at the height of its fame, and I saw there an unforgettable performance of Synge's *The Playboy of the Western World,* with Sara Allgood, Maire O'Neill and the Fay Brothers. In that setting it was one of the most enjoyable experiences in the theater that I have ever known.

Many fine writers were at work in Dublin at that time—W. B. Yeats, "A.E.," Oliver St. John Gogarty, George Moore, Lennox Robinson and Lady Gregory, to name the outstanding ones—and many of them were friends of my father's. The extraordinary Lady Gregory, who played an important part in the running of the Abbey Theatre, was also one of the leaders in the campaign for the return to Dublin of the Lane collection of pictures. But my more immediate interest in her was through her only son, whom I had met while he was serving as a pilot in No. 40 Squadron, under Robert Loraine, at the airdrome in France from which I had just come. He was killed later in the war.

There was also in Dublin a lively school of painters, and it was then that I first met William Orpen, who was a particular friend of my father's. He visited me later in France during one of his tours of the Front as an official war artist. Among others, he painted a fine portrait of James McCudden which is now on view in the Imperial War Museum.

Along with many people, I cannot help feeling that it is a dreadful pity that the splendid artistic and literary inspiration that came to life in Dublin in those days seems now to be pretty well extinct. It was of the greatest importance in British art, literature and drama. When Southern Ireland cut itself off from Britain, the artistic and the literary creativeness of its people seemed to wither. While we were together, we were able, in some strange way, to help each other, for the role of the Irish, the Scots and the Welsh—the Celtic fringe—is to act as an inspiration to the rather dull and prosaic English.

I do not mean that as a derogatory comment on the character of the English: they are a wonderful people in so many ways—even if those ways appear at times to be very contradictory—and I am quite sure they are a greater people than those of what I have called the Celtic fringe. But they are solid, even stolid, and rather unimaginative: steady and intent on making their own way, and with a firm sense of purpose. The Irish before and during the First

World War were like a gadfly on the back of a somewhat dull host which delighted in stinging that host into action. But once the gadfly cut itself off from its host it languished.

It was remarkably stimulating for me to be able to meet so many of those fine creative Irish artists and writers and thinkers at just the time that I did in 1917 because I was too close, in my own life as an airman, to death and destruction. One of those who made the strongest impression on me was the renowned Professor Mahaffy, who was at that time Provost of Trinity College. He was a distinguished classical scholar, and he had been for several years President of the Royal Irish Academy. As professor of ancient history, his particular field was the Silver Age of Greece, and his books, which have become standard authorities, were the ones I had used at school. He had played an important part in the Easter Rebellion of 1916 when he directed the defense of the college; and in recognition of his services and his great career as a don he was later made a G.B.E.

It was perhaps only natural that I should have looked up to Professor Mahaffy, then seventy-eight, with something approaching veneration, all the more so because he was in appearance a noble and impressive figure with snow-white hair and twinkling eyes. On one occasion my father and I were invited to dine with some people who lived on the outskirts of Dublin, and since Mahaffy had also been invited we gave him a lift in our car to the house. At dinner I drank green Tokay for the first time, and I noticed that Mahaffy imbibed a considerable quantity. When the time came for us to leave, he went with us. It was a cold, crisp night with a bright moon, and as soon as the clean, sharp air hit him, and before we even got as far as the car, the old professor fell flat on his face on the pavement. He was out cold, and my father and I had the rare experience of escorting the venerable scholar back to his lodgings over the front gate at Trinity College and putting him to bed.

During the summer of 1917, and right at the time I was either in the hospital or on leave in London, the Germans staged the heaviest of their daylight air raids on the capital, the largest coming on June 13. In all these raids the enemy used their large twin-engined Gotha, which had been developed from an early version of an airplane designed by us which had unfortunately fallen into the hands of the Germans; and the name of the Gotha, along with the Zeppelin, came to have about it an evil ring in the minds of many on the home front. Public opinion ran high, and there was an outcry against these German terror raids. Such was the indiscriminate nature of their bombing that the raids could not be regarded as anything but an effort to strike terror into the minds of our people. Public reaction was understandably one of anger, particularly since the casualties of that day numbered nearly six hundred, including forty-six infants who were killed when a bomb demolished a Council School in Poplar. This was the beginning of another aspect of the use of the air that was later to become all too familiar.

Although the people at home were disturbed over the casualties, and rightly horrified that the Germans should have staged these raids, I did not find that the home front was in any way shaken. The civilians found the raids a hard blow to accept, coming as they did on top of the dreadful casualty lists that had appeared after the battles on the Somme; but on the whole they stood firm. The Government became agitated over the effect that the bombing might have on civilian morale, and elaborate measures for defense were introduced. There is even on record an official statement about a lapse in civilian morale; but I did not know from my own experiences of any undermining of the dogged determination of our people to see the war through.

There were instances that I heard of in which men and officers of the Royal Flying Corps were attacked by irate civilians for not putting a more effective stop to the raids, but such an experience was never mine. In fact, I always found that the civilians were particularly sympathetic toward the Royal Flying Corps and, later, toward the Royal Air Force, which was probably one of the reasons why our sessions of leave in London were spent in such an agreeable fashion. It would be stupid if I were to say that we in the Flying Corps did not know that in the eyes of the public we were young heroes. Some of my friends in the R.F.C. undoubtedly were heroes, and I was proud to be associated with them. I knew that we were thought of as dashing, devil-may-care types, and I must confess that we often took the bit between our teeth.

By the early summer of 1917 I had disposed of my leave in a way that, if not exactly edifying, was well in the fashion of our lives. I had almost completely recovered from the shaking-up I had had in the crash in France, and after a medical board I was passed fit for light duty. The job I was then given turned out to be a particularly interesting one, and it led me straight back to Ireland.

Early in 1917 it had been decided that the Royal Flying Corps should be expanded to 106 service squadrons and 97 reserve squadrons. This called for a big increase in the training program. Six months later, in June, after the coming of the German daylight bomber raids on London, there was a sudden demand for what has been described as "a formidable expansion" in the whole of the training of the Flying Corps, and the Government then decided to increase the service squadrons to 200.

The job I was given was that of traveling all over Ireland with the object of selecting eight sites for airdromes on which the Royal Flying Corps could establish some of their training schools. There were no airdromes at all in Ireland at that time, and the Lands Officer at Irish Command had picked out for me what he thought might be some likely sites. It was left to me to inspect them and to make any recommendations that I saw fit. We were looking for grass fields which would give us good runs of about five to six hundred yards in any direction.

Before I left for Ireland, I was told that a car and a driver would be provided for me by Irish Command, but I was thinking in terms of the air. An airplane would not only provide a much better means for inspecting potential sites: it would also save a lot of time. I was given permission to use a B.E.2c, and I started off for Dublin by way of Stranraer and Larne, making the narrowest possible sea crossing over the North Channel. When I got over Northern Ireland I ran into thick cloud, part of which I knew was stuffed with the "mountains of Mourne that run down to the sea." But I managed to avoid them at the last moment, and I arrived safely over Dublin. I landed in Phoenix Park, and I left my aircraft outside the gates to the Viceregal Lodge, solemnly warning the two sentries on duty there that they were to guard it with their lives. The troubles of only a few months before were still fresh in my mind, and I was being cautious about sabotage.

But severe though the troubles had been, I was being over-cautious, for the way I was treated throughout my tour of inspection gave me no cause at all for alarm. Most of what are today the principal airdromes in Eire and Northern Ireland were selected by me on that trip during the early summer of 1917; and they included such places as Colinstown, Baldomell and Aldergrove. I also found a site for an airdrome near Fermoy, and another one at the Curragh. I would fly over the sites that had been suggested to me, weigh up their possibilities from the air, and then go by car to make inspections on the gound.

Whenever I made any journeys by road, the "corner boys" lounging at the street corners in the villages almost invariably scowled at me, and a few of them even threw some stones. The sight of the uniform of the British Army was becoming an increasingly unpopular one. But such is the extraordinary, and at times rather touching, illogicality of the Irish mind that when I flew anywhere and landed in a field near some village or other I found that the young men would come running out on to the field cheering and shouting wild Irish cries and throwing their hats in the air, all because most of them had never seen an airplane before. I often wondered how many of them had thrown stones at me when I had passed through the villages in my car.

On the completion of this survey, I flew back to London. I made my report, and it led to airfields being established at most of the sites that I had selected, along with training schools for pilots and observers. In itself that sounds cut and dried enough as a record of what I had been able to do, and as far as I knew, I had dealt in a satisfactory manner with a fairly straightforward assignment. But there was more to it than that. I had taken yet another step forward in broadening my experience, and if, through being away from the Front, I was not adding my name to the roster of great fighters in the air, I was nevertheless laying a further foundation for what was ahead. I was also learning still more about the value of making the most of the opportunity offered by the moment. Such were the hazards of our existence at the Front that we never knew, from one moment to the next, just what was going to happen to us, or if we would even survive that moment; and so we came, through sheer necessity, to watch it, to live for it, and to extract from it all that we could, and not to worry about any moments that did not call for immediate attention. All in all, I have since found that a fairly reasonable way of life.

Although no effort had been made to summon me for another medical examination, and I was therefore not fit, officially, for operational flying, on my return from the Irish mission I was instructed to take command of a new fighter squadron that was in process of being formed. This was No. 84, and it was stationed at the airdrome at Lilbourne, near Rugby. "Daddy" Nicholl, with whom I had served in No. 8 Squadron two years before, had been organizing the squadron, but it was felt that he was rather on the old side for fighters, and that it was a job for a younger man. So I was given command.

I was particularly pleased with this new job because I was very keen to have a single-seater squadron. My experience at the Front up to that time had all been in two-seaters. I was also delighted to find that we were to be equipped with S.E.5's. We were the second

squadron to have these fine new fighters—by that time No. 56, the
first to be equipped with them, had already been doing very well in
France, covering itself with glory, in fact. We were under orders to
get into fighting trim as soon as possible because we were badly
needed out in France.

There is an old saying among those whose interests are in aviation that if an airplane looks right, then you can be pretty sure that
it will fly. Of all the hundreds of different types of aircraft that
have been designed and built since man first took to the air, the
S.E.5 must surely be one of the most attractive in appearance.
There are many who will assert with more than fondness that it is
the most beautiful airplane that has ever been built. For a long time
I felt the same way, but nowadays I am inclined to award the
crown for sheer beauty to the Comet IVB used by British European
Airways.

During the early years of this century, most of the pioneering in
the development of aircraft was done at the Royal Aircraft Factory—as it was then called—at Farnborough. By late 1916 they
had produced the first S.E.5 (the intials standing for "Scout
Experimental," and the number for roughly the fifth version). It
was this which, with certain modifications, was to become the
famous S.E.5a, usually referred to as the S.E. or the S.E.5. It was
a trim, sturdy little biplane, the fuselage and wings of which were
made of spruce and ash with plywood and fabric covering; and it
was powered by a two hundred horsepower Hispano-Suiza engine.

By the summer of 1917, the S.E.5 was undoubtedly the finest
fighter that we possessed, and in performance it was approached
only by the Fokker D VII which was brought into use by the
Germans in the summer of the following year. But even the Fokker
could not match in appearance the splendid lines of the wonderful
little S.E.5. It was a very strong airplane, and even under the most
ham-fisted and violent handling it never caused us the slightest
apprehension about the possibility of its breaking up in the air. It
was fast for its time, with a top speed of 127 miles an hour; and
although that sounds almost ridiculous by modern standards—or
even by the standards of the fighters of the Second World War—it
was then the fastest thing in the sky over the Western Front.

The armament of the S.E.5 was also most effective. It consisted
of a Vickers gun mounted on the fuselage, firing through the
propeller, and a Lewis gun on a quadrant mounting on the top
plane. Normally we used the Lewis gun in its fixed position for
firing straight ahead, the trajectories of the two guns, fired together
from a trigger on the joy-stick, meeting at a range of about one

hundred yards; but some pilots, Ball and McCudden in particular, made a special use of it. They would creep up underneath a high-flying two-seater, pull the gun down on its mounting so that it pointed at an angle upward, and then send a burst of fire into the belly of the aircraft above.

For the sighting of our guns, the backsight was made up of a metal ring of about four inches in diameter with smaller rings inside it, with the foresight consisting of a short, thin metal rod with a bead on top of it. Later we were issued telescopic sights which gave us a closer look at our targets; but in any case, all the sights that were then in use were quite primitive. We always tried to get right behind the aircraft we were attacking so that we could get a straightforward and dead shot from behind. But if we were attacking somebody from an angle, we had to use our judgment— which was based on hard experience—in measuring off on our ring and bead sights just how much deflection we would have to allow.

Our guns were the same Vickers and Lewis machine guns as those used by the infantry on the ground: they were merely adapted for mounting in an aircraft. The former was fed from a long belt of ammunition, and the latter with drums which had to be replaced in the air. When we fired, there was surprisingly little vibration. The guns were not heavy enough for that (they compared in no way with the heavy armament of the fighters of the later war).

The .303 ammunition that we used in the first war was also the same as that used by the infantry, except that it was specially screened so as to avoid as much as possible any likelihood of stoppages through jamming. Our armorers would always go carefully through all the ammunition, round by round, before filling the belts and the drums. But even then there was far too much jamming of the guns in the air, which was one of the most frustrating experiences we had to endure. We had solid lead bullets interspersed with tracer—I used tracer about one in five—with some Buckingham (incendiary tracer) added if we were going to attack balloons. The tracer gave us a chance to see where our fire was going, but it was not as accurate as the solid bullets. It used to wander a little, and for that reason it was not used any more than was absolutely necessary.

We very soon learned to follow what had already come to be accepted as a basic rule for fighting in the air: there was no point at all in firing in long bursts. That merely used up a lot of ammunition, and one might easily run out of it before the patrol was over. We had found that it was a much better practice to fire in very short bursts of about ten rounds and then resight before firing again.

Although I was all for new methods of attack, I found that pushing the Lewis gun back into the fixed position while flying in the open cockpit of the S.E.5 at high altitude called for an almost superhuman effort. We had no supply of oxygen in those days, and I found that my strength at height fell off very considerably. It was difficult enough to change the double drum of ammunition on the Lewis gun without having to manhandle the gun into position for an attack and fly the airplane all at the same time. There were others who had the same difficulty: and more often than not, we had to dive down to a lower altitude before we could reload. It was the price we had to pay for not being superhuman.

The S.E.5, in addition to all its other good qualities, was a great pleasure to fly. We sat in quite a roomy and well-padded wicker seat with—since we had no parachutes—a cushion in it, and we were fairly well protected from the blast of the slipstream. In front of us, under the padded rim of the fuselage, there were assembled the instruments, above which was a small, solid windshield, with the gunsights in front of that. We were strapped into our seats with a broad belt around our waists attached to the back of the seat in such a way that while we were secure we still had quite a fair amount of movement.

Except for that one occasion when I crashed early in 1917, I always flew strapped in. It was vitally necessary that we should be secure in fighters because we were constantly and rapidly changing our aspect: we might suddenly find ourselves on our backs in the involved maneuvers to which we had to resort quite often. I always dreaded the thought of falling out—which was not an uncommon occurrence in those days.

Since the fighter pilot had to keep as sharp a lookout behind as he did ahead, it was essential that he should have as much freedom of movement as possible, and that was where the waist strap had it over the shoulder straps that were brought into general use after the war. We had to watch our tails all the time—it was fatal to overlook doing that—which was another reason why, with our open cockpits, we wore goggles all the time. Quite apart from the blast of air full in our faces from the propeller, protected though we were to some extent by the tiny windshield, all sorts of odd drafts would trickle into the cockpits. We were fairly comfortable as long as we crouched down in the seat well behind the windshield and out of the slipstream; but there were many occasions when we had to swivel our heads about to keep that sharp lookout, and goggles were essential. We became so used to wearing them that we gave no thought to them, and I never felt that my vision was in any way restricted.

The engine of the S.E.5 was a comparatively quiet one, stationary, water-cooled, and in line with long exhaust pipes, and there was little of that nauseating smell of burnt castor oil that came from the exhausts of the rotary engines of those days, and that was so apt to affect pilots whose bowels were easily moved. The in-line engine well tucked away into the airframe afforded us a good view all around, and the aircraft maintained its good performance at high altitude. In the rough and tumble of the fighting in the air that we were called upon to do we had no time to worry about the smoothness or finish of our flying, particularly at height; and in the stress and excitement of battle the S.E.5 proved to be very steady. For one thing, we could be quite sure of our ability to take careful and proper aim when diving to the attack.

The S.E.5 was also a quieter aircraft in its actual flying, and much more so than those with rotary engines, although there could still be heard when the engine was shut off the rush of air through the flying wires and the struts. When we came in to land in the 1½ Strutter, we used to correct our angle of approach by switching our engines on and off, blipping them with the switch control of the throttle in much the same way, only more sharply, as racing cars are handled on the starting grids of today. It could be very easily overdone, and in its way it revealed how effective the pilot was in his judgment of the right approach to landing, and for that reason too much of it was discouraged. With the stationary engines, such as the Wolseley Viper and the Hispano-Suiza with which the S.E.5 was powered, there was no need for this blipping. We flew much more easily into a landing.

All the experience I had gained the year before in the long-drawn-out business of forming No. 43 Squadron enabled me, during the summer of 1917, to tackle with far more assurance the job of bringing No. 84 Squadron up to a level of operational efficiency; and this assurance, backed by a prompt supply of new aircraft and my being allowed to keep the pilots I was training, led to our being ready to go to France in a reasonably short time. But I was very nearly outmaneuvered in one important posting to the squadron.

By the late summer my father had his work as director of the National Gallery in Dublin well under control, and, not to be outdone by any of the younger men in serving his country, he had then returned to England and his job in the Army. Quite unknown to me, but undoubtedly inspired by all that I had been telling him about the Royal Flying Corps, he then applied for a transfer from the Royal Army Service Corps to the R.F.C., and he asked specifically for a posting as adjutant to No. 84 Squadron.

When I heard about this extraordinary wangle, I quickly realized that, for all my fond respect for my father's spirit, having him as my adjutant would create a thoroughly impossible situation. I was twenty-three and he was fifty-four; and quite apart from the close relationship of a father and son, there would always be the embarrassment of that great difference in our ages. Such was the nature of his work that the squadron adjutant was expected to receive, and in fact did receive, brickbats of all shapes and forms from nearly everybody in the squadron, and particularly from the commanding officer.

As soon as I heard what was brewing I lodged a strong protest, but it was not until I finally took the unorthodox step of telephoning the chief personnel officer at R.F.C. headquarters that I was able to make sure that the threatened posting was canceled. As might have been expected, my father took a very poor view of what I had done; but the risk of what that might do to our relationship was much less than it would have been in having him as my adjutant. Always a romantic, my father made this gesture in his own particular fashion, which, I am quite ready to admit, was much more colorful than mine.

As far as the rest of the officers and men were concerned, by the time that we were ready to go overseas, I had what I felt, with a justifiable pride, was a good squadron, and there were some new boys who were already showing promise of becoming outstanding pilots. My senior flight commander, upon whom I was going to have to lean heavily for support on the flying side, was Captain K. M. Leask, who had been serving in my brother's squadron at the time of his death. Leask was later to become an Air Vice-Marshal in the Royal Air Force.

In the middle of September we flew across to France, and we settled down at the airfield at Estrée Blanche, which was one of those airfields lying behind the northern part of the Front. It was only a very short distance to the southwest of Treizennes, but in more open country. (Although it was one of the better-known airfields from which we flew during the First World War, I was disappointed, on my tour of the old Front in 1959, at not being able to locate it, despite a careful search.)

Estrée Blanche was a larger airfield than most, with two or three

other squadrons there, including No. 56. Since we were the second
squadron to arrive at the Front with S.E.5's—No. 60 had been re-
equipping with them in France at the same time, but they were not
as far along as we were—it was expected of us that we would be
on our toes. We had before us the splendid example set by No. 56
Squadron, which had been doing very well, and I knew to my
gratification that my own pilots were keen to accept the challenge.

Just before we arrived at Estrée Blanche, the strength of No. 56
Squadron had been greatly increased by the posting to it of James
McCudden as a flight commander. By that summer Albert Ball
was dead, and Edward Mannock was only just emerging. Mc-
Cudden was our foremost fighter pilot. He had been hard at it
almost from the very beginning of the war, and when he asked for
a posting to No. 56 Squadron they were only too happy to have
him. His arrival in the middle of August is recorded in the
squadron history as "a valuable reinforcement." That speaks as
well for the spirit of the men in No. 56 Squadron as another
squadron's later refusal to have him as their commanding officer
because he had come from the ranks condemns them for arrogant
snobbishness—a state of affairs which made my blood boil when I
heard about it.

Of all the men I came to know well during the years of the First
World War, from Boom Trenchard himself down to the hard-
working airmen of my own squadrons, it was Jimmy McCudden
who made the strongest impression upon me, and I have always
been proud of our friendship. Just over a year younger than I was,
McCudden was born in Kent, but there flowed in his veins a
mixture of northern and southern Irish and of French blood; this
gave him alertness and enthusiasm and lightheartedness without
his having for a moment to resort to flamboyance: qualities that
came to be so well appreciated by those of us who knew him well.
He also had, greatly to his credit, the best qualities of the young
soldier who was proud of being a professional. In appearance
McCudden was boyish, with a frank and unaffected manner. But
then, so many of the pilots were scarcely more than boys. Mc-
Cudden was just over twenty-three years of age when he was
killed.

Jimmy McCudden had indeed come from the ranks, and in the
best tradition. At the age of fifteen he had followed his father's
example and had joined the Royal Engineers as a bugler. He
transferred to the Royal Flying Corps in April, 1913, and he
arrived in France right at the beginning of the war as a mechanic
in No. 3 Squadron. During the summer of the next year he became

an observer, and early in 1916 he learned to fly. Posted back to France as a sergeant pilot in July, 1916, McCudden shot down his first German early in September, over the Ypres Salient. As a D.H.2 pilot with No. 29 Squadron, he went down to the Somme, and it was then that he began to establish a reputation for himself as a fighter pilot. In October he was awarded the Military Medal; and in November, while still on the Somme, he and two other pilots from his squadron had one of the first of the serious encounters with the new Albatros fighters that the Germans had just brought into use. For twenty-five minutes, he and his companions fought six of the Germans, and McCudden got back with twenty-four bullet holes in his aircraft: the most severe peppering he was ever to receive.

Commissioned in January, 1917, Jimmy McCudden received a Military Cross almost immediately afterward, and he returned to England for a spell as an instructor. After serving on home defense against the invading Gothas during the early summer of 1917, he returned to France, and for a short time he flew with No. 66 Squadron, which was equipped with Sopwith Pups. By then McCudden had an enormous amount of experience flying many different types of aircraft.

During all this time I had heard a great deal about the progress that Jimmy McCudden was making, and the name that he was acquiring as a fine pilot and a keen fighter; and when I came to know him better I also learned to appreciate his views about the future of the rapidly evolving tactics of air fighting. We thought alike about the way in which our work as fighters should be done; and when I found, on our arrival at Estrée Blanche, that McCudden was there, it was an added incentive to me to examine still further the way in which we should conduct this new dimension of fighting in the air.

From the moment he joined No. 56 Squadron, McCudden had rapidly increased the rate at which he was shooting down Germans; and since we were equipped with the best fighters on either side of the Western Front, there was no lack of opportunity to put to the test the theories that were evolving. During the next six months McCudden scored another fifty victories in the air, and to the M.C. and the M.M. that he had already received there were added a Victoria Cross, the D.S.O. and bar, and a bar to his M.C.

There were occasions when Jimmy McCudden would still practice going up on his own, seeking out and shooting down the lone high-flying German reconnaissance aircraft that came over our lines. But his main interest was in developing his original ideas—original enough, that is, for those early days of fighting in the air—about the tactical use of fighters in flights and squadrons; and I shared that interest with him. The Germans were already working along the same lines, as we had discovered earlier in the year, but they were going in for larger formations than we thought either necessary or feasible. Having been a mechanic, McCudden also took the greatest interest in the airplane in which he was to fly, and he was meticulous in the care and the sighting of his guns, which he insisted upon doing himself.

By that summer of 1917 we who were using S.E.5's were already practicing the basic plan of flying on patrol as squadrons in three flights of five aircraft in each. Jimmy McCudden insisted that in their fighting the pilots of his flight should stick to him like glue, and that they should never, unless prevented by an accident, become separated from him. He no longer believed in the dog-fighting that had been going on almost from the beginning. It had enabled some of the exceptional lone-wolf pilots to accumulate the most impressive scores; but McCudden stressed the view that when the new and inexperienced pilots tried to operate on their own, they were more often than not picked off and shot down in their early encounters with more experienced German pilots. McCudden always put the two least experienced pilots in his flight at the back of the formation of five with instructions that if they were attacked from the rear they were to dive for protection underneath the aircraft in front, rather like young chickens rushing to the safety of the cover of the hen. This sound plan soon put a stop to unnecessary casualties among the new boys. It also helped to give them the experience that was so vitally necessary.

From all this evolved the use of the flight as one individual unit. The result was that the leader, in this case Jimmy McCudden himself, shot down most of the Huns while the rest of the flight looked after his tail; and a lot of Huns were shot down in this way with very few casualties. There was some criticism of McCudden in No. 56 Squadron on the grounds that he was being selfish and trying to bag all the glory for himself. Such criticism was natural enough from those who were overeager to get into the limelight; but those who had had longer and more varied experience at the front realized that McCudden was right. He was a very good pilot, a most accurate shot, and an experienced leader; and I felt that it was up to those who would follow in his footsteps to prove themselves by learning from him.

A little later Jimmy McCudden and I shared a further interest when his young brother, Anthony, joined my squadron as a pilot. Anthony McCudden was very keen and, as I soon discovered, overanxious to follow in his brother's footsteps. McCudden had seen that while the nineteen-year-old youngster was still under training at home, and he was always worried that his brother would suffer from being overconfident. "That always spells trouble for the fledgling," he commented. He often spoke to me about his brother and this eagerness of his, and since he was so worried about him I kept as sharp an eye as I could on young Anthony McCudden.

Earlier in the year, when I had crashed at Treizennes, Wilfrid Freeman had intervened in what happened immediately afterward and, against my wishes, had done me a great service by giving orders that I be shipped back to England. Shortly after I got back to France some five months later, this time in command of No. 84 Squadron, he did me another service when he saw to it that I remained in France. My right to be there was questioned when it was discovered by the people who handled the records that I had not been passed by a medical board as fit for a return to operational flying. The bits and pieces of paper had come to rest on somebody's desk, and this technicality had developed until there was talk about my being sent back to England. That would have broken my heart because I was terribly keen about my squadron and the work we were doing; and it was unthinkable that I should have to give it all up. Fortunately for me, Freeman intervened on my behalf, and after an examination by the wing medical officer I was passed as thoroughly fit for operations.

Wilfrid Freeman had been back in France for some time as a wing commander, and he had written to me earlier in the summer, before I had taken command of No. 84 Squadron, and he had spoken about the fortunes of No. 43 Squadron. After pleasantly thanking me for "the work you did out here under somewhat trying conditions," he went on to add, a little sadly I thought, that "your old squadron is doing well, but I am afraid there are not many of the old originals left. I only wish there were—they were a good crowd you collected."

It was from that letter of Wilfrid Freeman's that I received the final and conclusive proof that the German pilots with whom I had had such a brisk encounter going on for two years before, while I was flying from Marieux with No. 8 Squadron, were indeed Oswald Boelcke and Max Immelmann. Freeman had managed somehow or other to get hold of a copy of a German printing of Boelcke's diary. "It has now been translated," he wrote. "Here is the bit about yourself!" And he sent the full extract from the diary for the day of December 29, 1915.

It was amusing, and to some extent flattering, to read what such a notable adversary as Boelcke had had to say about my flying at the end of 1915. By the time of my arrival back on the Western Front in September, 1917, for what amounted to my fourth tour of operational flying, I could fairly claim that I was a very experienced pilot. And being at Estrée Blanche meant that we were on an important part of the Front in good time to take part in and observe from the air the worst of what I have always felt was the most terrible battle of the First World War: the Third Battle of Ypres. The Somme of the year before had been bad enough—after that we had felt that the lesson of the futility of mass attacks must surely have been learned. But it was not learned, and less than a year later our Army was called upon to embark on an offensive that in many ways was even more terrible than the Somme.

Although Douglas Haig had been forced by the requirements of the French to launch his earlier offensives further south, on the Somme and at Arras, he had long been planning for a campaign in Flanders. Pressure had been brought to bear on him to push the Germans back from the Flemish coast, from which the Germans were launching part of their unrestricted submarine strangling of communications with Britain. That gave Haig at least one strategic objective, which was something he had found so lacking in the other campaigns. He had decided that the place to make his drive was in the Ypres Salient, and that it should be preceded by an attack on Messines Ridge, the narrow stretch of higher ground just to the south of Ypres.

A couple of weeks before the first contingent of the American Army arrived to take its place in the fighting in France, this attack at Messines was launched. It was made in the small hours of the morning on June 7, and the noise from the gigantic mines that were exploded under the Ridge was heard even in London. At first the attack was a success; but before Douglas Haig could proceed with the launching of the main attack in the Salient he had to embark on yet another round of disputes with the politicians at home. Six weeks of magnificent weather in the height of the summer were wasted before the attack on the Salient was allowed to get underway, and by that time the Germans, well placed in the higher ground surrounding and looking out over the Salient, were well aware of what was coming. They moved up formidable reinforcements, even thinning out their defenses against the French to the south, for the French were in no state to do anything more than lick their wounds. At the end of July the Third Battle of Ypres was launched. It was the beginning of what was to become for those on the ground a long and indescribable misery.

lorem..., even thinning out their defenses against the French to
the south, for the French were in no state to do anything more
than lick their wounds. At the period during which the Third
Ypres was launched, it was... ...
for those on the ground a long and inexorable misery.

10 / Passchendaele

THE DELAY that was allowed to occur during the
spell of fine weather between the storming of the ridge at Messines
and the opening of the larger offensive that became the Third Battle
of Ypres was to cost us very dearly. The weather broke, and August was the wettest known in that part of Flanders for as long as
the local inhabitants could remember. Our extremely heavy artillery
bombardment, which was supposed to open the way, merely left
the land over which the fighting was to take place pockmarked with
holes, all of which rapidly filled with water. In the Salient itself,
which is in very low-lying country, there were occasional dry spells,
but all the drainage systems were smashed in the opening bombardment, and eventually the whole area became clogged with mud.

Over this devastated area which had been reduced to the state of
a quagmire, attack after attack was launched, but so many of them
were to flounder in the mud; and the blood bath of Third Ypres
was underway. The state of affairs in the Salient after the first
month's fighting has been described by Cyril Falls as "taking on
the aspect of a nightmare: casualty-clearing stations with helpless
patients under shell fire by day and air bombing by night; horrible
scenes in horse-lines and on the tracks." For communication there
were only the rough tracks which wound their way almost aimlessly
across the mire, and wandering off them led to drowning. The
Germans welcomed the rain as "our strongest ally." During September there was some improvement in the weather, and the
ground, although still a tortured and horrible sight, dried out a
little. But three days before our arrival at Estrée Blanche, on the
eve of the launching of yet another attack, the weather broke
again, rain set in, and there was an early start to the autumn.

What with a combination of the weather, the battle that was
being waged, our new aircraft, and having a brand-new squadron,
on my return to France I was glad to be able to compare notes
with my opposite number: the commanding officer of No. 56
Squadron. He was a man of extraordinary drive and enthusiasm by

the name of Major R. G. Blomfield. He had given McCudden and the other flight commanders in his squadron full rein in developing their ideas: as a result, he had met with great success.

Another attribute possessed by Blomfield was his shrewd eye for publicity, and one of his stunts was the formation of the No. 56 Squadron orchestra, which became famous throughout the Flying Corps on the Western Front. In addition to pulling all sorts of wires and resorting to every kind of trick in bargaining and trading, Blomfield had even raided London in recruiting and gathering together in his squadron a group of airmen who were musicians as well as basically tradesmen in the Flying Corps; and no social occasion in the life of the squadron was celebrated without the orchestra's being in attendance. In its way, this could be looked upon as the peak of the efforts made by the R.F.C. to say it with music. Maurice Baring wrote in his book of hearing the orchestra play on one occasion Mendelssohn's "Spring Song"; and on another visit to Estrée Blanche during the time I was there he stated: "The favourite tunes of the Squadron at this time were 'Hullo, My Dearie,' and 'Someone Has Got to Darn His Socks.'"

Late one afternoon, a couple of days after our arrival at Estrée Blanche, I was with some of the pilots of No. 56 Squadron watching Jimmy McCudden and his flight of S.E.5's as they landed from a patrol over the Salient. We joined them as they got out of their aircraft, and they told us about the scrap in which they had just been involved. It was a fight that was to become recognized as one of the most gallant exhibitions of courage ever seen in the air; it is now recorded as a particularly colorful episode in the history of flying.

After attacking and destroying an enemy two-seater, Jimmy McCudden saw another S.E.5 having a scrap with one of the new German fighters, the Fokker triplane, over Poelcapelle in the northeastern corner of the Salient. He led his flight into the attack, and it immediately became apparent that the German upon whom they had pounced was somebody quite out of the ordinary. Exhibiting the greatest skill and daring, he took on all seven of our pilots, and for ten minutes he fought them in a manner which McCudden described as "wonderful to behold."

All our S.E.5 pilots waded into the scrap with this one German. In a description that he later wrote about the encounter, McCudden said: "The pilot seemed to be firing at all of us simultaneously, and although I got behind him a second time, I could hardly stay there for a second. His movements were so quick and uncertain that none of us could hold him in sight at all for any decisive time." Another German, in an Albatros, then joined in, and he was followed by the arrival on the scene of a formation of six more Albatroses. But they were prevented from making an attack on the S.E.5's by a formation of our Spads.

The German triplane continued to hold off and even attack our S.E.5's without making any effort to escape. "At one time I noted the triplane in the apex of a cone of tracer bullets from at least five machines simultaneously, and each machine had two guns," Mc-Cudden reported. They were by then low down, at only about one thousand feet. The single Albatros had been disposed of, and the German triplane was again on its own. Lieutenant A. P. F. Rhys-Davids, one of the deadliest fighters in No. 56 Squadron, slipped into a favorable position. He had already poured a great deal of fire from his Vickers and Lewis guns into the triplane.

"I got in another good burst and the triplane did a slight right-hand turn, still going down," Rhys-Davids stated. "I had now overshot him, zoomed, but never saw him again."

But McCudden saw what happened after Rhys-Davids made his attack, and of that he wrote: "I noticed that the triplane's movements were very erratic, and then I saw him go into a fairly steep dive and so I continued to watch, and then saw the triplane hit the ground and disappear into a thousand fragments, for it seemed to me that it literally went to powder. Strange to say, I was the only pilot who witnessed the triplane crash, for even Rhys-Davids, who finally shot it down, did not see its end."

This German pilot, who had fought so gallantly against such great odds, crashed on our side of the lines. When the body found in the midst of the wreckage was examined it was discovered that it was Werner Voss, who was at that time second only to Richthofen in the number of successes (his total stood at forty-nine). He was then twenty years old—the same age as Rhys-Davids— scarcely more than a youth.

"As long as I live I shall never forget my admiration for that German pilot, who single-handed fought seven of us for ten minutes, and also put some bullets through all of our machines," McCudden stated. "His flying was wonderful, his courage magnificent, and in my opinion he was the bravest German airman whom it has been my privilege to see fight."

When Rhys-Davids was told the next day that he was credited with having destroyed Werner Voss, he exclaimed, "Oh, if I could only have brought him down alive." Rhys-Davids was a very intelligent and good-looking young man, and he had a particularly charming manner. Maurice Baring, who visited us frequently at

Estrée Blanche at this time, recorded that he always flew with a volume of William Blake's poems in his pocket. On one occasion Rhys-Davids made the succinct comment to Baring: "The Buddhists have got a maxim, 'Don't be stupid': that is all that matters in life."

Only a very short time before, Rhys-Davids had been captain of the school at Eton. A month after making that comment to Baring, and with twenty-three enemy aircraft destroyed to his credit, he was dead. How Rhys-Davids was killed is not known. He disappeared after chasing some Germans back over their lines near Roulers, to the northeast of the Salient, and they merely reported that he was shot down. "He had told me the last time I saw him that he was quite certain he would be killed," Baring wrote a little later.

Three weeks before Rhys-Davids was killed he had made yet another contribution to flying history when, at a special dinner in the mess to celebrate some new awards made to the pilots of No. 56 Squadron—including a D.S.O. for Rhys-Davids himself—he had asked all of those present to rise and drink to "Von Richthofen, our most worthy enemy." In this incident there is an indication of the spirit of the Flying Corps of those days, a spirit that can really be understood only by those who have come to fly. All the pilots present drank to the toast. The only person who refused to do so was a nonflying officer who, according to McCudden, stated, "No, I won't drink to the health of that devil."

At that particular time the health of Manfred von Richthofen was probably not of the best. Early in July, an offensive patrol of our fighters made up of six F.E.2d's of No. 20 Squadron, two-seater pushers, and four Sopwith triplanes of No. 10 (Naval) Squadron got into a scrap over our part of the line with Richthofen and his Circus of forty fighters. One of the F.E. crews did a splendid job in sending down out of control four of the enemy aircraft. They then set about another, an all-red Albatros; but they did not claim it because, although it went into a spin, they did not see it crash.

That particular Albatros was being flown by Richthofen, and one of their bullets had hit him across the left side of his head, severely creasing his skull and splintering the bone. Blinded and for a few moments paralyzed, he had fallen out of the sky, recovering just in time to make a safe landing and climb out of his aircraft before collapsing. Richthofen was in the hospital for a while, but he insisted on returning to the Front as soon as possible, even though his wound had not completely healed and he was far from fit. Only six weeks after being wounded, he was flying again over the northern part of the Front.

The fighting in the air during those weeks of the summer and the autumn of 1917 reached a stage that must have appeared quite as spectacular from the ground as it was to those participating in it. The Germans were re-equipping with the Fokker triplane, a formidable fighter, and Richthofen's Circus was given every opportunity to try it out against our S.E.5's. There was constant fighting over the Salient between formations of fighters of both sides, and there were serious losses to both.

In Jimmy McCudden's book, *Five Years in the Royal Flying Corps* (edited by C. G. Grey and published shortly after McCudden's death), there is a particularly good description of what it was like in the air over the Salient at this time. It is at the beginning of his account of the fight that led to the death of Werner Voss. "As soon as we crossed Hunland I noted abnormal enemy activity," he wrote, "and indeed there seemed to be a great many machines of both sides about. A heavy layer of grey clouds hung at 9,000 feet, and although the visibility was poor for observation, the atmosphere was fairly clear in a horizontal direction. Away to the east one could see clusters of little black specks, all moving swiftly, first in one direction and then in another. Farther north we could see formations of our own machines, Camels, Pups, S.E.'s, Spads and Bristols, and lower down in the haze our artillery R.E.8's."

All this heavy fighting meant that those who survived were becoming very experienced. When we in No. 84 Squadron started flying from Estrée Blanche late in September, 1917, we immediately found ourselves up against the tough Richthofen and his Circus. It was for me yet another encounter with them, and from then on, whenever either they or we were moved, it seemed that we were still up against each other, either stalking or being stalked.

It was the lot of No. 84 Squadron, because we had S.E.5's, to be sent quickly from one battle to another. For the same reason, Richthofen and his Circus invariably popped up in opposition to us. In our encounters with them we tried to take every precaution against being pounced upon by Richthofen. We knew only too well that that would be fatal. When we saw the Circus approaching, we would climb as hard as we could, if possible up into the sun; then we would try to take them from above and behind and out of the sun. The superior performance of our S.E.5's enabled us to do this more or less with impunity. We allowed ourselves to be under

Richthofen only when we had to go to the rescue of one of our own people—usually an artillery cooperation aircraft.

Although fighting in the air had taken on a definite form by this time, the chases and the scraps that we got into—the dogfights—were quite different from those of the second war. For one thing, it took us longer to close with our adversary than it did in the fighters of 1939–45 because our speeds were so very much slower. On the other hand, when we did catch up with each other, things were not nearly so straightforward as they were later. Our maneuvers were confined to quite small areas for the actual fights and were much more complex, and there was a great deal more jockeying for position. In the second war it was more a matter of hurtling in from quite long distances and getting in a quick squirt at the enemy before you were again miles apart. In the earlier war we swirled around and over each other—never under if we could help it—trying to line up the enemy in our gunsights; and all the time we were watching to make sure that nobody was swooping around on our own tails.

In those contortions of ours, confined as they were by our low speeds and great maneuverability to a fairly small area once we had joined in combat, we gave no thought to our aspect in relation to the ground or the sky. The individual combat was usually over in a few minutes, although a dogfight between two formations might last longer, from ten minutes up to half an hour or more. Our opponents would maneuver for position and we would go after them, and then they would go after us and we would have to take avoiding action even if it meant standing on our heads. Aircraft would be whirling around in all directions trying to get at each other.

The attitude of our aircraft did not matter as long as it was still under control. Our one object was to get our gunsights on the enemy, and if it meant that we went over on our backs and were upside down, that did not matter greatly as long as we were still on the attack and had the enemy in our sights. There were times when we found ourselves in the most astonishing positions, and there was always the danger of collision. I saw quite a few collisions, and there were several that I managed to avoid only by the skin of my teeth.

When we were flying high up, our actions were always hampered to a certain extent by the cold and by lack of oxygen. Winter or summer, it was pretty cold in our open cockpits. I used to wear a lot of flying kit topped off with a thick leather flying coat—it was

larger than a mere jacket—that I had bought quite early on in the
war. It has been displayed in the Imperial War Museum in London. I used to wear a muffler around my neck. For further protection against the cold some even wore mufflers—quite often in the
form of one or two of their girl friend's stockings—around their
mouths. We all used an antifrostbite ointment, particularly in the
winter, which we smeared over our cheeks below our goggles, thus
protecting the only parts of our faces left uncovered. The rest of
our heads and faces were protected by flying helmets and goggles. I
never covered my mouth because I was never troubled with
cracked lips, as some were.

On occasions I did manage, by pushing things hard, to get my
S.E.5 up to a height of just over twenty-two thousand feet, usually
in order to get into a position from which I could dive down
unseen on the Hun. That height was not possible with the rotary
engines of the 1½ Strutter or the Camel; even the SE.5 became
very sluggish and difficult to control, and seemed only too ready to
fall out of my hands. Any exertion at such a height without oxygen
left me gasping for breath, but that and the cold were the only
discomforts I ever suffered. I was one of those fortunate enough
never to be bothered by airsickness. Being in an open cockpit and
having plenty of fresh air helped. As I became more experienced I
found that lack of orientation did not enter into any of my
sensations.

Being a new squadron, we suffered fairly heavy casualties at the
outset. Because of that, we had to learn fast. I insisted on putting
into practice the ideas that were expressed and demonstrated to me
by Jimmy McCudden, and I refused to listen to the criticism
expressed even by some of the other pilots of his own squadron.
No. 56 Squadron was made up largely of a number of brilliant and
experienced individualists, some of whom were still looking with
disfavor on what McCudden was preaching. I did not have such
knowledgeable fighters under my authority, and I was well supported by my young pilots in my efforts to adopt McCudden's
ideas about fighting in formation. The outstanding of these youngsters in my squadron was a young South African by the name of
A. W. Beauchamp-Proctor. He was to have a spectacular rise to
fame. Scarcely more than five feet tall, Beauchamp-Proctor was an
extraordinary young man who, despite his size, had already shown
that he was made of iron. There was always a bit of a mystery
about where he came from, and even about his exact age. After
leaving school in Cape Town he had studied for a while for a

science degree in engineering at the University of Cape Town. In 1915 he joined the Army, in South Africa, and he served as a signaler in the campaign in German Southwest Africa.

That grueling experience in the deadly climate of the German colony was enough to test the endurance of any man, but Beauchamp-Proctor appeared to be none the worse for it, and when it was over he volunteered for service with the Royal Flying Corps. He was sent to England, and after his initial training he was one of the original pilots sent to me for No. 84 Squadron. He was a wiry little man with black hair, a swarthy complexion and snapping dark eyes, and from the very beginning he showed that he was both courageous and a first-rate shot. He was so small that we had to make special adjustments to the rudder-bar and the seat of his S.E.5.

Beauchamp-Proctor reveled in the ideas that McCudden had put forward and which I was adopting, and it was in his use of them that he eventually achieved such great success, because he became an extremely good formation leader. The moral effect of his enthusiasm on the rest of my squadron was worth his weight in gold, and for that reason I very often let him lead the squadron, being content myself to go along as deputy leader.

When I say that we flew and fought in formation I do not mean that we were able to move in the rigid and very impressive patterns executed by the aerobatic teams of the Royal Air Force of today. We did not have anything like the power that they have, and our formation flying was designed primarily for fighting, not exhibition. When we were not actually going into an attack or being attacked, we flew in rather loose formations; but as soon as action was imminent, we closed up and flew in quite as tight a formation as the fighters of the second war. We had no radio whereby we could talk to each other and give and receive instructions, and the leader would waggle his wings to draw us in and even, in an emergency, shoot off a red Verey light to call in the stragglers. Then we would be very close to each other, with the whole formation moving as one unit.

Our arrival at the Front brought us into the Third Battle of Ypres at the stage known as the Battle of Polygon Wood. This started on the morning of September 26. The battle was planned as a jumping-off point for a direct assault on the ridge that had as its focal point the village of Passchendaele. To all those involved in the fighting in the Salient at that time, on the ground and in the air, that name, the Third Battle of Ypres, is really scarcely more than the textbook term for the campaign that will always be known to us as Passchendaele.

At first we were sent off on offensive patrols up and down the road between Menin and Roulers, just behind the German front lines and running along the Passchendaele ridge. There were swarms of aircraft in the air. On the whole, the Germans were more experienced pilots than we were; they rarely came over our side of the lines and therefore suffered fewer casualties. We suffered casualties because we were a new, raw squadron and we had not yet adopted the right tactics. As soon as we learned the advantages of sticking close to each other, we found that our casualties fell off and our successes increased, even in facing Richthofen and his formidable band.

With the start of the attack on Passchendaele itself, on October 9, after two days of continuous and heavy rain, our work was changed to that of carrying out low-flying attacks against enemy concentrations on the ground. It was supposed to be an effort on our part to assist our troops, who were struggling in what had become nothing more than an appalling morass. In this job there was very little fighting in the air, and since we were flying at heights of only two or three hundred feet, we were supposed to be able to see plenty of what was going on below us. What I saw was nothing short of horrifying. The ground over which our infantry and light artillery were fighting was one vast sea of churned-up muck and mud, and everywhere, lip to lip, there were shell holes full of water.

These low-flying attacks that we had to make—for which most of my young pilots were quite untrained—were a wretched and dangerous business, and also pretty useless. It was very difficult for us to pick out our targets in the morass because everything on the ground, including the troops, was the same color as that dreadful mud. Quite often when we went diving in to the attack, we found ourselves unexpectedly peering slap down the muzzles of a score of German machine guns. Even from our point of view in the air, it was all grim and bloody and pointless; and how our men on the ground could live under such appalling conditions, much less make the advance that was expected of them, was utterly beyond my comprehension. The pluck and the pertinacity of our infantry won our greatest respect. Although they did manage to inch their way forward, it was quite obvious to anyone viewing from the air this dreadful battleground—if ground it could be called, for it was mostly awash in mud and slime—that any chance of a major advance or a breakthrough was quite out of the question.

The weather continued to be foul, and almost every day it rained heavily and at times continuously. We all came to feel that somewhere or other, by somebody or other, there had been committed in the ordering of more attacks the grossest of blunders. It was understandable enough that the British had to attack heavily at this time in order to keep the Germans busy and so relieve the pressure on the French, who were in a sorry state of unrest and mutiny. But as I watched from the air what was happening on the ground there were presented to me some terrible questions. Why did we have to press on so blindly day after day and week after week in this one desolate area and under such dreadful conditions? Why was there not some variety in our strategy and tactics? The questions that I asked then are the questions that have continued to be asked ever since. The answers have never ceased to be most painful.

A lot has been written about the lack of firsthand knowledge back at Douglas Haig's headquarters, and the ignorance of the Staff officers about the actual conditions under which the soldiers were having to fight in the Salient. The Staff, it seems, very seldom visited the front lines. *In Flanders Fields,* a book on the fighting of 1917 published in the late 1950's and written by Leon Wolff, an American author who had served in the United States Army Air Forces in the Second World War, recounts in detail the story of the Third Battle of Ypres. Of one incident, which involved no less a person than Douglas Haig's Chief of Staff (the father of a boy with whom I had been at school at Tonbridge), Wolff wrote:

The following day Lieutenant-General Sir Launcelot Kiggell paid his first visit to the fighting zone. As his staff car lurched through the swampland and neared the battleground he became more and more agitated. Finally he burst into tears and muttered, "Good God, did we really send men to fight in that?"
The man beside him, who had been through the campaign, replied tonelessly, "It's worse further on up."

Some years after the end of the first war I wrote a staff paper about the superiority of our fighters over the Germans in the autumn of 1917. In it I said: "There is little doubt that the S.E. was the most successful of any of the single-seater fighters that we employed during the war." Repeating this now will cause howls of anguish from the pilots who flew the Sopwith Camel; but it was a fact that the S.E.5 maintained, in a large measure, its performance at high altitudes, which the Camel did not. And since the S.E.5

was very steady in a fast dive—which nine times out of ten was
our way of attack—this was an additional advantage over the
Camel. The faster we dived in the S.E.5, the steadier the aircraft
became as a gun platform. The Camel, on the other hand, being an
unstable machine, would vary its angle of dive at high speed in
spite of all the pilot's efforts to keep it steady; and because of its
rotary engine there was also a good deal of vibration when diving
fast, which made good shooting difficult.

But even our reliable S.E.5's were not yet altogether trouble-
free. As with all new types of aircraft, there had been some difficulties over the engines, although we had been in luck and escaped
a great deal of trouble. But one morning toward the end of
October an engine failure left me in what could have become a
tight spot. I was leading a flight (we were still in our basic formation) on an offensive patrol up and down our familiar beat over
the road between Roulers and Menin. After a while my engine
started to play up—popping and banging and dropping in revs. It
was not actually failing, but it was not developing the power that it
should, so I signaled to the others that I was leaving the flight, and
I made off for home.

I was down near Lille and still some distance behind the German lines when I spotted a lone enemy fighter, an Albatros, preparing for an attack. He came down on me out of the sun trying to
take me by surprise, but I had been keeping a sharp lookout and I
saw him coming. Despite the loss of power from my engine, I
managed to maneuver around him and to get my sights on him,
and I gave him a burst from both guns. The Albatros promptly
dived away. I think I hit him, but I could not claim that I had shot
him down. If my engine had not been playing up, I would have
tried to finish him off; but I could not risk that, and I had to nurse
the engine along as it spluttered its way back to Estrée Blanche.

The stiffest opposition put up by the enemy in the fighting over
the Salient came from the Fokker triplane, which was still being
developed, and the Albatros and the Halberstadt single-seater
biplanes. When we were flying level with them in our S.E.5's and
wanted to get out of range—to clear a jammed gun, for instance—
all we had to do was go into a dive, keeping the engine running at
full throttle. Although later the Fokker D VII was slightly faster
than the S.E.5 in level flight, the S.E.5 would pick up speed in a
dive much quicker, and for a few precious seconds we were sometimes able to draw out of range of the enemy. Then, with the fine
zoom that the S.E.5 had even at high altitudes, we could return to
the attack. In the low-flying attacks that we carried out at Pas-

schendaele, this zoom often enabled us to rocket up to comparative safety when we came across an unexpected machine-gun nest.

All through October we were engaged in flights up and down the Menin-Roulers Road and over that ridge that has become so well known, and the casualties in my squadron went on being heavier than I had expected. There was still quite a lot of argument about how we should operate, and whether we should fight in flights or in squadrons made up of flights. But bitter experience is a quick, as well as a hard, teacher. I came to feel with increasing conviction that the flight was not strong enough to operate unsupported on a fighting patrol, and I started insisting that my squadron work as one unit made up of three flights of five aircraft each. I was one of the first squadron commanders to do that.

There was bound to be some opposition from the individualists in the squadron. Since the Flying Corps was made up so largely of individualists I found that my pilots did not hesitate to argue and to press their views. Eventually I had to give strict orders that no pilot was to leave the formation on any account, even to take on what looked like an easy opportunity to shoot down an enemy aircraft. The initiative in any attack, I ruled, was to rest wholly in the hands of the leader. If he dived to the attack the whole squadron was to dive with him; and when he zoomed away after an attack—even if he had failed to shoot down the enemy machine that they were attacking—all his pilots were to zoom away with him, still keeping formation. Being the most experienced of all the pilots, the leader was the most capable of shooting down the enemy quickly and effectively; and with the squadron behind him and acting as a buffer against any attack from the rear, he could afford to concentrate all his powers on the destruction of the enemy without having to peer over his shoulder all the time. This was also the method adopted by Richthofen.

Another lesson that my inexperienced pilots soon had to learn was that there were occasions enough when it was quite wrong to accept battle. I had to din into them that they must always strive to take the enemy at a disadvantage, and, equally important, that they must not be taken at a disadvantage themselves. Quite often this meant deliberately refusing to accept the challenge and cautiously retiring so as to get into a better position. The only permissible exception to that rule was if they saw other Allied aircraft, of any number, being overwhelmed by superior numbers of the enemy; and then, whatever the odds, they must accept battle. But under normal conditions—if such a business could have the word normal applied to it—I stressed that we should force the fight upon the enemy, and not wait until he could force it upon us.

Out of the unique experience we were gaining under the conditions of actual war, it had come to be an accepted fact that—contradictory though it may sound—the pilots who got good scores were not necessarily good pilots. Those who shot down the enemy were those who knew how to use their guns and had taken care to see that their sights were properly lined up. They were good shots and they were not concerned with the excellence of their flying. If, for instance, a pilot went about making a correct and properly banked turn, he could waste a lot of time, whereas if he just flipped the aircraft around in a flat turn, bad flying though it might be, he was taking the shortest cut to getting his sights on the Hun.

As far as my own skill was concerned, I knew that I was a good, correct pilot, and that I could fly in no other way; and that was probably one of the main reasons why my own score of enemy aircraft destroyed was not a large one. I see from certain records that it is given as six, in addition to those probably destroyed or damaged, but I never kept a record. I do not know what my final score was because, for some reason I do not understand, it did not particularly interest me. I was more interested in my squadron's score.

A very good example of the way in which a pilot could become engaged in all-out fighting without worrying about his flying was in the great battle between the pilots of No. 56 Squadron and Werner Voss. It was extraordinary that Voss should have managed to stay alive as long as he did and, at the same time, to put holes in all the aircraft that were attacking him. He achieved it by sitting on his tail and firing in one direction and then sharply swinging around without any attempt at proper or orthodox turns—just a flat turn with his nose in the air—to fire at another of his attackers. He was not concerned with good flying, and he had no time to think about it. He was fighting for his life, and the reason he survived as long as he did against such formidable odds was the sheer excellence of his shooting and the way he used his aircraft as a platform for his guns.

Toward the end of October, just before the final capture of Passchendaele, my squadron was transferred to the 13th Wing, which was working with the Fourth Army. This transfer took us from Estrée Blanche down to the south to the airfield at Izel-les-Hameau, a few miles to the west of Arras. We got there in time to

take part in another battle that was just about to be staged; but I
had no objection to that because I was only too glad to get away
from the Salient at Ypres.

It could be argued with some justification that we in the Flying
Corps were lucky in not having to live in the midst of all the filth
and the squalor of the destruction on the ground, and that we had
a better time of it because we were able to return after our patrols
to the comforts of our airfields well behind the lines. That is true,
and it was, when one paused to think about it, quite astonishing to
notice the startling difference between the havoc of the battlefields—particularly in the Salient around Ypres—and the undisturbed countryside behind the lines, where most of the airfields
were situated.

Our lives were unquestionably a great deal more comfortable in
a physical sense in the Flying Corps than in any other branch of
the Army; but that did not mean we were not under a strain. Many
times over the years I have been questioned about the physical
details of our lives as fighter pilots on the Western Front. The
questions express a natural enough interest. For a short period we
were able to live and work in a way that man had never known
before and would never know again in quite the same way.

In the second war, what with the more highly organized and
efficient system, the greater speeds of the aircraft, the modern
communications (in the form of very good radio telephone backing up the early warning given by radar), the close control from the
ground, and the enclosed cockpits, actual flying was a much more
mechanical performance. During those years of 1914–18 we were
not only experimenting the whole time: we were pioneering as
well. Our airfields in the first war, for instance, were still just fields
with temporary wooden hangars, small ones, and huts and tents
scattered around the edge of the area of grass used for taking off
and landing; and many years were to pass before there came into
use such things as runways.

If we were warned for the early patrol, the fighter pilots' day
started just before dawn, when we would climb into the thick cloth-
ing that we all wore, summer and winter, for protection against
the cold in the upper air. It never became even warm in our aircraft
—and that was quite different from what happened in most of the
enclosed cockpits of the aircraft of the second war. We would
make our way through the first light of dawn to our airplanes, the
engines of which had already been warmed up by our mechanics.
We would climb into our open cockpits—which allowed at least
our heads to be above the fuselage—strap ourselves in with our

waist belts, start up the engines, and then taxi out into position for our take-off.

Not being enclosed, we were able to look around quite easily in every direction, and we would take off in formation and climb to the height we needed while still well behind our own lines and out of sight of the enemy. It usually took time for us to get to a reasonable height, and all we had to think about then was our flying. When we reached the height we wanted, we would turn and, still in formation, fly out over the trenches. Then we would start taking notice of all the signs of war on the ground and in the air.

There is a very great difference between what one sees of the earth when one first starts flying and the way in which one looks at it after the solid experience of many hours in the air. On my first flight as an observer early in 1915, I had been utterly confused by what I saw of the strange patchwork of the ground below me; but with experience I learned to spot an extraordinary variety of the sights to be seen on the ground and to recognize almost instinctively all the features of the earth over which I was flying. In a way, it is a matter of progressing, through the intelligent reading of a map, from confusion to an instinctive understanding. After one reaches that last stage, one feels just as much at home in the air in relating one's position in it to the ground as one does in walking over the fields or along the roads.

The trenches over which we flew were quite clearly marked as they snaked their way across the desolation of the battlefields. They resembled a broad, ugly stream several miles in width which wandered from horizon to horizon across the normal green countryside. When we got over the enemy lines, their archie would start rushing up at us, bursting with the black smudges of high explosive and usually not very effective. We might pass one of our own bombing formations, and we would wave to each other and they would wave back—such were our speeds in those days that we had time for that sort of exchange—and they would go on their way.

Our penetration of the enemy territory usually took us well beyond the area of the actual battlefields, and the archie would tail off. The sun would be up by then, and we could see longer distances. The early patrols of the enemy fighters would appear, at first scarcely more than specks in the sky, ready to object to our intrusion. They might be above us, so while there was still time we would turn away and start climbing, working our way around to get between them and the sun and above them. There was no blind rushing at them. We stalked them, just as they, if they saw our formation, would go about stalking us.

When our relative positions were to our advantage, we would dive down on the enemy, following closely behind our leader, holding our fire until we were close enough to be able to bring to bear the most effective burst from our machine guns. The enemy formation would turn in an effort to attack us, and we would turn with them. In a few seconds tracer might come whistling past one's ears, indicating all too clearly that the enemy had managed to get behind and was on the attack. If that happened it meant that we had lost out in the preliminary tactical maneuverings. In such a case we might find ourselves in the middle of a dog-fight, with aircraft of both sides hurtling around in all directions and often separated by distances that could be measured in yards. The tracer was warning enough that one was being attacked, and a quick kick on the rudder and pulling the stick back enabled one to climb for a moment out of harm's way, glancing back at the same time over one's shoulder to see where the attacker had gone to and forward to avoid a possible collision. At this stage we would often have to indulge in very strenuous aerobatics confined to quite a small area.

We always looked for the Hun who had become separated from his friends, and when we found him we wasted no time. We would pounce and give him two or three short bursts, and if our shooting was up to scratch, he would start the long fall to earth, sometimes on fire. Whenever I saw that happen I always knew for a moment a feeling of something approaching sickness. A fellow human being had died, or was dying, and it had all happened so quickly. But that reaction was only momentary, and the protective jelly around one's mind that came with experience blotted out any more thoughts about what had happened.

What mattered was that we were still intact. Looking around we would see that the fight had been broken off, and that the two sides had separated. Our leader might be firing a red Verey light as a signal for us to form up on him, and we would return to our formation. Perhaps our time on patrol was up, and fuel and ammunition were running low, so we would turn back for the lines, with more archie being flung up at us as we crossed them. We would mutter complaints or make rude comments to ourselves, and then we would be across the lines and gliding down to a landing on our own airfield.

There was some exhilaration in being back all in one piece. We were relieved at being safe and perhaps even a little overstimulated after the fight, and it was a pleasant letdown as we wobbled back over the uneven ground to the hangars. Then would come the reports on the patrol. followed by breakfast. It was only the start of yet another day, and although we might feel that we had already done a day's work there would be more patrols with the same thing happening all over again.

Whenever I went into a scrap I knew, as everyone else did, a tightening of my nerves, an awareness or anxiety that caused some fear; and once clear of the fight I usually felt only too glad that I was out of it and still intact. Because of the nature of my temperament I did not know the wilder sense of exhilaration that was experienced by some; and when I got back and landed, I always seemed to be too busy to have time to sit back and think about what had happened and possibly fret about some close shave or other. I never knew what it was to fret about things, even when I was a junior pilot with no other responsibility.

When later I became a squadron commander, there was always my desk waiting for me, with reconnaissance and combat reports put in by my pilots to be checked and passed on, my recording officer and all his papers to attend to, and the mass of other administrative work entailed in running a squadron. Although I knew quite well that there were those whose nerves were strained —the semihysteria experienced even by the great Mick Mannock was proof enough of what could happen—I think that generally the effects of that strain have perhaps been overplayed in certain books and films. On the other hand, it might have been my good fortune that, in being physically robust and of a temperament not easily disturbed, I had plenty of padding for the nerves.

Ours was a strain of a new and peculiar temper that even now is hard to analyze. In some cases the abrupt change from the quiet of our way of life on the ground to the heat of being in a scrap in the air over the front lines, often in a matter of only a few minutes, led to a tension or strain that, I must admit, had severe effects on the nerves. Stomach ulcers became one of the hallmarks of our trade, and insomnia and nightmares sometimes made a mockery of sleep; and there were young pilots who broke under that particular strain and had to be sent home as unfit for further service at the Front. They were not listed as officially wounded, but they were, nevertheless, still casualties, and some of them were wrecked in health for the rest of their lives.

Our airfield at Izel-les-Hameau was only about ten miles to the southwest of Vimy Ridge, and in the work that we did, we quite often flew over the Ridge on our way to support the Army in their next attack, which was the Battle of Cambrai. Launched on November 20, within only a few days of the end of the campaign in the Ypres Salient, it came as a surprise for the Germans because there was no softening up by our artillery, which had been such a feature, and a warning, of all our previous attacks. And for the first time our tanks were used in full force as a weapon. For these reasons it was one of the more interesting battles of the war, and at first there was a promise of great success.

The role played by my squadron throughout this battle, which took place in the northeastern reaches of what had been the scene of the Battles of the Somme of the year before, was the protection, by means of offensive patrols, of our low-flying and contact-patrol aircraft. The weather for most of the time was unfavorable for flying, with fog, mist and a drizzle of rain, and it was impossible to work in larger formations than the flight. There were even times when I had to send my pilots off singly or, at the most, in pairs, which nullified my fine new theories about flying in formations of a reasonable size.

The attack at Cambrai started in the early morning with a large number of our tanks opening the way ahead for the infantry. Spectacular advances were made, including a breaching of part of the defenses of the Hindenburg Line. The heavy tank assault broke through the enemy positions into relatively clear and dry ground, and there was a great chance for a further advance. But, yet again, there were no reserves available, partly through a lack of foresight by those who had done the planning, but mainly because most of the available reserves had been used up to no purpose in the fighting for Passchendaele and the other points in the Ypres Salient. Before we could do anything about getting reserves up, the Germans recovered and counterattacked.

During the rest of the rapidly changing fortunes of the Battle of Cambrai—it lasted just a little over two weeks—the Germans, after the first forty-eight hours, put up quite a large number of contact-patrol and reconnaissance aircraft. These were supported by plenty of their fighters, because three days after the battle started, our old opponents of the Richthofen Circus were brought down in a hurry from the north, with Richthofen himself in command of all the German fighters. But such was the state of the weather that all our fighting was done at an exceptionally low altitude—anywhere from three hundred to two thousand feet, and never higher than that—and the arduous apprenticeship that my squadron had served on the Salient bore its first fruits. We shot down five or six of the enemy without loss to ourselves.

The operational orders given to me, and to all the other S.E.5 squadrons, for the Battle of Cambrai were that I should have ready "from zero hour onwards throughout the day" approximately eighteen machines. I was given instructions about which particular patrols we were to fly and which enemy airdromes we were to cover, and I was further told that "as the situation develops patrols will be pushed farther out." These orders came from Headquarters, 3rd Brigade, which was commanded by Brigadier-General J. F. A. Higgins, a well-known Flying Corps character who was sometimes referred to as "Josh" but much more often as "Bum and Eyeglass." The orders were relayed to us by our wing commander, George Pretyman, by then a Lieutenant-Colonel. (At Upavon, nearly two and a half years before, he had given me my final examination for my wings.)

But for all our interest in the Cambrai offensive, it was an unsatisfactory sort of battle, mainly because the weather gave us so little opportunity to put into effect the formation-flying techniques that we had been practicing. It was also an unsatisfactory battle from the point of view of the tanks and the infantry because their initial successful advance came to nothing. In the words of Cyril Falls: "They had at last found ideal ground, an all-weather, unscarred tank battlefield which offered strategic results better than those on which they had fought to please the French Command." The war had come out of the trenches and into the open; but when we found that we did not have the reserves ready to exploit the great tactical success that had been achieved at the outset, everybody had to go slinking back again into their holes in the ground.

With thrusting counterattacks, the Germans succeeded in regaining most of the ground that they had lost. There echoes in my mind now the wish that was in the minds of so many at that time who thought about what was happening: if only the Battle of Cambrai had been fought a month or two earlier, with sufficient reserves available to exploit the early success of the tanks and the infantry. As it was, the battle died out in a withering blizzard, and the snow drove everybody to seek cover. Although it had lasted only two weeks, the figures of the casualties again leave the mind boggling: about forty-five thousand on each side. We took eleven thousand prisoners, and the Germans captured nine thousand of our men. There were to be no further major assaults on our part of the Western Front during the rest of that winter. As far as its influence on the future was concerned, the Battle of Cambrai was to have an effect on military thinking that was of more importance in the Second World War than all the other clashes of the first war put together.

Although we had been severely hampered during the actual battle by the wretchedness of the weather, the strength of the Royal Flying Corps assembled for it had been particularly impressive. By this time specialization in our flying was well established. If what I have said about the air sounds as if only the fighters were involved, that is only because I was by then concerned only with fighters; my role was exclusively that of fighter pilot and commander of a fighter squadron. But, bumptious though the fighter pilot might have become, our task in providing protection for all the other squadrons left us in no doubt that there were many others busy in the air on less spectacular and far more hazardous work.

In any consideration of the First World War, it should never be overlooked that the pilots and the observers who flew the reconnaissance aircraft and the early bombers of those days were men possessed of the very highest order of courage. It was all well and good for the fighters to go dashing around, getting mixed up in all sorts of scraps that, although deadly enough, were still eye-catching because they were spectacular. From these early air battles, there emerged the rather brash type that has ever since been recognized, and often caricatured, as the fighter pilot. But for all our colorful exploits in the air, there were so many who had to proceed on their way in a much less spectacular fashion. They did not have the stimulation of the limelight. All they had was the sure knowledge that there was a job to complete, and that it had to be done with no chance of barging off out of it if the going became too hot. And more often than not, they had to fight their way to and back from their targets.

My command of No. 84 Squadron at the Front lasted for over a year, and whenever my turn for leave came around I was as eager as the rest to get back to England for a few days. Every leave that I had during the First World War at least started in England, which usually meant London. My family and most of my friends were there. It was during 1917 that I first came to know Gertrude Lawrence—she was, at the time, if I remember right, in one of Charlot's revues—and from time to time over the years we continued to see each other. The last time was in New York in 1953, when she was playing the part of the attractive widow in *The King and I*. Although she was then obviously far from well, she seemed pleased to see me again; two weeks later she died from cancer.

The theatre continued to provide me with a great deal of pleasure whenever I was on leave, and there were many good

shows that I was able to see. There were also the very popular
night spots that we haunted, and their names will always remind
those of us who were in the R.F.C. of some of our livelier
escapades: Murray's, the Grafton Galleries, and Rectors. They are
only names now, but they are almost a part of the history of the
Royal Flying Corps. And there was always the Cavendish Hotel, in
Jermyn Street, owned and managed by an extraordinary woman
named Mrs. Rosa Lewis.

I sometimes stayed at the Cavendish when I was on leave in
London. Rosa Lewis was a wonderfully warmhearted woman with
a free-and-easy outlook on life. Every evening she used to have a
party in her sitting room on the ground floor of the hotel that she
had started back at the turn of the century. The champagne
flowed, and she particularly liked having around her young officers
of the Flying Corps and attractive young women. She was always
very generous if any of us happened to be hard up. There were
occasions when Rosa refused, as she did with others, to let me
have a bill for my stay in the hotel, and only very rarely were we
allowed to pay for the champagne which we nearly always drank.
Rosa used to tell us that she had charged it up to her wealthier and
older customers, and she would assure us that they would not
mind; but I always had an idea that she paid for it herself.

Rosa Lewis lived on at the Cavendish until the early fifties,
when she died at the age of eighty-five. The obituary notice
that appeared in *The Times* after her death must have stirred
a warm and fond memory in the hearts and minds of many
of our older pillars of society, no matter how crusty they might
have become. One evening just before her death I walked along
Jermyn Street on my way home from my London office in Lower
Regent Street. As I passed the Cavendish I noticed that the cur-
tains had not been drawn, although the lights were on in Rosa's
sitting room on the ground floor. It was many, many years since I
had been in there. I glanced in as I passed and I saw Rosa sitting
in front of the fire with a shawl around her shoulders. She looked
very old. I hesitated for a moment, and I felt a strong impulse to
go in and see her; but I was already late for an appointment, so I
hurried on. I have always regretted that I did not go in and make
myself known to her.

11 / March Retreat

With the ending of the Battle of Cambrai and the onset of winter at the end of 1917 there came a damping down of any further major clashes on the Western Front. It was to be another hard winter. Our flying became more routine in nature, and during the next three months we were busy probing the strength of the enemy. There was reason enough for us to be on the alert, because the collapse and withdrawal of Russia from the war earlier in the year had released the German and Austrian troops on their Eastern Front, and they were being moved to the west. The Germans were also able to transfer to their front facing us huge quantities of stores and guns and other materials of war.

Our military leaders knew all about this, and they also realized that the instability of the French and the mauling that the British had taken during the latter part of 1917 were leaving us in a weak and difficult position. That caused them finally to reverse their way of thinking. Our leaders began to think about the ways in which our armies should be used along more defensive lines— instead of being always on the attack, for which we had been almost exclusively trained.

As might have been expected, this way of thought did not appeal at all to Boom Trenchard. Early in the new year of 1918, he made it clear that no matter how defense-minded the Army might become, the offensive in the air must be kept up. In its way that was fair enough. We were the eyes of the Army, and it was our job to keep a sharp lookout for any sign of the enemy preparing for an attack.

Early in 1918, my squadron was again on the move. We were sent still farther south to an airfield at Flez, on the Somme.It was in open, rolling country about ten miles due west of St-Quentin, and on the outskirts of what had been the village of Guizancourt. We were in the middle of the devastation left by the Germans when they had retreated, nine months before, to the Hindenburg Line.

Our move was not an uneventful one because we ran into quite a lot of trouble with our engines. There is a note in the squadron records about one of my flight commanders whose "expression of his opinion on such engine troubles was warming if not comforting to his pilots." Five days after our arrival at Flez, however (as a start to what was to become over the next eight months such a magnificent score), Beauchamp-Proctor shot down a German two-seater.

Shortly after that, another South African pilot, Second Lieutenant Hugh Saunders, joined my squadron. He was straight out of a training school, and he was later to become very well known in the Royal Air Force as "Dingbat" Saunders. A large, burly man and as steady as a rock when things were going badly, he has changed over the years less than almost anyone I know. He is now a retired air chief marshal. These two South Africans, Beauchamp-Proctor and Dingbat Saunders, were to become the backbone of my squadron during the spring and the summer of 1918. They were entirely different in almost every way: Saunders the very solid and imperturbable type; and Beauchamp-Proctor the mercurial and highly strung little eager beaver. But they got along very well together, and they were excellent foils for each other.

Being at Flez put us directly under Lieutenant-Colonel F. V. Holt, who was in command of the 22nd (Army) Wing, and whose headquarters was also at Flez. A red-faced and at times somewhat choleric individual, but for all that an excellent wing commander, Holt had been the first commanding officer of Peter Portal's squadron, No. 16, on its formation in February, 1915. Holt had done his full share of fighting in the air, even having been credited, earlier in the war, with shooting down an enemy aircraft with a rifle.

Tony Holt had good and original ideas on tactics which he did not hesitate to try out with the squadrons under his command. There were occasions when I found myself mixed up in some pretty violent disagreements with him, but I nevertheless respected him for his ability as a leader and, for all his irascibility, as a man whom one had to admire. Our work for the next three months was to fly in support of the operations of the Fifth Army, which was under the command of General Sir Hubert Gough. We were slap in the middle of the area of the Somme held by them, and right behind the front lines of the St-Quentin sector, and I still flinch a little when I think of that.

It became known to us during February that the Germans were being strongly reinforced, and there were plenty of indications that they were preparing for an offensive that would probably be launched on the Front of the Fifth Army, and so against us. We were quite well briefed about what was likely to happen, and we received very detailed instructions from brigade headquarters about what our action in the air was to be in the event of a German offensive. "The S.E.5's will patrol the area of operations for the purpose of attacking hostile formations," those instructions stated.

From all the reports that were passed on to him by the squadrons under his command, Tony Holt could not help taking note of the large number of new airfields that had been brought into use by the Germans immediately opposite us. He then organized some combined bombing attacks on some of these airfields. On the 9th and on the 17th of March some of the squadrons went in low down and did their bombing, while the S.E.5 squadrons, including my own, sat stepped-up above them acting as a protective cover. I took part in the first of these two raids, leading the top flight of the fighters. Our targets were the enemy airfields at Busigny, Bertry and Escaufourt.

Our intrepid wing commander flew well above all of us, keeping an eagle eye on the way we were doing our jobs. While Nos. 48 and 54 Squadrons—who were equipped with Bristol Fighters and Camels, and who shared with us the airfield at Flez—did their bombing of Busigny and Escaufourt, "84 sat in the heavens and kept ward," the squadron record states, in a somewhat lyrical description of the way in which we provided the others with air cover. They had been practicing for just such an attack, and I watched them as they scored direct hits on the hangars and the other buildings, all the time keeping a weather eye out for any enemy fighters that might come on the scene. But none appeared, and all our aircraft got away unharmed. I led my squadron back to Flez without even having fired my guns.

On the second of these two raids it was a very different story. During the raid and the patrols in the afternoon of the same day, No. 84 Squadron was particularly successful. We ran into Germans, there was a lot of fighting, and we shot down ten of their aircraft, bringing the score for the squadron during the six months that we had been at the Front to a total of ninety-seven. That evening we received from Jack Salmond (who had taken Trenchard's place as the General Officer Commanding the R.F.C. in France when Trenchard had returned to London to help form the Royal Air Force) a signal which read: "Best congratulations on brilliant success to-day." At the same time I made an entry in the squadron records that the enemy were getting wise to the fact that we were increasing the size of our fighting patrols.

The buildup by the Germans for the offensive against us in March, 1918, was of proportions that were well-nigh fantastic. From the air we could see, for all the efforts that they made to hide what they were doing, that it was going to be a very big affair. Their object, in Ludendorff's words, was to smash through our front "before the Americans can throw strong forces into the scale."

Despite all the warnings that this offensive by the enemy was imminent, and that it would take place on our Front, when it did come it was launched with an unheralded crash of astonishing ferocity. Spoken of in official military history as "The German Offensive in Picardy," it has become better known to us as "The March Retreat." On the nineteenth, after a long spell of dry weather, there was rain, and after that a heavy mist settled everywhere. By the night of the twentieth the mist had thickened, and it had become just plain fog. All sight and sound were muffled by it, and the enemy, after some artillery fire, had become quiet. "The unusual silence was oppressive," H. A. Jones wrote of conditions that night, "and, with the fog, combined to produce an atmosphere of the macabre." It had been a dull day as far as flying was concerned, with very little for any of us to do, so, feeling rather bored, I had gone to bed early in my small hut on the edge of the airfield.

Shortly after half past four in the morning of March 21, I was suddenly awakened by the shattering noise of a colossal and extremely noisy bombardment, with tremendous reverberations of sound. It was the beginning of the most intensive bombardment by artillery staged so far in the war. I leaped out of bed and hurriedly dressed, but as soon as I got outside I saw that the airfield was shrouded in thick fog. The Germans had launched their attack, and our position in the St-Quentin sector placed us right in the middle of it.

Although we did not know it at the time, we were pretty heavily outnumbered by the German Air Force on this part of the Front. We had a total of 579 aircraft, of which 261 were single-seater fighters. The Germans had managed to keep hidden from us the full extent of the buildup of their Air Force. When the battle started they had available 730 aircraft, of which 326 were single-seater fighters. But what with the fog, and the conditions that were to develop, we were not greatly concerned with their numerical superiority in the air. It very quickly became clear to us that our job was going to be working in closest possible support of the troops on the ground.

No flying was possible that morning, and the German assault made rapid advance, so rapid, in fact, that by the afternoon, when the fog had lifted and it was possible to fly, we were given orders to harass the advancing hordes with low-flying attacks. This was a far cry from the offensive patrols against enemy fighters—the "hostile formations"—that had been detailed in our earlier instructions; but already, by the end of the first day, it was realized that there were clear indications of a possible disaster. The Germans, by sheer brute force employed with a shrewd cunning and an even shrewder appreciation of tactics, appeared to be headed for an overwhelming success.

"The R.F.C. was displaying magnificent courage and self-sacrifice," Cyril Falls has recorded with a warm generosity. "It had been told to take 'all risks,' to fly 'very low,' and to 'bomb and shoot everything they can see on the enemy's side of the line.' It did all these things."

This was the introduction of the pattern that our operations were to follow for the next two weeks. We did what we were told, even if it was a job that we had rather disliked in the past. All our thought and training had gone into how to chase and destroy German fighters in the air, usually at fairly high altitudes. Now we were having to carry out, as we had in the Ypres Salient, very low-flying attacks with bombs and machine guns on the enemy troops on the ground.

The onslaught from the German Army was both massive and new in concept. It was little wonder that I was nearly flung out of bed by the noise in the early hours of the morning of March 21 because their surprise artillery bombardment was made without any prior registration, and it came from a massing of a huge number of guns. The Germans also made free use of gas, and our troops had to wear their gas masks through most of the first day, and what with that and the fog, they were very severely handicapped in trying to cope with the infiltrations of the enemy.

New tactics had been worked out for the German infantry. The leading troops were to feel out and penetrate the weak points in our defense, with their reserves quickly backing up wherever the infiltrating troops had been able to make progress. Through sound reconnaissance there was a quick dissemination of reports on the progress being made, and the leading troops, the storm troops, worked ahead of the lines of attacking infantry. Equipped with automatic rifles and machine guns and light mortars, they penetrated wherever they cound find openings, leaving it to the larger masses of the infantry to follow up and deal with the rest of our defense. No effort was made to keep a uniform line in the attack, and the speed of the advance was that of the fastest and not the slowest.

Of the position on the Fifth Army Front the official military historian has said: "Never before had the British line been held with so few men and so few guns to the mile; and the reserves were wholly insufficient." We in the Fifth Army had to cover a length of forty-two miles of the front line, and for that purpose we had twelve divisions and three cavalry divisions. The Germans opposed us with forty-three divisions. Our Staff thinking and planning, after so long spent brooding over trench warfare, had been much too static to be able to cope all of a sudden with the German attack, and we were suddenly called upon to improvise in every way.

From the moment on that first day that the fog cleared enough for flying to be possible with observation of the launching of the German attack, activity in the air was intense. Large numbers of German aircraft were at work on contact-patrols and in support of their advancing troops. They had fighters flying higher up, but we were far too busy attacking ground targets to be able to worry about them. In the histories of the German Army published after the war it is revealed that their infantry was greatly harassed by the weight of the attacks that we delivered. Their historians even went so far as to criticize their own Air Force for not being there to ward off our efforts to stop the advance on the ground.

Despite all the resistance that we offered on the ground and in the air, the Germans made rapid progress; and right opposite us, at St-Quentin, there was a quick breakthrough. The last of the Fifth Army's scanty reserves were absorbed, and since counterattacks were out of the question there had to be given a general order to retire. My squadron, along with the others on this front, was busily at work during the afternoon making low-flying attacks with our machine guns and twenty-five-pound bombs, all of which, the Germans later admitted, were very effective. One of their historians speaks with respect of "the way in which these airmen came down to twenty metres in order to throw their bombs."

All the same, these attacks were not effective enough to halt the onrush of the enemy. But we persisted with them, and during the afternoon twelve aircraft of my squadron dropped forty-five bombs on a concentration of the enemy which had reached the village of Holnon, to the west of St-Quentin and an uncomfortably short distance from Flez.

Later in the afternoon I was told to move my squadron quickly out of Flez and back to an airfield at Champien, which was just to the east of Roye and about fifteen miles away. I gave instructions for our equipment and stores to be loaded onto our motor transport, and I sent all the aircraft off immediately after they had finished their last patrols so that they should be safely out of the way. I kept only my own S.E.5 standing by. Earlier I had sent some of my motorcyclists off down each of the roads that converged on Flez from the east, giving them instructions to return every hour or so and report to me the position of our front line and how far the enemy had advanced. The situation was becoming very confused, and I had no wish to be caught in the onrush of the German Army.

One of these cyclists of mine, a mechanic named A. M. Knight, was attacked by a low-flying Albatros. Knight dived into a ditch, and as the German fighter passed overhead at a height of about a hundred feet he fired back at it with his rifle. To his astonishment the engine of the Albatros stopped, and the pilot made a forced landing nearby. Knight came rushing back to me with the news that he had shot down a Hun, and although I felt highly skeptical about his claim, I sent off a party in a Crossley tender to investigate. Sure enough they found the Albatros just where Knight had said it was. Although there was no sign of the pilot, there was one hole in the aircraft, slap in the engine. They set fire to the machine, and Knight was given the credit for what, in the words of the squadron records, was "believed to be the first instance of an R.F.C. cyclist bringing down a Hun, a good but amusing show." It sounds like a tall story, one might say, but it was quite true.

By dusk the last of our motor transport was leaving the airfield, and I was just about to hurry off to my airplane when the telephone rang. Tony Holt had managed to get through, and he was speaking from his new headquarters some miles back. The instructions to evacuate Flez had come from him in the first place, and now he wanted to know how things were going. My motorcyclists were all back with the most disquieting reports, and I knew that I had no time to spare. Everybody else had left, and I told Holt that I was just about to leave myself. He insisted on knowing if all the motor vehicles had got safely away, and I told him that I could see the last of them driving off.

But there was no satisfying my eager wing commander, and he went on giving me instructions that I was to stay at Flez until I was absolutely sure that everybody had left. Since I knew that they were all on their way and that the Germans were not far off, I was in no mood for any argument. It was also rapidly getting dark, and

I told Holt that I was not wasting any more time. Our argument became heated, and eventually I had to slam down the phone and rush out of the hut and into my airplane. I took off in a great hurry, and a few minutes later I landed at the airfield at Champien. It was by then almost dark, and it was a good thing that I had made my getaway when I did. Four hours later the airfield at Flez was engulfed in the German advance, with the enemy infantry swarming all over it. I heard nothing more from Holt about the near insubordination of which he had accused me on the phone.

During the second night it was realized that such was the vigor of the German attack that the enemy were massing in even greater strength, and our own weakness became still more apparent. The next day was spent by us trying to help the Army in their retreat, and we were in the air as soon as the fog cleared and hard at it with more of our low-flying attacks. But the Germans continued to make a formidable advance. Early in the afternoon twelve of us from No. 84 Squadron found, just south of the airfield at Flez that we had evacuated, and right in the valley of the Somme, columns of advancing German troops. We promptly dived on them. There were enemy troops everywhere, and we went about shooting them up until we were all out of ammunition. Only an hour or two later the squadron went off again. We immediately found a great many more targets than we could ever cope with, and again we waded into the attack until we were completely out of ammunition and bombs.

The Germans were advancing literally in hordes, and since they were not taking any particular precautions against attack from the air, we found that our low flying against them was not as dangerous as we had anticipated. My pilots almost wept with joy as they fell upon these massive targets, and it gave them a terrific boost to be able to feel that they were doing something solid to help stem the enemy advance. I have always felt that the work done by low-flying fighters of the Royal Flying Corps during the March Retreat of 1918 has not received the full credit that it deserved. Those attacks produced a very real effect in helping to delay and eventually to stop the enemy advance; and there is enough authority for this belief in the numerous enemy documents which tell of the death and destruction that we inflicted on the German troops during that critical time.

Our stay at the airfield near Roye was only a short one, but it was enlivened by the splendid spirit of my pilots in tackling their work. If ever any men went about "pressing on regardless," as the expression went in the Second World War, my pilots did just that, even to the extent of unintentionally disregarding the safety of their commanding officer, as I discovered shortly after our arrival at Champien. I was standing by the hangars one afternoon when I saw a German aircraft diving straight toward me. He seemed to be firing his guns at me, so I very quickly ducked out of the way. When I looked up again I saw that an S.E.5 of my own squadron was right on the tail of the German; it was his bullets and not those of the enemy that were whistling around my ears.

Still blazing away at the German two-seater, that pilot of mine, Lancelot Duke by name and a Canadian by birth, followed it right down and sent it crashing in a field at the back of the hangars. We rushed over and made prisoners of the pilot and the observer. In that curious custom of the German Air Force, the former was an N.C.O. and the latter an officer, and when I made the observer give me the binoculars which he had slung around his neck, he protested that it was all against the rules of war. It might have been, although I could not see that a prisoner-of-war would ever be allowed to keep his binoculars. I made him give them to me, and I kept them for my own personal use for the rest of the war.

Three days after the Germans launched their attack, it was found that they stood a good chance of driving a wedge between the Fifth Army and the Third Army to the north of us. The area of the Somme was again alight. That day the Commander-in-Chief, Douglas Haig, issued a special order in which we were all told that we had again reached a state of crisis in the war, and that the enemy were "aiming at the destruction of the British Army."

By then I was unavoidably out of touch for quite long periods with even our wing headquarters. Telephone communications had broken down completely. Tony Holt did his best to visit us every other day or so, but it was impossible for him to give us regular and detailed orders about our work. I was left to use my own judgment about what should be done, and I sent off patrols as I saw fit, working on such scanty information as came my way.

There was plenty of work to do, and it was not difficult for me to get on with it even if it did mean that I was filling the role of the wing commander as well as that of the squadron commander. We simply put our backs into making a maximum effort to stop the Hun. Since office work was at a discount, Tony Holt having very sensibly told me not to bother trying to make any official returns, I was left to get on with supervising our flying. We kept our squadron record book going, but apart from that, all the usual returns, combat reports, and other accounts were allowed to lapse. Later I was to learn that the same applied to all the squadrons in the hard-pressed 22nd Wing, and that is why the records of the achievements by the squadrons in the wing at that time are so incomplete. It could also be one of the reasons why full credit has never been given to the effectiveness of our operations.

On the third day of the German attack—which was also launched, although with less spectacular success, to the north of us—there was some return to air-to-air fighting at higher altitudes, even though much of it took place at under five thousand feet. In No. 84 Squadron we still had our noses down on ground attacks; but in what Harold Balfour described as "a boom of prosperity" my former squadron, No. 43, saw some extraordinary action. They had been re-equipped with Camels some months before, and they were working from the airfield at La Gorgue, on the River Lys. The flight commanders in the squadron were Harold Balfour, J. L. Trollope, and H. W. Woollett. Although Balfour admits that they knew the German "crack scouts had been moved south," Trollope nevertheless put up a fine record that day by being the first to shoot down six enemy aircraft in one day. Only three weeks later, Woollett, whom I knew quite well, equaled that record, shooting down six Germans in one day over the area around Estaires.

The worst reverses that the British suffered, and the greatest advances made by the Germans, were on our part of the Front, and by March 25 the line in front of us was developing an ominous bulge. Shortly after that, I was given instructions to move my squadron still farther back, and for a short time we operated from an airfield near Abbeville, not far from the coast. All along the Front, as far as we could make out, the whole line seemed to be crumbling; but it appeared that the main thrust from the enemy was now to be against the Third Army, just to the north of us.

Urgent orders were sent to the squadrons of the R.F.C., and those flying over the Somme were told to "bomb and shoot up everything . . . on the enemy side . . . very low flying is essential . . . all risks to be taken. . . ." That led to our working more to the north, and by the early morning of March 26 we were flying up and down the straight road that runs between Albert and Bapaume, making continuous attacks against the German troops who were swarming along it.

Our old adversary Richthofen had also appeared again, and he and his Circus had gone into action over that road and that area a few days before we arrived on the scene. On March 24, Richthofen claimed the destruction of an S.E.5 of No. 56 Squadron; on the 25th, a Camel; on the 26th, another Camel and an R.E.8; on the

27th, a Camel and two Bristol Fighters; and on the 28th, an Armstrong-Whitworth. That was an impressive rate of scoring, and it is little wonder that Richthofen called the Somme his happy hunting ground.

After all the early confusion caused by the unexpectedly massive aggression on the part of the Germans, it began to look as if they might be making a dead set at the important railway center of Amiens. On March 26, five days after the start of their attack, there was held at Doullens, just behind our Front, a conference of the Allied leaders; it was agreed that the situation generally was a grave one, and that every effort should be made to save Amiens. It was then decided that the French General Foch should be put in charge of the coordination of all the Allied armies on the Western Front.

As one who was a close participant in all that happened on the Front to the east and to the south of Amiens, I have always thought that our Fifth Army, handicapped as it was, did very well. From the outset it was hopelessly weak in numbers for the task that it was called upon to perform. By March 27, six days after the start of the German onslaught, the position appeared to be well-nigh hopeless. But still our men held on, and the official air historian has recorded: "In view of what the Fifth Army had suffered from the day the German offensive opened, the conduct of the troops on the 27th, grey with utter weariness, was magnificent." With that I agree in every way. Despite all the violent battering that our men had been taking, they did manage to maintain some sort of cohesion, and they did delay and eventually stop the enemy advance. The very next day, as we were to learn later, the German commanders themselves were in a state of consternation over the way in which they had been brought to a halt.

A week after the German attack started, we were still hard at our low-flying attacks, disregarding the upper air in order to give our Army on the ground the maximum support. R.F.C. losses were high, mainly because of our refusal to be deterred by the fire from the ground that was withering at times. Nearly all our losses were due to that. Then we heard the astonishing news that our Army commander, General Sir Hubert Gough, had been relieved of his command. This decision was to spark a controversy that became one of the most heated of the First World War, and one which grossly overshadowed the splendid achievements of the Fifth Army.

We who were on the spot and a part of Gough's Fifth Army

were puzzled and angry. From the outset we all felt that Gough was being made a scapegoat. I had come to know him slightly because he had visited my squadron a few times, and what we in the R.F.C. appreciated about him—apart from the fact that he was the youngest general in the British Army—was that he seemed to know and care more about the activities of the Flying Corps than most of the senior generals we had run across.

A very experienced commander, Hubert Gough had participated in all the battles of any importance on the Western Front: Mons, the Marne, Loos, the Somme, Arras and Third Ypres. In his book *The Fifth Army,* published in 1931, I am proud that my squadron is listed among those of the R.F.C. in the Order of Battle for March 21, 1918.

The row that blew up over Hubert Gough's dismissal contains in it yet another glaring example of the way in which intrigue in high places during the years between 1914 and 1918 came to have such grossly unfair results. Even now, after so many years have passed and so much has been said about this affair, it is more what has not been said that is most revealing. There are excuses and explanations, but in all the material that has been published it is the blank spaces that have come, with the passing of time, to give some indication of what should have been said.

How close the Allies came to defeat in March, 1918, as a result of the German onslaught was known at the time by some, but it was not until long afterward that there was a general understanding of the disaster that so nearly overwhelmed us. When I look back on it now and recall what it was like to be right in the thick of it, I know that I was not particularly scared. I was anxious, as we all were, and we would have been stupid if we had felt otherwise. But we had on our side the resilience of our youth, and it enabled us to face that very serious setback with a determination that was at least buoyant.

It is clear now that the same could not be said of some of our leaders. Of the Prime Minister, Lloyd George, for instance, who was on a visit to France at that time, right on our part of the Front (even if well behind it), Douglas Haig wrote: "The P.M. looked as if he had been thoroughly frightened, and he seemed still in a funk. And he appears to me to be a thorough impostor." There are opinions that contradict that, but what is of interest is the astonishing difference between that statement and the feelings of the commanders-in-chief toward Winston Churchill in the Second World War. I was a C.-in-C. myself in the second war. For all that has been said about Churchill, and indignant though some of us became at times over the way he drove us, there was not one of us who could ever have accused Winston Churchill of being "in a funk."

By the spring of 1918 I had had a great deal of experience fighting in the air, and I had thought enough about it to have formed what I considered some pretty sound opinions. I had come to believe that, of all the different ways in which the R.F.C. operated, the work of the fighters was the most interesting, the most exciting, and—even if it does sound odd to put it this way—the most amusing. It was interesting, I believed, because it was all so new. There was a novelty about it, with no hard and fast rules such as there were, for instance, in infantry tactics, which had been built up as a result of centuries of experience. It was exciting for reasons that are obvious; and it was amusing because we were young and had a youthful sense of humor.

We were in a very new branch of the forces, but we were at this time still in the Army. While it was recognized that everybody was entitled, within certain limits, to express his opinions, there were nevertheless certain restrictions. But most of us in the Flying Corps voiced our opinions pretty freely—as has been done in the Air Force ever since—and we argued about them, and we even quarreled. At that time, with our tactics in such a very early stage of development, it was impossible to be dogmatic and to lay down any rigid rules for fighting in the air.

During the first war the pilots who were successful fighters employed methods that differed slightly from one another's; but running through all those methods was a tenuous thread of principles that we were just beginning to understand. The application of those principles of air fighting might be different in nearly every case, but it was those differences that provided us with the grounds for debate. And, as with everybody else, we in the air service found that anything that was debatable was also unquestionably of interest.

Another reason why air fighting had become of such interest was because success in it depended, far more than in any other forms of fighting, on individual skill, nerve and courage. In fighting on the land or at sea it was largely a fluke, dictated by pure chance, whether one came through with a whole skin or fell by the wayside. One sat in a hole in the ground on land, or behind a sheet of armor plating at sea, and it was purely a matter of chance whether a bullet or a shell hit you or the man standing next to you. But that was far from being the case in fighting in the air. If you

were alert and watchful and able to think a split second faster than
the man against whom you were fighting, and if you could shoot a
shade straighter and with an ounce or two more nerve, then ninety-
nine times out of a hundred you were able to beat your opponent.
It was up to the individual—chance played only a comparatively
small part in the encounter.

It was my experience by then that in fighting in the air I was
often comforted by the thought that success depended almost
entirely on my own skill, and that I was on my own in the way that
I used it. In common with most people, I did not particularly mind
being beaten by a better man in a fair fight; but I did object
strongly to the imposition of any flukes. And since I also objected
strongly to being killed through pure chance, as so many were on
the ground, I found that conditions in the air were a great deal
more congenial. I felt that if I were killed in the air it would be
very largely because of my own stupidity or lack of skill.

Being so young at the time, I also found, as many others did,
that there was a curiously amusing side to fighting in the air. It was
challenging: rather like a very dangerous game of rugger. I do not
mean to say that I was never frightened. I do not know anybody
who has ever flown under conditions of active service who will
claim that he has not known fear. I certainly knew it, and quite
often. But it did not occur so much during an actual fight. It was
in the minute or so before a fight that I knew the feeling of fear,
during the time when the enemy airplanes developed from small
black specks in the distance into something that one could recognize, and then came closer and closer, and I knew that in a
moment or so I would be in the middle of them. Then I knew, in
my fear, the temptation to cut and run.

Once I was in the middle of a fight and had to fly with all the
skill that I could summon up, I knew a certain sense of elation,
almost of inspiration; and as I twisted and turned and dived and
zoomed and fired and was shot at, I sometimes found myself
shouting absurd battle cries and even singing at the top of my
voice. Earlier in the war, when I was flying in two-seaters, I had
for a while as my observer a large Canadian, and he would roar
out the rudest of epithets as he plastered the Huns with his Lewis
gun. It all helped to relieve the tension, and it was done in a
fashion that was quite involuntary. There is no way we can ever
know again the innocence of such experiences—it was not even
known in quite the same way in the second war—because the
fighters now fly at such fantastic speeds and have to be operated
with such deadly and cold-blooded precision. We who were fighter

pilots during the years between 1914 and 1918 knew an emotional experience that was unique, and we lived it to the full. It was the highlight of the most colorful period that flying has ever known.

It would be presumptuous of me if I were to try and overstress any skill that I may have had as a young fighter pilot; but I can rightly say that I had my moments. My one big failing was that, although I was a good enough pilot, I was not, for some unaccountable reason, a good shot, and good shooting, as I have already stressed, was essential for any outstanding success in putting up a score. On the other hand, it would have taken a very smart Hun to get his sights on me. Even Hermann Goering, good as he was, could not bring that off on the occasions when we did set about each other in the air.

As it turned out, my contribution to the role of the fighters in the first war was in finding out through firsthand experience how they should be used, and in developing tactics. But there were always the odd occasions when even our carefully thought out tactics had to go by the board. One of those occasions came during those hectic days of the March Retreat when I found myself in the thick of a free-for-all of an old-fashioned dogfight. We were on a low-flying patrol, intent on strafing the advancing German infantry, when we ran into a bunch of German fighters, Pfalzes, at an altitude that was too low for the use of any of the tactics that we had evolved. After a few moments of pretty hectic whirling around I managed to get on the tail of one of them—they were biplanes similar in appearance to the Albatros—and I gave him a couple of good bursts of fire, and he went down and crashed just the other side of the German lines. It was seemingly all over before I even had a chance to think.

As one of the pioneers, if I may so call myself, in fighter tactics, I was only too eager to learn as much as I could in the school of firsthand experience, and learn we did in that spring of 1918. A year before, we had taken such a beating in the air that all we could think about then was saving our necks; but by the spring of 1918 our S.E.5's had put us on top, and we were then able to consider more carefully how we could exploit to the utmost that superiority.

At the height of the German offensive in March, 1918, the commander-in-chief of the British Expeditionary Force recorded in his diary: "Our Flying Corps did wonders yesterday. They crashed sixteen enemy machines and we only lost one. They too had marvellous targets; masses of infantry on roads, horses, guns,

etc. Into these they fired with machine-guns, and spread consternation and disorder."

It was a handsome tribute that Douglas Haig paid us, and it was
a splendid experience for me, as a young squadron commander, to
see the way in which my pilots and mechanics, inspired by the
occasion, worked themselves to a standstill. Those targets which
Haig described as marvelous were wide open to attack, even if the
word that he used so glowingly was not exactly appropriate. There
is nothing marvelous about slaughter. For the first time we were
presented with near-perfect ground targets: troops marching in
fours along the roads, and batteries of guns and ammunition
wagons all moving in the open.

We could see very plainly what we were attacking. What is
more, we could see the exact effect of our machine-gun fire and the
bombs that we dropped, all from such low heights. The troops
would scatter into the fields leaving the killed and wounded lying
prostrate in the roads; and wagons would be overturned and horses
thrown into confusion. One of my pilots even managed, to his
immense delight, to see his attack cause an enemy general's car to
run into a ditch and turn over. Hard and difficult as the great
retreat was for our Army, as far as we in the Flying Corps were
concerned it turned out to be something of a picnic, and during the
whole of that strenuous fortnight, I had in my squadron, to my
great relief, only one casualty.

The method of attack that we evolved against these ground
targets was first of all to fly over the enemy, always in formation,
at a height of between eight and ten thousand feet. At that height
we presented to the enemy guns fast-moving targets that were
difficult to hit, and we were too high for their machine guns to be
effective. On the other hand, we could scan wide stretches of
country in search of suitable ground targets. Having slected his
target, the leader would dive at it, but not too steeply—flying down
to it from a distance with engine full on. When we were within
range, we opened up with our machine guns; and at about two
hundred feet away from the target, we dropped our bombs.

Immediately after our attacks, we zoomed up as hard as we
could go, usually turning at the same time. In the dive we would be
doing between 150 and 180 miles an hour, and in the zoom that
followed we rocketed up to about a thousand feet. We would go on
repeating that performance until we were out of bombs and
ammunition; and so much practice did we have against those live
targets that we were able to plant our bombs with an accuracy that
surprised us—being fighter pilots and not bombers.

After two weeks of hectic activity and mass movement over the large area to the east and the south of Amiens, the Germans were finally so extended in their advance that they had to come to a halt. By then, any examination of a map which purported to show the positions of the front lines led one to the feeling that they were so smashed and scattered that the map looked as if it had become covered with pieces of broken spaghetti. But for all the retreating that we had been compelled to do, the Germans had by no means had it all their own way. "It may be predicted that when all the facts have been made known and studied, and the last word has been said, the retreat of the Fifth Army will be the subject of a glowing page in military histories," H. A. Jones wrote seventeen years later.

One must be careful, I know, not to indulge in too much of the British inclination to speak of defeats as strategic withdrawals and of routs as glorious episodes of momentary setbacks. We heard quite a lot about all that sort of thing in the Second World War. But that retreat of March, 1918, was nevertheless a memorable experience for those of us who participated in it. It is the fashion with many of our younger writers of today to decry so much of what we, the British, have achieved in the face of adversity—a fashion, I should add, that I find deplorable. These writers, being in many cases very young men, have not had to face adversity, and they have not known what it is to have to fight for their lives and their country with their backs to the wall. Such an experience over a period of time can go a long way, as many older men know, toward strengthening the backbone.

By tiring the enemy as they did over the wide stretches of the Somme, the Fifth Army greatly reduced the verve of the attack that the Germans had launched to the north in their offensive in the direction of Arras, and in the battles in the basin of the River Lys and in Flanders. As soon as the Germans found themselves brought to a halt, still without having captured Amiens or broken through at Arras, and still contained in the bulge in the line farther south (which had been threatening to break in the direction of Paris), they tried to strengthen this attack to the north. It was a massive attempt, and at first they gained ground; but their plan of breaking through to the coast failed, for after about three weeks of very heavy battering our line still held. During those weeks the casualties to both sides, the Germans on the one and the Allies on the other, were about the same: very nearly three hundred and fifty thousand each. It was for us an extremely anxious time; but for the Germans it was the beginning of the end.

12 / The New Service

BY THE SPRING of 1918 the sheer weight and intensity of the personal experiences of the past three and a half years had made us feel, without even thinking about it, that the war had been going on for an inordinately long time. To that there was added the knowledge that it had also been raging in the grimmest fashion to the south of us—particularly around Verdun—and on the Eastern Front in Poland and Russia, on the fronts in Italy and the Balkans, and in the Middle East and at sea. But so preoccupied were we with our own affairs and the actual day-to-day waging of the war that we scarcely had any thoughts about the future. Perhaps that was why the rush of the events of the last six or seven months seemed to bring the war to an end so much more quickly than any of us expected.

There was still plenty of hard fighting ahead, and in my own case I was in the thick of it right up until the day before it actually ended. All my thoughts were directed solely to running my squadron. It was not until much later that I came to realize that the last six months of the war saw three outstanding developments in the air. The first was the formation of the Royal Air Force; the second was the infusion of new blood that we received from overseas, particularly from the United States; and the third was the grim reminder to the air services as well as to those fighting on the ground and at sea that the heroes also die.

It has been said that by the spring of 1918 air power had come of age. It was a forced maturity—forced by urgent necessity—but it was unquestionably true that the air had changed the whole nature of the waging of war in so many ways. No matter how reluctant they might be, the Army and the Royal Navy were compelled by circumstance to acknowledge the full development of the third dimension. But in that acknowledgment there was born an unfortunate and unhealthy competition in the protection of what the older services regarded as their own interests; and this

218

unnecessary rivalry, which developed with an unwholesome intensity, led in turn to muddle and waste. An answer to that had to be found. For once the politicians did manage to steer the right course: they planned in such a way that out of the confusion finally emerged a sound and constructive proposal.

On April 1, 1918, the Royal Air Force came into being. Although this event (which we airmen consider somewhat noteworthy) was achieved only after a great deal of argument among the politicians and the generals and the admirals, the impression that it made upon those of us in the middle of the bloodier battle at the Front did not amount to very much. We were far too busy with our flying to pay much attention to it, and it was not until some weeks later—when our friends in the Royal Naval Air Service changed their ranks, and some of the boys appeared in the new, and rather startling, uniforms—that we really appreciated that the R.F.C. and the R.N.A.S. had been amalgamated, and that we were now in a Service of our own, quite apart from the Army and the Royal Navy. It was the first time that any country had formed an entirely separate and independent air force.

At first even Boom Trenchard himself was against the formation of this separate Service; and as late as August 28, 1917, Douglas Haig was writing in his diary: "The War Cabinet has evidently decided on creating a new Department to deal with Air operations, on the lines of the War Office and the Admiralty. Trenchard is much perturbed as to the result of this new departure just at a time when the Flying Corps was beginning to feel that it had become an important part of the Army. The best solution would be to have one Minister of Defence with the three Officers under him, viz., Admiralty, War Office, Air."

In saying that, Douglas Haig was expressing a sound and prophetic thought. Nearly four months later, on December 17, 1917, he wrote in his diary a comment about a visit that Trenchard made to his headquarters (Trenchard had by then been selected as the first Chief of the Air Staff). Of the Air Ministry that was in process of being formed, Haig recorded that "T. stated that the Air Board are quite off their heads as to the future possibilities of Aeronautics for ending the war. I told T. that it was evidently necessary that he should become C. of S. of Air, much as I regretted parting with him."

Ten days after that Trenchard addressed a letter to all ranks of the Royal Flying Corps, and in it he told us that he had been "appointed Chief of the Air Staff in England," which, he stated, would "undoubtedly interfere with my close personal touch with the Flying Corps in France." For three years Trenchard had been in very close touch with us; this was what led him to say: "The morale, which is a most important factor, has always been of the highest, and I would like to let everyone know that it is a great blow to me to sever my close personal connection with the splendid fighting force that I have had the honour to command."

If ever the high morale of the R.F.C. originated in any one man, it was surely in Trenchard himself; but we were also singularly fortunate in having as our new leader in France a man who was all that we could ask for. His name was John Salmond, and at the time that he took over from Trenchard, he was already an experienced major-general, even though he was still only in his middle thirties. One of the earliest of the Army officers to transfer to the R.F.C.—he had been in the Royal Lancaster Regiment—Salmond was in command of No. 3 Squadron when the R.F.C. first went to France. He had progressed rapidly up the ladder in appointments in France as a wing commander and a brigade commander and on the staff in London.

The Royal Air Force has always felt for Jack Salmond the warmest admiration. The most sympathetic and human of all the senior officers I have ever known, he was always ready to listen to what we had to say, and we knew that there was no need for any hesitation in talking to him quite frankly about our problems. His career in the Air Force was a particularly distinguished one in every way, and today Sir John Salmond is the senior Marshal of the Royal Air Force, having been promoted to that rank over thirty years ago.

The path that Boom Trenchard was to tread, following his appointment as our first Chief of the Air Staff, was a tortuous one, and it was to end in an extraordinary reversal of all his plans. The Air Council had been formed at the beginning of the year of 1918, with Lord Rothermere—the newspaper proprietor and brother of Lord Northcliffe—as Secretary of State. How much that appealed to Trenchard is revealed by Haig in his comment in his diary entry of January 26, when he wrote: "General Trenchard came to dinner. He could think and talk nothing else but the rascally ways of the politicians and newspaper men."

The dissatisfaction felt by Trenchard was more than just an objection to the way in which the affairs of the Air Force were being handled. As Chief of the Air Staff he was directly responsible to the Secretary of State for Air—who was both a politician and a newspaperman—and it was small wonder that he and Lord Rothermere were soon quarreling. Trenchard was inarticulate and, at times, bumbling in his ways; but he was a fearsome man in an argument. Because of the high esteem in which he was held in the Service he also carried a great deal of weight with the other members of that first Air Council. It was natural enough that he, the expert, should believe that he knew more about the air than the civilian to whom he was responsible, and such was the clash between Rothermere and Trenchard that a showdown was inevitable.

On March 19, 1918, just before the official birth of the RA.F., Trenchard handed in his resignation. There had developed by then the full unwholesome fury of the quarrel between the politicians on the one hand and the military on the other; in this wretched atmosphere Trenchard found his resignation accepted. On April 15, only two weeks after the R.A.F. had come into existence, Trenchard's place was taken by Major-General F. H. Sykes, a pioneer aviator and, as far as the politicians were concerned, a more amenable character.

The politicians were scoring heavily, for by this time all three Service chiefs had been replaced: Jellicoe at the Admiralty, Robertson at the War Office, and now Trenchard at the newly formed Air Ministry. The astonishing nature of the views held by these politicians is all too clearly revealed in a letter written by Rothermere to Bonar Law at the time of his own resignation (which came only shortly after Trenchard's). "In getting rid of Trenchard I flatter myself I did a great thing for the Air Force," Rothermere wrote. "With his dull unimaginative mind and his attitude of *Je sais tout* he would within twelve months have brought death and damnation to the Air Force."

The "death and damnation" that Trenchard did, in fact, bring to the Service was of a nature that we in the Air Force seemed, perversely enough, to thrive upon; in the annals of the R.A.F. it is the name of Trenchard that lives. Officially, the whole affair has been dismissed in our history with the cautious statement: "There appeared grave differences of view between the Chief of the Air Staff and the Secretary of State . . . it is clear, also, that there were differences of temperament." But the actual record of the facts gives a much more vigorous account of the birth of the Royal Air Force, difficult though it may have been. Rothermere felt that he had occasion to flatter himself for what he had done to Trenchard; but the truth is that Rothermere is forgotten. It is the name of Trenchard that has survived and is particularly bright in the memories of those of us who served under him on the Western Front and who later grew up with him in the Royal Air Force.

On the lighter side of the formation of the Royal Air Force was the appearance in the spring of 1918 of our new uniforms. One of the most incongruous sights that any fighting service could ever have presented was the way in which we dressed in the Royal Flying Corps. It was all done quite correctly, but the uniforms represented those of different countries as well as the different branches and regiments of the Army from which we came, to say nothing of the Royal Navy. It was a common sight to see the pilots in a squadron wearing an astonishing variety of uniforms, all the way from the rather smart double-breasted wrap-over jacket of the R.F.C.—which was known to us as "the maternity jacket"—to the tartan trews and short jackets of the Scottish regiments, with caps ranging from the fore-and-aft of the Flying Corps to glengarries and even the boy scout hats of the Americans.

When the R.A.F. was formed, the uniforms designed for the new service were at first a source of rude hilarity, although we soon became reconciled to them. I even acquired one of them myself. They were of a somewhat impractical shade of a lightish blue with rank stripes in gold lace. While we made no effort to wear the new uniform at the Front, C. G. Grey has rather aptly commented: "At home it did much to heighten the dullness of the wartime streets and places of entertainment." The same authority records that in a melodrama on the London stage at that time, a half-witted British soldier who had managed somehow to escape from a German prison camp literally threw a fit when he first saw the fanciful new uniform adopted by the Air Force. For general wear, most of us went on using our old khaki Army and R.F.C. uniforms until the R.A.F. uniform that is still used today was introduced, shortly after the war.

Twelve days after the Royal Air Force came into being the onslaught from the Germans on the Western Front had become so threatening that Douglas Haig felt compelled to issue an order of the day that has since become famous. It finished with the words: "With our backs to the wall and believing in the justice of our cause each one must fight on to the end. The safety of our homes and the freedom of mankind alike depend upon the conduct of each one of us at this critical moment." It was a stirring message, but as far as most of us could see, our problem was to find the wall. That it was found and that our line held together were the factors that led to a change in the whole course of the war.

The first order received by the Royal Air Force from the newly appointed overall commander-in-chief on the Western Front—the

French General Foch—had read: "At the present time the first
duty of fighting aeroplanes is to assist the troops on the ground by
incessant attacks, with bombs and machine guns, on columns,
concentrations, or bivouacs. Air fighting is not to be sought except
so far as necessary for the fulfilment of this duty."

But immediately after that order was given, the Germans started
appearing in quite large formations, flying high over us as we went
to work making our attacks on ground targets. On one occasion a
formation of about thirty Albatros and Pfalz single-seater fighters
came swooping down on us. Our own formation was made up of
twenty-seven Camels and S.E.5's from No. 65 and my own
squadron. For about an hour there was a merciless fight. It took
place at various heights up to about fifteen hundred feet over the
area around one of the forward flying fields used by the Germans
near Rosières, a village to the south of the Somme that had seen a
great deal of fighting, including a stand made by remnants of the
Fifth Army. We had outstanding success in this scrap; between us,
Nos. 65 and 84 Squadrons either destroyed or crashed five enemy
aircraft and drove off the rest without any losses or injuries to our
side.

As soon as the lines on our part of the Front became more
stabilized, with the opposing armies again sinking back into the
ground in a general state of exhaustion, I received orders to move
my squadron forward from the airfield near Abbeville to the
airdrome at Bertangles, which was some five miles northwest of
Amiens. We were close to the Front, and from Bertangles we
could see the shells bursting over the lines, particularly in the
vicinity of Villers-Bretonneux, to the southeast, where there was
continued heavy fighting. But our line was holding, and the
Germans got no farther west than that.

With the exception of St-Omer, the name of Bertangles is
perhaps better known to the Air Force than that of any other
airdrome on the Western Front during the First World War. It was
located in the middle of pleasant, open country, and Amiens was
within easy reach. The months that I was to spend there during the
summer of 1918 provided for me one of the most interesting and
enjoyable periods I knew during the war. I pitched my tent in a
coppice alongside the airfield, and it seemed that the wood was
packed with nightingales. I have never heard so many of them
singing together in such a small space. At first, their combined
song at night used to keep me awake; but when I became
accustomed to it, I found in the song a relief from the other,
sharper sounds of war.

By this time my squadron was a sound fighting unit and very experienced in the system of formation tactics that we had evolved, and our score of Huns was rapidly mounting. We had excellent N.C.O.'s, and the airmen were all keen to do their best to support the pilots. Such was the progress made by my two South Africans, Beauchamp-Proctor and Dingbat Saunders, that I had had them both made flight commanders.

The effect that Beauchamp-Proctor had on the morale of the squadron was tremendous, and quite apart from his genial nature, he seemed to excel in everything that he did in the air. He was a very good formation leader, and at long range his eyesight was extraordinarily keen. He seemed to be able to spot an enemy aircraft much farther away than any of the rest of us. He also had great courage, and he had developed a particularly good sense of tactics. After he had sighted the Huns he would proceed to stalk them with the greatest skill and patience, eventually taking them unaware and with the advantages all on our side. Although I still led the squadron at times, I was happier flying as Beauchamp-Proctor's deputy leader, for in the air he was what the boys in the second war would have called "wizard."

Our flying from Bertangles during the weeks that lay ahead was in support of the Australian Corps, which was holding the line directly in front of us. This enabled me to see at first hand the work done by these rugged troops, who were under the command of one of their own people: a remarkable man by the name of Lieutenant-General Sir John Monash. His headquarters was in the large chateau on the outskirts of the village of Bertangles, overlooking our airfield. Through my contacts with the Australians during that summer I came to know and to understand something of their character.

Among the officers serving on Monash's staff at that time was a young major named Richard Casey. Even then Dick Casey's appearance and manner were distinctive, quietly assured and always attractively attentive, and stamped with the style that he bears today as the well-known Lord Casey, the foremost diplomat produced by Australia, and the present Governor-General of that country. We often met after the day's work; Casey would come to see me in our mess, or I would visit the Australians at the chateau. Out of this developed a friendship that has continued down through the years.

It would be asking a lot of the imagination, I know, if I were to suggest that at Bertangles in the early summer of 1918 the example set quite unintentionally by the Australian Corps commander pointed the way for several of the younger Army and Air Force officers who were there. But it is nevertheless of interest that quite a few of us did achieve senior and even high rank and title in the course of our future careers. On the other hand, perhaps we were lucky: we were the ones who happened to survive.

In my own squadron I had Dingbat Saunders and Beauchamp-Proctor, both of whom went on to make great names for themselves as fighter pilots. Commanding No. 209 Squadron, which had Camels and which shared the airfield with us along with No. 48 Squadron, was a fiery little pilot named J. O. Andrews. During the Second World War, Jock Andrews became one of my group commanders, an air vice-marshal, when I was myself commander-in-chief of Fighter Command. "Pussy" Foster, who had been one of my flight commanders in the early days of No. 43 Squadron, before we went to France, was also in No. 209 Squadron as a flight commander, and he eventually became an air chief marshal.

In command of No. 48 Squadron—equipped with the Bristol fighter, which had proved itself after its early difficulties and had become our best two-seater aircraft—was a tall, slim New Zealander, a pronounced individualist, who had got into the Air Force the hard way and against all orders. Today he is well known as Air Chief Marshal Sir Keith Park.

When the war broke out in 1914, Keith Park joined the New Zealand Artillery as a gunner. He was a corporal when they made their landing at Gallipoli in April, 1915, and he served there until the evacuation eight months later. He was commissioned in the field during that time; and after that he served with his battery during the battles on the Somme in 1916. Seriously wounded and returned to England on a stretcher, Park was passed as permanently unfit for active service. To his intense disgust he was made an instructor in gunnery.

"I heartily disapproved of a cushy job in England when all my friends were in France," he has said in describing his adventures, "so I wangled a transfer to the R.F.C. as a ground officer. Immediately my transfer was effected I further wangled a course as a pilot, although I was officially medically unfit for flying or any active service. In fact, I was still an out-patient at the Woolwich Hospital when I began my pilot's training."

Part of the reason for Keith Park's success in getting around a hopelessly adverse medical category was that all the War Office papers on his case were lost. It was typical of the man whom so many Battle of Britain pilots will remember that he made good use of that mishap. He joined No. 48 Squadron as a pilot in June, 1917, becoming a flight commander by the end of the year, and commanding officer of the squadron in February, 1918. It was then that I first met him: we were sharing the airfield at Flez. Although I did not always agree with Park's way of doing things, he was an outstanding commanding officer, and he used to do a great deal of flying himself, leading his squadron very successfully.

Another of those serving at Bertangles as a pilot in No. 48 Squadron that summer of 1918 was a tall youngster who is now known as Air Marshal Sir Charles Steele. He did not leave school— he was at Oundle—until the middle of 1915. After going to Sandhurst and then learning to fly, he was a pilot with No. 15 Squadron during the battles on the Somme less than a year later. He joined Keith Park in No. 48 Squadron during the time we were at Flez—although it was not until we were at Bertangles that I came to know him at all well.

Charles Steele was another of those who appeared to be so very, very young (which in fact he was). He has retained a smile that is still cheerful and boyish. During those early days he shared with Harold Balfour a rather highly strung temperament, but he always managed to keep it under control. Charles Steele is one of the most likeable of all the men I came to know well in my Air Force career.

The month of April, 1918, saw delivered to the German Air Force one of the heaviest blows they could have suffered. It was of such importance that it made flying history. On Sunday, the twenty-first, just over a couple of weeks after we arrived at Bertangles, Manfred von Richthofen was shot down and killed in a fight that took place over the River Somme, only a few miles away from us. The weather had been bad, with heavy storms; and the high winds, blowing from the east for a change, put the German pilots at a disadvantage. After taking off from Bertangles in their Camels for a morning offensive patrol over the lines, the pilots of No. 209 Squadron got into a scrap with Richthofen's Circus, which was flying from the airfield they occupied at Cappy, right beside the river and due east of us.

In that scrap our pilots were outnumbered by the Germans. One of the new boys of No. 209 Squadron was a Canadian named Lieutenant W. R. May, and he carefully followed the instructions that had been given him before take-off by his flight commander, a fellow Canadian named Captain Roy Brown, with whom May had been in school. When the fighting became too hot, May did his best to get out of harm's way, and he dived down into the valley of the river and smartly made off in the direction of Bertangles.

But the young Canadian found that he had a German flying a Fokker triplane stuck on his tail. Although he did not know it, that German was Richthofen. May went through every maneuver that he could think of in his efforts to get out of the way of Richthofen's fire, but the German kept after him until they were low down over the River Somme itself, and almost over the trenches of our front lines, which were occupied by the Australians. Seeing the fix that May had got into, Brown dived to the rescue, and the German pilot was caught in the hazardous position of being fired at, low down, by a Camel from above him and by machine gunners from the ground.

Apparently unaware that Brown was on top of him, Richthofen was concentrating on trying to shoot down May. He had to his credit, by then, eighty of our aircraft destroyed, the last two of which had been Camels that he had shot down only the day before. Brown opened fire and scored an immediate hit. Richthofen's triplane seemed to falter in the air, and then it fell in a clumsy way to a very rough landing in a field just behind our lines and near a large brickworks. The close proximity of the crashed aircraft to the lines brought it under artillery fire from the Germans, but the Australians nevertheless managed to get to the wrecked machine, and they found that the pilot was Richthofen. He was already dead when they got his body out of the cockpit: one bullet from Brown's fire had passed clean through his chest, and it must have killed him instantly.

Because I was on the same airfield and closely associated with the pilots of the other two squadrons there, I knew Roy Brown. He had been in the Royal Naval Air Service until the formation of the R.A.F. only three weeks before, and he was a tired and rather sick man who had seen a great deal of fighting. When he returned to Bertangles that Sunday morning he put in a report about the combat, but he did not know until afterwards that it was Richthofen whom he had shot down. By then the excitement was intense, and when the remains of the Fokker triplane and Richthofen's body were brought in, there was immense curiosity about them.

In the customary fashion (one that I have always found somewhat repulsive), the souvenir hunters were quickly at work, and in a very short time the triplane was stripped. Eventually various bits and pieces of it came to be distributed to the four corners of the earth. The engine can now be seen in the Imperial War Museum in

London. The Australian War Memorial in Canberra has the compass and the joy-stick and some other items, as well as the flying boots that Richthofen was wearing and a walking stick made from a piece of one of the blades of the propeller. The seat from the aircraft and more pieces are in the Royal Canadian Military Institute in Toronto. Quite a number of other relics of Richthofen's career which were kept in a museum in Berlin were lost when it was destroyed during our air raids of the Second World War. The many relics and records belonging to Richthofen's family fell into the hands of the Russians when they ransacked his mother's home late in 1944.

The only suitable place in which to keep the body of Richthofen was a canvas hangar belonging to my squadron that happened to be empty. He was laid out in the hangar on a small raised platform, and many of us went to see him as he rested there more or less in state. It was a curious experience, after all that we had heard about him, to see him lying there. The next day he was buried with full military honors in the local cemetery at Bertangles, alongside the airfield. The escort and the final salute were provided by the Australians, who were claiming that their people had shot down Richthofen from the ground.

It was with mixed feelings that I watched the burial of the great German ace; it was impossible not to feel a little emotional about it. Richthofen was the most successful, in actual scoring, of all the fighter pilots of the First World War. I thought about what he had achieved, and I wondered, as I have many times since, just what sort of man he was. Richthofen was undoubtedly a gallant pilot, although he always fought with the utmost caution—except for his very last scrap—and he never hesitated to avoid a fight or pull out of one if he thought that the odds against him were too great. He always had his highly trained Circus behind him, protecting him from attack from the rear and enabling him to devote the whole of his attention to shooting down his victims. It is possible that this lack of attention to what was happening behind was the reason he did not see Roy Brown coming down on him.

I did not disapprove of the tactics employed by Richthofen because in many ways they were similar to those developed by Jimmy McCudden. But Richthofen operated almost entirely over his side of the lines, waiting there for British aircraft to come to him rather than forcing the issue by coming over our side of the lines to find suitable targets. In that lay the main difference between the German and the British methods of operating fighting patrols. Only a few days before Richthofen's death, one of my pilots had been hit and killed by our own antiaircraft fire as he was returning from a low bombing and strafing raid. He crashed on our side of the lines. The squadron records state that he was "the only member of the squadron to meet his death in the air on the British side of the lines."

We were all glad enough, in our hearts, that Richthofen was out of the way. He had been a thorn in our sides for such a long time, it seemed. After his death, his place as leader of the Circus was taken by Wilhelm Reinhard, an Army officer from before the outbreak of war who had seen a great deal of service and had been severely wounded at least twice. Two months later Reinhard was killed in a flying accident while testing a new type of fighter, and the Circus was then placed under the command of Hermann Goering. That led to our continuing to engage each other, as we had for some time past, in further brisk exchanges in the air.

During the weeks immediately following the death of Richthofen, it was the turn of the Royal Air Force to be dealt not one but two staggering blows. Within the short space of just over two weeks—it seems to me now that the two disasters happened all at once—we lost both Jimmy McCudden and Mick Mannock. In company with Albert Ball they made up our great trio of outstandingly successful fighter pilots, and each was a master in his own fashion. By the summer of 1918 they were all dead, killed in ways that were not the result of direct combat in the air: Ball, so far as could be ascertained, by antiaircraft fire; McCudden through a crash on taking off; and Mannock by machine-gun fire from the ground.

Of the three, the one I came to know best was Jimmy McCudden, who had kept in touch with me because of his concern about his younger brother Anthony. McCudden had reason enough to feel worried about him because Anthony had made up his mind that, no matter what the cost might be, he was going to follow in his famous brother's footsteps. But he went about doing it in entirely the wrong way. Jimmy McCudden knew that. He talked to me about it, and he warned Anthony about his recklessness. "He was far too brave and headstrong to make a successful fighting pilot, for he was in the habit of doing daily over the enemy lines the most hair-raising things," Jimmy McCudden commented.

Anthony McCudden was far and away the most impetuous youngster in my squadron. Jimmy McCudden came to see me several times about putting the brakes on young Anthony, and I did my best to restrain what was so obviously a rashness that was bound to land him in trouble. I warned him many times to exercise more caution; but he would not listen, and he even met with such success that quite early in his career in the squadron I felt bound to put him up for a Military Cross, which he received in March, 1918. By then he had shot down several Huns and some balloons —his score is given as eleven victories—but almost immediately after he got his M.C. he was shot down himself while the squadron was escorting some of our bombers on a raid over enemy territory.

Toward the end of March I received a letter from Jimmy McCudden written from the R.F.C. Club in London, which in those days was in Bruton Street. In it he asked if there was any further news that I could give him about his brother. He had just heard that he was missing. He also commented in that letter on having seen one of my flight commanders who was on leave "doing the heavy over here, with a string of ribbons that damn near blinded one." Considering that the letter was written only a couple of weeks before McCudden went to Buckingham Palace to receive from the King all at one swoop his Victoria Cross, his Distinguished Service Order and Bar, and a Bar to his Military Cross, I could not help thinking, in an amused way, that his own chest was covered with ribbons that far outshone those of any others.

Another thought that Jimmy McCudden expressed in his letter to me revealed how anxious he was to get back to France. "I suppose you are at present fighting like the devil," he wrote. "I only wish I were out there." A few weeks later—after it was established that young Anthony McCudden had been killed when he was shot down over thirty miles behind the enemy lines, and that he was buried near Le Cateau—McCudden was given his first command of a squadron, and a crack one at that: No. 60, equipped with S.E.5's.

By then Jimmy McCudden had to his credit fifty-seven victories; and he had been hard at it for a long, long time. He was promoted to the rank of major, and on July 9, 1918, he left for France to join his new squadron. He flew out from England, and on the way he landed at the airfield at Auxi-le-Château, which was between Abbeville and St-Pol. As he was taking off from there on the last leg of his journey, he made a mistake that, although trivial enough, was to cost him his life.

During the five months he had spent instructing in England— which he had been doing since leaving No. 56 Squadron on a rest from operational flying—McCudden had become accustomed to flying aircraft without having a full war load on board. As he was taking off in his S.E.5 from Auxi-le-Château the engine failed; and in one vital second he must have overlooked the critical fact that he was in a heavier aircraft. He made the mistake of trying to turn back, and instead of responding as he expected it would, the aircraft sideslipped and crashed, and McCudden was killed. He was buried in the small cemetery nearby, at Wavans, which is only five miles or so to the east of one of the most famous battlefields in our history, Crécy, the fourteenth-century battle site.

A few weeks after the death of Jimmy McCudden, an understanding tribute was paid to him by Jack Salmond, his squadron commander at the beginning of the war in 1914, his General Officer Commanding in 1918. Of the early period during which McCudden had been one of his mechanics, with the rank of what today would be a corporal, Salmond said: "He was at that time one of the best engine fitters we had. . . ." Over the next four years McCudden was to achieve more than any other pilot; and in the end Salmond said of him: "He fought with his head as well as with his great heart."

Just before he was killed, Jimmy McCudden gave to C. G. Grey the completed manuscript of the book he had written. In editing it and preparing it for publication, Grey described it as "a faithful personal record of five years in the Royal Flying Corps . . . an extremely valuable historical document." The book first appeared soon after McCudden's death in 1918, and it bore then the title *Five Years in the Royal Flying Corps.*

That first title given to this important book was, I know, a somewhat unimaginative one; but when the book was reissued in 1930 it was given the dreadful title of *Flying Fury,* and it is by that title that it has since become quite well known. Nothing could be more misleading than to credit McCudden's flying with any fury. There was no fury at all about him: he was remarkably cool and calculating in his fighting, and he went about the job of shooting down Huns in a very level-headed and businesslike way, going to infinite trouble to see that his machine was absolutely right in every respect. He took particular care over his guns and gunsights. Always approaching his dangerous work with a sane caution, he also took care to avoid unnecessary risks. It was entirely wrong to infer that there was any special fury about McCudden or his way of doing things.

It was in Mick Mannock that there was anger. Right from the beginning he displayed a temperament that was as emotional as any of those of the leading fighter pilots I came to know. One of his friends in No. 40 Squadron at Treizennes recorded a comment

made by Mannock during the summer of 1917, before he became
at all well known, that reveals all too clearly the nature of his
highly strung temperament. "That's the way they're going to get
me in the end—flames and finish," he said; and the friend who
placed that comment on record added: "Poor old Mick. He was so
obviously in a highly strung emotional state." For that reason
alone Mannock always carried a revolver in the air, explaining that
it was "to finish myself as soon as I see the first sign of flames."

That was in the beginning, when Mick Mannock's start was
slow. His lack of success was getting on his nerves, and he knew
that the others were watching him, wondering why he was so slow
to get off the mark. By the end of the year, when he was sent back
to England for a badly needed rest, he had a score of only six
destroyed, although there would probably have been many more
added to that had he been sharp enough in his claims. But
Mannock, in the words of Larry Callahan, one of the Americans
who flew with us, "was not a headhunter." He spent three months
flying at Biggin Hill and in instruction at London Colney, and then
he returned to France as a flight commander in No. 74 Squadron.

No sooner was Mannock back on the Western Front than he
started shooting down Huns at a fantastic rate. Despite his faulty
left eye he had, as Beauchamp-Proctor had, extraordinarily good
long sight. After only a few weeks he was promoted to the rank of
major and given command of No. 85 Squadron, taking over from
Billy Bishop. "Edward Mannock was a great formation leader who
had the gift of inspiring those who flew with him," H. A. Jones
wrote in the official history. "He had a keen, analytical mind, and
the pilots who served under him have testified that he was always
thinking out schemes for the tactical handling of a fighter formation."

One of the schemes that Mannock worked out when he took
command of No. 85 Squadron was to set himself up as a decoy to
draw the German fighters down on him, keeping the rest of his
squadron somewhat dispersed and well above and out of sight. He
selected Larry Callahan as the one to fly with him in this particular
plan. "He would always be the low man, not high man: that's
where I always admired Mannock," Callahan has explained. "He
was always low, and I knew it because I was with him. When a
bunch of Huns came along he would goad them into attacking
him while the rest of the boys were off in the distance, waiting. It
worked magnificently. Mannock was such a hell of a fighter and such
a good shot that he could afford to get himself into the worst

position and still shoot his way out. He was a highly imaginative pilot, and the best shot that I ever saw in my life."

Mick Mannock was a remarkably good leader, and he used to nurse his pilots along carefully and sensibly; many times he even set things up for them. His success resounded throughout the Air Force. In No. 85 Squadron Mannock flew most of the time with Larry Callahan. Of Mannock's frame of mind then Callahan has recalled: "He was determined to win. He hated the Huns and he wanted to kill all of them. He wasn't interested in just killing them himself. He wanted a lot of them killed, so he trained us how to do it. That was why, on several occasions, Mannock made way for a new pilot to come in and finish off an enemy aircraft that he had already winged. It was to give the new boy confidence."

In going to such lengths to help his own pilots, Mannock was exceptional; and it was after doing just that in the early morning of July 26, 1918, that he was killed. There was in No. 85 Squadron a young New Zealand pilot by the name of Donald Inglis. Although keen enough, Inglis had not had any success in his fighting, so Mannock went off with him to try and find a German they could tackle together. The squadron was then flying from St-Omer.

Just to the west of Laventie, over the enemy side of the lines, Mannock and Inglis ran across a German two-seater. Mannock opened fire and hit it, and then he turned away, giving Inglis a chance to go in and finish it off. Inglis did that, and together he and Mannock watched it crash. They were very low down by then, only a few hundred feet from the ground: and then Inglis saw that flames were starting to spurt from the side of Mannock's S.E.5. The aircraft fell to the ground just to the south of Merville, and it blew up in a burst of fire. Mannock must have been hit by enemy machine-gun fire from the ground. He died, as he had always imagined he would, in flames.

No grave for Mannock was ever found. When I was in France in 1959 I was shown the only memorial there is to his name. Along with many others it is on a pillar in the large Commonwealth War Graves Cemetery on the outskirts of Arras which commemorates the names of airmen with no known graves. Mannock was awarded the Victoria Cross posthumously. He had already received the Distinguished Service Order and two bars and the Military Cross and bar; and his score of seventy-three victories put him at the top of the list of all the British fighter pilots.

13 / War Birds

ONE OF THE REASONS the Royal Air Force has always enjoyed a certain broad-minded outlook—and been all the better for it—has been the early infusion it received of a vigorous brand of cosmopolitan humor. We were never cramped or parochial in our attitudes. In the early days there were, through circumstance, only two services that provided the young men of the British Empire with the opportunity to fly: the Royal Flying Corps and the Royal Naval Air Service, which merged in 1918, and became the Royal Air Force. The Australians formed their own Flying Corps at the beginning of 1918, which absorbed many of their pilots who had been flying with us, but there were still quite a few of them who remained in the Royal Air Force. And we continued to be greatly strengthened by the Canadians and South Africans and New Zealanders who were with us. The Canadians seemed at this time particularly good at producing great fighter pilots.

Long before the United States came into the war, there were quite a few young Americans who had felt, for reasons that ranged all the way from stern principles to a hotheaded zest for adventure, that they must find their own way across the Atlantic and get into the fray. Many of them joined the air services of Britain and France.

As early as the beginning of 1917 I had acquired some knowledge of the way the minds of these men worked. An American youngster by the name of Frederick Libby had joined me at Treizennes as a pilot in No. 43 Squadron at the time of the Battle of Arras. Disguised as a Canadian, Libby served with the Royal Flying Corps during the worst period in our fortunes. Not long after joining us he shot down an enemy aircraft one afternoon which crashed just to the east of Vimy Ridge.

It seemed that many of the first pilots in the infant air service of the United States in 1917 came from fairly well-to-do families. For some curious and inexplicable reason, financial independence seemed to produce men who were strangely addicted to an odd

sort of violence. That was noticed not only by us: even some of
the Americans themselves commented upon it.

Almost by chance, these vigorous young men of unpredictable
action contributed to the early life of the Royal Air Force a bond
that must surely be one of the strongest that has ever existed
between the fighting services of two different countries. Before
the American air service could become operational, large numbers
of the first of their pilots and mechanics were attached for experience to Royal Flying Corps squadrons. From then on, our lives
were never quite the same. In a way that was unique and at the
same time both touching and revealing, the Americans themselves
placed on record the origin of the bond that was established. For
that, we of the Royal Air Force will always be grateful. That record
is to be found in a book entitled *War Birds*.

Possibly there have been books about flying in the First World
War that are better than *War Birds* from a purely literary point of
view, but no book can touch that one for its splendid and heartwarming story, and for the rugged manner in which that story is
told. In the minds of all of those who participated in the war of
1914–18, *War Birds* will always be the great classic of flying. It
was written by Elliott White Springs and first published in the
United States in 1927; and it was a tremendous success. I have
always felt I was particularly fortunate in the close association I
enjoyed with the vigorous young Americans who contributed to its
making.

When the United States came into the war, ground schools for
future pilots were formed at several of the American universities,
including Princeton. Shortly afterward 210 of these cadets from
ground school were sent to England for further training with the
R.F.C., and a large number of them were billeted in Exeter College, Oxford, which is right next to Lincoln, my own college. "We
have the whole college to ourselves," Springs wrote. Exeter and
Oxford itself, for that matter, must still be haunted by the ghosts
of those spirited cadets.

The *Diary of an Unknown Aviator,* as Elliott Springs preferred to
call *War Birds,* is purported to be by one of a trio made up of
Springs and his two closest friends: Larry Callahan and Mac Grider.
It is in the form of a diary by Grider; but it was in fact written by
Springs. Right at the outset, at the time they left America to come
to England, he stated: "I haven't lived very well but I am determined to die well." That could have been the battlecry for that
undaunted trio: Springs, the son of a wealthy cotton mill owner

from South Carolina, Mac Grider from Arkansas, and Larry
Callahan from Chicago.

When I recall now the names that appear in *War Birds* of the
first members of the American Army who came to serve with us
and to share so completely our lives, an almost riotous flood of
memories is summoned up. They were such a joyful and high-
spirited band of men. Julian Stanley, today a stockbroker in New
York, is the Jake Stanley of the book, and I always spend some
time with him whenever I am in his part of the United States. I met
Elliott Springs again at Stanley's home on Long Island, only a
short time before he died in 1959. Larry Callahan, now a stockbroker in Chicago, had been in London on a visit only just before
that, and we had met again then. Their humor was unimpaired,
and their enthusiasm was as keen as ever, and our talk was of
George Vaughn and Bim Oliver and Alex Mathews and Earl Hammer and Sam Eckert and Mort Newhall and a host of others who
became as well known to me as they did to Springs and Stanley
and Callahan, and to all those who have read *War Birds*.

That happy band worked hard and flew hard and brawled and
drank their way through their training; and yet, for all their high
spirits, Springs could still pause to make the comment: "These
Englishmen sure have a funny idea of a party. They want to smash
everything." It was a penetrating observation, and just as shrewd
as his comment when he learned to fly and found that his first
instruction was to be on "the awful looking bus," the Maurice
Farman Shorthorn. "They say that you test the rigging by putting a
bird between the two wings," he wrote. "If the bird gets out,
there's a wire gone somewhere."

All their moments off duty the Americans spent as we did—and
more often than not with us—in London and joyfully at play in the
fashion of the R.F.C. They acquired a house in Berkeley Square
which I visited quite often while they were there, and they staged
what seemed to be a never-ending party there and at Murray's and
the Grafton Galleries and all the other night spots. And the shows
in town were enlivened with the attentions they paid to the young
actresses of that time.

A month or so before we in No. 84 Squadron left for France,
Billy Bishop started forming a new squadron, No. 85. It was
intended orginally that they be equipped with Dolphins, the latest
of the single-seater Sopwith fighters. Instead they were equipped
with S.E.5's. Bishop, who was by then one of the top-scoring
fighter pilots with a Victoria Cross and a whole lot of other

decorations to his credit, gathered together as cosmopolitan a bunch of pilots as one could imagine, including Elliott Springs, Larry Callahan and Mac Grider.

It is in describing that move in the fortunes of the Americans that Elliott Springs' book comes into its own, for his descriptions of life in No. 85 Squadron, on duty and in their off moments, provide as good a picture of what all our lives were like (except, perhaps, for the drinking) as anything that has ever been written. "If these boys can fly two-bladers like they can fly fourposters, there'll sure be a shortage of Huns before long," Elliott Springs commented at the time that No. 85 Squadron proceeded to France in May, 1918; and his description of the departure of the squadron from Hounslow is, in his own words, "a scream."

The pilots were given their final instructions by Billy Bishop before an assembled crowd which included wives and sweethearts. "He told us that Lympne would be our first stop and to be sure and take a good look at the wind sock and to land squarely into the wind," Springs wrote. "But he didn't call it a sock. He called it by the name we always call it on the field when there are no ladies or gentlemen present. He turned red and the ladies lowered their parasols . . ." Farfetched as it is, that note is nevertheless a natural one in a book written with such gusto.

There is only one fault I have to find with *War Birds,* and in all fairness, I must place it on record. The drinking done in the R.F.C. and the R.A.F. was not nearly as strenuous nor as constant as Springs leads one to believe, hilarious though the effect is in the book. I am able to say that because of my own long experience of conditions at the Front. Normally very little alcohol was consumed, for the simple reason that we had discovered in the beginning that we could not indulge in heavy drinking and fighting in the air at the same time. I do not mean to imply that we were teetotalers, or that we were against drinking. We were all for it in the right place and at the right time; but if we had been at the bottle as constantly as Springs makes out, we would all have been in our graves very quickly.

When the occasion for a party—or a binge, as we used to call it in those days—did blow up, we were not slow to take advantage of it. There was one such occasion in our lives at Bertangles during the summer of 1918 which was well in the *War Birds* tradition, and which could very easily have let us in for disastrous results. Our wing commander also had his headquarters at Bertangles, and he started the sensible custom of releasing from duty some of his squadrons as soon as he could in the afternoon, sometimes as early

238   COMBAT AND COMMAND

as five o'clock. When that happened, it was understood that the
squadron would definitely not be called upon to do any more flying
that day.

On occasions such as this—which came our way about once
every two weeks—I used to arrange for a squadron guest night. To
this party we invited pilots from other squadrons and Army
officers such as those on the staff of the Australian Corps at the
chateau. It was a way of providing some light relief from the
tension of our continuous and somewhat nerve-racking flying. On
these occasions I used to let the boys go, and there was then some
pretty solid drinking. But we only got caught out once, and then it
was scarcely our fault.

On instructions from our wing commander we had been released
early, and the party we had organized was well underway. We were
all feeling better for the drink and the letup, when I was called to
the phone. I was told that the squadron would have to take off
immediately for an offensive patrol over the lines. It appeared that
there were a lot of Huns about, and no other squadron was free to
chase them away. What I should have done, I realized afterward,
was explain that under the circumstances none of us was really fit
to fly. But my spirits were well stimulated, and being young and
confident I was all for taking on the enemy regardless of our
condition. I called all my pilots together and gave them their
orders. Full of fight I prepared to lead the patrol myself.

Somehow or other it seemed to take us much longer than usual
to get ourselves sorted out and into the air. By the time we
managed to join up, our formation was a pretty ragged one. We set
off for the lines, but when we did finally arrive over them there was
not a Hun in sight. Dusk was falling, but we went on chasing about
the sky for a while looking for the enemy. It was just as well,
under the circumstances, that we did not find them. Since it was
getting dark I thought that it was about time we started back, so I
turned for home and gave the signal to the squadron to go down
and do a bit of ground strafing on the German side of the lines on
the way. Things were quiet at the moment on the ground, and my
pilots eagerly went about stirring them up, albeit in a very disorderly fashion. I myself set about shooting up an enemy ration
party that I found on the way up to their lines with what must have
been the evening meal.

Our luck was in. Although we had a good bash at the poor
devils of Germans on the ground, none of us received any injuries,
and we arrived back safely over the airdrome at Bertangles. It was
very nearly dark by the time we got there, and some of the land-

ings made were at least peculiar, although there were no crashes. I
had my own back on our wing commander by roaring down and
beating up the wing headquarters, giving everybody there a good
rattling. It was not exactly a clever thing to do, but nothing was
said to me about it. The only result achieved by the patrol was that
it did sober us up; and the only near casualty suffered was when one
of my flight commanders had a bullet from the ground whip up
through the floor of his aircraft between his legs and whistle past
his face. That shook him a bit, and when he landed he was very
sober.

At the time No. 85 Squadron arrived in France, early in 1918,
Elliott Springs recorded that the pilots were made up of "three
Americans, two New Zealanders, two Australians, one South
African, six Canadians, two Scots, one Irishman, and six Englishmen." My own squadron, No. 84, consisted of nearly as wide a
variety of nationalities. Two of my three flight commanders were
South Africans, and I had several Canadian pilots. And then
suddenly I had one whole flight taken away from me and replaced
by Americans, pilots and mechanics, about fifty of them all told.

At first I was not at all happy about my squadron being broken
up in this way, but very soon after the Americans arrived I found
that they were as fine a lot of men as I could have wished for.
They were all members of the United States Army, and they
remained so. They stayed with us and worked as part of my
squadron for about three months in order to get experience before
going off to help form new American squadrons. Their places were
then taken by a fresh batch of American pilots and mechanics.

It was in this way, in 1918, that I first came to know the
Americans as a whole. After that I disliked having to part with
them, particularly the pilots. They were cheerful and courageous,
and I soon realized that the effect they were having on my squadron and its morale was all to the good. That early experience with
the Americans went a long way toward helping me to an understanding of my father's action when he himself became an American citizen after the Second World War.

New to us—and a never-ending source of amusement—was the
way the Americans faced up to the discipline of the Royal Flying
Corps. Their reaction reflected their particular brand of humor. In
getting away in his S.E.5 from a hectic encounter with six Germans south of Courtrai, Elliott Springs dived and raced back to his
own airfield, but in doing it he tore loose most of the fabric of his
top wing. He was still in such a high state of excitement when he

landed that he taxied slap into Billy Bishop's S.E.5, and locked wings with it. Then came an expression of the irrepressible American humor, and in *War Birds* we read: "The major was all set to bawl him out but Springs walked up to him and ran his finger across his row of ribbons and said, 'You see these medals?' Bish nodded. 'Well,' says Springs, 'I just want to tell you that you are welcome to them!' With that he walked on into the bar."

His sense of humor was robust enough for Elliott Springs to be quite ready to tell a story against himself. One of these was of an encounter that he had with his own people while he was still serving with the R.A.F. Billy Bishop had been recalled to England for staff work, and as many of the pilots of No. 85 Squadron as possible went to Boulogne to see him off. At lunch, Springs recorded, they ran into some officers of the American Army who had just arrived in France. Of what happened then, he wrote:

> There were two officers at the next table to us at lunch. One of them saw my R. F. C. wings and wanted to know why I was wearing a crown above my wings. I told him because I was a qualified R. F. C. pilot.
>
> "Well," says he, "you can wear a crown if you want to. But as for me,—I can't get enough eagles on. I just want eagles all over me."
>
> They had on funny belts. I said, "Where'd you get the funny Sam Browne belts?"
>
> "Sam Browne belts?" said one of them. "These ain't Sam Browne belts. These is Liberty belts!!!"
>
> That gave the squadron a laugh. They've been kidding us about it ever since. They call us the Liberty Boys and want to see our eagles.

Among the American pilots who first came to me were Lieutenants S. B. Eckert and M. Newhall. They were older than most, good steady chaps, and they left me after only a few weeks to take command of Nos. 17 and 148 Fighter Squadrons, two of the first Camel squadrons formed in the American Air Service. After them I had with me Bim Oliver, whom Elliott Springs mentions quite a lot in his book. He was a tiny man, no taller than Beauchamp-Proctor, most amusing, and a character in his own right with a dead-pan humor that was typically American. He was with me in No. 84 Squadron for some months before going off to become a flight commander in Mort Newhall's squadron. Another of the "war birds" who came to my squadron was Earl Hammer. He was in many ways the most attractive of all the Americans we had with us, handsome, charming and gay. Unhappily he was shot down and killed while flying with us.

The most successful of all the Americans who served under my command was Lieutenant G. A. Vaughn, who was one of my pilots for about four months. He had come over with Elliott Springs, and his name also appears frequently in *War Birds*. By the end of the war George Vaughn was the second most successful of all the American fighters—Eddie Rickenbacker was the first—who survived.

George Vaughn had been at Princeton University with Elliott Springs, and he also received his early training there. He was a thoroughly pleasant man in every way. He was a very good shot in the "Dead-Eye Dick" fashion; and on the first patrol he made with us over the enemy lines, he shot down a Hun which fell out of the sky in flames. It was a very difficult shot, because Vaughn had to do a quick turn and at the same time take a pot shot at the Hun as the latter climbed away.

In one scrap we got mixed up in a little later, George Vaughn pulled up his S.E.5 underneath a Hun until he was hanging on his propeller and on the point of stalling. Not until then did he open fire and, from a quite impossible angle, shoot down the enemy aircraft. He went on shooting down more of them while he was with us until he had six to his credit, as well as several balloons; and in September he received the British Distinguished Flying Cross which I had put him up for. It was one of the first to be awarded to an American Army pilot. So much did Vaughn come to like the S.E.5 and his post with us that he was quite upset when he had to go on to Camels in the American squadron to which he was sent as a flight commander.

As we had discovered earlier, the Americans soon found that flying in wartime, particularly in fighters, was something done best by those who were, first and foremost, individuals. The most successful of all the American fighter pilots in the First World War was Captain E. V. Rickenbacker. He was not one of Elliott Springs' war birds, but if ever there was an individualist that man is Eddie Rickenbacker.

A prominent and very successful racing motorist before the war, Rickenbacker started out on his Army career as chauffeur for General Pershing, Commander-in-Chief of the American Army in France. Although he was getting on toward thirty by the time he got to France, he insisted on learning to fly. He was trained in France, and the Americans then tried hard to put to the fullest use his great knowledge of engines by making him a senior engineering officer. But Rickenbacker insisted on a more active form of service. He was on the very first operational patrol flown by an American fighter unit in the First World War, and a little later he was in command of their well-known 94th ("Top Hat") Squadron.

I met Eddie Rickenbacker only once during the first war, and although I found him then a little brash he was obviously a man of parts, with his head screwed on the right way. To the people of the United States he became a national hero, and he was the only one of the four pilots who received the Congressional Medal of Honor —the American equivalent of our Victoria Cross—to survive the war.

To the astonishment of many people, Eddie Rickenbacker was to achieve more distinction in the second war, during which I had several amusing and at times downright curious encounters with him. Since then I have come to know him well as one of the foremost of the American civil airline executives. I have also learned to appreciate the strength of his unusual character. While being a deeply religious man, Eddie Rickenbacker has always been a hell-raiser and a dynamic law unto himself.

A lighter aspect of our association with those stalwart Americans who served in my squadron was the way they joined us and plunged—I use the word advisedly—into playing rugger. There is a vague similarity between American football and our game—the former, I believe, having grown out of the latter—and since we had quite a good team in the squadron, some of the Americans were only too ready to participate in our matches. In place of knowledge of the rules of rugger, they had their own uninhibited brand of enthusiasm.

One of the American mechanics sent to me had a great reputation, we were told, as an American footballer. Since he was a huge fellow and very strong (as is apparently the case with all those who play the American game), we played him in the pack. There he was a tower of strength, and during one game he was seen to pick up in his arms the opposing scrum half, a diminutive chap, complete with the ball.

"What shall I do with him?" he roared as he stood looking around.

We were delighted with that. "Throw him away!" we all shouted.

With that, our huge American did just what he was told, and he literally threw away his opponent, ball and all, and the game went on.

Another source of amusement was provided for us during the short time that No. 85 Squadron spent at Bertangles. We found

that the British members at least lived up to the spirit, if not quite
the speed, of the Americans who were serving with them. Although
I had met them before, it was then that I came to know well both
Elliott Springs and Larry Callahan. Mac Grider had been killed a
little earlier in a scrap that he and Springs had had with a German
two-seater over Armentières. Springs and Callahan were flying in
"Nigger" Horn's flight in No. 85 Squadron. They could not have
been in better hands, because Horn, who figures prominently in
War Birds, had previously served in No. 60 Squadron, from which
had come so many good fighter pilots.

If Elliott Springs ever intended that there should be a hero in
War Birds—I use the word cautiously, for want of a better
one—that hero must have been Larry Callahan. A slim, tallish,
rather slow-moving young man in his early twenties, with a
quizzical gleam in his eye and a magnificent sense of humor,
Callahan had two main interests in life: flying and playing bridge.
Springs says that he "takes his fighting just like his bridge." Since
Springs admitted that they were apparently "the only Americans in
Europe that are really enjoying this war" and since there was
plenty of bridge and even more flying, Callahan was at least kept
busy. "He's the best natural pilot we have," Springs recorded.
"Nigger says he has the smoothest hand on the stick he ever saw."

Set against the subtlety of Larry Callahan's nature, that of
Elliott Springs was of a more vigorous humor. Physically a robust
man, he was of about the same age as Callahan. His disdain for all
rank and all forms of class consciousness was nothing short of
superb. Life for Elliott Springs was to be lived to the full, and he
flew in the same way, not hesitating to take on anybody and everybody. If Callahan's sense of humor was sharp—and to this day he
can see the ridiculous with an astonishing alertness—then Springs'
humor was almost flamboyant. And yet he, too, could be extraordinarily perceptive. There was not a thing that missed the shrewd
eye of this dynamic character. If by chance anything did, then
Callahan was there to remind him about it. "He and Springs argue
for two hours after every patrol," we are told in the book.

One night at Bertangles, Keith Park had a cinema show in one
of No. 48 Squadron's wooden hangars. Charles Steele invited me
over to see it, and I took with me some of my pilots, including
Alex Mathews, one of my cheerful Americans. Larry Callahan and
Nigger Horn and Elliott Springs from No. 85 Squadron were also
there. The show had been going on for some time when a bomb
exploded slap on another of No. 48 Squadron's hangars nearby,
setting it on fire. A German night bomber had crept over the

airdrome, and they must have seen a chink of light coming from somewhere or other and aimed at it.

The orderly officer came rushing into the hangar in which we were sitting and called for the Fire Party. Just as the audience was giving him a rather rude reply, another bomb fell very close by, and then a lot more came down. I was one of those sitting in the front row, and I dived under the piano which was standing in front of me while all the others flung themselves on the floor. But we did not stay there more than a few moments because the fire attracted the attention of other German bombers, and they started unloading their bombs on it and shooting us up.

By then the whole place seemed to be erupting, and several of the other wooden hangars were also ablaze. Everybody made a rush to get out, and Charles Steele and I dashed off for some trenches that he said had been dug near the mess about a hundred yards away. The fire was blazing and quite out of control, and that was attracting even more attention from the German bombers. Then they started dumping light antipersonnel bombs on us and machine gunning everything they could see. I ran faster than Steele, and managed to get to the trench just before the next load of bombs came down. Although Steele threw himself flat on the ground, he was hit in three places, and had to spend the rest of the war in the hospital. No. 48 Squadron had many casualties that night, wounded and killed; and to my deep regret we lost Alex Mathews, who was killed by machine-gun fire from one of the German bombers as he also started to run away from the fire.

From the shelter of the trench, I could see that the raiders had hit and set on fire one of the hangars of my own squadron on the other side of the airdrome. I shouted to our people to join me, and we all rushed across to the burning hangar, and did what we could to save our aircraft. Although we suffered no other casualties, we did lose one of our S.E.5's when the roof of the wooden hangar fell on it and broke its back. The rest of our machines we managed to drag out to safety.

In his account in *War Birds* of that night's happenings, Elliott Springs records: "Alex Mathews is dead." As one reads his book one is struck by the way he has to record the deaths, one after the other, and with an awful frequency, of those who had started out with him from the United States such a short time before. In that he was sharing the experience that had been ours for what seemed such a long time.

Five German bombers attacked Bertangles that night. Although it was stated officially that "an inconsiderable number of bombs" were dropped, they certainly did enough damage. No. 48 Squadron lost five hangars and nine of their Bristol fighters with a sixth hangar, the last one, partly destroyed and two more Bristol fighters that were in it damaged. Another Bristol fighter which was standing outside was destroyed by a direct hit, and the squadron offices and stores huts and some tenders also went up in flames. So heavy were the all-round losses to Keith Park's squadron that it had to be withdrawn from the line and re-equipped. With a commanding officer of the quality of Park, however, they were back on the job within forty-eight hours.

Another of the Americans I met in rather a curious way at Bertangles in the summer of 1918 was John G. Winant. He was also a Princeton man, and from the university had found his way into flying and had become a pilot (although he was not among the happy warriors of *War Birds*). Winant was nearly thirty years old by then. One afternoon as I was at work at my desk he suddenly arrived in my office: a black-haired, beetle-browed pilot, a lieutenant in American uniform looking rather like a young Abraham Lincoln. I did not have the faintest idea who he was, but he introduced himself, after smartly saluting me in a very correct way, and asked if I would let him fly one of my S.E.5's. He told me that he was with an American Army cooperation squadron working from an airdrome nearby, and flying R.E.8's.

There was something appealing about the way Winant put his case. He was quite intense in his manner and yet so earnest and persuasive in his ambition to fly an S.E.5, asking me most courteously if I would be so very kind as to allow him to do just that. Rather against my better judgment he won me over, and I took him to one of my aircraft and sat him in it, showing him all the taps and explaining the controls. Then I sent him off. Winant flew around quite happily for about half an hour; then he landed in a respectable way, thanked me in that genuine and sincere manner of his, and disappeared.

I did not see or hear anything more of John Winant until shortly after he took up his appointment as the American Ambassador to England in February, 1941, in place of Joseph P. Kennedy—an appointment of which he made such a great success. There was no hint then in his quiet and courteous manner of any reason for the tragic way in which he was to die only a few years later.

In contrast to these older men, we had so many in the Air Force who looked like mere schoolboys—indeed, many of them had been just that only a few months before. When the Americans came in, they also had many youngsters. One of the most youthful in appearance who came to me to fly with No. 84 Squadron was Lieutenant E. J. Boudwin. He came from Washington, D.C., and he was a delightful boy, but no more than a boy, which was why we dubbed him "Child Yank."

In appearance Boudwin seemed to be about fifteen, although he was in fact about eighteen or nineteen; but he was a very gallant young pilot who stayed with us almost to the end of the war, when he went off to join an American squadron, No. 25. He was another of those who genuinely enjoyed his time with the Royal Air Force. A few weeks after the end of the war, following on my promotion, I received from him a rather touching letter which I still have. It was written in a schoolboy hand, addressing me as "Colonel Douglas," and signed "Child Yank." There was in it an expression of the same feeling for the British that Elliott Springs wrote about.

"So you are back in good old England," Boudwin said. "Oh! how I do wish I could get back again as I never had a better time anywhere. We few Americans who were trained and went out with the British certainly were lucky. I enjoyed every minute of it, and the next war I am coming to the R.A.F. tout de suite, so if England goes to war soon I will look you up."

The Americans, being of more volatile temperament than we were, and less self-restrained, seemed to burn themselves out quicker than we did, in some respects. They were never lacking in guts, and they went about their fighting in the air with an enthusiasm that won the admiration and respect of all those who ever came in contact with them. Perhaps it was that enthusiasm, as well as their high-spirited drive in everything they did, that exacted such a heavy toll on their endurance. This strain, coupled with the very heavy losses they were forced to suffer, did contribute toward sobering them up to some extent. But they accepted all their troubles in a way that was just as touching, I felt, as their earlier, apparently unquenchable eagerness to get into the fight.

All that sadder aspect of flying was handled so well by Elliott Springs in *War Birds*. The best part of the book is toward the end. There Springs wrote with an unexpected depth of understanding about the effect on a man's nerves and his spirit of all the flying and the fighting, of the hairbreadth escapes from disaster, and of the friends' deaths that we all had to endure. Springs never spared himself. He was in the thick of a lot of fighting, and he was shot up

and shot down and injured and generally put through the mill in a
very short space of time. And he scored his full share of victories,
for which he and Larry Callahan, who also did splendidly, received
our Distinguished Flying Cross at about the same time that George
Vaughn got his.

"I have learned many things, especially that discretion is the
better part of valor," Elliott Springs wrote in a soberer tone. "And
in this game, not only the better part, but about ninety-nine per
cent of it. When there are more than two Huns above you and your
immediate vicinity is full of lead, well, my boy, it is high time to go
home. Never mind trying to shoot down any of them. Go home
and try again to-morrow."

Our American companions were working themselves hard, and
the strain was telling. I think that what Springs had to say then was
quite honest and certainly sincere. "I'm all right in the air, as calm
as a cucumber, but on the ground I'm a wreck and I get panicky,"
he wrote. "Nobody in the squadron can get a glass to his mouth
with one hand after one of these decoy patrols except Cal and he's
got no nerve,—he's made of cheese. But some nights we both have
nightmares at the same time and Mac has to get up and find his
teeth and quiet us. We don't sleep much at night. But we get tired
and sleep all afternoon when there's nothing to do."

Toward the end of the book there is an account of a typical
encounter with the enemy which Elliott Springs credited to the
time that No. 85 Squadron was flying with us from Bertangles.
"I'm not feeling very well to-day," he stated. "I fought Huns all
night in my sleep and after two hours of real fighting to-day, I feel
all washed out. Yesterday produced the worst scrap that I have yet
had the honor to indulge in." He then gave in detail a description
of the way in which a fighter pilot acts and reacts in the heat of a
scrap. It is one of the best I have ever read, and it must surely
sound a sharply responsive note in the minds of every pilot who
ever flew on operations in either of the two world wars. "Before I
got back I was shivering so I could hardly land," he finished. "And
I haven't been feeling right since. My heart seems to be trying to
stunt all the time."

It is the great heart of *War Birds* that gives to Elliott Springs'
book the quality and the appeal of a classic. A few years after it
first appeared, T. E. Lawrence, who had been serving in the
R.A.F. for some eight or nine years by then, wrote to Elliott
Springs, describing it as "a permanent book and a real and
immortal part of our war with Germany. The British Air Force of

today is very grateful to you for 'War Birds,' and proud of having carried off, through your writing, so many of the spoils of war . . ."

By the time the Allied armies were on the move for what was to become our final advance, the Americans had already lost many of their pilots. These casualties occurred in their own squadrons which were serving with us, as well as among those who came to fly in our squadrons. Many were killed and others became prisoners-of-war; among the latter was Jake Stanley, another American air service pilot who had been sent to serve with British squadrons. Stanley was flying Bristol Fighters when he was shot down and taken to a German hospital. "It gives me a dizzy feeling every time I hear of the men that are gone," Elliott Springs wrote. "And they have gone so fast I can't keep track of them; every time two pilots meet it is only to swap news of who's killed."

Most of the pilots and observers who survived the war managed, after a reasonable period of time, to regain their equilibrium; but there were quite a few who were never again the same as a result of their experiences. That is also true of the air crews of the second war. But whichever way we went, all of those who flew under the stress of war will understand what Elliott Springs meant—and he was no weakling—when he stated at the end of the book:

I'm all shot to pieces. I only hope I can stick it. I don't want to quit. My nerves are all gone and I can't stop. I've lived beyond my time already.

It's not the fear of death that's done it. I'm still not afraid to die. It's this eternal flinching from it that's doing it and has made a coward out of me. Few men live to know what real fear is. It's something that grows on you, day by day, that eats into your constitution and undermines your sanity. I have never been serious about anything in my life and now I know that I'll never be otherwise again. But my seriousness will be a burlesque for no one will recognize it. Here I am, twenty-four years old, I look forty and I feel ninety.

After the war this more serious frame of mind led Elliott Springs to make a great success of being a writer, for all the opposition that came from his wealthy father. He published several other books about wartime flying that were quite good, although none of them came up to the high standard of *War Birds*. Then he settled down to a career in his family's business: the Springs Cotton Mills of South Carolina. He also made a great success of that, the more spectacular side of which is reflected in his last book, *Clothes Make The Man.* Only Elliott Springs would have thought of adding to the book the subtitle *How to Put the Broad in Broadcloth.*

Elliott Springs served during the Second World War with the United States Army Air Force as a colonel in command of a station in North Carolina. His son, Leroy, joined the U.S. Air Force while still a freshman at Princeton University, and he qualified as a pilot and was completing the training of his bomber crew when the Second World War ended. In May, 1946, Leroy Springs and another pilot were flying in a B.T.13, an American aircraft, towing a glider in which his father and another man were riding. They were only three hundred feet off the ground when something went wrong—it was never determined just what happened—and the aircraft towing the glider crashed, caught fire, and was burned out. The glider cut loose in time, but it also crashed with minor injuries to the two occupants. Leroy Springs was killed. "It was a pretty harrowing experience for any father to have to witness," Elliott Springs' widow, Frances Springs, commented some years later.

When Colonel S. B. Horn—the Nigger Horn who figures so prominently in *War Birds,* and who knew so well the three musketeers of the book—heard of the death of Elliott Springs in 1959 he said: "I think, without reservation, he was one of the bravest men I ever met, a brilliant pilot and staunch friend. His sense of humour and light-heartedness were legendary." In saying that, Horn spoke for all of us. That legend, for which we must thank the Americans, was to play a part in the forming of the tradition of the Royal Air Force that was not unimportant.

14 / Onslaught

NOT ALL THOSE who flew in fighters in the First World War worked in the broad light of day. As happened in the second war, there were a few specialists of rather different temperament who worked better in the dark, and they became the pioneers in fighting at night, particularly during the last few months of the war. Very little had been discovered about the way in which we should tackle the enemy bombers at night, although one squadron, No. 151, had been formed and equipped with Camels, which were painted black, with the sole object of exploring the best methods to employ against these night raiders.

By that summer of 1918 the pilots of No. 151 Squadron were tackling the Gothas and the Giants of the German Air Force that came prowling around at night. The latter was an enormous aircraft with five engines and a crew of nine. The squadron did very well, and in only five months they shot down twenty-six German bombers without suffering a single casualty. Two of the bombers they shot down were destroyed on the night of the raid on our airfield at Bertangles.

One of the great difficulties about night fighting has always been to get into the right place and the right position to start looking. Without some assistance in that, the pilot is pretty helpless. It was not until some time after the start of the second war that we found the answer, and it came during the time when we were having to combat the heavy bombing of the night blitz. We had learned by then that it was impossible to intercept any enemy bomber at night with only the naked eye unless there was a good moon above the horizon. The answer came in the form of airborne radar.

But in the summer of 1918 we had no aids whatsoever, and we had to rely solely on our own eyesight. In our night flying we had not even been able to work out any satisfactory methods of making full use of the light of the moon. The main target that the German bombers were aiming at then, on our part of the Front, was Amiens, and since our airdrome, which was well known to the

250

Germans, was only a few miles away, we also received their attention.

The persistence of these German attacks became annoying, so we in No. 84 Squadron decided to try our hand at shooting down these intruders. My squadron was neither equipped nor trained for night flying, but I thought that if we could get into the air about half past three in the morning, and if we were prepared to stay up for about an hour or so, we might be able to catch the German bombers as they were returning from Amiens. We would also have at least the first light of dawn to help us land back again at our own airdrome. Getting off in the dark was simple enough; landing was another matter altogether.

We had first tried out this plan as early as the middle of May. The squadron records have a somewhat stilted entry about the first patrol stating: "The squadron was very early astir. Three S.E.5's headed by Major Sholto Douglas ascended at 0325 with the object of intercepting enemy bombers bound for Amiens." Beauchamp-Proctor was with me that morning, and what was not so stilted was his complaint about being blinded by "a convergence of search-lights." This was a complaint that I was to hear only too frequently from my pilots in Fighter Command in the second war. Our intention was good, and our execution of the plan went well enough; but we day fighters in our S.E.5's were never able to intercept any of the German night bombers.

Just before the deaths of Jimmy McCudden and Mick Mannock, the Germans had started introducing on the Western Front a new fighter, the Fokker D VII, a single-seater biplane fitted with a new B.M.W. engine—a name that will give the pilots of the second war cause to reflect. It was one of the best airplane engines produced by either side up to that time. Fortunately for us, one of these new Fokkers was captured intact not long after it first appeared, and we were able to try it out against our own S.E.5. I was one of those who flew it, and we found that our own machine was a shade faster in level flight, by about two or three miles an hour, but it did not have such a good rate of climb. The Fokker D VII was also slightly more maneuverable than the S.E.5, but we still had an advantage in being able to pick up speed more quickly in a dive.

The new German fighter was not a particularly attractive-looking aircraft, but it was a very good machine for those times. We found it a much tougher opponent than the Albatros and the Pfalz scouts or even the Fokker triplane, against which we had been fighting for the past few months. This stiffer opposition from

the enemy was quickly noted by our wing and brigade commanders, and they started planning to use even larger formations
of fighters. Holding the views that I did, these new plans were very
much to my liking. The rise in our casualties which had started
with the appearance of the D VII was checked, and our own
successes began to pick up again.

The offensive patrols that we flew out over the Somme during
the summer of 1918 were hardly ever executed by less than several
squadrons working in formation. Only when the weather was such
that the maneuvering of any large formations of aircraft was
difficult or impossible did we fly in smaller formations, and then
one flight would be sent out with a roving commission. But on
many occasions we were able to stage patrols made up of two and
three squadrons—up to fifty aircraft—flying some distance over
enemy territory. The S.E.5's would fly at fifteen to seventeen
thousand feet, with the Bristol Fighters (which were good in both
attack and defense and were thus able to protect the rear of the
whole formation) flying at up to about eighteen thousand feet.

It became the custom about this time—at any rate, in the wing
to which my squadron belonged—for the bombers to be escorted
by fighters. The targets for the bombers were never more than
twenty to thirty miles behind the enemy lines. Although I believed
generally in fighter escorts for the bombers, I thought that such
close escorts were often unnecessary. Quite adequate protection
for the bombers could have been provided by a careful arrangement of offensive patrols with the fighters left free to attack the
enemy as and when they found it convenient, and under conditions
which were of their own choosing. A fighter squadron tied rigidly
to escort duty was rather like a boxer fighting with one hand tied
behind his back: he could not freely accept any opportunities
presented for attacking his opponent because his one free hand
was employed solely in defending himself. On close escort duty all
that we, the fighters, could do was to wait until the enemy
launched their attacks, and then do our best to parry them.

Soon after we started on this escort work I came to the conclusion that for these short-range operations the bomber formations—which were made up of machines with a good performance
flown by pilots who could operate in close formation and manned
with observers who could shoot straight—could fight by themselves very successful defensive actions even against superior
numbers of enemy fighters. It was, of course, entirely different
from the type of operation in the Second World War when the
American bombers operated from England in daylight. They had

to fly great distances to get to their objectives, and they needed all
the protection that their fighter escorts could give them.

There was one occasion in the middle of July, 1918, when I
wished fervently that we could have been let off the leash. It was a
good example of the way in which the planners were taking double
precautions in protecting the aircraft doing the bombing, while at
the same time wasting the time of the fighters. Wing headquarters
ordered a raid on the German airdrome at Foucaucourt, the way
to which was indicated by the perfectly straight road that runs due
east from Amiens to St-Quentin. By air it was less than thirty miles
away, and the instructions given to the five squadrons involved
were that they should carry out "the destruction of hangars and
machines and the infliction of as many casualties as possible."

We set out, three of the five squadrons coming from Bertangles,
with the S.E.5's providing the fighter escort for the Camels which
were to do the bombing and ground strafing. On this occasion I led
the fifteen S.E.5's of No. 84 Squadron. The fighters were stepped
upward in the sky to a height of about eighteen thousand feet. In
many ways the whole operation was a forerunner of the fighter
sweeps that we were to stage over northern France in the second
war twenty-three years later.

When we arrived over the airdrome at Foucaucourt, the Camels
dived down on their targets, dropping their bombs and generally
shooting up everything within sight. My job was to keep my
squadron up as top cover for the escort, and we sat up there
watching the havoc being caused by the attacking Camels. I saw
two direct hits by bombs on some hangars and at least six more
hits on various huts, and I saw a Fokker biplane on the ground
demolished by another direct hit.

During all this I was keeping a sharp lookout for German fighters
because I fully expected that the Huns would be stirred up enough
to try and retaliate by jumping on those low-flying Camels. But for
once not a single Hun appeared. Even archie was pretty innocuous, high up, because the German gunners were paying most of
their attention to the squadrons lower down. I had rather looked
forward to being able to leap on the Huns, since we were at the
top of the escort, with my squadron packed in behind me. When
none appeared I longed to go off and find them. But there we had
to stay, high up and looking on, just waiting.

That was the first precaution that had been taken in protecting
the Camels. The second, I realized later, was in the choice of the
timing of the raid. It was deliberately staged at an hour when all
the Germans, being the methodical people that they are, would be

at their lunch; and apparently that included the German fighter pilots. Shortly afterward it was realized that it was a waste of time and effort for the fighters to engage in close escort duty on such short-range raids, and the practice was discontinued.

Another aspect of the work in the air over the actual battlefields that was of particular concern to the fighters was the extensive use made throughout the war of large numbers of observation balloons. These floated from the cables by which they were tethered on both sides of the lines. As the need arose, they could be raised and lowered quite rapidly. They were of great value in providing a means for seeing what was going on, but the occupation of the observers who worked with them was a decidedly hazardous one. It was also an almost equally dangerous experience for those of us whose job it was to try to shoot them down. Balloon-busting came to be a fair part of every fighter pilot's experience; and there were even a few who preferred it to all other forms of activity. The Americans had one pilot—described by Larry Callahan as "that cock-eyed boy who would go out all by himself and take on the whole goddamned German air force any time anybody wanted, and he got killed doing it"—who specialized in destroying balloons. His name was Frank Luke, but he was better known as the "Balloon Buster," and his activites won for him the Congressional Medal of Honor. His spectacular career on the Western Front lasted only seventeen days, which, even by the standards of the worst time we went through, was short enough. There were occasions when he destroyed two and three balloons in a day. One of the outstanding specialists in the R.A.F. was Beauchamp-Proctor, who eventually destroyed sixteen balloons.

These tethered balloons had baskets suspended from them, in which the observers worked; and for protection from attack they relied on antiaircraft fire from guns and machine guns, and on patroling fighters. These all provided reasons enough why it was not as easy to attack balloons as might be expected. We were always experimenting and trying out new and safer methods of attacking them. It was never easy to get through their defenses in the first place; and it was quite often just as difficult to set the wretched thngs on fire. Many pilots had the disappointing experience of pumping tracer ammunition into the envelope after diving on it only to see the tracer go straight through with no fire starting up.

After a great deal of experience, we found that one had to get very close to the balloon, at a distance of fifty yards or even less, before firing with tracer and Buckingham incendiary ammunition, because no matter how good the shooting might be, the balloon rarely, if ever, caught fire if we opened up beyond that range. The state of the weather was also an important factor. If it was raining or the atmosphere was moist, it was almost impossible to set fire to the balloon.

In our attacks we tried out all sorts of different approaches before we found the one which was the most effective. If we dived from a good height onto the balloon as it was hauled down— which almost always happened when the enemy realized that we were about to attack—our angle of approach became steeper and steeper. In the end, it would become so steep that not only was good shooting difficult but, owing to the speed of the dive, one was in effective range of the target for only a very brief period. We found that the most effective method was to dive steeply to a point about a half a mile away from the balloon and level with it, and then to flatten out and go straight for it with all the added speed that we had picked up in the dive. At a range of two hundred yards we would take a sighting shot with our Vickers machine gun, and at fifty yards we would open up with the Lewis gun. We would carry straight on to within twenty yards of the balloon, firing all the time, and then hop over it and zoom away.

When the observers in the baskets of the balloons found themselves being attacked, they quite often got safely away in their special type of parachute. They were the only ones who had parachutes at that time. All the pilots and their observers had to fly without them because, I understood, there were none suitable for use in airplanes. I often wondered why some fairly ingenious scientist had not devised a free-falling parachute that could have been used in an aircraft. To put it mildly, it would have been a great comfort to us in those days to have had such a means of escape to rely on in emergencies, and it certainly would have saved many men from horrible deaths. It was not until only a couple of years ago that I learned to my disgust that the reason why we did not have them was an astonishing policy adopted during the First World War that deliberately denied us the use of parachutes.

In his Science Museum book *The Aeroplane,* the erudite historian Charles Gibbs-Smith gives a full account of the way the free-falling parachute had been developed and was in use in the United States well before the war broke out and even before the formation of the Royal Flying Corps in 1912. "That this device was not immediately and universally taken up is one of the deeper mysteries of aeronautical history," he states. He further says the official reason why aircraft personnel were not equipped with parachutes was that "pilots would be encouraged to abandon their machines." He describes this viewpoint as "disgraceful."

"There was no excuse whatever for not having produced a satisfactory pack parachute, the problems being relatively simple and already having been solved," Gibbs-Smith concludes. When I learned about that, and I thought about what we had had to endure and recalled how so many men had died in such agony—all because certain individuals had thought so little of us that they believed that providing us with parachutes would encourage us to abandon our aircraft—my anger was roused in a way that is unusual for me. It was indeed a "disgraceful" reason for arriving at such a contemptible decision.

The Germans were apparently slightly ahead of us in the use of the parachute. On my very last operational flight in France, two days before the end of the war, I saw a German pilot escape from his aircraft with the help of one. It was the only time I ever saw such a thing happen. We were operating as a squadron and just underneath a layer of cloud when, all of a sudden, we found ourselves by pure chance flying in formation behind a squadron of German fighters. Without wasting a second we all started shooting at a straggler at the rear of the formation, and we quickly set his aircraft on fire. The pilot jumped out, and a moment later I saw, to my astonishment, a little pink parachute open out. The pilot was attached to it, and he was floating safely down to earth.

Part of our routine work when we were on patrol was to watch over our own balloons. While doing that I became involved one day in a most unfortunate misunderstanding. I was leading the squadron when I spotted a balloon that was flying in a rather suspicious way almost slap over our front-line trenches. I could not make out at first whether it was one of ours or a German, so I went down to take a closer look. I saw that it was one of our own, and satisfied with that identification I sheered off. But a few moments later, when I looked over my shoulder, I was horrified to see the balloon going down in flames. I turned back and dived at top speed toward it, and when I got closer, I saw a German fighter sneaking back very low down over the enemy lines.

By that time I was over the spot where our balloon lay blazing on the ground, and as I pulled out of my dive I lost sight of the enemy fighter. I turned and flew out over Hunland searching for it, but I could not find it, so I continued with my patrol. When I got back from that and landed at my airfield I was told that the leader of an S.E.5 squadron had shot down one of our balloons, and that there was more than a suspicion at wing headquarters that I was the culprit. To make matters worse, the observer shot down was Lieutenant-Colonel W. F. MacNeece, the commander of the local balloon wing, and he was badly injured when he had had to bail out at a low altitude.

I realized at once what must have happened. The German fighter had sneaked out very low over his own front-line trenches, and he had popped up just long enough to shoot down our balloon. When I appeared a few seconds later diving like a madman over the burning balloon in pursuit of the Hun our people on the ground somewhat naturally thought that I had shot it down. They promptly reported that, and from then on there had been trouble in store for me. Fortunately the fact that my guns had not been fired at all on that particular patrol proved my innocence; but it was not until I produced a certificate to that effect from my squadron armament officer that I was able to clear my name at wing headquarters.

I went over to the local hospital to see poor MacNeece, who was in bed with a bad concussion. I did my best to assure him that I was not the one who had shot him down, and I explained to him how the misunderstanding had come about. But he was in no fit state to be able to take in what I was saying, and for years afterward he went on believing that I was the one responsible for this unhappy incident. It was not until we were serving at the Air Ministry together in the middle 1920's that I was able to sort the matter out with him, although even now I am not altogether certain that Air Vice-Marshal MacNeece Foster (as he later became) was ever really convinced by my arguments that I did not shoot him down on that summer day in 1918.

On the Front well to the south of us, which was held by the revitalized French Army reinforced by the gathering might of the Americans, the Germans had made one last bid in the middle of July for a breakthrough, but they were repulsed. Hard on the heels of that was launched the start of what became almost continuous Allied offensives. The French attacked on their front, with the newly arrived Americans joining in, and the thrust against the Germans started there spread up the line to the north. By the first week in August we who were on the Front around Amiens were poised and ready to make our attack.

When the opportunity came, after the war, to make a sober study of the events of the last three months of the fighting in France, it became quite clear to the historians that the day the

German High Command realized that the war was lost was August 8, 1918. On that day we caught the Germans completely by surprise, threw them off balance, and started our advance. If I had been fortunate, from a professional point of view, in being able to participate in all the major actions on the Western Front up to that time, then I was even more fortunate, for a variety of reasons, in being where I was when we started that final advance.

One of the main reasons for our success was the very efficient secrecy of our planning. We had heard about what was happening to the south of us, and we knew by the end of July that something was afoot; but diversions and other camouflage fooled the Germans about what we were up to. Our attack was launched with a Canadian-Australian spearhead on a front of about fourteen miles, and we who were flying from Bertangles in support of it were on the left prong of that spearhead.

During the afternoon of August 7, just before the attack, all squadron commanders were able to brief their air crews about what was going to happen; and I was able to tell my own pilots, from a memorandum prepared by our brigade commander, something of the plan of the battle that was to be fought. Of this unusual advantage the official air historian has said: "This appears to be one of the few occasions so far as can be judged from the official records when a formal considered attempt was made to take the pilots and observers into the confidence of the General Staff."

Zero hour was twenty minutes past four in the morning, an hour before sunrise. Our bombardment of the enemy positions east of Amiens was followed immediately by the tanks and the infantry moving forward. As had happened on March 21—when the Germans had started their advance against us—there was a thick ground mist, and although this was of great value as a screen for the troops on the ground, we who were to support them in the air between the River Somme and Villers-Brettoneux were of no use until about nine o'clock. But as soon as we were able to get into the air we found that the Germans had been caught completely by surprise and were in a fine state of confusion. We also had overwhelming superiority over the German Air Force. The 5th Brigade of the R.A.F. on our short stretch of the Front had in it eight fighter squadrons in additon to nine squadrons doing other work: a total of 332 airplanes.

The main targets for the R.A.F. were the bridges across the River Somme. As soon as the enemy realized what we were up to they rushed in reinforcements in the air, and at last the German pilots were forced to give battle by going on to the attack. It is only fair to record that they fought very hard.

The Richthofen Circus itself was brought into the thick of things; but just before the opening of our offensive, Hermann Goering, who was in command, had gone on leave, handing command over to Lothar von Richthofen, the younger brother of the founder of the squadron. A few days later young Richthofen was wounded, and his place was taken by Ernst Udet, who was to remain in command until Goering returned from leave a couple of weeks later. We were up against many tough, seasoned fighters.

The vigorous attacks made by our aircraft on the bridges crossing the River Somme were not as successful as we had hoped for, and the Royal Air Force suffered heavy losses. For one thing, the German fighter airdromes were close by these bridges, and in some cases within sight of them, and our bombing aircraft were pounced upon as soon as they appeared. The bridges themselves were the bottlenecks of the enemy lines of retreat, and the Germans had to keep them intact or perish. The pilots of the German Air Force, I must admit, showed no reluctance to sacrifice their lives in their efforts to keep them open.

After four days of heavy fighting the first stage of the advance—the Battle of Amiens—was completed just short of the devastation of the battlefield of two years before. The first objective had been achieved: Amiens, the important rail center, was safe from enemy artillery fire. Ten days were to pass in a lull before the Second Battle of the Somme opened up and we were called upon to help our Army and support its further advance. Hermann Goering had by then returned from leave to resume command of the Richthofen Circus, but they had already, in the words of our official history, "been fought almost to destruction."

At the time when that history was written (1937), H. A. Jones was concerned only with the part that Goering had played in the air in the First World War. Comparing him with Richthofen, Jones wrote of Goering that he was "a leader of proved worth," and that he "was possibly gifted with a temperament more offensive in quality than that of his predecessor." This remark was obviously not intended as it could now be interpreted. From my own experience of meeting the Richthofen Circus and Goering in the air at that time, I would go further than Jones did and say that it was Goering's lack of caution that led to his squadron being finally decimated. He was brave enough and dashing enough, and he appeared, even then, rather to relish having his back to the wall.

It was the custom of the Germans, particularly in the Richthofen Circus, to allow each pilot to have his aircraft painted in striking and variegated colors of his own selection. The object of this, I can only assume, was to intimidate us. We had a standard and rather drab khaki color for all our aircraft, with R.A.F. roundels and red, white and blue stripes on our rudders. If the enemy thought that they were frightening us with their fanciful color schemes they were entirely wrong. With the ribaldry that was so much a part of our humor, we merely made even ruder remarks about our opponents. At the same time we used their color schemes as a means of identifying them. Richthofen's aircraft were all painted a solid scarlet; and Goering adopted, as far as I can remember, green and purple, one color for the fuselage and the other for the wings.

During those last days of August, 1918, I encountered Goering quite a few times in the air, chasing him around the sky when he was not chasing me. But neither of us was ever able to get his gunsights on the other, even though Goering had a score of twenty-two destroyed to his credit and had been awarded the Pour le Mérite. Whatever his subsequent crimes, Goering as a young man was undoubtedly a brave and good fighter pilot. I have wondered many times to what extent the course of history might have been changed if, in one of our encounters in the air at this time, I had managed to draw a bead on him long enough to finish him off. It would have saved the world, and me, a lot of trouble many years later.

In the lull between the Battle of Amiens and the resumption of the fighting across the desolation of the Somme which became known as the Battle of Bapaume, our wing commander issued a statement of policy that was both very sensible and human. In it he called to our attention the role that the fighters were to play. "After the first rout of the enemy a time comes when he will organise his defence and our progress will slow down," he stated. "This is a time when low-flying scouts must be sparingly employed, and then only on reliable information. Indiscriminate low-flying must cease at this period, or casualties will be excessive . . . the physical powers of the pilots must be taken into consideration, as no pilot can stand an excessive strain of low-flying."

For a week during the end of August and the beginning of September the battle raged across the Somme. By this time the Front had also been exploding to the north as well as to the south of us, and the general advance of the Allies along the whole Front was well underway. The Germans had been tough opponents for a long time, and any advances that our armies had made—when they were made—had been negligible. But now the enemy was close to being in full retreat, and it was the speed with which the Germans were collapsing that rather surprised me.

The weather was fair, and at times during the day it was really hot. Our targets were easy to see and to hit, while the enemy's antiaircraft defenses were disorganized through being constantly on the move. Again, but this time in a reverse movement, the Germans became demoralized by the low-flying attacks that were hurled at them by our aircraft.

But we who were doing the actual flying were not the only ones in the Royal Air Force who were being worked hard. In the records of No. 84 Squadron there is a comment that I wrote which provides a revealing picture of the conditions that our hard-pressed ground crews were having to put up with. "It was quite common during this period," I stated, "for mechanics to get no more than two full nights' sleep a week eked out with an occasional nap when their machines were in the air."

For all the hard fighting, there was by now in our minds a much surer note of success; and with the beginning of this second stage of the advance, Douglas Haig issued to all commanders instructions that contained an indication of that note. "Risks which a month ago would have been criminal to incur ought now to be incurred as a duty," he stated. "It is no longer necessary to advance in regular lines and step by step as in 1916–17 battles."

At the end of August there came the ferocious assault by the Australians on Mont St-Quentin and Péronne, which led to the capture of the last natural commanding position left to the Germans. Mont St-Quentin is a rounded hill two miles to the north of Péronne. It dominates all the surrounding country, and it had to be captured; but the Germans had turned it into a gigantic fortification, and their crack troops were under orders to hold it at all costs. We watched from the air as the Australians under the command of General Monash fought their way up to it; and the result was the spectacular success which earned for them the right to name Mont St-Quentin as one of their finest achievements during the First World War.

Opposite us the Germans retreated to the last great stronghold of their fortifications: the Hindenburg Line itself. During all this time my squadron was still based at Bertangles, but we had already started using advanced landing fields to the east, right up behind the troops at the Front. For a few days we worked from a

field at Proyart, about a mile or so from the airdrome which had
been used by the Germans at Foucaucourt and which we had
attacked in a heavy raid only a short time before. We would fly up
to these advanced fields at dawn, and then go about the day's work
on orders from our wing headquarters. In the evening we would
return to Bertangles.

A few days after the capture of Mont St-Quentin and Péronne,
at the end of August and the beginning of September, five aircraft
of my squadron made a patrol that has since been offered as an
outstanding example of the flying that we were all doing at this
time. Led by Beauchamp-Proctor, our S.E.5's took part in a low
reconnaissance over the German lines. After completeing that task,
Beauchamp-Proctor took his flight farther into enemy territory and
flew over Roisel, a few miles to the east of Péronne. From a height
of about a thousand feet he noticed that there was very little road
movement and only slight and inaccurate antiaircraft fire from the
Germans, so he went down to investigate. Flying fifty feet above
them he found only three small groups of the enemy; and although
the Germans fired at our aircraft with machine guns, our men
noticed that the Germans were not there in any strength.

Contour-chasing—or hedge-hopping, as it later came to be
called—at about twenty feet, Beauchamp-Proctor and the others
flew south along the German lines to Hancourt, and then on to
Mons-en-Chaussée, where they crossed the straight road that runs
due east from Amiens. They discovered that the trenches were
only lightly held by the enemy. When they were about a mile or so
to the north of the airfield at Flez, which we had used earlier in the
year, a German field gun opened fire at them, so they went to work
on it with their machine guns, destroying the crew.

Turning to the west, and still flying very low, Beauchamp-
Proctor then spotted an enemy machine-gun team waiting in a
sunken road for our advancing infantry. The flight attacked and
killed all the Germans. When Beauchamp-Proctor flew over our
troops, he was given an indication that there were more Germans
up ahead, so he led his flight down to only ten feet above the
ground, and they flushed some more of the enemy out of one of the
trenches. They attacked them and some more machine-gun nests
with their own machine guns, and that paved the way for our
infantry to move forward and capture the remaining Germans.

It is a far cry from the exuberance of the American book *War
Birds* to the stately dignity of the official history of the Royal Air
Force, known as *The War in the Air,* and it would scarcely be

thought that one could become linked with the other. But as we might have expected of him, Elliott Springs made such a step; in doing that, he had his name recorded in our history.

Just to the north of us, in support of the Third Army, an American squadron, the 148th, equipped with Camels, was serving as a part of the Royal Air Force. Elliott Springs had become a flight commander in that squadron under Mort Newhall, and he was trying hard to overcome his dislike of the Camel after having flown so much in the S.E.5. On the morning of September 2 the 148th Squadron and three of our R.A.F. squadrons tangled with a formation of German fighters. Offering the combat report written by Elliott Springs "as an example of its kind . . . of interest as showing British and American pilots in action together," the official history quotes:

At 11.45 A.M., with three machines I attacked four Fokker biplanes on the Arras-Cambrai road about four miles south-west of Haucourt. Three more came down out of the clouds and we were forced to withdraw. Seven more enemy aircraft came up from the north-east, and after some manœuvring I attacked another enemy aircraft south-east of the road, but we, in turn, were attacked by a large number. Succeeded in drawing enemy aircraft closer to our lines and went in again. Our top flight attacked from above us and a dogfight ensued. We were badly outnumbered. Took one enemy aircraft off tail of a "Camel" and was, in turn, attacked from above. Saw one enemy aircraft attack an R.E.8. and attacked him. Assisted by a Bristol attacked another enemy aircraft very low. We succeeded in preventing enemy aircraft from attacking R.E.8, and eventually drove them all east. Enemy aircraft finally disappeared in clouds over Cambrai. Very heavy clouds of 4–5,000 feet, but visibility good underneath. Fokker pilots very good, but poor shots. About 25 enemy aircraft seen.

One can only offer the approving comment that this combat report was written in the fashion typical of the man. Elliott Springs and George Vaughn—who left my squadron to become a flight commander in the 17th Squadron of the American air service, which was also equipped with Camels and was with us on our part of the Front—continued to fight alongside us and to add to their laurels. But just before the end of the war, both squadrons were taken away from us and sent to join the other American squadrons supporting the United States Army.

Away to the southeast of us, the Americans were engaged in hard fighting in the Argonne, and what was left of the Richthofen Circus was sent down there from our part of the Front. The Circus, which was still under the command of Hermann Goering, had suffered very heavy losses but continued to put up a good fight. However, Goering's men were then fighting in desperation, and this was something they had never done during their time under the command of Manfred von Richthofen.

There was never any question about the willingness of our old adversaries to go on fighting, and Ernst Udet and Hermann Goering—between whom no love was lost—and Goering's great friend Bruno Loerzer and a few others of the more case-hardened Circus pilots gave the Americans as severe a mauling as they received themselves. But the odds were overwhelming, for the German Air Force on the Western Front was now facing the full weight of the Royal Air Force, the rapidly expanding American air service, and the powerful French air force.

Throughout the war the French had produced aircraft and engines that, both in quality and in quantity, were a notable contribution to the war in the air. They also had the men to fly them, and the names of their great pilots—men such as René Fonck, Georges Guynemer, and Charles Nungesser, to name only three of the most successful—rank with the best airmen who emerged during the years between 1914 and 1918. We saw quite a lot of them during the war because they frequently worked alongside us.

The most successful of all the top-scoring Allied fighter pilots was René Fonck, who had learned to fly in the Caudrons at Le Crotoy two or three weeks before I was there in 1915. When the war ended he had to his credit seventy-five victories in the air, two more than Mannock. He was also the highest scoring of all the pilots on both sides who survived the war. But of more appeal to the public, largely because of the somewhat romantic figure that he presented, was Georges Guynemer, who had fifty-four victories, ranking next to Fonck among the French aces. I met Guynemer on several visits that I made to his squadron. He was a thin, delicate, intense young man whose health, never good, was, at the end, very poor. Guynemer refused to give up his flying, even after having achieved great fame as a fighter pilot, and eventually he was killed fighting over the Ypres Salient.

As happened with several other famous fighters, the exact way in which Georges Guynemer met his death is not known, and nothing was ever found of his aircraft or his body. The Germans claimed that they shot him down over their territory; that is all that is known about his death. On my visit to the Western Front in 1959 I went to the small village of Poelcapelle. It stands in the northeastern part of the old Salient, and it is said that over it Guynemer apparently met his death. In the center of this village (which was obliterated in the fighting of the first war) is a monument to him in the form of a tall column which has on the top of it a stork in flight, a reproduction of the well-known emblem of Guynemer's squadron. It is flying to the east.

In the course of the retreat the Germans had made on our part of the Front during the spring of the year before, when they had gone back to the immensely strong positions that they had prepared between Cambrai and St-Quentin, they had carried it out with an orderliness and a precision that had caught us by surprise. Now it was to be a very different story. They were being flung back, and we were poised in confident readiness before their last great line of fortifications. But the approaches to the Hindenburg Line, as we were able to see from the air, were still formidable: deep canal-trenches filled with water and wire that made the job of getting the tanks and the troops across immensely difficult, and acres upon acres of thick and impenetrable wire, and massive concrete and other earth fortifications of all descriptions and in great depth. It was up to the artillery to pave the way for the infantry, and they went about their task with a fury that was staggering.

On the evening of September 26, while all the attacks on the other parts of the Front were actually getting underway, a bombardment by our guns began on that part of the Fourth Army Front over which my squadron was flying. It was to last for fifty-four hours, and it was a stupendous operation, the scale of which only a view from the air could bring into anything approaching the right perspective. Then came the great moment that we in the Fourth Army had been waiting for. The spearhead of our attack was made up of English, Australian and American divisions, and the object was to smash through the solid defense system held by the Germans in their Hindenburg Line. The attack was launched at five-thirty on the morning of September 29 in fog following storms during the night. By the end of the day a great wedge had been driven into the German positions, and the enemy were forced into a large-scale retreat.

As soon as the mist and the smoke of the artillery bombardment cleared sufficiently for us to fly (around ten o'clock), we went to work carrying out the orders that we had received to destroy the enemy's observation balloons. The whole squadron set about the task, one flight making the actual attack while the two other flights stood by giving protection against intruders. It was as well that they were on guard, for no sooner was our attack launched on the balloons than ten Fokkers swooped down on us. As soon as that happened, down came the other two flights of my squadron. They kept the German fighters so busy that the pilots of the first flight were able to shoot down in flames five of the enemy balloons.

In this engagement one of the attacking Fokkers was shot down by us and it crashed in flames, but I lost one of my pilots, who was shot down from the ground and crashed behind the enemy lines. Of the five balloons destroyed that morning, Beauchamp-Proctor accounted for two, rapidly shooting down one after the other. In the afternoon we destroyed four more balloons, making our score for the day a total of nine.

Another part of the orders given to us stated: "If in course of a low-flying attack an enemy battery is encountered in action in the open, it will be justifiable to leave all in order to attack it: this should be particularly impressed." Since we had already become rather expert at this sort of attack, we set about carrying out that order also, although the weather was by then becoming increasingly difficult for flying, particularly in the mornings.

It was during this time that Beauchamp-Proctor's brilliant career on the Western Front was brought to a close. In a scrap in the air he was shot through the arm and was finally compelled to come off flying and return to England. He had been showing an extraordinary zest for attacking the enemy at any height and under any conditions, and in a manner that had become the talk of the Air Force. He had had only one spell of leave during the entire time that we had been in France—by then over a year—and he had always been most persistent in his wishes to remain with the squadron. For all his size, that little man had the guts of a lion.

Immediately after Beauchamp-Proctor was wounded and taken off flying, I proceeded, with the help of a few stiff drinks, to work myself into a sufficiently inspired mood to sit down and do justice to the writing of a recommendation that he be awarded a Victoria Cross. About three weeks after the Armistice, when I was also back in England, the *Gazette* announced that the V.C. had been awarded to him; and I then had the pleasant experience of reading in the citation the results of my efforts to express the very high regard that I had for Beauchamp-Proctor's prowess as a fighter pilot.

"In all he has proved himself conqueror over fifty-four foes, destroying twenty-two enemy machines, sixteen enemy kite balloons, and driving down sixteen enemy aircraft completely out of control," it stated. "Captain Beauchamp-Proctor's work in attacking enemy troops on the ground and in reconnaissance during the withdrawal following the battle of St. Quentin from March 21st, 1918, and during the victorious advance of our armies commencing on August 8th has been almost unsurpassed in its brilliancy, and as such has made an impression on those serving in his squadron and those around him that will not be easily forgotten."

In successfully and so rapidly smashing through the Hindenburg Line, the Fourth Army carried off the laurels of the whole advance. The night before that happened Ludendorff told his chief, Hindenburg, that it was obvious that the situation, as far as they were concerned, could only become worse, and that efforts must be made to obtain an armistice as a prelude to a peace offer. Hindenburg agreed with Ludendorff, and he informed his government that in order to save Germany from a catastrophe there must be an immediate armistice. But the politicians in Germany, although in agreement with the military leaders, took their time about finding the answer, and the fighting went on.

But it was fighting for which the Germans now had little stomach, although in the air we found that their pilots went about their business with resolution enough. The morale of the German Army was shattered by the reverses that they had suffered, and by the reports of the events that were happening on their own home front, where starvation and political chaos were rife. As every commander knows, if there is in the minds of those who have to do the actual fighting no longer any wish to fight, and no belief in what they are being told, then no brave words or grandiose planning will stir them to any action other than to rid themselves as quickly as possible of the confusion that is besetting them.

By early October, the length of the Front occupied by the Fourth Army was only about eight miles, and over that area nine single-seater fighter squadrons were operating. Of these, my squadron was one, and our instructions, stressed as "essential," were to fly offensive patrols to protect our reconnaissance and bomber aircraft. From early in the morning, whenever the weather permitted, formations of two and three squadrons went off together on patrol. Thick cloud from two thousand feet up helped the German pilots in the hit-and-run tactics which they were now having to employ. This thick cloud and the worsening weather meant that we were also called upon, whenever we were not part of the large offensive patrols, to do a great deal more low flying.

Owing to the rapidity of our advance and the bad weather, often with fog, communications between the Front and the various headquarters were strained, and repeatedly broken. Our Army commander was often left with no information about the positions of his forward troops. It was then that my squadron was able to be of help in a way that was later described by the official air historian as "a novel form of low reconnaissance," and in doing it we "adopted an ingenious plan."

Because of this need for information—and possibly because I was feeling more adventurous than usual—I went about working out my own special form of reconnaissance. The Corps squadrons had their hands full, so I invented for use under these conditions of bad weather and fog a method for locating the forward enemy positions. The mist was quite thick at times and the visibility was very limited, and in order to remain in sight of the ground I had to fly at heights of only two or three hundred feet.

On one occasion I brought my scheme into use when our troops were just in front of Le Cateau. Visibility was only about four hundred yards, and the cloud base was down to about three hundred feet. I took off and flew just above the treetops down the long, straight road that ran from north of St-Quentin to Le Cateau. There were three or four roads running out of Le Cateau to the east, and I flew along each of these in turn until I found myself being shot at from the ground, at which point I rapidly turned around. After marking on my map the spot where I had been fired at, I made my way back to Le Cateau and repeated the process along the other roads. Having collected this information, I then groped my way back to my own airdrome by contour-chasing with my map on my knee. When I got there and gave the information to our intelligence people they were able to join up the points that I had marked; and through that they were able to gain quite a fair picture of the location of the German front line.

Since the flying in this operation was both useful and exhilarating, I continued with it for several days. I rather flattered myself that through my long experience as a pilot I had become quite good at finding my way across country at very low altitude with visibility literally of only two or three hundred yards. It was mainly a question of following roads marked on my map: second turning to the left, turn right at the next crossroads, and so on. Le Cateau was not too difficult to find by this method, even in bad visibility. With that as my working base, it was simply a question of taking the right turnings.

It was for work of this nature, among other things, that I was awarded a Distinguished Flying Cross, the citation for which appeared in due course in the *Gazette* and read in a fashion that I felt was decidedly overgenerous. In placing it on record I hope that the fulsome reference made to me will be overlooked because I offer it as an official accounting of my squadron's success. It read:

A very gallant officer and brilliant leader to whose personal influence and example is mainly due the fine record of his Squadron which, since the 21st. 9. 17, has destroyed 201 and driven down out of control 149 aircraft. On the 17th, 18th and 19th October last, Major Douglas carried out most successful reconnaissances of the enemy front at exceptionally low altitudes (at times descending to twenty feet owing to dense cloud) and in face of intense hostile rifle and machine-gun fire.

During the last few weeks of the war all our flying was in weather that was difficult and at times downright bad. The Fourth Army was through the Hindenburg positions, and the Germans were retreating in ever increasing confusion; and by the beginning of the last week in October, they had reached a line that ran along the western edge of the large Forest of Mormal and, to the south of it, the Sambre Canal. We were very nearly back to the positions just to the south of Mons where the fighting had taken place at the beginning of the war over four years before.

Toward the end of October we had to leave our pleasant nest at Bertangles, where we had been based for the past six months, and I moved the squadron up to an airdrome which the Germans had been using at Bertry, about five miles to the west of Le Cateau. "Not a bad place," the squadron records state, "and we are all in good billets in the village." For the first time for months we had permanent roofs over our heads, and I was allotted the billet that had formerly been occupied by one of the German squadron commanders. We also took over the hangars on the airfield that had been built there by the Germans and which they had left intact.

A few days after we got settled in at Bertry I took off alone in my S.E.5. on what the squadron records described as an "aerial sentry." While flying low over the lines near Englefontaine, on the western side of the Forest of Mormal, I could see that a heavy artillery engagement was going on. From the gun flashes I judged that the Germans were hidden in some trees on the edge of the forest, so I flew over it at a height of fifteen hundred feet to see if I could find out just what was happening.

I was by then about three miles inside enemy territory, and suddenly three Fokker D VII's jumped on me. The squadron records state somewhat wryly: "Douglas at once turned west, put his nose down and contour chased back to our lines, kicking his rudder." I certainly did kick that rudder. It would have been committing suicide to have flown straight and level even for a few seconds with three of those dangerous Fokkers on my tail; and my contour-chasing was flying right down as near as I could get to the ground.

The three German pilots were all blazing away at me, but as we approached the lines two of them turned back. The third kept on attacking, even chasing me about a mile over our own side of the lines. Feeling that the odds were now more in my favor, I turned on him, whereupon the German smartly whipped around and started back over his own lines. My S.E.5 had it over the Fokker slightly in speed, and I was able to close in on him until we were only fifty yards apart. I then opened up with both my machine guns. I must have scored an immediate hit because the Fokker's nose went down and the machine crashed into a clearing near the far, eastern, edge of the forest. I did not hang about to make any more investigations, but simply turned away and, to repeat the expression that we used at that time, "contour-chased home."

On October 30, only a few days before the end, the German Air Force made an unexpectedly tough stand in their fight against us. It was a day of many hard combats with severe losses to both sides, and when the whole picture was assembled, we found that it was the most successful day that we had had, in terms of enemy aircraft destroyed, during the entire war. On the British front alone, sixty-seven German aircraft were destroyed, two of my own pilots contributing to that score.

Although one is compelled to quote them, mere statistics alone provide a somewhat lop-sided view of things; but it will, perhaps, give some idea of the scale of our operations on that day by comparing it with what happened on the famous day of September 15, 1940, which is now remembered as the climax of the Battle of Britain. That day in 1940 had a greater splendor; but October 30, 1918, saw heavier losses. On that Sunday in 1940 the Germans lost sixty aircraft: seven less than the number that they lost to us on the British Front alone on October 30, 1918. In the first war, the R.A.F. lost in action on that October day forty-one aircraft, with three pilots killed, eight wounded and twenty-six missing. The figures for September 15, 1940, were twenty-six fighters lost, with thirteen of our pilots killed.

On November 4, 1918, the Fourth Army launched its attack against the enemy positions along the Sambre Canal. After the morning mist cleared, our part in the air was fought with even increased intensity; but on that day the enemy resistance on the ground broke down completely, and all along the Front the German army fell back in an open and general retreat. In the words of Cyril Falls: "Everyone was marching." The whole of the Allied attack was on the move, eastward by us and northeastward toward the Ardennes by the Americans and the French. Our job in the air was to tackle the retreating columns of the enemy troops with bombs and machine guns, and they were only saved from what might have become a large-scale slaughter by the weather closing in again with rain and mist, thus hampering our flying.

The plight of Germany had become by then an impossible one, although there was not the utter chaos that marked that country's affairs on the home front at the end of the second war. Despite Ludendorff's appeals to Hindenburg over a month before for an armistice, the fighting had gone on, and Ludendorff had even changed his mind and gambled on trying to save the day. But his gamble failed, and late in October he resigned before he could be given the sack. At the same time came the mutiny of the German Navy at Kiel which sparked off a revolution that was to affect the whole of Germany. On October 30 the Turks signed an armistice; and on November 3 the Austrians did the same thing. On November 7 the German government named their delegates for discussions about an armistice; on November 9 revolution seized Berlin; and on November 11 came the Armistice. The fighting was brought to a halt. We had been at war on the Western Front for four years and three months.

Because of all that I had known and seen of the German Air Force during those long years of the war, it was impossible for me not to admire the way they conducted themselves at the time of their final defeat. They certainly went down fighting. The Richthofen Circus alone was still, as far as morale was concerned, a sound enough unit, even if it was greatly reduced in strength; and all the pilots fought well right up until three days before the end of the war. Then Hermann Goering received orders that they were to be demobilized; but since there was so much confusion and the orders could not be confirmed, he stood firm and waited.

When the Armistice was declared, Goering received further instructions to deliver his aircraft to the Americans. He refused to do that—although he surrendered readily enough to the Americans twenty-seven years later—and instead he flew the squadron back to Germany. But time had run out for the once deadly Circus, and Goering was forced to disband. With that, he and Ernst Udet—

who had a final score of sixty-two victories—and Bruno Loerzer and the others who had fought so well went their separate ways.

During the last week of what has been rather stupidly called the Kaiser's war, we were at work helping to chase the Germans back across the very same fields over which they had so successfully chased us in 1914. Then orders came through for me to return to England. I was to be promoted to the rank of lieutenant-colonel, and I was to take command of a flying wing at home. My successor arrived on November 8, and I spent the next two days handing over to him the squadron to which I had become so greatly attached.

The break that I was now making was not an easy one, and as I packed my gear and prepared to leave I found it hard to realize that the war upon which we had embarked with such light hearts and with such an anticipation of exciting adventures would all be over in a matter of a few hours. I recalled the spirit of four years before and the enthusiasm that had possessed us. I could not help comparing that with what we had been through, and of what we had come to know—those of us who had survived.

The years of the First World War provided us with an experience that was so extraordinary that it was impossible to understand immediately what it all meant, so profound that it was to alter the whole course of our lives. We had scarcely begun to know what living meant, but we knew all about dying; and for many the experience was so disturbing that it was to leave the deepest of scars. It is said of our experience that it was traumatic; but we who went through it have other names for it. We were young in years, and we had learned to present a front that was high-spirited and apparently carefree; but in other respects we were indeed old before our time.

My own feelings when the fighting came to a close were not so simple as to be able to think along just one line. In fact, I found those feelings decidedly mixed. Underneath them all, and in my case pretty deeply embedded because I am not by temperament given to showing my feelings, I was definitely tired and weary of war. It had been a long spell of strenuous physical and emotional experiences for which none of us had been prepared. I had been commanding fighter squadrons in the new realm of the air for the past two and a half years, since the age of twenty-two. Through commanding men in this hard way I had learned some very valuable lessons in leadership.

By the end of the war I was a pretty good pilot, and I was

definitely keen on flying; and I was going off on promotion to command a wing. I was twenty-four years of age, nearly twenty-five, and I had been awarded a Military Cross, a Distinguished Flying Cross, and a French Croix de Guerre, and I had been mentioned in Dispatches three times. But about the future, my own future, I found that I was doubtful and even vague. I did not seem to be able to feel the enthusiasm or the interest that I had expected would come with the ending of the war.

I left the airfield at Bertry on the morning of November 10, and, traveling via Boulogne, I arrived back in London that evening. As soon as I got there I rang up my favorite girl friend and we dined together at the Comedy Restaurant in Panton Street. For us that was the start of the celebrations that were to explode with the signing of the Armistice. The next morning I slept later than I intended. When I awoke it was to hear the shouting and cheering of the crowds swarming through the streets as they rejoiced over the coming of the Armistice at eleven o'clock on that morning of November 11, 1918.

At last the war was over. With that, the lid that had contained our emotions flew off with an almighty bang. The scenes in London on that first night of peace almost beggar description; it seemed to me that nearly everybody was drunk either from the drinks that flowed so freely or from an immense sense of relief that caused people to give vent so wildly to their feelings.

15 / Hand of Chance

THERE WERE enough aspects of the Great War of 1914–18—man's first war in the air—to give everybody reason to feel perplexed over what happened. Ever since that time people of all types and ages have been asking questions about those calamitous years. But discussion and sober examination have not led a tapering off of all the controversy that has been stirred up; instead there has come with the passing of time an increasing general interest, or curiosity, in the course that history took during that early part of the century, plus a deep desire to know what went wrong in the affairs that affected all our lives.

It was so much more than just something "going wrong." That war was in many ways a new kind of war. Methods of waging it were employed that were new; and for perhaps the first time, people were more generally informed about what was happening. There was openly revealed the astonishing distrust that existed between those who were supposed to be working side by side— between the political and the military minds, for instance—and over so many issues there came to light a state of astonishing muddle and confusion. Of more importance even than that was the way life as we had known it had disintegrated in a curiously silent fashion—for all the noise of the war—leaving us in a void of bewilderment.

I was far from being alone in my difficult frame of mind. There can be few who have returned from the wars after actual participation in them for any length of time who have not been thrown off balance in some way or other by what they went through. Those who had known, as I had, the intensity of the experience of having to find out what fighting in the air meant and demanded of us were in a state of mind that even we could not fully understand. In my own case, I was by no means approaching exhaustion, but I was, I realize now, in a confused and unhappy state.

A great deal has been written over the years about the conditions of the minds of those who returned from the Great War, and it must be difficult for many of the younger people of today to understand why there was so much distress. The overall answer to that is to be found, I think, in the fact that we had lost so much. The whole way of life we had only just discovered before August, 1914, had changed so completely. Whether one approved of that life or not is beside the point. When we returned home we found conditions that were very different from what we had expected they would be. We did not know where or how to make the adjustments that were going to have to be made if we were to fit in. Some never did adapt themselves, and for the rest of their lives they were misfits. At least I was spared that, although for a while I felt that I was at loose ends in a way that was not at all to my liking.

On my return to England I was given a couple of weeks' leave, which I put to good if somewhat exhausting use in what seemed to be an endless round of celebrations; then, in a state of depletion in every sense of the word, I took myself off to my new job at the airdrome at Cranwell, in Lincolnshire. Just over a year later, this was to become the site of what is now the Royal Air Force College. It had been established by the Navy early in 1916, and during the war a large number of naval officers had been trained there as pilots for the Royal Naval Air Service.

By the end of 1918 the airdrome at Cranwell had become a very large station of over three thousand acres in area. It was under the command of a colonel in the Royal Air Force who was still referred to as "the Captain." He was, in fact, an ex-naval captain. The whole atmosphere of the place was strongly impregnated with the influence of the Navy, and a large proportion of the officers and men still wore naval uniforms. Whenever any of the men talked about leave, they asked for permission to go ashore, and the R.A.F. tender which took the men going on leave to the nearest railway station was known to everybody as "the liberty boat."

In the wing which I had under my command were three flying training schools at Cranwell and a fourth at Digby, some ten miles away. One of the instructors on my staff was Charles Steele, who had spent the past four months in the hospital recovering from injuries he had received in the bombing at Bertangles. Since I had in my wing a school for the training of pilots in flying the Handley Page bomber, the twin-engined 0/400, Steele and I decided that we fighter pilots should broaden our experience. So we went about learning to fly the much bigger aircraft. Although at first we found its enormous size a little staggering, we came after a while to handle the 0/400 competently enough, and we did quite a little flying in it together.

The history of the Handley Page 0/400 is a short but important one, and after my long experience of fighters it came to play an unexpectedly interesting role in my life. First introduced into service with the Royal Naval Air Service in April, 1917, it was the one standard heavy bomber used by our Air Force in the First World War. It was flown by five squadrons of what was called the Independent Force, which had been created in May, 1918, and placed under the command of Boom Trenchard after he had resigned from the post of Chief of the Air Staff. His aircraft carried out the long-range bombing of strategic objectives, and it had been intended that he should have under his command French, Italian and American squadrons as well as those of the Royal Air Force. As Commander-in-Chief, he was given, in the words of the official historian, "full control of the tactical employment of his force."

This rather vague name given to Trenchard's force was not a good one. It is little wonder that it caused the French to view its establishment with some concern, and one of their generals to ask of whom it was intended to be independent. "Of God?" the Frenchman is said to have demanded. Knowing Trenchard as I did, I should imagine that the question rather tickled his sense of humor. In fact, his force came under the direct orders of General Foch, the Supreme Commander.

The Handley Page 0/400 was a good airplane, a large twin-engined biplane. Even if its speed was only a shade under eighty miles an hour, it had an endurance in the air of eight hours. Its use in the Independent Force was solely for strategic bombing, which made of that force the forerunner of Bomber Command as we later came to know it. Trenchard had been working hard for a strong bomber policy, and from the time that the force first came into existence, in the summer of 1918, until the end of the war, its main objective was the same as the later command: the heavy bombing of targets in Germany itself.

The period right after the end of the war was a generally unhappy time for most of those in the services. The Armistice had been signed, and although technically that did not mean that peace had come, it was enough for the men to feel that the war was over. They could see no reason why they should not be demobilized and allowed to get back to their lives and their work as civilians. But that was not the view of the Government, which appeared to believe that the armed forces should remain in being until the peace treaty was actually signed and ratified. Some time passed before plans for the demobilization of the services were produced, and when they became known they appeared to contain anomalies which only led to the men's feeling that they were being treated very unfairly. Discontent soon became rife, and there were mutinies at several Air Force stations.

When this disaffection struck at Cranwell, it caught me in a mood for strong action, and action I took. One morning the men refused to appear on parade, some even skulking in their huts. I harangued them and reminded them of their duty, telling them that I would do my best to help get a move on with their demobilization. And then I suddenly remembered that there was to be a pay parade that afternoon. How legal a step it was from the point of view of military law I did not know, but I told them that if they did not appear on parade that afternoon they would not get their pay. No doubt it seemed to them to be rough justice, but it won the round for me. They appeared on parade, and they continued to parade without any further trouble.

But the men were not the only ones who were discontented. There were persistent and ugly rumors about the future of the Service itself, and many of the officers were also wondering what was going to happen to them. No plan had yet been produced for the establishment of regular officers through the granting of permanent commissions in the new Royal Air Force. When I considered my own case, I had to admit to myself that I felt doubtful about being able to appreciate Service life in time of peace; that, plus the reaction that had set in after my long period of active service, only added to my own unhappy frame of mind.

This general reaction was possibly the most difficult to cope with in all the problems that confronted me. Life now seemed to be so dull and uninspiring. I was restless and did not seem to be able to bring my thoughts to settle constructively on anything in the way of plans for the future. I thought about going back to Oxford and trying to complete my work there for a degree. My other brother, Bobbie, had served throughout the war in the Royal West Kent Regiment in India and Mesopotamia, and he was a captain at the end of it. As soon as he could get out of the army he took up his Classical Scholarship at Christ's College, Cambridge, with the intention of getting his degree and trying for the Indian Civil Service. Gordon Alchin, my closest friend from my schooldays, had survived the war as a pilot and had been awarded an Air

Force Cross, and he went back to Brasenose, at Oxford, to continue working for his degree in law.

Others who had been through even more strenuous and disturbing experiences than I had known were making their plans for a return to civilian life. I knew that they were right in what they were doing; but having been a fighter pilot and for so long in command of squadrons in action I felt quite incapable of settling down to an academic life and of studying again as an undergraduate. But I was faced with the necessity of having to earn a living, and it was imperative that I make up my mind about what I was going to do.

Those serving in the Royal Air Force who had been regular officers in the Royal Navy and the Army could but wait with patience for confirmation of their appointments in the new service —and let it be recorded that the patience of some of them was very sorely tried. Fortunately for the Air Force and its future, Boom Trenchard was reappointed Chief of the Air Staff in February, 1919. It was a shrewd move brought about by Winston Churchill, who had become Secretary of State for War and for Air only a few weeks before. Together they set about the tremendous task of organizing the permanent Royal Air Force.

But for all the effort that Trenchard made to hold together the Service about which he felt so deeply, it was very nearly bled to death. In the House of Commons in March, 1919, there were introduced the Air Estimates for the coming year. They gave the first peacetime establishment for the Royal Air Force, and that filled many of us with feelings of despair. At the end of the war the Air Force had consisted of 30,000 officers and 300,000 other ranks. This was to be cut to a strength of 5,300 officers and 54,000 men. Most of those who had been in the Air Force wanted to get back to their lives as civilians, but there were still many who wanted to stay on in the new Service and make a career out of it as professional airmen. But such ruthless surgery, performed in the way that it was, caused a great deal of apprehension.

As with so many of my friends, the only real qualifications that I could claim and which might help me to earn a living were in flying. I was still keen enough about that, and about airplanes and aviation in general; but there was something about the prospects of Service life in peacetime that did not appeal to me. I thought about it all a great deal, and I worried about it, and then there came to my mind an idea that, I felt, might provide an answer. Why not become a civil pilot?

There was not much doubt in the minds of those who could see beyond their noses that aviation, after the boost that it had received during the war, was something with a future in it. Here was a chance for me to get in on the ground floor. I was young, and I felt the need for more than just a routine occupation, to use a drab but fitting word. As I thought about the future, it seemed to me that the one job that showed promise of having some zest in it was that of a test pilot. I started trying to make some plans, and I wrote and asked several aircraft manufacturers if they had any vacancies. There was some interest expressed, and at one stage I very nearly got a job as a test pilot with Blackburns, but at the last moment it fell through.

Shortly after that I heard one day that Frederick Handley Page—who must surely have been the outstanding individualist of all our aircraft manufacturers—was starting a civil air transport company using the Handley Page 0/400. I went down to the company's offices at Cricklewood, on the outskirts of London, and I had a talk with Handley Page. I asked him for a job, and he appeared to be fairly impressed by my record and interested in my views; but, because he was the man he was, there had to be some pretty shrewd dickering.

Eventually I was offered the job of chief pilot in Handley Page's newly formed Air Transport Company. It sounded important and promising enough, even if the salary was a somewhat meager £500 a year, and I accepted it. There was no trade union for pilots in those days. If there had been such a union I do not doubt that I would have come under the heading of sweated labor. When I compare my meager wage in 1919 with the princely salaries paid to the airline pilots of today I cannot help feeling a retrospective pang of envy.

Frederick Handley Page was an extraordinary man in many ways, and I always felt quite a warm affection for him, even if I was not altogether happy as one of his employees. He started designing airplanes as far back as 1910, and right up to the time of his death in 1962 at over seventy years of age he was still very much the active head of the affairs of his company. He was a man of courage and original ideas; he had considerable wit and was known as a most amusing after-dinner speaker.

Immediately after the Great War came to an end, Handley Page showed splendid enterprise, as well as a staunch belief in the future of civil aviation, in forming three companies for civil airline operations in Europe, South Africa, and India and Burma. He also tried to start air services with the use of flying boats in Brazil and

Peru. All of these ventures, with the exception of the company in
England, failed. The English one, known as Handley Page Air
Transport Limited, was one of the three companies—the other two
were Air Transport and Travel Limited and S. I. Instone and
Company Limited—that were created in 1919 and later amalga-
mated to form Imperial Airways, the forerunner of B.O.A.C. and
B.E.A.

When the opportunity to be demobilized presented itself to me
in April, 1919, I promptly took it. I left the R.A.F. and I joined
Handley Page in the middle of the same month; and in becoming
the first chief pilot of the Handley Page company, I was one of the
very first in the profession known today as that of civil airline
pilot.

Civil aviation came into existence officially in this country on
May 1, only a couple of weeks after I joined Handley Page. The
first thing I did was to get one of the new licenses as a commercial
pilot. I wanted to try and get license No. 1, but I started off badly
that first day in May, 1919, by allowing myself to become involved
in one of the arguments my father and I so often indulged in. I was
staying with him at his house in London, and because of our
argument I was later than I had planned in getting to the Air
Ministry, and when eventually I arrived there I found that three
pilots of Air Transport and Travel had just beaten me to it by
about five minutes. When my turn came to be issued with my
official license as a "pilot of aircraft carrying passengers for hire or
reward" it was No. 4.

Later that first day on which commercial flying became officially
recognized I made what has been described as the first transport
flight between London and Manchester. Using one of our Handley
Page 0/400 aircraft, I flew eleven "passengers for hire or reward."
The trip took me three hours and forty minutes flying in the face
of a vicious head wind; and that day's work alone, I should think,
entitles me to the claim that I was perhaps the very first to
participate actively in civil aviation as it has since become known
in England. During the next few days I made several other flights
with passengers, going as far afield as Carlisle and Montrose and
Aberdeen.

Flying those large Handley Page 0/400's loaded with passengers
and freight was very different from the livelier work that I had
done for so long in fighters on the Western Front, but I enjoyed it
because I had the feeling that I was in at the birth of a new

industry. Our aircraft were large enough to provide for a cabin which could hold fourteen passengers, and they were the best commercial transport aircraft of that time. We were all enthusiastic about our work and keenly interested in finding out for ourselves how things could be done, and more often than not, all the experimenting and making do with the limited facilities that were provided suited us very much better than mere dull routine.

We were the first of those who are now known as civil airline captains. I am afraid that the captains of today, who are rightly jealous of their standing, have been at times rather shocked when they have heard stories about our alleged lack of respectability in those days of forty-odd years ago. Perhaps they overlook the fact that we were all young and, if I may say so, trying to find our way in a newly established profession. Quite a few of us continued to live in the carefree fashion to which we had become accustomed during the war, and thoughts about respectability never entered our minds. If in appearance and behavior we seemed to be light-hearted and perhaps even irresponsible, it was only because we were carrying on with the front that we had learned to adopt in a very hard school.

In much the same way we had done during our time on the Western Front, we often had to fly at a moment's notice on all sorts of unexpected jaunts. On Rose Day in June, 1919, for instance, I took off from Cricklewood with a load of passengers, and over Hyde Park we dropped a bouquet of roses for Queen Alexandra, who before the war had started this annual appeal for funds for the hospitals. I then made an additional gesture by flying low over and around Marlborough House, the home of the Queen, as a result of which Handley Page received a telegram expressing her pleasure and thanks for what we had done.

A great deal of our flying during 1919 was on charter work. In this we made the first use of the air for the distribution of newspapers, dropping them by parachute. The *Daily Mail* people—who have always been staunch supporters of new ventures in the air—asked us to fly bundles of their newspapers from Manchester to Dundee and Aberdeen. It was a publicity stunt, but it was an imaginative one. We dropped the bundles onto local golf courses. The expert responsible for the use of the parachutes came along with me on our first trip, bringing with him his secretary, a young woman. On our arrival over Aberdeen he himself dropped by parachute onto the golf course, intending to visit some friends. We watched with delight the comical spectacle he presented as he floated down to earth with a small suitcase in one hand and an umbrella in the other.

It had been planned that we should indulge in yet another publicity stunt when we arrived back over Manchester—that the secretary should make an exhibition jump with a parachute over Alexandra Park. At the last moment the poor girl got cold feet, and she hesitated about jumping. While the arguments were going on behind me, I had to circle around, but eventually she was helped to make up her mind by what has been described as a wink from me to her helpers, and down she went.

Early in July of that first year after the war, I flew the first cross-Channel commercial flight ever made from this country to Brussels when, on charter, I took some freight across in one of our 0/400's. A few days after that, I was instructed by Handley Page to fly one of his V/1500 bombers to Amsterdam so that it could be shown at the first international exhibition of aircraft that was ever organized anywhere in the world.

The V/1500 was an even larger aircraft than the 0/400, for those days a huge machine, and the largest British bomber built during the First World War. It was also the first to have four engines, and it was designed to fly to Berlin and back from airdromes in East Anglia. The war ended just before the first squadron of these aircraft could become operational, and Berlin was spared the bombing that London had had to endure. Although never used on operations, the V/1500 was nevertheless important in the history of the Air Force in that it was the first bomber designed for strategic bombing from bases in England.

This huge airplane was also called the Super Handley. It had a rugged undercarriage, described by its makers as "a massive affair of four large wheels and their struts," and it was of the usual wood and plywood structure of those times, covered with fabric. It had four Rolls-Royce Eagle VIII engines, each of 375 horsepower, mounted in pairs, back to back, the front engine driving a two-bladed propeller, while the rear engine drove a four-bladed pusher propeller of slightly coarser pitch. But it was the vast wing span of this biplane that was the most impressive feature of its appearance: it was 126 feet across, nearly five times the wing span of the little S.E.5. Flying the V/1500 called for a crew of between five and seven, depending on operations, and it could stay in the air for seventeen hours at a cruising speed of over eighty miles an hour.

As was the custom with nearly all of these early aircraft, the pilot of the V/1500 sat in an open cockpit behind a large wind-

shield, with a great wheel in front of him for the controls. There
were no engine instruments in the cockpit. They were mounted on
panels on the frames between the wings holding the radiators of
the engines, and the pilot could just see them through the whirling
discs of the propellers.

Flight engineers of today will wince at the thought that petrol
from the two-thousand-gallon fuel tank in the body of the aircraft
was fed to the four engines by wind-driven pumps. But they would
feel even greater sympathy with their predecessors if they knew
what demands we pilots had to make on the engines of all our
aircraft of those days. It was always surprising to me how well
those engines stood up to the caning we gave them. When we
opened up the throttles to take off, there was no easing them back
after we were airborne. We left them there at full power because
we needed all that we could get out of the engines in order to keep
going. Part of every engineer's tool kit was some chewing gum and
insulating tape for quick repairs to the water jackets of those
engines. They always seemed to be springing leaks, and the gum
was chewed and then plugged in the leak and secured with the
tape.

Before I could make the flight to Amsterdam for the exhibition
of the V/1500 I had to go up to the airdrome at Bircham Newton,
in Norfolk, where the squadron which had them had been getting
ready for the bombing of Berlin. I flew one of the aircraft down to
Cricklewood, and a few days later I set off for the Continent. I
went first to Brussels, where I demonstrated the machine to the
Belgian Air Force. King Albert of the Belgians was at the airdrome, and he asked me to take him up for a flight, which I did;
then I flew from Brussels to the Dutch military airfield at Soesterberg. From there I was due to fly the V/1500 to a field near
Amsterdam alongside which they were staging the exhibition.

Arrangements for this show were in the hands of Lieutenant
Albert Plesman, of the Dutch Army, and he was at Soesterberg
when I arrived there. Always an enthusiast and very efficient,
Plesman was to contribute a great deal to the development of air
transport in the years that lay ahead. He was the founder of the
great Dutch civil airline K.L.M., of which he was chairman for
many years.

But of greater interest to me in my visit to Soesterberg at that
time was the opportunity that it provided for my first meeting with
the Dutch aircraft designer Anthony Fokker. It was he who had
been responsible for producing some of the best of the fighters

used by the Germans, against which I had done so much flying and fighting. Fokker was a much smaller man in stature than I had expected; he was pleasant enough in his manner, and we were able to talk quite freely about aircraft design and performance.

As soon as Albert Plesman and I started making plans for the next day, he warned me that the field at the exhibition upon which I was supposed to land was only a small one, and that the surface was very soft. He seemed to be rather overawed by the size of my aircraft, and he was apprehensive about my being able to get into the field with anything as large as the V/1500. Plesman made out a plan of the field for me, and he marked with a cross the exact spot where I must be sure to touch down because, he explained, the surface of the rest of the field was so soggy that I might very easily find myself bogged down.

When the time came for me to take off from Soesterberg the next morning, I saw Anthony Fokker sprawled out on the ground some hundreds of yards ahead of me waiting to check on how much of a run I would have to take before I was able to lift the aircraft into the air. He was apparently quite satisfied to stay there lying flat on his stomach, relying entirely on me not to run over him. There were probably many of those who had served in the R.F.C. and the R.A.F. who would not have blamed me if, in hurtling along toward Fokker, I had kept the wheels on the ground just a little bit longer.

It was only a short flight to the small field near Amsterdam on which I was supposed to land, and I found that Plesman had been quite right about its size. I checked everything very carefully, and then I put the aircraft down right on the precise spot indicated on his plan. The field was wet because it was by the side of a canal, and I had run scarcely more than a hundred yards when the four great wheels, each of which stood five feet in height, broke through the thin surface crust and sank down to their axles in the mud. The huge aircraft very nearly tipped over on its nose, but I just managed to right it without any damage being done, and it was then hauled to a harder standing.

We found that my V/1500 was so large in span that it was much too big to go into the exhibition hall. But Albert Plesman was not the man to allow that to defeat him. He had the front of the hall, which was a large hangar, almost completely removed so that we could get the aircraft in, and then he had two enormous slots cut in the walls to take the tips of the wings which were allowed to protrude outside. The visitors to the show were most impressed.

After that first visit to Amsterdam, I made other flights in the V/1500 around Holland and Belgium demonstrating the aircraft, in the hope that we would get some orders for Handley Page. At the same time, demonstrations of the Handley Page bombers were being put on by my pilots throughout Scandinavia, and one was even taken to Madrid to show to the Spanish authorities. Others were taken to Portugal for demonstration. But instead of getting orders, Handley Page was receiving only cancellations of government contracts, and the future on the manufacturing side was far from bright. I am tempted to expand on that unhappy theme because it sounds with such a recurring note of frustration in so much of what has happened ever since then; but it is too long and sorry a story to compress into just a few words.

By July, 1919, our government had reached an agreement with the French about starting commercial flying between our two countries, and the competition between the Handley Page company and Air Transport and Travel Limited to be the first into business on the London-to-Paris run became pretty brisk. It was my responsibility, in addition to selecting and training the crews and testing the aircraft, to make all the necessary arrangements abroad for the proper handling of our aircraft on the ground, and for supplies of petrol and oil.

There seemed to be so many difficulties that stood in our way, no matter how carefully we might plan, and each pilot was rather a law unto himself or, perhaps I should say, a master of ceremonies. As soon as he took off from Cricklewood, he was in complete charge of the aircraft, the plans for the flight, and all the ground arrangements at the other end, as well as the care of the passengers in the air and on the ground. We found that those early passengers entered fully into the spirit of what was very much an adventure. Quite a number of them would even ask to be dressed up in flying suits, helmets and goggles so that they could sit in the two open seats in the nose of the aircraft, in front of the pilot, rather than take the more comfortable seats in the cabin. They at least got better views of the country over which they were flying than passengers do today.

Our competitors on the Paris run beat us to it by a few hours, but our first flight with fourteen passengers from London to Paris was still made with a Handley Page 0/400 on the day on which it had been agreed that such commercial flying could start: Monday, August 25, 1919. A week later we had a regular service in operation. It was a comfortable enough flight in our 0/400's provided that we did not run into strong head winds, for when that happened we were rather outpaced by any trains that we might happen to follow. There were also occasions when, it was said, we even failed to keep up with the red buses running along the Edgware Road, which we followed in the very first stage of the route that was to take us to Paris; and it was not unknown for us to pass over Marble Arch at a height of only five hundred feet as we made the slow climb into the air.

Our successes and our failures during those first commercial flights of the London-to-Paris air service—our fare for which, one way, was fifteen guineas—were well recorded in the press, and some of the reports were distinctly amusing. Perhaps the most colorful was an item in the New York *Herald,* which spoke of the 0/400 that flew to Paris on September 3, 1919, as a "Handley Page Pullman Aerobus." The account described the way in which "the big ship sailed down on the field at Le Bourget," and stated that "the passengers united in describing as glorious" our flight from London. Since I was the pilot, I was relieved to hear that the airplane "rode it gracefully." Expanding on the heading about the "aerobus," our aircraft was described as "a Pullman palace on wings." That particular flight from London, including a forced landing that I had had to make near Abbeville because of trouble with the fuel supply, had taken four and three quarter hours; but, the report stated, the passengers "agreed that battling against air currents is far preferable to being tossed about on the waves of the Channel."

But not all our flights were quite as straightforward as that. On one occasion I ran into weather that could hardly have been worse. The story of the flight I made that day offers a good example of what we had to contend with in those early days of civil aviation. There was low cloud, a strong southwesterly wind was blowing with torrents of rain, and visibility was down to a minimum. I took off from Cricklewood at ten o'clock in the morning, and set course to the northeast. Over the docks lining the Thames I followed the river as far as Gravesend, and then I turned off and set course for Paris. It took me an hour of strenuous flying to get as far as Dungeness, and even then we were at a height of only three hundred feet.

Out over the Channel we went, still very low down, and I tried not to think about how unattractive the sea looked; and on the way across France I had to keep a sharp lookout with constant

changes of course in order to avoid the high ground, hidden in the
cloud, of the Beauvais ridge which stood between us and Paris.
Three hours after leaving Cricklewood we arrived over Chantilly.
Ahead there was a solid wall of cloud right down to the ground, so
I decided to play for safety and land on the racecourse below us.

But even in trying to get back to earth, I was handicapped
because, as I came into land, I found that hurdles had been placed
halfway across the course, sticking out alternately from either side.
It called for a lot of tricky maneuvering at the last moment; and
then we had to sit there on the racecourse and wait for the cloud to
lift. When it did, we started off again, and I had to do a lot of
kicking on the rudder-bar to avoid the hurdles on our take-off. But
we made it, after catching our breath two or three times, and we
completed the last twenty miles of our journey to Le Bourget,
arriving there four and a half hours after leaving Cricklewood. The
time taken today by the aircraft of British European Airways in
the flight from London to Paris is about forty minutes.

Most of the pilots flying now in British European Airways were
not even born when I was making those flights from London to
Paris in the summer of 1919, and I hope that they will not take it
amiss if I call attention to the vast difference between the working
conditions for the air crews when I first started and those of today.
I have the greatest admiration and respect for the air crews of
today and for the way in which they are doing their work. I should
like to think they know that I appreciate what a heavy load of
responsibility they so readily carry, and that because I was once
one of them I understand them.

In the very beginning, those early days of civil flying had shown
a definite promise for the future; but after too short a time a
situation developed that was hard to understand. The Government
seemed slow, even reluctant, to foster aviation, and we seemed to
be working not only in a hand-to-mouth fashion but without any
firm plans or official encouragement. It became very difficult to see
ahead, even if, in theory, it was obvious enough that civil aviation
would develop. Added to that unrest there was in my own mind
the thought that the salary of five hundred pounds a year that I
was receiving as chief pilot was very small for the responsibilities
that the work entailed.

I also found, to my surprise, that the flying I was doing as a civil
pilot was becoming monotonous, and that the fun had gone out of
it; and there crept back into my mind the restlessness which had

caused me to leave the Air Force and take on the challenge of the new world of civil aviation. But even now, after all these years, and with what I hope is a more balanced understanding of myself, I am still not at all sure what it was that made me decide to give up my job with Handley Page—for that was what I did.

Perhaps the most important reason for my state of unrest, and one that I by no means understood at that time, was that I was suffering from what so many of us experienced after the war. It was a malaise of the spirit that has come to be given a wide variety of names, all the way from downright bloody-mindedness to the terms bandied about by the psychiatrists. The mood that I was in was an extension of the frame of mind that had made me leave the Air Force. For all that they may say about it today, it seemed then to defy analysis. We who had participated so actively and so eagerly in the war over such a long period of time had been subjected to an overstimulation that was now exacting its toll. In many different ways we were run down to a state that approached a standstill.

It was a rash thing to throw up my job with Handley Page as I did, but such was the depressed state of my mind that I simply could not go on with it. I was very short of money, and I had married only a few months before, in the summer of 1919; but I had come to feel that I had no prospects in flying, and, what was even worse, I appeared to have little ambition at that time to make anything out of it. I seemed to have reached a wretched state of being completely at loose ends. It was a thoroughly hateful experience, and I did not seem to be able to find any way out of it. But I had to support myself and my wife, and I also had to keep going a furnished flat that we had taken in the Temple. The more I thought about it, the more muddled I seemed to become, and the only thing that remained clear was that somehow or other, at something or other, I had to earn a living.

My thoughts turned again to the possibility of finding some way to go back to Oxford, but I did not like at all the prospect of being a married undergraduate. Strangely enough, for a man of his perception, my father was not very helpful at this time with any ideas that could be regarded as constructive, although he did help me out financially. But that was understandable enough. He had the responsibility of a new family by his second marriage—another boy, Roderick, and two girls, Katherine and Rosemary—and they were young and making quite enough demands on his attention.

During a talk one day with my father, in an effort to find an answer to my problems, I struck on the idea of possibly joining him in his work as an art dealer. He was by then well known and firmly established; and since I had always been interested in art and pictures, and fascinated by the work of the critic and dealer, it seemed to me that this was something I would enjoy. I suggested the idea to my father, but he was not exactly enthusiastic about it, although he did not discourage me. But when he saw that I was becoming genuinely interested—he could not have helped being aware of the negative state of mind I had been slipping into since the end of the war—he began to help in a more constructive way.

"You'd better start off with the easiest school, the Dutch school," he advised, taking a thoroughly practical view.

Under my father's guidance I went about doing a great deal of reading, tackling all the authorities on the Dutch and the Flemish school of painting. During that winter I spent a month in Holland going around the galleries, including the Mauritshuis in the Hague, the Rijks Museum in Amsterdam, the Boymans Museum in Rotterdam, and the museum in Haarlem. I also met some of my father's contemporaries in the world of art criticism and history, and I had long and helpful talks with them, chiefly with Dr. C. Hofstede de Groot, who was a very pleasant and kind old man. And so I went on reading and trying to educate myself in the Dutch school of painting.

It was all interesting enough, and I enjoyed my studies in Holland; but when I got back to London I had to face the cold and sobering realization that I was completely broke and entirely dependent upon my father. It was a most unhappy state of affairs, and it worried me greatly. With that, all the wretched uncertainty in my mind began again, dominating all my thoughts. In common with many other ex-servicemen I was what we used to call "nervy"; and being so utterly dependent upon my father left me with a feeling of humiliation, unnecessary though that might have been.

Within a very short time I became so disgruntled that I even gave up the idea of following in my father's footsteps. Off I started again on another search, hunting around for some sort of job that would at least enable me to earn a living. There even started to form at the back of my mind a vague idea that I would like to emigrate to the United States. Among my father's many friends and acquaintances were rich patrons of the arts whom he advised on their buying of pictures, and some of these were prominent American businessmen. Having decided that I would rather like to go to the United States and try my luck there, I asked my father if he would give me some introductions. He told me that one of those to whom he was acting as an adviser was the financier J. P. Morgan, Jr., of New York, and he said that he would ask his advice.

Described as "one of the most powerful financiers in Christendom," Morgan happened to be in London on a visit to the English firm of Morgan, Grenfell and Company, which at that time he controlled. My father spoke to him about me, and I was asked to go to see him at the Morgan, Grenfell offices in the City. I knew nothing whatsoever about the strange world of high finance, and all that I really knew about Morgan was what I had read somewhere or other about his banking house being so influential that during the war it had acted in America on behalf of the British and the French governments.

At my first meeting with J. P. Morgan early in 1920, I found myself facing a man who was most impressive in appearance, and yet quite affable in manner. For all the formidable aura that attended his name, Morgan was very kind to me, and at the end of quite a long talk we had together he offered me a job with a company he had just acquired in India: Andrew Yule and Company, jute merchants. He explained that I would have to settle in Calcutta. Considering that I was young and that I had no qualifications whatsoever, the salary that he named—£700 a year—was quite a generous one.

If I had been offered a job in the United States I probably would have jumped at it; but the thought of India, for all that J. P. Morgan was offering, left me with some indefinable feeling of doubt. I asked him if I could have twenty-four hours in which to think things over. Morgan agreed to that, and he told me to come and see him again the next morning. Just what it was that was holding me back I could not say, except that, as with almost everything that I tried to think about at that time, I was having such difficulty in making up my mind.

I was a member of the Bath Club in those days, and after leaving Morgan's office I went there for a quiet lunch by myself to think things over and to try and arrive at a decision. I was really conscious of only one thing, and that was that I was facing a most important turning point in my life. The time had come, I knew, when I was going to have to make up my mind about what I was going to do, and after I had done that I was going to have to stick to it.

After I had thought about it all for a while, I came to realize that there was something weighing on my mind that was of even greater importance than my dislike of the idea of having to live in India. In its simplest terms, it was that I would be cutting myself off for good from the world of aviation. Admittedly I was unemployed, and the prospects of finding any work in flying were remote; and even if I were able to get some sort of work in aviation I still had to face the fact that conditions were such that it would be of a very precarious nature. But deep down in my own mind I knew that flying had come to mean a very great deal to me. It was the only thing that I could do reasonably well; and what was possibly more important, it was in a world in which I felt that I really belonged. Why throw it all up? I went on with my lunch, sitting alone and pondering what I should do. At the end of it I had still not reached a final decision.

The more I thought about the predicament I was in, the more I realized—or so it seemed to emerge from the confused state of my thinking—that there was no one to whom I could turn for advice. Now I was really on my own, and the time had come when I was going to have to make up my own mind. I decided to go for a walk, just to see if that would help. Then there occurred one of those fortuitous events that can so curiously change the whole course of a man's life. As I was leaving the club, right on the doorstep in Dover Street, I ran into Boom Trenchard, who was on his way in. He was by then firmly in the seat as the all-powerful Chief of the Air Staff.

"Hullo, Sholto!" he exclaimed in his gruff and kindly way; and almost as if he read my mind he asked: "What're you doing now?"

That was all I needed. Trenchard was the one man to whom I could talk, and talk I did. I told him all about the offer I had just received from J. P. Morgan, and what a difficult time I was having in trying to make up my mind about accepting it.

"Oh . . . don't go to Calcutta," he said without a moment's hesitation. "You come back to the R.A.F."

The instant that Trenchard said that, I knew that I had found the answer. It was as if he understood instinctively—as he so often did—the right solution to the problem. But I was still a little dazed from the effort of having racked my brain so strenuously over the offer from Morgan. Hesitantly I asked if the suggestion that he was making was really possible.

"I'll see that you're taken back, and in your old seniority," Trenchard replied.

Any final doubts that I might have felt were promptly swept

aside. My luck was in, and I knew it, and I accepted Trenchard's suggestion without further delay. He told me to see his secretary, and that all the details for my rejoining the Service could be worked out the next day.

Now I had to face the interview with J. P. Morgan, which had in it the prospect of being rather an embarrassing one. I felt a little guilty about having to tell him, after all the kindness and the consideration that he had shown me, that I was turning down his offer, but I knew I would have to go through with it. The next morning I went to the City and I saw Morgan again. I told him that I was regretfully declining his generous offer because I had decided that I would go back into the Royal Air Force.

"You are a fool," Morgan said. "What are your prospects in the British Air Force? You will always be a poor man. If you were to go to Calcutta for me you would be a rich man in twenty years, and be able to retire."

As far as actual riches are concerned—if one is to define riches in terms of money—Morgan was right in taking such a gloomy view of my prospects. Instead of accepting his generous offer and his forecast of those riches to come, I chose a career in the Services; and in those days Service life was notorious for being very poorly paid and nothing, financially, to compare with the offer from Morgan. I was married, and I was going to have to make do on a meager pay. My future in the R.A.F. was quite impossible to predict, and even if I did manage to climb to a reasonably senior rank, I knew that so far as money was concerned I would never have very much.

But considerations of financial gain were not and never could be the whole story. Money alone is not wealth, and I have never been at all impressed by the all-consuming pursuit of it which is such a dominant influence in the lives of so many. By returning to the Royal Air Force I was acquiring a wealth that could never be measured in such terms. My life in the Air Force, I fully realized, might not yield much more than the right, when eventually the time came for me to retire, to be addressed as a group captain or an air commodore or, stretching things a bit and with luck on my side, an air vice-marshal. What was important to me was that I was going back to flying. That in itself was sufficient wealth, because in flying I felt that I would find happiness and a satisfactory way of life. All other prospects for the future would have to depend on that.

When I think now about my experiences and the mood that I

was in during the early spring of 1920 I recall that I gave very little consideration to the element of luck, which might or might not play a part in what lay ahead. I was concerned more with practical thoughts about the work that was in store for me, and the life that I would be able to lead in doing that work. The uncertainty in my mind that had been pestering me since the end of the war was past. I was eager to make the most of the opportunity that was presenting itself, with the prospect of being able to do my best in that which I knew and liked the best.

16 / A Hard-won Freedom

SO FAR AS the infant Royal Air Force was concerned, the years of our experience during the First World War were short enough in time, but they were rich in knowledge and in experience. We were an independent Service—the first independent air force ever formed in the world—and in starting from scratch with scarcely anything more than our "perfect instruction," the R.A.F. was in a good and healthy condition and able to act for itself. That aspect of the future of the Service was given the closest personal attention by the Chief of the Air Staff, and Trenchard was determined that the morale of the new Service should be of the highest quality.

In his endeavors to make sure of that, Boom Trenchard had taken it upon himself to decide personally about who should and who should not be offered commissions in the R.A.F., and he kept his eye on all matters of selection, relying on his own knowledge of all the men who had served under him. Andrew Boyle, his biographer, has spoken of that, commenting: "It was the way he had always ruled, autocratically but very personally. To him the air force was not a faceless entity but the sum of its living parts."

The extent to which this autocratic and personal control was exercised by Boom Trenchard over everything concerning the R.A.F., and through that over our personal lives as well, has been revealed by Mr. J. Morris, a former director of the Air Historical Branch of the Air Ministry. In 1925 a conference was called by Trenchard to discuss the work that was in progress on the writing of what was to become the splendid six-volume *The War in the Air,* the official history of the British Air Forces in the First World War.

In the course of the discussion Trenchard stated his views, with which one of the officers present was rash enough to express his disagreement. "Trenchard thereupon brought his fist down on his table with a resounding bang and characteristically boomed:

294

'While I'm C.A.S. I'm having things done my way. Gentlemen, the conference is now ended,' " Mr. Morris has recalled, adding that in expressing his views about the writing of the history, Trenchard stated to him: "I want a book dealing with the spirit of the Air Force." How magnificently Trenchard got his wish is now a matter of happy record.

The personal interest that Boom Trenchard took in gathering back into the Air Force in those very early days the men whom he knew and wanted for the new Service had resulted in my own return to the R.A.F. as a squadron leader with a temporary commission; and in March, 1920, I was posted to the staff of No. 1 Group, the headquarters for which were at Kenley, just to the south of London. My interest in speaking of that time now is mainly because it brought me directly under the command of Group Captain H. C. T. Dowding, who was in charge of the group and who was later to become the renowned Air Chief Marshal Lord Dowding of Bentley Priory. During the war he had risen to the rank of brigadier. But his commission in the Royal Air Force was only a temporary one, and after the war there was an unhappy prospect that he might have to return to the Army. Why Dowding should have been treated in that way was not revealed until many years later, and it does not reflect much credit on Trenchard.

During the war Stuffy Dowding had expressed quite forcefully his views about the way in which pilots were being rushed out to France without sufficient training, and this strong objection against Trenchard's plan for getting on with the war in the air almost regardless of cost—with which many of us disagreed—brought down on Dowding's head the strong personal disapproval of Trenchard. We all knew vaguely that no love was lost between the two men; but the way in which Trenchard obstructed Dowding's being given a permanent commission in the new Service was singularly petty for a man who was so big in every way.

I had known Stuffy Dowding slightly since the time when I had served as an observer with No. 2 Squadron on the Western Front in the spring of 1915, but I cannot say that I got to know him more than slightly because he was older than I was and much more senior in rank. In addition to that, he was not exactly the most approachable of men.

At Kenley, however, it was rather different, and I like to think that it was during our association there that Stuffy Dowding and I began to understand each other. We had both been through a strenuous war, and that gave us quite a lot in common, and during the time that I served directly under Dowding I grew to like and to respect him. And I also discovered why, although it was never his slightest wish or desire, Dowding became a figure around whom there has been a certain amount of unwelcomed controversy. He was always such a pronounced individualist, and never hesitant about expressing his views.

But for all the certain stiffness in his manner, Stuffy Dowding nevertheless showed that he had a warmly human side to his character, as well as what was to me a pleasantly sharp and ready wit. He was always most thorough and painstaking in his work, with a good head for detail, and he rightly insisted upon accuracy in all information that was given to him as well as the production of sound and proper arguments and reasons for any opinions that were put up to him. During the year that I served on Dowding's staff I learned a great deal from him about being an efficient staff officer and how to deal with staff duties, which, up to that time, had been to me rather a mystery. For one thing, he checked an inclination on my part, which was possibly a hangover from the war, toward being a little too slapdash in my paper work.

Despite the uncertainty about his own future, which must have been difficult enough for him, Stuffy Dowding was always considerate in his attitude toward his own staff, watching closely over their interests. Only a short time after I rejoined the Air Force, he saw to it that my own temporary status was changed to that of a permanent commission; and I have always understood that this was granted to me while he was still in doubt about his own position. But he was not without friends, and there were those among the senior officers who believed strongly in Dowding. One in particular took it upon himself to tell Boom Trenchard that he was only doing himself harm through his petty refusal to approve for Dowding a permanent commission, and eventually Trenchard was prevailed upon to see reason; and although it was still against his inclination at that time, he confirmed the commission for Dowding.

It was not until some years later, when Dowding was serving at the Air Ministry, that Trenchard came to admit that he had been wrong. He called Dowding to his office one day, and the atmosphere in the brief exchange that then took place must have been a curious one.

"I am not often wrong about men," Trenchard said to Dowding, "but I want you to know that I was wrong about you."

In that admission there is some indication of the largeness, for all that he had harbored in his mind, of Trenchard's heart.

Faced with the problem of presenting the new Royal Air Force to the tax-paying public in as favorable a light as possible, Boom Trenchard early brought into being as a shop window for the Service the annual R.A.F. Tournament which later became known as the R.A.F. Pageant and then the R.A.F. Display. The first of these immensely successful displays was staged at the airfield at Hendon in the summer of 1920, and it was the occasion for me to indulge, through a thoughtlessness that was quite inexcusable, in an exploit that was a very poor return on my part for all that Trenchard had done for me only a few months before.

When the news of the proposed air show reached us at Kenley, we were asked to make suggestions about any items that we thought might be of interest. During the previous year that I had spent out of the Service, mainly as a test and civil airline pilot, I had gained some experience of flying the Handley Page V/1500, the largest four-engined bomber then in service. I suggested to Stuffy Dowding that the sight of even a small formation of these huge bombers might make quite an impression. He promptly agreed to the idea, and gave me permission to see what could be done about it.

At the airdrome at Hawkinge, down near the coast of Kent to the southeast of Kenley, there were in storage several of these V/1500's. The station commander there was Keith Park, who was also a squadron leader. I talked with him about my idea, and Park arranged for three of the V/1500's to be made serviceable, and he and one of his pilots and I then proceeded to do some training in formation flying.

It was a feat for those days to fly these lumbering great machines in close formation—they must have been the largest aircraft in the world at that time—and it was difficult to think up anything more spectacular than just keeping them reasonably close together in the air. The three of us went enthusiastically about our practice in taking off and flying around together. I added a touch of sensation by arranging for a girl who was a parachutist, and who had flown with me during the short time that I was a civil pilot, to give the onlookers a thrill by making a jump from my aircraft.

On the day of that first tournament at Hendon, on July 3, 1920, we found that the wind was blowing directly over the airdrome from the Royal Box. It was known that King George V was not exactly well-inclined toward the air. He disapproved of much of what we were, and he had a firm dislike of airplanes and the noise and the smell that went along with them, and he was represented at the tournament by Prince Henry, one of his sons who is the present Duke of Gloucester. But in my thoughtlessness all that mattered to me was that we should make an impression on the crowd, and it occurred to me that it would be a most effective stunt if our three great airplanes took off together in formation straight toward and over the Royal Box. The fact that we would have to do it in any case in order to fly into the wind was only a minor technical consideration.

With Keith Park and the other pilot in their aircraft on each side of and slightly behind me I got our formation all lined up, and then we roared across the airfield straight toward the box in which the royal party and their guests were sitting. Feeling very pleased with myself for what I considered was an added touch of spice to the show, I held the formation down to what I believed would be for the crowd an intriguingly low height, and we thundered over the royal group, assaulting them with noise and the smell of burnt oil from our engine exhausts. We then went blithely about our formation flying, and we finished up with the woman parachutist making her jump and coming to earth in the middle of the airdrome.

When we landed I was all ready for a warm word of praise for what I felt had turned out to be a well-executed act; but all that I received was an order to report immediately to the Chief of the Air Staff. I did as I was told, and Boom Trenchard was waiting for me behind the Royal Box. He was very angry, and he demanded to know what the devil I thought I was up to, endangering as I had the lives of our royal guests. What would have happened, he wanted to know, if any one of the three aircraft, taking off as we did in a pretty tight formation, had had an engine failure? It was the first and it was to be the only time that Trenchard ever really went for me, and as soon as he started wading into me I knew that he was absolutely right and that I thoroughly deserved a ticking-off for being so thoughtless. Had there been an accident through an engine failure—and such failures were common enough in those days—there could have occurred a disaster of the greatest magnitude; and when I thought about that I shuddered.

In the first volume of the official history, *The War in the Air,* which was first published in 1922, only a couple of years after I had rejoined the R.A.F., Sir Walter Raleigh spoke about the tradition of our Service that was "to be handed down as an heirloom to the coming generation." To that he added the statement: "It will not fail to reach them. The Royal Air Force is strong in the kind of virtue that propagates itself and attains to a life beyond a life. The tradition is safe."

It is controversial ground to tread upon nowadays, but I must affirm my belief in the value of that tradition. It was proved so conclusively to me during the thirty-odd years that I was to spend in the Royal Air Force, and during two world wars. What was possibly of the greatest importance in helping to create it was that we who were in the Service were able to grow up together. The R.A.F., which had evolved from the Royal Flying Corps, was only a very small Service in those early days, and one inevitably got to know, or know about, everybody else. The Service was complete within itself, and not merely made up of so many different units. And we had all seen active service in the air, which was something that gave us a common bond of sympathy and understanding.

In any attempt that may be made to speak about the way in which the Royal Air Force had to struggle for survival during the early years after its creation in 1918, we who were young officers in the new Service were not perhaps quite as aware then as we might have been of what an uphill and personal battle it was for Boom Trenchard. We all owe a great deal to him for his strength, which was based very largely on his extraordinary personality, and not on the quality of his brains. In some ways Trenchard was inclined to be a little stupid; but that was of no importance when one considered the great driving force of his personality. Although largely inarticulate, with ungrammatical sentences booming out in his efforts to express himself, he could, and did, become wholly convincing in his arguments, and it was in those arguments that he won his battles.

During the early days after the war a paper was prepared by Trenchard in which he gave Winston Churchill, who was Secretary of State for War and for Air, his views about the way in which they should try to shape the future. It was a remarkably short paper of not more than about eight hundred words, but in it Trenchard included two enormously important factors in the future development of the Service: ". . . traditions, built up through four years of war"; and the need for specialized training.

It is of importance to note now that only a month after Boom Trenchard became Chief of the Air Staff of the Royal Air Force in the middle of February, 1919, a similarly dynamic character was making his mark in American military aviation. The explosive General William Mitchell became Assistant Chief of Air Service and Director of Military Aeronautics of the American Army. In his views on air power Billy Mitchell was to the Americans what Trenchard was to us; but he had to face opposition that was even rougher than that experienced by Trenchard. Of that, General H. H. Arnold, the "Hap" Arnold who was Chief of the United States Army Air Forces during the Second World War, has said: "Mitchell at once began the running battle which was to increase the Air Arm's vitality and lead, in the end, to his own elimination."

The "running battle" that was conducted by Boom Trenchard in his efforts to preserve the R.A.F. from the obliteration with which it was threatened by the politicians and the Royal Navy was done with more skill than Billy Mitchell was apparently capable of exercising, but even then Trenchard was reduced by the intrigue that went on in Whitehall to having to threaten at one time to resign. "Trenchard realised that the whole future of the R.A.F. now depended on his adroit handling of the Secretary of State," Andrew Boyle has stated. It is a fair enough assessment of what was happening at that time when there were such powerful influences at work trying to break up our independence.

Part of that "adroit" handling resulted in a very angry exchange between Boom Trenchard and Winston Churchill. It was purposely provoked by Trenchard, and out of it there came another paper, a longer one this time, prepared by Trenchard and his staff. Although the reception of this statement of what the Air Force believed that they needed was at first lukewarm, it soon became the keystone upon which the whole freedom and the future of the R.A.F. as an independent service were built, and it enabled Winston Churchill to fight the battle that Trenchard was hoping for in the corridors of Westminster.

In that memorandum of Trenchard's, which is today recognized as one of the most important documents relating to the history of the Royal Air Force, he gave his views on the needs for the new Service about which he felt so strongly. "To make an Air Force worthy of the name," he stated, "we must create an Air Force spirit, or rather foster this spirit which undoubtedly existed in a high degree during the war, by every means in our power." Trenchard was so absolutely right in what he said. His views were long-term, and during those years of the 1920's he carefully laid the foundations for an efficient air force, and it was done with a thorough understanding of the meanings of air power.

On the Continent during those years, planning of a different nature was being indulged in, and in Germany there was a state of discontent which, understandable though it was, gave to an unsavory Austrian nonentity just the opportunity that he was looking for. Described by one historian as "the frustrated artist now becoming the master propagandist," Adolf Hitler had started gathering around him a rabble of ex-service and other malcontents. Not all the people in this country were in the dark about the discontent in Germany. Officialdom knew well enough, and dispatches were being received by the Foreign Office from our Embassy in Berlin during the early months of 1920 which stated quite clearly that the Germans "with their strong sense of nationality and order may weld themselves into a nation which may again prove formidable to the world." To that there was added the grim warning that "a strong Government may be established which, even though democratic in form, will be autocratic in essentials." Adolf Hitler was casting his shadow before him; but for all the warnings, our leaders paid little or no attention.

I knew nothing about all that at the time. I was a young squadron leader in the Royal Air Force, and my thoughts and interests were almost wholly absorbed in my work. But when one looks back over the span of the years, the emergence of Hitler and the rise of the Nazi Party in Germany appear now as evils that were almost historical oddities, and it does not seem possible that so much could have happened in the short space of the twenty-odd years that passed uneasily between the two world wars. In those early days the swastika of the emerging Nazi Party meant little to me; and there was no possible way that I could know that I was destined to have to play a curiously personal part in helping to eradicate it.

Much has been made of what is now referred to as the gaiety of the 1920's; but when I think of those years I can still feel the clammy grasp of the frustration that dogged those of us in the Air Force who were conscious of what was happening in matters of defense. For a long time during those years we faced the threat of outright extinction as a service through the efforts of the Army and the Navy to absorb us; as well as frustration at the hands of successive governments which were too intent on following what they chose to believe was a desire on the part of the public for unilateral disarmament. It was touch and go, and we in the Service were reduced to a readiness to accept almost anything that would enable us to keep the Royal Air Force alive and intact as an independent service.

Frustration on the part of those in the Services who try to plan for the future defense of the country is a story that is familiar enough, and those members of the Air Staff who have to look ahead have always had the same problem in dealing with their political masters. But for all the raised eyebrows of recent years, it has never been as difficult as it was during most of the years between the wars. Then we had to endure naïve official statements such as the one which read "the government would view the situation with anxiety but for their earnest hope and expectation that the Disarmament Conference now in session at Geneva will bring about a reduction in air armaments." That statement was contained in the memorandum which was attached to the Air Estimates as late as the year 1933, only six years before the outbreak of the Second World War.

After spending a year at Kenley on the staff of No. 1 Group, I was posted to Manston, in Kent. It was the airdrome which became known to many Americans as well as to our own people who had to make emergency landings there during the Second World War. I was happier about being there than I had been on the staff at the group headquarters if only because as chief flying instructor of the new No. 6 Flying Training School that was just being formed there, I was back on flying duties.

There was also established at Manston a school for the technical training of Air Force mechanics, and that had been placed under the command of Keith Park, who joined me there. We also had with us a young flight lieutenant named Arthur Coningham who, although born in Australia, was a New Zealander by adoption. Like Park he had found his way into the R.F.C. from the New Zealand Expeditionary Force, and he became very well known during the Second World War as the "Mary"—a corruption of "Maori"—Coningham who commanded the Desert and the Second Tactical Air Forces.

Keith Park and Mary Coningham were both tall, handsome men with fine records as fighting pilots during the war. They were also curiously alike in their temperaments, which was what enabled them later to become such good tactical commanders. It might be exaggerating and a little unfair to say that they were flamboyant, but they did have a freedom from the inhibitions which put so much restraint on the style of our own people. Park and Coningham were both men of strong physical and moral courage, always hard-working and conscientious, and they were typical of the other Australians and New Zealanders, of whom we had a goodly share, who contributed a great deal to the unique strength of the Royal Air Force.

Our way of life on the airdrome at Manston was a pleasantly complete one after the duller and more routine staff life at Kenley. Robin Willock—always known as Bill Willock—who was then the squadron leader in charge of administration and who later became an air vice-marshal well known in America and in Australia, and Keith Park and I were all married. There had begun to form the social pattern of Service life as it was to be lived on all R.A.F. stations. One of the features of that life has always been the readiness of the people who live in the neighborhood to allow us to join in their own social lives; in our case one of the homes in which we were always made welcome was that of Freddie Lonsdale, the very successful writer of what has been described as "highly varnished comedy." His immensely successful play, *The Maid of the Mountains,* had been a great hit with all of us during the war when we were back in London on leave from France. In his home we met many people from the world of the theater, and since the theater has always been of great interest to me, this added to my own moments of amusement.

But we were not quite as senseless in our way of life as that of the twenties is often made out to be. In my own case I was on a fairly steady diet of quite serious flying. In order that I should not develop too casual an attitude toward life, the fates on one occasion arranged for a court martial to stare me in the face. One of my flight commanders had been killed when the Bristol Fighter in which he was flying crashed through engine failure, and the Court of Inquiry found that this failure was due to faulty maintenance. It was alleged that the orders given regarding that maintenance were inadequate. Our commanding officer, who was responsible for the orders, was away at the time, and since I was temporarily in charge of the unit it was decided that I was the one who was to blame and that I would have to face a court martial on the charge of neglect of adequate maintenance.

The Flying Training School at Manston was part of No. 1 Group under the command of Stuffy Dowding, and orders were received by him from the Air Ministry to proceed with my court martial. As might have been expected of Dowding, he felt very strongly about how unfair it all was, and he promptly exercised the prerogative of a group commander and refused to take any action. It was a courageous as well as an honest stand for Dowding to take because there was still doubt about his own permanent commission being confirmed, and it could so easily have jeopardized his own chances of making a career for himself in the R.A.F.

In sticking to his guns, Stuffy Dowding stated emphatically that he considered that it was quite unfair that the Air Ministry should go to such lengths in trying to find a scapegoat. I have always had a shrewd idea that Dowding also resented being told by the Air Ministry to take such a step because he considered it an intrusion. But whatever his motives may have been, I have always been very grateful to Dowding for the stand that he took on my behalf. He had the whole stupid affair quashed in his own decisive fashion.

It was in the year of 1922, four years after the end of the First World War, that Ferdinand Foch, the famous French marshal who had become the Supreme Allied Commander on the Western Front, made a statement on the use of the air that was to become noteworthy. "The military mind always imagines that the next war will be upon the same lines as the last," he said. "That has never been the case, and never will be. The greatest factor in the next war will obviously be aircraft. The potentialities of aircraft attack upon a large scale are almost incalculable."

That statement is now looked upon as one of the most significant in understanding the importance of military aviation at that time; and it should be remembered that it was made by a man who was a soldier of a country which, at that time, saw fit to maintain a very powerful air force. In comparison with the French air service, our own Air Force had been whittled down in strength to the point of almost utter insignificance. What with the shortsightedness of the politicians and the grasping attitude of the Royal Navy, our future life, even though we were a healthy young Service, was in a parlous state.

My own thoughts about the use of the air were given an opportunity during that year to develop in a way that was of great importance to my own future. Up to that time my experience, though extensive enough, had been devoted almost wholly to the practical aspects of flying. But in the early spring of 1922, Stuffy Dowding put forward my name as one of those to attend the first course of the newly created R.A.F. Staff College.

In the determined effort that he made to place training above all else, Boom Trenchard had already started, two years before, the Royal Air Force Cadet College at Cranwell. On April 4, 1922, there was opened at Andover, in Hampshire, this Staff College which was to provide such valuable instruction for those of us who were already well equipped in actual flying experience, but who needed to be able to sit down for a while and exchange views under suitable guidance and in a more academic atmosphere than could ever be found on an airdrome or in working on the staff. It was arranged that twenty Air Force officers, with additional students from the Royal Navy, the Army, the Indian Army and the Dominions, should attend each course, which was to last one year.

Those of us who had spent our time as more or less enthusiastic young amateurs in the rough and tumble of wartime flying were already discovering that being a regular officer in the Royal Air Force was very different from serving in the Royal Flying Corps during the war. The way of life in the new Service was being shaped in a mold that was a blending of the styles of both the Royal Navy and the Army. We were all quite prepared to play our part in that; but to it we added our own particular brand of light-heartedness, even if it did at times smack of irreverence. That was by then too deeply ingrained in us ever to be lightly discarded; and those who were responsible for shaping us and our way of thought were much too wise ever to try to erase it.

We who were at the Staff College in the beginning will always be thankful that one of our instructors was Wilfrid Freeman. He was then a group captain. If ever there was one man in the R.A.F. who could inspire the very best in creative thinking, it was Wilfrid Freeman, and we all benefited from that. Among the other young officers on the course with me who were eventually to become leaders in the R.A.F. were Keith Park, Richard Peirse, John Baldwin and Peter Drummond. But the outstanding student of our group was Squadron Leader C. F. A. Portal, who was known to all of us as Peter Portal. Even in those early days he showed that there must be a great deal ahead for him.

It is possible that we who remained in the Services after the war were more sheltered—I had known how cold and draughty it could be outside during the year that I had spent as a civilian—but I do not think that we abused the opportunity that was given to us to regain our senses. I know that I worked hard enough, particularly during my time at the Staff College, and I gladly took on extra work, part of which was trying to do more than just learn all that there was to learn about the way in which the Air Force was to be run. Carrying further all that I had learned from Stuffy Dowding during the time that I had spent on his staff, I came to feel that if one was to get ahead one must go as far as possible in learning to master the handling of paper work. I had been a good student from my days at school and up at Oxford, and while still young I had learned to read well and quickly; and while I was at the Staff

College I set myself additional tasks by writing various papers which enabled me to win some valuable prizes.

After completing the Staff College course I was posted for the first time to the Air Ministry. It was the beginning of what was to become a long experience of staff work there. Stuffy Dowding was by then Director of Training, and under him I was given the work of running Flying Training; the stress that was being laid on this meant that I was again fortunate in being so closely associated with the actual building of the new Air Force.

With that first appointment to the Air Ministry I also came more directly in touch with what was going on in the struggles for control of the Air Force. It was not a happy picture, for the Army and the Royal Navy were both out for our blood. Even those of us who were comparatively junior officers on the Air Staff were very well aware of the fight that was being put up for our survival; and we all seemed to spend a great deal of our time drafting papers for Trenchard to use as ammunition to fire, particularly at the Royal Navy.

By the spring of 1922 the issue over the retention of a separate and independent Air Force had become badly—and perhaps purposely—clouded through a great deal of gossip, speculation and whispering campaigns; and finally Winston Churchill was compelled to take the firm stand and point out that the Service did exist and that it would take a repeal of the Act of Parliament that had created the Royal Air Force in the first place to get rid of it. To Trenchard's great delight, that led to a definite statement in the House of Commons on Government policy about the air, and Churchill was able to say: "We consider that it would be a retrograde step at this time to abolish the Air Ministry and to re-absorb the air service into the Admiralty and the War Office." It was the beginning of the rout of what has been called "the unholy alliance" of the admirals and the generals and their supporters in their campaign against Trenchard.

There appeared in The Times at this period a series of articles which caused consternation in the minds of a great many people who should have been better acquainted with the facts. It was revealed that France had the most powerful and strongly equipped air force in the world. Coming right at a time when Westminster was embroiled in senseless arguments about whether or not Britain should even have a separate Air Force, this revelation—which was known well enough to the Air Staff—came as a timely warning, because the attitude then of France toward Germany left many shuddering over our inability to be able to do anything about it should that become necessary.

No sooner had I arrived at the Air Ministry at the beginning of 1923 to take up my new post as a young squadron leader on the Staff than France made a definite move. Under the cloak of the vexed question of the German default in payment of reparations, she occupied the Ruhr. "France's consuming passion for security clashed with Britain's policy of reconciliation," one historian has recorded. Ridiculous as it may sound, that forced us at the Air Ministry to start thinking in terms of a possible war, with France as the potential enemy.

During the past year or so I had found that my own personal interests in all that was happening had been widening. Largely as a result of my success in winning a prize for a paper on the value of aircraft in a naval action—about which I knew, in fact, very little—I became involved in this aspect of the use of the air in a way that was to continue throughout my Service career. And I could not help being intrigued, as well as stimulated, by the clash of the giants: Trenchard, our own Chief of the Air Staff, and Beatty, the First Sea Lord. One could scarcely call Field Marshal Sir Henry Wilson, the Chief of the Imperial General Staff at that time, a giant. He caused us trouble enough; but he was almost as much a misfortune to the Army as he was a thorn in the side of Trenchard.

There is something that is so sad about the struggle that was put up by the Royal Navy to try and wipe out the Air Force and grab for themselves their share of the air. Although they had a fine lot of aviators in the Navy, many of whom became part of the Royal Air Force, most of the admirals of that time understood very little about the air, for all the urgency of the problem. Trenchard knew that, and in his wisdom he said that although they were not yet ready for it, someday they would have to be given their share of the air.

But not all the admirals were blind. The toughest and roughest of the lot—the redoubtable old Jackie Fisher, the man who had been responsible for so much of the battleship thinking in the first place—had already gone on record with the statement: "By land and by sea the approaching aircraft development knocks out the present fleet, makes invasion practicable, cancels our being an island, transforms the atmosphere into a battleground of the future. There is only one thing to do to the ostriches who are spending these vast millions on what is as useful for the next war as bows and arrows. Sack the lot."

One would like to think that it was the chilling message about the future of the big ships that made the admirals and their supporters want a part of the air, and I believe that there were those who did think that way. But for all that, and for all Fisher's warning, the Navy went on thinking in terms of "spending these vast millions" on their big ships while the Royal Air Force was near starvation.

But we in this country were not alone in our struggles with the Navy over who was to have control of the air, for right at the time that all the wordy battles were going on in London, the same sort of scrapping was taking place in the United States. In fact, what was to become known as the Bomb versus Battleship argument was even more heated across the other side of the Atlantic, and I followed with the keenest interest the fight that Billy Mitchell was putting up for his own air service.

American naval thought was dominated by the same misconception that caused our own Royal Navy to be at that time so pigheaded. It was an insistence that an airplane would always be shot down long before it could ever reach the ships and drop its bombs, and that even if the airplane did get through it could never sink a warship. Added to that there was, in the case of the Americans, even less interest right after the war in military aviation than was shown by our people.

When the American Congress refused to have anything to do with either the Treaty of Versailles or the League of Nations, it meant that the American people withdrew from the rest of the world and relied on the oceans to the east and to the west of them for protection. Isolationism became their overriding state of mind, and with that they abandoned the air even more disastrously than we did. Billy Mitchell and other exponents of air power tried to speak up, but the response from the United States was just as reactionary as it was from the Royal Navy. Admittedly there were some American naval officers of the highest rank who understood what Mitchell was trying to say, but the forces against the air were formidable ones.

As early as 1921 Billy Mitchell had forced a showdown in the bomb versus battleship argument in the United States, and he had proved beyond all doubt what could be done with bombs dropped from aircraft by sinking a former German battleship of 27,000 tons which had been surrendered to the Americans after the war and which was considered unsinkable. But even that unpalatable proof to the die-hards of how wrong they were did little to further

Mitchell's ideas about the establishment of American air power. The United States was well protected by the oceans, the argument persisted, and the oceans could be taken care of by the Navy.

On both sides of the Atlantic the big ships went on being built, although some concession was made in the form of a few aircraft carriers. But no genuine attempt was made to listen to the few who were trying to make clear the real meaning of air power. It was of the greatest interest to me that there should be an even more exaggerated neglect of this in America than there was in this country. They got themselves into such a muddle that they even went to the extreme of crucifying Billy Mitchell in 1925 by court-martialing him and throwing him out of the Service.

The main difference between Billy Mitchell and Boom Trenchard was that Mitchell was a firebrand, and it was that which got him into trouble. Trenchard could be outspoken and he had a lot to say; but he knew better than Mitchell how to take care of himself when it came to any in-fighting. But out of Mitchell's sacrifice some good did come to the Americans. "Our Navy," Hap Arnold was later to write, "made a study of the entire affair and of all the incidents relating thereto, and became air-minded in a big way. They even went out of their way to find new means of using aircraft in naval operations."

In summarizing what happened in Britain during those early years of the period between the wars, the historian Michael Howard has said: "The story is of course a melancholy one of confusion and short-sightedness, arising from the stubborn refusal of the Government and nation to think at all seriously about defence once the first world war was over."

The story was indeed a melancholy one. During the four years between 1922 and 1926 that I was to spend at the Air Ministry, I was busy with the ordinary routine of helping to organize the flying training of the R.A.F.; but at the back of my mind all the time there was, as it was inevitable that there should have been, some knowledge of and feeling about what was happening abroad. If the politicians refused to think about it and the public was in no position to know about it, we who were on the Air Staff could not help knowing something about what was going on. It was our job to know and to advise, and for all the criticism that has been leveled at us, I think that was done. Beyond advising our political masters, we could not go; and we had to do what we could for our own Service with whatever weapons were allowed us.

When the air estimates were introduced in the year of 1923,

they amounted to £18,605,000. For the year 1965–66 the air estimates come to £503,800,000, with an additional £274,960-000 for the Ministry of Aviation. Thinking about disarmament was just as much in the minds of all people back in the early twenties as it is now; and which of the Services was to be the bastion upon which we were to rely should there be any necessity for that was, as it still is, the perplexing question.

After a final showdown in what the Secretary of State for Air—who was then Sir Samuel Hoare—has described as "the fierce battle of July, 1923," the Board of Admiralty was finally routed. The press had a field day, and there was the usual wild speculation. The Prime Minister announced that the reasons "that there should be a single air service must, in the opinion of the government be accepted . . ." With that Boom Trenchard had won for us our lasting freedom to make plans unhindered by the threat of annihilation.

17 / Home and Away

THE POWERFUL BOOST given to flying by the First World War, followed by the way in which public imagination was stirred by the deeds of the pioneers in long-distance flying during the years after the war, made the people of Britain conscious enough of the air. But with us, flying had come to be generally regarded as a medium for travel or as a sport rather than in its more lethal context.

In Germany flying was viewed in a very different light, and long before Adolf Hitler and Hermann Goering came to power, a determined move was made to find some means of evading the limitations imposed by the peace treaty. The Germans were forbidden to have any military air forces, but there was no prohibition against the manufacture and the possession of civil aircraft; and throughout the twenties they industriously went about developing and building aircraft which, although classified as civil machines, were designed with a sharp eye for adaptation to military use.

Aircraft designers with names that were to become very well known were given every opportunity to carry on with their undercover planning; and, through subsidies, there were built for them outside Germany factories where they could carry on with their work. While Hitler was still struggling for a foothold, Hermann Goering—who, right after the end of the war, had said to a gathering of his former brother officers: "I implore you to cherish hatred"—had come under his spell, and the courageous man against whom I had fought in the air over the Western Front was busy organizing for Hitler the rabble on a military basis. Despite the prohibition by the terms of the peace treaty, the Germans even then had a large mission in the Soviet Union which was helping the Russians in the training of their new air force, and, in doing that, at the same time helping themselves. Through careful planning, the German civil airline Lufthansa had established by 1926 a network of air routes, and it was operating in a manner that made it the foremost airline in Europe.

In Britain as in Germany there developed during those early years of the twenties a keen interest in light airplane flying; but whereas in Germany it was all part of a shrewd plan, in this country the movement was for quite some time distinct from what was meant by civil or commercial aviation and military flying. It was literally the flying of light airplanes purely for pleasure. Although anchored to a desk at the Air Ministry, I developed a strong interest in this type of flying, and over a period of four years I did a great deal of it in various competitions.

It was not until after the Germans had shown what could be done that our own light airplane movement received any official encouragement by the Government through the formation and sponsoring of flying clubs. This encouragement enabled a great many men and women to learn to fly and provided a reserve of pilots to call upon for further training in an emergency. My participation in the movement did not come until a little later; it was not official, and my own activities were limited mainly to racing.

In the summer of 1924 I heard that a competition for light airplanes was to be staged at the airfield at Lympne, in Kent. It was to be the first of three historic meetings over the course of the next three years in which many young men whose names are now famous in aviation tried out their ideas. I had the rare experience of participating, as a pilot, in all of these meetings. In that first year I made inquiries around the aircraft manufacturers, and I discovered that the firm of George Parnall and Company, a small outfit down at Bristol, had built an aircraft specifically for this competition. They were calling it the Parnall Pixie, and after a little lobbying I managed to induce them to let me fly it in the races.

This additional flying was quite apart from my routine duties in the Royal Air Force, and it all had to be done in my own time. There were a fair number of us in the Service who were interested in this meeting, and some even entered machines which they had built themselves in organized groups. In addition to the pleasure that was to be had in the actual flying, there was for all of us the added attraction of the valuable cash prizes which were provided by both the Air Ministry and private donors.

The Pixie was a good little single- and two-seater airplane, and it was easy to handle and to fly. The feature about it that was of particular interest was that it had been ingeniously designed so that it could be used as either a monoplane in speed tests or a biplane for slow flying. When needed, the additional plane, the top one, could be fitted in a matter of only a few minutes. As with all the other aircraft entered, it had an engine of only just over thirty horsepower.

The competitions were held at Lympne at the end of September and early in October, 1924, and about a dozen manufacturers entered aircraft for the varied and rigorous tests, which called for slow flying, landing in the shortest possible space, taking off over an obstacle, and a speed test around a triangular course. Parnall had entered three different versions of his Pixie; but after we got to Lympne the judges decided that they could not allow us to enter the airplane as both a monoplane and a biplane. We had to decide to enter it as either one or the other, so we put it in as a biplane, hoping to score so many marks in the landing and take-off events that we would build up a sufficient lead to offset the losses that were inevitable through having to fly the Pixie as a biplane in the speed contest.

Judged by the standards of today, or even by those of only a few years after these early competitions, the frequency of mechanical failures among all of the aircraft entered was fantastically high, and the ingenuity and patience of all of us were tried to the limit. But it was a challenge, and since none of us would have been there in the first place if we had not been of the type to relish challenges, we all had an exciting race of an unexpected kind seeing to it that the whole meeting did not come to a premature end through running out of aircraft.

Our expectations of success in slow flying were justified, and I won the landing and the take-off events against all comers; but when it came to the speed test, our Pixie, as a biplane, was much too slow. I could only barely maintain the minimum required speed of sixty miles per hour, and my engine was overheating and dropping revs because of my efforts to work up some speed by running it flat out. We did not get anywhere in the final assessments. But I had enjoyed the flying, and it gave me an opportunity to mix freely with and to come to know the test pilots, the aircraft designers, the engineers, and the manufacturers; some of these men were later to become good friends of mine and world famous in their work.

In the August Bank Holiday meeting at Lympne in the following year, 1925, I flew a D.H.53 which I had managed to persuade De Havilland's to lend me. By then I had already come to know Geoffrey de Havilland quite well and his engineers, Charles Walker and Frank Halford. It was the beginning of an association with the

De Havilland Company in which we were to grow up together, and it has continued for over forty years. Eventually it led to our close cooperation in the development of the Comet and the Trident during my time after the Second World War as chairman of British European Airways.

That early D.H.53 was one of the first of their light airplanes. It was a very small, low-wing monoplane, compact but robust, a single-seater with a good turn of speed. Starting from scratch I won my heat and finished second in the final of the Holiday Handicap, which was flown in pouring rain. Bert Hinkler, one of the legendary figures in the early days, was hard on my heels, coming in third. In another race I finished second by only two feet, the propeller of my D.H.53 having split during the contest. The next day I flew the same aircraft in another race, but this time my engine failed on the second lap and I had to make a forced landing.

By 1926 light airplane clubs subsidized by the government were springing up all over the country; and for the last of the three important years of the famous Lympne competitions, I arranged with the firm of A. V. Roe and Company—which was one of the great pioneering aircraft manufacturers in this country—to fly a fine little two-seater of theirs known as the Avis. The trials for that year included a series of races to Brighton and Eastbourne in order to attract the attention of the holidaymakers at the various popular resorts along the coast. But I did not do very well because the Avis, which was by then quite well known and had been flown by Bert Hinkler at the meeting the year before, was rather slow, and most of the time I seemed to run into strong head winds.

On the second day, while flying in a race to Eastbourne and back, my engine cut out near Winchelsea, and in the forced landing that I had to make, I ran into a shallow ditch. The undercarriage of the Avis buckled, and the machine had to be towed back to Lympne. Repairs were made, and a couple of days later I was flying again. But no sooner had I taken off from Lympne, heading in the direction of the sea, when again the engine failed. The ground beneath me was a hillside which sloped away quite steeply from the edge of the airdome toward Romney Marsh—it is the same airfield used today by the cross-Channel car-ferry service —and I found myself gliding with a dead engine toward what looked like an inevitable crash into the trees at the bottom of the hill. The only action that I could possibly take was to do something which we had always been taught was fatal. I whipped the aircraft right around down wind and with a dead engine and sailed straight toward the slope of the ground as it rose in front of me;

just as I was about to crash, I yanked the stick sharply back as far as it would go. The aircraft reared up for just the moment that was needed, and then it sat quietly down on the slope.

The machine was not damaged—the engine had failed through magneto trouble—and it was dragged through the fields and back to the airdrome, and again the Avro people managed to repair it. After a couple of test flights the next morning I went in for some more races; but I got nowhere at that meeting. In spite of the good handicaps that I was allowed, my aircraft was too slow.

The rate at which an officer receives promotion in the middle ranks in the Services is always a matter that hangs over his head like a guillotine, ready at any moment to come crashing down, putting an end to his career. By the end of 1924, while I was still at the Air Ministry, I had been a squadron leader for seven years. The regulations were such that it was not possible to become a wing commander before one was thirty-two years of age, and since I was only just coming up to thirty-one I was, even after seven years, too young for promotion. There should have been nothing for me to worry about in that. I was high up in seniority in the list of squadron leaders. But there were quite a few officers on the staff who, while junior to me in the work that we were doing, had been promoted over my head because their age had made that possible.

It was the sort of pinprick that is always present in Service life, and it can affect and slow down very seriously the course of one's career. Although I tried to bear it with patience, I found it an irritating stumbling block. There was in it the threat of being passed over later for more senior promotion and so being prevented from getting ahead. By then I was sufficiently experienced, and interested, to want to be able to make the most of my Service career. Eventually it was realized that the position that I was in was so ridiculous that the matter was brought up before the Air Council. They took pity on me, and by special dispensation I was promoted to the rank of wing commander on January 1, 1925. I was then just a week over thirty-one years of age.

Only a short time after that promotion I got myself involved in an incident of which I was not at all proud, and which again brought me under the eagle eye of Boom Trenchard. Arrangements had been made for him to inspect the Flying Training School at Sealand, in the Midlands, and since flying training was my responsibility at the Air Ministry, I was detailed to accompany the C.A.S. during his visit to the station. Knowing Trenchard as I did, I thought that it would be a wise move on my part if I made sure that I knew all the answers to the questions that he would be likely to ask, and the day before his visit I flew from Kenley to Sealand in a D.H.9a, taking a mechanic with me as a passenger.

I had not had much experience in flying the D.H.9a, which was the war horse of our light bombers during the war, and it seemed to me that, compared with most of the types of aircraft with which I was familiar, it was rather fast in its landing. Feeling that it would be as well to allow for all the room that I could get on the actual airfield, I came gliding in between two hangars. At the very last moment I found a wireless mast sticking up in the middle of the gap between the hangars, and I was heading straight toward it. There was no possible chance of avoiding it, and it was too late to open up the engine and go around again, and in a moment my starboard wings had slashed into the mast. The aircraft was flung violently around while still in the air and sent crashing onto the roof of one of the hangars.

The D.H.9a had an evil reputation for catching fire all too readily in an accident, and what with that and the possibility of sliding off the roof and crashing to the ground, both my passenger and I were out of it very quickly and helped to get down to safety. I was angry with myself as well as crestfallen because, with all my experience, I had been guilty of a bad error of judgment. I should have kept a much sharper eye on what I was doing, and I should have spotted much sooner the wireless mast that was standing in the way.

A crew of mechanics and fitters immediately went to work, and they got the damaged aircraft down from the roof of the hangar and out of the way before Boom Trenchard arrived the next day. I was grateful enough for that because I should have hated having to explain to him what had happened. But there was still quite a hole left in the roof of the hangar. It was covered over with a tarpaulin, and all of us prayed that the C.A.S. would not notice it. He did not seem to, and whether Trenchard ever heard about what had actually happened—he was the kind of man who always seemed to hear about everything—I never knew. He said nothing to me about it, and perhaps it was only my imagination which made me think that there was a slightly suspicious gleam in his eye as I accompanied him the next day on his tour of inspection.

Of all the light aircraft ever developed and built in this country, the most successful was the De Havilland Moth. It first appeared while I was on my first tour of duty at the Air Ministry, and, since I was particularly occupied with flying training in the Royal Air

Force, I was keenly interested in this fine airplane. The name of the Moth has become a legend, and countless thousands of men and women were to receive their first instruction in learning to fly in it. The airframe of the Moth was designed by Geoffrey de Havilland, and its engine by Frank Halford; and it was the first time that an effort by one coordinated team was able to produce a complete airplane in this way.

The Moth was first flown in February, 1925, but Geoffrey de Havilland cautiously held it back from too much competition flying until he was absolutely sure that he had the aircraft as he wanted it. At one of the flying meetings held at Bournemouth in 1926, Hubert Broad—who was the test pilot for De Havilland's— and I flew two Moths in the races. On December 28 of that year, I took Stuffy Dowding up in a Moth as a passenger. He was then the Director of Training at the Air Ministry and the head of the department in which I was serving, and he wanted to see for himself what this new aircraft could offer to the Service as a trainer. It was the start of one of the most important aspects of the Moth's success story that was to extend over the next thirty years.

In addition to the memorable Lympne meetings of the light airplane enthusiasts there were also meetings in other parts of the country, and as a pilot I participated in many of them. During the Easter break in 1927 I took part in a three-day meeting at Bournemouth for which the Avro people provided me with an Avian. A month later I took part in the Hampshire Air Pageant held on the airdrome at Hamble, near Southampton, which is now the site of the College of Air Training at which the pilots are trained for British European Airways and British Overseas Airways. At that meeting I flew again in an Avro Avian.

We were all unquestionably enthusiasts in this light airplane flying, and while it was of value to me to be able to mix with so many people outside the Service who were genuinely interested and concerned with aviation, there was always the tempting prospect of being able to pick up some of the prize money, which did help to put a little icing on the cake. It was also this extra money which I was able to earn that enabled me during the earlier part of the twenties to become one of those from this country who helped to turn the summer in the south of France into the holiday season. For many years the winter had been the season for the French Riviera; and very few ever thought of going there in the summer. It was considered to be much too hot, and those of us who did start going there in the summer were considered to be greatly daring and not quite right in the head.

But we had good reasons for our trips to the south of France in the summer, the main one being that at that time of the year the prices were at rock bottom and not, as they are now, up in the stratosphere. During one summer in the early twenties, my wife and I stayed at quite a decent pension in La Condamine, which, unbelievable as it may sound, cost us five shillings a day each, and that included bed, three meals a day, and a garage for our car. But by the late twenties the change was underway, with the seasons for going to the south of France becoming reversed. We who pioneered the holiday in the sun, and who later, through the air services that we developed, brought it within easy reach of the masses, also managed to spoil a lot of our own simple pleasures.

After nearly four years at the Air Ministry, which was a longer period for a young officer to serve there than was usual, I was informed that my repeated requests for a move to more active work had at last been granted. I was to be given command of the fighter station at Tangmere, in Sussex. It was a prospect that delighted me because fighters were still my main interest. But no sooner had I handed over my job at the Air Ministry to Arthur Tedder and got myself all organized for a move to the country than the plans were changed, and I was told that I was one of four officers from the Royal Air Force who had been selected to attend the first course of the newly created Imperial Defence College.

In a way I was disappointed in this change, but I was promised a fighter station immediately after I completed the course. I had to admit to a feeling of being a little flattered that I should be one of the first to be selected for this course at the entirely new inter-Service college. Its purpose was to give a final, almost postgraduate, polish to the education of carefully chosen staff officers from the three fighting Services, the Civil Service, and, as with the Staff College, the Dominions. That first course started at the beginning of January, 1927, and I was the youngest officer among those to attend it. Quite a few of those with whom I spent the next year in very intensive study were to become leaders in the Services during the Second World War.

The Commandant of the I.D.C. was Admiral Sir Herbert Richmond, who later became Master of Downing College, Cambridge. He was a pleasant enough man, but rather salty and not very interested in the air. We were all, instructors and pupils alike, feeling our way, and we spent our entire time working out together (and with all the Services being represented and working so closely together we were able constantly to exchange ideas) every conceivable situation which might develop in wars with France, Germany, Russia or any other possible opponents.

At one stage in our considerations, we prepared for a war with France, our immediate object being to work out how we would handle the French territories in the Middle East. True to form, our worthy commandant envisaged in this case a great naval battle with the French fleet out in the Mediterranean. Some of us, including all those from the R.A.F., made ourselves very unpopular with him when we suggested that the first thing to do would be to bomb the hell out of Paris and so force the French to come quickly to terms. The Admiral made it known that he considered that such a proposition was off-side. It spoiled all his dreams of a great naval action.

Among the students at the I.D.C. with me during that year of 1927 there was a Lieutenant-Colonel C. J. E. Auchinleck, as he was then, of the Indian Army. It was obvious to me from the beginning that Auchinleck was a man of strong character and will, and that he had a sound understanding of the uses of the Army in a tactical sense. Also on that course there was a lieutenant-colonel of the Royal Artillery named Alan Brooke. He made a very strong impression on all of us. Along with John Tovey and Ralph Leatham, who were then both captains in the Royal Navy, these were some of the men who were to become so well known in the years that lay ahead.

One of the questions that never ceases to intrigue and quite often to anger the later generations is how our political leaders came to follow the tortuous course in their thinking that they appeared to be compelled to take back in the years of the twenties and the early thirties. When in December, 1925, the Treaty of Locarno was signed, "there were great rejoicings," to quote Winston Churchill; and "after this memorable Instrument had received the cordial assent of Parliament, Mr. Austen Chamberlain received the Garter and the Nobel Peace Prize." Our Foreign Secretary may have received the highest of awards for his part in negotiating this security pact; but there are many today who will ask what "this memorable Instrument" was all about.

The signing of the Locarno Treaty raised all our hopes, and the meetings of the delegates from Britain, France, Germany, Belgium, Italy, Czechoslovakia and Poland which had produced it seemed to have found an answer that was going to provide us with a lasting peace. To quote again from Winston Churchill: "Thus did the Western European democracies agree to keep the peace among themselves in all circumstances, and to stand united against any one of their number who broke the contract and marched in aggression upon a brother land."

But for all that was intended by these fine words, my work as a professional airman was to think about what we should do in the event of war. Any personal loathing that I might have felt for war—and it was a strong one that was based on long firsthand experience of the Western Front of 1914–18—had to be pushed to one side so that I could maintain the correctly objective attitude that I had to adopt toward my work. I felt that I managed to achieve that while I was at the Air Ministry and the I.D.C.; but it was nevertheless a relief when the time came for me to return to the less complicated life that was to be found in operational Service flying.

The promise that had been made to me before I went to the I.D.C. was fulfilled, and with the completion of the course I was given command of the fighter station at North Weald, in Essex, a few miles to the north of Epping Forest, and still within easy reach of London. The wing there consisted of two squadrons which had been particularly well known to me during the war—Nos. 29 and 56—and they were equipped with Siskins, biplane single-seater fighters manufactured by Armstrong Whitworth. The Siskin was very much an aircraft of the transitional interwar period during which we changed from the use of wood to metal in basic structure. It was not as light and as agile as the fighters with which we had become so familiar in our flying during the war—the S.E.5a and the Camel, for instance—but it was better equipped, and above all else it was docile.

It was this last quality which enabled the Siskin to provide such colorful demonstrations in the air at the displays at Hendon, and it was the best aircraft we ever had for aerobatics. During the time that I had spent at the Air Ministry I had continued to take part in the annual displays, and one year, flying a D.H.53, I won the race for Air Ministry staff officers. At the display in 1929 I led a wing of three Siskin squadrons—my own, Nos. 29 and 56, from North Weald; and No. 19 from Duxford—in an exhibition of wing formation flying, our outstanding stunt being "threading the needle." While the aircraft of two of the squadrons flew around line astern in a tight circle, I led those of No. 56 in a dive, in squadron formation, through the middle of it. That was my last appearance in these immensely popular prewar air displays.

My tour of duty as station commander at North Weald was of importance to me personally through the firsthand experience that I was able to gain of our steadily, if slowly, developing system of home defense. We were a fully operational fighter station, and in

all our work we were part of what was later to become the
structure of Fighter Command with all its elaborate and splendidly
coordinated machinery for the defense of the United Kingdom.

The course that I was following in my career was a logical
enough progression, even if, at the time, I did not fully realize that
it was going to be an immensely valuable one. My command of a
fighter station came about ten years after the first war and ten
years before the second one. A great deal of thought was being
given by those concerned to our home defense, and there was an
ever-increasing awareness of the need for full preparedness against
air attack from the Continent; most of us were greatly concerned
over the inadequacy of our defenses. There was always in our
minds the report prepared by the committee under the guidance of
Jan Christian Smuts as early as August, 1917, in which it was
pointed out that the future held the threat that "aerial operations
with their devastation of enemy lands and destruction of industrial
and populace centres on a vast scale may become the principle
operations of war . . ."

We who were working in the new realm of the air during those
years of the peace between the wars may have been young, as was
our Service; but it can never be said that we did not know all about
the threat that lay ahead. Our efforts to make that clear, and our
struggles to find some form of adequate defense, were deeply
rooted in our realistic understanding of what could happen; and
that understanding was common to young pilots and senior commanders alike. We all grew up together with the knowledge that if
the blow should fall, the task of trying to ward it off would be on
our shoulders. For that reason alone we were always particularly
anxious about the need for the best possible air defense.

During all this time, Boom Trenchard was still strongly inclined
toward the offensive role as the best method of defense, and in
furthering that, he thought in terms of bombers as a deterrent. But
we who had to think more urgently of the moment—as all those
who were trained and experienced in fighters had learned to
think—were more concerned with the best possible use that we
could make of the weapon at hand. We had a fighter structure, but
we were still woefully short of aircraft, and we were totally lacking
in anything approaching an adequate warning system.

In the personal lives of my mother and my father, Robert
Langton Douglas, there was, for all the success that I was able to
achieve and which they both lived to see, a lingering element of
sadness for both of them as a result of their unhappy marriage. Of

the five children born to them during that marriage—which ended in divorce while I was still a mere child—two died within a very short time of their birth; my youngest brother, Archie, was killed on the Western Front while flying in the Royal Flying Corps; and my other brother, Bobbie, died in India in 1928. He had served in the West Kents out there and in Mesopotamia during the war, after which he had gone up to Christ's College, Cambridge, with the Classical Scholarship that he had won at Tonbridge before the war. Joining the Indian Civil Service, he had returned to India, and at the time of his death from cholera, he was a district commissioner.

My brother's death left me as the only surviving child of my father's first marriage. My mother did not marry again. From his second marriage there were for my father three more children; but that marriage also ended in divorce. In 1928 he married for the third time; and that marriage was one of the most sensible things that he ever did in his whole life. Already well-established as an art critic and historian, he was then aged sixty-four, and his third wife was a Scotswoman of only twenty-six years of age named Jean Stewart. She was attractive and intelligent, but at the time I was rather worried that the great difference in their ages might ruin the possibility of a happy marriage. In that I was entirely wrong. Jean was devoted to my father, and she provided him with just the right setting for his brilliant and, at times, restless mind, and her own alert intellect enabled her to be good company for my father and his friends and his associates in his work.

In addition to being the director of the National Gallery of Ireland in Dublin for six years—from 1916 to 1923—my father continued to enhance his reputation as a critic and historian. He added to his established work as a writer further studies of the Italian painters—notably Perugino and Leonardo da Vinci—and he continued to act as an adviser to a number of wealthy men, including Lord Duveen, in the buying of pictures for their collections. This meant that he was able to prosper financially in his canny dealing in pictures as well as being able to enjoy his more academic interests. By the time that I was commanding North Weald at the end of the twenties, he had acquired a pleasant house in Montagu Square in London, and he was enjoying the benefits that came to him from his mounting international reputation as a shrewd dealer in pictures and a sound art critic.

In my own way I was also establishing further my position in my own work in more than mere flying. The long experience that I had had at the Air Ministry and on Staff courses had stimulated my interest in the more academic side of my profession as an airman. I continued to read a great deal, as I have always done, and I was asked by the well-known military historian B. H. Liddell Hart to write an article on air fighting for the *Encyclopaedia Britannica*. He was then one of their senior editors on military matters, and I rather like to think that my article, which was published in the edition produced in 1929, was in its way a small hallmark on my name as an authority on the subject.

With less paper work on my hands at North Weald than had been thrust upon me at the Air Ministry, I was also able to devote a little time to writing about other Service matters, and in 1928 I again received the first prize in one of the official essay contests. The prize money came in handy, and the books that I received with it made a good addition to my own collection. Quite a few of those who, over the years, won these prizes were later to become senior commanders in the Service, and I was in good company.

The way in which the future of the Royal Air Force as an independent Service had become assured was displayed to us of the rank and file more in the way in which the morale of the Service developed and became more buoyant than in any political or official statements. In speaking of that many years later, Lord Templewood, who, as Sir Samuel Hoare, was Secretary of State for Air four times during the 1920's, paid a splendid tribute to Boom Trenchard. "It was only in morale that he demanded perfectionism," Templewood stated. "It was the superb morale that distinguished the Royal Air Force from the other air forces . . . In the face . . . of any formidable attacks, he held fast to his plans, and refused to abate his demands for long periods of training . . . It was obstinacy such as this that convinced the young men in the service that 'Boom' would not let them down."

How thoroughly Boom Trenchard established the character of our independent Service "as an essential part of the doctrine of the indivisibility of air power," as Templewood put it, was later seen in what happened to the French and German air forces. They were not thoroughly independent air services, and when the testing time came they failed through not being free from the control of Army authority.

By the summer of 1929 I had been station commander at North Weald for eighteen months, and I knew that the time was approaching for me for a tour of duty overseas. It was inevitable that I should have to face this as just another stage in my career, and the personal dislike that I have always had of being away from

England for any length of time could not be taken into account. What I had to try and plan for was a posting to some place which would be amenable and which would, at the same time, enable me to see some action. The latter was perhaps the more important consideration, for there was active service enough to be had abroad, and even in those times of peace some officers were making reputations for themselves. One pilot alone won during these years a D.S.O. and bar and a D.F.C. for his work in Iraq and the Aden Protectorate.

In thinking about the prospect of going overseas to any area where there might be unrest, there were several factors that I had to take into account. In the first place I wanted to spend as short a time as possible away from England. That ruled out India because it was a five-year tour of duty out there, and, in any case, it was a notorious command for always being starved of aircraft and equipment. Nor did I like the idea of Iraq, although they were seeing action enough out there. The Sudan seemed to offer the right solution, and I put in for that. It was a tour of only two and a half years, and it was a small, independent command where one would have more responsibility and freedom and be a long way from the headquarters of the Middle East Command in Cairo, under which it came for administration.

In August, 1929, I left England and in the leisurely fashion of those days I went out to Egypt by sea. For three months I was temporarily the wing commander on the air staff in Cairo of the Air Officer Commanding, Middle East; but at the end of the year I handed over what was rather a dull job to Bert Harris, that turbulent character who was to make such a great name for himself as Commander-in-Chief of Bomber Command during the second war.

My tour of duty in the Sudan, or the Anglo-Egyptian Sudan, as it was called in those days, turned out to be a much pleasanter experience than I had anticipated. We were in what might be considered a remote part of the world, although it has been brought to public attention enough today; and yet the Sudan is a country of vital importance if only because the River Nile, flowing from south to north, runs slap through the middle of it. In area it is ten times the size of the whole of the United Kingdom. Today it has emerged as one of the many independent African states, and it is enjoying, or suffering from, the same turbulent domestic life that has always been the lot of the mixed races of the country.

If names mean anything, perhaps listing those of the countries on the boundaries of the Sudan will provide some idea of the huge area that it covers. Libya lies to the northwest; Egypt to the north;

the Red Sea and Eritrea and Abyssinia, or Ethiopia, to the east; Kenya, Uganda and the Congo to the south; and the former French Equatorial territories of Ubangi-Shari and Chad to the west. But for the Nile, the Sudan would probably be nothing but a vast desert.

The types of the people of the Sudan vary as much as the nature of the country, and they never failed to intrigue me. Although we speak of them as Sudanese they are of many different origins, all the way from the noisy and unreliable Fuzzy-Wuzzies in the east to the proud descendants in the west of those who found their way there from Arabia; and down in the south there are the Negroid tribes. Our reason for being in the Sudan was to maintain, as Britain had been doing only in fairly modern times, some form of control over the tribes of natives who were notorious for their disrespect for both law and order. While we never actually had any small wars during the time that I was there, we were nevertheless called upon to give several demonstrations over some of the tribes when they started showing signs of their inherent restiveness.

My headquarters in the Sudan were in Khartoum, the capital, which stands at the junction of the Blue Nile and the White Nile right in the heart of the country. It was a pleasantly picturesque city, and only shortly before I arrived there it had become modern enough for a system of electric trams to be in operation. The waterways of the Nile rivers were developed so that they could provide better contact with the other districts of the Sudan, while a railway ran from Khartoum to Port Sudan on the Red Sea nearly four hundred and fifty miles away to the east. There were also means of traveling to Cairo nearly fifteen hundred miles to the north by rail and steamer. Because of the way in which the rivers converged at Khartoum, and because, in joining, they formed such a great trunk of a guiding line all the way up to the Mediterranean, Khartoum had also become an important staging-post for the flying that was done between Cairo and the Cape.

Our social life of those times was, as might be expected, true to the British pattern. The people with whom I associated were the Air Force officers who were serving under me, and the Army officers, and the civil servants, and they all provided congenial enough company. The climate of Khartoum was quite bearable, even in the hot weather, except for the dust storms—when the Haboobs, as they were known, came swirling in great black clouds across the countryside—and the enormous swarms of locusts which also occasionally darkened the skies. But for a month or two in the winter, the climate was ideal.

One activity that I indulged in which will come as a shock to many of those who think they know me well was the singing that I enjoyed in the male choir in the cathedral. Turned out in scarlet cassock and a surplice, being a member of the choir gave me a great deal of pleasure. I had always enjoyed choral singing, and as a small boy I had had quite a good treble voice. While I was still very young I used to sing in the choir of St. John's Church, Balham. Later I sang as a soloist in the Tonbridge school choir; and after my voice broke I sang in the school choir as a tenor. When I went up to Oxford I sang in the Bach Choir.

At a cocktail party one evening in Khartoum, Bishop Gwynne, who was the Bishop of Egypt and the Sudan, said to me: "Sholto, why do you never come to church?"

The Bishop was a charming old man, and I did not want to offend him, or cause any unnecessary argument on such an occasion by giving him my views on religion. The only way out, I thought, was to be facetious. "I never go to church unless I can both read the lesson and sing in the choir," I replied, hoping that that would stop him dead in his tracks.

"Right, my boy . . . you'll do both next Sunday," he retorted. "Choir practice is at six o'clock on Friday."

At the other extreme from singing in the choir in the cathedral there was my work as the Wing Commander, Sudan. I was the senior R.A.F. officer in the country, and I was responsible for advising on any air operation that might be necessary. For that work I had only one squadron, No. 47, with which to cover this vast parish, but we were equipped with aircraft which were well suited for the work: the Fairey IIIF. It was a largish biplane, a two-seater designed for general purpose flying in either reconnaissance or as a bomber. We had no need for any fighters.

During the rains in the summer we changed over and became partly a float-plane squadron by replacing the wheels of the fixed undercarriage with floats. The rivers and the lakes of the southern Sudan filled up during the summer floods, and many of our landing fields were apt to be put out of action through the rain and the resulting mud. With our floats we were able to retain our mobility and, almost regardless of conditions, cover the whole of the southern Sudan. We usually spent six months of the year working with floats and the other six months with wheels.

As a pilot I did several hundreds of hours of flying in our aircraft all over the Sudan, and I became quite skillful and experienced with the float-plane. From Khartoum we could fly out to the Red Sea; and we used to fly up either the Nile or the coast bordering the Red Sea on our journeys from the Sudan to Cairo. The distances we had to travel were very great for those days, and, since our aircraft had a cruising speed of not much over one hundred miles an hour, even in the air it often took us a long time to get anywhere.

On one flight that I made up the Red Sea from the Sudan, we decided to stop for the night at a spot about halfway along the coast between Port Sudan and Cairo where the coast itself sticks out in a point known as Ras Banas, which provides a gulf called Foul Bay. We landed on the water and taxied up to the beach. The coast of this desolate region is most inhospitable, and at any time of the year the heat is very trying. Inland, about two hundred miles due west, there is now being built on the Nile the Aswan High Dam. But the desert along the coast, for all the heat, can be strangely attractive; and to my delight that overnight stop was to provide me with one of my pleasantest memories of the time that I spent in that part of the world.

At the head of the gulf there is the very ancient little seaport of Berenice, which was named after the mother of one of the Ptolemys; in centuries gone by, it was a connecting link in the trade between India and Arabia and Egypt. My attention was attracted to the ruins of a temple which we found there, just back from the beach, standing completely alone in the desert. Later I learned that the inscriptions that we saw in the temple preserved the name of Tiberius, the Roman Emperor. We pitched our camp and cooked our supper and we slept the night on the beach, and the next day we flew on to Cairo. Later I made a point of again visiting that lonely and fascinating place.

The two years and three months that I was to spend in the Sudan brought me in contact with an entirely new world; and so far as flying was concerned I did more there than I have ever done in any similar time span. I reached then the peak of my efficiency as a pilot, even if the Air Officer Commanding, Middle East, did not think so. That appointment in the latter part of my time in the Sudan was filled by Cyril Newall, who was then an air vice-marshal.

On the first tour of inspection that Cyril Newall made of the Sudan, I flew him around myself in one of our Fairey IIIF's. He insisted on making it a very thoroughgoing tour, and I took him to Juba, not far from the Congo border, and the Sudd, deep down in Equatoria. Some of the low flying that I did then with Newall in the other seat caused him to tell me somewhat tartly after we landed that he considered that it was altogether too dangerous, and that I had run unnecessary risks. I had thought that I was giving him a particularly good view of the vast amount of wildlife that was to be seen down there, and I nearly took the routine dim view of the opinions of officers of air rank. My own brass hat might have been in the not too distant future, but the thought of that never entered my mind; and if anybody had suggested then that Newall and I should ever become as closely associated in our work as we did ten years later I would have greeted the idea with hoots of laughter.

It was down in the south that there occurred the only approach to any form of headache that we had during the entire time that I spent in the Sudan, and it came about in the southeastern corner of the Sudan and in northern Kenya. Marauding tribes of Abyssinians used to come sweeping down out of the mountains of their own country, and they would cross the border and run riot along both the western and the eastern shores of Lake Rudolf. Pouncing on the more peaceful tribes of northern Kenya, the intruders would kill and loot and steal their cattle and their women.

The government of Kenya appealed to the Governor-General of the Sudan for help, and a detachment of the Equatorial Corps of the Sudan Defence Force was detailed to march across country from Kapoeta, the farthest station in the southeast of the Sudan, and join up with the Kenya Regiment at Lake Rudolf, and together they were to try and scare off these raiders from Abyssinia. I detailed a flight of five aircraft from No. 47 Squadron to cooperate with our troops during their march of two or three hundred miles through country that was only very sketchily mapped.

It was not likely that I would leave myself out of what showed promise of being an interesting expedition, and I went along with the flight. We were down there for some weeks. We accompanied the troops throughout their march, and sometimes, when the terrain was suitable, we landed beside them. They were making their way through very rough country that was at first only slightly inhabited and then completely uninhabited and which was, for the most part, a steaming equatorial jungle. Finding our way about in the air was not easy, and on this expedition we explored from the air two ranges of mountains with a deep, heavily wooded valley between them, to the west of Lake Rudolf. They were marked in only the vaguest and most inaccurate fashion on our maps; and some fifty miles east of Kapoeta, in Equatoria, we came across a lake that nobody seemed to know anything about.

The officer who was in charge on that expedition was Charles

Steele, an old friend from the war and just after it, and of whom I saw a great deal in Khartoum, where he was one of those under my command. We were flying alongside each other when we spotted this great lake of which there was not the slightest indication on any of our maps, and around which were hordes of wild game of every variety. We could also see that there were a few native huts at isolated points around the edge of the lake. We had heard a great deal about the big game and the wildlife that were to be seen in Kenya; but on those flights over the southeastern corner of the Sudan we saw countless numbers of giraffes, rhinoceros, deer, buffaloes and elephants.

Our discovery of the lake prompted the Governor-General, when I got back to Khartoum and put in a report on our expedition, to suggest that it should be called Lake Sholto. But that can be no more than an ephemeral claim to fame because I am not so sure that the lake, for all its size at the time when we saw it, was always there. Vast areas of the marshes and swamps that extend for miles in that part of the country become flooded with the rains, and on quite a few occasions I landed on floats on water at places where, according to our maps, there should have been no water at all.

Our orders for that expedition were to help chase the marauding Abyssinians back across the border, but we saw no indications of what it was reported had been going on before we arrived, and we had to be satisfied with being merely explorers. In all our flying, we were largely showing the flag, and whenever any of the naturally rebellious natives refused to pay their taxes, or started playing up and raiding their neighboring tribes, we would arrive on the scene and, after due warning, stage demonstrations of flying. It appeared to be an effective enough way of keeping the peace; but that was in a world and an age that were both very different from what we know today.

During the twelve years that had elapsed since the end of the war, I had followed with great interest the accounts of the exploits of another of my former adversaries in the air over the Western Front: the famous German ace Ernst Udet. He had probably been the most active in his flying of all of us, and he had achieved a great reputation as a pilot who was ready to take on any sort of flying, the more hazardous the better, particularly if it had anything to do with the making of films. The flying that he did in 1929 among the mountains of Switzerland for the film *The White Hell of Pitz Palu* will always be some of the finest that has ever been placed on record.

Late in the following year Ernst Udet spent three months in Tanganyika with a company that was filming the lives of the natives and the big game, and during that time he had continued with his own brand of hair-raising flying. There was nothing that he would not take on. When the season of the rains came and the company prepared to leave, Udet and a cameraman flew out in his light airplane, heading north. After refueling at Kisumu, they set off again, still heading north, the cameraman shooting film of the herds of the various wild animals that they could see so easily from the air. They had some trouble on the way when the fuel tank broke away from its brackets, but Udet managed to get to a small airfield in Uganda. After making repairs he flew on to Juba, in the southern Sudan, where he refueled again, and then he started off for Malakal.

We had heard, in Khartoum, that Udet had been down in Tanganyika and Kenya, and we had also been told that he had started in his light airplane on his way back to Germany. We knew well enough from our own experiences that he was going to have to fly, on his way from Juba to Malakal, over a vast area of swamp and marsh some two hundred miles long by one hundred miles wide. It was a desolate and treacherous stretch of country, and we knew that there were only a few dry spots where the ground rose above the level of the water-soaked swamp through which the White Nile flows to the north.

After a day had passed with no news of Udet since the time that he left Juba, the news that he was missing broke in the world's newspapers. He had become too well known a figure in the public eye for it to be anything but a sensation, and there was a brisk demand in Khartoum for news, with telephone calls pouring in from all over the world. As soon as it was quite clear that he was overdue at Malakal, I sent three of my aircraft down to the southern Sudan to do a square search of the area to the north of Juba. At the same time, Campbell Black, a very experienced pilot who later made a big name for himself in long-distance flying, took off from Juba, after letting me know what he was doing, to join in the search.

Three days passed with no news, and then there came a message from Juba that Campbell Black, who had been flying over that area for some years and knew it very well, had found Udet and his companion and their airplane beside a rough track that ran through the area of the swamp connecting up the dry spots. The airplane was quite undamaged, and they had been forced down when all their fuel had drained away through a leak in the petrol tank. Udet and his companion had been able to do nothing more than sit and wait by their airplane, hoping that searchers would see it, and they would have been hopelessly lost in that desolate part of the southern Sudan but for the good sense that Udet had shown in landing beside the track. It was that which led Campbell Black to them.

We flew some of our mechanics to the spot where Udet had been found, and they went about repairing the leak in the tank; and then Udet flew his airplane out and came on to Khartoum. For a few days he stayed with me in the house that I had there. During the war we had heard that he was a decent, likeable man; and in the talks that I had with him in Khartoum I came to appreciate his honesty and his sincerity. I also liked his rather swashbuckling attitude toward life, and I felt that he enjoyed being well liked by everybody. I was glad that my part in helping to rescue him had led to our being able to meet.

While Ernst Udet was staying with me, we naturally talked a great deal about our two countries and the war—it was before there was any need to be guarded in any talk about the political state of affairs in Germany—and we compared the experiences that we had had during the times when we must have fought each other in the skies over the Western Front. He made an amusing reference to that, linking it with his rescue in the southern Sudan.

"I never thought that I would know the day when I would be glad to see the roundels of the R.A.F. flying over my head," he commented in a way that stressed the relative positions which we had always tried so hard to maintain in our fighting in the air.

18 / The Slow Awakening

THE ENGLAND that I had left in the summer of 1929 was part of a world still dominated by the aftereffects of the war that had ended eleven years before. When I returned home in the spring of 1932, it was to a country that was changing almost without its knowledge from a weariness over what was past to an awareness of the future: from a postwar condition to one that was uneasily prewar.

The strain of the economic collapse in the United States after the stock market crash in 1929 had only added to a situation in Europe that had been in a parlous enough state ever since the end of the war in 1918; and in Germany there was a confusion that provided fertile ground for the opportunists. Adolf Hitler found all that he needed in that soil to implant the "weird mixture of the irresponsible, megalo-maniacal ideas . . . the glorification of war and conquest and the absolute power of the authoritarian state . . . the contempt for democracy and humanism," as the American writer William Shirer has described the origins of the thinking which produced the creed of the Nazis.

My return to England after the two years and three months that I had spent overseas was pleasant enough, but the full enjoyment was lost to me through the collapse of my first marriage. But even the preoccupation of such personal problems could not exclude thoughts about what was happening in Germany. Political violence and murder stalked the streets during the spring and the summer and on into the winter of 1932, and we heard disquieting enough reports of what was going on there. By the end of January, 1933, to quote Shirer again, "The former tramp from Vienna, the derelict of the First World War, the violent revolutionary, became Chancellor of a great nation."

There has been a great deal of high-spirited, if not heated, argument during the past few years among even the most erudite of the historians about where the responsibility rests for the eruption of the Second World War. It is not easy to hang it neatly

332

on any one hook; but can there be any doubt about the major part played in that responsibility by Adolf Hitler? There are those who will argue in a way that sounds suspiciously like argument for argument's sake that he was only one of those who was to blame, and that he did no more than some others who helped to steer the course that led us to the second war. So far as those of us whose work was the hard-headed and practical maintenance of this country's armed forces were concerned, by 1932 we had a fair enough indication that something diabolical was afoot, even if we did not realize that it would take only seven years for the "megalo-maniacal ideas" to bear fruit.

With my arrival back in England in March, 1932, I came to the end of my time in the Royal Air Force as an active, operational pilot. In the sense of a Service career I had my foot well placed on the lower rungs of the ladder, and from then on I was to start climbing it with increasingly important appointments which brought with them a fairly rapid promotion. I had already been promoted to the rank of group captain while I was still out in the Sudan, and on my return I was posted to the Imperial Defence College as the Royal Air Force instructor. The Army instructor was Alan Brooke, who had been a student with me on the first course five years before and who had become a brigadier; and for a time the naval instructor was Captain Bertram Ramsay, Royal Navy.

Alan Brooke was, as always, first rate in his work. He had brains which he was not afraid to use, and he was a man with a strong character. Although he was ten years older than I was, the experience that I had of working so closely with him at the Imperial Defence College was the beginning of a friendship that was later to be of the utmost importance to both of us. In the words of Arthur Bryant: "His diversity of experience was un-rivalled in any of the Services."

Of the same age as Brooke—and also ten years older than I was—Bertie Ramsay was another man of distinct character, and in the years that lay ahead he was to turn what looked at first like a personal failure into a very great success. He had a rather over-quick temper which was inseparable from the unorthodox nature of the man, and his mind was of a brilliance not typical of the naval officer. I intend no slur on the Royal Navy in saying that, because I greatly admire their senior officers; but in the senior Service they have a style that is all their own, and it is a style to which most of them seem to feel that they must conform. Bertie

Ramsay, with his quick mind and sharp intellect, would not conform. Because of what lay ahead I was fortunate in being a member of that triumvirate at that particular time. Brooke and Ramsay and I worked well together, and while I contributed my share on the air side I also continued to learn from them a great deal about matters of inter-Service cooperation later to be of exceptional value to me. We also became close friends in a personal way.

In all our work at the I.D.C. we had available a fair amount of confidential information about what was happening in international affairs, and I always made a point of trying to keep myself as well informed as possible. There was also the additional reading that I was able to do of intelligence files at the Air Ministry. Through all these sources I became fairly well aware of what was happening in Germany during the early thirties, and my interest was naturally spiced with the personal eye that I kept on the activities of my former adversaries in the air.

As one of the early stalwarts of the Nazi Party and a German war hero, Hermann Goering allowed his name to be well exploited when Hitler became the German Chancellor early in 1933, and he received appointments to very high offices, becoming Minister of the Interior for Prussia and the head of the newly formed Air Ministry. At first there did not appear to be anything wrong in that, and I was rather inclined to like the way in which he promptly gathered around him his closest friends from his days as a pilot in the First World War and as the commanding officer of the famous Richthofen Circus. Karl Bodenschatz, who had been the adjutant of the Circus, became Goering's personal assistant and adjutant at the Air Ministry; Bruno Loerzer, Goering's oldest friend and fellow pilot, was put in charge of the training of pilots in the "German Sports Flying Club"; and Ernst Udet, the most successful Circus pilot of them all, and the most technically minded while being the least politically minded, was appointed to an important post in the German Air Ministry.

There was now money at the disposal of the Nazi Party, and Ernst Udet's first act in those early days of the new regime was to hurry off to the United States, where he bought some aircraft with which he wanted to experiment. He went on devoting all his time to flying, and he made use of the American aircraft in developing some ideas that he had about powered diving which later became all too well known to us.

During this time of the establishing in power of the Nazi Party, the pioneer aircraft designers in the new order of German aviation were being carefully briefed by Goering in what was expected of them, and the names of Junkers, Focke-Wulf, Heinkel and Dornier came to the fore. Another pilot whose devotion and loyalty to Hitler led to his becoming one of the most important figures in the Nazi Party and the government was Rudolf Hess. In the words of one authority: "He came to be regarded as the man most linked with the Party objectives and organisation . . . from then on he took part in the preparation of all decrees of the Fuehrer."

The work upon which Alan Brooke and Bertie Ramsay and I were engaged as instructors at the Imperial Defence College during the years of the middle thirties was mainly in fighting on paper together with our students every possible major war; and we did it all without any great disagreements in the compiling of our staff solutions. The officers from the Royal Navy, the Army and the Royal Air Force who came to us represented the best that the Services had to offer, and since they were all well known to us, we were working in harmony with a great wealth of past experiences, many of which were personal, that had been shared at some time or other with each of us. It was the close, personal understanding that we gained of each other as instructors and pupils (many were later to become prominent leaders in the Services) and the problems which each of the Services faced together that enabled us to work so well together in the years of the war which lay ahead of us.

But even by the middle 1930's there still lingered on in this country the climate of pacifism in public opinion that had existed ever since the twenties. It was something quite different from the mood of today, which is based largely on a fear of nuclear war. Back in the 1920's there had developed a genuine belief in the minds of a great many people in Britain that war was stupid—as it undoubtedly is—and that it should be abolished, and we pinned our hopes for that in the League of Nations.

But for all the excellence of the theory, there was so much more to it than that. The disarmament talks which were conducted went on for years, and although everybody hoped that they would come to something, there was nothing but failure. From the point of view of the Air Force, it was even worse than that. Through all the ineffectual talking that went on, the rebuilding of the R.A.F. was held up at a time when there was such a great need for it to be brought up to what should have been at least a reasonable strength.

The pacifism that was in people's minds in those days was more emotional than it is today. The feeling now is a more hard-headed one dominated by the deep fear that the world might be blown up or, at least, that civilization might be destroyed. That has tended to twist people's minds in their thoughts about war as we have known it in the past. Now those thoughts have been narrowed down to a consideration of mere survival in the face of the threat from nuclear annihilation, and it is not always remembered that we still have to cope with the possibility of the more conventional forms of warfare.

Being an island people still imbued with a profound belief in the protection that had always been provided for us by the Royal Navy, we were also quite sure during the twenties and the early thirties that we were a country safely apart from the Continent. In believing that the strength of the Royal Navy was enough, Britain had pursued a course of unilateral disarmament, and that only caused us to talk far too much about setting an example to the rest of the world. In that we were led by the muddle-headedness of many of the so-called intellectuals in their bleating about the virtues of unilateral disarmament.

Another of the reasons why we had not made saner efforts to rearm in the face of threats from abroad was the deliberate policy of the government of the times to avoid upsetting the balance of our industry and its ability to export. That in itself was a desirable enough aim because we were, as we still are, so dependent on the output of our industry in relation to exports, and rearmament, it was felt, would throw that all out of gear. It was primarily because of that, and not because of any high ideals, that the government had allowed our position so far as the armed forces were concerned to deteriorate in such a shocking way. By 1932 the Royal Air Force had shrunk until, unbelievable as it may sound, it occupied only about the fifth position in strength in the air forces of the world, even lagging behind Italy and Japan.

It was all becoming a merry-go-round except that there was nothing very merry about it. In addition to the three Service instructors at the I.D.C. we also had on the staff an instructor who was an expert in economics. In that sphere he kept us all on our toes, and since he was Clarence Fayle, the recognized authority on his subject, there was a good rounding-out of the overall picture for us in our general considerations. I learned a great deal from working with Fayle, which was one of the reasons why I came to appreciate what J. F. C. Fuller said later about our "trade war" with the United States, particularly during the years between 1925 and 1931.

"To gain time and disguise this fact, [our] statesmen indulged in an intensive propaganda for disarmament," Fuller has written. "They proclaimed that another war would wreck civilisation, and that the sole means of preventing such a calamity was collective security. Thus it came about that by the time Hitler gained power, the British people were so completely doped that had a British Government proposed rearmament, it would have been turned out of office."

Working in this tormented atmosphere of political uncertainty, we found it our duty at the Imperial Defence College to consider the best uses that could be made of our armed forces as they existed, and to instruct our students in that. In the course of that instruction, which was backed by our own time as students at the I.D.C., Alan Brooke and Bertie Ramsay and I had to exercise our minds on the ways and means of facing every possible war that might come about, including war with Germany, Italy and Japan. For the purposes of those exercises during the early and middle thirties, we had to build up on paper to a much larger extent the forces which the Germans, for instance, might have at their disposal than what they actually possessed during the years between 1933 and 1935. Such was the nature of our planning that it turned out that those forces which we had credited to them in theory were very similar in numbers and composition to those actually possessed by them in the reality of 1940.

In our exercises we came to the conclusion that, with the forces that we had allowed for, the Germans would be able to advance through Belgium and northern France as far as the Channel ports, but that the French would still be in the war with their land forces facing north from a position on the Seine. The problem that we then had to face was to try and figure out what the Germans would do in that situation. Would they proceed with a full-scale invasion of France and try and knock her right out of the war? Or would they stand fast where they were in France and devote all their forces, land, sea and air, to an all-out attempt to defeat Britain? The staff solution on which Brooke, Ramsay and I agreed was that the correct course for the Germans to follow in such a situation, and their best chance of winning the war, was to go flat out against Britain with everything that they had, and to deal with France later and at their leisure.

Our studies at the I.D.C. during those uneasy days also gave us cause to devote a great deal of thought to the possibility of a war with Japan. Although we foresaw a speedy loss of Hong Kong, from the information that was available to us we thought that we would be able to hold on to Singapore. But what would happen after that? Would we still be in a position whereby eventually we would be able to bring Japan to her knees and force her to sue for peace? It would be a long-term and very difficult business, and in all our thinking we could not figure out any way of bringing it off without the full support of the United States of America.

Those of us in both Britain and the United States who had access to the best that our intelligence had to offer could not help but be aware of what was going on in Germany in the buildup of their armed forces. We already knew that for a long time past the Germans had been sending experienced pilots to Russia to keep up their training in military aviation. The story of all these developments has since been placed freely on record by Adolf Galland, who was to become one of the foremost German fighter pilots of the Second World War. He has spoken of a talk that he had with Hermann Goering in the spring of 1933. "The secret training of German pilots in Russia, used as a temporary expedient, must now come to an end," Goering told him. To that Galland added: "We now had the opportunity of training our fighter pilots with the Italian Air Force. In order to avoid international complications for Italy as well as for Germany, the whole affair had to be treated with the greatest possible secrecy and carried out under rigorous camouflage."

After Hitler came to power in 1933, the Germans conducted their training schemes more cunningly under the cloak of civil aviation and sporting flying. Of his own qualifications after training at that time, Adolf Galland has said: "Although to all outward appearances I was a civilian, I was also an almost perfectly trained fighter pilot." He was then flying as a pilot for Lufthansa. On March 9, 1935—by which time I had been an instructor at the I.D.C. for three years—Hitler made the open statement that Germany had an air force that was equal in strength to our own.

For all the advantages that the Germans must have enjoyed in being able to start from scratch with new equipment in the building of their new air force, there must nevertheless have been many difficulties that Hermann Goering and his associates had to face, not the least of which must have been the creation of a staff made up of men with real hard-headed knowledge of military aviation. Goering had plenty of eager youngsters like Adolf Galland who had become, or who wanted to become, pilots, but he had only very few men who could fill the role of commanders. The Royal Air Force had been in existence without a break right from the very beginning, and it was the world's first independent air service with a thoroughgoing and tested knowledge of what its function must be in the overall scheme, and an uninterrupted system of training for those who were to become its commanders.

The German Air Force came into being with quite a number of pilots trained through their undercover schemes; but its structure at the top was slight. Goering surrounded himself with his friends, trying to fit them into positions of high command; but for all his experience as a pilot in the First World War, he was himself only a political general, and he was far from being a trained and experienced Air Force commander.

Those years between 1932 and 1936 were for all of us years of something approaching various stages of an awakening, and we lived through what can only be described, in the light of history, as an unhappy awareness of a slide toward the edge of the cliff. During all that time we heard right on our own doorstep repeated warnings that there was trouble afoot. Winston Churchill was the man who saw to that. His voice was raised in the House of Commons, alone and unafraid, time after time, calling for action.

By 1934 the expansion of the Royal Air Force had become a necessity that could no longer be denied. But the "belated and inadequate" proposals, as Churchill described the plans that were then put forward, were, in his eyes, a clear enough indication that the Air Ministry was at fault. "There seems no doubt," he wrote, "that these experts and officials of the Air Ministry at this time were themselves misled and misled their Chief. A great air power, at least the equal of our own, long pent-up, had at last sprung into daylight in Germany." In that statement he was exaggerating, for no one was then able to get at the truth about the strength of German air power.

On the one hand there was our official Air Staff intelligence, which was the guide in our thinking; but, on the other hand, Churchill had his own personal intelligence service. How that operated was known only to Churchill and to those who were intimately concerned with it. On the whole it was perhaps the better of the two. We rather tended to throw cold water on the estimates—and very detailed ones they were—that Churchill offered in the House of Commons on the strength of the German Air Force. How or why that should have happened I do not know, but as a result we did underrate the German capacity for expansion. We were finding considerable difficulty ourselves in expanding the R.A.F., and we mistakenly imagined that the Germans, in having to start from scratch, would have even more difficulty. Instead, they went ahead much more quickly than we did, which was something for which we did not make sufficient allowance.

Of all the speeches that were made in the House of Commons, the ones which naturally intrigued me most were those in which Winston Churchill agitated, almost alone, for an expansion of the Royal Air Force. Early in February, 1934, he declaimed: "The crash of bombs in London and the cataracts of masonry and fire and smoke will warn us of any inadequacy which has been permitted in our aerial defences." And he issued the warning: "This cursed, hellish invention and development of war from the air has revolutionized our position." As a seasoned practitioner in that "cursed, hellish invention," I was able to appreciate the important difference between war in the air and "war from the air."

At first we all thought that Winston Churchill was laying it on a bit thick; but as time passed—and with the rush of events it seemed to pass so quickly—we had to realize that there was a great deal in what he was saying. A little later in the same year he made a statement on the subject of disarmament that rings with just as much truth now, over thirty years later, as it did then. "It is the greatest mistake to mix up disarmament with peace," he said. "When you have peace you will have disarmament, but there has been during these recent years a steady deterioration in the relations between different countries, a steady growth of ill-will, and a steady, indeed a rapid increase in armaments that has gone on through all these years in spite of the endless flow of oratory, of perorations, of well meaning sentiments, of banquets, which have marked this epoch."

My time as the Air Force instructor at the Imperial Defence College lasted a year longer than was usual in this appointment. There did not seem to be any particular reason for that, and I had no objection because the work that we were doing against the background of the political developments in Europe was all of intense interest. When the time came for me to give it up, my place was taken by Peter Portal, who had returned to England after an overseas tour of duty in Aden.

In June, 1936, I was promoted to the rank of air commodore; and immediately after that, in the summer vacation, I was sent to Italy as the official Air Ministry observer at the maneuvers of the

Italian Army. I went there in company with General R. H. (later Sir Robert) Haining, who was then the Commandant of the Imperial Defence College. An able, genial man and a good traveling companion, Bob Haining was the official representative of the War Office.

The maneuvers which we attended took place in the mountains in the vicinity of Bolzano in northeastern Italy. It was a magnificent setting for the exercises, and I was impressed by the quality of the Italian troops, especially the Alpini, although the signals organization of the Italian Army struck me as being particularly inefficient. To my surprise, the Italian Air Force scarcely put in any appearance at all. It was not until later that I realized that they had been fully occupied in their odious adventures in Abyssinia, and that they were preparing for further exploits in the conspiracy about the future of Spain.

After Bob Haining and I had spent three days unobtrusively watching the maneuvers, we were told that Benito Mussolini, the Italian dictator, had asked that we should spend the next day with him. I rather welcomed the opportunity of at least meeting this man whose reputation had already won for him so much notoriety, and I was curious to find out for myself what I could about his character through such a personal contact. Mussolini appeared at our hotel at six-thirty the next morning, driving himself in a bright red, open Alfa-Romeo with a chauffeur sitting beside him. Bob Haining and I were smartly placed in the back seat of the car, and off we started on an astonishingly rapid and extensive tour of inspection.

With his brutal conquest of Abyssinia under his belt only a month before, Mussolini was cock-a-hoop and on the crest of the wave of popularity in his own country. I realized from the moment that we set out on the tour that we were to make with him that we were in for an awkward and anxious time. Neither Bob Haining nor I had sufficient command of Italian to understand just what the dictator was saying; but I could not help noticing that the name of England was introduced many times in the course of the orations that he made to his people.

It seemed when the day was over that the entire time was taken up by Mussolini in harangues launched at the Italian civilians and troops with a cunningly varied tempo. Whenever we got to one of the townships which he was due to visit, he would make his way rapidly to the rostrum that had been set up in the main square and around which there were already gathered crowds of people. The

Italian leader would then proceed to put on one of his fiery acts, delivered in stentorian tones, and he would quickly arouse in his audience a great pitch of excitement.

In a way that I later came to realize must have been craftily planned, Mussolini insisted that Bob Haining and I should stand on either side of him while he roared away at the crowds; and he was no doubt purposely leading them to assume that the presence beside him of a senior general of the British Army and an air commodore of the Royal Air Force meant that he had England eating out of his hand. But to what extent he was doing that we could not say, and, in any case, there was nothing that we could do about it.

In that brief but vivid encounter that I had with him it was pounded home to me that above all else Mussolini was such a flamboyant actor. We could not help noticing that everything that he said and did while he was in the public eye was calculated for effect, and that it was all laid on with a skillful use of the trowel. When it came to addressing the troops I noticed that he was much more restrained in his style than he was when he thundered at the civilians. Then he would become the stern soldier addressing his legions. But in haranguing the civilians he threw himself about, waved his arms, and shouted. When he spoke to his troops he held himself erect and still, and he spoke quite differently, apparently adjusting his whole personality to what he thought they expected of him.

After Mussolini stepped off the rostrum his whole attitude would change yet again. He would become quite a pleasant and, in fact, jolly companion, joking with us, and apparently enjoying trying out on us the little English that he was able to speak. He kept us with him, one sitting on either side of him, at a hearty official luncheon, after which we continued with the tour of inspection; and in the evening he delivered us back at our hotel. In addition to the exertions of everything else, he had done all the driving of that red Alfa-Romeo throughout the entire day.

The only time when I did come to feel quite strongly that a policy of appeasement was practiced by our government during the thirties was at the time of that Italian aggression against defenseless Abyssinia. We could very easily have put a stop to it by simply refusing to allow the Italians the use of the Suez Canal. Such a move by us over the Canal might have been contrary to the international agreements about its use, and it might even have brought on a very serious quarrel involving Germany as well as

Italy, but we should have risked that. As it was, we came badly out of the whole wretched business, and that only helped to pave the way for harsher trouble.

The year of 1936 was the year during which, having been awakened, we had to get out of bed and go to work. The final act of throwing off the bedclothes, or of having them ripped off, was possibly the march made by the Germans into the demilitarized Rhineland in the early spring of that year. The astonishing effect that this further violation of the Treaty of Versailles—and of the Treaty of Locarno as well—had on the German people was summed up by William Shirer, who was working in Germany at the time. In his description of the way in which Adolf Hitler's announcement about what they were doing was received by the assembled members of the Reichstag in Berlin he wrote:

All the militarism in their German blood surges to their heads. They spring, yelling and crying, to their feet. Their hands are raised in slavish salute, their faces now tauted with hysteria, their mouths wide open, shouting, shouting, their eyes burning with fanaticism, glued on the new God, the Messiah.

Years later William Shirer was to comment again on that move of Hitler's with the statement: "That the Allies at this time could easily have overwhelmed Germany is as certain as it is that such an action would have brought the end of the Third Reich in the very year of its birth." That is what people are given to calling a sobering thought.

The immediate reaction of France was to consider forcing the Germans back, and such was the relative military strength of France and Germany at that time that they could have done it. Hitler's own appreciation of that is contained in the statement that he made afterward. "If the French had then marched into the Rhineland," he said, "we would have had to withdraw with our tails between our legs, for the military resources at our disposal would have been wholly inadequate for even a moderate resistance."

But the British government would not support the French, and the whole affair became nothing more than a tortuous argument. "The forty-eight hours after the march into the Rhineland were the most nerve-racking in my life," Hitler later stated; and it is even recorded that he contemplated suicide in the event of failure. But instead of failure, his bluff paid off in a way that had even his own generals gaping with astonishment.

On my return from the Italian maneuvers, I was posted back to the Air Ministry, this time in the appointment of Director of Staff Duties. That brought me into a much closer and more personal touch with all that was going on in the development of the Royal Air Force. In addition to the great changes in the structure of the Service and its reorganization at home into the four principle commands that have lasted to this day—those of Bomber, Fighter, Coastal and Training—the prototype of the Spitfire had made its first flight only two days before the Rhineland affair; and the prototype of the Wellington first flew three months later. During the summer of the year before, the first practical demonstrations had been given by the scientists to a select few in the use of the Radio Direction Finding which was later to become known as radar; and in November of that year of 1935 the prototype of the Hurricane had made its first flight.

Much has been made of Hitler's statement in 1935 that by then Germany had an air force as strong as the Royal Air Force, and that he was aiming at parity in the air with France. But there is in that claim, in hard fact, scarcely what could be called parity with us. There is nothing whatsoever on record to substantiate what was scarcely more than a claim made by Hitler in talking with some of our statesmen in Berlin, and our official historians have seriously contested the truth of what the German leader was trying to scare into us.

By 1936 we in the R.A.F. were not exactly dragging our feet. At the display at Hendon in June that year, we had on view, among other older aircraft, the new Hurricane, Spitfire, Wellington and Lysander. But counting heads is only one way of comparing strengths, and it can never provide the whole answer. One must surely consider the spirit of the people whom one is trying to evaluate, and it is now so obvious that for all that our political leaders were telling us they were grossly lacking in a sense of realism when they tried to understand the German leaders, let alone the spirit of the people.

During the Nuremberg Trials after the Second World War, evidence was introduced about Hermann Goering's announcement on March 10, 1935, that Germany was building a military air force, and a statement which he made to Ward Price, who was for so long a well-known foreign correspondent. "In the extension of our National Defense [Sicherheit] it was necessary, as we repeatedly told the world, to take care of defence in the air,"

Goering stated. "As far as that is concerned, I restricted myself to those measures which were absolutely necessary. The guiding line of my action was, not the creation of an aggressive force which would threaten other nations, but merely the completion of a military aviation which would be strong enough to repel, at any time, attacks on Germany."

It is dangerous to offer quotations of what the Nazi leaders said as any indication of what they thought, but we have to be guided to some extent, as the judges were at Nuremberg, by these statements. When Ward Price asked Goering if the German Air Force would at that time be capable of repelling attacks on Germany, Goering replied: "The German Air Force is just as passionately permeated with the will to defend the Fatherland to the last as it is convinced, on the other hand, that it will never be employed to threaten the peace of other nations."

In the normal course of my life in the Service up to and including the years that I spent at the Imperial Defence College, I had always been able to enjoy regular periods of leave, which had been quite liberal, and which provided opportunity for either extra work or travel. With the increasing tempo of the expansion of the R.A.F. from 1936 onward, however, leave so far as the senior members of the Air Staff were concerned was not so easily come by. I managed fairly well for a couple of years, and I did get a good free spell of nearly three weeks in the summer of 1938, which I spent in Monte Carlo, mainly because it had continued to be a favorite haunt of mine. That was the last spell of good leave that I was to have for a long time. I intended to go back there again the following year; but the trouble that glared at us during 1939 resulted in my getting only one long weekend in August at Le Touquet.

On the Air Staff at the Air Ministry we gradually worked up to longer and longer hours each day, and after a while it seemed that less and less attention came to be paid to the days of the week. Under that increasing pressure we also learned to abandon all the routine habits that had been ingrained through long usage of working to set hours, with weekends off. We were always on the job, with an ever-increasing load of responsibility.

My return to a desk in a more senior appointment at the Air Ministry also brought me into a closer firsthand contact with the other senior officers of the Air Staff. Important changes were taking place, and there were beginning to emerge as senior officers the men who were to play important roles in the Second World

War. On Boom Trenchard's retirement at the end of 1929 his place as the Chief of the Air Staff had been taken by Jack Salmond. Next to Trenchard he was our outstanding leader in the First World War, and today Sir John Salmond is our senior Marshal of the Royal Air Force, having been promoted to that rank as far back as 1933.

On Jack Salmond's retirement, his place as C.A.S. was taken by his brother Geoffrey. But he died within only a few weeks of taking office, and he was succeeded in May, 1933, by Edward Ellington. A quiet and rather shy and retiring man—as a result of which he was not particularly well known in the Service—Ellington was a very able staff officer. He had been Air Member for Personnel at the time that I had gone through the crisis in my personal affairs on my return from the Sudan, and he had been kind to me and had given me sound advice about my divorce.

A feature that struck me as so curious about Edward Ellington after he became the Chief of the Air Staff was the way in which he opposed the expansion that was first proposed for the R.A.F. in 1934. That seemed to me to be looking a gift horse in the mouth. I could understand his fear that the Air Force might expand too rapidly, which would cause efficiency to fall off, with a consequent damage to morale; but I thought that that was an altogether too timid approach. Here we were with the longed-for chance to expand, and it was a chance that should have been seized with no thought being given to trying to cut it down or advise that the rate should be slowed up. It was then, while I was still at the Imperial Defence College, that I began to feel that I had reached a stage in my own career where I was able, through experience and seniority, to think in the bigger terms, and that I was in a position that now enabled me to express my own views more openly and with more likelihood of having them receive attention.

By the middle thirties there were still at the top those who had been our senior commanders during the first war. When the Royal Air Force was reorganized in 1936 into the commands in which it still functions, nearly thirty years later, Stuffy Dowding, after a great deal of experience at the Air Ministry in research and development, became the first Commander-in-Chief of the newly created Fighter Command. It had been thought that in due course he would take Edward Ellington's place as Chief of the Air Staff; but Cyril Newall was appointed C.A.S., and Dowding was kept at Fighter Command.

Although it would unquestionably have been pleasant for him if he had been able to fill the most senior appointment in the Service, it was at Fighter Command that Dowding belonged. When he first went there, I was doubtful about how he would get on with the fighter boys, for his nickname clung to him, and if there is one thing that fighter pilots cannot be accused of it is being stuffy. I was very glad to be proved so wrong in my assessment. Quite apart from all that he achieved as C.-in-C. Fighter Command, Stuffy Dowding became very popular among the pilots, and today he is venerated by those who served under him.

Between the time of his return from the Middle East, where I had served under him, and his appointment early in 1937 as Chief of the Air Staff, Cyril Newall had been the Air Member for Supply and Organisation, and at the Air Ministry I naturally continued to come into close contact with him. Newall had done well as A.M.S.O., which must have had a great deal to do with his appointment as Chief of the Air Staff.

But the most important personal contact that I had on the Air Staff was with Wilfrid Freeman, who took over from Stuffy Dowding as the Air Member for Research and Development. He had had a long tour of duty in Palestine while I was in the Sudan, followed by two years as commandant of the R.A.F. Staff College. He became a member of the Air Council a few months before I returned to the Air Ministry, and that brought about a renewal of our old friendship, and from that time on we were to work very closely together. It became increasingly my concern during the next four years to support him in the laying down of our requirements to the technical staff of what we wanted in aircraft and armaments.

As a result of a very great deal of experience in the management of men of all types, it has become my conviction that for all the routine education that one may receive—and I do not question that it is imperative that one should receive as broad and as general an education to start with as possible—it is the work that one does on one's own, the self-education based on the formal, acquired education, that is of the most permanent value. So far as becoming senior executives, or leaders, is concerned, I am convinced that that education must be broad, and certainly much broader than is generally the practice today, in this age of specialization, if one is to become a leader.

My years at the Imperial Defence College were the last experience that I was to have of the more or less academic life, and I had made the most of my time there. By the time that I returned to the Air Ministry, I realized that opportunities greater than I had anticipated lay ahead in my own profession, and I was interested enough in both the opportunities and the profession to want to take full advantage of what was being offered to me. I had married again, and having a much more settled domestic life I was able to bring to bear all that I knew and all that I had been trained for and which I had experienced; but I had also come to appreciate by then that no matter what I did, or how far I progressed, I would always go on learning.

The title of Director of Staff Duties that was mine was a bit of a misnomer. Although I was responsible for all of the training of Staff officers, the most important part of my work was in taking care of the operational training of the R.A.F. By 1937 the expansion of the Service was gathering momentum, although it was still not with the speed that some of us on the Air Staff would have liked. But after Hitler perpetrated "the rape of Austria," in the spring of 1938, "a new earnestness marked our preparations," Denis Richards has recorded. "Economy ceased to exert its malign spell, and the Cabinet withdrew the principle of 'no interference with the course of normal trade.' "

It was high time. The politicians, after their hesitancy of the years before, began urging the Air Ministry to enlarge the Air Force at a greater rate than the Air Staff was prepared to accept, and we had the odd situation in which the politicians were urging us to expand with the Air Staff putting on the brakes. The reluctance at the Air Ministry to fall in line with the new political thrust was due largely to the caution advised through the fear that if the Air Force expanded too quickly it would become, through dilution, defective in its efficiency and morale. The Air Staff also had to think in terms of orders for new types of aircraft rather than to go on placing orders for aircraft which, although in production, were already out of date.

The views generally held by the Air Staff were right up to a certain point; but I was more inclined toward a somewhat Machiavellian policy in that I would have preferred at least an acceptance of the figures put to us by the Cabinet. Holding back in the way that we did was a mistake, and we should have tried harder and earlier for the fullest possible program of expansion. The production of new and more modern aircraft was well underway, and it could have been speeded up, and we need not have worried about the older types.

The French attempted an expansion on obsolete types. That certainly turned out to be a disastrous mistake, and it left the French Air Force equipped at the time of the outbreak of the

Second World War with a large collection of obsolete aircraft that could not even begin to hold their own against the German Air Force. We did at least make our plans so that we had the eight-gun fighters—the Hurricane and the Spitfire—ready in some quantity to take their part in the Battle of Britain; and we had laid the foundations for the production of the four-engined bombers—the Halifax, the Stirling and the Lancaster—which later became such a big factor in the defeat of Germany.

But actual expansion was not the only problem with which we were faced. Of particular interest to me—as it had been ever since my time as a fighting pilot in the First World War—was the study of air tactics. In time of peace we had more opportunity for careful study of the problems involved even if we did not have much firsthand opportunity to put our theories to the test. But our thinking was still based very largely on what we had learned in the years between 1914 and 1918, and we were not sure how far those lessons would apply in the changed circumstances of another war in the future. The aircraft would certainly be three times faster than those with which we had fought in 1918, and with more than four times the fire-power.

I was always conscious of what little background we had to work with in those thoughts about air strategy and tactics. Compared to the Army and the Navy, we were such a new Service, albeit potentially a very powerful one. But how were we to use that power? Perhaps it was because of the demands that were made upon us for new and original thinking that we in the Royal Air Force were kept so much on our toes. We had to be flexible, and we had to welcome innovations; and we knew that in our adaptability lay our strength.

19 / The Faces of Reality

SUCH WAS THE gathering momentum of the expansion of the Royal Air Force during that short and crowded period of the years of the late 1930's, just before the outbreak of the Second World War, that most of us who had attained by then fairly senior rank came to know in our promotion an unexpected acceleration. Only eighteen months after becoming an air commodore I was myself promoted, at the beginning of 1938, to the rank of air vice-marshal; and with it I fully expected that I would be posted to an operational command. I had been a staff officer in London for the past five and a half years, and it was time for me to gain some more practical experience of higher command.

But instead of a command of my own there came, with what I had to admit to myself was a certain personal feeling of satisfaction, my appointment to a new post at the Air Ministry that had only just been invented: that of Assistant Chief of the Air Staff. In this I was to be directly under Cyril Newall, the Chief of the Air Staff, and I was to be responsible to him for the work of the Directorate of Staff Duties—of which I had already been the head for the past two years—and the Directorate of Operational Requirements.

The work done in Operational Requirements was to arrive at decisions about the actual needs of and the specifications for all the aircraft in the Service and their equipment, including such things as guns and bombs and radar, which was then only just out of its infancy. These decisions were passed by me to the Air Member for Supply and Research, who was a member of the Air Council; and it was his job to make provision for all that was asked for by the Air Staff. There was a great deal of give and take between the departments concerned, and through free discussion we were able to make sure that the Air Staff requirements were both technically feasible and of the best possible quality. In a business sense we were highly organized and experienced professionals, with thorough and intensive training.

350

As Assistant Chief of the Air Staff from the beginning of 1938 until the early spring of 1940, I had a great deal to do with these operational requirements of the R.A.F. in new types of aircraft and equipment. On the lower level of Director of Staff Duties I had been immersed in a great mass of detail, but in becoming A.C.A.S. I emerged from that on to the broader level which dealt more with policy, and I was then given the opportunity to view the overall picture with a much better perspective. Even then we were dealing with the development of the new multi-engined bombers such as the Manchester, which later became the Lancaster, the Halifax and the Stirling, and the new fighters were in actual production.

At this time I also began to come more closely in contact with the Americans. We started having discussion with them about the fighters that they were manufacturing, trying to find out if we could make any use of them. The Americans were naturally anxious to sell them to us, but we came to the conclusion that they were not as good as our own eight-gun Hurricanes and Spitfires. What we did like about what they had to offer was the twin-engined aircraft developed by the Lockheed people in California which we came to call the Hudson, and we placed with them quite a large order. That led to a devil of a rumpus with the unthinking and the ill-informed, who did not hesitate to air their opinions that it was entirely wrong to have in the Royal Air Force any aircraft that were built outside our own industry. They did not seem to be able to realize that our own industry was already working flat out, and that we had to go abroad for the extra aircraft demanded by the expansion of the Service.

Our own new fighters were by then in production, and we knew that we had in them attacking aircraft that were quite formidable; but we had only very few of them in service. That was serious enough, but our anxiety about their hitting power led us to considerations about the armaments which could make them even more formidable. In the beginning the Hurricane, the first of the breed to exceed three hundred miles an hour in speed, was designed as a four-gun fighter. Almost casually somebody asked one day why it should not have eight guns instead of four, and from that the Hurricane became equipped with the eight Browning machine guns with which it was later to fight so well. We did the same thing with the Spitfire.

Although the Americans tried hard to interest us in their new fighters, there was no doubt in our minds that we were well ahead of them. At a later stage in our negotiations, their famous aircraft designer Alexander de Seversky came over from the United States with a fighter that he had produced, and in the course of our negotiations I got to know him quite well. He was an extraordinarily interesting man whose life story held more appeal for me than the aircraft that he was trying to sell to us. Born in Russia, the son of the first man ever to own and fly his own airplane in that country, De Seversky was trained at the Imperial Naval Academy and the Military School of Aeronautics, and by 1915 he was serving as a pilot with the Russian Navy in the Baltic. He was shot down, crashed and lost a leg. Despite this physical disability he got back to flying, and he went about creating for himself a great reputation as a fighter pilot.

Sent to America as a member of a Russian military mission at the time of the Revolution, De Seversky stayed in the United States, and after the war he became an American citizen. From a start as a test pilot he went on to designing aircraft, and then to the formation of his own company. The fighter that he was trying to interest us in was designed by him for the United States Army Air Forces, but we were able to prove to him that the fighters which we were producing were better. Out of our discussions there came his plans for further developments to his fighter, and he then designed the Thunderbolt, which was to become one of the foremost of the American fighters in the Second World War, and for which the Royal Air Force placed a fairly large order.

If any war between two or more nations is rightly looked upon as an ultimate stupidity, then surely civil war between the people within one country must be something in the nature of a sacrificial tragedy. In any reading that is made of the history of the 1930's there can be only heartache over the terrible way in which Spain was ripped to pieces by the civil war which the proud people of that country endured between the years of 1936 and 1939. Tempers became inflamed enough, and rightly so, over what happened then; but my concern, as a professional airman, was with the situation as it developed in the air.

A full use was made of the battleground that smeared itself over Spain, and in the air as well as on the ground the dictators grasped at the opportunity to test in every way their newly found strength. It has been recorded that the Italians sent between sixty and seventy thousand troops to Spain, as well as vast quantities of supplies. The Germans themselves have freely admitted that on their participation in the civil war—a participation that went on from start to finish—they spent half a billion marks. Facing these forces of the Germans and the Italians, which were supporting the rebels, was the strong Communist aid from Soviet Russia.

Adolf Galland has written in detail of his own experiences, and of what, late in 1936, those in the German Air Force thought of ". . . Spain, where World War II was being rehearsed on a small scale." By the early summer of 1937 Galland was flying there, with many Germans, as a fighter pilot, and he was soon in command of a fighter squadron. Galland spent two years openly fighting in Spain with the German Air Force, and, as with many other German pilots who were later to become thorns in our sides, he gained a tremendous amount of very valuable experience. Of even more value to the Germans in a technical sense was the way in which they were able to try out their new fighter, the Messerschmitt 109. They also introduced the result of Ernst Udet's experiments in power-diving, the Junkers 87: the dive-bomber known as the Stuka which earned for itself a name that came to be dreaded by so many people.

As the possibility of a larger war in Europe appeared to loom up over the ill-defined horizon, we who were at the Air Ministry became increasingly anxious about the state of the Royal Air Force. Try as we might, and drive as we did, it seemed that we were only too obviously being beaten by the Germans in the race to rearm; and by the time of the Munich crisis in the summer of 1938, I was among those who became very alarmed over our unpreparedness should we be forced to go to war with Germany in the immediate future. This apprehension was universal among the senior officers of the Air Staff. We were the ones who were responsible for the effectiveness of the Royal Air Force, and in trying to figure out the right answers for our political masters, we all went through an extremely anxious time.

There has been a great deal of sloppy thinking and loose and ill-informed talk and writing about what has been called appeasement, particularly in its relationship to what happened at the time of the Munich crisis. The politicians have had to bear, at one extreme, the brunt of that attack; but there has also been, at the other extreme, an inclination on the part of some people to think of the senior officers in the Services as a pack of saber-rattling warmongers. So far as we in the Services were concerned (with only very few exceptions) nothing could be further from the truth. We knew through firsthand and, in many cases, very bitter experience just what war meant, and we wanted none of it. Whenever these accusations start being made, it is almost invariably the case that the more vehement our accusers became the less they themselves know about any personal participation in active service under conditions of war.

The main problem over the Munich crisis itself was a much simpler one than all the argument has since made it appear to be. That the appeasement that was indulged in before the time of Munich contributed largely to the development of the crisis is true enough, but that time of the crisis itself can be considered separately, and not as an indivisible part of the whole. Even if one takes into account all that has been revealed since that time in the way in which attempts were made to influence public opinion, we can still come down to some hard and inescapable facts.

The whole matter of what we, the British, could or could not do at the time of Munich hinged very largely on the state of the preparedness of the Royal Air Force and whether it was in a fit condition to fight a war. At the Air Ministry we knew exactly what could be done in the defense of this country, and we had to think almost solely of defense. We were naturally bound to silence, on the grounds of security, so far as any public utterances were concerned. But of all those involved we were the realists because the actual fighting—if it should come to that—would be in our hands; and in the final, personal analysis it was we who would have to face the music in any attempts that might have to be made to defend the people of this country.

What we at the Air Ministry knew beyond all doubt was that Britain in the summer of 1938 was in very poor shape to be able to engage in any bargaining with Hitler. I was of the opinion that on the military side we had aimed neither high enough nor hard enough in our efforts to rearm. In speaking of the state of affairs as it was three years before, Winston Churchill had made the comment: "It is always dangerous for soldiers, sailors or airmen to play at politics. They enter a sphere in which the values are quite different from those to which they have hitherto been accustomed."

While I admit that there is a great deal of truth in what Winston Churchill said, I find that statement a very difficult one to reconcile with the role that we in the services were expected to play, particularly during the few years just prior to the Munich crisis. That our values were "quite different" from those of the politicians I readily agree, and I am equally sure that Churchill would have allowed that our values were simpler and more forthright even if, in the eyes of the politicians, they were more naïve. But we were expected by the politicians to advise them, and so long as they were our masters who can say where "playing at politics" started and where it stopped? Ours was a role that was secondary to the political considerations, but it was inextricably bound up with the political role.

In any attempt that may be made at an evaluation of the state of the Royal Air Force in the summer of 1938 there must always be borne in mind the effect that those political considerations had had upon our development. They were introduced in too many ways, and one of those who, while striving for our good, was guilty of that was Winston Churchill. As far back as the summer of 1935 he had become, although not a member of the Government and still reserving the right to criticize openly and as he saw fit, a member of the important Air Defence Research Committee of the Committee of Imperial Defence, and he had brought with him as his personal scientific adviser Professor F. A. Lindemann. Known to so many as the "Prof," he was later to become Viscount Cherwell.

Through direct personal experience I was to come to know only too well that that move of Winston Churchill's was more than enough to introduce into our important and secret deliberations an extraordinarily political and far from happy atmosphere. We on the Air Staff had our scientific faith pinned on Sir Henry Tizard, who was our official adviser, and who had been a pilot in the Royal Flying Corps. But Lindemann and Tizard, both brilliant scientists, were by temperament and for personal reasons quite incompatible, and the work that we were trying to do was all too often disrupted by the clash between these two exceptionally intelligent and gifted men.

Every form of abuse has been hurled, and continues to be hurled from within and without this country, at the British Government for what happened over the Munich crisis in September, 1938, in which we and the French were compelled to allow Hitler to have his own way in his demands, supported by his threats of force, for the return to Germany of a third of Czechoslovakia and its people. That it was shameful that we should have had to surrender in the fashion forced upon us by all that had gone before I do not deny; but I say without any reservations that we followed the only course that we could in the circumstances of the time.

Another line of thought that is advanced is that the year which we gained over the Munich affair was put to better use by the Germans than by us. Again the record, at least so far as the air is concerned, disposes of that. The rate of the expansion of the Royal Air Force during that year was greater than that achieved by the

Germans, and we definitely improved our strength relative to that of the German Air Force; and that position included the most vital items in the air defense of this country: fighters and radar. At the time of Munich we did not have nearly enough up-to-date fighters, and our radar warning system was not far enough along in construction for us to be able to face with any confidence the air attacks which we considered could have been launched against this country. A year after Munich we had enough modern fighters to make at least a stand, and that stand was supported by an effective radar screen.

It is a gross mistake to confuse appeasement with what had to be done right at the time of Munich. It is also a mistake to try and say that this or that political party was or was not guilty of the appeasement that led up to Munich. One of the reasons for the attitude of most people in this country toward the threat that was looming up in Germany was the strong influence of what used to be called funk. That is not a pleasant thing to have to admit; but at the Air Ministry we were influenced by the attitudes of those at the time of Munich who were affected by it.

There were altogether too many indications that if we failed in the air the whole country would suffer a major defeat. It could never be said that we got into a panic, for we had been hardened to that in the forge of fright over quite a long period of time; and in many ways it was that, in the face of the hysteria that did break loose in other quarters, which enabled us to remain realists about the immediate threat.

The problem that disturbed us most was what effect an air attack on Britain would have if it took the shape of the expected mass bombing. We had no great experience of the bombing of cities; but the reports that we were receiving about what was happening in Spain were enough to make us apprehensive. We were fully prepared to expect that great damage would be done and heavy casualties caused by the German Air Force if they launched an attack. It was a matter of facing something in which there was such a very large element of the unknown, a plunge into something that could only be understood by experiencing it; and it was natural enough that all our people should shrink from taking that plunge.

Not all those who rebelled over the way in which our affairs were allowed to be shaped were, I felt, exactly clearsighted. Winston Churchill later admitted that "throughout 1939 our position improved as more squadrons were remounted," and that "we began to overtake Germany and improve our own position"; but for all the soundness of his information and the shrewdness of his appreciation of it, he was the foremost of those who opposed the course taken by us at Munich. Anthony Eden had resigned from the office of Foreign Secretary some months before, but that was because of his general disagreement with the Prime Minister over foreign policy. More directly involved in the outcome of Munich was Duff Cooper, who felt compelled to protest by resigning from his office of First Lord of the Admiralty.

I had come to know both Anthony Eden and Duff Cooper some months before through meeting them with Oliver and Maureen Stanley, who were both old friends of mine. By chance I ran into Duff Cooper one day shortly after the Munich crisis. It was at lunch at a restaurant in the West End which we all frequented quite a lot. He was holding forth on the evils of appeasement, which was fair enough; but when I ventured to suggest that we were lucky to have managed to avoid getting into a war with Germany at that time he became quite red in the face, and we went on from there to an exchange of embarrassingly angry words.

For some reason that I cannot understand, those of the time, and of today, who would have had us risk a fight with Germany over the Munich affair seem to ignore the position so far as it affected or was controlled by the air. But there are available for them all to see exact enough statements about that position. There is, for instance, the telling record offered by Denis Richards, a record which speaks for itself of the state of the air so far as our defense was concerned.

"In September, 1938," Richards points out, "to oppose the German long-range striking force of some one thousand two hundred modern bombers, Fighter Command could muster, including all reserves, only ninety-three of the new eight-gun fighters. All the remainder of its six hundred and sixty-six aircraft were the outdated biplanes. No Spitfires were yet in the line; and the Hurricanes, being without heating for their guns, could not fight above fifteen thousand feet, even in summer."

With such harsh facts staring us in the face, I came to feel a steadily mounting alarm as the political negotiations with the Germans proceeded during those weeks of the summer of 1938. It was so obvious that if war should come at that time, then Britain, and in particular London, would be in for a terrible and probably a disastrous pasting from the German Air Force. In something approaching a mood of desperation I spoke up one day to Cyril Newall with much more than the customary frankness that marked the expression of my opinions to the Chief of the Air Staff. As forcefully as I could I told him of my own deep personal alarm over the way in which the future was being shaped.

In his position as the Chief of the Air Staff, Cyril Newall was subjected to great pressures from almost every quarter, and he stood up to them in a way for which he has not been given nearly sufficient credit. He knew far more than those of us who were serving under him about just what was happening; but he always listened in the attentive way that he had, and he never got unduly excited. In response to my outburst he quietly told me to go away and put down on paper in full all that I had just said to him. I gladly did as I was told, and I went back to my desk and composed what I thought was an eloquent plea in support of the theory that we should do all that we could to try and postpone the outbreak of war. I could not help believing in my heart that a war with Germany was inevitable, but I urged as strongly as I could that we should try and gain at least a year so that we might have a chance to catch up with the Germans in the air.

It was this state of our defense in the air that must have been one of the critical points at the back of the minds of our people in the negotiations at the time of Munich. The Chief of the Air Staff took the paper that I had prepared, and I have always understood that, along with the views expressed by other members of the Air Staff who were in agreement with me, it was a basis for the appreciation that he himself worked up and submitted to Sir Kingsley Wood, the Secretary of State for Air. After a great deal of discussion, Wood placed these views of the Air Staff before the Prime Minister and the Cabinet; and it was with this vital information in mind that Chamberlain had to play his hand in the tortuous game that was then enacted in Munich.

During the discussions that took place just before the final settlement was reached, Hermann Goering had talked freely with Sir Nevile Henderson, our Ambassador in Berlin, who then repeated all that had been said to Neville Chamberlain. John W. Wheeler-Bennett refers to this with the report: " 'If England makes war on Germany,' the Field Marshal had said, 'no one knows what the ultimate end will be. But one thing is quite certain. Before the war is over there will be very few Czechs left alive and little of London left standing,' and he had gone on to disclose how well Germany was informed of the unprepared state of Britain's air defences."

For all that bold front, we know now that Hermann Goering was not as confident as he appeared to be. After the whole transaction was completed, he was "obesely gloating," Wheeler-Bennett has recorded; but behind the scenes Goering made it known clearly enough that he did not want war. Even before going to Munich he stated to those with whom he was most closely associated—Karl Bodenschatz being one of them—that he would do everything that he could to avoid it.

There are many who have cited Winston Churchill as strong evidence in support of their denunciation of the Munich transaction, thereby adding fuel to the controversy that will never produce an answer upon which everybody can agree. But there was one statement that Churchill did make in the House of Commons a few days after the Munich crisis which was reasonable enough in its prophecy. "And do not suppose that this is the end," he said. "This is only the beginning of the reckoning."

In the early summer of 1938 there were important changes in the higher direction of the Air Ministry. After very nearly three years as Secretary of State for Air, Lord Swinton was succeeded by Sir Kingsley Wood. During the three important years which had passed while Swinton was in office, there had been a complete about-face in the political attitude toward expansion, and he had achieved a great deal in helping to foster the development of the R.A.F. Much of that had to remain on the secret list, and little has been made known to the public of what was achieved by Lord Swinton.

With the appointment of Sir Kingsley Wood as Secretary of State for Air there also came promotion in the political ranks for Harold Balfour, who was appointed to the post of Parliamentary Under-Secretary. This appointment was of particular interest to me personally because Balfour was an old friend of mine; and it was of importance to the R.A.F. because he had the finest possible Service background with long service as a fighter pilot in the First World War, during which he won an M.C. and bar.

With such a fine war record to his credit, Harold Balfour could have stayed in the Royal Air Force, but his restlessness led him into journalism and politics, and while I had been making my way up in the Service he had been climbing the political ladder. On one occasion after the Germans began to flex their muscles, he went out there to see for himself what was happening, and he met most of the senior officers of the Luftwaffe. When he got back he told us about what he had discovered. Through his political understanding and his Air Force experience, he was possibly the best informed of all of us at the time of Munich; and of what we gained in being able to bring our fighter force up to a reasonable strength after that, he has said: "It was a year of salvation."

Almost immediately after the full realization of what had happened in the Munich crisis had hit home, the Secretary of State for Air called for a thorough reappraisal of the whole situation so far as it affected the air. An important memorandum was produced for the consideration of the Cabinet, and out of that came Plan M, the most important one, and the last one, that was to be made before the eventual outbreak of war. It was a thoroughgoing study of all that we would have to do to rectify the mistakes and the inadequacies of the past.

One of the most important phases of the master plan was the decision to give the highest priority to the strengthening and equipping of Figher Command; and hard on the heels of that there was to be the re-equipment as soon as possible of Bomber Command with the new heavy bombers. These were scarcely more than just beginning to emerge from the factories; but their use, as well as that of the fighters, in the long-term planning for what lay ahead was well appreciated by those of us on the Air Staff who looked to the future with some imagination and, I might add, no little apprehension.

There can be very few of those who have risen to senior rank in the Royal Air Force who have not known, at some time in their careers, what it is to become involved in crashes in aircraft. We were all pilots, and flying itself was a hazard that we all had to face—quite apart from actual combat in the air in time of war— and a surprisingly large number were killed even after reaching air rank. It is also a solemn feature of the life of our Service that there are many who have attained senior rank only to know then the grievous loss of their sons either in action or in crashes. In these personal mishaps and losses there is an aspect of flying as a career that has given to the Royal Air Force a maturity which came about very early in its life as a Service.

In the course of my own Service career, I was to know a fair share of accidents, starting with some right at the beginning of my training as a pilot and including a very serious one that I had out in France as a squadron commander in 1917. But the closest encounter that I have ever had with death while flying came in the summer of 1939. On June 28 I was one of a small party accompanying Sir Kingsley Wood, the Secretary of State for Air, on an official visit to Belfast. Air Chief Marshal Sir Christopher Courtney, as he is now, who was then commanding Reserve Command, and I were the two Service representatives in the party. We were flying in a D.H.86, and we ran into some foul weather over the Irish Sea; and by the time that we approached what should have been the Irish coast we were flying blind. Somehow or other the pilot allowed the aircraft to go into a flat spin, and I could see from the altimeter in the cabin that we were rapidly losing height while there was still no sight of the ground.

I began to feel with a tightening of the throat and a rather clammy certainty that I was about to face my last moment. But the pilot managed to regain control of the aircraft only a few hundred feet above the ground, and as he pulled out of the spin I saw the tops of the trees flash past just beneath us. It then appeared that we were flying straight toward the side of a steep hill; but the pilot had control of the aircraft by then, and he proceeded to climb up through ten thousand feet of thick cloud until he was on top of it, and then he turned back toward England. But he still had to make a decision about where and when he was to go down through the cloud in order to land at some airdrome. He decided to make for Blackpool, and he got a bearing for that from the radio station at Manchester.

Once again we started down through the cloud, expecting to find our way in over Morecambe Bay. But when we finally broke through the cloud we were at a height of only two thousand feet, and we were among what looked like mountains. There was very little petrol left, and there was no chance of having another go at finding our way out. The pilot decided to put the aircraft down as best he could at the nearest convenient spot, and we landed in a heap on a mountainside. Fortunately I was sitting toward the back of the aircraft, and as soon as we came to a stop I scrambled out of the wreckage as fast as I could, fully expecting that it would burst into flames. That should have happened, but, by a stroke of luck the wreckage did not catch fire, and we were given a chance to collect our scattered wits.

At first glance I appeared to be the only one who had escaped without some injury or other. Sir Kingsley Wood had received such a crack on the head that he had been knocked out; his Parliamentary private secretary, Sir Edward Campbell, had a broken wrist; the pilot was injured in some way or other, and the second pilot had had his head knocked about and had broken an ankle; and Chris Courtney had some sort of leg injury which later turned out to be a broken kneecap. How he managed it I do not know, but he had crawled out of that wreckage almost as quickly as I had. Being an old hand at flying he knew as I did that there was every possibility of fire.

There was a thick mist over the mountains, and we had no idea where we were. But we had to get help, and being the only one who was undamaged I set off at random, making my way through the wet heather that covered the sides of the hills. After going only a quarter of a mile or so, I realized that I was losing my sense of direction, and then suddenly I found myself standing at the top of a steep declivity which led down into a valley. At the bottom there was a stream, on the banks of which stood a stone hut with smoke coming from its chimney. Scrambling down the slope, I made my way to the hut and banged on the door, and when it was opened I found three shepherds sitting around the fire inside. I explained what had happened, and they told me that we were in the mountains of southern Cumberland about five miles north of Ulverston. One of the men immediately set off for Ulverston to get help, and the other two came with me, and we scrambled up the slopes back to the crashed aircraft.

It began to rain, and very soon we were all soaking wet. We managed to get those who were injured back into the shelter of the broken cabin of the aircraft and in some little comfort. We waited for quite some time for help, and finally the police arrived, and then an ambulance managed to crawl up a mountain track to within about a mile or so of where we had crashed. Our biggest difficulty was in carrying Chris Courtney, a tall, well-built man, through the waist-high heather in the pouring rain down to the ambulance. But eventually we reached it, and we were all taken into Ulverston.

Throughout this unpleasantness Sir Kingsley Wood had remained calm and in good spirits, and he took what must have been for him a great deal of punishment without any show of being unduly disturbed. It was a nasty crack on the head that he had received when we crashed, but he was nevertheless back at his desk at the Air Ministry the next day. Chris Courtney was the one who was out of luck. His broken knee put him out of action for quite some time, and that, as it turned out, was to change the whole course of his career. But for the moment in which he received those injuries, a moment over which he had no control whatsoever, Courtney would have been Commander-in-Chief of Fighter Command at the time of the Battle of Britain, and it would have been his name and not Stuffy Dowding's which would have become associated with the Battle of Britain, and I would never have had the opportunity of becoming Dowding's successor in time to fight the Blitz. It was yet another case of the unpredictable reaching out of the hand of chance.

In planning for the future, the Air Ministry had decided as early as 1938 that Chris Courtney should succeed Stuffy Dowding as Commander-in-Chief of Fighter Command when Dowding's tour of duty there came to an end in 1939. Courtney was informed officially about that appointment, and at one stage he was even posted to the headquarters of Fighter Command to sit in as Dowding's deputy; but after only a very short time at Bentley Priory he found that he had little or no work to do. Courtney then asked the Air Ministry to make other plans for his immediate future, and he was then appointed to command Reserve Command.

When he had partly recovered from his accident, Chris Courtney was sent to Canada to get the first training scheme organized there, and on his return to England, at the beginning of 1940, he was appointed the Air Member for Supply and Organisation. We were by then already well known to each other, but from that time on we became close friends.

It is perhaps not generally realized what a great debt the Royal Air Force owes to the Royal Navy for the way in which the Navy spurned, in the early days of flying, men who were of outstanding character and ability. Chris Courtney was only one of the many former naval officers who was treated in this way, and he came to play an important role in the growth of the Royal Air Force. He started his Service career as a naval cadet in Britannia in 1905, and after some years of sea service he applied to join the incipient naval air service. That was looked upon with such disfavor by the Lords of the Admiralty that he was smartly sent off to sea in a battleship. But he persisted with his interest in flying, and eventually he was posted to Eastchurch, where he took his pilot's certificate in 1912. He was the Admiralty's official observer at the first Schneider Cup Race which was flown at Monte Carlo in 1913.

By the time that the First World War broke out, naval flying was more or less accepted, and Chris Courtney's early start in the new arm gave him an opportunity to gain a great deal of practical experience in both wartime flying and in staff appointments. On the formation of the Royal Air Force in 1918 he became an officer in the new Service, and later that year he was appointed to command a brigade in the Independent Force under Trenchard. As a brigadier-general at the age of twenty-eight, he was surely the youngest ever known in the Service. "I opted for the new Service," he has said, "because of the lack of understanding displayed by the Admiralty towards aviation matters."

As Air Member for Supply and Organisation during almost the entire Second World War—from January, 1940, until the end— Chris Courtney was one of those who served in an illustrious back room, and in that he did exceptionally well. His good, clear mind, his wealth of experience in the Service, and his breadth of vision and readiness always to listen enabled him to use to the full his first-rate powers of organization throughout a long period of severe strain; and he emerged intact from that grueling experience with all the genial good humor and aplomb for which he has been so well liked and respected. He was one of the most admired of the senior officers in the R.A.F., and a fair share of credit must go to Courtney for the way in which Fighter Command was able to fight the Battle of Britain, for it was his job to see to it that the supply of aircraft and equipment was maintained in the waging of the battle.

All too often in the studies that have been made of the year that was to pass between the time of the Munich crisis and the actual outbreak of the Second World War on September 3, 1939, there is overlooked one vitally important factor. That the state of affairs which led to Munich should never have been allowed to develop can never be denied; but it did develop, and it had to be faced with realism. What must never be forgotten, or overlooked, is that in the year that followed it, we were provided with just enough time in which to bring the Royal Air Force up to a state that, we felt, would at least enable us to put up a fight.

There are too many who argue about Munich and its aftermath in a way that puts the air, in disregarding it, in a regrettably false position. William L. Shirer, for instance, has made the sweeping statement: "As Churchill, backed by every serious Allied military historian, has written, 'the year's breathing space said to be "gained" by Munich left Britain and France in a much worse position compared to Hitler's Germany than they had been at the Munich crisis.' As we shall see, all the German Military calculations a year later bear this out, and subsequent events, of course, remove any doubts whatsoever."

Laying claim to such powerful backing in support of a certain view of what happened is one thing; but looking soberly at all the hard facts is another. It is true that Winston Churchill did make that statement, but even he, for all the agony of mind that he suffered over the way in which the Munich affair was settled, qualified it with a reference to the air which should be kept much more firmly in mind. "There is however one vital sphere in which we began to overtake Germany and improve our own position," he wrote; and he went on to describe how "throughout 1939" we greatly strengthened our Air Force "as more squadrons were mounted."

While this admission can scarcely be called a grudging one, even Winston Churchill's assessment does not give with sufficient emphasis the true value of that improvement. It was a desperately critical time for the air, and it was the air that was important. Through the improvement that we managed to achieve we were able to bring to "subsequent events" an interpretation that was quite different from that offered by those who would insist upon our continuing weakness in comparison with the strength of Germany. In the air in 1938 we had practically nothing; during 1939 we went a long way toward catching up; and by 1940, "when the test came," as Churchill has put it, we were in a position to be able to wage successfully the most vitally important battle that has ever been fought in the air.

20 / On Borrowed Time

DURING THAT last year before we became embroiled in the Second World War, I found that when my mind was not devoted to my work it was all too often preoccupied with gloomy thoughts about the disastrous way in which the international state of affairs was sliding into chaos. The humor of that time was one of unrelieved crisis, and in a way it was even worse than an actual state of war. Many times I wondered how it had come about that, with one great world war still fresh in our memories, we could again proceed with such grim inevitability toward another attempt to settle our differences by force. I knew some of the answers to that; but had we learned so little in the past twenty-five years?

It is considered that war is a stage in the development of national policy, and if that is true then the final determination of the broad policy in war must rest in the hands of the politicians. The Service chiefs can advise the politicians according to the circumstances, and they must tell them in terms of the actual waging of war what is possible and what is not possible; but they must always remain subject to political control. At the same time, the politicians must give the Service chiefs the ways and the means for the winning of war—the sinews of war—and, from the strictly military point of view, they must not interfere unduly with the conduct of the actual fighting once it has started as a result of political planning, or the lack of it. It is the lot of the military to carry the can in a variety of ways, and none of them is pleasant.

There have been occasions when I have been asked to express my views on the theories of war, and my answer has always been a short one: I have views on war, but I have no theories about it. War, so far as I am concerned, is a practical problem that has to be faced with a practical outlook. I always thought of myself, in my role of military airman, as a realistic practitioner of war; and I am not a theorist. It is a thorny enough subject upon which all the experts disagree in any case, and even if one were able to get a universal agreement about theory, no one would be much the better for it. Foch always used to say in any question that might be raised about the waging of war: "What is the problem?" War so far as I am concerned is a series of practical problems to which one must find the right answers, and from the point of view of the military mind, I do not think that one can go beyond that.

During the time that I spent at the Imperial Defence College with Alan Brooke and Bertie Ramsay we never discussed, in our work as instructors, what might be called the principles of the theory of war. We worked with facts and with the solving of practical problems through the right planning; and we did not waste our time on any highfalutin pretensions about theory. To us the object of war was to win it as quickly and as economically as possible.

And so it was that, no matter which way I looked at the situation during 1939, I could not seem to banish from my mind these depressing thoughts about how stupid we seemed to be in our handling of it. I recalled the ghastly carnage of the earlier war throughout which I had served. All the horror of that had occurred not so very long before, and it was unthinkable that we should have to go through it all again. And yet there it was, staring us in the face.

Of what we gained in a practical sense during the year after the time of Munich, one of the most important assets was the creation of an effective radar screen. This enabled us to know at all times and under any conditions everything that was happening in the air for many miles beyond our coastline. No longer were we solely dependent, as we had been throughout history, on what we could see with our eyes and hear with our ears. We had this invisible electronic screen around our coast which gave us a magical vision, and on instruments we could follow the movements of all aircraft that approached us from the Continent. We knew where they were in space, their height, the courses that they were following, their speed, how many of them there were, and even if they were our own or those of an invader.

The idea for such a screen, following the success of the early scientific experiments, was approved as far back as September, 1935. Planning for the construction of the many transmitting and receiving stations that would go to make up the chain which would raise this invisible screen came in August, 1937. The screen itself was in operation and a part of the air defense of this country well before the outbreak of war. In the words of Denis Richards: "It may be doubted whether any project of equal complexity was ever evolved from untried theory to practical application on so large a scale within so short a time."

My own knowledge of radar, which was a scientific achievement in which Britain was well ahead of the rest of the world, and which was the greatest of all our early secrets—just as the atom bomb was the greatest of the later ones possessed by the Allies—dated from those days of its beginning in the middle thirties, and I had rather grown up with the idea as it was developed by the scientists of this country. As Assistant Chief of Air Staff in 1938 it was part of my work to determine what use we would be able to make of the screen around our coast. This called for a fairly thorough knowledge on my part—short of the more technical aspects—of what had been going on, and what we might expect of Radio Direction Finding, as it was known before we adopted the American word radar later in the war.

Although I never ceased to marvel at the way in which radar had developed, I was fortunate in being able to accept it gradually over a period of time and so to understand it more for its practical value than as a mysterious and awe-inspiring contraption. In that respect I was one of the small group on the Air Staff who could see what tremendous possibilities there were in the use that could be made of it, and I gave my support in every way to its development.

Years later Sir Robert Watson-Watt, the British pioneer in the work done in radar, was to state in his book *Three Steps to Victory:* "If I were given the invidious task of naming the Royal Air Force officer, outside the little group of those engaged wholly on radar duties, who did most to ensure that radar became an effective weapon of war, effectively wielded, I think I should name Air Chief Marshal Sir W. Sholto Douglas . . ." I quote that now not so much for the generous compliment that is paid to me as for the reference that is made to radar as "an effective weapon of war." In what lay ahead I was to make great use of that weapon.

In addition to the radar warning system that we were able to develop, we also in that year of borrowed time became definitely stronger in the air. At the time of Munich we had had only ninety-three modern fighters. When the war came, a year later, we had ready for operations over five hundred modern fighters. In that alone we had at least surpassed the Germans in the rate of expansion, and we were in a position to fight, even if it was against a deadly opposition.

One of the aspects of the air which was held back in its development during the latter part of the interwar years was the use that was to be made of aircraft against warships. I became involved in the arguments that developed with the Royal Navy over this through being the Air Ministry representative on what was known as the "Bomb versus Battleship" subcommittee of the Committee of the Imperial Defence. From the outset I had strongly in mind the results of Billy Mitchell's views about the use of the air against warships and his arguments which he had been able to support with such devastating proof as far back as the early twenties. My encounters at committee meetings with the representatives of the Royal Navy, headed by Tom Phillips, an admiral who was a gallant and delightful little cock-sparrow of a man, were at least lively enough in our exchanges if not conclusive in the results. All the views about the air that were held by the Royal Navy in the years up to even just before the war were astonishingly lopsided, and of a cussedness that inspired Jack Slessor to remark: "With great respect I believe this to be nonsense."

In our efforts to prove yet again to our sailors all that Billy Mitchell had already demonstrated so successfully to the Americans, we conducted some trials a year or so before the war with attacks by aircraft of the R.A.F. on ships of the Royal Navy. I organized the air side of these trials, and it was a relief to be able to put on some practical demonstrations of our claims instead of sitting interminably round a table haggling about them. But even though the air won the day, the Navy continued to be loath to accept hard facts, and it was only when they were brought face to face with the reality under the conditions of war that they finally agreed to our views. For many of those good, if misguided, men it was then too late.

Even by the late thirties there were still many senior officers in both the Royal Navy and the Army who seemed to be unable to accept the Royal Air Force as a quite separate and equal service dealing solely with the air. By then we had been in existence for twenty years, and we were just as professional in our understanding of the air as they were of the sea and the land. That the Royal Air Force, through its work in the Middle East and in India, had been continuously in action of some description or other ever since the start of the First World War was of tremendous advantage to us in a widening of our experience and a testing of our men, machines and ideas; and down through the years the Air Staff had developed with an unbroken continuity.

From the all-wood and fabric biplanes which we had flown for so long it seemed that we suddenly spurted in the late thirties and early forties into a new world of complex all-metal monoplanes powered by engines which provided astonishing performances. It was a growth in the development of the airplane that has not been exceeded by any other period, and we went all the way from the last of what may be described as the simple flying-by-the-seat-of-the-pants biplanes—when, in fact, flying was a great deal more fun—to the beginnings of being hurled through the air by jets.

British engineers, headed by Frank Whittle, were able to achieve a great deal during those years in the pioneering development of the jet engine, but it is a matter of sad record that Whittle had to fight an uphill battle to get support for his ideas. During the middle 1930's there was even a statement about jet propulsion made by the Under-Secretary of State for Air that: "We do not consider that we should be justified in spending any time or money on it . . ." That official attitude was typical of the way in which aviation, both military and civil, was viewed by the governments of this country from long before then until long afterward. In the case of the jet engine, that lack of intiative at government level led to its being produced by the Germans before us: their first jet flew in great secrecy on August 27, 1939. Whittle's first engine was flown by us on May 15, 1941. The Americans flew their first jet-engined aircraft on October 1, 1942.

But if the fighters were becoming increasingly elaborate and complex in their design and operation, their growth was nothing compared to what happened with the bombers. Their development, about which we could naturally make no public statements, was a great leap forward, and specifications were laid down by one of the departments for which I was responsible for all the new four-engined bombers which later became so well known as the Stirling, the Halifax and the Lancaster. There were a multitude of problems which we had to resolve, including power-operated gun turrets, bombsights, and the use of airborne radar.

This particular department, the Directorate of Operational Requirements, was in the hands of R. H. M. S. (now Air Marshal Sir Robert) Saundby, who was a thoroughgoing professional airman. Five years before, he had been one of my students at the Imperial Defence College. As with all of us, Saundby had been an operational pilot, specializing in flying at night, in the First World War; and during the second war he became the senior air staff officer and deputy to the Commander-in-Chief of Bomber Command, Bert Harris, in whose squadron he had served as a flight commander in Iraq back in the early 1920's.

In speaking of the work done by Bomber Command during the Second World War, Bert Harris refers to Sandy Saundby as one of the hardest workers he had ever served with, and with "less side than almost anybody I have known." Harris also reveals that Saundby was a keen fisherman, "which was why all the main German towns that were our targets had the names of fish for code names." But when Saundby later took up collecting butterflies and moths he found himself rather stumped for names because, as Harris somewhat dryly explains, "it would obviously be inconvenient to use words like Broad-Bordered-Beehawks."

During the feverish spell just before the disaster of the war descended upon us, the Air Ministry had taken what were considered precautionary measures, and a reserve operations and intelligence center had been organized at Garston, just to the north of Watford, and some twenty miles northwest of London. This center was located in the buildings of what had been the Building Research Station, among whose activities, one of my staff rather delightedly told me, was the study of, as he put it, "the way in which bricks die." It was intended that Garston should be a standby headquarters from which the war in the air could be directed should London itself be as badly bombed as we expected.

Just before an actual state of war came about, I was instructed to move with my staff to this reserve center. I was in charge of the whole show, and I was to exercise operational control over the R.A.F. should the Air Ministry in London be blown to smithereens. With the move to Garston I took with me the Directorate of Staff Duties, which was under Bill Willock, an old friend from my days in the early twenties at Manston; but there was not room for the whole of my staff, and the Directorate of Operational Requirements, under Sandy Saundby, had to move into some elementary school buildings near Harrow.

While I was prepared to grant that it was possibly a wise enough precaution to move out of London, it was an awkward and unsatisfactory arrangement, and being so far away from the rest of the Air Ministry was bad for my work and the efficiency of my staff. At Garston we also had a standby war room, a duplicate in every way of the war room at the Air Ministry in London, which could immediately be brought into use if Whitehall and the Chief of the Air Staff and all his various staff officers were knocked out. We seriously thought that that might well happen, through the heavy bombing that we expected from the Germans.

The Services had become fully mobilized on September 1. Two days later I paused in my work at my desk at Garston to listen to the Prime Minister's broadcast on that morning of Sunday, September 3, 1939. Everybody who ever heard that broadcast which announced that we were at war with Germany has memories of his or her own personal thoughts and reactions. My own I can still recall quite vividly. "My God . . . we've got to take those bastards on all over again," I thought. "We finished them off twenty years ago. Why do we have to start off all over again." The answer was simple enough, and I knew it; but I felt that I could allow myself at least the one last luxury of asking it.

One of the most interesting aspects of the differences that existed between the First and the Second World Wars must surely be the strong contrast that was so clearly displayed in the moods of the people at the time of the outbreaks of those wars. In my own case, it could not have been greater. In August, 1914, I had shared with everybody else the almost burning eagerness and enthusiasm to get to grips with the enemy, and a view of war as something in the nature of a crusade to be waged with the flags flying and the bands playing and a proud clutch at the heart as one thought of all that it meant to be privileged to fight for King and country. In September, 1939, there was unquestionably resolution enough to fight, but it was with a somber anger that made me, as with many other people, feel that this evil that had been thrust upon us must be destroyed, even if the task that lay ahead was so obviously going to be a dirty and horrible business.

On that Sunday morning my own heart was heavy enough, and in my mind there were questions that could never be answered. What, I wondered, were my former adversaries in the fighting in the air of the first war thinking about it. I knew, of course, that Hermann Goering was now at the top. He had visited England at the time of the Coronation of King George VI, hoping to be among those present, but he had only got as far as the German Embassy in London before being hustled back to Germany by his own people. Only hours before war was declared, he had tried to get to London in an attempt to conduct further negotiations, but he had been rebuffed. In view of all that lay ahead, it was as well that we never actually met, other than in combat in the air during the first war.

On the other hand, I regretted that I had not been able to meet again the gallant little Ernst Udet. He was a major general and chief of the Technical Section of the German Air Ministry when he had come as a member of an official mission to this country in 1938, but I did not meet him on that visit. We had heard that he had been the first to fly the revolutionary new Me. 109 as far back as 1935, and on that visit to England he had accompanied General

Erhard Milch, who was then a sort of Secretary of State for Air in Germany. They were even shown the original shadow factories of our aircraft industry around, of all places, Coventry and Birmingham.

In the course of the various functions which took place during the visit of the Germans I did meet Erhard Milch. He was an inconspicuous pilot in the German Air Force in the first war, but during the interwar years he had done a great deal in helping to form and operate the very successful German airline Lufthansa. But his advancement had been more through playing politics, in which he had worked his way up to the position of becoming Goering's deputy. With Goering and Udet he made up the trio which shaped and formed the German Air Force in the prewar years. He was a thickset man with an obstinate air about him which was far from easy to penetrate.

At one of the cocktail parties which I attended, I got into conversation with Erhard Milch's A.D.C., who was a bright young fighter pilot. At first he was keenly interested when he found that I had myself been a fighter pilot during the First World War. But when he heard that I had actually fought against Richthofen, Goering, Boelcke, Immelmann and Ernst Udet in the skies over the Western Front he seemed to think that I was showing a somewhat unseemly audacity in even daring to be alive to tell the tale.

While I was still turning over in my mind this odd conglomeration of thoughts about those who were again our enemies, the air raid sirens sounded the first alarm of the war. We had all been thoroughly instructed about what we were to do, and since we fully expected that the Germans would immediately launch an attack upon us I promptly joined everybody else down in the air raid shelter. We all sat around there looking rather stupid and waiting for the Germans to start knocking the hell out of us, but after about ten minutes there came the all-clear signal, and we filed out and returned rather self-consciously to our offices. The only evidence of anything definite having happened was the state of the work being done in boarding up the windows of our improvised war room. The air raid siren had not only caused the workers employed on the job to down tools to a man: they had all smartly gone home and they were gone for the rest of the day.

When I inquired about the warning, I was told that the responses on our radar screen had produced a blip that could not be identified, and playing safe until such time that it could be identi-

fied, the warning had been sounded. It was then discovered that
the radar blip which had caused the plots on the unidentified
aircraft to appear on the operations room tables of Fighter Command was in fact from a French aircraft on its way to Croydon
with some French officers on board. No warning about this flight
had been passed to Fighter Command, and they were not going to
be caught napping.

But for all our alertness and anxiety about being bombed and
gassed, the war at the start turned into something quite different
from what we expected, and we were subjected instead to the
monotony of doing little more than stand guard. So far as the
Services were concerned, instead of being allowed to get on with
the war now that it was upon us we were held back, and we had to
put up with the last thing that I had ever expected: the demoralizing phony war, as it came to be called. I believed then, and I still
believe, that our political leaders were wrong to allow that to
happen. I had expected that the R.A.F. would be given instructions to start attacking Germany immediately, and I still believe
that that was what we should have done. Instead we seemed to be
prepared to allow German policy to dictate what our activity
should be, and that resulted in precious little of it.

A large part of the German Air Force was engaged in the
violent assault on Poland, and I have always believed that the
Poles would have held out much longer than they did if we had
attacked in the air, and even on the ground, from the west. Had we
taken prompt action we could have given a great deal of help to
Poland, although, I must admit, we could not have saved her. By
bombing Germany's western frontier right from the moment of the
outbreak of hostilities, we and the French could have waged a
much more effective war, because the one thing that the Germans
had always been apprehensive about was a war on two fronts.
Instead we allowed Germany to fight a war against Poland on one
front with practically no interference from our side. Poland was
our ally, and I think that she had every right to expect action from
us. As it was, the Royal Air Force was restricted to the ridiculous
and humiliating business of dropping senseless leaflets over Germany, a performance which achieved nothing whatsoever.

It was all a continuing hangover from, or an aftermath of, the
policy of appeasement or conciliation, not to mention a fear of
retaliatory bombardment of London by German bombers. I could
only assume, with a feeling of the bitter frustration that was shared
by all of us on the Air Staff, that the Prime Minister and the
Cabinet were still thinking that they might be able to come to

terms with Hitler after he had smashed Poland. In refraining from more direct action we gave Hitler time to regroup his forces after he had defeated Poland, and time to concentrate everything in the west for an attack upon the French and upon us.

But if the British frame of mind so far as policy was concerned was one of being decidedly backward about coming forward, we were positively thrusting compared to the French. Just before the outbreak of war I had gone to France with the Chief of the Air Staff for discussions with the leaders of the French Air Force, and what we had learned during our talks at Rheims and what we had seen as we were shown around had shocked and horrified us. The once mighty French air service had fallen on evil days.

That the French had made only very little progress in aircraft design was already known to us, but I had never expected to find such an atmosphere of defeatism. Their fighters were nothing to compare with the Hurricanes and Spitfires which we had in large-scale production, and their bombers were practically nonexistent. On paper they had quite a lot of squadrons, but they were made up of almost worthless, outdated aircraft. We had had our doubts about the worth of our ally in the air, but after that visit we had to come to the unhappy conclusion that in the event of war we could not expect much help from the French. To me it was a particularly sad situation because in the air in the First World War the French had acquitted themselves with great distinction.

No sooner was the war upon us than, as we had rather feared, the demands from the French for additional air support began to increase in such a way that they became the main issue of the next eight months. And it was upon the way in which that issue was handled by us that the outcome of the whole war depended. So precarious was the position in which the French found themselves that even on the night before we went to war with Germany, and before issuing their own ultimatum, they started asking us for more and more support, including the use of our home-based bombers.

"As far as air policy was concerned, severe differences of opinion between France and Britain existed," Charles Webster and Noble Frankland have stated about the position at the time of the outbreak of war in their official history of our bombing offensive. During the next year I was deeply involved in all Air Staff policy, and I would go even further than these eminent historians in weighing up our relationship with the French over matters of the air. The "severe differences of opinion" quickly became piteous cries for help which, for all the searching that we did for appro-

priate answers, developed into increasingly difficult and troublesome conflicts.

Within a few days of the outbreak of war, and while we were
still at our reserve headquarters at Garston, there started the
demand from France for more of our fighter squadrons to be sent
out there. I was instructed to approach Stuffy Dowding about
getting them from his Fighter Command squadrons. In providing
squadrons for the Air Force that we sent to France he had already
made a large contribution from his resources; and this latest
request was the beginning of what was to become one of the most
trying problems that we had to face during the months that lay
ahead.

The headquarters of Fighter Command at Stanmore were only a
few minutes' drive from Garston. Feeling in need of a little moral
support for what was obviously going to be a tough nut to crack, I
took Bill Willock with me, and we drove over to Stanmore, where
we bearded Dowding in his office in Bentley Priory. I stated the
Air Ministry's case, and, almost as I expected, I got a smart rebuff.
It became an increasingly difficult struggle in the efforts that we
made to cope with the French demands while at the same time
helping Dowding to nourish his own strength.

It did not take long for everybody concerned with the effective
running of the Air Ministry to realize that splitting up and moving
the departments under my control from central London to Garston
and Harrow was interfering seriously with our work. We stayed at
these reserve headquarters for only a few weeks, and then, since
the war in the west showed promise of proceeding along the
quietest of lines, we were moved back to the Air Staff headquarters
in and under King Charles Street, Whitehall.

One of my particular interests during the days just before the
war started had been the formation of the Operational Training
Units. These were to provide a means whereby pilots and other air
crews would receive their final training in the flying of operational
types of aircraft before going off to join the fighting squadrons. I
felt very strongly about the value of these O.T.U.'s because of my
own experiences in the First World War. For too long in that first
war we received in the squadrons at the Front raw pilots straight
out of the Flying Training Schools at home with scarcely more
than a few hours of flying to their credit. We had to devote
precious time and effort in the squadrons to giving them their final
training, and no matter how hard we tried they were still only half
trained when they went into battle. As a result of that we suffered

very heavy casualties. I was determined that that should not happen again, and when my chance came as a senior officer on the Air Staff, I pressed hard for the formation of these final training units.

In making our plans for this we also evolved schemes for equipment that contributed greatly to the later development of the elaborate simulators which are in such universal use today, both in the Services and in the civil airlines. In these a pilot can go through every conceivable experience in the flying of an aircraft of any nature without ever leaving the ground, and all the time he is under the watchful and critical eye of an instructor or an examiner testing his ability. In those days we called them synthetic trainers, and I had Bill Willock, who was also in charge, under my control, of the Directorate of War Training and Tactics, impress upon the Treasury the urgent need for approval of these plans. His comment to me after he came back from the meeting at which it was agreed that we should have the necessary funds was brief and to the point.

"It's unheard of," he said, "but they approved everything without a word of objection. For once they realized all too clearly that it was a case of money being well spent."

There were problems enough, however, in getting our Operational Training Units started. For one thing, as a result of the rapid expansion in the number of the front-line squadrons that we were aiming at, we ran into difficulty in getting our hands on enough operational aircraft and the experienced crews that were necessary for the proper functioning of the scheme. But by begging, borrowing and stealing, we did gather together a sufficient number of both to get it underway. The Commander-in-Chief of Bomber Command, who was then Air Chief Marshal Sir Edgar Ludlow-Hewitt, was greatly in favor of the scheme; but to my surprise the one who objected, and went on objecting, was the one from whom I least expected opposition: the Commander-in-Chief of Fighter Command.

Stuffy Dowding wanted to build up his first-line squadrons, and so far as he was concerned—and to a point it was understandable —the formation of the Operational Training Units meant diverting aircraft and pilots from those squadrons. I thought that Dowding was wrong because without the O.T.U.'s it would have been quite impossible for the operational squadrons to have coped with the influx of new and still untrained pilots straight from the Flying Training Schools. Not only would the newcomers have had to be trained in the flying of the operational aircraft, but they would also have had to be trained in tactics, formation flying, and everything else that goes into making up the full qualifications of operational air crews.

Another reason why I found that objection of Stuffy Dowding's rather curious was because I knew just how keenly he felt about casualties. That was with him a concern that was more heartfelt than it was in the case of any other commander in the Service, and, as I well knew, it went back to what had happened in the days of the First World War. Dowding had always strongly opposed the use on operations of any pilots who had not received the fullest possible training. But for all his objections to our scheme we went ahead and organized these O.T.U.'s, and we were finally able to convince him that they would be to his benefit.

As the phony war in the west dragged itself sluggishly through those bitterly cold and miserable months of the winter of 1939–40, there were all too few occasions upon which I was able to pry myself loose from my desk for visits to the Air Force in the field. But there was one such occasion which started and came very near ending almost immediately in disaster on New Year's Day, 1940. It occurred when Harold Balfour and I decided to go together to France on a visit to the Royal Air Force, which had out there the Advanced Air Striking Force and units of the Air Component of the British Expeditionary Force.

When we got to Hendon, from which we were to fly to France, we found that the airdrome was shrouded in a thick fog, with visibility down to not more than fifty yards. The pilot of the twin-engined aircraft in which we were to fly was an experienced veteran of Imperial Airways, and he told us that from the weather reports it appeared that the fog was fairly local and not very thick, and that he had decided that we could make a start.

After only a short run the pilot lifted the aircraft off the ground, and no sooner were we free from it than we were immediately enveloped in dense fog, with no visibility at all. And then, just as we were in the air with an urgent need for all the power that we could get, there was a sudden loud bang from the port engine. I quickly looked out, and to my horror I saw that the top of one of the cylinders was sticking up above the engine cowling. At the most critical moment of take-off the pilot suddenly was faced with only one good engine. The immediate prospect of what might happen in the next few moments was only too obvious. Hendon was not a large airdrome, and it was enclosed by houses with the ground sloping upward in the direction in which we were heading.

We were hanging on with only one engine working when we
needed all the power that both engines could give, and we were in
thick fog. Balfour and I looked quickly at each other, and since we
were both very experienced pilots I had a feeling that we read in
each other's eyes the thought that we both had in mind.

At a time like that it takes only a split second for a disaster to
happen, but fortunately for us we were in the hands of a very
capable as well as an experienced pilot. He controlled the aircraft
most skillfully, holding it well and maintaining a slow, steady
climb. But I still shudder when I think of the narrow margin by
which we missed the roofs of the houses over which we passed on
the edge of the airfield. By the time that we got up to about a
thousand feet we were clear of the fog and in bright sunshine.
There was no way in which we could turn back and try and land in
that fog on one engine, but we were told on the radio that Shoreham was clear, so we staggered down to the coast and landed
there, changed to another aircraft, and then went on our way to
France.

After several days spent visiting the various units of the R.A.F.,
Harold Balfour and I agreed that it was impossible to feel at all
reassured by what we saw and heard. The morale of the personnel
of the Advanced Air Striking Force and the Air Component was
sound enough: it was the light bombers with which the A.A.S.F.
was equipped that was troubling everybody. There were a few
squadrons that had Blenheims, but most of them still had outdated
Battles, in which none of us could feel any confidence at all.

Designed in 1933, the Battle first flew in 1936, coming into
service in the Air Force a year later. It was a single-engined, low-
winged monoplane, very slow, underpowered, and sadly lacking in
defensive fire-power. Against fighter attack from the rear it had
only one Lewis gun on an out-of-date mounting which was
scarcely more than what we had had in the First World War. Some
of the Battles had a gun fitted in the floor of the aircraft which
could be brought to bear if an enemy fighter should make an attack
from underneath the tail, but that was an awkward and primitive
arrangement.

My own experiences in the First World War led me to feel a
deep sympathy for the air crews who were flying those Battles,
which had become quite unsuitable for daylight operations unless
they had fighter escorts. All that I feared for them then was to
come to pass when the Germans did start their move in the west at
the end of the phony war. The Battles were simply mowed down
by the German fighters. The first two Victoria Crosses to be

awarded to members of the R.A.F. in the Second World War were made posthumously to the pilot, Flying Officer D. E. Garland, and the observer, Sergeant T. Gray, of a Battle of No. 12 Squadron for a low-level bombing attack that they made in northern Belgium on May 10, 1940.

On that same day, another of the pilots of No. 12 Squadron, the well-liked William Simpson who is now the chief public relations officer of British European Airways, was extremely badly burned when his Battle was shot down by antiaircraft fire during a bombing run, as a result of which he became one of the stalwarts of the Guinea Pig Club of East Grinstead. Bill Simpson has written with a moving balance about his experiences in being so badly injured, and the opening pages alone of his book *I Burned My Fingers* reveal with great clarity how the lives of those who fly can be so rapidly changed by that hand of chance.

The casualties suffered by the Battle crews in low-level bombing in daylight were appalling, and those young men won for themselves the highest respect for the magnificent way in which they faced up to almost certain death: "A rate of loss," Denis Richards records in the official history, "which, taking no account of aircraft merely damaged, was forty per cent of sorties on 10th May, one hundred per cent on 11th May and sixty-two per cent on 12th May." When those squadrons were put to the test and suffered so disastrously, I could not help feeling with the deepest regret that it would have been so much better if, some years earlier, we had developed a dive-bomber along the lines of the German Ju. 87 instead of devoting so much of our resources to the design, the development and the production of those wretched Battles.

The hours of hard work that we who were often stiflingly employed upon in London were long and, for some, even nerve-racking, and there were more than one might suspect who soon began to show signs of the strain. Perhaps I was fortunate and spared from the deadening effects of routine in not having to stay too long in any one appointment. I had been Assistant Chief of Air Staff only just over two years when I was appointed, toward the end of April, 1940, to the post of Deputy Chief of the Air Staff. That further step up came just as the phony war ended, and when Hitler finally turned his attention to the west.

As Deputy Chief of the Air Staff, I was more closely concerned with actual operations than I had been in any other appointment that I had held at the Air Minstry. I was responsible for the day-to-day operations of the whole of the R.A.F., and I had under my control the directorates of home, overseas and naval operations, of military cooperation, and of intelligence. Again it was through the long years of experience and development that there was the clearly defined staff procedure for all the work that I was to do, and which was executed through an established system and not through reliance only on committees.

The broad policy in the use that was to be made of the R.A.F. was decided by the War Cabinet, from which would come instructions to the Chief of the Air Staff. So far as operations were concerned, he would then discuss with me the directives or orders that would have to be sent to the various Commanders-in-Chief. This meant that I was very closely in touch with the C.A.S., seeing him personally all the time. I would have drafts of the directives prepared by my staff which I would then discuss again with the C.A.S. When they had received his final approval, I would see to it that they were issued officially to the Commander-in-Chief concerned. There would then usually be further discussion with him and with the C.A.S. In fact, a great deal of this work was done through personal discussion.

There was enough to worry about because we now knew more about the strength of the German Air Force and the way in which it was being used, and I was particularly anxious and, indeed, worried about the strength of our own Fighter Command. My thoughts were constantly occupied with questions about whether we had enough fighters and if our force of them was powerful enough to fend off the attacks of the German bomber force which were bound to come. The period of waiting for Hitler to strike had come to an end, and with the launching of his attack in the west it was all too clear that it would soon be our turn to have to face the fury that had so quickly disposed of Poland in the east.

21 / Security of the Base

S O FAR AS the generally accepted principles of Air Staff doctrine were concerned, I had always been more of a heretic than a conformist. That was clearly understood, and appreciated, by those whom I regarded as my friends and with whom I had to work; and in many ways I was fortunate that, in holding unorthodox views, I was able to make the progress that I did eventually achieve in my Service career. Few fighter pilots attained the positions of the highest command in the Service, or even served on the Air Council, before and during the Second World War, and that may have been because fighter pilots as a race are inclined to be of the somewhat harum-scarum type which does not take very kindly to orthodoxy.

The Air Staff attitude toward the role of the air had rested, over a long period of time, in the virtues of the bomber, and all other considerations took second place to that. Up to a point the doctrine that emerged from that attitude had some considerable merit, but too much was sacrificed to it in the years immediately preceding the Second World War. Starting from the generalization that offense is the best form of defense, the doctrine approved by the Air Staff had called for the emphasis to be placed on the importance of bombers and bombing even at the expense of fighters and their role in the air. Anyone who pressed, as I did, the claims of fighters and the importance of Fighter Command could not escape the charge of heresy. It was thought, and it continued to be thought, that the bombers would win the war; but that was too sweeping an opinion for me to be able to accept. First things had to come first; and I had firmly in my own mind the view that Alan Brooke had expounded during the time when we had worked together at the Imperial Defence College. "It is no good launching an offensive from an insecure base," he would say. "You must make your base secure before you start launching an offensive." In terms of the air that meant that one must have adequate fighter

382

defenses before one could ever start thinking about an effective bomber offensive.

The great fear that had come almost to obsess me from well before the time that the war broke out was that we were not taking sufficiently vigorous steps to make sure that we had a secure base. I also felt that too many highly optimistic theories were being entertained in Air Staff thinking about the way in which bombers could be used and the effects that they were likely to have on the enemy in our bomber effort to gain that security. It smacked far too much for my liking of a hit-first-and-worry-afterward school of thought. There even persisted a conviction that our bombers would have little or no trouble in bombing Germany in daylight without fighter escorts.

There was a great deal about the overenthusiasm of the bomber barons that I did not like, and which I could not bring myself to trust. Their reasoning I found too glib, and lacking in realism. On one occasion I even had to contend with the opinion expressed by a very senior officer that the bomber would always be able to shoot down the attacking fighter because the latter would be firing up wind while the bomber, using its rear guns, would be firing down wind, and the bomber's fire must inevitably reach the fighter before the fighter's bullets reached the bomber! Puerile as this blimpish theory may sound, it was the cause of a great deal of trouble for me, and I had to spend hours in conference trying to convince this particular officer and his supporters that their views were all a lot of nonsense.

The difficulties that I had to face in my arguments with the bomber supporters were not based on any disagreements over the quality of the bomber aircraft which were by then planned for use by the R.A.F. I believed, as they did, that we were about to have in our hands some very formidable aircraft, and I anticipated that our crews would make good use of them. It was in the basic planning for that use that I felt at odds with the views held by those who seemed to be so blindly devoted to the bomber. I felt that we needed a much broader approach in our thinking to the use that was to be made of all types of aircraft.

With the ending of the phony war, my ideas about the necessity for securing one's base and for fighter escorts for the bombers were both quickly put to the test. Although I was proved to be right, the results nevertheless provided a series of brutal shocks. First of all it came to some fundamental re-thinking about the way in which the bomber was to be employed. It was found that, no matter how fast and well armed we might think they were, sending bombers over enemy territory in daylight without fighter escort resulted in prohibitive losses. With that sharp lesson digested, our bombing offensive was switched to the cover of darkness.

But it was not only among those of the Air Staff that there existed these erroneous theories. Even after the war broke out we still had difficulty in convincing the Army and the Royal Navy— particularly the latter—that they were going to need fighter cover. They were finally compelled to change their ideas through the losses that they both suffered; but by then it was too late because the R.A.F. simply did not have enough fighter squadrons to give all the fighter cover that was demanded of it.

So far as the Army was concerned, it was the experiences of the soldiers in France and in Norway in 1940 which convinced them of the need for fighter cover. So stern was their lesson that they then tended to go to the other extreme, and they started making demands for what they erroneously came to call a "fighter umbrella" at all times. They overlooked the fact that a fighter umbrella could only be produced at the most extravagant cost of keeping strong standing patrols in the air all the time from bases which were reasonably close to the area over which the so-called umbrella was required.

The German dive-bombers which had been developed by Ernst Udet were particularly effective against the troops on the ground in the campaign in France in 1940. In addition to practical results, their important contribution was the shocking effect that they had on morale. Being dive-bombed by the German Stukas was a terrifying experience, and they played an important role in the early stages of the war in France. On the other hand, the dive-bomber was a slow and inefficient aircraft, handicapped by the very characteristics that were demanded of it. So long as our fighters were not about they were effective enough; but in level flight they were easy prey. Our fighter pilots almost wept with joy whenever they ran across any Stukas.

But even the day of the dive-bomber soon passed, and after a while there was evolved the fighter-bomber: an aircraft which could be used either as a straightforward fighter or for low-flying attacks against enemy troops. In its way it was reverting to the use that we had learned to make of our fighters in the First World War. But the Army was still slow to appreciate that, and even as late as 1942 I was subjected to a heavy attack during a lecture that I gave to the Army Staff College at Camberley over what the soldiers

COMBAT

Lincoln College, Oxford, 1914. Stroke (nearest camera), Sholto Douglas.

October, 1914. British artillery moving through a French village. This is the same thirteen-pounder gun with which Sholto Douglas' unit was equipped.

Captain W. S. Douglas, Royal Flying Corps, Summer, 1916.

The Pulpit in which Sholto Douglas flew as a pilot. Note that the observer's seat is curiously mounted in front of the propeller.

The Caudron in which Sholto Douglas was given his initial training as a pilot, in France in 1915.

This is the B.E.2c, in which Sholto Douglas flew as an observer in No. 2 squadron and as a pilot in No. 8 squadron, and in which he had his fight with Boelcke and Immelmann in December, 1915.

Major J. B. McCudden, V.C., D.S.O. and bar, M.C. and bar, M.M.

BELOW LEFT:
Captain A. W. Beauchamp-Proctor, V.C., D.S.O., M.C. and bar, D.F.C.

BELOW RIGHT:
Major "Micky" Mannock, V.C., D.S.O. and two bars, M.C. and bar.

IMPERIAL WAR MUSEUM, LONDON

ABOVE LEFT: Lieutenant A. P. F. Rhys Davids, D.S.O., M.C.

ABOVE RIGHT: Captain Albert Ball, V. C., D.S.O. and two bars, M.C.

THE WAR BIRDS

BELOW LEFT: Left to right: Elliott White Springs, Mac Grider (wearing R.F.C. wings on his American uniform), Larry Callahan.

BELOW RIGHT: 85th Squadron, St-Omer, June, 1918. Larry Callahan and Elliott White Springs are fourth and fifth from the left.

PHOTOGRAPH PROPERTY OF MRS. FRANCES SPRINGS   IMPERIAL WAR MUSEUM, LONDON

Fokker E.III, as flown by Boelcke and Immelmann in their fight with Sholto Douglas, December, 1915.

Hauptmann Oswald Boelcke.

Left, Rittmeister Baron von Richthofen, after his 62nd victory. September, 1917.

Left to right, Loerzer, Fokker, Goering.

Oberleutnant Max Immelmann, standing beside the wreckage of his seventh victim.

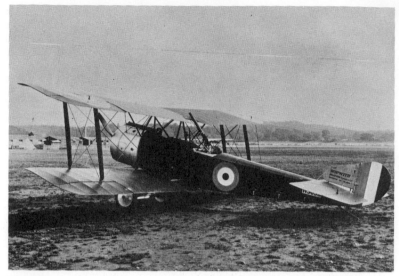

The 1½ Strutter flown by Sholto Douglas while he commanded No. 43 Squadron, 1916–1917.

The S.E.5a.

Major Sholto Douglas, C.O., No. 84 Squadron, Summer, 1918.

Peace: Sholto Douglas' civil pilot's license. Note that it is No. 4.

COMMAND

The Sudan, 1930. Wing Commander W. S. Douglas is the center figure, holding the map. The lion cub was a pet kept in the Officers' Mess in Khartoum. Float planes of the No. 47 Squadron are moored on the banks of the Nile, at right. AIR MINISTRY

BELOW LEFT: Air Commodore W. S. Douglas at the Italian Army maneuvers, 1936 (second from right, with stick under his arm). Mussolini is talking to the King of Italy, whose back is toward the camera.

BELOW RIGHT: Headquarters, Fighter Command, 1941. Air Marshal W. S. Douglas, center.

BRITISH AIRCRAFT

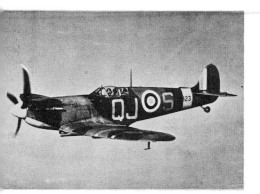

Spitfire Mark V, 1941. Hurricane, 1941.

A Beaufighter of No. 604 Squadron, Fighter Command, 1941.

BELOW LEFT: Mosquito Mark II, night fighter, 1942.

BELOW RIGHT: A Mosquito of Coastal Command attacks a U-boat.

IMPERIAL WAR MUSEUM, LONDON

ABOVE LEFT: Sholto Douglas and "Boom" Trenchard, Western Desert, 1943.

ABOVE RIGHT: The Cairo Conference, 1943. Air Chief Marshal Sir Sholto Douglas, Winston Churchill and Field Marshal Sir Alan Brooke, Chief of the Imperial General Staff.

Tripoli, 1943. Left to right: General Sir Bernard Montgomery, commanding the Eighth Army; Air Chief Marshal Sir Sholto Douglas, commanding the R.A.F. in the Middle East; General Sir Henry Maitland ("Jumbo") Wilson, Commander-in-Chief of the Army in the Middle East; and Air Chief Marshal Sir Arthur Tedder, commanding the Allied Air Forces in the Mediterranean. IMPERIAL WAR MUSEUM, LONDON

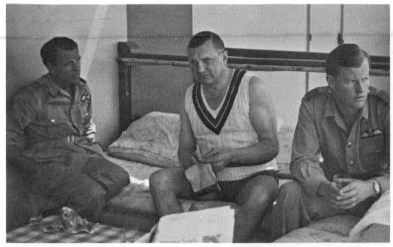

Max Aitken, Sholto Douglas and John Grandy in Alexandria, 1943.

Cairo, 1943. King Farouk, center. Behind him, at right, Sholto Douglas; at left, General Sir Henry Maitland Wilson.

IMPERIAL WAR MUSEUM, LONDON

The authors, Berlin, 1946: Robert Wright (at left) and Sholto Douglas. Wright was Personal Staff Officer to Douglas, who was then Military Governor and Commander-in-Chief of the British zone of occupied Germany.

Germany, 1947. Marshal of the Royal Air Force Sir Sholto Douglas and Field Marshal Lord Montgomery.

London, 1965, Westminster Abbey. Lord Douglas, on right, in his robes
as a Knight Grand Cross of the Order of the Bath.

considered was a woeful lack of a dive-bomber in the Royal Air Force.

As patiently as I could, I pointed out that the day of the dive-bomber belonged in the past, and that we in the Air Force were convinced that the fighter-bomber was the answer for the future. Among those who listened to my lecture that day was my old associate Alan Brooke, who had by then started on his brilliant course as the Chief of the Imperial General Staff. He had had experience enough in France in 1940 of the terrors of the dive-bomber; but on that day at Camberley two years later it provided me with a little solace to find, when I came under attack, that he agreed with me over the views held by the R.A.F.

With many thoughts and, as yet, largely untested ideas burgeoning in my mind, my appointment as Deputy Chief of the Air Staff came in the middle of the ill-fated campaign in Norway in the spring of 1940: the "Scandinavian Misadventure," as the official historian calls it. I became quite deeply involved in the affairs of that campaign, and I was to learn a great deal from what happened; and the results, which were in nearly every way disastrous, went a long way in providing support for some of the ideas that I had been putting forward about a more realistic approach to the use of the air.

Between the middle and the end of April, 1940, we launched a counterstroke against the German invasion of Norway that had just taken place by attempting too much with too little. Quite a large part of the country was already in the hands of the Germans, and right from the beginning, when our Army formations went ashore at Aandalsnes, on the coast of central Norway, Namsos, farther along the coast to the north, and Narvik in the extreme north, there was a desperate need for fighter cover. But in addition to the problems that had to be faced in setting up at very short notice a ground organization for the R.A.F. in Norway, there was also a great difficulty in finding airdromes or suitable sites from which our fighters could operate.

That problem had been anticipated right from the beginning, and the task of finding sites for fighter bases had been placed in the hands of a young Auxiliary fighter pilot named Whitney Straight. The story of his brief but hectic venture into Norway has in it clear enough indications of the makeshift way in which we asked our men in the field to go to work, and the splendid way in which they responded; but there is also in it a glaring example of how, at that time, we relied altogether too much on our native liking for improvisation. In what Straight attempted he demonstrated the powers that were peculiarly his for getting the most out of anything that he might attempt to do. This ability of his was later to receive fuller recognition, and it was eventually to lead to his becoming a prominent figure in civil aviation; today he is the deputy chairman of Rolls-Royce.

At the time of the Norwegian venture, I knew Whitney Straight only through having met him a few times socially in London; today, over twenty-five years later, I like to think of him as one of my best friends. He is one of those who, while not a regular officer, found in the Royal Air Force a way of life which gave full rein to the compulsive individuality of his outlook. He was to share that with quite a few others, including Max Aitken. Straight and Aitken were to serve under me during the second war in a way which proved that they were men of distinct and unusual character. They both became outstandingly successful young commanders, and it was in achieving what they did that they gave me, their Commander-in-Chief, a service that had in it a loyalty which was to lead to understanding and lasting friendships between us. For that reason, if for no other, their stories, as well as those of a few others who served me in the same fashion, are so much a part of my own, and without some account of what happened to them, anything that I might have to say would be incomplete.

An American by birth, Straight's wealthy New York family had strong ties with Britain. He was up at Cambridge, and after some considerable time spent on the Continent he became a British subject in 1936. By then he was already well known in this country as an enthusiastic civil pilot and racing-car driver, and he had begun to lay the foundations for his own civil airline. He was looked upon as a bright young spark in civil aviation.

One of the pilots in the exuberant company of No. 601 Squadron of the Auxiliary Air Force at that time was Max Aitken, the son of the late Lord Beaverbrook, who is also now a close friend of mine. Aitken and Straight had become well known to each other, and it was through Aitken that Straight joined the squadron in March, 1939. Straight was the sort of man who was at home in the devil-may-care atmosphere of the Auxiliary Air Force. He already had to his credit a great deal of flying as a pilot, and he was known to be a man with pronounced views of his own and a vigorous sense of humor. "He was just the type for us," Aitken has since commented.

It was his broader concern with getting on with the waging of the war that caused Whitney Straight to become more restless than most over the inactivity of the phony war. For all his great experience of flying and aviation in general, Straight was only a junior pilot in the squadron—his rank was that of flying officer—and he was there to do as he was told. But at that time there was little or nothing to do, other than fly routine convoy patrols over the English Channel, and Straight has never been a man to sit around doing little or nothing. He started making inquiries at the Air Ministry about the possibility of some more aggressive role than the phony war appeared to be able to offer to a fighter pilot.

The response to his inquiries was quicker than even Whitney Straight had anticipated. He was summoned to the Air Ministry, and in confidence he was told about the anticipated German invasion of Norway. He was given the job of going to Norway to help in the destruction of the airfield at Stavanger, in the southern part of the country, should the Germans show signs of trying to capture it. But the Germans got there before us, and Straight had to sit and wait for further instructions. They came when it was realized that his knowledge as a civilian of the building of airfields was just what was needed to find airfields for the air support that we were going to send in with our own invasion of Norway. It was decided that landing grounds in the wild, mountainous country could probably be made out of the surfaces of some of the frozen lakes. Promoted from flying officer to squadron leader, he was sent in by sea with the Royal Navy to find suitable lakes, and to clear them for this purpose.

Landing at Aandalsnes, Whitney Straight set off on his search. He found what he was looking for at Lake Lesjaskog, inland in central Norway from where he had landed. It was large enough in area, but its frozen surface was covered with thick snow. But the Norwegians were willing helpers, and with their eager cooperation, large bands of workers were organized, a road to the lake was prepared, and a start was made in clearing away the snow and making a runway. But the Germans were making rapid advances, and it was a race against time.

In searching for other possible sites for landing strips, Whitney Straight put to good use his prewar experience of skiing; and he also flew in a Tiger Moth—"a very frozen passenger in the front seat"—which was fitted with skis, and which was piloted by the commanding officer of the Norwegian Air Force. They were on a reconnaissance flight, and they went through the ridiculous (even if it was terrifying) experience of having a very warlike Heinkel 111 make a brief pass at them and then procced on its way.

In that Norwegian expedition of 1940 there were also young regular officers who showed that they had every bit as much drive and sense of purpose as any of those who might have thought of themselves as being less shackled by Service controls. One of them was a squadron leader known as "Bing" Cross who is now Air Marshal Sir Kenneth Cross, and another was Wing Commander R. L. R. (now Air Marshal Sir Richard) Atcherley. They were both embroiled in the flying in Norway in a way which, because of the tragedy that befell their eager forces, called for the utmost initiative and self-reliance, and both Cross and Atcherley showed that they had a full measure of those qualities.

In our effort to provide fighter cover for our expedition into Norway, we arranged to fly off a whole squadron of Gladiators, No. 263, under the command of Squadron Leader J. W. Donaldson, from the aircraft carrier H.M.S. *Glorious* as she was lying off Aandalsnes. It was the first time that the pilots of this squadron had ever performed such an operation, and they had to make their way to the landing strip organized by Whitney Straight on Lake Lesjaskog. The whole operation was performed without mishap, and for just one day the squadron flew from this site under the most appalling conditions and with the utmost gallantry. But working conditions that were well-nigh impossible, as well as the vastly superior enemy forces in the air, were against them. It was so freezingly cold on the site that the controls and the wheels of the aircraft became locked, and the engines could be started only after herculean efforts. They nevertheless got into the air and fought as best they could; but the heavy German attacks and bombing left them at the end of the very first day with only four out of the eighteen aircraft that had landed on the ice, which had by then been broken up by the repeated bombing.

Far to the north, Dick Atcherley had been preparing sites for fighters in the same way that Whitney Straight had been doing in the south. He managed to clear some runways on airfields in the vicinity of Narvik, and from these a Hurricane squadron, No. 46, commanded by "Bing" Cross, and a re-equipped No. 263 Squadron continued to operate during the month of May. But the Germans made an all-out attack, and in the end we had to order evacuation.

After the abandonment of the site at Lake Lesjaskog, Whitney Straight had made his way back to Aandalsnes. He found the place in ruins, and still under heavy air attack. The next morning, as he was helping with the final evacuation of his party, a bomb fell alongside a lorry that he was himself driving, and when he recovered from the blast he found that he had been hit. He was so shaken that he could do no more than stumble to a dressing-station, from which he was taken on a stretcher to one of the ships of the Royal Navy. He had severe head injuries and a hole in his back, and he was promptly grounded by the medical people. But he was also awarded a Military Cross and the Norwegian War Cross; and he was back to flying officer in rank, having been a squadron leader for just twenty-five days.

In the last hours of the final evacuation from northern Norway a month later, the effort made by No. 46 Squadron was one of the greatest ever staged by a fighter squadron, and it was all to end in disaster. The Gladiators of No. 263 Squadron were told to fly off from their airfield and land on H.M.S. *Glorious,* which they did. But it was not considered that the Hurricanes of No. 46 Squadron could be landed on the deck of the aircraft carrier, and orders were given that they should be destroyed. "Bing" Cross and every one of his eighteen pilots pleaded to be allowed at least to try and get down on the carrier with the ten Hurricanes that they had left. Permission was granted, and after a day of very heavy fighting in the air with the pilots suffering from near exhaustion, and for all their lack of experience in never even having made so much as a carrier landing before, every one of the aircraft was landed safely on *Glorious.* It was a magnificent achievement.

Then came the disaster. The German battle cruisers *Scharnhorst* and *Gneisenau* were on the prowl off Norway, and they found *Glorious,* and from long range they sank her with shell-fire. All the pilots except "Bing" Cross and one other were lost, as well as all the aircraft. When that news reached me at the Air Ministry I was badly shaken. The loss of all those precious aircraft was serious enough; but the deaths of so many gallant young pilots under such awful circumstances was a terrible blow.

There can never be any doubt about the grave faults in our planning for the whole operation in Norway. From the outset we knew that the air side was going to be very chancy, but for all our pleading, no one would take the air situation seriously enough. There was too much vague optimism about the whole venture, too much self-assurance about getting our troops and stores and supplies ashore and being able to keep them there. Did not our own Prime Minister announce only a few days before the Germans

invaded Norway that Hitler had missed the bus? We were the ones
who missed the bus, and in allowing it to happen we lost so much.

The immediate repercussions from our dismal failure in Norway
shook Parliament into doing something about the political leadership of the country. We had become bogged down in the hands of
an ineffectual government that was a hangover from the days of
peace, and there was a crying need for a change. We got it, and on
May 10, 1940, Winston Churchill became Prime Minister. And
with that change, Sir Archibald Sinclair—who had been Churchill's second-in-command of a battalion on the Western Front in
the earlier war—became Secretary of State for Air. Under Churchill's guidance, we all came to know a leadership that was both
dynamic and inspiring, even if it still causes some of us to consider
a little ruefully the bruises that we suffered from it.

While we were still in the process of being kicked out of Norway
there came the start of the German invasion of Holland, Belgium
and France. In the early hours of the morning on which that
onslaught was launched, I was called on the telephone in my flat in
London by a member of my staff on duty at the Air Ministry. The
German armies were on the move, I was told, and I hurried down
to my office. An hour or so after I got there—it must have been
about half past six—the Dutch Ambassador arrived asking to see
the Chief of the Air Staff. Since I was the senior officer on duty at
the moment, he was brought to my office, and the talk that we had
then was acutely difficult for both of us. The rapid turn of events
had left the Ambassador—who had apparently been up all night—
quite distraught, and he begged me to order that squadrons of our
fighters should be sent at once to Holland to try and stop the
German invasion.

There was nothing that I could do about it, and I had to point
out to the Ambassador as fairly as I could how utterly impossible
it was to grant his request. We had no prepared bases in Holland
from which our fighters could operate with assured supplies of
ammunition, petrol, oil and all the other items that would be
needed. I could not very well remind him that only a short time
before we had asked his Government if we could discuss with them
proposals for setting up a skeleton organization for the operations
of our fighters in Holland, and that they had refused even to talk
about it. All that I could tell him was to assure him that we would
try and cover the west coast of Holland from our own fighter bases
in England. To my great dismay, the poor man, who was by then

in an acute state of distress, dropped his head forward on his arms on my desk and burst into tears.

Such was the tension under which we were having to work at that time that the way in which this happened—I fully understood the Ambassador's distress, and I felt for him the deepest sympathy —was not as uncommon an occurrence as one might imagine. In the privacy of our offices at the Air Ministry, some of our most senior commanders were known, as a result of overstrain and worry and near-exhaustion, to come very close to the breaking point. They would not have been human had they behaved otherwise, and it reflects only credit upon them that they should have taken so much to heart the awful reverses that we suffered during the first part of 1940.

During that time of intense crisis no man was more conscientious in the performance of his duties than Cyril Newall, the Chief of the Air Staff. He had been filling that most arduous of posts since September, 1937, and he had had to weather some ferocious storms. He and Stuffy Dowding had fought together many a battle in the interests of the R.A.F. and, in particular, fighter defense. As Deputy Chief of the Air Staff, I was the servant of the C.A.S., and the channel for communications between him and the various Commanders-in-Chief. During most of 1940 I worked closely with Cyril Newall and Stuffy Dowding, both together and apart. For a younger officer of lower rank—I was then an air vice-marshal—it was in itself an experience of intense interest and value; and I knew at firsthand exactly how hard they drove themselves in their work.

At one time Cyril Newall ruled that because of the threat from bombing, all senior Air Staff officers at the Air Ministry would have to sleep on the premises. There had been built in the basement of the building in King Charles Street a series of horrible little concrete dungeons that were fitted up as sleeping quarters. Newall was probably the hardest worker of all of us, and he was in his office every night until about two o'clock. He would then have only four or five hours of sleep in one of the dungeons before starting work again in his office in the morning, and he went on with that exacting routine for weeks on end, maintaining over himself the most rigid and exhausting control.

Such were these demands on our time and nervous energy that I was in my own office every night of every day of the week until about midnight, and sometimes later. But I detested the idea of the dungeons for sleeping, and Richard Peirse, who was Vice Chief of the Air Staff, felt the same way about it. I was quite prepared to take my chances in my own bed in my flat in Lowndes Square, for it meant at least a change of scene for a few hours of each day. Peirse and I went to the C.A.S. together, and we suggested to him that we should be allowed to take it in turns to sleep on the premises every other night. Newall agreed to that, but he went on sleeping in the dungeons himself, and he never seemed to leave the building other than to go to conferences elsewhere in Whitehall.

So far as the fortunes of this country were concerned, those weeks of the early summer of 1940 seemed, as the days rushed by, to be lived through an endless and unrelieved story of one disaster after another; and at the Air Ministry all this caused us to view things with a very real alarm. The Germans quickly occupied Holland and most of Belgium; our own Army was beaten back to the sea at Dunkirk; and Hitler's panzer divisions roamed about northern France almost at will.

During the months of May and June, the R.A.F. lost just short of 1,000 aircraft, of which 477 were fighters. In order to try and keep the morale of my staff at the Air Ministry up to scratch, I arranged that we should all meet at nine o'clock every morning for a briefing by our own intelligence people on all that was happening. I thought that it would be better if we heard the dismal story as a team rather than let each one try and digest the reports separately in the seclusion of his own office, and I hoped that this would stimulate discussion and that there would be engendered a greater mutual confidence. I also knew that it was part of my responsibility to present a brave front in the face of the disasters that were befalling us, and I soon found that the mere fact that I had to do that helped greatly to keep up my own spirits.

As a people the British have always relished eccentrics, and that has often included those whom we look upon as rebels. It was the rebellion which becomes so marked in our people whenever we are subjected to any threat to our freedom that led to the great upward surge in our morale when Winston Churchill became Prime Minister. At this very time of the fall of France, I had the most conclusive demonstration of our strength in a comparison that I was forced to make with the defeatism which was so unhappily eating away at the hearts and the minds of the French. It occurred early in June, when I was called upon to make what was to be my last visit to France until after the war was over.

On instructions from the Chief of the Air Staff, I flew to Paris with the Deputy Chief of the Naval Staff, Admiral Sir Geoffrey Blake, to discuss with Admiral Darlan and General Vuillemin, the

Chief of the French Air Force, what action the Royal Navy and the Royal Air Force should take when Italy came into the war, an event which, it was anticipated, would happen within the next few days.

We knew that a bitter feeling of defeatism was rife in the French Army and Air Force. From the vantage point of his important post in Paris as the particularly well-informed military liaison officer between us and the French, General Sir Edward Spears made the statement: "This lethargy of the French Air Force is extremely disquieting." That report was connected directly with our visit for talks with the French.

When Geoffrey Blake and I landed at the military airdrome at Villacoublay, just outside Paris, we rather expected that, in view of the importance of our mission, there would at least be somebody there to welcome us. To our astonishment the only soul in sight was Douglas Colyer, our air attaché in Paris. We got out of our aircraft, and just as we did so, a little man wearing a tin hat and with a gas mask bouncing on his backside came dashing out of a dugout nearby. He shouted at us to take cover because in a minute or two the Germans would be starting their bombing of the airfield.

With the nature of our welcome so quickly determined, Douglas Colyer and Geoffrey Blake and I rushed off to the nearest air raid shelter. It was a not very reassuring mound of sandbags and corrugated iron, and just as we got to it the first bomb came down, bursting on a hangar about thirty or forty yards away. And then came a whole salvo of bombs which fell all over the airdrome and the hangars. Later I was to learn that that day, June 3, 1940, was the one on which the Germans staged their one and only large-scale raid on the French capital during the whole of the Second World War.

There were some fifty or sixty fighters of the French Air Force standing parked around the airdrome, and we saw a number of them blown up in the raid. Just as we were landing, I had seen three of the French fighters take off, but so far as I could ascertain these were the only fighters that attempted to go into action from Villacoublay that day. There could be no excuse for such a lack of interest in trying to get at the enemy because our Air Staff had obtained reports through our own intelligence, only a day or two before, that the Germans were planning a big raid on Paris, and that information had been passed on to the French.

After the raid was over, Geoffrey Blake and Douglas Colyer and I made our way to the officers' mess, and there we found all the French pilots—with the exception of the three who were airborne—sitting down quietly having their lunch, and so far as we could make out they were not at all interested in what had just happened. I could not help thinking what a striking contrast their attitude offered to that of the French pilots whom I had known in the First World War. It was an impression that unhappily stayed with me, and it was not until some time later, when I had Free French pilots directly under my command, that I found that there were those Frenchmen who could be as keen and as gallant as one could ever wish for.

After the all-clear was sounded at Villacoublay, we drove in to Paris, passing on the way the Citroën factory, which had been bombed and part of which was ablaze. But there were no great signs of any widespread damage. We had lunch, and then we were taken to the French Admiralty, and we started our discussions in Admiral Darlan's office.

Much has been said and written about Admiral Jean Darlan and the role that he played in the Second World War up until the time when his life was brought to an abrupt end through assassination at the end of 1942. His position in the French Navy was the equivalent of that of our First Sea Lord; but he had achieved it more through the politics that he always played rather than through any ability as a sailor. He was salty enough in his manner, and at our meeting he was full of fire and spirit over what he was going to do to the Italians. The French fleet, Darlan declared, would go out and bombard La Spezia and other naval bases on the Italian coast, and he would see to it that the torpedo-bombers of the French Navy went in to attack the Italian fleet. In temper his style was glowing and warlike.

After this encouraging reassurance from the head of the French Navy, we went on to another meeting at which we had discussions with General Vuillemin, the Air Force chief. He told us that he had given orders for the French Air Force to prepare to bomb factories in northern Italy. That was even more reassuring. I told him that the R.A.F. could not do a great deal to help in that because of the distances from our bomber bases in England. But I did tell him that if the French were prepared to provide us with the use of a couple of airdromes in the south of France, somewhere near Marseilles, we would send a force of Wellingtons to be based down there so that they could also bomb the Italian munition and aircraft factories at Turin and Milan. I further promised that we would send a force of Whitleys from English bases which could be refueled in the Channel Islands for the long flight to Italy and back.

With all these arrangements completed for such satisfactory cooperation with the French both at sea and in the air, I talked on the phone with Air Marshal A. S. Barratt—later to become Sir Arthur, but always known to us by his nickname of "Ugly"—at his headquarters in northern France. He was the Commander-in-Chief of the British Air Forces in France, and I arranged with him for a ground party and a wing headquarters from his Advanced Air Striking Force to be sent down to the airdromes which the French had allocated to us for our use near Marseilles. After that I arranged with Peter Portal—who had been appointed Commander-in-Chief of Bomber Command early in April, just before I became Deputy Chief of the Air Staff—for the Wellingtons to be flown to these French airdromes. Encouraged by this offer of cooperation from the French, Barratt and his staff made a great effort, and they quickly had a party organized and on the way south by road with ammunition, bombs, and all the other paraphernalia which would be needed to launch an air attack on Italy from the French airdromes.

Only those of us who were trying to make sense out of the way in which the war was going so that we could, in turn, make sound plans for it knew just what a state of chaos developed during this period. By the time that I got back to my desk at the Air Ministry in London and had been able to report on our talks and the arrangements made with the French, I felt that so far as the air was concerned the planning showed great promise. It had already been decided by our Government that the moment that Italy made a declaration of war—and Mussolini's intention so far as that was concerned was clear enough, with such a declaration being expected at almost any moment—the R.A.F. would commence bombing operations.

Our force in the south of France was under the command of Group Captain Roger Field, who was an experienced pilot from the time of the First World War and a contemporary of mine, and it was given the code name of "Haddock." But when the time came for action, the flavor of this venture, which had been so readily agreed to in theory by our Allies, was found by the French to be anything but appetizing. Italy's declaration of war became effective at midnight on June 10, as a result of which a squadron of our Wellingtons arrived in the south of France on the afternoon of the next day. Their task was to be the bombing of Turin that night, and the target selected was the Fiat Works.

But no sooner were our Wellingtons in the south of France than all hell broke loose, and it was not through any hostile action that we were able to take. To our astonishment, all the various French commanders there took it upon themselves, one after the other, to ring up Roger Field and tell him that on no account whatsoever must his bombers be allowed to attack Italy because that would only invite reprisals against Marseilles, Lyons, Toulon and other cities in the south of France. They stressed that there were no fighters for defense in that part of the country, all the French fighter squadrons having been transferred to the north for the battle that was going on there.

It was not long before General Vuillemin did his about-face and started adding his weight to the protests. A call from him on the phone came through to the Air Ministry in London. He wanted to talk to the C.A.S., but he was put on to me. Making no bones about the French change of mind, Vuillemin asked me to issue an order that the Wellingtons should not bomb Italy that night. I told him that I could not possibly give such an order as the operation had been approved by the Prime Minister, but after further protests from him I said that I would speak to the C.A.S. about it. Winston Churchill was at that moment in France, and when, a little later in the afternoon, he was consulted about the French protests he gave firm instructions that we should continue with the operation.

The final instruction to proceed as planned was passed on to Roger Field, and he briefed his crews, and they got ready to take off for the raid on Italy. During the time that this was going on, Field was being deluged with instructions from the French commanders that under no conditions whatsoever must he continue with the operation. Field was thoroughly experienced in the handling of foreign officialdom through having served during the years between the wars as air attaché at several of our embassies abroad, and he was not likely to be deterred by any undue interference with his orders.

The Whitleys were already on their way from the Channel Islands for their bombing of Italy when our Wellingtons started to taxi out, just before midnight, toward the runway of the airfield in the south of France. Right at the moment that they did this there appeared out of the darkness a horde of French lorries. They were driven to positions right across the airdrome that were obviously prearranged, and which completely blocked the path that our aircraft would have to take if they wanted to get off. It was impossible for our bomber crews to do anything about that. Field wisely decided not to risk a stand-up scrap with the French, and he canceled the operations for that night.

With the situation now such a political one, I could only sit at my desk and wonder at the way in which wars come to be fought. But a day or so later the Prime Minister managed to sort things out, and he persuaded the French Government to allow the Wellingtons to operate in the manner that had been planned and agreed upon. We were then able to go ahead, and the Wellingtons and the Whitleys did some bombing, but it was not very effective. A couple of days after that the French Government capitulated, and with that there came the tragic collapse of France.

The urgent problem that then faced me at the Air Ministry was how to get the "Haddock" force back home. It was a simple enough matter to fly the Wellingtons back across France. They could do that at night without being molested. The difficult task was how to get the ground personnel back. I consulted the Admiralty, and I was told that there were some of our merchant ships still in Marseilles. Arrangements were made for these ships to wait there for a short time, and I issued instructions for our people in the south of France to be told to make their way as best they could and as quickly as possible to Marseilles and on to the ships waiting for them. Unfortunately it meant that they had to leave all their equipment behind them, but they were able to get to the ships; and although there was a threat that the Italians might intercept them on the way to Gibraltar they all eventually arrived safely back in England.

During all this feverish activity I had to spend a great deal of time in long distance discussions on the phone, and connections, which were not good at the best of times, became hourly more difficult. Those with our various headquarters in France, which were over the lines of the civilian telephone network and which, with the rapid change in events, I was using several times a day, were very bad and most unreliable, and it was always extraordinarily difficult to hear what was being said from the other side of the Channel and, in turn, to get across my own messages. There were all too many occasions when the conversations that I had with Ugly Barratt finished up with making little or no sense at all.

Just before the fall of France, when we scarcely knew what was happening to our people out there, one amusing exception did occur in the almost constantly wretched state of the telephone communications, and it had to happen just when, for all the urgency of the situation, there was nothing much to talk about. It was around midnight, some time early in June, and I was at my desk in the Air Ministry clearing up some paper work. The phone rang, and over the line, as clear as one could wish, came the voice of Air Vice-Marshal P. H. L. Playfair, who was in command, under Ugly Barratt, of the Advanced Air Striking Force. So clear, in fact, was Pip Playfair's voice that I immediately asked: "Where are you? How did you get back from France?"

"I'm still in France," he answered. "I'm sitting here in a chateau while the staff load everything into lorries for our getaway."

France was being over-run, and everything was in a state of turmoil, and yet here, by some strange fluke, Pip Playfair and I were able to talk with each other just as if we were in the same room. I had only just sent Bill Dry, my personal staff officer, off by air to France with an urgent letter for Ugly Barratt telling him that he should plan for a rapid withdrawal of all his forces, and later I was to learn that there was a letter from him on the way to me asking for those very instructions. If I had tried at that time to get him on the phone it would have taken a miracle even to establish contact.

Pip Playfair explained over the phone that the chateau from which he was speaking was on the bank of a river. If I remember right, he said it was the Loire. He explained that the Germans were on the other side of the river, and I could even hear various bangs from what I assumed were guns and bursts of machine gun fire.

"Is there anything I can do for you?" I asked, feeling pretty helpless.

"No," he said. "I've only rung up because I felt rather lonely and I thought I'd like to talk to somebody at the Air Ministry. I'll be off in my car in a few minutes and will try and get to the coast."

We talked pleasantly for a few minutes, and I wished him luck, and then he went back to his war while I sat in the quiet of the night in the Air Ministry in London and tried to find some answers to the demands that were being made by the French political and military leaders. They were bound to make a strong impression on us, and particularly, because of the nature of the man, on our own Prime Minister. We gave their appeals the most earnest consideration; and Winston Churchill hoped up until the very last moment that somehow or other, and in some shape or other, we would be able to keep the French in the war, even if they had to continue the fight from North Africa.

If there was one thing about these demands that we at the Air

Ministry knew would be absolutely fatal it was to agree to go on pouring fighter squadrons into France. It would mean that Fighter Command, from which the fighters would have to come, would be drained away to no purpose at all. But from the time when the Germans started their advance to the west these demands from the French were incessant. Day after day General Vuillemin was on the phone asking for the C.A.S., and if he or the Vice C.A.S. were busy at Cabinet meetings or conferences he would speak to me, which he did quite often, about what he wanted from us.

There was naturally very strong opposition from the Air Staff to these demands from the French, and I gave the C.A.S. every support that I could to resist the pressure that was brought to bear. No one opposed the sapping of the resources of Fighter Command more strongly than its Commander-in-Chief, and Stuffy Dowding fought like a tiger against anything that would reduce his already limited strength. In that he was perfectly right, and in fighting so hard for his command, even before the time of the testing of its strength, he rendered to the cause of the free world the highest service.

On the insistence of the Prime Minister we had to send some reinforcements; but we found that the odds were such that it was all too often the case that a Hurricane squadron sent to France at that time would be reduced within the space of only a few days to two or three aircraft and half a dozen pilots. Wastage at that rate would soon have decimated Fighter Command. We would then have been left wide open to defeat in the air battle against Britain which we felt so sure was about to be launched by the Germans.

There have been comments at various times about the tension that, it is alleged, existed in the relationship between Stuffy Dowding and the Air Ministry over matters other than the operational control of his command. Of this, since it was none of my business, I knew nothing; but I was very closely in touch with Dowding in the matter of operations during this entire period, including the whole of the great air battle over Britain, and I was fully aware of the strain that he was under and the devotion that his single-mindedness about the efficacy of his command inspired in him. Whatever other stresses there may have been, the relationship between us personally could not have been better. We had known each other for a very long time, and we understood each other, and I had for Dowding both as a commander and as a man the highest admiration and respect.

Less than two weeks after the war broke out, Stuffy Dowding

had addressed a long and very detailed official letter to the Air Ministry in which he had reminded us that the Air Council's estimate of the number of fighter squadrons that would be needed for the defense of this country was fifty-two. It must be stressed that this figure was based upon the assumption that the Germans would be operating from their own bases in their own country, and that we would have to face raids from unescorted bombers. It did not allow for the possibility of the enemy bombers coming from nearer bases only just across the Channel, and accompanied by swarms of escorting fighters.

Of his actual strength on the outbreak of war, Stuffy Dowding had called attention to it as "the equivalent of thirty-four squadrons"; and of that strength he stated: "This, although much below the Air Council's estimate of requirements for home defence, was, in my opinion, sufficient to cause such heavy casualties to an attacker that in a comparatively short space of time his attacks would be brought to a standstill." But so soon after the outbreak of war, demands made for fighter squadrons for service in France reduced even that strength to such an extent that, Dowding pointed out, in a few months' time it would be down to only twenty-seven squadrons. Of that situation, he made the comment: "This is a grim prospect."

The Chief of the Air Staff always gave Stuffy Dowding his strongest support, knowing full well that it would have been utter folly to have agreed to all of the French demands. But even then, we received instructions from the War Cabinet in the second week in May, 1940, to send more fighters to France. This was at a moment when French resistance was rapidly approaching a state of collapse. Dowding then made a stand that was of the utmost importance.

A Cabinet meeting was called—they were meeting then several times a day—on May 15 to consider this further request from the French Prime Minister that ten more of our fighter squadrons should be sent to France. Stuffy Dowding's reaction to that was bound to be a most vigorous objection. Our squadrons in France had taken a terrible beating in the first few days of the fighting, and he knew, as we on the Air Staff knew, that sending more squadrons out there would be tantamount to throwing them away. There has always been a great deal of conjecture about the personal reactions of those who were present at that Cabinet meeting. On our side, it was attended by the Secretary of State for Air and by Cyril Newall, and, at his own request, by Dowding.

At the time I had no firsthand knowledge of what actually went on at that meeting, but we realized by late that night that Stuffy Dowding must have put up a stern battle to win them over to his views. It is recorded that at the critical point of the meeting, which was "originally hostile to his opinions," as Denis Richards put it, Dowding—who had the figures of the fighting of the past few days on a piece of paper in front of him—said to the Prime Minister: "If the present rate of wastage continues for another fortnight, we shall not have a single Hurricane left in France or in this country."

Among those present at the meeting there was a man with whom I had been at school at Tonbridge before the First World War. Now Air Chief Marshal Sir William Elliott, he was in attendance that day in his capacity as a wing commander on the staff of the secretariat of the Cabinet. Many years later, Elliott told me that the atmosphere was tense, and that it was one of the most highly charged emotionally that he had ever known. He described Stuffy Dowding as being white in the face with strain; but, he added, when Dowding came to make that statement of his it was put so ably and sincerely, and with such feeling, that there was no room left for any further discussion. It was decided that no more squadrons should be sent to France.

22 / Account Rendered

OUR SALVATION in the battle that was to come has earned for Stuffy Dowding the deepest gratitude of the people of this country, if not of the whole world. What is not generally appreciated is the way in which, in his own wisdom, Dowding fought so hard to maintain the strength of his command long before that battle began. We on the Air Staff saw all too clearly how vitally necessary it was to secure the base; but it was upon Dowding's shoulders that there fell the heavy load of responsibility to make absolutely sure of that before he was ever called upon to fight from it.

On May 16, the day after the Cabinet meeting at which Dowding had made such a decisive stand, he wrote an official letter to the Air Ministry that is now in the category of an historical document. It was a long letter, and its contents are of vital importance to a full understanding of what had happened at that Cabinet meeting and immediately afterward. For these reasons, all that he said must be considered in full when he wrote:

I have the honour to refer to the very serious calls which have recently been made upon the Home Defence Fighter Units in an attempt to stem the German invasion on the Continent.

I hope and believe that our Armies may yet be victorious in France and Belgium, but we have to face the possibility that they may be defeated.

In this case I presume that there is no one who will deny that England should fight on, even though the remainder of the Continent of Europe is dominated by the Germans.

For this purpose it is necessary to retain some minimum fighter strength in this country and I must request that the Air Council will inform me what they consider this minimum strength to be, in order that I may make my dispositions accordingly.

I would remind the Air Council that the last estimate which they made as to the force necessary to defend this country was 52 Squadrons, and my strength has now been reduced to the equivalent of 36 Squadrons.

Once a decision has been reached as to the limit on which the Air Council and the Cabinet are prepared to stake the existence of the country, it should be made clear to the Allied Commanders on the Continent that not a single aeroplane from Fighter Command beyond the limit will be sent across the Channel, no matter how desperate the situation may become.

It will, of course, be remembered that the estimate of 52 Squadrons was based on the assumption that the attack would come from the eastwards except in so far as the defences might be outflanked in flight. We have now to face the possibility that attacks may come from Spain or even from the north coast of France. The result is that our line is very much extended at the same time as our resources are reduced.

I must point out that within the last few days the equivalent of 10 Squadrons have been sent to France, that the Hurricane Squadrons remaining in this country are seriously depleted, and that the more Squadrons which are sent to France the higher will be the wastage and the more insistent the demands for reinforcements.

I must therefore request that as a matter of paramount urgency the Air Ministry will consider and decide what level of strength is to be left to the Fighter Command for the defences of this country, and will assure me that when this level has been reached, not one fighter will be sent across the Channel however urgent and insistent the appeals for help may be.

I believe that, if an adequate fighter force is kept in this country, if the fleet remains in being, and if Home Forces are suitably organized to resist invasion, we should be able to carry on the war single handed for some time, if not indefinitely. But, if the Home Defence Force is drained away in desperate attempts to remedy the situation in France, defeat in France will involve the final, complete and irremediable defeat of this country.

During the time of the collapse of France, my contacts with our Commanders-in-Chief were both close and constant. In the case of Stuffy Dowding, it was part of my work to know what he was thinking, and to be thoroughly familiar with the plans he was making for Fighter Command. There were many occasions when, on his visits to the Air Ministry, he came to my office, and we would talk about the affairs of his command, and at times we would discuss the drafts of letters and reports that he was preparing before he actually sent them to us.

It was no very great surprise to me that Dowding should write as he did; but the strength and the clarity of the thought behind it which that letter of his contained filled us all with admiration for its writer. It was the one great word of sanity in the midst of a most perplexing situation, and it stood out like a beacon light in what happened immediately before and immediately after Dowding came to write it.

At the Air Ministry there flowed across my desk a mass of reports and documents which gave me a comprehensive view of all that was happening in the war. By the middle of May it was a sorry picture, and so far as the air was concerned I was greatly worried. In Norway we were taking a devil's own thrashing, and all we could think about in operations there was how best to get out of the country. On May 14 the Germans launched an air raid on Rotterdam which was made with no consideration whatsoever being given to the Dutch declaration that it was an open city. In France on that same day we had the heavy casualties in our air attacks against the advance being made by the Germans across the Meuse.

"Any hopes that the Germans might apply a code of morals in the West different from that which Poland had experienced in the East were quickly shattered by the mass bombing of Rotterdam," the official historians Charles Webster and Noble Frankland have stated. It was a brutal attack, and if we had needed bringing to our senses with a hard realization of what we were going to have to face, that first assault in the west did it. At the time it was reported that between thirty and fifty thousand civilians had been killed, and that naturally generated a great deal of anger. Later we learned that that figure was an exaggeration. But it was no exaggeration to say that the city was subjected to a most barbarous assault.

At a Cabinet meeting the next day it was decided that we should hold back no longer from bombing Germany, and Bomber Command was let off the leash. On the night of May 15, 1940, there began what is now known as our strategic air offensive against Germany, an operation that was to continue without interruption and with a mounting fury for the next five years. It was one of the most formidable operations of the war, and from that slight beginning in the middle of May, 1940, it grew into something that many of us eventually came to view with thoughts that had in them an unanswerable question. It was possibly that which was at the back of his mind when Winston Churchill made a remark that was so typical of his humor when he heard of the results of the trials at Nuremberg after the war. "If you get into a war, it is supremely important to win it," he said to Lord Ismay. "You and I would be in a pretty pickle if we had lost."

It was at the Cabinet meeting only a few hours before that raid was made on Germany that the decision had been reached not to send to France the ten squadrons that had been asked for by the French. But on the very next day, for all the impression that Stuffy Dowding had made upon them, I had to pass on to him the unpalatable instructions that we had received from the Cabinet to send immediately to France eight half-squadrons. The actual Cabinet instruction to us had been for four squadrons; but I managed to get an interpretation of that approved in the form of the eight flights. It was my thought that by doing it in this way we would at least preserve in this country the nucleus of the eight squadrons, and the draining away of the strength of Fighter Command would not be so severe.

On that day, May 16, and it is a day to remember, Winston Churchill saw the French Prime Minister in Paris, and what he learned then about all the disasters that were overwhelming the French shocked him very deeply. He later recorded clearly enough the astonishment that he experienced when he found how badly their high command had handled the battle. "I was dumb-founded," he has said. "What were we to think of the great French Army and its highest chiefs?" The "mortal gravity of the hour," as he described it, and his great affection for the French and his anxiety to keep them in the war, then compelled Churchill to take a step that led to a serious state of confusion which, particularly for us, was corrected in London by one of the most vitally important decisions taken in the whole course of the Second World War.

A message was sent from Paris by Winston Churchill to the Cabinet in London asking that six more fighter squadrons should be sent immediately to France. With the eight half-squadrons already agreed to, these would have given the French the ten squadrons that they had asked for, and Dowding's great struggle against that at the Cabinet meeting of the day before would have been in vain. It would appear that the Cabinet, which met late at night, was at first inclined to agree to Churchill's request.

But Cyril Newall took a firm stand against any such obvious frittering away of our forces, and in doing that he saved the day. He pointed out that there were available in France neither enough airfields nor the facilities to accommodate these extra squadrons; and that, in addition to the consideration of the drain that it would impose upon our resources, led the Cabinet to decide against sending these precious squadrons to France. Instead it was agreed to keep them based in England, and to operate from those bases out over France.

It was not until a long time afterward that it was realized that in the request made by Winston Churchill from Paris he was laboring under a most serious and well-nigh disastrous misunderstanding of our fighter strength. Even now it is not generally understood that through that misunderstanding we came perilously close to losing the Battle of Britain before it was even fought. But it has since gone beyond that, and has even led to something being accepted as a truth which is, in fact, quite the opposite, and it rests in Churchill's grave misunderstanding of something that he claimed Stuffy Dowding had said to him about the minimum number of fighters that would be needed for the defense of this country.

The massive six volumes of Winston Churchill's *The Second World War* are rightly accorded a position of the greatest importance in the annals of that war. It is nevertheless a feature of these books that at times he recounts in great detail the record of events as they happened up to a certain point, and then, for some odd reason, he does not complete it. In this curiously inconclusive way, Churchill records as a fact in the second volume, so admirably entitled *Their Finest Hour,* the agreement of the Cabinet to his request telegraphed from Paris for six more fighter squadrons to be sent to France. He does not say anything about the vitally important way in which this was dealt with by the Cabinet. He has nothing to say about the decision that the squadrons should not go to France but should operate instead from forward airfields in Kent, from which they could work over France, merely landing at French airfields to re-arm and refuel.

The reason for Winston Churchill's apparent belief that we could spare these squadrons and send them to France, which was the source of this misunderstanding of his, is revealed in his statement: "Air Chief Marshal Dowding, at the head of our metropolitan Fighter Command, had declared to me that with twenty-five squadrons of fighters he could defend the Island against the whole might of the German Air Force, but that with less he would be over-powered."

Any acceptance of this patently incorrect figure of twenty-five squadrons as our minimum requirement is quite inexplicable; and when one considers that it was accepted by, of all people, Winston Churchill, who was in a position to be so well informed, it leads to bewilderment. How did it ever come about that Churchill could

ever accept this, try to make his plans believing it, and even go so
far as to credit it to Stuffy Dowding?

These were the questions which exercised our minds when
Robert Wright and I came to examine together so many years later
the details of my involvement in the story of those days just before
the start of the Battle of Britain. Bob Wright was on the staff at
the headquarters of Fighter Command at that time, and he knew
Dowding and he had for him, as I had, the greatest respect and
admiration. So strongly did we come to feel about what we were
discovering that we agreed that he should ask Dowding if he would
be so good as to let us have his views. In their talk together Wright
found that Dowding listened with such care and consideration to
the views that we held that I was then prompted to write to
Dowding and tell him that we did not want to distress him in any
way by stirring up unhappy memories. We wanted to get the facts
right, I told him, and at the same time to do what we could to
correct what we considered was a grave injustice.

For all the many years of having worked so closely with
Dowding, and knowing him as well as I did, I found his reaction to
what we were asking of him warmer and more understanding than
even I had expected. I was deeply touched when, in the forthright
way that has always been so typical of him, Dowding not only gave
us a correct answer to our questions: he also gave us a very
complete one, with permission to quote it in full. In this important
comment he stated:

How Mr. Churchill, as he was then, ever came to put such an absurd
statement into my mouth I simply do not know. I had just been waging
a desperate battle in the Cabinet to be allowed to retain the equivalent
of 36 squadrons against the 52 squadrons which was the Air Staff estimate of my requirements. Is it reasonable to suppose that I then told
Mr. Churchill personally that 25 would suffice? The suggestion is ridiculous. Furthermore, there was no opportunity for me to have given
any personal estimate of my requirements to Mr. Churchill before the
Cabinet meeting and his departure for France. I had no contact with
him at all. It is not for me to speculate on the origin of this mistake; I
can only repeat categorically that I did not make, and in fact could not
have made, such an absurd underestimate of the requirements of my
Command.

It can now be seen that it was this misunderstanding on the part
of Winston Churchill—which, revealingly enough, was not corrected in his book when it was first published in the summer of
1949 and was not corrected in any of the later editions—that must

have led him to believe that we could help the French far more than was possible. But what is so astonishing is that this totally incorrect figure put forward by Churchill has now come to be so generally accepted as an exact statement of the minimum requirement put forward by the Royal Air Force for the defense of Britain. No less an authority than *The New Cambridge Modern History* offers it in Volume XII—*The Era of Violence*—which was published in the summer of 1960. Air Chief Marshal Sir Arthur Longmore contributed to that the section on "Air Forces," and in that he makes the unequivocal statement: "Twenty-five squadrons of Hurricanes and Spitfires was the figure decided upon as the minimum necessary for the purpose."

This inexplicable distortion of fact provides an impressive example of the way in which a mistake made by authority can so easily become treated, because of the importance of the authority, as an historical truth. In his book, *The Third Service,* published as long ago as 1955, Air Chief Marshal Sir Philip Joubert credited no less an authority than Air Marshal Sir Richard Peck, who was one of the stalwarts of the Air Staff, with having told him "that Hugh Dowding had thought twenty-five fighter squadrons more than sufficient to ensure security against air attack from Germany." Joubert then commented: "If this statement was truthful, and there is no reason to suppose that it was not, then Air Chief Marshal Dowding was at fault."

Statements such as these are extremely difficult to understand because they contain in them the most unfair and unjust criticism of Stuffy Dowding. At the same time they reveal a perplexing lack of understanding of what was required so urgently at that time: a full appreciation by all those concerned of what was needed to secure the defense of Britain.

During our expulsion from France at the time of what we refer to now as Dunkirk, my mind turned so often to the exercises on paper that Alan Brooke and Bertie Ramsay and I had worked out together at the Imperial Defence College in the early thirties. We had thought then, and I continued to think, that in the circumstances the most effective way in which the Germans could achieve an overall victory was to have a go immediately at Britain. I am not suggesting that I thought that a German invasion of Britain would have been successful, but I do think that, from the German viewpoint, Hitler should have tried an immediate assault. Fighter Command would still have been a tough nut to crack, and the

German invasion forces would have been vulnerable to attack from both the air and the sea as they crossed the Channel in the improvised landing craft which would have been scarcely more than barges. But once they were ashore in England there was—immediately after Dunkirk—very little that we had on the ground with which to stop them.

A great deal of criticism was hurled at the Royal Air Force by the Army during and after the evacuation from Dunkirk, and there developed quite a lot of ill-feeling. Somewhat understandably, the Army wanted to know why they had been subjected to so many attacks on the beaches from the German Air Force, and they were bitter about what they considered was the absence of the R.A.F. It was naturally difficult for them to appreciate that our fighters were hard at work holding back, inland and out of sight, a much larger and heavier onslaught that the Luftwaffe were trying to launch at our poor bedeviled troops on the beaches.

Winston Churchill was fully aware of all this, and he became very disturbed at the time over the criticism that was being expressed of the R.A.F. Later he was to say of the part that the Air Force played in the evacuation: "They bit into the German fighter and bomber squadrons, taking a heavy toll, scattering them and driving them away. Day after day this went on, till the glorious victory of the Royal Air Force was gained." In the Commons on June 4, the day on which the evacuation at Dunkirk was completed, he stated: "We must be very careful not to assign to this deliverance the attributes of a victory. Wars are not won by evacuations. But there was a victory inside this deliverance, which should be noted. It was gained by the Air Force."

It was also in the course of that statement in the House that Winston Churchill posed, on the eve of what was to become, without any of us knowing it, the Battle of Britain, the superb question: "May it not also be that the cause of civilisation itself will be defended by the skill and devotion of a few thousand airmen?"

For all our agreement about what the Germans would do next, to our surprise Hitler acted in an entirely different fashion. Instead of having a go at us immediately after the fall of France, he turned to a more complete subjugation of that unhappy country, with plans for the invasion of England to come later. In that he made one of his great mistakes. For one thing we were granted an invaluable breathing spell of a few short weeks in which we were able to reorganize our forces on the ground; but of more importance than that it enabled us to rally our strength in the air, and to give to Fighter Command the greatest possible nourishment.

In all my own thinking about the part that would be played by the air, I took some little pride in the belief that in the practice of my profession I was a realist. On several occasions I became deeply shocked when I found that there existed, in the thoughts of the less military-minded civilians, ideas which, so far as I was concerned, were downright foolish. On one such occasion I got into quite hot water over my objection to what I considered was a lack of realism in the civilian mind.

In the course of discussion over dinner one night at the home in Westminster of Oliver and Maureen Stanley, I listened with some surprise to the views expressed by one of the other guests who happened to be a well-known and influential Member of Parliament. The conversation had turned somewhat naturally to what was going to happen now that France had fallen. In reply to what was being said, I expressed the view that it was certain that the Germans would launch an air attack on Britain, and that our cities, particularly London, would be the objectives. To my utter surprise, that precipitated a heated dispute. Somebody or other said that the Germans would never sink so low, and somebody else commented that even if they did, the amount of damage that they would be able to do would never be severe enough to bring us to our knees.

This ridiculous lack of any apparent ability to face the facts, particularly after all that we had only just had so blatantly proved to us in the course of the past few weeks, made me very angry. I said that I thought that they were all underestimating the effect of bombardment from the air on a civilian population, and that in my opinion there was the strongest likelihood of tremendous damage being done, and even, in that, a possibility that we might be forced to sue for peace. By then tempers were becoming frayed, and perhaps I was rather more emphatic than I should have been in my objections to what I considered was some very woolly thinking.

As a result of this brusque exchange over a dinner table, I was reported by the Member of Parliament to the Prime Minister. I was accused of defeatist talk and of being an alarmist, which, it was considered, was particularly unfortunate in anybody occupying as important a post as that of the Deputy Chief of the Air Staff. Before I knew what was happening, and without my even having heard that the Prime Minister was asking for a report, Archie Sinclair was brought into the matter. I have him to thank for the staunch way in which he defended my character and my courage.

His loyalty and understanding convinced the Prime Minister that it was all a storm in the coffee cups, and with that the matter blew over.

Far too little has been recorded about the intense loyalty toward the R.A.F. that was felt by Archie Sinclair, and his enthusiasm for the Service toward which he always displayed the keenest sense of responsibility. When Winston Churchill appointed him Secretary of State for Air in the Cabinet that he formed in May, 1940, it was for more than purely political reasons. Churchill knew Sinclair well, and he liked and trusted him. But even then, and for all his loyalty, I am not sure that Sinclair was always able to carry sufficient weight in the rougher sessions of Cabinet meetings. At some meetings at which I happened to be present, I saw Churchill brush him rather harshly to one side. Nor do I think that Sinclair was quite as shrewd a politician as Harold Balfour, who, as Under-Secretary of State for Air, joined him in watching over the affairs of the R.A.F. throughout the war.

It was unquestionably Harold Balfour's firsthand experience through having been a pilot in the Royal Air Force which enabled him to serve us so well. Balfour was always a very astute politician, and because of that he was well aware of making the right impression. During his long time as a Member of Parliament he gained a great deal of valuable experience, and after he became Under-Secretary of State he handled his side of the battles with skill and imagination. Through our long friendship and knowledge of each other, I never hesitated about discussing our problems with him, and he never failed to give me his full support.

Some weeks after Archie Sinclair had stood up so well for me in the silly little matter of a dinner-table squabble, I was present at a meeting in the Cabinet Room at No. 10 Downing Street when I saw him under attack from no less a forceful character than Lord Beaverbrook, the Minister for Aircraft Production. We had received at the Air Ministry an urgent signal from Air Chief Marshal Sir Arthur Longmore, who was then the Commander-in-Chief, Middle East, asking for some modern fighters. He had for his use out there only the already outdated Gladiators, and he asked for some Hurricanes to be sent immediately to the Middle East. At a meeting to which we were summoned by the Prime Minister I was called upon to support my own Minister, the Secretary of State for Air. Winston Churchill was in the chair, but he occupied it rather in the manner of a highly interested if not amused spectator while

Archie Sinclair and Beaverbrook, the two Ministers directly concerned, battled it out.

With the hard facts of the Battle of Britain, which was then in progress, staring us in the face, we at the Air Ministry had not decided lightly about agreeing to Longmore's request for aircraft which we could ill afford to send out of the country. But we had agreed that he should have some of our precious supply of Hurricanes. That brought the Minister of Aircraft Production roaring into the attack. Churchill sat back listening, and obviously enjoying, the arguments.

I could not help feeling sorry for Archie Sinclair. Sticking loyally to his guns in defending our decision to send these Hurricanes out to the Middle East, he was also defending our position in the face of Lord Beaverbrook at his most aggressive. Beaverbrook had a good enough point, which was that every aircraft available was needed for the fighting of the battle that was taking place over Britain. But we at the Air Ministry had to consider the broader aspects of the use that was to be made of the Royal Air Force in all the different theaters in which we had to operate.

In an effort to support my Minister I put in my two-penny worth of technical opinion, but that only seemed to provoke Beaverbrook into an even more violent attack. With the somewhat restrained Service way of exchanging views to which I was accustomed, I found it hard not be believe that there was something personal in the way in which Beaverbrook was expressing himself. But mine was not a political mind; and for all the thrashing that he was taking, Sinclair stood his ground, and much to Beaverbrook's disgust won support for the Air Ministry decision.

Almost immediately after winning that tussle, we were told by Middle East Headquarters that perhaps the Hurricanes would not be needed after all. It appeared that the pilots out there had found that the Gladiator was more maneuverable, and because of that it was more to their liking! That was one occasion when I felt that young fighter bloods should be seen and not heard.

In all that happened during that fateful year of 1940 there were three of the most senior of the Air Force officers who, under the direction of the Chief of the Air Staff, rendered to England in the time of its greatest peril such service that it was truly of an outstanding nature. Stuffy Dowding was brought right to the fore as the commander of Fighter Command during the Battle of Britain, and in all that he did he received every support from Cyril Newall. But Bomber Command was also called upon to play its own important part in the battles that raged throughout the spring and summer and on into the early autumn of that year, and it must never be overlooked that Peter Portal was Commander-in-Chief of Bomber Command from April 3 until October 5 of that year of 1940. It is proper that we should remember that during the critical period of the fall of France and the Battle of Britain our two most important air commanders were Dowding and Portal.

Behind the scenes, in charge of development and production, stood Wilfrid Freeman, who was so shrewd and so able in the support that he gave to the operational commanders and to the C.A.S. and the Air Force as a whole. Shortly after the outbreak of war, Freeman's department was moved from London to Harrogate, and once a week I used to go up there with Sandy Saundby. Freeman, Saundby and I would go over the position so far as production was concerned, and decisions would be made about what plans should be prepared for further production of aircraft and equipment and for the continuing expansion of the Air Force.

These meetings and discussions were always splendidly stimulating, and the inspiration unquestionably came from Wilfrid Freeman. He was always looking ahead and planning with a particularly astute and long-term understanding of our needs. Even before then Freeman had been laying the plans, and bringing them into operation, for the splendid production of aircraft that was to take place by the time he got the Ministry of Aircraft Production, under Lord Beaverbrook, into high gear. Many years later, Lord Beaverbrook himself spoke generously about that, saying that Freeman was among those who "had never received the credit they deserve."

"In my opinion, as regards industry Wilfrid made his major contribution in the 1937/8/9 expansion," Lord Hives, the head of Rolls-Royce, stated in a letter to Jack Slessor after the war. "It was the expansion which was carried out under his direction at that time which enabled the Battle of Britain to be won. Without that foresight and imagination, no efforts in 1940 would have yielded any results. Our big Rolls-Royce expansions . . . were only achieved by the inspiration and encouragement and criticism we received from Wilfrid." Hives stated that he also thought that "Wilfrid Freeman's contribution . . . has never been sufficiently recognised."

That contribution of Wilfrid Freeman's was not limited merely to the production of fighters. He had a multitude of problems with which to cope in seeing to it that the R.A.F. had the right aircraft and equipment for all the various duties that it was called upon to perform. Freeman was just as concerned with the production of bombers as he was with fighters; but the full results of all his work with the bombers did not become apparent until after a great deal of desperate trial and error, but even then there was an astonishingly rapid expansion and development of the striking power of the R.A.F. from the air. Just as the fighters had come into their own in the First World War, so did the bombers come into their own in the second war.

But during the early years of the Second World War, our bombers achieved very little that was really effective, and during my time as Deputy Chief of the Air Staff, and particularly while I was working so closely with Peter Portal during his time as commander-in-chief of Bomber Command, I was very perplexed over their failure. The Battles out in France proved to be much too vulnerable and weak to be able to carry out any effective bombing in daylight. To a lesser degree that applied also to the Blenheims. When our heavier bombers were let off the leash and sent over the Ruhr at night, they achieved surprisingly little. The precise art of finding and pinpointing targets at night had not then even begun to develop in the way that was to become so effective in the latter part of the war. Also, in the beginning, the weight of the bombs was too light and the types of bombs themselves that we dropped did not have very much effect.

Of all the senior officers on the Air Staff at the Air Ministry during that summer of 1940, I was possibly the only one whose flying on operations on the Western Front in the First World War had been exclusively in fighters. That long and invaluable experience as a fighter pilot and a commander of fighter squadrons enabled me to understand to the full the problems faced by the man who was in overall command of the fighters in 1940 as well as the young pilots themselves. It was inevitable that, as I sat at my desk in the Air Ministry, my thoughts should turn so often to what those youngsters were facing in the skies overhead.

One of the more sobering aspects of attaining senior rank is the way in which it brings with it a sharper understanding of the attitude adopted by the young pilots in the squadrons. They so often tended to look upon officers of air rank as a race apart. To them we were old and desk-bound, and it was hard for them to understand that in our time we had known all that they were experiencing, including their ribaldry about the effects of age. Just as we of an earlier generation had thought of those over the age of the middle twenties as old fogies, so they looked upon such aging

gentlemen as "clapped out," usually adding to that one of those
select and incisive words which are always so abundant in Service
vocabularies. We knew what there was in their hearts and in their
minds, and we thought all the more of them for it.

At the time nobody could see further than the blow-by-blow
course of the battle, and it was not until afterward that we came to
know that the greatest air battle that had ever taken place, or is
ever likely to take place, had been fought and won in the skies over
Britain. And it was won by men and not by machines, by young
men of many different types who shared one great characteristic:
an ability to understand the tradition that had been handed down
to them.

It was not the shortage of aircraft that was the great problem in
the Battle of Britain. That did exist, but it has been rather overstressed. The great problem that Stuffy Dowding had to face as the
battle proceeded was a shortage of pilots. There were aircraft
available, limited though the supply was, but casualties among the
pilots was the cause of grave concern even after we had pulled out
a certain number from bomber and army cooperation units and
hurriedly converted them to fighters.

We also knew that the squadrons were below the established
strength in the number of pilots which they were supposed to have,
and that those who were surviving in the grim fight that was taking
place were becoming physically and mentally exhausted. The
forces that we had available were limited to standing guard against
the onslaught of the German Air Force, and what we should have
done without the help of the radar warning system in that I do not
know. The German Air Force would probably have smothered us.
But with it our fighters were able to stay on the ground and con-
serve their strength when there was nothing hostile approaching
the country instead of having to maintain constant and exhausting
patrols on guard in the air; and it also enabled them, when they
were sent up at the first signs of anything coming in, to be placed
in the most advantageous position for attack. That helped enormously in relieving what would otherwise have been an utterly
intolerable strain on the pilots.

We know now that, through being so surprisingly ill-informed,
German intelligence both before and during the Battle of Britain
was astonishingly ineffective. The Germans failed almost completely to appreciate the hidden strength that was given to the
Royal Air Force by our radar screen, as well as by our very
efficient system of controlling our fighters by radio once they were
in the air on information that went on being supplied by that

screen. The Germans could not seem to understand the reason why our fighters were always so well placed to attack them whenever they appeared, and they were perplexed over the nature of the orders which they could hear our controllers on the ground passing by radio telephone to the fighters in the air.

During the latter part of the First World War, I had had, as a commander of fighter squadrons, a great deal of experience in the early development of fighter tactics, and one of our aims then had been to develop ways of fighting with squadrons in formations of wings. In achieving that we had met with a great deal of success, and ever since that time we had tended, in any consideration of tactics in large-scale fighter operations, to think in the use of wings made up of three or more squadrons. By using large formations of fighters we believed that we would stand a much better chance of inflicting severe damage on any large enemy formations. But that called for the time that would be necessary to get the squadrons formed up into these wings and ready to launch their mass attacks.

In thinking, back in 1940, about the most suitable tactics that might be employed, it seemed to me that the object to be arrived at in stopping an enemy offensive was to shoot down such a large proportion of his bomber force that he would be compelled to diminish the scale of the offensive and finally to call it off. If, for instance (and to oversimplify the issue), the enemy started off his offensive with one thousand bombers and we could shoot down ten per cent of them each day it would mean that very quickly he would lose the lot. Obviously no air force could stand that rate of destruction, and the enemy would be compelled to reduce his effort and attack every other day, or one day in three, or in reduced numbers.

It was apparent that the most effective way of causing such a heavy casualty rate as this to an enemy bomber force was to meet him with large, and even superior, numbers of fighters operating in a cohesive pattern: in wings made up of three or more squadrons. But here that element of time came into play: the time that it would take to form up into wings. It was naturally desirable, in fact imperative, that we should attack the enemy bomber formations before they could get to their objectives and drop their bombs; but all too often there was not sufficient time, for all the excellence of our early warning system, to get the fighters formed up into wings. Then we had to attack in smaller numbers. That resulted in fewer casualties to the enemy and greater losses to the attacking fighters. While in the short run that might reduce the effects of the accuracy of the enemy in their bombing, it did not have the effect of destroying so many of the enemy aircraft that he could not continue with the attacks. Only larger formations of fighters could bring that about.

The problem facing Fighter Command was to get at the enemy bombers as quickly as possible and at almost any cost, and to break up the attacks before they reached their objective. That was the short-term view, and the right one, and it naturally had to govern the day-to-day operations. Good though the radar warning system was, it still could not provide sufficient time for the squadrons to the south and the east of London to be able to get satisfactorily into wing formation, and all too often the squadrons had to be hurled into the attack with only a very narrow margin of time.

Every effort also had to be made to preserve the fighter airfields and their operations rooms, particularly in these southern areas; and that definitely meant getting at the enemy before his bombs could get at them. As it was, the Germans gave some of our fighter airdromes a severe plastering, but they were never able to knock them out altogether. Our air defense did become depleted, and it was under the most severe strain, but it held together. And if there was one thing that the Germans did realize it was that they would have to destroy that air defense before the way could be opened up for an invasion.

For the purposes of history it is recorded that the Battle of Britain started on July 10, 1940. Each and every day from then on the Germans were on the attack. At times large fleets of their bombers and fighters came over, and there were days when it seemed that the climax must surely have been reached. Fighter Command was stretched, but such was its resilience that its control over the battle never once gave way. We know now that the high direction of the attacks by the Germans, massive though they were, suffered from amazingly indecisive and unimaginative planning. They had an objective, but they never seemed to know what they were doing in trying to achieve it.

No one German commander was more responsible for the serious lack of any firm direction during the onslaught on Britain than Hermann Goering, and it was in the way in which he played around with the powerful force that he had at his disposal that he revealed his own rank amateurism. Goering was never a professional airman. When I came to realize that, I recalled that he had conducted his command of the Richthofen Circus against which I had fought in the air in the First World War in much the same way. He had all the flamboyant qualities of the death-or-glory

fighter pilot, with none of the mature power of command that
develops with experience.

On September 15, 1940, there came what we were to know later
as the climax of the Battle of Britain. It was the day upon which
the Germans were compelled finally to change all their planning.
At the Air Ministry we were aware of the intensity of the fighting
in the air over the south of England as the enemy made repeated
efforts to break through our fighter defense. We had all the reports
pouring in from the headquarters of Fighter Command at Stanmore, where they were working with the more detailed information
coming from the radar chain and the Group Headquarters. We
were fully informed almost blow by blow about the progress of the
battle.

"It was one of the decisive battles of the war, and, like the
Battle of Waterloo, it was on a Sunday," Winston Churchill later
stated. His description of the visit that he made that day to No. 11
Group Headquarters, which was the most deeply involved of all
the groups of Fighter Command, has been quoted as one of the
most moving accounts of the events of that particular Sunday. In
the bombproof operations room at Uxbridge, on the outskirts of
London, and fifty feet below ground, he sat and watched the
course of the battle. He saw the way in which Keith Park, who was
by then the Air Officer Commanding the group, acted on the
information passed on from the headquarters of Fighter Command, and how he supervised the flow of orders being given to the
sector controllers, who, in turn, were giving information over the
radio to the pilots of our fighter squadrons in the air. The group
controller that day who was working directly under Keith Park was
an Auxiliary Air Force pilot by the name of Wing Commander
John Willoughby de Broke: the Lord Willoughby de Broke who is
now particularly well known as a steward of the Jockey Club.

The air battle that day reached a climax when all the squadrons
in No. 11 Group were engaged. "What other reserves have we?"
Winston Churchill asked Keith Park.

"There are none," Park replied.

In recording their conversation in that way, Winston Churchill
has given a one-sided impression of the true state of affairs. Park's
reserves were possibly exhausted, but there were still the other
groups with their squadrons standing behind him and ready to
back him up with their support. That Churchill was keyed up and
emotional over what he had seen and heard is amply proved by
what he said after he left Park's operations room. On that visit to
No. 11 Group he was accompanied by his wife and General Sir

Hastings (later Lord) Ismay, and the latter has spoken of what happened in his own *Memoirs*.

"We left by car for Chequers," Pug Ismay has recorded. "Churchill's first words were: 'Don't speak to me; I have never been so moved.' After about five minutes he leaned forward and said, 'Never in the field of human conflict has so much been owed by so many to so few.' "

Therein is the origin of the public statement that the Prime Minister was to make a little later and which has since become so famous.

Although regrettably as well as incorrectly overstressed, there did occur during the course of the battle a difference of opinions over the way in which the fighters were being employed. One of the contributing factors to the way in which this controversial matter developed was the clash between the personalities of the two principal group commanders concerned: Keith Park at No. 11 Group, and Trafford Leigh-Mallory at No. 12 Group. I had known both men very well from the time when we had served together as young squadron commanders on the Western Front, and I knew that they were both men of the greatest ability, but of vastly different temperaments. They also held widely differing views about the way in which the air battle should be fought.

It was this clash of personalities more than anything else which led to an unnecessarily heated argument one afternoon between Keith Park and Trafford Leigh-Mallory at the Air Ministry. Because I was myself at heart a fighter pilot, quite apart from being the Deputy Chief of the Air Staff, I naturally took the keenest interest in their differences of opinions even if I was not then actually involved in the disagreement. But from that time on I became drawn into their argument, and just as Stuffy Dowding's name has become linked in it with Keith Park's, so mine has become associated with Leigh-Mallory's. Neither Dowding nor I have ever been at all happy about that.

It was Leigh-Mallory's rather overforceful contention that the air battle should be fought with formations made up of these wings of from three to six squadrons in each, his object being to outnumber the enemy. Up to a point, he had a good idea. Park's view on the way in which he had to operate was that because of his closer proximity to the attacking bombers he did not have time for his squadrons to form up into wings. He had to fight with units of squadron strength or less because the squadrons took off as such and were ready to fight as soon as they were airborne and at sufficient height to operate most effectively.

The urgency of Keith Park's position meant that he had to get his squadrons into the air and at the enemy as quickly as possible and before the raiders could reach their targets. This resulted in his squadrons quite often going into action one at a time and even piecemeal, and there were times when they were defeated in detail by larger formations of enemy fighters. The snag about Leigh-Mallory's tactics was the obvious one that it took time to gather the squadrons together into a wing. If Park had followed these tactics it would have meant that, on far too many occasions, the enemy would have had a free run at their targets before they were intercepted by the wing which had had to take time to form up. But since it was obvious that better results in the number of enemy aircraft shot down would be obtained if attacks upon them were made in superior numbers I felt that there was surely room for both methods.

In theory I agreed with Leigh-Mallory and I would have preferred to have seen the fighters operating in wings; but I could also appreciate the urgency with which Keith Park was faced. In the official history entitled *The Defence of the United Kingdom,* Basil Collier states of my views that I "had shown where [my] sympathies lay in this controversy by declaring that 'it does not matter where the enemy is shot down, as long as he is shot down in large numbers.'" Collier further makes the statement about my views: "he made his attitude still clearer by announcing that he had 'never been very much in favour of the idea of trying to interpose fighter squadrons between enemy bombers and their objectives.' He would rather, he said, shoot down fifty of the enemy when they had bombed their target than ten forward of it." Such an appreciation of the views that I held in this highly controversial matter is much too simple, and even blunt, in its approach, and what I thought about it was much more subtle and elastic than that.

It is quite clear that Stuffy Dowding, the one man to whom the main credit belongs for winning the battle, was not as deeply involved in what has come to be called "the wings controversy" as too many writers would make out. He has since told Bob Wright that at the time he knew little about it, and that he was far too busy to pay attention to unnecessary arguments. That must go a long way in answering those who have so firmly lined up Dowding and Park on one side and Douglas and Leigh-Mallory on the other. There was no such firm alignment, even if some of us did hold certain views. On the other hand, I do know that there was no lack of pressure in the expression of their views by some of the more enterprising young squadron commanders in No. 12 Group, to the north of London, led by that dynamic character Douglas Bader.

There was a lot of good sense in what these young commanders were proposing; but they were not faced with quite the same pressure as those in No. 11 Group. Having spent such a long time myself as a young squadron commander on active service in time of war, I know how strongly one can come to feel about tactics. Leigh-Mallory felt the same way, and he gave his young commanders his full support, and since he was also an exceptionally forceful character that support carried a great deal of weight. But Keith Park did the same thing, naturally backing his use at squadron strength, and he had his young commanders supporting him. By the very natures of all of the men involved, there were bound to be clashes, and had it been left at that I do not think that the argument would have gone any further than a vigorous exchange of views, with each fighting well in his own way.

But these two groups were alongside each other, and each was called upon to support the other. The full blast of the battle fell on Keith Park's group, No. 11, but Leigh-Mallory's Group, No. 12, was right there in the background, always eager to leap into the fray. I did come to have a feeling that Park was rather inclined to resent, even without his realizing it, the way in which the squadrons from Leigh-Mallory's group at times came into his area uninvited, and looking for a battle with the enemy. That feeling of mine came about through one occasion when I actually heard Keith Park complain that No. 12 Group was, to use his word, "poaching." It sounded to me as if he was talking about his local shoot, and it struck me as rather surprising that he should look at what was happening in that way.

But one had to see Leigh-Mallory and Keith Park actually facing each other to realize how strong the clash was between these two forceful personalities. They were both such able commanders, and each was right in his own way. I think Park was right to get his squadrons off the ground and at the enemy formations as soon as possible; but he should have had a better liaison with No. 12 Group so that they could have had their larger formations of fighters—which had had time to form up—ready to back up the early efforts of No. 11 Group. Leigh-Mallory should have been more understanding in that matter of liaison, and readier to give Park quick and effective support regardless of any theories about the way in which the battle should be fought.

It would have been ideal if we could have had the best of both

worlds, with the squadrons of No. 11 Group attacking the enemy
on the way in, and the No. 12 Group wings tearing into them as
they were retreating. But some lapses in liaison—as happens all
too often in times of peace as well as in war—interfered with that
and prevented it from becoming fully effective. To some extent the
responsibility for these lapses must rest on the shoulders of the
staff at the headquarters of Fighter Command. In the final analysis
it was up to them to see to it that there was the closest cooperation, through proper liaison, between the groups which went to
make up the Command.

The Battle of Britain was fought against the threat of a German
invasion, and the Germans were defeated. It was an event that is
unique in military history, and it was a great British triumph. The
operations of that battle and what we have come to call the Blitz
overlapped; but the Germans planned and executed their night
bombing after the Battle of Britain for reasons that were altogether
different. As the attacks by day diminished, the severity of the
bombing by night increased. And with that there came about a
very big change in the course of my own career.

Toward the end of October we were already having to change
our line of thought from defense by day to defense by night, and it
was at that time that Peter Portal was moved from Bomber Command. He was appointed Chief of the Air Staff in place of Cyril
Newall, who had had an exhausting experience in that office for
over three very trying years. Promoted to the rank of Marshal of
the Royal Air Force, Newall went to New Zealand as Governor-
General.

With the appointment of the new C.A.S. there was obviously a
general post going on, and I began to wonder what would be
happening to me. I was told by Cyril Newall just before he left that
I would shortly be in for a change, and after the long time that I
had been at the Air Ministry—by then very nearly five years—I
was quite pleased with the idea. Newall had said that I would
probably be appointed to command one of the groups in Bomber
Command. I told him that I would rather have a group in Fighter
Command because I knew much more about fighters than I did
about bombers.

Within the space of only a few days there was a sudden and
totally unexpected development in my own affairs. In the course of
a casual discussion with Harold Balfour—we were old enough and
close enough friends to be able to speak to each other with
complete frankness—he told me that instead of being given a

group, I was to become the Air Officer Commanding-in-Chief of Fighter Command. I was to take the place of Stuffy Dowding, who was to retire; and a day or so later there was an official announcement about it.

This very important appointment caused in me a quite unexpected turmoil of feelings. In the first place, it was so much more than I had ever expected, and a much bigger step forward. I was naturally pleased and proud that I should have been selected for such a responsible post, and I had sufficient confidence in my own ability to believe that I could make a good job of it. But at the same time I could not help feeling a little overawed by the importance of such high command. To a large extent the fate of the British people would be resting in my hands.

One of the announcements of my new appointment was on the front page of *The Daily Telegraph* for November 20, 1940, along with a photograph that had been taken outside the Air Ministry, with the caption "Fighter Command New Chief." On the same page there were solid headlines stating that there had been a "Stream of Bombers over Midland Town" the night before. For security reasons the town was not named. It was Birmingham. There was also a short item on the front page stating that "Air Ministry experts are concentrating in the first place on steps to check night raiders," and that "those in a position to know predict with some confidence that mass raids by moonlight will become so costly that the enemy will be largely forced to abandon them as they have the large-scale daylight attacks."

At that time I was not one of those predicting "with some confidence" that we were going to force the enemy to abandon anything: I was much too keenly aware of the difficulties of the task that lay ahead of us to indulge in any such unwarranted optimism, valuable though it might be as propaganda. On the other hand, as I eventually stated in my dispatch on the first year that I spent as Commander-in-Chief of Fighter Command, I knew very well that "the defeat of the night bombers must be one of my main tasks."

23 / Fighter Command

IN ALL THAT HAPPENED during the summer and the autumn of the year of 1940, when for the first time in their evil designs the Nazis were sharply brought to book, the freedom of mankind was saved by the young air crews of the Royal Air Force backed up by the people of Britain. There was quite a lot of unsavory and defeatist criticism of us, but we fought alone against formidable odds; and the rest of the world would do well to think about that when they talk so glibly about their own freedom.

If there are any who would question our right to be proud of what we achieved let them read through the list of the names of the R.A.F. air crews who fought in the Battle of Britain. There were with us some gallant Canadian and Polish squadrons with pilots who had the guts to join us; but note must always be most carefully taken of the way in which the vast majority of those who fought in the air have the word "British" appearing after their names. They were all members of the Royal Air Force and the Fleet Air Arm of the Royal Navy.

The Battle of Britain and the night Blitz which followed it are not isolated incidents in the war: they are part of an overall pattern. Those battles were the physical signs in the sky of the clash between the Germans and the British in the effort made by the Nazis to launch their invasion of this country. Before they could swarm across the narrow English Channel and try their hands on our beaches, they had to make sure that they had smashed the air defenses of this country. They were beaten in the air, and at the last moment the Germans had to postpone the launching of their seaborne invasion of Britain. But for that defeat in the air, we would have been invaded, and what would have happened then to the rest of the world is something that is enough to give cause for every thinking man to ponder over the meaning of freedom.

The sharp edge of the sword wielded in 1940 by the people of Britain was the Royal Air Force. I am proud of the part that was played by my own Service. And in the years that have passed since then, years which have brought with them an ever-increasing understanding of the importance of that one particular year, I find myself becoming more and more deeply touched by the part played by those young air crews. For that reason alone the moment of becoming Commander-in-Chief of Fighter Command in November, 1940, immediately after our fighters had put up the greatest battle ever fought in the air, was an experience about which I will always feel very strongly. I was responsible for the operation of a magnificent and battle-seasoned command.

While I was fully aware of, and at times overawed by, the weight of the responsibility which I was going to have to carry, in my heart and mind I was able to accept that weight with a reasonable eagerness. I knew the breed of the men whom I was going to command through having been one of the first of them. I understood them, even if, in the arrogance of their youth, they might at times look with disdain on the "scrambled eggs" on the peak of my cap, for I knew that it was particularly in the tradition of fighter pilots to look upon all authority with a pronounced irreverence.

I do not doubt that many of those young bloods who served under my command during 1941 and 1942 thought that I did not understand the inclination which they showed toward a certain flamboyance in manner, and that the style of the cynicism which they appeared so casually to adopt was a mystery to me. The truth of it was that their outlook and spirit were expressed in just the same way as that known to those of us who had started it all not so many years before.

My departure from the Air Ministry and my arrival at Bentley Priory to take over from Stuffy Dowding happened so quickly that the actual transfer of command was effected without any time element being involved at all. Dowding kept very much to the point. But I had known him too well and for too long for him to be able to hide from me his very natural and understandable distress about having to give up his great command. He had striven so hard to create it, and now that the test was over, it was proudly displaying its first splendid battle honor, and giving it all up must have been for Dowding a terrible wrench. He was never the kind of man who invited any expression of personal feelings, but I would have been quite insensitive if I had not felt for him in my heart a deep sympathy.

There has been a great deal of unnecessary discussion, and

somewhat unpleasant speculation, over what has been referred to as the way in which Air Chief Marshal Sir Hugh Dowding, as he was then, was treated over his relinquishment of Fighter Command, and his subsequent retirement from the Royal Air Force. It is long overdue, and only fair to him, that the whole story should be placed in a much clearer perspective. Having been so personally involved through being the man who took his place, I am in a position to be able to provide a few of the facts, all of which are in Dowding's favor.

But for the outbreak of war, Stuffy Dowding would have relinquished his command in 1939, at the end of the usual period of service as an Air Officer Commanding-in-Chief. But the aircraft crash in which Chris Courtney and I were involved with the Secretary of State for Air early in 1939 resulted in an extension of the time which Dowding was to serve at Fighter Command. Coupled with the tremendous demands that the year of 1940 made upon him, these were the only factors which led to his retirement at the end of that year. That Dowding was by then a very tired man, and that he had come near to working a miracle, was clearly understood by all of those of us who had been close to him. We knew through the actual experience of working with him how very much he had given of himself, and we understood what a strain it had all been on him. No matter what there may have been in the way of conflict between Dowding and other branches of the Air Ministry, so far as we on the Air Staff were concerned his retirement was honorable in every conceivable way.

What I have always found not so honorable was the way in which, for some reason that has never been explained, no mention whatsoever was made of Stuffy Dowding's name in the immensely successful and widely read official "The Battle of Britain" pamphlet which was published by the Ministry of Information for the Air Ministry immediately after the battle was over. The name of Hermann Goering appeared repeatedly in it. The names of Marshal Ney, Kellermann, Napoleon, Samuel Pepys, Hitler and Goebbels were all dragged in, and even the printer was named. I should imagine that the excuse would be made by officialdom that for some policy reason or other none of our people was named; but a rigid application of anonymity which freely permits the naming of the losers but cannot at least name the man who led the victors is as ridiculous as it is unjust.

Throughout my Service career I had worked closely, and with surprisingly few breaks, either under or with Stuffy Dowding; and from the time of the outbreak of the war I had been in close

contact with him during his days of trial and triumph at Fighter
Command. He had a great deal of influence upon the course of my
own career, and I knew that that influence had been never-failingly
good. The word dedication has lost some of its value through the
way in which it has been so bandied about; but Dowding was truly
dedicated to the defense of the United Kingdom through the best
possible use of the command which he had created and which he
brought into action in war.

When it came to handing over to me, and all that that meant in
bringing to an end his Service career, Stuffy Dowding was perfectly
proper in every way, and for all that he must have been experiencing he was polite even if, as always, rather short and abrupt in his
manner. But he was quite reasonable about the whole business,
and we understood each other and our work too well for a need for
any elaborate gestures. In any case neither of us was by nature
given to being demonstrative.

Any gestures that were to be made had to come from those who
had in their hands the bestowing of public recognition, and in that
there was a grievous fault. Dowding's elevation to the peerage was
delayed far too long; it was over two years before this high honor
came to him. He was created a G.C.B. during the Battle of Britain,
while he was still at Fighter Command; but his departure was
allowed to occur in a way that reflects no credit whatsoever on those
who should have expressed at the time a public recognition of his
great achievements.

It was just over three weeks after the ending of the day Battle of
Britain that I became Commander-in-Chief of Fighter Command.
Twenty-two years had passed since I had finished my own wartime
operational flying as a fighter pilot: since, in the lingo of the fighter
boys now under my command, I had been "one of the chaps."
With that, and with further promotion to the rank of air marshal, I
was relieved forever of any further experience of service in the Air
Ministry itself. With that command of my own—which was the
culmination of all my work with and interest in fighters—my world
became at once much more intense and personal, and at the same
time, and of necessity, narrower in its outlook.

During the years which I had spent at the Air Ministry, I had
been able to look at the world and all that was happening in it
from a fairly broad point of view, and to absorb in a general way
all the events of the times. But as the C.-in-C. of Fighter Command, I had a specific and very exacting responsibility for the
defense of the country. I was no longer just part of the machinery
of the Air Staff: at forty-six years of age I was on my own and

entirely responsible for the operation of the most important command in the R.A.F. at that time. In a way I knew again the feeling that I had had when, as a young pilot, I had returned to the Front during the First World War, to the narrower but much more exciting world of direct action, and what was happening outside that world seemed to recede into a rather remote background.

The headquarters of Fighter Command was physically in two parts: one above ground, and the other well below it. What everybody could see above ground was Bentley Priory, a rambling and historic old building standing in its own extensive grounds between Stanmore and Bushey, twelve miles to the northwest of London. It was first occupied by the R.A.F. when it was taken over in the late 1920's for the headquarters of what was then called the Inland Area, which, in turn, became part of the early air defense of Great Britain.

In 1936 Bentley Priory became the headquarters of the newly formed Fighter Command, and as the signs at the entrance now proudly proclaim, it is still the site for this important headquarters. During the war the old building stood there for all to see; but in those days only those who were allowed past the heavily guarded entrance knew just what went on in the enormous block of operations and filter rooms and offices which were buried well underground alongside Bentley Priory, all of them having been built just before and brought into operation just after the outbreak of war. In those days that great underground block—known inevitably to all of us as "the Hole"—presented to the newcomer at first sight a picture that was almost Wellsian.

Of immediate concern to me on my arrival at Bentley Priory to serve as its second Commander-in-Chief was the important matter of the officers who would be directly supporting me. The air officer in charge of administration had been in that post under Stuffy Dowding for the past eighteen months, and for personal reasons, in addition to every other one, I was particularly happy to have him continue as my A.O.A. He was Air Vice-Marshal H. R. (later Sir Hazelton) Nicholl, and he was an old and trusted friend whom I had known well ever since the days when we had flown together as pilots in No. 8 Squadron on the Western Front during the summer and autumn of 1915. Known in the Service as "Daddy" Nicholl, he was a kindly and understanding man. He had an exceptionally thorough understanding of his work through many years of varied experience which had even included service in Australia for a time before the war as a member of the Air Board of the Royal Australian Air Force.

The senior air staff officer, and my righthand man in running the operational side of the command, was Air Vice-Marshal D. C. S. (later Air Chief Marshal Sir Douglas) Evill, who was known to all of us as an exceptionally intelligent and capable staff officer. He had been one of my students at the Imperial Defence College in 1933. Born in Australia of English parents, Strath Evill had come to the Royal Air Force from the Royal Navy. He and Arthur Longmore, who was also born in Australia, were first cousins, and Evill had been an R.N.A.S. pilot during the First World War, having learned to fly after leaving the Royal Naval College at Dartmouth. Evill had won a Distinguished Service Cross in 1916, and an Air Force Cross in 1919.

On the outbreak of war in 1939, Strath Evill had gone out to France as the senior air staff officer of the British Air Forces in France, and after the collapse there he was one of the last to make his way back to England. He was sent shortly after that to Fighter Command as senior air staff officer, and he had served under Stuffy Dowding throughout the stress of the Battle of Britain. I greatly admired Evill for the quiet control of his manner, which was a feature about him that won for him the affection of everybody with whom he came in contact. It was particularly noticeable to all of us at Bentley Priory in the way in which he conducted himself when his son, who was scarcely more than a boy just out of school, was killed in 1941 on one of his early raids as a bomber pilot over Germany.

All the other senior officers on the staff of Fighter Command were known to me either personally—one, Group Captain D. O. Mulholland, had been a pilot flying with Mick Mannock from the same airfield at Treizennes from which I had flown in 1917—or as a result of knowing about them through the routine channels of our lives as regular officers in the Service. But such was the demand made for officers through the rapid expansion of the various staffs that by the second year of the war most of the junior officers were those who had volunteered for war service. Quite a few of them were men who had seen service in the first war, and who had rejoined the Air Force on the outbreak of the second; but many of them were of the interwar generation: too young for the first war, and too old, or not fit enough, for flying duties in the second war.

There was one quality that had always been so much a part of the spirit of the R.A.F. which was amply demonstrated at the headquarters of Fighter Command. Daddy Nicholl and Strath Evill both had links with the Commonwealth, but there were some members of my staff who had even stronger ties. When Nicholl left my staff just over a year later, his place as my A.O.A. was taken by Air Vice-Marshal H. W. L. (now Air Chief Marshal Sir Hugh) Saunders. He was a South African who was very well known to me personally through having been the Dingbat Saunders who was one of my flight commanders in No. 84 Squadron on the Western Front in 1918.

In one appointment to my staff that was of a purely personal nature, I had to work rather in the dark. As my personal assistant I had to have somebody upon whom I could rely to a far greater extent, under the conditions of war, than would have been usual in peacetime. There was no longer any need for the P.A. to be my personal pilot—as had been the prewar custom—and I did not want an officer who would be burdened down with social activities. I needed someone who could run my office for me, and who could, with discretion and good judgment, spare me from the mass of detail, particularly in the paper work.

It had been the custom of Stuffy Dowding to use young regular officers who were also pilots as his personal assistants, but their inclination had been, understandably enough, to get back to flying. For a while during the latter stages of the Battle of Britain he had had in this personal appointment Robert Wright, who was then a flight lieutenant in the Volunteer Reserve, and who had previously been working in radar in the underground filter room. Dowding suggested to me that I might like to keep Wright on as my P.A.

When I came to look through Bob Wright's personal file, I found that although he was English by birth he had spent practically the whole of his life abroad. He later said of himself that through having actually lived and grown up in the countries which he knew so well he was an Anglo-South African-Australian-New Zealand-Californian. In talking with him I learned that when war broke out he had returned to England from the United States, where he had been living for some years, under his own steam, and with the express purpose of trying to join the Royal Air Force. He was a writer by profession, and through having lived so much abroad and on his own he had an independence of mind and a rather prickly dislike of red tape. Since that was in tune with my own outlook, I had him appointed as my personal assistant.

In the course of all the work that we have since done together, Bob Wright called to my attention the book *Fighter Command,* which was published a few years ago. It was written by Peter Wykeham, who was a distinguished fighter pilot during the second

war, and who is now an air marshal. In a state of some glee,
Wright pointed particularly to two things that Wykeham had to say
about me at the time during which I was C.-in-C. of Fighter Command.

"Swallow them if you can," Wright said. "They describe you in
a way that is almost the opposite of what you were."

Despite the excellence of Wykeham's book—it is one of the best
that has been written on the subject—I did find it difficult, for
reasons which I hope will be obvious, to gulp down the more
personal things that were said about me. In describing my appearance then, he wrote: "He presented a formidable picture to the
world. Not tall, but burly, immensely strong and of a commanding presence, his face often set in a scowl of concentration that
wanted only the dueling scars to rival the appearance of the most
ferocious German general that ever glared out from under a steel
helmet." Although he admits that I was "most friendly and
approachable," Wykeham goes on to say about me that "he found
it difficult to convince his officers that he was really a mild-
mannered man."

I was shaken by this unfortunate impression which I appear to
have given at that time; but Bob Wright then pointed, with even
more amusement, to a remark recorded by Wykeham that I made
in reply to a complaint from one of my squadron commanders. He
had claimed that his squadron was forgotten and unloved, and that
annoyed me. Wykeham wrote: " 'What the hell do you mean,
nobody loves you?' shouted Sholto furiously. 'I love you! Get that
into your thick head: I love you!' "

My main concern as a Commander-in-Chief was to plan for the
future, and an essential part of that planning had to be a careful
evaluation of the personalities of all the senior officers whom I
would have under my command. Because of the nature of its work,
the strength of the Royal Air Force, as with its weakness, rested
even more firmly in the individual than it did in either of the other
Services. And again, in considering the personalities of the senior
officers in my command other than those on my headquarters staff,
there was such clear evidence of the contribution that had been
made by the Commonwealth to the building of the R.A.F.

At the time when I was appointed Commander-in-Chief, it was
also decided that there should be some changes in the group
commanders. I had nothing to do with these decisions, and only a
couple of weeks after I took over the Command, Keith Park, the
New Zealander of whom it could be said that he possessed in full

the fighting qualities of the All Blacks, was relieved of the command of No. 11 Group in a way that has since been the cause of a great deal of controversy. He had been senior air staff officer at Fighter Command and Air Officer Commanding No. 11 Group through a very difficult period from well before and right through the Battle of Britain, and he had distinguished himself as a very able commander. And then it appeared as if he was suddenly banished to a flying training group in a manner which, coupled with the retirement of Stuffy Dowding, led Denis Richards to comment: "Their translation to quieter spheres, though doubtless wise in itself was not perhaps the most impressive immediate reward that might have been devised for the victors of one of the world's decisive battles."

The new Air Officer Commanding No. 11 Group was Trafford Leigh-Mallory, who was moved from No. 12 Group. I knew that Leigh-Mallory was exceptionally capable, and I was quite happy about having him as one of my senior officers; but I also knew that his strong and rather overbearing personality led him to be somewhat self-opinionated, and while not himself particularly prickly he did have the habit of raising the hackles of other people. Some found him arrogant and apt to lay down the law on his own assumption that he always knew the right answers. He was the brother of the famous mountaineer who made climbing history and lost his life in his attempt to reach the top of Mount Everest in 1924; and perhaps he shared with him that rugged determination which had led G. L. Mallory to make the remark "because it is there" when he was asked why he felt compelled to climb Everest.

There was also to be found a good indication of the continuity in our Service careers as professional airmen over the long span of the years in a comparison of what most of my group commanders—all air vice-marshals—and I, their Commander-in-Chief, had done in the First World War. During my time at Fighter Command, Keith Park, Trafford Leigh-Mallory, Quintin Brand, Jock Andrews, E. J. Kingston-McCloughry and R. E. Saul were all Air Officers Commanding groups in my command. By the last year of the earlier war, all seven of us were serving together as young majors in command of squadrons on the Western Front.

A further personal link between the staff at Fighter Command and my early career in the Air Force was revealed to me with a quite unexpected discovery when I arrived at Bentley Priory. I found that Air Vice-Marshal Sir Tom Webb-Bowen had come out of retirement and that he was serving as an air commodore on the staff in the underground operations block. It was a far cry from the time in 1915 when I had been a young observer in No. 2 Squadron of the Royal Flying Corps on the Western Front and he had been my commanding officer, and he had, during the spring of that year, recommended me for training as a pilot.

In addition to Fighter Command, I also had under my operational control for the air defense of Great Britain the Anti-Aircraft Command of the Army, and our own Balloon Command, and the Observer Corps. Balloon Command had been formed in 1938, and with its headquarters in Stanmore, nearby, it was under the command of Air Vice-Marshal Sir E. L. Gossage, who had been Keith Park's predecessor at No. 11 Group. He had also been out on the Western Front with us in 1918, as a lieutenant-colonel in command of a wing. The role of the balloons was by the very nature of their purpose a passive one, and those called upon to operate them had a dreary and unrewarding job which was nevertheless a useful one in raising the morale of our own people and in lowering that of the enemy raiders.

The task of the Observer Corps, which had been formed back in the early 1920's, was to keep track of and to report to Fighter Command all raiding aircraft after they had crossed in over our coastlines, backing up the information already supplied by the radar screen on the approach of aircraft from the sea. The volunteers who manned the Observer Corps posts performed an unspectacular duty which was at times also a very lonely one; but they were all extraordinarily keen and, as I was to discover on one particularly interesting occasion, very reliable in the way in which they went about their work. Official recognition of that was made when it became known as the Royal Observer Corps.

The relationship between Fighter Command and Anti-Aircraft Command could all too easily have produced difficulties between the Air Force and the Army, and it was due to the loyalty and sound common sense of General Sir Frederick Pile, the General Officer Commanding-in-Chief, Anti-Aircraft Command, that the two commands were able to work so well together. On its formation in April, 1939, Anti-Aircraft was first commanded by Alan Brooke, but about three months later he handed over to Tim Pile, who was a small, alert little Irishman for whom I learned to have the highest respect. He was to remain in that appointment throughout the Second World War.

The headquarters of Anti-Aircraft Command were in a large building within a very short walking distance of Bentley Priory. By the time that I arrived at Fighter Command, Tim Pile had had a great deal of experience, and he was both senior in rank to me and older. He was a wise little man, and while of a determined disposition he was always reasonable, and I could not have received from him firmer and at the same time more understanding cooperation. Whenever I asked him to do anything with the guns or the searchlights—which were also under his command and our control—Pile was always ready to listen and to do all that he could, and I never knew of a single instance of a serious clash in what we proposed to do in our joint efforts toward providing the air defense of the country, which was by then mainly at night.

During the two years of 1941 and 1942 which I was to spend as Commander-in-Chief of Fighter Command, there was action enough for my day fighter squadrons, and their operations involved me in not a little controversy. But it was what happened under the cover of darkness that was my biggest problem. Stuffy Dowding had fought the daylight Battle of Britain and the beginning of the enemy night offensive over this country, the Blitz. In trying to combat the latter, he had done a great deal in urging on the development of the radar-equipped night fighters. By the time that I stepped into his shoes, the Blitz was in full fury, and there fell squarely on my shoulders the task of fighting the battle at night. That task alone was mammoth and worrying enough; but I was soon to appreciate more fully something that I had sensed from the way in which Stuffy Dowding had conducted himself as a Commander-in-Chief: I was in for some quite strenuous tussles with Whitehall.

Even though I was to some extent prepared for those struggles, I was nevertheless surprised at the difference in the atmosphere between serving on the staff at the Air Ministry and having an active command all of one's own. My experiences of the past year or so in dealing directly, on behalf of the Air Ministry, with the various Commanders-in-Chief had indicated to me that when the time came for me to become an operational commander, I would be in the firing line in more ways than one. But the crossfire to which one was subjected was never more intense, I found, than when one came to occupy the most senior of all operational appointments. Outside influences, including political ones, had a great deal to do with it; and in my own case it was particularly strong over the uses that were to be made of radar.

While it was inevitable that the night bombing of Britain by the German Air Force had to come, the actual nature of the bombing, which was contained in the name Blitz, was the result of a mistake. On the night of August 24, 1940, some of the German bombers out over England blundered badly in their navigation, and bombs were dropped indiscriminately on London, the first time that the city had been bombed in that way since 1918. We naturally believed, at the time, that this bombing was deliberate, and the very next night we did the same thing to Berlin, and for the first time bombs were dropped on the German capital.

One of those who was in Berlin that night and who was actually doing a radio broadcast at the time to the United States was William Shirer, and he wrote in his diary: "The Berliners are stunned. They did not think it could happen. When this war began, Goering assured them it couldn't. He boasted that no enemy planes could ever break through the outer and inner rings of the capital's anti-aircraft defense. The Berliners are a naive and simple people. They believed him. Their disillusionment today therefore is all the greater. You have to see their faces to measure it."

Violent propaganda was launched against us by the Nazis for being cowardly and piratical, and it led Hermann Goering into making another of his great mistakes in strategy. Early in September he altered the nature of the attacks being made by the Luftwaffe, and they started the heavy bombing of London by day and by night, and that marked the beginning of the Blitz. In allowing that to be done it was Hitler's hope that he would bring us to our knees without having to resort to an invasion.

By the end of 1940 the effects of the Blitz in its full force were being felt by all the people of this country, and it was vitally necessary that we should find some way of dealing with the enemy night bombers. It was all too apparent that we were not gaining with our own fighters the success that was needed and which was expected of us. I had my own views about what the answer to that would be, if we could ever get it to work, and that was the fighter equipped with airborne radar; but there were many other theories and even actual devices floating around which I knew that I would at least have to try out. Any of them might turn up trumps.

The defeat of the German night bomber was clearly my first responsibility. The safety and welfare of the country depended on that. But by the end of 1940 we had found no answer. None of the devices was worth anything, and airborne radar, although in operation, had yet to prove its worth. I was convinced, however, as Stuffy Dowding had been, that this airborne radar, linked with radar on the ground, would provide the answer. The system that was fitted to the twin-engined aircraft which we were using as night fighters—first the Blenheim, and then the new and more powerful Beaufighter—was showing promise, but it was still too unstable and unreliable, and the necessary type of radar control from the ground had not yet been worked out. For these reasons I could not put all my eggs in one basket, and I had to pay attention to other means of coping with the night raiders.

From early in September the Germans had kept up incessant night raids over this country, paying particular attention to London. Other cities had suffered, and Coventry, for one, had been heavily and scientifically bombed on the night of November 14. The raid continued throughout that night, and the city was devastated, and although Fighter Command put up over a hundred aircraft they were unable to intercept any of the raiders. The guns were able to claim two shot down. It was a powerful and skillful attack by the enemy, and our defense was obviously as ineffective at night as it was effective by day.

Some answer to this night bombing had to be found, and it had to be found quickly, and it was made clear to the Air Staff that the government was becoming very concerned about the effect that this continued and heavy night bombing was having on the morale of the civilians. During the two months before I took over from Stuffy Dowding, London alone was attacked quite heavily night after night, the weather of November generally helping the raiders. Immediately after the first heavy raid in September, a special committee was set up under Sir John Salmond which included Wilfrid Freeman, Philip Joubert, Arthur Tedder and myself, and we had decided on a number of urgent measures having to do with night defense, one of them being the recommendation that all possible use should be made of the single-engined fighters.

During the last year of the First World War, I had made a tentative effort, as a young squadron commander, to find out what use we could make at night of our single-engined fighters against the German bombers which were attacking our airfields on the Western Front. I had not met with any success. There were a few pilots who found that they could operate at night; but during the years between the wars little or nothing had been done about developing night fighting. On the other hand, the fighters of 1940 were much more sophisticated and lethal than those of 1918, and I felt that since airborne radar was not yet, for all its promise, working satisfactorily, we should do all we could with the single-engined fighters.

So strongly had Stuffy Dowding come to believe in his radar-equipped fighters that he had become a little blinded, I felt, to the more simple hit-or-miss, trial-and-error use of the single-engined fighters. I agreed that it was a primitive effort to throw what were really day fighters into the darkness of the night skies in the hope that they would be able to see something. But I felt, and in this I was supported by the other members of the committee and the Chief of the Air Staff, that the effort had to be made; despite his strenuous protest Dowding was given instructions to make more use of his Hurricanes and Defiants at night.

Commenting on that decision, the official historian, Basil Collier, has said: "Whatever the ultimate value of the Hurricanes as night-fighters, they could scarcely hope to accomplish much in such conditions as must be expected on many nights throughout the winter." I agree that the outlook for their success looked bleak, but we had to try, and that was the main consideration then as well as after I took over Fighter Command. There were very experienced pilots who thought that something might be achieved. One of them was Air Vice-Marshal Sir Quintin Brand, the A.O.C. of No. 10 Group. As early as 1918 he had succeeded in shooting down quite a number of enemy bombers at night, flying in a single-seater fighter. I could never agree with Collier's statement: "The prevailing opinion was that the slender chance of intercepting bombers in the dark with ordinary day-fighters scarcely justified their diversion from normal duties unless conditions were exceptional." That is being wise after the event, and as was shown by the findings of the Salmond Committee, "the prevailing opinion" at the time was just the opposite. We did not know then what could be achieved, but we had to do all that we could to find out.

I have never been at all happy about the way in which Basil Collier has spoken in the official history about what he describes as the "important differences of outlook between Dowding and the Air Staff," any more than I have liked being described by him elsewhere as Dowding's "ex-officio critic." There is in these statements a serious lack of understanding of the relationship with Dowding that I had known and valued over a period of many years, as well as an insufficient appreciation of the way in which Commanders-in-Chief conducted their official relationship with the Air Staff.

In these relationships there was a great deal more give and take and understanding between us than is implied in the expression "ex-officio critic." As with the controversy over the use of wings, too much has been made of the difference that did admittedly exist at times in our opinions. If I managed to advance my own opinions in a way which won support, that did not mean that I was unduly criticizing Dowding, any more than it meant that he was unnecessarily criticizing me. We were much too experienced and we had much too keen and profound an appreciation and respect for each other for that.

Our early neglect of the problems of night fighting meant that by the autumn of 1940 we still did not even know to what extent fighters which were not equipped with radar would be able to make interceptions at night. For that matter, we were still far from sure about how effective the results would be with those which were being equipped with radar. After a great deal of effort, which continued for quite a time after I took over Fighter Command, we did find, however, that it was well-nigh hopeless for the single-engined fighter pilots to make contact in the dark with the enemy bombers, other than by chance, unless the moon was well above the horizon. In the moonless periods they were blind in every way. But when there was a reasonable amount of light from the moon some of the pilots were able to see far enough to spot the raiders, and contacts were made with the enemy and some of them were shot down.

During this period of groping for the answer to the raiders which made the nights of the winter of 1940–41 so torn with strife, the scientists were telling us that they thought that they could produce a radar set for the single-seater fighter which would give the pilots the ability to see in the dark. They were also on the verge of a breakthrough in effective radar control of night fighters from the ground. Earlier Stuffy Dowding had made it clearly understood that he much preferred the idea of a radar-equipped twin-engined night fighter with a pilot and a navigator: the former concentrating on the flying of the aircraft, and the latter on controlling the interception through the use of his radar set.

Shortly after the Germans launched their Blitz, the Prime Minister set up the important Night Air Defence Committee. We were all greatly puzzled and worried over what to do, and after I became C.-in-C. of Fighter Command I continued to attend all the meetings, along with Tim Pile and many others. We would thrash out every conceivable idea that came to us or which was thrust upon us. Winston Churchill was nearly always in the chair at these meetings, but on one occasion Clement Attlee, the Deputy Prime Minister, took it, and to my surprise I discovered that he was a particularly good chairman, and even better than Churchill, who could all too easily be led off along some sidetrack by visions of the spectacular.

In all the meetings of this committee the one who was most

guilty of sidetracking was Professor F. A. Lindemann. The "Prof" was a past-master at laying trails which delighted Churchill, and which spurred him on to the chase which too often led nowhere. But in fairness to Lindemann, he was not the only culprit. Other fertile minds came up with fanciful ideas which Churchill, with his addiction to imaginative prospects, would ride almost as if he had found a hobby-horse. Off he would race in hot pursuit, and while in doing that he was always interesting and quite often amusing, he all too often wasted time and eventually came a cropper.

That Professor Frederick Lindemann had a brilliant mind no one would ever attempt to deny. "I knew nothing about science, but I knew something of scientists, and had had much practice as a Minister in handling things I did not understand," Winston Churchill once stated, and he coupled that with his tribute to Lindemann, who "was my trusted friend and confidant" and who "could decipher the signals from the experts on the far horizons and explain to me in lucid, homely terms what the issues were."

Professor Lindemann was Winston Churchill's personal advisor in scientific matters for a long time before and throughout the war, and his attitude toward his fellow men has been summed up by Lord Ismay in his statement: "He seemed to have a poor opinion of the intellect of everyone with the exception of Lord Birkenhead, Mr. Churchill and Professor Lindemann . . ." In accepting Lindemann's deciphering of the signals, Churchill has further said that he was able to make sure "that some at least of these terrible and incomprehensible truths emerged in executive decisions." In that statement there is sufficient explanation of the way in which Lindemann's ideas were fostered.

It was one of the ideas thought up by Lindemann for night air defense that was to give Fighter Command a particularly acute headache. Almost rammed down our throats because of Winston Churchill's very strong wish—the wretched thing could almost be described as having been, for a time, his favorite project—it was a scheme rejoicing in the unenterprising code name of "Mutton," or the Long Aerial Mine. This fanciful idea called for the sowing from an aircraft of aerial mines suspended from parachutes at the end of two thousand feet of piano wire.

This particular piece of gadgetry was supposed to enable the aircraft to drop a curtain of these mines in the path of the incoming bombers, and we were even driven to having a squadron specially equipped for this work. It was in operation in the West

Country for a year, and the skeptics saw the prospect of the countryside being festooned with miles of wire and parachutes and unexploded bombs. The whole scheme was much too impractical and difficult to operate, mainly because the defending aircraft had to be placed in exactly the right position to fly at right angles directly in front of the oncoming enemy bombers. That in itself was asking for far more than could then be achieved by the controllers on the ground.

We were compelled to go on with this ridiculous scheme long after it was proved to be a complete waste of time and effort, and long after a normal radar-equipped night fighter squadron flying from the same airfield had proved that its methods were infinitely more effective. Lindemann was too skeptical for too long about the value of airborne radar in fighters, while we at Fighter Command were sure that it would turn the trick. It took us a whole year of frustrating experiments before I was finally able to convince the Prime Minister that the idea of "Mutton" was worthless and he agreed to abandon it.

Another of the bright schemes thought up for us was the free balloon barrage. This one originated in some fertile brain in the Royal Navy, and it called for the use of a whole lot of balloons with mines attached to the end of considerable lengths of wire. They were to be released from the ground in the path of the oncoming enemy bombers. It was much the same as "Mutton" in its idea, but the great snag here, apart from the impracticability of the device, was a meteorological one. We were entirely dependent on the wind conditions being such that they would allow the balloons to rise in an effective way in the faces of the enemy bombers. But we had to try it out, and over a period of months we released the barrage on several nights without any apparent success, and eventually that also was abandoned.

A more promising idea upon which there were spent a great deal of money and time and effort was an extension of the use of airborne radar. Known as Turbinlite it called for the combined use of radar and an airborne searchlight. This special type of high-powered light was fitted into the nose of the Havoc, a twin-engined American light bomber which was built by the Douglas people in California and which we had adapted for use as a night fighter. The Havoc became a radar-equipped aircraft, and it was accompanied by a Hurricane flying in formation with it.

The object aimed at with Turbinlite was to place the two aircraft behind the enemy raider. The Havoc would detect it with its radar and illuminate it with its searchlight in such a way that the

Hurricane could then close in for the kill. But the weight of all its equipment and the obstruction in its nose slowed up the Havoc too much in pursuit of the enemy bombers to be attacked. There were also technical difficulties which were hard to overcome, and although quite a number of Turbinlite Flights were formed, in operation they were surpassed in effectiveness by the straightforward radar-equipped night fighter.

Throughout that winter of the blitz and on into the spring of 1941, we who were concerned with the defense of the United Kingdom were groping in the dark in more senses than one, as well as in more ways than were ever suspected. There were times when I could not help feeling that we were trying out altogether too many schemes, and that we were getting to the state where we were rather casting around in desperation. It would have made life a little easier if I had known that the answer was not so very far off.

24 / From Defense to Offense

IT WAS human curiosity that led inevitably during the unique period of the Battle of Britain and the Blitz that followed it to Fighter Command attracting to its headquarters, the nerve center, a great many visitors of all descriptions and of almost all nationalities, other, perhaps I should add, than those of our enemies. Bentley Priory was the place from which the higher direction had come, and was continuing to come, for the vital fighting in the defense of the country. Of particular pleasure to me, and, I do not hesitate to state, a source for a feeling of personal pride, was the occasion when Boom Trenchard took it upon himself to come out to Bentley Priory for a talk only shortly after I had more or less settled in, and we were able to discuss the way in which the work of my new command was progressing.

In the most invigorating way, Trenchard drew me out, and we talked earnestly about the difficulties which we were having over our radar-equipped night fighters. There were the usual teething troubles in the functioning of the new aircraft and equipment, I explained to him, but with the latter there were additional problems in its actual manipulation as a weapon. We were finding that this called for exceptionally careful and tricky maneuvering, and a very close cooperation between the pilot and his navigator. Trenchard clearly understood how anxious I was about our lack of success in the night battle, and I shall always recall with warmth the reassuring comment that he made about that. It was offered in the way that was so typical of him.

"Never mind, Sholto," he said. "You take my word for it . . . a man will arise."

After our talk in the seclusion of my office, I took Trenchard into the mess for lunch, and his presence there attracted from my staff the closest attention; since he was in a particularly revealing mood, there was a great deal that he had to say which we all found of extraordinary interest. In the entry in his diary which Bob Wright made about that luncheon he recorded a particularly

442

intriguing comment that was made by Trenchard. It was about Hermann Goering, and Wright's diary reads:

He explained that he had paid a visit shortly before the war to Goering at a veritable palace that Goering had in the Black Forest.

"I wanted to find out whether he was genuine or a mountebank," Trenchard explained. "There were a hundred guests to dinner, and he held them all."

Afterward, outside the palace, there was a concert and entertainment. Then, from behind the hills, there came noise, unadulterated noise, deafening and bewildering.

"What was the reason for that?" the C.-in-C. asked.

"The reason!" Trenchard exclaimed. "You know the German character. You know the way their minds work. Cannon, guns, trench mortars, everything . . . all blazing away together."

And then Trenchard spoke very earnestly about Goering, although he seemed to be slightly puzzled. "He's vulgar and coarse and brutal . . . but he's a great man," he said. But he sounded worried.

It has always been my conviction that Boom Trenchard was himself one of our great men. Even in those last years of his long and immensely interesting life he was still able, in the strange way that he had, to make what were almost predictions about the future. That was shortly to be proved to me in what he had said about a man rising to the challenge in night fighting.

While I appreciate the credit which Sir Robert Watson-Watt so generously gave me for the part that I had played in helping with the development of radar, there were people on Stuffy Dowding's staff who had also played important roles. Right from the outset I knew, from the great amount of experience that I gained while I was at the Air Ministry, that Fighter Command in particular was going to have to make the greatest possible use of radar. But the details of its technical development so far as the night fighters were concerned had become problems which were being dealt with more directly by those on the headquarters staff at Bentley Priory, and to them and to the scientists with whom they were associated must go a great deal of the credit for what was achieved.

Two of the officers who had been on the headquarters staff for a long time and who were directly and intimately concerned with the use of radar in Fighter Command were Wing Commander R. G. (later Air Marshal Sir Raymund) Hart and Squadron Leader W. P. G. Pretty, who is now Air Marshal Sir Walter Pretty. Hart was a pilot in the first war, and he had won a Military Cross on the

Western Front while he was still very young; and Pretty was a Cranwell cadet of the interwar years. They had both become specialists in radar, and they were to continue to exert a great influence in developing still further the refinements in its use.

As early as 1936, Raymund Hart was working closely with a brilliant young scientist named Dr. E. G. Bowen on the development of airborne radar, and together they were the first men ever to see in the air a blip on the cathode ray tube of an airborne radar set. It had been constructed by Taffy Bowen. That important development had occurred as far back as two years before the war broke out, and from then on there had been constant pressure from Fighter Command for Taffy Bowen to press on with this work in this entirely new field.

By late 1939 we were operating a few night fighters using Blenheims equipped with an elementary form of airborne radar which was notable more for its temperament than its efficiency; and during the first year of the war such good progress was made that it seemed that we were constantly on the verge of a breakthrough. And there we remained, stuck with a brilliant promise. The radar sets in our aircraft were altogether too unreliable, and our radar control of the aircraft from the ground was primitive; but there were those of us who remained firm in our belief in radar, and that it would work with the efficiency that was being demanded of it.

In July of 1940 the crew of a Blenheim from an experimental unit in Fighter Command completed the first successful interception ever made of an enemy aircraft with the use of radar at night, and they shot it down. By the autumn of that year we had re-equipped the night fighter squadrons with the Beaufighter, which was a powerful and heavily armed aircraft fitted with the first reliable form of airborne radar. There was also coming into use by then the new control of the fighters by radar from the ground which had been developed. On the night of November 20, 1940, the Germans staged the second of three nights of heavy raids on Birmingham. Of the night fighters up that night one of the Beaufighters of No. 604 Squadron, which was stationed at Middle Wallop, in Hampshire, and which was flown by John Cunningham, then a young flight lieutenant, with Sergeant John Phillipson as his navigator, intercepted and shot down a Junkers 88.

This first success of John Cunningham's was also the first occasion in the whole exciting history of radar upon which a night fighter of an operational squadron intercepted and destroyed an enemy aircraft with the assistance of airborne radar; and it had occurred three weeks before Boom Trenchard had come to see me at my headquarters. On the night of December 20, nine days after Trenchard's visit, Cunningham and Phillipson shot down another raider. This time it was a Heinkel that was one of a heavy force of enemy bombers which attacked Liverpool and Birkenhead.

On Sunday, December 29, my wife and I spent the morning flat-hunting in Stanmore. There was an official house provided for the commander-in-chief, but we had found it much too large and gloomy for our liking. After that we had lunch with Oliver and Maureen Stanley, and in the afternoon I returned to my head-quarters for talks with Trafford Leigh-Mallory and my staff about the tour of inspection that I was to make the next day of some of the stations in his group. I was not giving any particular thought to the work of the night fighters, but Bob Wright recorded in his diary that at the end of our discussions I suddenly said: "I want Cunningham, who has shot down those two Huns . . . a damn good show . . . to get the D.F.C."

During that month of December the main target of the German bombing of this country was London. At the conclusion of the conference at my headquarters on that Sunday, December 29, I was told that there were indications that the Germans were plan-ning yet another raid on the capital for that night. The enemy were then using an effective system of coming in on their own radio beams which originated from across the other side of the Channel, and they had in operation a special squadron of trail-blazers which marked with incendiaries the targets to be bombed. Our own scien-tists had done a great deal of sound research on these radio beams, and as soon as they started up, our own reception of them enabled us to know pretty accurately what the target was to be for that night.

By the evening of that day the weather was not at all good. Up to that time what has been described by the official historian as "rain, snow, fog, ice and thick clouds" on the Continent had inter-fered with the operations of the German Air Force. But on that dark Sunday night they were able to operate, despite cloud and high winds, and they staged a raid that turned into the most spectacular of all the raids that were ever made on London. The Heinkels of the trail-blazing force bombed very accurately on instruments, and they hit the heart of the City with a great shower of incendiaries; and hard on their heels came the high explosives. The strong winds caused that onslaught to drift a little to the south of the river, but by then it seemed that the whole of the center of London was already ablaze.

The attack of that night was not the heaviest raid ever thrown at London, but that night the capital burned in a way which none of those of us who saw it will ever forget. "It was an incendiary classic," Winston Churchill has stated; and Tim Pile has described it in more detail as "a great fire raid upon the City, a spectacular and devastating attack which swallowed up in flames great areas around St. Paul's Cathedral." The fires spread alarmingly, and there was added difficulty in fighting them through the River Thames being at its lowest ebb right at the time when there was the greatest demand for water. Our defense against what Churchill called "this clatter and storm" was still depressingly ineffective.

While the immediate problem facing us at Fighter Command in the new year of 1941 was to defeat the German bombers in their night attacks, there still loomed in the background that threat of an invasion in the spring. What we knew then about the German intentions amounted to little more than shrewd guesses based on the sound thinking of our intelligence people. It was not until the major war crimes trials that took place at Nuremberg after the war that there was revealed to us what the Nazis had in mind.

So far as the Prime Minister's thoughts about invasion at that time were concerned, he has revealed that he had rather hoped that the Germans would try it. "Personally, on purely military grounds, I should not have been averse from a German attempt at the invasion of Britain in the spring or summer of 1941," Winston Churchill has stated. "I believed that the enemy would suffer the most terrific defeat and slaughter that any country had ever sustained in a specific military enterprise. But for that very reason I was not so simple as to expect it to happen. In war what you don't dislike is not usually what the enemy does."

Since the whole of our thinking in the Royal Air Force had always been that offense was the best form of defense, the work of Fighter Command in the defense of this country after the Battle of Britain was not confined merely to the waging of the night battle against the German bombers. That daylight battle had secured the safety of this country from the threat of a German invasion in 1940. Immediately after that, we started making plans for a change in the use that was to be made of the day fighters. By the time that I arrived at Fighter Command, they were about to go on to the offensive, and to be given a chance to hit back at the Germans over their own territory in Occupied France.

Shortly before I left the Air Ministry to take over from Stuffy Dowding, the possibility of the use of our day fighters on these offensive operations had been introduced into our thinking and our planning for the future. Peter Portal had become Chief of the Air Staff in place of Cyril Newall on October 25, a month before I left the Air Ministry to go to Fighter Command, and he sent for me one day soon after that to talk about this plan for the future use of the day fighters. He told me that Boom Trenchard had just been in to see him, and that Trenchard had suggested that since the heavy day fighting appeared to have come to an end it was now time for Fighter Command to go on to the offensive. Trenchard had told Portal that he thought that we should now "lean towards France," and he advocated a system of offensive sweeps of fighters across the Channel which was along much the same lines as that used by us in our operations over the Western Front in the First World War.

When Peter Portal asked me what I thought about this idea, I had to tell him that I was very doubtful about the value of such a proposal. I pointed out that our offensive fighter policy on the Western Front in the years between 1914 and 1918 had been very expensive in casualties, although I had to admit that, for the most part, it did enable us to maintain air superiority. But I could not help feeling that the casualties which we would be likely to suffer in offensive operations across the Channel would be too severe for the results that we would be likely to achieve. I told Portal that I was not in favor of Trenchard's suggestion.

In that quiet and wise way of his, Peter Portal did not attempt to argue with me. Instead he merely said: "Go away and write a paper sustaining your point of view."

Since by this time I was very experienced at this sort of staff work, I welcomed the opportunity of being able to get all my thoughts down on paper. I wrote a very full appreciation with the object of proving that a policy of offensive patrols over northern France was not a good one. But after I had completed my paper and I had had a chance to think more carefully about it, I had to admit to myself that my arguments were pretty feeble. If it proved anything at all it was that, in the circumstances then prevailing, an offensive policy for fighters against the German Air Force in northern France was the right one. I then told Portal that I had had to change my mind, and that I was now in favor of Trenchard's idea.

But there was still at the back of my mind when I got to Fighter Command the thought that we would have to exercise some caution in sending our fighters over Occupied France, and not just go belting over there looking for trouble. A directive had been issued by the Air Staff to Fighter Command even before my talk with Peter Portal to prepare for these offensive sweeps, and Keith Park had been eager to employ wings of three squadrons to attack any German formations which could be found over the Strait of Dover. I was quite willing to get on with this plan, and soon after the middle of December, 1941, my fighter pilots started carrying the war to the enemy, with our bombers adding their weight.

Right from the beginning, the whole plan for these offensive operations was very carefully worked out with the intention that the air sweeps should all be part for some time to come of a continuous operation. "The objectives were manifold," Denis Richards has explained. "To destroy enemy machines in the air or on the ground, to shoot up and bomb airfield buildings, ports and communications—all these were within their province. The chief motive underlying the offensive, however, was not so much to cause direct damage as to force the enemy to maintain strong air defences in the west. At the same time powerful moral advantages would accrue as our pilots grew accustomed to exercising the initiative, and as the enemy became thoroughly imbued with the idea of our superiority in the air."

In speaking of the results achieved during the first six months— up until the time of the German attack on Russia—Denis Richards is too inclined to pour cold water on what we were able to do, and I cannot agree with his reference to "the completely ineffective mass sweeps at high level by fighters without bombers." This is overlooking altogether the tremendous value of the experience alone which was gained by our pilots, and which he has admitted, quite apart from the actual operations themselves.

After the Germans attacked Russia in June, 1941, it became of even more importance that we should keep up the pressure over France and so prevent the enemy from moving their Air Force in very large numbers to the Eastern Front. At the time this was not altogether clear to us at Fighter Command. Leigh-Mallory had written to me pointing out that our casualties in the sweeps were becoming such that he doubted if they were paying off. After thinking that over I wrote to Peter Portal, and I advanced the same doubts, and I asked for a review of the whole idea. As had happened when I had expressed my doubts before, the answer that I got from Portal was a balanced and wise appreciation of the whole situation. The important point that he emphasized was one

that Leigh-Mallory and I had already discussed: the value of our
offensive operations in helping the Russians.

The Germans had the bulk of their Air Force in operation on
their eastern front against the Russians. We immediately stepped
up our day offensive, with more bombers escorted by fighters
operating within the maximum reach of the latter. Large formations of fighters alone were also sent out over France. Our losses in
those operations during the next two and a half months were
admittedly heavy, although mere statistics did not give the complete picture. I have always felt that totting up the number of
aircraft shot down by either side and so trying to strike a balance
is a very shortsighted way of delivering judgment on the results of
an air operation. On the other hand, some indication of the
severity of our losses alone on these offensive operations can be
found in the figures of the casualties among our fighter pilots for
the year of 1941. Four hundred and twenty-six of my pilots were
killed, missing or taken prisoner, which was just slightly more than
the number of pilots killed in the Battle of Britain.

The advantages that we gained from these sweeps—advantages
which, for all the doubts that I had expressed, fully justified the
policy which had led to our going on to the offensive—have been
rather played down. It was good for the morale of the fighter
squadrons to be able to go on to the offensive, and it helped to
inculcate in them the offensive spirit. Our leaning into France put
us out over enemy-occupied territory. It has been reported that
the German Air Force rather welcomed that, and when I first heard
about this reaction there immediately came to my mind the
thought that their fathers had felt the same way in the First World
War. During those years between 1914 and 1918 we had spent by
far the greater part of our flying time on the Western Front
operating over the areas behind the German lines. Twenty-three
years later the pattern was the same, and it was that which enabled
us to attain air superiority.

The second important aspect was that these sweeps gave Fighter
Command invaluable experience in operating in large formations.
This was by no means an easy task, and it called for a great deal
of hard training and practice. It also prepared us for what was to
be done later in the invasion of Europe, when large formations of
fighters were employed in the air over the invasion area.

It was not long after we started our large-scale day fighter
operations out over France that I was very forcibly reminded of
my own experiences as a fighter pilot on the Western Front during

the First World War. The casualties among my pilots indicated that the Germans were by no means accepting our intrusion without offering some stern resistance, and there came to me a flow of reports about the rigorous fighting that was having to be faced by our pilots. There was one opinion that I could get which I thought might be of value, and I sent Bob Wright down to the airdrome at Ford, near Arundel, to have a talk with Gerald Maxwell, and to get his views.

An old friend of mine, and for a short time on my staff at Fighter Command headquarters, Gerald Maxwell had been a very successful fighter pilot in the earlier war, during which he had flown S.E.5a's in Jimmy McCudden's flight in No. 56 Squadron. We had worked together a great deal in our flying during those earlier days, and I valued his opinion as a tactician, which was why I had placed him in command of a special unit for testing on operations new aircraft and equipment. Maxwell and Wright knew each other well. They went to Tangmere and to its satellite airfield at Westhampnett, and they watched the fighters as they returned from operations, and they listened to the reports on what had been encountered. When Wright told me about what he had seen and heard, the story was almost identically the same as that which I had known as a young squadron commander in 1917. There was no questioning the morale of my pilots; but the opposition being faced by them did raise grave doubts about the quality of the aircraft with which we were asking them to fight.

As had happened almost throughout the first war, so I found in early 1941 that we and the enemy were on a seesaw over the performance of our fighters. By the early spring of that year the Germans had brought into use a new version of their well-tried fighter: the formidable Me.109f. With this they were able under certain critical conditions to outfight our Spitfires—the Hurricanes were already past their prime, and were being reserved for special tasks—and our pilots were not liking it in the sweeps which they were being called upon to make over the northern part of Occupied France, both alone and as escort for our bombers.

Trafford Leigh-Mallory had also spoken to me about this, complaining that our Spitfires were being outclassed in both speed and rate of climb. I had the whole problem most carefully examined by my technical staff, after whch I wrote officially to the Air Ministry, lodging a complaint about the technical inferiority of our fighters compared with those of the Luftwaffe. I asked that the performance of the Spitfire be improved; and I allowed myself what I thought was the justifiable liberty of making the comment that it seemed to me that in the matter of aircraft production quantity was being placed before quality.

In the tone of the official letters that a Commander-in-Chief has to write, there must always be a firm note of assurance; and it was in this vein, feeling confident of my own decision, that I always wrote to the Air Ministry. Peter Wykeham has commented about the temper of my letters at this time, bringing them into relation with the example set by Stuffy Dowding, and saying that "the Chief of the Air Staff may well have wondered if there was something in the air of Stanmore that produced this acid tone from those who sat in the chief office at Bentley Priory." Many years later Peter Portal was to tell Bob Wright that he had always found me, as one of his Commanders-in-Chief, particularly reasonable and ready to try and understand his point of view, which makes Wykeham's comment a little wide of the target. But if he had made it about the reaction to my views from the Minister of Aircraft Production, he would have scored a bull's-eye.

In speaking about the appointment on May 14, 1940, of Lord Beaverbrook as Minister of Aircraft Production, Jack Slessor has said that "Mr. Churchill's decision . . . was undoubtedly right." With that I entirely agree. Slessor then goes on to say: "There is, however, a rather widespread impression that this reorganisation and the appointment of Lord Beaverbrook came in the nick of time to bring about an industrial miracle and save this country from the disastrous consequences of the inefficiency of the Air Ministry. That is entirely untrue." With that I could not possibly agree more, and a great many other senior officers in the Royal Air Force at that time feel exactly the same way.

On June 3, 1940, Winston Churchill recorded in a minute to the Secretary of State for Air the comment: "Lord Beaverbrook has made a surprising improvement in the supply of aeroplanes, and in clearing up the muddle and scandal of the Aircraft Production branch." That was yet another unhappy example of Churchill's "genius for self-deception," as Jack Slessor has put it, as well as being a ridiculous and unfair remark to make on two counts. First, it was ridiculous because no one man could possibly have brought about such a change in the course of the mere three weeks during which he had been in office. And second, because it was quite wrong about and most unfair to the splendid work which was done by Wilfrid Freeman over a long period of time.

Wilfrid Freeman had taken over from Stuffy Dowding as Air Member for Research and Development at the Air Ministry on April 1, 1936, when the latter had gone to Stanmore to create

Fighter Command. Freeman's title had been changed to that of Air
Member for Development and Production on August 1, 1938. On
May 14, 1940, the Ministry of Aircraft Production was formed,
with Lord Beaverbrook as the Minister, from Freeman's department at the Air Ministry. Freeman remained with the Ministry
until November 1, 1940, right through the period of the Battle of
Britain.

Most of the invaluable work that Wilfrid Freeman did in the
equipping of the Royal Air Force was accomplished in the four
years prior to the formation of the Ministry of Aircraft Production,
and he was therefore the one responsible for the production of the
aircraft, the armament, and all kinds of equipment for the expansion of the R.A.F. from 1936 until well on into 1940; and for all
the fine work that he did then he deserves the highest praise. In
that period the eight-gun fighters, the Spitfire and the Hurricane,
were developed and produced, as was the all-important radar, and
plans were laid down for our great four-engined bombers.

The foundations for the production of the Hurricane and the
Spitfire were in being long before Lord Beaverbrook ever appeared
on the scene, and the answer to Winston Churchill's most unjust
accusation of "muddle and scandal" is to be found in the cold
figures recorded in the official history. There it is clearly revealed
that even before the creation of the Ministry, the production of
eight-gun fighters had already begun to soar. In April, 1940, the
planned production of fighters for the month was 231: the actual
production was 256. The planned production for the month of
May was 261: the actual production was 325. "As the substantial
rise in output during April and May indicates, some of the worst
production difficulties had already been overcome before the creation of the new Ministry," Denis Richards records. "And the
magnificent achievement of June, July and August was of course
the achievement of the aircraft industry as a whole . . ."

There has come about an unfortunate blurring of the credit for
this achievement which has dimmed the fine contribution that was
made by Lord Beaverbrook as well as by Air Chief Marshal Sir
Wilfrid Freeman in producing the aircraft which we needed for the
Battle of Britain, just as we owe to Stuffy Dowding so much for
having won, through the use that was made of those aircraft, the
battle itself.

We who were "bloody Air Marshals," as Lord Beaverbrook used
to refer to us, all had, from time to time, our differences and
disagreements with him, and the occasion upon which I was

subjected to my particular onslaught from him came over the letter that I had written to the Air Ministry about the performance of our fighters early in 1941. A few days after sending it off I was asked to go and see Lord Beaverbrook in his office at the Ministry of Aircraft Production. I had no idea what it was that he wanted to see me about, and when I was ushered into Beaverbrook's office I found him sitting in such a way that he seemed to be crouching behind his enormous desk. There were no papers whatsoever upon it, but there was a row of telephones of various colors in front of him, and to one side there was a battery of push buttons, also in different colors.

"Good morning, sir," I said as I entered the office.

My civil salutation met with nothing more than a glowering silence. Whipping open the top righthand drawer of his desk, Beaverbrook pulled out some sheets of paper, which he slapped down on the desk in front of me. "Did you write that?" he growled.

When I looked at the papers I saw that they were a copy of the letter that I had sent to the Air Ministry. "Yes," I said, "I wrote it."

That was just what was needed, apparently, to touch off the explosion. The little man started to roar and shout and wave his fists in the air, and for several minutes he set about roundly abusing me, Fighter Command, and everything to do with us. At first there was nothing that I could do but listen; but after a while I began to feel my own temperature rising. There were echoes in my mind, and this outburst sounded to me altogether too much like the political browbeating of the military about which I had heard so much but of which this was my first experience.

It takes a great deal to make me lose my temper and control of myself to the point where I make any physical demonstration; but the way in which Beaverbrook was going for me was stretching things, I began to feel, altogether too far. All said and done, I reminded myself, I was the Commander-in-Chief of Fighter Command, and a high-ranking officer in the Royal Air Force. But here, in the face of what I, as the completely informed and responsible commander, had stated in an official letter about a fact which we all knew was perfectly correct—that our fighters were inferior in performance to the German fighters of the day—I was being subjected to a humiliating display of extraordinarily bad temper.

But I knew that I was right, and there came into my mind one simple question. Why the hell should I take this outburst lying down? With that I promptly lost my temper. I went what felt like being red in the face, and started thumping Beaverbrook's desk with my fist and shouting back at him. It was all quite stupid. But there we were, a Cabinet minister and a Commander-in-Chief: each trying to shout the other down.

All of a sudden, and to my astonishment and even bewilderment, Beaverbrook threw himself back in his chair and lifted his head, and the shouts of anger gave way to an outburst of the extraordinary but infectious cackle of laughter which was characteristic of him. I was quite taken aback by this abrupt change, and thrown right off my stride. And then the little man started to play a fandango on the panel of multicolored pushbuttons at the side of his desk, which smartly brought into the office on the run a whole lot of rather frightened looking civil servants.

"Here is the Chief of Fighter Command," Beaverbrook announced. "He says that his fighters are not good enough. His boys are being shot down." He pointed to one poor wretch and demanded: "What are you doing about it?"

The unfortunate underling singled out for this interrogation started to make some stuttered explanation for which he promptly had his head bitten off. There were more stammered explanations all round, and no doubt many of them were perfectly valid ones; but Beaverbrook would have none of them. Angrily he told them all to go away and to improve without further delay the performance of the Spitfire, and with that the company shuffled out.

"I think you'll find it will be all right now," Beaverbrook said, and he smiled in the broad, cheerful way for which he was so well known.

A few days later E. W. (later Lord) Hives of Rolls-Royce ("H.S.," as he was known) came to see me in my office at Bentley Priory. Another of the unsung giants behind the scenes in our war effort, Hives was a genius in engineering while at the same time being one of the pleasantest men whom one could ever wish to know. He had joined Rolls-Royce back in 1908, only two years after the company had been formed, and when he was twenty-two years of age; and he was to remain with them for the next forty-eight years. He drove their first experimental cars and supervised much of the early development work that was done on their engines, and he was a loyal supporter of both Charles Rolls and Henry Royce. Hives contributed a great deal to the development of aero engines in the first war; and after the second war he was elevated to the peerage just before he, who had started with Rolls-Royce as a mechanic, became chairman of that world famous company.

In the quiet and modest way for which he was so well liked, Hives told me that he had heard that we were having trouble over the performance of the Spitfire. But for all his quietness of manner, Hives was always to the point in anything that he had to say, and I was able to speak to him with equal frankness. After I had stated our case, he asked me how I would like to have a certain very desirable increase in the power of the Merlin engine with which the Spitfire was equipped.

"What will be the effect on its performance?" I asked.

The answer given me by Hives was just what we wanted, and out of his assurance there came the Spitfire V, which proved as soon as we started using it that it was fully capable of taking care of the latest Messerschmitt being flown by the Germans.

During the few hectic minutes of my altercation with Lord Beaverbrook, one of the points about which I had felt most strongly, and which had made me so angry, was that, whether he at first realized it or not, we were arguing about the lives of my pilots. That might have been the point which hit home hardest with Beaverbrook, and which caused him to do such a rapid about-face in his attitude toward me. It was not until after I had left his office and I was on the way back to Stanmore that I suddenly thought of this point and realized that, without intending it, I had scored very heavily. Beaverbrook's own son, Max (now Sir Max) Aitken, was at that time one of my pilots in Fighter Command, although he was no longer with the day fighters.

Known for quite a long time to so many as "Young Max," Beaverbrook's son was a fighter pilot molded in the finest tradition as well as being a chip off the old block. Only just before he died in 1964, Beaverbrook paid a public tribute to young Max which I felt had in it a perception that was both acute and very touching. In the course of a published interview he was asked:

"What are you most proud of in your life?"

"Well, I'm very proud of my son," Beaverbrook replied. "He's a fine fellow."

The interviewer then recorded that "the mood instantly changes from gay to sad," with Beaverbrook adding: "He's a nicer man than ever I was. A much, much nicer man."

A measure of the feeling that Max Aitken had, in turn, for his father was revealed shortly after the death of Lord Beaverbrook. In an agreeably commendable fashion, Aitken renounced the title which he had inherited, and it was not done for any political

motives. His explanation was simply that so far as he was concerned there could be only one Lord Beaverbrook.

While I knew by name many of the fighter pilots who had
achieved so much in their fighting during the Battle of Britain, and
some of them I had even come to know personally, it was not until
I became the Commander-in-Chief of Fighter Command that I felt
that I was able to make myself known more fully to them. Among
those who had impressed me while I was still at the Air Ministry
were both Max Aitken and Whitney Straight.

Born in Canada, Max Aitken bore, even as a young man, a
strong resemblance in appearance to his father. But for all the
position that Lord Beaverbrook was able to assure him, young
Aitken was never satisfied with merely sitting back in the mighty
Fleet Street shadow of his father, and he made his own way,
particularly in flying in a manner that was uniquely his own. At
Cambridge he had made a name for himself as a footballer and a
golfer, and he had joined the Auxiliary Air Force in July, 1935,
becoming a pilot in No. 601 Squadron. But service in the squadron
was not the only flying that he did during those years. Piloting an
aircraft of his own, he flew a great deal in the United States, and
also over most of Europe.

The company with which Max Aitken was associated in No.
601 Squadron was of a nature that was flamboyant and gay, and
indeed reckless, and as harum-scarum in some ways as the Service
has ever known. They were a happy band of playboys; but when
the heat was on, they became in the most effortless fashion one of
the most gallant and courageous of our fighting squadrons. Just
before the outbreak of war, No. 601 Squadron was re-equipped
with twin-engined Blenheims. On September 3, 1939, the first day
of the war, Max Aitken flew with the squadron from Biggin Hill on
its first operational patrol over the Channel.

In the new year of 1940, No. 601 Squadron was moved from
Biggin Hill to Tangmere and again re-equipped, this time with
single-engined Hurricanes. When it was arranged in May, 1940,
for half-squadrons to go to France to help out, No. 601 was one of
those called upon to contribute a flight, which was to fly from the
airfield at Merville. There was in that a strong personal appeal for
me because one of the young pilots in No. 601 Squadron was a
youngster named William Rhodes-Moorhouse. In 1915 his father,
as enthusiastic an amateur airman then as his son was to become
later, had been my pilot for a while in No. 2 Squadron when I first
became an observer in the Royal Flying Corps, and we had flown

together in our B.E.2's from Merville. The father had died winning the first Victoria Cross ever awarded to an airman.

By June, 1940, only a couple of weeks after Lord Beaverbrook had become Minister of Aircraft Production, Max Aitken was in command of No. 601 Squadron. Within days he was demonstrating his ability in night as well as day fighting, in which he had already started scoring, by shooting down a Heinkel 111 at about midnight. He led the squadron with gusto into the Battle of Britain, and he was awarded a Distinguished Flying Cross. He was also to know to the full, as I had, the meaning of personal loss in combat.

William Rhodes-Moorhouse had become Max Aitken's closest friend in No. 601 Squadron, and he was one of Aitken's flight commanders. They had done a great deal of flying together all over Europe before the war. "He was an exceptional pilot and a delightful companion," Aitken has said. They shared an interest in golf, and Rhodes-Moorhouse was so good at skiing that, as Aitken has put it, "he could have easily skied for England if he had so wished."

Of the spirit shown by Rhodes-Moorhouse in his fighting in the air, Max Aitken has commented: "I was always worried by his utter disregard for his own life." It was that gallant disregard which was to lead Rhodes-Moorhouse to his death, just as had happened in the case of his father twenty-five years before. He had already won a Distinguished Flying Cross, and he was a very experienced combat pilot. Right in the thick of the Battle of Britain he attacked one day an Me. 109. "Although he knew he was being fired at from behind he continued to press his attack home," Aitken has recalled. "He shot the Messerschmitt down, but in turn was killed before he could turn." The sense of loss felt by the members of No. 601 Squadron in 1940 must have been exactly the same as that which we had known in No. 2 Squadron when this young pilot's father had died after pressing home his attack in the same way in 1915. They did indeed share in the air the poet's commendation: *Dulce et decorum est pro patria mori.*

From the rough and tumble of the air battle, Max Aitken found himself transferred to a desk in the Directorate of Operations at the Air Ministry, and it was at a meeting there in the autumn, while I was still Deputy Chief of the Air Staff, that I first met him. Under the chairmanship of Wilfrid Freeman a conference was arranged at which the more experienced and rather older fighter pilots who had fought in the Battle of Britain were called upon to

discuss which type of new aircraft we should develop for use in
night fighting.

A few weeks before this, Adolf Galland, who had fought hard
against us in the Battle of Britain, had been asked by Hermann
Goering what he required most in the way of new equipment.
"Some Spitfires," Galland replied, thereby shocking even Goering
into an angry silence.

At our conference at the Air Ministry, one of the redoubtable
Atcherley twins came up with much the same idea in reverse.
When he was asked for his views about which aircraft we should
use for night fighters he suggested the twin-engined Messerschmitt
110. The difference between the German reaction to Galland's
sharp comment—which he later described in a rather stiff-necked
way as "such brazen-faced impudence"—and ours at the Air
Ministry to that made by Atcherley provides a good illustration of
the difference between the nature of the basic humor of the
Germans and the British. The Germans were angry with Galland.
At the Air Ministry we guffawed at Atcherley, and there was
chalked up to his credit another of the remarks that were so typical
of him.

Even before I left the Air Ministry, I had known that there was
going to be a need for a careful selection of the right type of man
to take command of the radar-equipped night fighter squadrons. It
was going to call for specialists in a type of flying about which we
still knew very little. After I got to Fighter Command I could not
help feeling, in its own amusing way, the subtle pressure to get
these appointments that was brought to bear by experienced young
pilots who were sitting behind desks at the Air Ministry. Men such
as "Zulu" (now Air Marshal Sir Douglas) Morris—a South
African who is now himself commander-in-chief of Fighter Command—and Max Aitken, to name only two, made determined
efforts to get back to flying, and this time at night. I welcomed
them to Fighter Command, and early in 1941, after having been
off operational flying for six months, Aitken took over No. 68
Squadron, which he was to command for the next two years on
night flying operations from Coltishall, in East Anglia.

There was always a friendly rivalry between the day and the
night fighters. They flew from the same airfields, and they shared
the same mess life, the day fighters handing over to the night fighters at dusk, and, in turn, coming back on to the job at dawn. But
they were of quite different temperaments, and they thought and
worked in different ways. Max Aitken was one of the few who
adapted himself to, and did well in, both spheres.

But that was only the beginning of the wide and varied experience as an operational pilot that Max Aitken was to gain in the equally varied commands which lay ahead for me. With the various changes of command that I was to make during the rest of the war, there always came a prompt request from Aitken for a posting to my new command. Long afterward Bob Wright asked him why he had always shown such a firm wish to serve with me.

"Because Sholto was the one man who could always be relied upon for decisions," Aitken replied.

25 / Swings and Roundabouts

IT WAS OUT OF the question that we should let the public know anything at all about the progress that we were making in our various uses of radar. It was then our great secret that had to be kept a secret, for it was one of our most effective weapons, but its use was shared with us by the Army and the Royal Navy. There were many of these uses; but the most spectacular was the way in which it finally turned the trick for our night fighters.

In giving to the public the story of our successes in the air, or as much of the story as we could give them, we had to be sure that we did not reveal anything of our secret, and the official subterfuge that was employed had one amusing side effect. We could not very well explain that the real reason for the success that came to John Cunningham, the first of the outstandingly successful night fighter pilots, was due to the way in which he and C. F. (Jimmy) Rawnsley—his prewar gunner in the Auxiliary Air Force who had learned how to handle the new weapon—had used their heads and became an expert team in the use of airborne radar. As a cover-up, a story was put out for public consumption that Cunningham had exceptional night vision, and as a result of that he promptly became known in the press and to the public as "Cat's Eyes" Cunningham. In fact, Cunningham's vision was no more than average, and the nickname which became attached to him and which has continued to this day is something which he detested right from the start.

Through my long association with the De Havilland people— Hereward de Havilland had been my pilot for a time on the Western Front in the early days of the First World War, and I had known Geoffrey de Havilland for many years—and my own high hopes for airborne radar, it was of interest to me to find that John Cunningham, who was then only twenty-four years of age and who looked even younger, was so enthusiastically at work as one of the pilots in No. 604 Squadron. He was even then a thoroughgoing

professional airman, having studied at the De Havilland Technical
School and learned to fly with them, and he had become one of
their test pilots before the outbreak of war. After the war, when
Cunningham returned to De Havilland's, the interests that we
shared continued through the work that was done by him in
developing both the Comet and the Trident for British European
Airways.

It was John Cunningham's professionalism as an airman and
Jimmy Rawnsley's enthusiasm and skill as a radar operator which
enabled this team to produce the results with airborne radar that
we had been hoping for, and their success was to pave the way for
the success of many other teams. That was also helped along when
we introduced the new and powerful Beaufighter, although at first
it won for itself the reputation of being unmanageable. But Cunningham proved that while it certainly called for sound and shrewd
handling by the pilot, it was nevertheless a very effective aircraft,
and that its armament of four cannon and six machine guns provided it with a devastating fire-power.

With Jimmy Rawnsley handling the magic of the radar night
vision, John Cunningham set about the enemy raiders in a fashion
that gladdened the hearts of those of us who had pinned our faith
in the radar-equipped night fighter. The faults from equipment that
all too often produced squints which had the pilot looking anywhere but where he should have been looking were largely
resolved by the scientists; and there was overcome the early
tendency of the sets to give up and hide shamefacedly in clouds of
smoke. The radar operators learned how to manipulate the sets
and how to cooperate with their pilots by telling them in a succinct
fashion what was to be seen and how to get at their airborne
targets. The crews of No. 604 Squadron in particular began to
produce results, but there were also others who were beginning to
go about this new trade in an effective fashion.

Early in the new year, with Jimmy Rawnsley now fully trained
and settled down as his navigator, John Cunningham began to step
up his rate of scoring, and with the increased efficiency in the
assistance of radar control from the ground he was able to help
greatly, along with the others who were also beginning to score, in
the formulation of more definite tactics in this new and largely
scientific business of night fighting. Hermann Goering was still
confident that the German Air Force could bomb us into surrendering, and they continued with their heavy raids on this
country; but the toll exacted by our night fighters was beginning to

tell. During the month of January they had managed to shoot down only three of the enemy raiders, and in February only four. But by the end of March the total for the month was twenty-two; and for April it was forty-eight. And during May they destroyed ninety-six, and that total did not take into account those enemy raiders which were damaged or probably destroyed.

The progress made in the use of airborne radar during those early months of 1941 was something in the nature of a sudden spurt, and it was in an altogether new venture in the business of fighting in the air. Calling on his own firsthand experience as a fighter pilot, Peter Wykeham has written of night fighting: "It was not face-to-face combat, but from the pilot it demanded a higher standard of skill and a far greater degree of patience, cunning, imagination and delicacy of touch. The radar navigator was a new creature altogether, combining the concentration and skill needed to wring the last ounce from his capricious apparatus."

With the night fighters coming into their own, there were the usual requests from various officials, both Service and civil, to be allowed to see how this new magic was being performed. We warded off most of these requests as best we could, but there was one which we would never have thought of trying to brush aside. The greatly improved performance of the night fighters led His Majesty King George VI to ask to be allowed to see at first hand how they were operating, and on the night of May 7 we were able to provide him with an unexpectedly good and complete view of how it was all done. It would have been well in the routine course of events if His Majesty had had to stay where we took him for nights on end with nothing happening; but such was the unwitting cooperation of the Germans that a ringside seat was provided for him in what we all came to call a Command Performance.

When I was told that His Majesty had asked to be taken to one of the night fighter squadrons, I arranged that he should go to Middle Wallop and spend the night there with No. 604 Squadron. As a result of the keen interest that Bill Elliott had shown in matters of night air defense during the time when he had been an assistant secretary in the Cabinet offices I had asked for him, and I had sent him to Middle Wallop as the station commander. I was told that Winston Churchill had been rather cross about losing Elliott's services, but he could not very well stand in the way of his Service career, and Elliott had been doing valuable work at Middle Wallop in urging on the development of night fighter tactics. He was a highly qualified pilot—during the First World War he had won a Distinguished Flying Cross—and he was particularly good at picking the right men, which was one of the reasons why, after a great deal of varied experience as a senior commander during the war, he was to become the first postwar Commander-in-Chief of Fighter Command.

During the late afternoon and early evening, the King was taken by us around Middle Wallop on a more or less formal inspection of the station and No. 604 Squadron. He was able to meet the pilots and navigators, and for a while he talked with Cunningham and Rawnsley. Immediately after that the squadron went to readiness for the night's operations, and the first aircraft were taking off for their patrols as we drove off by car to take the King by road to one of the ground radar stations from which the aircraft were to be controlled.

The station, which was one of our best, was at Sopley, in southern Hampshire. It was run with outstanding skill by Squadron Leader J. L. Brown, who was known to everybody as Brownie, and who was as much of a genius as a controller with the radar on the ground as Rawnsley was with it in the air. After only a very brief description of what he and his airmen and airwomen were doing, and the equipment with which they had to work, Brown pointed out to us that a blip had just come up on the large cathode ray tube of his radar set which indicated that an aircraft was on the way in.

On that particular night the Germans sent in their bombers for raids on the Midlands. Their force had been considerably reduced through withdrawals from the west for operations on their forthcoming eastern front, but they nevertheless sent over 166 aircraft to bomb Liverpool and Birkenhead, and 72 to attack Hull. At Sopley we were watching one of the first to appear.

"It's a bandit," Brown said. "John Cunningham's up there. I'll put him on to it."

The approaching enemy aircraft was still well out to sea, and through the instructions that he gave on the radio, Brown had time in which to maneuver John Cunningham into the right position, and at the same time to explain to the King what he was doing. I began to feel that it was all too good to be true. After some minutes we heard Cunningham's voice state over the radio that they had radar contact; and from that moment on, Brown was silent, and all we did on the ground was stand and watch the two blips on the cathode ray tube. They began to come closer together as Rawnsley guided Cunningham in toward their target. They were still over the sea when they had picked up the enemy aircraft on their own radar, and since there was a bright moon behind them, and shining on the sea, Cunningham made a cautious approach so as not to be seen by any German rear gunner who might be on the alert. He caught sight of his target, but he waited until they were both just over the coast, and less likely to be spotted against the darkness of the ground, before he closed in for his attack.

By then they were not very far from where we were watching the whole affair on the radar set at Sopley. There was a marked tenseness in the atmosphere as we stood gathered around Brown, and we watched intently as the two blips moved across the cathode ray tube. Several minutes passed, and then suddenly Brown suggested that we should all step outside and see for ourselves what was about to happen. Just as we did that, the sound of aircraft engines was interrupted by the thunder of cannon as Cunningham opened fire, and in the sky not very far to the west of where we were standing we saw an aircraft coming down in flames.

We drove back to Middle Wallop, and when we got to the mess, in which there was an excited gathering, we found John Cunningham waiting there for us. He was able to give the King a detailed report of the way in which he had shot down the enemy bomber, a Heinkel 111, which was his twelfth victory. It was a rare experience for a Commander-in-Chief to be able to set before the King such an impressive demonstration of his wares.

Although by May, 1941, the Germans had moved quite large numbers of their bombers from France to the Balkans and to their eastern front in preparation for the attack that they were to make on Russia, they continued to mount heavy night raids against this country. In addition to the problems with which we were faced in our defense against that bombing, we also had a great deal of detail to attend to in our planning for the daylight offensive operations, which were by this time in full swing. Part of the activities of my day fighters was in escorting our bombers in their daylight raids over France; but there had developed some conflict over the purposes of these "circuses," as they were called.

In the joint effort that we were making to operate out over France, Bomber Command believed that the primary object was to smash up the invasion bases on the French coast, and to put the Germans on the defensive. We at Fighter Command looked upon the presence of the bombers more as bait to lure the German fighters into a battle. It was not long before being considered merely as bait led Bomber Command to make a somewhat natural objection, and it took a meeting between the two commands and an Air Ministry decision before the idea of the "Circus" operation was more clearly defined as an effort to force the Germans to fight under conditions that were favorable to our fighters, with our bombers inflicting enough damage to make it impossible for the Germans not to retaliate.

In addition to that, we had also been sending over France for some time large formations of our fighters on high level sweeps, as well as continuing with the use of our fighters on low-level attacks against ground targets. These were both further developments of the flying which I had done in single-engined fighters in the First World War, so that in all my thinking I had a fair background of firsthand experience upon which to rely in arriving at any decisions now that I was a Commander-in-Chief.

After spending Saturday morning of May 10 in my office, I had lunch at my flat on Stanmore Hill, and then I went up to London. Ronald Squire, the actor, who was an old friend of mine, had arranged for us to go to the theater, and we saw the play *No Time for Comedy,* starrring Lilli Palmer and Rex Harrison. I was back at Bentley Priory by late afternoon, and I was then greeted with the news that the German beams had come on. The target for that night was London.

The attack on the capital of Saturday night, May 10, was to be the last heavy raid that London had to face. For seven hours in bright moonlight, over five hundred German bombers did their damnedest in an all-out attack, and they inflicted a great deal of damage. But so far as I was concerned, that night was to provide an experience that had nothing to do with that raid, and which, as it unfolded, rather overshadowed what was happening to London.

From eleven o'clock onward the activity at my headquarters at Bentley Priory was intense. There was the heavy raid on London which most of those on duty had to contend with; and it was the night upon which Rudolf Hess made his astonishing flight from Germany to Scotland. Such was the general activity that I was in the crowded and busy underground operations room myself from late evening until somewhere between five and six o'clock the next morning; and since we were intimately concerned with what happened as it was going on, I was in the exceptionally good position of being able to obtain as full a picture as anybody of the whole of the Hess escapade.

Not long after it became dark, radar plots began to go down on our filter room table—plots which were passed immediately to the operations room table—of the track of an aircraft that was behaving in an entirely different way from the others which were being seen. It had come out from Holland, and it was heading in a northwesterly direction across the North Sea. Since all the other tracks of the raiders were heading for London and none was heading for the north of England, this one stood out like a sore thumb. At first it was watched with an interest that was more of perplexity than anything. It continued across the North Sea in the direction of the south of Scotland, apparently heading for the mouth of the Forth, and as it approached the coast, the radar people in Northumberland reported that from their responses it was definitely a single aircraft.

The behavior and the speed of this one lone aircraft were presenting us with a mystifying picture, and when it came in over the coast and continued on across Scotland to the south of Edinburgh, I asked for a report from the Observer Corps in that area. They came back with the information that they had spotted it, and that it was an Me. 110. Identifying an aircraft like that at night sounded like an extremely good effort on their part, but for two reasons the claim seemed to me to be suspect. I knew that the Me. 110 did not carry enough fuel for a long flight from Germany, or even from France, to Scotland and back to wherever it came from; and I felt that being able to recognize such a small high-flying aircraft at night was a most extraordinary feat. I asked for a check on the report, and the Observer Corps came back with the confirmation that it was definitely an Me. 110, and that they had recognized the silhouette against bright moonlight.

The German aircraft continued to be plotted by the Observer Corps as it flew westward across Scotland, and shortly after eleven o'clock, just as the main onslaught started on London, we received a report that it had crashed some miles to the southwest of Glasgow. This report was followed almost immediately by another stating that the pilot had bailed out. About two hours after that there came a telephoned report that the aircraft which had crashed was indeed an Me. 110, and that the pilot who had bailed out was being held a prisoner.

The intense activity of the German raid that had by now built up over London, and the need to get as many of our night fighters into the air as possible, banished from my mind for a while the information about that German aircraft and its pilot in Scotland. We had both single-engined fighters—one of which, a Hurricane, was flown by Whitney Straight—and the radar-equipped Beaufighters in the air. Tom Pike, who is now a Marshal of the Royal

Air Force and a former Chief of the Air Staff, was on patrol in a Beaufighter of the squadron which he was then commanding, and he made a radar interception of a Heinkel coming in and blasted it out of the sky. Other successful combats were also being reported, and I began to feel that at last our fighting in the air at night was about to come into its own.

About an hour or so went by, and then my attention was diverted from the battle over London by a report from Scotland that had us all gasping with astonishment. I was told that the pilot who had bailed out of the Me. 110 was claiming that he was Rudolf Hess, and that he was asking to see the Duke of Hamilton.

It all sounded so incredible, and I found the story impossible to believe; but there was one step that I could take which would quickly sort it all out. The Duke of Hamilton was at that time a wing commander in the Auxiliary Air Force, and he was serving as the sector commander at one of my fighter stations at Turnhouse, near Edinburgh. I got through to Hamilton on the phone, and I talked with him in his operations room about what had happened. I asked him if he knew Rudolf Hess. He told me that he did not know him. I asked Hamilton to drive over immediately to see this man who was claiming to be Hess, and to report back to me if he had anything worth saying. The hours dragged by, and finally there came a phone call from Hamilton. He said that he had seen the man, and that he might be Hess, but he could not be sure, although the prisoner certainly looked like the Nazi leader.

With this added information I then had the whole incident reported, in the early hours of the morning of Sunday, May 11, to our intelligence people at the Air Ministry. They in turn consulted an official at the Foreign Office, who suggested that Hamilton should fly down to London as soon as possible and make a personal report to the Foreign Office. Hamilton did that; his report was in the hands of the Foreign Office later that day, and on the Sunday evening he reported to Winston Churchill. For some reason which is still not clear to me, the Foreign Office took no effective action for the best part of twenty-four hours; and at the time I got the impression that they seemed to think that the whole affair was something in the nature of a mare's nest.

It was not until the morning of Monday, May 12, that, as has been revealed by Sir Ivone Kirkpatrick, the Foreign Office began to take action. But even Kirkpatrick, who had known Hess before the war, and who came to play such an important part in the affair,

later made the comment that "the Hess episode was comedy from
the beginning to the end." He also admitted, in a nonchalant
fashion, that a long period of time did indeed elapse before the
Foreign Office got on with the job of finding out what it was that
had led Hess to making his flight to this country.

Winston Churchill said of this weird incident: "I never attached
any serious importance to this escapade." In addition to his view
on what he called the "comedy" of the incident, Ivone Kirkpatrick
stated: "Hess was a simple, stupid soul with a strong streak of
fanaticism and some eccentricity." I cannot feel that there was
ever anything at all funny about the Hess episode. Nor can I agree
with the view that Hess was nothing more than a stupid man. No
one could be stupid who could prepare so carefully and make so
skillfully the long flight—most of it at night, and doing all his own
navigation as well as flying a complicated twin-engined fighter—
that Hess did in that Me. 110 from the airfield in Augsburg, in
southern Germany, to within only a few miles of his objective in
Scotland.

There can be no doubt that Hess was quite often muddled in his
thinking, as well as fanatical in his outlook; and he apparently
suffered from more delusions than were normal for even a Nazi
leader. The reason for his flight—it was the fourth attempt that he
had made at it—is proof of that: he thought that he personally
could negotiate a peace. As with the others who were convicted at
Nuremberg, in the official consideration that I was later called
upon to give to the appeals against the sentences I had to weigh up
carefully the state of Rudolf Hess's mind, and one of the features
about that which I had to consider very carefully was that he had
moments when he was bright enough to hold his own in the company of some pretty thoroughgoing and quick-witted scoundrels.
But Hess undoubtedly went through periods when he was de-
ranged; and that was something that I also had to bear in mind in
my personal consideration of his case.

The Hess affair was the cause of great embarrassment to Hitler.
He gave orders that if Hess ever reappeared in Germany he was to
be shot, and he replaced him as the deputy leader of the Nazi
Party with Martin Bormann, whom William Shirer has described
as "a more sinister and conniving character." For Hermann Goering, who was summoned by Hitler to Berchtesgaden, it was as
agitating an affair as it was astonishing to me in London. Adolf
Galland has spoken of it as "one of the most mysterious affairs of
the war." He has described in some detail the way in which Goer-

ing telephoned him, and how he was ordered to take off with all his fighters and stop Hess, who, Goering stated, "has gone mad and is flying to England in an Me. 110. He must be brought down." Galland commented after receiving this order from Goering that he was far from sure about just who it was had gone mad.

In the course of the few weeks that followed the flight of Rudolf Hess from Germany, decisions were made by the Nazi leaders which had far-reaching effects, and which were to result in the evidence that was presented at the war crimes trials at Nuremberg being so shocking in its nature and so overwhelming in its effect. During May and early June, Hitler and his henchmen completed their plans for the German attack on Russia. By then, their interest in trying to crush us had subsided, at least for the moment, and the bombing of this country slackened off as the time approached for the opening of their onslaught on the Eastern Front.

After the big raid on London on May 10 there was only one other sizeable raid on this country for that year of 1941. It was on Birmingham, six days later. With that the Blitz virtually came to an end. During the time of its operation—between September 7, 1940, and May 16, 1941—London had received by far the heaviest blows: seventy-one major raids by the bombers of the German Air Force.

When the Germans called off the Blitz, they nevertheless continued with their offensive operations over this country, although with smaller and more irregular raids. The main force of their bombers had by then been moved to the east for use against the Russians. But our night fighters were getting into their stride, and they were shooting down the enemy raiders in enough numbers to prove that we were on the right path, and that we had at last got the answer. It was of comfort to all those on the ground when the Blitz did come to an end, and one of the reasons for our existence was to help in providing that comfort. But it was a little hard on the enthusiasm of the air crews who had worked so hard to bring this entirely new and involved and highly technical business of night fighting to the pitch where we could be assured of a reasonable success. Just as we thought that victory in a broad sense was within our grasp, Hitler withdrew the bulk of his bombers, and for the enthusiasts the targets became scarce.

Quite early in the evil planning for that brutal attack on Russia, and a good six months before it took place, Hitler had stated: "In view of the present political developments and especially Russia's interference in Balkan affairs, it is necessary to eliminate at all costs the last enemy remaining on the Continent before coming to grips with Britain." The military elimination of Russia was one thing; but the brutal annihilation of the people of that country which—as we were later to learn—the Nazis had in mind was something altogether different.

"I know that the necessity for such means of waging war is beyond the comprehension of you generals," Hitler told the senior officers of the German armed forces. "German soldiers guilty of breaking international law . . . will be excused. Russia has not participated in the Hague Convention and therefore has no rights under it."

It was this statement that was to become of such importance in the proceedings at Nuremberg because it posed a vitally important question. Should all the German soldiers, sailors and airmen, and any others involved in aggression and war crimes, have blindly obeyed the orders given them by Hitler to commit these war crimes, or should they have observed the dictates of their consciences? They chose to obey Hitler, and the results were as frightening as anything that has occurred in the long history of mankind. "The ruthlessness of the German treatment of the occupied territories in the east was not fortuitous," the historian Alan Bullock has pointed out; "it was part of a methodical system of exploitation and resettlement planned in advance and entered upon with a full appreciation of its consequences."

The German attack on Russia was launched in the German fashion, without any of the customary warnings—although it was generally anticipated by us and by the Americans—at four o'clock in the morning of June 22. A month later, Hitler's Chief of Staff, Field-Marshal Wilhelm Keitel, issued in the Nazi leader's name an order calling for "the spreading of such terror by the occupying forces as is alone appropriate to eradicate every inclination to resist amongst the population."

In all the terror that was let loose, Hermann Goering was one of those who deliberately planned it and saw to its execution both on the ground and in the air. The days of the strength of the Luftwaffe were past, but Goering, for all his waning interest in it, still maintained the posture of being the head of his Air Force. He even told Tim Pile, who talked with Goering while he was on trial at Nuremberg after the war, that, to quote Pile, "he had flown over London in the First World War and again in this, and that, thanks to me, the second time was a very unpleasant journey." While I grant, from my personal experience of flying against him in the first war, that Goering was a dashing enough young fighter pilot, there is no evidence whatsoever to support the truth of his statement about having flown over London in either of the wars. By the middle of the second war Goering's mind was already swamped with the self-delusions which were so marked a feature of the Nazi leaders and their way of thought.

A few weeks before the Blitz came to an end, and a couple of months before the Germans launched their attack on Russia, one of the visitors to Bentley Priory whom I was particularly glad to see was General H. H. Arnold, the Chief of Staff of the United States Army Air Corps. Hap Arnold was in England for general discussions with the Royal Air Force, and we were under orders to speak openly and frankly with him, and to show him everything. This genial and forthright character and pioneer airman had to his credit the unique honor of actually having been taught to fly—he was one of the very first of the U.S. Army officers to learn—by the Wright brothers as far back as 1911.

Through this early association with them, Hap Arnold knew both Wilbur and Orville Wright very well, and in speaking of the discussions which took place in those very early days of flying he revealed that there were in the natures of these two men qualities which I have known well in the pioneers in flying in this country. "Their presence in the hangar always made the sessions different," he once stated about the Wright brothers. "Despite their mild, retiring way of listening until everyone else had made his speech about this incident or that phenomenon, or what the exact future of an air development would be, you always felt them there. They were usually so courteous, almost diffident, really. Wilbur, for example, often hesitated to give an opinion without first consulting the little black note-book of aeronautical data he always carried with him."

In the long course of his career as a military airman, Hap Arnold had been at the center of all the quarrels, and being passionately devoted to the air he had known all the frustrations to which the American air service had been subjected. They would appear to have been even more irritating and stupid than all that we had known. At the time of his first visit to my headquarters, he was a major general, but he was dressed, being a neutral, as a civilian, and he was accompanied by his aide, Major Elwood ("Pete") Quesada.

While of a younger generation, Pete Quesada had already made quite a name for himself as an American Air Force pilot, and in the course of the next eighteen months he was to rocket up in rank in the American service from major to major general. After the war he was to play a big part in American civil aviation during the time when I was chairman of British European Airways.

Our American visitors made it quite clear to us that they were fully aware of what Fighter Command had achieved in the Battle of Britain only a few months before, and of that Arnold was later to write: "In many ways, in all history there was never such a battle fought. It was not only the first all-air battle in the world, it was perhaps the most epic. Suddenly, the inept, the pursued, became the foxy killers; not merely the defenders, but the hunters. Air Marshal Dowding's long, mousy preparations, the great warning system, the movements of fighters back from base to base as the South England dromes were bombed out, the air-ground control system, the tireless morale of the British pilots, their skill and courage, and the Spits and Hurricanes, paid off. At the peak of its triumph, Goering's Luftwaffe was suddenly demoralized—not merely out-fought, but out-thought."

If Hap Arnold's assessment is not altogether as accurate as one would have wished for, and his choice of words sounds at times a little strange to our ears, there is nevertheless generosity and sincerity in his tribute. He did not hesitate to express the same genuine feelings when he first came to see us at that time when America was not yet in the war. In talking with him I found him eager to benefit as much as he could from the actual experiences of the fighting in which we were engaged in the air.

"After the Battle of Britain, we rushed more air officers to Britain to learn everything we could," Arnold said later. From that time on he pressed even harder for the creation of the training system which eventually enabled the Americans to get into a position where, to quote him again, and to indicate the vast scale of their planning, "before the war was over, in 1945, we were graduating pilots at the rate of 105,000 a year."

In view of the difficulties that were later to develop over the conflict of ideas which came to be held by the Americans and by us in the use that should be made of the air, it is of particular value to consider Hap Arnold's opinion of Peter Portal, our own Chief of the Air Staff, and his opposite number. "He was one of the most brilliant of the British Chiefs of Staff," Arnold stated. "He had a remarkably agile and logical mind. He was far-sighted in his military planning, and on the many problems we had in common we worked extremely well together."

Of the way in which Peter Portal conducted himself in the tussles which our Chiefs of Staff had with the Prime Minister, and about which so much has been written, it is also of interst to have the opinion of someone who was on the outside. Hap Arnold was able to speak from the personal experience of seeing them in action. "Portal handled himself brilliantly," he stated, "and was able to hold his own in the conversation with the Prime Minister, in spite of the many quips the Prime Minister made, either seriously, or in a joking way, about the Air Force."

The Royal Air Force was not altogether ignorant of the ways of the Americans as individuals. We had known them well in the first war, and as early as October, 1940, while I was still at the Air Ministry, we had decided to form separate fighter squadrons with pilots from among those Americans who had volunteered for service in the R.A.F. Just as there had been those who had seen fit to come over and join the Royal Flying Corps in the First World War, so there were eager young Americans who could not wait once the second war had started, and there were some who were with us early enough to see action in the Battle of Britain. One of them was Billy Fiske, who, like Whitney Straight, came from a well-known and wealthy New York family, and who had been up at Cambridge. He volunteered for service with the R.A.F. two weeks after the war broke out. By July, 1940, he was flying under Max Aitken's command in No. 601 Squadron and in time for action in the Battle of Britain. He was killed during the course of the battle while flying from Tangmere.

Among the other Americans there were three who came to us after making unsuccessful attempts to join the French Air Force, and although the United States Embassy in London was discouraging American citizens, who were neutrals, from getting mixed up in the war, they found their way into the R.A.F. and flew in the Battle of Britain with No. 609 Squadron. They survived the battle, and they were the first three pilots in the all-American squadron formed by us.

This first Eagle Squadron, as we officially named it, was in operation under my command by March, 1941. By November of that year we had three Eagle Squadrons in operation, Nos. 71, 121 and 133, and by the time in September, 1942, that they left us to become part of the United States Army Air Forces, they had seventy-three enemy aircraft destroyed to their credit. They had also had their own casualties, and by then the first three founder members of that first Eagle Squadron were all dead.

Right from the beginning I had heard rumors from the R.A.F. station where the Americans were working up their first Eagle Squadron to an operational status that they were a pretty wild lot. Our station commander there, a regular officer in the R.A.F., was a giant of a man, well over six feet in height and built to match it; and I had heard that his method of dealing with the frisky new-comers when they got out of hand was to reach out and take them by the scruff of their necks and bang their heads together. In the circumstances that seemed to me to be fair enough. I recalled my own experiences in coping with the exuberance of the Americans when I had had them serving under me in my squadrons in the first war, and I knew that that was just the sort of treatment that they understood. It got results, and that was what mattered. When Hap Arnold came on to see me, after visiting the Eagle Squadron, he had no comments to make about the way in which the Americans were being treated, so I gathered that everything had gone off quietly enough.

After showing our visitors around our headquarters, I took them on to the airdrome at Northolt, which was one of our main fighter stations for the defense of London. Just as we got there one of the fighter squadrons was scrambled to intercept some intruders. It was almost as if the whole thing was being stage-managed, but I was able to assure Arnold that it was the real thing. That was quite enough to bring a gleam into his eyes, and of the experience he later wrote: "That afternoon gave me detailed, inside information about what air defence really meant—something we in the United States had been getting piece-meal."

One of the other squadrons then stationed at Northolt was No. 601, and I took Hap Arnold over to their dispersal hut on the edge of the airfield, and I introduced all the pilots to him. They then did a demonstration scramble for him, taking off in formation. When we got to the operations room a few minutes later, Arnold shook everybody by asking if he could speak to the squadron over the radio as they went about their patrol. I agreed, and Arnold said a few crisp words of thanks and good wishes. As I listened I wondered what the Germans, who monitored all our radio com-munications, would make of that, and if it would dawn upon them that the voice that had come up on the radio was none other than from the chief of the then still neutral American Air Force.

There crossed my mind that afternoon at Northolt a thought about what Whitney Straight must have been thinking when he had been introduced to Hap Arnold. He was by then one of the flight commanders in No. 601 Squadron, and I wondered as they shook hands if Arnold knew who he was, but he gave no sign of recognizing Straight's name. There was no reason why he should have done so, but it was of interest to see these two men facing each other, and it seemed to drive home to me how close the link was between our country and the United States.

After he had recovered from the beating that he had taken in Norway, Whitney Straight had spent a short time behind a desk in the plans department at the Air Ministry, and then he had been appointed personal assistant to the Duke of Kent. But as with so many others, Straight had his heart set on getting back to flying, and while I was inclined at the time to feel that perhaps he treated the Duke in rather a cavalier fashion (a feeling of which Straight has always been well aware), his eagerness to get back on to operations was understandable when one realized that his squadron had been in the thick of the Battle of Britain. It was not until much later that I learned that I was wrong in what I had felt. Straight was interested in his work with the Duke of Kent, but, as he has explained it, "naturally as soon as I was fit I wanted to get back to the squadron."

By the time that Whitney Straight was fit enough for operational flying, the day battle was almost over. He had rejoined No. 601 Squadron when it was down in the West Country at the airdrome at Exeter, which a company that had been founded and which was owned by him had built and operated under lease before the war. All the hangars and other buildings had been built under his supervision. Shortly after his arrival there, Straight scored his first victory by shooting down a Heinkel 111. That was just after I became C.-in-C. of Fighter Command, and it was from then on that I came to know him quite well, and to be impressed by him as a man with outstanding personality and courage.

In these qualities Whitney Straight shared with Douglas Bader, and not a few others, an unquenchable spirit for wanting to get on with the job, and, as had happened in the Norwegian affair, a compulsion to go after the stickiest assignment. Bader had had to relinquish command of his squadron, No. 242, when he became a wing leader at Tangmere; but only a few days after that, the new commanding officer who had taken his place was killed. I realized that as a C.O. the squadron needed somebody who was quite out of the ordinary if there was to be maintained the spirit which had been fostered by Bader, so I had Whitney Straight take over No.

242. His comment on his new command—the squadron was a very experienced one made up of an extraordinary collection of pilots, including Canadians, Australians, French, Poles, Czechs and Norwegians—was to describe it as "a bloody marvellous outfit."

One of the various offensive operations conducted by Fighter Command which my pilots did not exactly relish, but which was of the greatest importance, was a business that went under the name of "Roadstead." In this we had our fighters acting as escort for light bombers—Blenheims and Beauforts of Bomber and Coastal Commands—in attacks on enemy shipping in the Channel. The object was to make sure that the Channel was closed to use by the enemy, and we were supporting in the air the work being done at sea by the Royal Navy. Attacks were kept up on all forms of enemy shipping which could be found at sea between the Dutch coast and Cherbourg.

The reaction on the part of the enemy was a vigorous one, and the casualties among our bombers became very heavy, with the fighters also taking a severe beating. The low-level attacks that had to be made became recognized as most hazardous, and since Whitney Straight was already known to us as the man for difficult jobs, we arranged for his squadron to be one of two that were to specialize in providing this particular type of fighter escort for the bombers. The enemy shipping had their own fighters escorting them, and they were also protected by heavily armed flak ships.

As an example of what these pilots had to face there was an engagement in which No. 242 Squadron became involved on July 27. It occurred between Calais and Dunkirk, and the squadron, which was led by Whitney Straight, provided fighter cover for our M.T.B.'s for an attack on a German destroyer and five of their E. boats. In bad visibility, and with the cloud base down to eight hundred feet, the squadron found the enemy ships, which suddenly appeared out of the gloom. They also found four Me. 109's orbiting above them, but also low down.

"I fired at all four," Straight reported, and he hit one hard, and heavy black smoke was seen to be pouring out of it; but it disappeared into cloud. For fifteen minutes the Hurricanes and the Me. 109's continued the fight only just above the sea and the coast. Straight eventually got in a long burst of fire at almost point-blank range at one of the Me. 109's which he had already damaged. With black smoke and liquid pouring out of the engine it also disappeared into cloud. Although both the enemy fighters were flying in such a manner that they must have crashed, the claim made by Straight could only be for two probably destroyed. Out of ammunition and short of petrol, the squadron had to return to its base at Manston. When they left the scene the destroyer appeared to be on fire.

On the last day of July, and, for all that they were suffering in casualties, still firmly on the offensive, Whitney Straight led his squadron as they escorted some Blenheims on an attack on some enemy shipping in the Channel between Le Havre and Fécamp. Opening the attack from low down, Straight went for some flak ships, trying to silence them at the outset. It was as pure an example as one could ask for, if one may put it that way, of the roles of aircraft and antiaircraft fire, each blazing away at the other, and it was a hazardous venture at the best of times, even if it was the sort of challenge which few fighter pilots could resist.

Late that afternoon we received at Bentley Priory a report from No. 11 Group headquarters at Uxbridge about what had happened to No. 242 Squadron. "There was very heavy pom-pom fire from escort vessel and E. Boats," it read. "S/Ldr. Whitney Straight was seen to break off in the middle of his dive. His aircraft put out white smoke consistent with a hit radiator. He was heard to say, 'I have been hit, am going to force land in France.' He then told the Squadron to return to base. All except one pilot had then attacked."

Some little time was to pass before we heard that Whitney Straight was uninjured in his forced landing in German-occupied France; but it was a long time before we heard the full story of what happened to him after that.

Only just over a week after the disappearance of Whitney Straight, the door of my office flew open one afternoon with an unaccustomed violence, and Bob Wright came rushing in clutching a piece of paper.

"Douglas Bader's missing," he said.

"Oh, God, no!" I exclaimed.

I knew that a sizeable fighter sweep had been in operation that day, and all the time I had to be prepared for casualties. But this, coming on top of the loss of Whitney Straight, was a severe setback. Bader was one of my best wing leaders, and, by virtue of his incredible exploits in the face of severe handicaps, he had attained an enormous reputation as a stern fighter and a very great leader.

A Cranwell cadet, Douglas Bader had lost both his legs in an aircraft crash before the war, and yet, for all that the handicap of his artificial legs imposed upon him, he had become a far more capable and fit human being than most of his fellow men. His record as a fighter pilot was a formidable one, and he had already shot down a sizeable bag of enemy aircraft. I knew what a blow his loss would be to the morale of my pilots. One of those flying with Bader at that time was Johnnie Johnson, who was to finish the war as the top-scoring Allied fighter pilot, and who is today an air vice-marshal. Of Bader he has said: "He had taught us the true meaning of courage, spirit, determination, guts—call it what you will."

In his diary Bob Wright recorded that I was as agitated over this news of the loss of Douglas Bader as he had ever seen me up to that time. He handed me the report, and I took it from him as I got to my feet. I glanced at it, and I then went through to Strath Evill's office where I talked with him about what had happened. The story was far from clear. Two squadrons of the Tangmere wing had been led by Bader over the area of Béthune—a part of northern France so well known to me from my own flying in the first war—and he had taken them into an attack, diving onto some Me. 109's.

"Twenty-three pairs of eyes had watched the wing leader launch his attack," Johnnie Johnson has said; and then they were all "into a confused, savage nightmare of twisting Spitfires and cannon-spitting Messerschmitts." When our pilots emerged from that nightmare, they found that Bader had disappeared. But no one had seen him go.

A couple of days later we heard that Bader was safe and in the hands of the Germans, and then we heard more about what had happened. He had had to bail out when he was rammed by an Me. 109, which had chopped off the tail of his Spitfire, and he had landed near St-Omer. On August 13, four days after his disappearance, I received a signal from No. 13 Group headquarters which reported having picked up a wireless message broadcast by the Germans. The signal stated that the first two lines of the message received were corrupt, and it then went on to say: "Wing Commander Douglas Bader, taken prisoner on 9/8/41 lost his right leg while bailing out. Bader requests that a new leg be sent. German permission granted to drop it by parachute. Communicate day and time of delivery by radio. Place of delivery will then be specified from here. Delivery aircraft granted safe conduct."

It was not generally known even to higher authority that we used to keep an S O S channel open between ourselves and the Germans so that we could tell them when any of our pilots were

floating in the sea off the French coast, and similarly they could
tell us when any German pilots were down in the sea just off our
coast. By this means we could pick up each other's pilots before
they were drowned. It was on this channel that we had received the
message from the Germans.

It was not likely that we would acknowledge receipt of this
message. We had no intention of making any deals with the
Germans. I rang up Trafford Leigh-Mallory at Uxbridge, and he
agreed that we could not allow the Germans to get away with their
talk about "permission" to deliver the leg and "safe conduct."
Instead we laid on an operation whereby a spare leg would be
dropped by parachute from one of the Blenheims over the German-
occupied airfield at St-Omer on the normal daylight bombing raids
before they went on to their target for that day.

A large fighter escort for the bombers was planned in the usual
way for August 19, with Bader's wing from Tangmere close in. It
has been said by some of those who flew on that mission that over
the airfield no flak was flung up at them, but Johnnie Johnson has
recorded that "heavy flak bracketed the bombers when the parcel
dropped out." The box containing the leg with a parachute attached was dropped from a height of ten thousand feet, and Leigh-
Mallory had had attached to it a message addressed to the
commandant of the Luftwaffe at Longuenesse airdrome at St-
Omer in which he stated: "Please accept my thanks, both for your
broadcast message and for anything you can do to ensure that this
new leg is delivered to Wing Commander Bader as soon as
possible."

When we heard that a message had been received that the leg
had been dropped we sent a signal on the S O S channel telling the
Germans that it had been delivered, and we asked for acknowledgment of its safe receipt. They promptly made an acknowledgment
of our signal.

That special delivery gave Douglas Bader legs to spare because
the Germans had already repaired the two artificial legs which he
had been using, one of which he had bent when he had landed by
parachute. The other was found very badly damaged in the
wreckage of his aircraft. By the time when we were dropping the
extra leg for Bader, ten days after he had arrived in German
hands, he had even managed to escape, and was in hiding. But he
was caught again almost immediately, and he had to endure being
a prisoner-of-war until it was all over in 1945.

One of the first to make himself known to Douglas Bader after he wound up in the hospital at St-Omer was Adolf Galland. They had been vigorously fighting each other in the air, and later Galland was to say of Bader: "This man had terrific will power. He refused to stay in the single room which had been allocated to him, but wanted to be in the same room as the other British pilots in the hospital. He set the tone, and upheld the spirit and the comradeship."

It is to Galland's credit that he arranged for Bader to be taken on a visit to one of their airfields, and even to sit in an Me. 109 and get the feel of what it was like; and it has been recorded by Galland that Bader then asked if he could fly it "just one circle over the airfield." For somewhat obvious reasons Galland refused; but that did not discourage Bader from escaping from the hospital almost immediately afterward.

As soon as we received from the Germans their acknowledgment of the receipt of the leg for Douglas Bader, I allowed our public relations people at my headquarters to put out the story of what had happened. In this story they told of the German broadcast to us, and then stated: "The R.A.F. requires no permission from the Luftwaffe to operate when and where it pleases over the occupied territories of northern France." The response from the Prime Minister to the story of the delivery of the leg was prompt and to the point. He phoned me the very next morning.

"You are fraternising with the enemy, Douglas," Winston Churchill stated. "I won't have it."

That was a rather stiff accusation, I thought, and I was not prepared to accept it. "You may call it fraternising, sir," I replied, "but after delivering Bader's leg we managed to shoot down some Me. 109's and damaged several others. That doesn't sound very fraternal to me."

There was a grunt from the Prime Minister, and without saying anything more he hung up, and at no time did he ever speak to me again about this incident.

One of the valuable lessons that I had learned through the intensive years of staff work at the Air Ministry had been the knack of dealing quickly with paper work. There were always great piles of it which had to be dealt with, and that seemed to increase rather than diminish when I became a commander-in-chief. It was inevitable, and in time I came to hear that my staff thought that I coped well with their files. Perhaps they did not realize that it was my way of making the greatest possible use of them.

From time to time there would appear among the official papers and files which Bob Wright guided across my desk some quite unofficial pieces which he thought might be of interest to me. Early in July one such item was a clipping which Wright had extracted from *The Times Literary Supplement* in which there appeared the comment: "These are bewildering times: nothing is constant but the unexpected, nothing sure but change. There is a point to which truth itself can be carried where it becomes deception, a point where tolerance becomes connivance. There is mystery in it."

A couple of days after reading that, the unexpected caught up with me. When I tried to get up one morning I felt so groggy that I had to go straight back to bed. The strain of the long hours and days and weeks and months of intensive work had finally caught me out. I had had no proper leave whatsoever since the time of Munich, nearly three years before, and even my robust constitution was reduced to a state of rebellion. I gave strict instructions to my wife and to Bob Wright that they must not say a word about what had happened, but Archie Sinclair, the Secretary of State for Air, got past the evasive answers that Wright was giving, and on the phone he ordered me to take some leave.

It had just been announced that I had been appointed a Knight Commander of the Order of the Bath, and among the congratulations that I received while I was still in bed there was a pleasant note from James Child, who had been my observer in 1915 during the fight which we had been in together over the Western Front with Oswald Boelcke and Max Immelmann, and for which we had both received the Military Cross. Such is the long arm of coincidence that Child was then living in a pleasant house in Bushey only a few hundred yards away from the entrance to my headquarters at Bentley Priory.

After the few days I spent in bed in my flat on Stanmore Hill, I attended an investiture at Buckingham Palace, and immediately after that I went off for a week's holiday in Scotland, trying for a short time to lose myself in the peace and quiet of the highlands. That was pleasant, but of all the more personal experiences of that time, the one that touched me most was when I was elected an honorary Fellow of Lincoln College, my college at Oxford. It seemed to bring to my mind an even stronger appreciation of the link which I had always felt with Oxford. I was born there, and for a year before the First World War I had been up at Lincoln as a classical scholar. Now, in the midst of a hectic and responsible period of turmoil as a senior Service commander in time of war, I was welcomed to the atmosphere of the academic life which, I must confess, has always had for me a particular attraction; and in its own way that was a pleasant relief from the sterner considerations which were being pressed upon us.

26 / The Spice of Variety

MY ENTIRE LIFE has been devoted to aviation, both military and civil, but there has always been in the background of my mind the strong influence of my father's work as an historian and art critic. By the time of the outbreak of the second war he was an internationally recognized authority in his work, and he was prospering in it. He had then a house in Montagu Square, in the West End of London, and he welcomed there with his many friends and associates in the art world all his children, the youngest of which were scarcely more than infants.

During the Blitz, the defense against which was of such personal concern to me, the house was bombed, and my father lost all the private papers which had to do with his work. That was a serious loss to him, and it was quite enough for him to make the wise decision to depart for the United States. With his wife and two young children he settled in New York. He was then seventy-six years of age, and he set about creating for himself yet another career in the new world. He was already quite well known there, so he was able at least to build on a sound reputation.

It was through my father's connections and interests as far back as the days of the First World War, when I was still a young man, that I had come to be quite well acquainted with the work that was done then by the official war artists. As a result of that, it was with particular pleasure that I welcomed to my headquarters at Bentley Priory, in the spring of 1941, the distinguished artist Eric Kennington. He had been commissioned by the Air Ministry to do a series of portraits of various people in the Royal Air Force, and he spent some weeks at work in Fighter Command. During that time, Kennington did a portrait of me which I have always liked, and which I thought was better than the one which was painted at the same time by James Gunn.

All of us at Bentley Priory were both amused and touched by the happily unaffected way in which Eric Kennington, who was a charming man, worked while he was with us. He chose to do it in

483

Bob Wright's office, which was the outer office to mine. Although I offered Kennington any and every facility to help him in his work, he merely asked for two chairs to be placed in one corner by the window of the outer office. On one of these he propped up his drawing board, to which he attached the paper on which he was going to work, and he sat on the other. For several days he worked there, unassuming and perfectly at ease, and quite undisturbed by the general activity of the office; and at night he stayed in our mess and appeared to enjoy talking with the officers of my staff.

Now and again during the time that Kennington was with us, Bob Wright would relay to me interesting and often amusing comments that Kennington had made, particularly in their talks together about T. E. Lawrence. Kennington had been a close friend of Lawrence's, and he had provided the magnificent illustrations for Lawrence's book *Seven Pillars of Wisdom*. One afternoon I found Wright with his head buried in one of the rare manuscript copies of Lawrence's later book *The Mint*. It was Kennington's own copy of the original, unexpurgated script. Wright passed it on to me. I read it, but when I returned it to Kennington I could not bring myself to tell him just what I thought of it.

Although I had seen him while he was serving in the R.A.F., I had not had the opportunity to talk to T. E. Lawrence; but his story was known well enough to me, as it was to every other senior officer in the Royal Air Force. That was after his *Seven Pillars of Wisdom* was published, and had brought him such fame, and I was naturally curious about the man. *Seven Pillars of Wisdom* is considered to be one of the most interesting books of our age; but in the light of subsequent knowledge it is what I would be rather inclined to call a good specimen of well-written "line-shooting."

In the case of *The Mint,* I found the book thoroughly poisonous. In voicing that opinion I am referring to the original version, and not to the emasculated, pallid edition that was published in 1955. It was quite understandable that a man of T. E. Lawrence's age and background should be unhappy as a recruit in the company of much younger men at the R.A.F. depot at Uxbridge; and it was only to be expected that he should feel like a fish out of water. How could a man of his temperament and upbringing and experience and, to boot, an Oxford don of about thirty-five years of age and a former colonel in the Army feel otherwise? He was masquerading as a raw recruit in the Air Force, and naturally the routine and the physical training and the drill and the coarseness of the life were distasteful to him. But he had deliberately chosen to live a life designed not for a highly educated man who was approaching middle age but for young men of nineteen or twenty years of age, many of whom were by no means bright and were certainly not well educated, and most of whom were straight from civil life.

The way in which T. E. Lawrence chose to write about the R.A.F. depot at Uxbridge was mean enough in spirit; but what I found quite inexcusable was the spite and the vicious unfairness with which he wrote about the commandant of the depot at that time. Lawrence made him out to be a brute and a sadist. I knew that officer well, and he was on my staff at Bentley Priory at the very time when Kennington came to stay with us. He had a good record in the First World War, in which he had been very severely wounded. He was a strict disciplinarian, but that was exactly the quality most needed in the commandant at a recruit training depot. The impression that *The Mint* made upon me was that, in some perverse way, Lawrence was trying to get his own back on the R.A.F. because he had found the life at the depot so hard and distasteful.

In the long run many of us came to feel that T. E. Lawrence, so far as the R.A.F. was concerned, was scarcely more than a nuisance. To appreciate that, one has only to imagine the difficulties that he created for the more junior officers under whom he served as an airman. They knew that he was writing personal letters direct to Air Vice-Marshal Sir Oliver Swann, the Air Member for Personnel, and to other senior and distinguished officers, and even to the Chief of the Air Staff, Boom Trenchard himself. Toward the end of his time in the Service, Lawrence flattered himself that he exerted a strong influence in the design of our high-powered motorboats. I do not believe that. The design of and the modifications to the boats were in the hands of specialists who had a great deal more experience and technical knowledge than Lawrence could ever have known.

That the exploits of T. E. Lawrence had a background of some achievement in the Middle East during the First World War cannot be denied, but that background was not nearly as important as he tried to make it out to be. Nor was it in any way as high, wide and handsome as the story that has been recorded in the spectacular, colorful and preposterous film *Lawrence of Arabia,* which has been so eagerly swallowed by the gullible public. When one makes the effort to cut through the spurious glamour of the legend that, down through the years, has come to be attached to the name of

T. E. Lawrence, it is very difficult to avoid coming to the conclusion that the man was, for all his gifts, in many ways a charlatan.
But that is only my own personal opinion. Eric Kennington did not
feel that way.

On a few occasions when I was given an opportunity to work
quietly at my desk at Bentley Priory, I was joined in my office by
Gordon Alchin, who had been my closest friend at school at
Tonbridge and up at Oxford, and who had also served with me as
a pilot in the Royal Flying Corps. He had gone back to Oxford
after the first war, and by the time that I became C.-in-C. of
Fighter Command in the second war he was already a county
court judge. But Alchin's heart was not in practicing law, although
he did well enough at it. He had always had an inclination more
toward being an artist, with a keen interest in sculpture.

During those visits that he made to Bentley Priory, Alchin would
go on with the bust that he had started of me some time before,
and while I would work at the papers on my desk he would
continue quietly at the task that he enjoyed, sitting over by the
windows, and with nothing being said by either of us. But the bust
was never finished, and what has since happened to it I do not
know. Alchin died some years after the war.

It became the inclination of old friends of mine such as Gordon
Alchin, men who had known me well and who understood the
liking that both my father and I had always had for the company
of attractive women—and who can question the wisdom quite
apart from the pleasure of such a taste?—to pull my leg about the
large number of girls of the Women's Auxiliary Air Force who
were working at the headquarters of Fighter Command. They were
mainly in the watches which were maintained right around the
clock in the filter and operations rooms in the huge underground
block, and there were also many girls at work at the group and
sector operations rooms as well as out on the sites of the radar
stations. Quite often these visitors would make remarks to me
about the attractiveness of what we used to call our beauty chorus,
and they were not wrong in noticing that our girls were unusually
attractive. I would not like to offer a firm opinion about whether
that was because they were also an exceptionally intelligent lot of
women, but intelligent they were, and many of them were later
commissioned and went on to other responsible work as officers in
the Air Force.

In addition to our beauty chorus, Fighter Command also seemed
to attract several well-known actors who showed that they had more

than just a fleeting interest in appearing in the uniforms of the armed forces. In the operations room when I arrived at Bentley Priory I found Clifford Mollison, whom I had known from before the war. He had served in the Army in the First World War, and had been badly gassed while he was still a youngster in the fighting in the Ypres Salient. Having learned to fly before the war, he tried, when the second war in his life broke out, to join the R.A.F., but he was told that he was too old for flying. He promptly rejoined the Army, and as a captain he was at Fighter Command as the liaison officer for Home Forces, and he served there throughout the second war. Reginald Tate, who had been an observer in Peter Portal's squadron in the Royal Flying Corps during the first war, was back in the R.A.F., and he was also in the operations room with Mollison. Later Tate became an active sector controller at two of our foremost fighter stations, and he also served throughout the war.

A few months after I had settled in at Bentley Priory, Ronald Squire, who was one of the great characters of the theater life of the West End, and who was an old family friend, came to see me about joining the R.A.F. I had known him well for many years, and I had always found him an amusing companion and quite a wit. He was a brilliant actor in light comedy, to which he brought his own air of amusing and cynical disillusionment. It was because of our long friendship that he saw fit to come and see me about joining up. Squire was nearly sixty years of age by then, and there was no need whatsoever for him to take such a step, but he was quite sincere in his eagerness to do something more active in the war effort. In order to make clear to him just what he would be letting himself in for in giving up, even temporarily, his very successful and lucrative profession, I called Bob Wright into my office, and with Squire listening I shot a direct question at him.

"What is the pay of a nonflying Volunteer Reserve pilot officer?" I asked.

It was quite clear to me that Bob Wright sensed what there was in the wind, and with a gleam in his eye he replied that it was something only a little more than ten or twelve shillings a day. We both saw a look of something approaching horror flick over Ronnie Squire's face, and he had to resort to his inevitable snuffbox. But after a moment he pulled himself together, and he declared that he still wanted to join up.

Since there appeared to be no way in which I could discourage my old friend, I handed him over to Bob Wright, who completed all the formalities. Following my instructions, he arranged for

Squire to join my headquarters staff as an air raid warnings officer, which meant that he also went to work, along with Clifford Mollison and Reginald Tate, in the underground operations room. It was not long before I heard that Squire was distinguishing himself there mainly through his utter inability to be able to give orders to any of the Waafs without adding, in the usual theatrical fashion, the word "darling," and addressing his brother officers as "dear boy."

Along with his extraordinarily puckish sense of humor, that only endeared Ronnie Squire all the more to everyone but the crustier old diehards. Their views on actors were as prejudiced, in any case, as their objections to having around them the young women of the W.A.A.F. But the rigors of watch-keeping eventually proved too much for Squire, and he was invalided out of the Service. It was possibly just as well. He returned to the theater, and he rendered us a far greater service in Terence Rattigan's play *While the Sun Shines.*

Within the short space of a few weeks the young Waafs at my headquarters were given sufficient cause for distraction by the appearance, among the many other visitors who wanted to see how things were done, of Leslie Howard and David Niven, and the American film actor Robert Montgomery. Howard and Niven came to talk to me about a film which was being planned on the life of R. J. Mitchell, the designer of the Spitfire. Bob Montgomery not only visited my headquarters but even, quite voluntarily and for the sake of the experience, went on watch in our naval liaison section in the underground block months before the United States came into the war. He had joined the United States Navy—one of the first of the actors in Hollywood to join the American armed forces—early in 1941, and by the spring of that year he was a lieutenant and serving as an assistant naval attaché at the American Embassy in London.

The idea of the film which Leslie Howard and David Niven proposed making had a strong personal appeal to me because I had known R. J. Mitchell, and I had been one of those at the Air Ministry who had been directly concerned with his work in producing the Spitfire. The film that was to be made was to be the story of his struggle to develop his ideas and the building of the aircraft, and its use in the air battle over Britain. For the filming of the Spitfires actually in use we arranged for Howard and Niven to have the use of one of our airfields in Hampshire, with the squadron stationed there playing real-life parts. The result was the film *The First of the Few.*

While the film was being made I received reports that the pilots of the squadron with whom the film people were working were basking with immense delight in their roles of part-time film actors. Knowing my fighter boys I could not help shuddering at first at the thought of what that might be doing to them, but we had to let them enjoy their moment. I need not have worried. Taking note of the style of the professional actors, they were soon, with their tongue in their cheeks, bandying around the suggestion that "you must see my latest film." There was no pulling the wool over the eyes of those young pilots. They faced reality too often for that.

While some of these young pilots of mine were romping around in their off moments with this harmless film acting—they were still an operational squadron ready at any moment for action in the air—I was myself becoming familiar with a form of acting that was of a far greater importance and a much deadlier seriousness. I was given the opportunity on several occasions to see intimately and at firsthand how Winston Churchill filled so dynamically the role of Prime Minister. It started not long after I took over Fighter Command, when I received the first of the calls that I was to have from time to time from then on to spend the night as one of Churchill's guests at Chequers. Those nights were to provide for me experiences which were of intense interest; but, at the same time, they were nearly always something in the nature of ordeals.

It was Winston Churchill's practice to ask the various Commanders-in-Chief of the Services to spend the night with him at Chequers at fairly frequent intervals. At these sessions he would gather around him other close associates, and we would all be able to exchange views freely and candidly about our thoughts on an astonishing variety of subjects. Those evenings, or nights, that I spent at Chequers were in so many ways of more than mere interest: they were at times downright exciting. And they were nearly always exhausting. There were usually quite a number of other people staying there who were at least fascinating personalities to meet, such as, even before America came into the war, Harry Hopkins and Averell Harriman; and the hours of the night would pass in extraordinarily stimulating discussions.

Quite often Winston Churchill would come down to dinner in what has been described as his "half-comical and thoroughly practical siren suit"; and after dinner he would usually add to the color of the scene by donning his gorgeous Oriental dressing-gown. He would show us with a happiness that was almost a childish glee some present or other—nearly always boxes of cigars or magnums of champagne—that somebody had sent to him. These presents appeared to be of immense importance to him, and he would hold them gently in his hands after reaching out with, again, an almost childish eagerness to pick them up. I found very touching the unaffected and warmhearted delight that he showed in these presents.

After dinner we nearly always had shown to us some film or other, and Winston Churchill always made it quite clear that, no matter what we saw, the one which he liked best above all others was the one produced by Alexander Korda about the affairs of Horatio Nelson and Lady Hamilton. It is a questionable choice, but there it was, revealing yet another facet in the strange and wonderful mixture that went to make up the man who was so spurned in peace and yet to whom we all turned so eagerly for guidance when we were under duress. After these film shows—and it would then be late at night—we would all settle down to discussions about the problems with which we were faced; and then would begin the sessions that would go on until the small hours of the morning, with all of us sitting around in armchairs, and some of us trying not to give way to the demands for sleep.

There were occasions during these sessions when Winston Churchill would suddenly electrify us with something that he would say, and quite often he would start composing some part of what would later become one of his famous speeches. It was then that we would see him at work as he strode up and down the drawing room talking away at us until, his great gifts for composition gaining the upper hand, he would start haranguing us as if we were in the House of Commons. Then the words would pour out in almost a torrent; and later we would read in published reports of the proceedings in the House of Commons what had been said, by then transformed into such inimitable prose. A secretary would always be at hand, taking down all that was said, and quite frequently Churchill would stop and ask our opinions or check back over some statement that he had just made, and then alter a passage by redictating it. It has always been known that he took infinite pains over the composition of his speeches, and it was of intense interest for those of us who happened to be present to watch him and to listen to him actually at work on one of them.

One of those who was almost always present at these gatherings at Chequers, quietly there in the background, was Winston Churchill's scientific advisor, Professor Lindemann. So far as I was concerned, and in strong contrast to all that I have heard of his behavior on other occasions, the Prof was always charming in his manner and, oddly enough, quite gently spoken. I was not greatly impressed by the value of his scientific judgment, but that opinion was possibly colored by the experiences which I was then having in trying to make sense out of his idea for the wretched "Mutton" scheme for the aerial mines.

As I watched and listened to Professor Lindemann during those sessions at Chequers, it did not seem possible that this quiet and pleasant man could have been one of the protagonists in the violent quarrel that had split the scientific world wide apart some years before the war broke out. The story of that terrible quarrel between Professor Lindemann and Sir Henry Tizard echoes down the corridors of Whitehall to this day, and it still has the power to arouse passionate argument.

The quarrel between these two brilliant men, who had once been good friends, and who were both recognized as among the foremost scientists of their time, was, in the words of Lord Birkenhead, a "terrible feud" and "a naked struggle for power between the two men." It was quite extraordinary in its ferocity, and to those of us who knew about what happened it was fantastic that two such intelligent minds could turn on each other with such violence.

The background for the explosion was an Air Ministry committee which was set up in 1935. Known officially as the Committee for the Scientific Survey of Air Defence, its object was to make a technical study of ways and means of combating raids on this country from hostile aircraft. Tizard was appointed chairman, with other scientists of note such as Professor A. V. Hill and Professor P. M. S. Blackett as members. It has always been known as the Tizard Committee, and my connection with it came in January, 1938, when I was made Assistant Chief of the Air Staff. But at that time the full violence of the quarrel, with which I could not help being familiar, was temporarily in abeyance.

When Winston Churchill was brought, in a semi-official capacity, into the inner sanctum which was the debating ground in matters of defense, he insisted that his scientific adviser, Professor Lindemann, should also have a voice. That voice was to sound in the Tizard Committee in a way which caused startling friction, and what was perhaps even worse, it was to influence Churchill in the complaints that he was to make at higher levels.

One of the sadder aspects of the clash between these two men was the element of confusion that it produced in the scientific development of radar. On the one hand we had Sir Henry Tizard, who was the official adviser to the Air Ministry. Right from the beginning, he supported the possibilities shown by the early experiments in radar, and it was mainly through his energy and drive that we had the radar chain functioning by the time that the war was upon us. It has been said that Professor Lindemann never really believed in the claims that were being made for radar, and that he did very little, if anything at all, to encourage it. But no less an authority than Sir Robert Watson-Watt himself has supported the claim that Lindemann did believe in radar. It would appear that what Lindemann did not want was a reliance entirely upon radar alone.

Along with the rest of the Air Staff, my support went to Sir Henry Tizard, and for that reason I agree with Lord Snow's statement: "I believe, along with a number of Englishmen who are interested in recent military-scientific history, that Tizard's was the best scientific mind that in England has ever applied itself to war." But Lindemann, "a genuine heavyweight of personality," as Snow has put it, "a gadgety scientist, inventive, on the lookout for ingenious tricks," had that powerful support from Winston Churchill which he did not hesitate to use in a curiously obstructive way.

With both Sir Henry Tizard and Professor Lindemann serving as members of the Tizard Committee, a battle for power took place that was to amaze us, and which made me wonder at the time what it was that made Churchill give Lindemann such strong support. Since then Churchill has given us his reasons, and they have been further developed by Lord Birkenhead, who has attacked with vigor the views expressed by Lord Snow with the statement: "He has used the most questionable artifice to produce an impression of Lindemann that is as odious as it is false."

So far as Winston Churchill was concerned after he became the Prime Minister, it appeared to many of us that the one priceless asset possessed by Professor Lindemann was his knack for being able to produce colored statistical diagrams which illustrated very well some important aspect or other of the war. In a way he was giving to Winston Churchill the same valuable service that, it is said, he had been able to provide in producing for Churchill before the war the figures which he used to quote in the House of Commons about German rearmament, and which had so confounded the Air Ministry. This was the one great service that Lindemann rendered to Winston Churchill, and in my experience it was much more valuable than his advice, for all his brilliance as a scientist, in scientific matters. There were times when I noticed that at the meetings at Chequers.

After a full and exacting day's work at my headquarters—there was no recognition of any set days or, for that matter, hours for rest—these late night sessions at Chequers were always tiring, and by three o'clock in the morning I would find my mind drooping with fatigue. I am one of those who needs normal sleep, and I am not given to trying to think clearly in the small hours of the morning. But at that unholy hour Winston Churchill would still be quite fresh, and he would go on vigorously discussing some problem or other having to do with the war, picking our brains, or, treating us as his audience, giving his mind to the composing of a speech.

Among those whom I met on some of the visits that I made to Chequers before the United States came into the war (and also when he came to see me at my headquarters), the one who made the strongest impression on me was Harry Hopkins, the friend and confidant of President Roosevelt. So far as I could make out, Hopkins had no special title or official position in the United States Government. His biographer, Robert E. Sherwood, has spoken of him as having lived for years "as a guest in the White House" and as "the Presidential aide" who "was in large measure Roosevelt's own creation."

There were times during my talks with Harry Hopkins when I found myself wondering at the extraordinary confidence that was placed in him by both the President of the United States and our own Prime Minister. So far as I knew he never once abused that confidence. He was in many ways a first-rate liaison officer functioning at the highest level. It was obvious that Harry Hopkins was a man with a remarkably alert intelligence; and although he had always been a civilian he had a firm grasp of the military problems of war, as well as an equally clear understanding of strategy.

The success of Harry Hopkins' ability in liaison was clearly proved in the way in which he got on so well with Winston Churchill. No secrets were withheld from him, and I used to talk quite frankly with him at my headquarters about my own problems, and although his name may now have faded into the shadows it should not be allowed to vanish. He was a good friend to the people of England in our hour of need, and of the effort that he made to help us even before America came into the war Jack Slessor, who was serving in Washington at the time and was in a position to know about what happened, has said: "He was almost a fanatic on the subject of aid to Britain . . ."

During one of the late night, or early morning, sessions which I attended at Chequers the discussion turned to the vulnerability of the R.A.F. airdromes in Britain, and questions were asked about how we would handle a surprise attack by enemy parachutists. That was before the R.A.F. regiment came to be formed, and it was at a time when the airdromes were guarded on the ground by detachments provided by the Army. It was a task that was not entirely congenial so far as the Army was concerned, and I was none too happy myself about the possibility of what might happen if we were suddenly faced with surprise attacks from parachute landings. But my loyalty to my own command demanded of me that I should insist, in the answers that I gave to Churchill's questions, and in the face of his expressions of what I regarded as skepticism, that I did not think that the enemy would get much change out of any attacks of this nature.

When the time came for me to leave Chequers the next morning, Winston Churchill asked me to drive with him back to London. On the way he raised again the matter of airdrome defense, and as we came up to the R.A.F. station at Northolt he suddenly gave orders to the driver to turn into it. Before I could quite realize what he was up to, we had reached the station headquarters, and there Churchill demanded that the alarm should be sounded for a parachute raid on the airdrome. He wanted it to be raised immediately, as if it were the real thing, so that he could see for himself just what would happen.

The result of the sounding of the alarm left me feeling rather red in the face. When it went off there was a great deal of what appeared to be aimless running about, and nobody seemed to be at all sure about what was expected of them. The Prime Minister strode about watching closely everything that was going on, and with feelings of no little embarrassment I dutifully accompanied him.

At one stage of this tour of inspection Winston Churchill went poking around behind one of the hangars. We found there a rather scruffy little airman crouching down with a rifle clutched in his hands in a manner that was not at all reassuring.

"What are you doing?" the Prime Minister demanded.

"I'm watching for the parachutists, sir," the airman replied.

"What would you do if they came?"

The little man did his best not to be defeated on that score, and he promptly stated: "I'd shoot them."

But the man's lack of assurance must have caught the experienced eye of the former soldier because Winston Churchill then asked: "Have you ever fired that rifle?"

"No, sir," the airman answered. "I've never fired a rifle at all."

That one incident alone was testimony enough to support the skepticism about airdrome defense which had been expressed earlier by Winston Churchill; but there was more to come. We walked together around the perimeter track, making our way to the dispersal points at which the Spitfires of the squadrons of the Polish Fighter Wing were kept in a state of readiness. By the time that we got there we found the Polish airmen standing right up on top of the high embankments which were built around the dispersal bays. They were eagerly peering up into the sky, and they paid no attention to us.

"Come down . . . come down at once!" Churchill shouted in indignation. "You should never stand on a skyline when the enemy are about!"

Since the Poles had no great knowledge of the English language, the shouts from the Prime Minister had little effect on them, and they stayed where they were, paying far more attention to the sky than to him. Being Poles, and so possessed of feelings about the Germans which had reason to be far more deadly than ours, this warning of the approach of parachutists was a promise of a chance to shoot down some of their hated enemies, and no civilian shouting at them was going to stop them.

Although he went on shouting at them, there was nothing that Churchill could do to get the Poles down from the high banks, and he had to give up. By then he was in a pretty bad temper, which was not improved by what he saw when we entered one of the dispersal huts. We found the Polish fighter pilots sitting around reading and smoking, with one group at a table playing cards. The squadron commander got up as we came in, and he came forward to meet us.

"Don't you know that at this moment there is a raid on by enemy parachutists?" Churchill demanded, his indignation beginning to boil over.

It was then that the Prime Minister got what I was beginning to feel was coming to him.

"Oh, no, sir," the officer replied, sweeping all such foolishness aside. "We know it's a false alarm. If it were not, we'd have been ordered into the air by now." Quite unperturbed by the famous Churchillian glower, he then produced a beautifully bound book, and politely he asked: "Will you please sign our visitor's book?"

Although he continued to look sulky enough, and was obviously disgruntled, Winston Churchill signed the book. And such was the delight that was expressed by the Poles over having acquired his autograph that the good humor of the Prime Minister showed signs of being restored. He knew what a gallant band of fighters these Poles were, and what with being able to talk with them, and proving to me the point that he wanted to make, when the time came for us to leave he was in a much pleasanter mood. Such was the magnanimous nature of the man that, as with the other dust-ups that I was to have with him, he never again mentioned this incident at any further meetings that I had with him.

At the southeast corner of the airfield of the R.A.F. station at Northolt, where the great main road from London to Oxford branches off to the right, there stands a memorial to the Polish Air Force and their fighter squadrons which flew from Northolt during the Second World War. During the fifteen years which I spent as chairman of British European Airways after the war, I passed that memorial every time I made the journey between my home at Denham and the B.E.A. offices in Ruislip. So familiar did it become to me that most of the time I would not notice it; but there were occasions as I drove past when it would catch my eye, and then it would remind me of all that it stood for, adding to my interest in the whole story of what had happened at Northolt in my own personal contact with this airfield over the past fifty years.

After the annihilation of the Polish Air Force by the Germans in the blitzkrieg in 1939, quite a number of Polish airmen made their way to England. After their arrival here they were given the opportunity to form squadrons of their own which operated as part of the Royal Air Force. Two Polish fighter squadrons fought in the Battle of Britain. They later formed more squadrons, and the wing of fighters from Northolt came to play an important part in the fighter operations out over France.

One of our own pilots who was most closely associated with the Poles, both in the Battle of Britain and later at Northolt, was Group Captain J. A. Kent, as he was when he retired from the R.A.F. a few years ago. A Canadian by birth, Johnny Kent had come to this country and joined the R.A.F. in the thirties, and by the time of the outbreak of war he was an experienced experimental and test pilot. But as happened with so many others, Kent wanted to get into the fight, and he did, first as a flight commander in one of the first Polish fighter squadrons, then in command of a squadron of his own, and by the summer of 1941 as the leader of the Polish wing from Northolt.

In the description that Johnnie Johnson has given in his book *Wing Leader* of the way in which the various wings of fighters formed up before the great armadas proceeded out over France, he said: "The Polish wing from Northolt would arrive in a rigid, impeccable formation as if their leader expected the rest of us to scamper out of his dignified path." It was suggested on one occasion to Johnny Kent that it would be worth having a record of what it was that he said on the radio which could produce such excellent formations. He chuckled and retorted: "In my Polish?"

During the whole of the time that I was to spend as a C.-in-C. of three different commands during the war it seemed that scarcely a day passed without there being brought to my attention some form of personal effort that was being made by men of such a widely differing variety to get either on to flying or back to it. It ranged all the way through a whole string of naturally keen staff officers who were experienced pilots, many of them regular officers in the R.A.F., and it extended to many who were not physically fit but who nevertheless tried to find some way around that.

One important aspect of any consideration of this compulsion to get into the fighting in the air lies in the fact that all air crews of the Royal Air Force were volunteers. These men were essentially individualists, and they chose for themselves the course that they wanted, or had, to follow. And that is possibly why I find now that when I think about my time in the Royal Air Force there is one memory of both wars which dominates all others. It is the memory of the men themselves, and it is not possible for me even to think about my experiences without thoughts about these men coming to life in such a vivid way.

While I was serving out in the Sudan in the early 1930's, one of my pilots was a character—I use the word advisedly—named Murray Payn. One day in the spring of 1941 he arrived with very little warning in my office at Bentley Priory bringing with him Prince Bernhard of the Netherlands, to whom he was acting as equerry, and whom I had only met casually in London. It was the first time that I had a chance to exchange views with Prince Bernhard, and it was to be the beginning of a long personal friendship. He has always been known as a direct, forthright man, and on this occasion of our first meeting at the headquarters of Fighter Command he did not fail in coming straight to the point. He explained that he felt a little doubtful about his standing in the eyes of the British public because, even though he was now Dutch, he was by birth a German. But he had an idea which, he thought, might help to establish his position more in the respect of our people.

"Would you have me taught to fly a Spitfire?" he asked.

It was common knowledge that Prince Bernhard had made a gallant stand on behalf of Holland and the Dutch royal family, even to personal combat, when the Germans had invaded the country which, since his marriage, had possessed his complete allegiance. I also knew that he had already done several hundreds of hours of flying as a pilot of light aircraft.

"Have you talked with the Air Ministry about it?" I asked, aiming the question more at Murray Payn than at Prince Bernhard. "This is really something that only the Chief of the Air Staff can decide."

Murray Payn was not the sort of man who could ever be put off his cheerful, if rather mad, stride by any formalities or red tape. But he had to admit that they had not approached the C.A.S. Moreover, Prince Bernhard added, the Air Ministry officials whom they had approached had refused to consider the idea because it was thought that, as a member of the Dutch royal family, his life was much too precious to risk learning to fly a modern fighter, and, in any case, his eyesight gave them cause to worry because he had to wear glasses.

Prince Bernhard had a pleasantly persuasive way about him. Ably supported by Murray Payn, he made such a strong appeal to be allowed to learn to fly fighters that I finally had to give in. But I agreed to it on only one condition, and that was that he should go to one of our Operational Training Units, and that, along with all the other pilots who were under training, he should do the full course. I was not going to have any playing about, and I explained that it would take several weeks of concentrated studying and flying. It was not to be a matter of merely learning to fly Spitfires at any spare time that might come up. He would have to go through the whole course with all the ground training and lectures as well as the actual flying.

The delight expressed by Prince Bernhard at the prospect of being able to do all that I had said must be done was more than I had expected, and it convinced me that he was genuinely eager to become at least a fully qualified fighter pilot. All the arrangements were made, and he and Murray Payn went to the Spitfire O.T.U. at Aston Down, in the West Country, where they both went through the whole gamut of the fighter pilot's course. At the end of it Prince Bernhard was passed out as a competent Spitfire pilot.

Having grown up with the breed, and, I suppose, having myself developed in their fashion, I was well aware that one of my responsibilities as Commander-in-Chief was to keep a tight rein on the natural exuberance and forcefulness of my fighter pilots. Of all of them, no more colorful characters could be imagined than the Atcherley brothers: Dick, generally known as "Batchy," and David. They were twins, and so alike in appearance that it was difficult, until one came to know them very well, to tell them apart. They were both exceptionally fine pilots, and they became well known during the thirties both at home and abroad for their astonishing feats in aerobatics; but their force of character, or the ways in which they expressed it, were always getting them into scrapes which on several occasions resulted in first-rate rows and losses of seniority.

Dick Atcherley was perhaps slightly the better pilot of the two, but in the seniority lists of the Royal Air Force, the brothers always managed to stay level as they progressed up the ladder of promotion. Eventually they both reached air rank. And then, some time after the war, David Atcherley disappeared on a flight in a jet fighter over the Mediterranean on the way to Cyprus. Dick Atcherley went on to become an air marshal with a knighthood before he finally retired from the Service after being Commander-in-Chief of Flying Training Command.

While I was at Fighter Command, I gave Dick Atcherley command of one of our night fighter stations which was located at Fairwood Common, in south Wales. He promptly set about devising a new system of airfield lighting at night which was a distinct improvement over anything that we then had in use. A little later I put him in command of the day fighter sector station at Kenley. At the same time I arranged for his brother David to take over from him at Fairwood Common. Only very shortly after that, David Atcherley lined himself up in front of me in my office at Bentley Priory and lodged a vigorous protest, asking if I was trying to perpetrate some sort of joke. His complaint was that, because he and his twin brother were so alike, no one at Fairwood Common, it seemed, knew that there had been a change in station commanders.

The antics of the Atcherley twins were always the subject of amused comment throughout the Service. Even though he must have been by then in his middle thirties, Dick Atcherley could still fly an airplane better than almost anyone in the Royal Air Force or, for that matter, in any air force. He was naturally anxious to pit his skill in combat against the enemy, and no sooner was he in command at Kenley—he was by then a group captain—than he saw to it that he was flying a Spitfire as just one of the pilots in the Kenley wing on their offensive sweeps over occupied France. A few weeks later I called in at Kenley during a tour of inspection, and while I was there I received word that the commanding officers of the three squadrons which made up the Kenley wing wanted to have a word with me. Their spokesman was Paddy Finucane, a rather wild Irishman who was making a name for himself as one of our outstanding fighter pilots of that time, and who was killed not long afterward.

"We are devoted to our group captain," Finucane stated, "and we fully appreciate that he is a splendid man, and that he flies very well." He paused for a moment, and then he blurted out: "But will you please tell him not to come with us so often?"

It was not at all necessary for Dick Atcherley to join in these fighter sweeps. His job was to run the sector on the ground. But I knew what it meant to him to be able to fly with the squadrons in the wing which was part of his overall command. When I asked Finucane why he did not want the station commander with them, I was told bluntly that it was mainly because of Atcherley's eyesight.

"He does not seem to be able to see the enemy aircraft quickly enough," Finucane explained. "He is being surprised by them, and then we have to go in and pull him out of the mess."

The others agreed with what Paddy Finucane was saying, and they all felt that the wing would be able to do better if they were able to concentrate on their job and not to have to worry about looking after their group captain, even if in actual flying he could still run rings around them. I could understand what it meant to both sides, but I had to think of the efficiency of the wing; and awkward though it was, I had to speak to Atcherley about it. I told him that he was not to go out on the sweeps so often, and that he should do it only as an occasional treat. I tried to soften the blow by pointing out that even if he was the best pilot on the station, he was nevertheless getting a bit long in the tooth for the high speed of the air fighting that was then taking place by day. Atcherley admitted that he had found himself slow in spotting the Huns, and he agreed to do as I asked of him.

To my surprise and annoyance it was reported the very next day that Dick Atcherley had been shot down on a sweep, and that he was floating around in his dinghy in the middle of the Channel. He was picked up, and on the following day, on my orders, he presented himself at Bentley Priory to receive the ticking-off that I had ready for him for so rapidly disobeying my instructions. But over the years Atcherley had become more or less immune from these reprimands.

In his manner Atcherley was contrite enough, and he freely admitted that an Me. 109 had got on his tail before he saw it. The German pilot had put a cannon shell from the rear right through the cockpit of Atcherley's Spitfire, and it had exploded in the instrument panel. But it was not being shot down that seemed to irritate him. Only a week before, he explained to me, he had bought himself an expensive gold watch, and the cannon shell that had ripped through his Spitfire had grazed his wrist, flicking off the watch and throwing it away into the sea. That loss he seemed to find distinctly annoying. Since it reminded me that the only trace of a wound that I had received as a fighter pilot in the first war had been when a bullet had grazed my wrist, I suddenly felt that there was nothing more that I could say.

Just what one should do about discouraging those who were more suited for administrative posts than they were for operational flying I was never quite sure. As a Commander-in-Chief I was entitled to give firm instructions; but as a man I knew what they were facing, and they had my sympathy. I had had such a good innings myself, and on the purely personal level it seemed unfair to stand in the way of a man trying to do what he felt that he must do in order to know for himself what it was to have to cope with the odds of active service. Along with many others, Bob Wright had come to feel very strongly about that, and from the time when the night fighters had come into their own in the spring of 1941, he had kept up a steady pressure on me to let him become one of the new race of night fighter navigator.

At first I felt that it was ridiculous that anyone who had become as experienced as Wright had in a good staff appointment should want to go off and start all over again in something for which it was quite possible that he would be totally unsuited. Moreover, I pointed out to him, he had already failed for any air crew medical category through poor eyesight. But against my advice he insisted upon having another medical board, and through some wangle or other he managed to get himself passed as fit for flying, and with that there came an increase in the pressure in his campaign.

It was then that I began to understand more what it was that Wright was looking for. Although he knew nothing about flying, and was not even particularly keen on it, we had talked a great deal together about my own experiences in the First World War, and he explained to me that this was his one chance to know for himself a little of what I had experienced in operational flying. I finally agreed to let him go, and after a year spent with me, Wright went off to do his training before going, through another pretty wangle, to No. 604 Squadron, which was by then commanded by John Cunningham. There he learned his trade under the guidance of Cunningham's navigator, Jimmy Rawnsley. After the war Rawnsley and Wright joined forces, and out of their experiences they wrote the book entitled *Night Fighter*. Wright's place as my personal assistant was taken by Flight Lieutenant R. A. G. Edwards, a charming man who had been working for some time in the filter room, and who was by profession a stockbroker.

Just over halfway through November, 1941, the German wireless broadcast an item of news which contained in it for me the cause for a distinct personal sadness and regret. Ernst Udet, it was announced, had been killed in a flying accident. A little later the same day, the Germans made the official statement: "The General in charge of Luftwaffe Supplies, Colonel-General Ernst Udet, was killed on Monday the 17th of November, 1941, testing a new weapon. He died of his injuries on the way to hospital. The Fuehrer has ordered a state funeral for this officer who died in so tragic a manner while in the performance of his duty . . . ."

Several days later there was a memorial service for Ernst Udet in the Air Ministry in Berlin, and that was followed by a state funeral. Both of these occasions were staged with all the pomp that was so dear to the hearts of the German people, and which was so cruelly exploited by the Nazis. In view of what actually happened, what Udet himself would have thought of it all beggars description.

For an indication of the way in which Hermann Goering conducted himself over the death of his old friend there is on record the ostentatious invitation card for the service and the funeral which was sent out in his name. It reads:

The Reichsmarschall of the Great German Reich and C.-in-C. Luftwaffe has the honour to invite you on Friday, the 21st November, 1941, at 11 o'clock in the Hall of Honour of the Air Ministry in the Wilhelmstrasse, to attend the state funeral of the late-lamented General of Luftwaffe Supplies, Colonel-General Ernst Udet.

At the service Hermann Goering spoke about his erstwhile comrade in the Richthofen Circus. It has been reported that he was overcome with emotion, and that he had difficulty in concluding his speech. Well he might have been, for he was one of the few who knew the truth of what had happened, and why it had happened; and if Goering had had a conscience there would have been weighing upon it the treacherous part that he had played in contributing to Udet's death.

There was speculation enough at the time about the manner of the death of Ernst Udet, and later it was confirmed that, no longer able to tolerate the iniquity of the ways of Hermann Goering and Erhard Milch, under whom he was serving in the Luftwaffe, he had committed suicide by shooting himself. Such a miserable ending to the life of a most likeable man, a great airman, and one of the genuinely popular German generals was not as unusual as might be expected because under Hitler no senior officer's head rested at all securely upon his shoulders.

Suicide among the Germans, and particularly among those who were Nazis, was a common practice: there was something in their way of thinking which seemed to compel them, under certain circumstances of stress, to destroy themselves. In war we also knew compulsion, but because of what we are as a people it was of an entirely different temper from that which leads only to self-destruction, even it could, in its effort to reach for the stars, bring us at times crashing to the earth. In our own fighting services I had long been familiar with the compulsion that drove men of every conceivable type to volunteer for operational flying, or service in submarines or tanks or any other hazardous action that is to be found in time of war. It is an age-old manifestation of the spirit that drives us in all human endeavor, and it should never be lightly dismissed, as too many are inclined to do nowadays, as nothing more than some form of aggressiveness. Without it, we are nothing. It has in it an intensity and purity of spirit to which Cyril Falls has referred; and in that spirit there is no mere love of war: it is beyond that. More often than not I have found that the men who have been possessed most strongly with that spirit have genuinely hated war.

It is difficult enough for the hearty, robust, simple-minded enthusiast to take in his stride the stresses of active service. For the intellectual these stresses become, because of the element of imagination alone, a far more insidious strain. And yet, for all that one might so mistakenly expect of them, we found the young intellectual well represented among our air crews in the Royal Air Force. One in particular with whom I came in quite close contact was Richard Hillary.

There were several reasons why I felt a strong sympathy for Richard Hillary. When the war broke out he was up at Oxford, as I had been when the earlier war came about. He had been, as I had, a keen oarsman, and, just as I had, he had also stroked his college boat. He learned to fly with the University air squadron, which enabled him to become a fighter pilot in time for the Battle of Britain, during which he was shot down and badly burned. That led him through a long session of plastic surgery in the hospital at East Grinstead. Some time after that, he appeared as a flight lieutenant on my headquarters staff.

Richard Hillary was typical of the intellectual who becomes a fighter pilot. That in itself sounds formidable enough, because the qualities of both must produce in a man obsessively strong traits of individuality. By the time that he arrived at Bentley Priory, the whole force and expression of Hillary's character had become rather excessively individualistic. It was known that he was exceptionally talented and highly strung. That was clear enough from a reading of his remarkable book *The Last Enemy,* which had been published only a few months before. He had also been a handsome young man; but now his face was disfigured with scars, and his hands were like claws. But it was not this physical disability which caused him to have what appeared to so many to be such a chip on his shoulder. He was much too intelligent for that. I found him charming, forthright and tart. My liking for him might have been because I have always preferred that a man should have some bite in his character.

In Richard Hillary's case there was some inner devil goading him on which none of us could really quite understand. He seldom spoke about it, but the result of that goading was to be seen in his manner. From the moment that he arrived at my headquarters, he started nagging at everybody about being allowed to return to operational flying. He had been through a hard and trying time, and many people went out of their way to help him; but Hillary simply could not reconcile himself to having to stay on the ground. He spoke to me several times about getting back to flying, and each time I told him that I simply could not recommend it. But he kept pestering me, and in the end I gave in with a rather foolish suggestion.

"If you can get the doctors to pass you," I told him, "you can go back on ops."

I said that because I felt quite certain that the doctors would never pass him as fit for any sort of operational flying. But I had not counted on Hillary's pertinacity and persuasiveness; and one day he appeared in my office triumphantly waving a favorable medical report, and he called upon me to live up to my promise. I felt in honor bound to keep that promise, even though I believed that, for all that the doctors might say, he was not really medically fit for operational flying. But I did tell him that I considered that it would be impossible for him to go back to single-seater day fighters, and that instead he should go to an Operational Training Unit with a view to becoming a night fighter pilot, in which the flying was not as rough and tumble as it was in the day fighters.

My proposal was accepted gratefully enough, although I sensed that Hillary was a little disappointed, and he went off to a night Operational Training Unit, with plans at the back of his mind that would enable him to join Max Aitken's squadron. I heard nothing more until there came the news some weeks later of his death in a crash at night early in 1943. I had only just left Fighter Command when it happened, and I was on my way overseas.

There have been many times when, in thinking about what happened, I have reproached myself for having allowed Richard Hillary to win me over. I should never have made him that promise. Perhaps in doing what he did he found something of whatever it was that he was looking for. But there was an additional feature about his death that has always troubled me. There has never been a full explanation of the reason for the crash in which this talented young man died. That was sad enough; but in it the young navigator who was training with Hillary was also killed. That adds to my own feeling of regret about having, through a rash promise, allowed Hillary to have his own way.

27 / The Broadening Fronts

IN A WAR that was to provide us over a period of nearly six years with shocks, blows, disasters and triumphs in an array that was at times so bewildering, the Japanese attack on the Americans at Pearl Harbor, in Hawaii, on December 7, 1941, was one of the most shattering. Many of those of us who were in responsible positions in Britain had felt for quite some time that sooner or later the United States would be in the war, even though the pattern for the future was far from clear.

At the time when the news of the disaster in the Pacific reached us at Bentley Priory, Jack Slessor, who was then in command of a bomber group, was with me on a visit to my headquarters, and it was of great value that I was able to exchange immediately with him views about what had just happened. Slessor had been back from the United States for about seven months after his work over a period of some time in Washington. During that time, he had, as he has expressed it, "to put across to the Administration the need for largely increased production in America of aircraft of types fully suited to our operational requirements . . ."

Through that experience of working so closely with the Americans, Slessor was as close as anyone I knew to American opinion, and as well as exchanging thoughts about the importance that the news meant to the whole future of the air I was able to talk with him about the immediate fighter situation, which was again causing me some concern. During the time that Slessor had spent in Washington in such close liaison with the Americans, one of the subjects debated in great detail was which of their fighters should be developed for future use.

At the time when I had been able to get down to good talks with General Arnold about what they were building, we had exchanged detailed views. In one respect the exchange even developed into a somewhat vigorous argument. Through our own vast experience I tried to urge Arnold to go for our own Spitfire, which I naturally thought was the best fighter in the sky; but he was far from being convinced of that. Arnold had some other fighters up his sleeve, such as the Airacobra and the Lightning which he was keen on seeing brought into service.

We had had some experience of the Airacobra, and it was all dismal, and I told Hap Arnold that; but I added that the most encouraging reports were coming to us from our people in Washington about the new Mustang that had been designed and was being built by the North American Aviation people to our specifications. The prototype was flying in September, 1940, having been built in the record time of just over three months. The R.A.F. was delighted with it, and a large number of them had been ordered, but the American Allison engines with which they were equipped were not up to what we wanted. I had stressed to Arnold our view that the Mustang with a Rolls-Royce Merlin engine might well turn out to be an exceptionally fine fighter.

But Hap Arnold did not seem to be at all keen about that, and he had talked about standardizing on their Thunderbolt, which had been flown for the first time some months before. Because of our much greater experience, that rather touched me on a raw spot. The Thunderbolt was indeed a thundering great aircraft in size alone, and in the R.A.F. we had no great liking for it, and I told Arnold that if he did not want the Spitfire he should certainly avoid the Thunderbolt. Back we came to the Mustang, which I firmly believed, on the information that I had received, might lead into something even better than the Spitfire. Eventually it turned out that the Mustang, after it had been equipped with our Merlin engines—which were also built under license in the United States— became one of the finest and most versatile of all the fighters that were produced during the Second World War. Arnold was to admit that later, when he made the generous statement: "It may be said that we could have had the long-range Mustang in Europe rather sooner than we did. That we did not have it sooner was the Air Force's own fault."

When one studies now the statements made during the war by the Nazi leaders, which, all said and done, were the only reflections we had of what they were thinking, it seems that they were convinced that they were always right on the verge of pulling off some great victory or other. They were such experts at self-delusion. It is possible that their thinking had become conditioned by the extraordinary successes which they had achieved during the first year of the war. Adolf Hitler and Hermann Goering, to mention only two, were always so sure that within a few weeks the courses which they had chosen to follow were bound to be capped with success.

But by the winter of 1941–42 the results of the German onslaught on Russia were, for all its earlier successes, far from what the Nazi leaders had forecast. The German generals on that front saw all too clearly what was happening, and it was during that winter that there came about the turning-point in both Hitler's power and that of the Nazis; and from that time on, although we were not then to know it, there came the slide down the hill which, even though it was to take another three and a half years, ended with their plunge into the horrifying abyss that was of their own making.

In his preoccupation with the wrath that he had drawn down upon his head on the Eastern Front, Hitler did not have much time left to worry about being particularly aggressive toward us in the west. But we had no intention of leaving him alone and merely waiting for him to strike again. By the new year of 1942 we were well into our stride in our air offensive against the Germans. In addition to the night bombing being done by Bomber Command, it continued to be the task of Fighter and Bomber commands to carry out strikes by day at objectives which were within range of the escorting fighters; and from the point of view of the fighters it quite often went beyond leaning into France and became almost a stretching into France.

The industrial area around Béthune, Lens and Lille—which was so well known to me from my own flying over it in the first war—was considered to be the most sensitive spot for attack by air in daylight from England, and we hoped that these daylight raids would induce the Germans to concentrate their own fighters in northeastern France. These combined circus operations led our fighters to the limit of their endurance, and one of the serious problems in our planning was that such long flights did not allow very much time for actual fighting over the area once it was reached. The fighters always had to make sure that they had enough fuel left to get back to their bases in England. It was the same problem all over again that we had faced in the first war when we had always been reaching out over the German areas behind the lines on the Western Front in our pursuit of the enemy, only to have to battle our way back to our own lines with an anxious eye on the fuel gauges.

In our offensive fighter operations out over France, we were finding that both the multiplicity of the actual operations as well as the stiff German defense were calling for strenuous fighting on our part. As the months passed in our pursuit of this offensive role, it became even more vicious and costly, and at one stage late in 1941 I received orders, based on a Cabinet decision, to put a brake on large-scale operations. So many times, when I read or listened to the reports of what was happening to my fighters out over France during 1941 and 1942, I was reminded so strongly of my own experiences as a fighter pilot on the Western Front, particularly during the spring of 1917. Into my mind there would come thoughts about what we had faced then in our early efforts to try and work out the best use that could be made of the air, and about the heavy price that we had paid for that early knowledge. Now we were planning with an understanding based on many years of study and experience, and a much surer knowledge of the uses that could be made of the fighter in the various types of escort, sweeps, support and cover which were called for in the execution of our plans.

All these fighter operations were conceived with far more in mind than just a day's outing for our pilots. For all my experiences as a fighter pilot in the first war I was never one of the death-or-glory boys. As Commander-in-Chief of Fighter Command, it was my duty to wage an offensive battle with vigor, but it must always be for a purpose. Fighter and Bomber commands were then the only two forces able to take the war continuously to the Germans, and it became my overriding concern to see that my command was equipped with aircraft and manned with pilots which would enable us to make the greatest possible use of it.

The value of the operations in which our bombers and fighters worked together, as well as our massive sweeps of fighters alone, continued throughout 1941 and on into 1942 to be the subject of a lot of argument and discussion. But it was obvious that after the day and night air defense of the United Kingdom, which was my command's first responsibility, we must continue with these operations. In them we were already waging, along with the Bomber Command offensive at night, a war on a second front. Although an air war, it was both strenuous and deadly, which was something that seemed at times to be overlooked in the political arena, when Britain was unfairly accused of not pulling her weight.

At one stage, Richard Peirse, who had taken Peter Portal's place as Commander-in-Chief of Bomber Command, expressed his doubts about the value of the circus operations in which my fighters were escorting his bombers on daylight raids. Since the whole object of our operations was to bring such pressure to bear on the German Air Force that they would have to engage us, I pointed out that we would have to have the bombers with us. That might have sounded, I admit, as if the bombers were being looked upon as bait, and I suppose they were; but we had to lure the Germans into battle. I was supported in this by Peter Portal, and these operations continued, with expanded forces, until at times we were sending out great swarms of hundreds of fighters.

But even then, it had become clear to us by the late summer of 1941, that our offensive against the Germans in the skies over France was not inducing them to withdraw their Air Force in any great numbers from the Russian front. We then reversed our policy and went about trying, by delivering our own attacks over wider areas, to make the enemy spread out their fighters along the coasts of France and the low countries. This brought continued action in engagements with the German Air Force, but we also suffered quite substantial losses, and the overall results were not as good as I would have liked, even if the experience that we were gaining was later to be of the greatest value.

But with the expanding state of the war, and the demands that were being made for aircraft for the other theaters, we had to draw back. When the Americans came in, our need was to plan with them for operations on a larger scale, and to make of Britain the great platform that it would have to become for launching air attacks against the German throttle-hold on Europe. And to make those attacks effective we would have to have a superiority in the air which was not likely to be granted lightly to us by the Germans.

In the introduction of new aircraft with improved performance it was still, as always, a seesaw, with first one side and then the other gaining the upper hand. With our improved Spitfires we had caught up with the Me. 109f. The struggle remained on equal footing until toward the latter part of the summer of 1941. And then we were caught flat-footed. My pilots reported seeing over Amiens a new type of radial-engined fighter. It was in the course of one of the circus operations, and there were some particularly experienced pilots flying in the wings from Kenley, Tangmere and Northolt. Our intelligence people ridiculed the idea. But what the pilots reported was correct: they were seeing for the first time the Focke-Wulf 190.

So far as night operations were concerned, which were mainly defensive against the occasional raids, the Beaufighter was being replaced by the summer of 1942 with the splendid Mosquito. Along with the greatly improved techniques which were by then being employed by the night fighter crews, that was quite enough to cope with any of the enemy bombers. They had not been improved at all, and with our more effective night fighters the Germans had cause to be cautious about making heavy raids. But these improvements in our own aircraft had not come about in any easy fashion: they were the result of incessant pressure from my headquarters, and some firm assessments on my part.

By the spring of 1942 I was preparing for a renewed effort by Fighter Command over the skies of France, but in our planning we found ourselves having to look very carefully at the number of aircraft that we had available in reserve. The Prime Minister himself expressed his anxiety about this to the Chief of the Air Staff, pointing out that while the circus operations could pay dividends, we should nevertheless watch our losses.

At the same time that we had this particular problem on our minds, I was yet again urging upon the Air Staff at the Air Ministry the need to consider most seriously all the problems of my command. In a letter that I had written early in 1941 to Peter Portal about this, I had stated clearly how concerned I was about the attitude of the Air Ministry. "This attitude is difficult to define," I had said, "but it presents itself to me and my staff as an atmosphere of 'Fighter Command is quite all right. We don't have to worry about them.' "

Over a year later, with the superiority of the Focke-Wulf 190 all too well established, the position was such that I was still having to hammer away at the Air Ministry. "It is scarcely necessary for me to emphasize the point that quality is more important than quantity in the production of fighters," I stated in a letter dated July 17, 1942. "We are now in a position of inferiority." The channel that I employed in expressing such an opinion—my letter was addressed officially to the Under-Secretary of State for Air—had in it what might be considered a certain piquancy, for the U.-S. of S. was Harold Balfour, upon whom I knew I could rely for a sympathetic hearing. Early in 1917, while serving as flight commander in my squadron in France, he had known only too well what it was to have to fight with inferior aircraft.

In expressing my views as firmly as I did I also called attention to statements that had just been made in the House of Commons by the Minister of Production, who was then Oliver Lyttelton, and the Minister of Aircraft Production, Colonel J. J. Llewellin. "They appear to find it difficult to believe that we have really lost our lead in fighter performance," I stated. "There is however no doubt in my mind, nor in the minds of my fighter pilots, that the FW 190 is the best all round fighter in the world today."

By that time Wilfrid Freeman had returned from the Ministry of Aircraft Production to the Air Ministry, and he was the Vice-Chief of the Air Staff. In response to my letter to Harold Balfour—a copy of which I had sent to him—Freeman sent me a copy of a paper which Peter Portal had just submitted to the Secretary of State for Air. Portal had registered a protest at the same time that I was making mine against the statements made by the Minister of Aircraft Production in the House of Commons that "the newest British aircraft now coming out of production was better at nearly every height than the two new German planes, and was as good at any height."

Once again Rolls-Royce came to our aid. They improved still further the performance of the Merlin engine, and with that we received the Spitfire IX. With that fine aircraft our fighter pilots were able to hold their own with just a little in hand against the Focke-Wulf 190. And a new fighter altogether, the Typhoon, which was being produced by the people who had manufactured the Hurricane, was beginning to emerge from its teething troubles and was proving quite a match for the FW 190 at lower heights.

In February, 1942, the energetic, forceful and at times so controversial Bert Harris became the Commander-in-Chief of Bomber Command, and with that there inevitably came about an acceleration in the expansion that was eventually to bring that command into being as one of the most powerful weapons in the west. Of the situation when he took over the command, Harris has since commented: "I had to regard the operations of the next few months not only as training or trial runs from which, and only from which, we could learn many essential lessons, but also as commercial travellers' samples which I could show to the War Cabinet."

In testing out new techniques and equipment, Bomber Command made a heavy attack a month later on the ancient German town of Lübeck, on the Baltic, causing a great deal of destruction; and in another attack three weeks later the similarly ancient city of Rostock, also on the Baltic, was almost completely destroyed. "Sir Arthur Harris was fired with a burning conviction that the strategic air offensive was the only means by which the war could be won in reasonable time and at bearable cost," the official historians Charles Webster and Noble Frankland have stated. These attacks were to cause some of our people to question our bombing policy; but Bert Harris' answer to the criticism of the destruction of the two cities, which were both perfectly legitimate military targets, was to comment: "There is the possibility that the destruction of

two towns of considerable size, and the mass evacuation which
followed, gave the enemy a jolt which he badly needed."

That is one way of looking at it, and it is a sound one, but the
reaction which it brought from Hitler was such that my own
command was called upon to cope with a sudden lashing out at
this country of what became known both to the Germans and to us
as the Baedeker raids. They lasted for six months during the
summer and autumn of 1942, and the German leader gave orders
for "terror-attacks of a retaliatory nature," aimed more at civilian
morale than any military targets. In them the German Air Force
made vicious night raids on the older and more well-known of our
country towns and cities which were of no military importance
whatsoever.

There also came other types of attacks such as the "tip and run"
raids from fighter-bombers which would come tearing in at high
speed gained from having started at a good height, fling down their
bombs, and then go belting out again very low down. Through this
element of speed alone, our day and night fighters on home defense
were kept constantly on their tiptoes. "We always seem to be going
down hill" was one of my pilots' comments on the flying that was
done by our day and night fighters over this country at that time.

In writing about the origins of the First World War, the historian Cyril Falls has spoken about "blunder and destiny, twin
sisters who walk about the world with arms entwined and resemble
each other so closely that they are often confused . . ." During
the second war those sisters continued to amble through history all
too often, and within a few weeks at the end of 1941 and early in
1942 they embroiled us in two affairs at sea which caused us the
utmost confusion, and which were both of personal concern to me,
one indirectly, and the other very directly.

When the United States Navy took such a terrible pounding at
Pearl Harbor it was yet further proof of what their own airmen
had been preaching about the effectiveness of bombardment of
ships from the air. At the time that it happened I could not help
thinking about the many arguments in which I had been involved
with our own people in the bomb versus battleship controversy,
when, as the spokesman for the R.A.F., I had crossed swords so
vigorously with those who were representing the Royal Navy.
Three days after Pearl Harbor, when we had only just caught our
breath, the news came that the Royal Navy had had to accept a
similar pounding from Japanese air power, and it was administered

in a way which was all that we, on the air side, had been predicting
could be done.

But there was no comfort whatsoever for me in being proved
right when the Japanese sank H.M.S. *Repulse* and H.M.S. *Prince
of Wales,* two of our finest battleships. Quite apart from the objective view of what a serious loss this was to us, there was in it, for
me, the grievous loss of a personal friend for whom I had the
warmest admiration. In the brief action that took place off the
coast of Malaya, Admiral Sir Tom Phillips was one of the many
who lost their lives when Japanese bombers, flying with a skill and
a precision which it had never been thought they could possibly
execute, sank our great warships. Not a sign of any of our aircraft
was to be seen in this action. Tom Phillips was a gallant and
charming little man, and it was he who had been my strongest
opponent in the arguments that we had had before the war when,
around the committee table, the Royal Navy and the R.A.F. had
discussed the ability of warships to protect themselves against
attack from the air. Captain S. W. Roskill, the naval historian, has
rightly commented of that action: "Rarely can a defeat at sea have
had such far-reaching consequences."

Whether Tom Phillips should have gone out as he did with his
two great ships to try and stave off the Japanese amphibious forces
which were creeping down the coast of Malaya has been the source
of endless discussion. At the outset he had been told that he could
not be provided with adequate fighter cover in the air, and he had
been warned that there were Japanese bombers about. In what
happened after that one can only look askance at the breakdown in
liaison. Phillips did not want to break radio silence, and he did not
ask for air cover when the Japanese attacked; and ashore his
people did not anticipate, in what was happening, what help he
might need. So he received no help at all, and the Japanese
achieved what was for them a notable victory.

But if there was a regrettable breakdown in liaison out in the
Far East, there was another serious one at home two months later
when some German warships made a dash for safety up through
the English Channel, and got away with it. While I could view
what had happened to the *Repulse* and the *Prince of Wales* with a
personal regret that had in it a certain professional detachment, the
exploits of the *Scharnhorst,* the *Gneisenau* and the *Prinz Eugen*
concerned me intimately; and none of us who was connected with
what happened in that affair can ever feel anything but uneasiness
and even embarrassment.

For centuries the English Channel had been at least our sphere of influence, if one may put it that way. Have we not given it our name? Of all the seas of which we have been so proud that we have ruled the waves, that small stretch of water between France and England has occupied in our minds the position of a bastion which we controlled, and heaven help anybody who played fast and loose with it. On February 12, 1942, the Germans did just that, and after the audacious step that was taken then by the German Navy we will never again be able to think of the Channel as something over which we have prior rights.

It had been known for months by everybody that the important German warships which were bottled up in the French port of Brest would eventually have to make a break for freedom, and it was even anticipated that they would make a dash up the Channel and try and get to the safety of the north German ports. Every time I heard the names of the *Scharnhorst* and *Gneisenau,* which were the two big ships tied up in Brest, I felt a chill run down my spine. They were the formidable German battle-cruisers which had sunk our aircraft carrier *Glorious* in the Norwegian campaign, causing such grievous loss to the R.A.F. We in the Air Force were desperately anxious, if only for personal reasons, to see the end of these two ships.

Adolf Hitler and his staff were always faced with the vital problem of providing adequate protection of German interests in the iron ore which they were receiving from northern Norway and Sweden. Hitler developed a hunch that we were about to make another attempt at an invasion of Norway. The fact that we had no such plan in mind has no bearing on what then happened. Hitler ordered that the German warships should be moved from Brest to German bases from which they could operate against our invasion forces; and he ordered, moreover, that the movement should be made through the English Channel. The German naval staff were shaken enough by this order, but it had to be carried out, and plans were made for it.

There was no lack of appreciation on our part of what might happen, although we could not know, of course, exactly what the Germans had in mind. But our own plans for such a breakout from Brest were made by the Royal Navy and the Royal Air Force to cope with the German ships as soon as their noses appeared from their resting place, and those plans became so exact, we thought, that by the second week in February they were even on a basis of a daily expectation. And then, at the last moment, the twin sisters, blunder and destiny, decided to give themselves a good airing, and they chose the English Channel as the scene for it; and their appearance caused our liaison between the Services, and within them, to fall apart.

The German warships set out from Brest late at night on February 11, and they started their run up the English Channel, evading by a most extraordinary string of circumstances that were particularly unfortunate for us any detection by the Coastal Command aircraft which were purposely placed on patrol outside Brest with the sole object of watching for any movements. From the time when there first came indications, about eight o'clock in the morning, that the ships had possibly started steaming up the Channel, the R.A.F. did not come out of the affair very well. Coastal Command, in particular, should have done much better, although they were handicapped in the initial stages by the unserviceability of their reconnaissance aircraft off Brest, and the failure of their airborne radar sets during the most critical period of their patrols.

I had received notification from my own radar people fairly early in the morning that something was brewing, and I went down to the underground Operations Room to see for myself what it was all about. The plots from our long-range radar stations started going down on the operations table in such a way that it was thought that there might be quite a lot of air activity at the extreme range to which radar could see to the southwest, well down into the Channel. The plots from the radar stations kept appearing and then quickly disappearing, which indicated that there might be a swarm of aircraft low down; but the whole thing was moving very slowly for aircraft. It might be a swarm of aircraft circling over something that was moving below them. But on the other hand it might be a fault in our equipment, which was also recording the reception of some very suspicious interference.

During the time that all this was happening, our controllers both at Fighter Command and at No. 11 Group were greatly perplexed in trying to interpret these evanescent indications. It was not unusual for such indications to appear in this inexplicable way off the enemy coast, and they could have been, as was known from past experience, either air-sea rescue operations or merely training flights. There was little that could be regarded as definite except that the whole thing did appear to be moving slowly up the Channel at about twenty to twenty-five miles an hour. All this was being reported to everybody concerned, but for a while it was generally agreed that the plots were no more than some freak in radar reception.

The wretched state of the weather that day prevented any

extensive air reconnaissance. In any case it was not the responsibility of Fighter Command because the patrols of our reconnaissance Spitfires were limited by their range to the area out into the
Channel only as far as the mouth of the Somme. And it was not
for me to interfere with any plans that might be under way by
Coastal Command. It was not until about eleven o'clock in the
morning that the first actual sighting of the German ships came
about, confirming that they were certainly on their way; and even
then it was a sighting that came about entirely by chance, and was
made by two of my particularly well-known fighter pilots.

The station commander at Kenley, Group Captain Victor
Beamish, and the leader of the wing from that station, Wing
Commander R. F. Boyd, both of whom had distinguished themselves in the Battle of Britain, had been on a quick intruder flight
in two Spitfires over France. On their way back they got into a
scrap with some fighters which were part of the air cover for the
German warships. What they saw below them made their eyes
nearly pop out of their heads. The big German warships and their
many smaller escorting ships were steaming up the Channel, and
the whole fleet had already arrived as far up as the mouth of the
Somme. Following instructions Beamish maintained the radio
silence that was rigidly demanded of all pilots, and he did not
report what he had seen until he landed back at Kenley. It might
have been excusable for him to have said something on the radio,
as it would have established the fact that the German ships were
on their way and it would have given their position and saved a lot
of time in helping to get at them. But Beamish did not know that
any movement of these warships was even anticipated.

Once we all knew for sure that the German ships were out, and
we had fixed their position, everything should have been fairly
plain sailing. But the Germans were in luck, with the weather
rapidly deteriorating. Added to that there was triggered off an
extraordinary chain of blunders and misunderstandings on our
part. So far as Fighter Command was concerned there was little
that we could do beyond providing radar information. But there
was not all that one could have wished for in the alert state of
liaison which should have existed between No. 11 Group of my
command and the corresponding groups of Coastal Command, as
well as between Bomber Command, the Air Ministry, the Admiralty, and the naval headquarters at Dover, which were still under
the command of Bertie Ramsay.

As the great German ships made their audacious passage

through the Strait of Dover, our Army gunners, who were severely
handicapped by the wretched state of the visibility, tried to get at
them with their big coastal guns, but without effect. There was also
an ineffectual attack by some M.T.B.'s from Dover. Then shortly
after midday, with the weather deteriorating even more rapidly, six
old and pitifully slow Swordfish of the Fleet Air Arm, flying from
the R.A.F. station at Manston, set out to make torpedo attacks.
Fighter Command undertook, despite a lack of adequate warning,
to try and provide them with five fighter squadrons for cover and
diversionary attacks, but it was all done in too much of a rush, and
only one squadron of Spitfires arrived in time to join up with the
naval aircraft. The rest got to the scene of the action as soon as
they could, but by then the Swordfish attack on the German ships,
which were through the Strait of Dover and off the French coast in
the vicinity of Dunkirk, had been attempted. It was made in filthy
weather, and although it was a complete disaster for the naval
airmen it was one of the most gallant efforts, and it stands greatly
to the credit of the Royal Navy.

Our own Spitfires were engaged by a vastly superior force of
escorting German fighters, and they were kept so busy fighting for
their lives that they were unable to be of any help to the unfortunate Swordfish, which had to plod on with their torpedo attacks in
the face of withering and devastating fire of all descriptions from
the German ships as well as from the enemy fighters. All six
Swordfish were shot down, and not one of their torpedoes hit
anything. Of the eighteen men who flew in those aircraft on that
attack only five survived. Their leader, Lieutenant-Commander
Eugene Esmonde, was among those killed, and for his extraordinary gallantry in leading the attack he was awarded a posthumous
Victoria Cross, which was the first to be won by the Fleet Air
Arm.

As the flag officer in command at Dover, Bertie Ramsay was
intimately concerned with this whole operation. Since he was such
an old and good friend of mine, it was all the more painful for me
when I heard about the strong protest that he made over the failure
of Fighter Command to provide the full escort which he regarded
as having been promised for the Swordfish. But time and the
weather were against us.

On the other hand, while those few Fleet Air Arm air crews so
willingly made the sacrifice of their lives against what they knew
were such appalling odds, there were failures for which the Air
Force must share a responsibility with the Royal Navy. The few
Coastal aircraft that were available were late in getting off, were

wrongly armed, and, it appeared, did not even know, through a misunderstanding in communications, what they were to do; and the Royal Navy seemed to go just as much astray. None of the M.T.B.'s, for all their determined efforts, succeeded in getting through the screen of German escorting vessels, and no hits were scored.

When destroyers of the Royal Navy were finally sent out from Harwich, they deliberately risked their necks and made their way through what was understood to be one of our own minefields in order to save time and get at the enemy ships that much quicker, only to learn later that the minefield did not exist. They made a determined attack in the filthy weather, but they were easily beaten off by the superior German forces. Bomber Command had plenty of aircraft available, but they carried the wrong type of bombs for the attacks that had to be made under the weather conditions then prevailing, which, in any case, severely hampered their operations. Their attacks resulted in fifteen aircraft being lost with no hits scored on any of the enemy ships.

At the time I was at a loss to understand the reluctance on the part of the Royal Navy to have available units of the Home Fleet ready to send out into the North Sea. I considered then that the prizes to be gained in an action with ships of the importance of the *Scharnhorst* and the *Gneisenau* and the *Prinz Eugen* would have been worth bringing some of our bigger ships into action in time to intercept the German warships before they could get within reach of the safety of their home ports. As it was, the enemy warships got away with it, even though they did hit some mines which failed to do more than slight damage, and they all made the safety of those home ports.

The German fighters which provided the air cover were under the overall command of Adolf Galland, who had by then been promoted to the position of general of the Fighter Arm. "The pilots of the R.A.F. fought bravely, tenaciously and untiringly," he has said, "but had been sent into action with insufficient planning, without a clear concept of the attack, without a centre of gravity and without systematic tactics." Unpalatable though it may be, there is a great deal of truth in that German appreciation of what happened that day.

So far as Fighter Command was concerned, we were put off our guard through a shrewd and effective use that was made by the Germans of some new techniques that they had evolved in their interference with our radar screen. Sir Robert Watson-Watt has made a spirited defense of our radar equipment, along with a detailed examination of the operations involved in that dash through the Channel. "If I am held to my reiterated statement that radar is not merely an equipment or a group of equipments, but a system," he has stated, "then the radar system did fail—but the electronics held out; the men behind the electronics were lamentably far behind."

The reaction from the British public to this apparent German success was what might have been expected, and I listened to and read some pretty harsh statements. "Nothing more mortifying to the pride of sea-power in Home Waters has happened since the 17th century" was the way in which *The Times* summed it up. The outcry was a noisy one, and, as might be expected, there was an official inquiry into the whole affair. It was surprisingly mild in its findings because of considerations which could not, at the time, be generally appreciated.

"Viewed in the after-light and in its larger aspects the episode was highly advantageous to us," Winston Churchill was to state after the war in summarizing the results of that day's activities. At the time our pride was hurt, and some searching comments were made; but Churchill's view proved to be the correct one. With the German ships effectively bottled up in their home port there was an immediate and widespread relief from the threat to the whole of the Atlantic that had existed so long as they remained in Brest; but in the flurry at the time, and again for reasons of security, the implications behind that, far-reaching though they were, could not be easily understood.

The last word on this affair probably rests in the opinion expressed afterward by Admiral Raeder, the Commander-in-Chief of the German Navy. It was a tactical success, he is said to have commented, but a strategic defeat. Nearly two years later, the *Scharnhorst* was sunk in an action in the Barents Sea; the *Prinz Eugen* was torpedoed off the Norwegian coast a short time after the Channel dash and had to limp back to its base; the *Gneisenau* never did put to sea again after getting back to Germany. Bomber Command reduced her to a wreck.

The broadening of the fronts in the world war brought about by the entry into it of the United States and Japan called for an immediate and effective linking of the Anglo-American efforts that were to be made against Germany in the air, and Fighter Command became closely involved in this. That brought a great increase in the number of visitors to Bentley Priory, and I welcomed the Americans because I liked them and I had high hopes that we would be able to work well together.

Some time before the United States became involved, their Ambassador to this country, John Winant, had visited my headquarters, and for a personal reason I was delighted that I was able to show him around. I had not seen him since the first and only other time that we had met. As a pilot in the American air service, he had come to see me one afternoon in the summer of 1918 at our airfield on the Western Front, and he had completely won me over in his earnest request to be allowed to satisfy his curiosity about it by flying one of the S.E.5a's of my squadron. He was then a lieutenant in the American Army, and he had made the unforgettable impression on me that he was to make upon everybody with whom he came in contact.

In the spring of 1942 there arrived at my headquarters as a colonel in the United States Army Air Forces none other than Larry Callahan. I had not seen him since those days when he had flown with us on the Western Front. He immediately attracted attention at Bentley Priory through his amiable and gently humorous nature, but more than that he was wearing the ribbon of our Distinguished Flying Cross which he had won while flying S.E.5a's with No. 85 Squadron on the Western Front in 1918. The mere sight of that ribbon alone—a rare enough one to see then on an American uniform—and the knowledge of his story were quite enough to open for him every door at our headquarters. That was one of the very reasons why he had been sent to us.

A stockbroker in Chicago during the years between the wars, Larry Callahan had been smartly brought back into the American Army Air Forces when they had come into the war. He was sent to England well in advance of the main body of the Eighth Fighter Command staff which was to operate here, and he was to learn all that he could from us. He joined the intelligence staff at my headquarters, and he also spent a great deal of his time visiting our fighter stations and talking with our pilots about the latest tactics in air fighting. There could have been no better man than Larry Callahan to carry out this early work, and apart from my own personal delight in welcoming him to Bentley Priory there was in his being with us a further reason for my hope that we would be able to establish the closest liaison between our two air forces.

It was to the credit of the Americans that they showed right at the outset such a felicitous understanding in their appreciation of the value of liaison. They also showed just as much imagination when the time came a few weeks later for them to establish at my headquarters an American Army Air Forces liaison section. The officer in charge—and as such a member of my staff—was Colonel J. C. Stanley, the "Jake" Stanley of *War Birds,* and an old friend of Larry Callahan's. He was also a stockbroker, from New York. As with the others in *War Birds,* he had learned to fly in England with the Royal Flying Corps, and he had been shot down, becoming a prisoner-of-war, while serving with one of the Bristol Fighter squadrons of the R.A.F. in 1918.

Through the prospect of actually working so closely with men such as Larry Callahan and Jake Stanley I came to form high hopes for the closest possible liaison which I felt was going to be so necesssary between the air forces of our two countries. The air was becoming increasingly important, and it was so necessary that we should work together, and Callahan and Stanley went a long way, in their understanding of us, in trying to achieve the unity of effort that was possibly of more importance in the air than in either of the other two Services.

In their planning after the United States came into the war, the first of the American fighter squadrons was due to arrive in England in the spring of 1942, and we had arranged to equip them with Spitfires. This was to be done at the airdrome at Atcham, in Shropshire, which was one of the first of the American air bases established in this country. The Spitfires and all the necessary equipment for the squadron were delivered to Atcham well ahead of time, and I decided to be there myself when the American pilots arrived so that I could personally welcome them to England.

At that time I was in the habit of flying around my command in a Percival Proctor, which was kept at the airfield at Northolt. It was a comfortable little two-seater, and for the visit to Atcham I invited Larry Callahan to come along with me as my passenger. The weather report for the day of our trip across England was not good, and I thought that I detected some signs of apprehension on the face of Larry Callahan from the moment when we started off on our flight.

There was reason enough for Callahan's feeling that way because almost immediately after leaving Northolt we ran into far too much fog and mist for my liking, and three times I was forced to land because of poor visibility. I did not do it intentionally, but I gave poor Callahan an awful fright in one of the landings I made, which was on a small grass airfield at Worcester. I came in rather fast, and we ended up with the propeller of the aircraft only about a yard or so from the hedge at the far end of the field. It was a testing time for him, but he cheerfully put a very good face on it.

When we finally got to Atcham we found that the Americans were delighted with the Spitfires which they had found waiting for them. During the afternoon the weather improved, and I was able to ease the pressure on Callahan's mind by flying an uneventful return trip to Northolt.

It took the Americans only a remarkably short time after the disaster of Pearl Harbor to establish in England a headquarters for their air forces which were to operate against Germany. They set up their Eighth Air Force Headquarters, under Major General Carl Spaatz, part of which was their Bomber Command under Brigadier General Ira C. Eaker, who was already known to me. As a colonel in the U.S. Army Air Forces, Eaker had first visited my headquarters during the previous summer, along with other American military observers.

One of the great men in American military aviation, Tooey Spaatz was in command of a fighter squadron in the American air service on the Western Front in the First World War, and by the time of the outbreak of the second war he was chief of staff to Hap Arnold. He was to emerge from the war as one of their great air commanders noted more for action than talking. How he came to acquire that odd nickname of his I do not know, but there is a good story that was told by Hap Arnold about what he called "the omnipresence" of Spaatz and his surname that has always stuck in my mind. An airman was in hospital for an examination, the story goes, and the doctor asked him if he could see spots in front of his eyes. "My God . . . do I have to see him in here too!" the airman exclaimed.

In the summer of 1942 I was promoted to the rank of air chief marshal, and while it was of personal pleasure to me to find myself at what I considered was the top of the tree—the final step to Marshal of the Royal Air Force was beyond even one's wildest dreams for that was a rank which was reserved for those who became Chief of the Air Staff—it did introduce from time to time some little embarrassment in our dealings with the Americans. By then we had been at war going on for well over two years, and seniority in rank in our greatly expanded armed forces had come through earning it the hard way. It was not possible for the Americans, while they were still at peace and with much smaller forces, to have senior officers with ranks equivalent to ours.

By April, 1942, agreement had been reached between the British and the American governments that joint planning should start for an attack across the English Channel against the German

occupation of France. The one man who was to become the most
responsible of all for that operation, Dwight D. Eisenhower, has
said of that agreement: "History has proved that nothing is more
difficult in war than to adhere to a single strategic plan. Unforeseen
and glittering promise on the one hand and unexpected difficulty or
risk upon the other present constant temptation to desert the
chosen line of action in favor of another. This one was no exception . . ."

While I was still Commander-in-Chief of Fighter Command I
was appointed, also in the summer of 1942, to act as the air
representative on the joint Anglo-American committee that was set
up to formulate the plans for our invasion of Europe. Just before
that, Major General Eisenhower, as he was then, had made his first
visit to Great Britain to examine, as a senior member of the
military staff in Washington, the "future organization and development of our European forces." Eisenhower was highly thought of
by the Americans, and from the start he made a very favorable
impression on Winston Churchill.

As a result of the report that Eisenhower made when he
returned to Washington after that first visit to London, he was
appointed commander of the American Army in the European
theater. With that he also became a member of our committee
which was directing the planning for the invasion of Europe. This
was the first step that was taken in building toward what later
became known as "Overlord": the invasion of Normandy. The
other members of the committee were Bernard Paget, the Commander-in-Chief, Home Forces, representing the British Army,
and, of particular interest to me personally, Bertie Ramsay, who
was responsible for the plans for the Royal Navy.

In those early stages of our planning we gave no thought to the
possibility of going into France through Normandy. For one thing
the range of our fighters in 1942 was not sufficient to be able to
give adequate fighter cover over the beachheads. We felt bound to
plan for an invasion across the narrow part of the Channel in the
Pas de Calais, with possible landings in the neighborhood of Calais
and Boulogne. From our discussions I soon formed, as did everybody else, a strong personal liking for Eisenhower. He was so
patently a genuine and honest man. It is true that he was not, as a
soldier, experienced in command in battle; but I think even then
that he had greater inherent qualities to offer in the role that he
was to play than just experience in actual fighting.

From the outset it was so clear that Dwight D. Eisenhower was
a man amongst men, that he had a positive attractiveness in his

character that was rooted in simplicity and sincerity, and that he was outstanding in his willingness to cooperate. It was apparent even then that he had a unique ability as a negotiator, which stemmed from the very sensible way in which he always seemed to be able to weigh up so well what was possible and what was not possible. Of all those of us who were concerned with that early planning it seemed to me that Eisenhower was always the one who had his feet most firmly planted on the ground. Even then he was showing his great ability to be able to hold a team together, and to extract all that there was to be had out of its members.

Of all those of us who were casting our thoughts ahead and trying to think in terms of breaking the stranglehold that the Germans had on Europe by making an invasion of France, no one was more eager for action than Winston Churchill. At one stage in our planning he made up his mind that as a first step to gaining a foothold on the Continent we should try and capture one of the Channel Islands. His choice was the island of Alderney. Bernard Paget, who had gained invaluable firsthand experience in the ill-fated Norwegian campaign, and Louis Mountbatten (by then head of Combined Operations), and I were formed into a working party quite separate from the other, bigger, committee, and we were instructed by the Prime Minister to evolve a plan for the capture of Alderney.

We all thought very carefully about the idea, and we felt compelled to point out to Winston Churchill that the island was quite stoutly defended by the Germans with a large number of coastal guns and a strong force of their occupying troops. It was also only twelve miles or so away from the nearest German airdrome, and any attempt at invasion on our part would be wide open to very heavy air attacks; and in order to keep it supplied we would have to maintain in almost continuous action very strong naval forces with powerful fighter cover.

But in spite of all our carefully considered objections, Winston Churchill insisted that we should go ahead and work out a plan. After a great deal of labor we managed to complete one. It was a plan by which, through a tremendous expenditure of effort, and with an anticipation of very heavy casualties, we thought that we might stand a chance of capturing Alderney. And then we asked ourselves a few pertinent questions. What were we going to do after capturing the island? What was the use of having it? Where was it all leading us?

When we came to present our plan to the Prime Minister we

plucked up our courage and we put these questions to him, stressing again that the plan would call for a continuous and major operation to keep the island, even if we were able to capture it, and to supply it with food and ammunition and everything else that would be needed. Without any further hesitation, Winston Churchill instructed us to abandon the idea. It is possible now to understand the nature of the pressures that were being brought to bear on the Prime Minister which could not be known by us, and at the time it seemed, in our more restricted view, that before he reached his decision—which in our eyes was a foregone one—there had been expended and wasted a great deal of time and energy on the part of senior commanders and their staffs.

In that sense this personal contact with the methods employed by Winston Churchill under certain circumstances leads me to sympathize so much with Alan Brooke over what, at times, he had to contend with, and to understand why he spoke with such feeling in his diaries about the time and the effort that he had to waste on detailed planning which in the end turned out to be so fruitless.

All of us who ever had any dealings with the Prime Minister could not help but become vexed at times with the way in which he would fly mercurially off on those tangents to which he was so addicted. That distinguished sailor, Admiral of the Fleet Viscount Cunningham, who was one of the great commanders produced by the Royal Navy, spoke feelingly about that in telling his own story; and Alan Brooke recorded in his diary that he attended one meeting with the First Sea Lord, over which Winston Churchill presided, with "dear old Cunningham so wild with rage that he hardly dared to let himself speak!"

But what would have happened to us without, in the words of Sir Arthur Bryant, "the man who rallied a defeated nation in storm and disaster: passionate, impetuous, daring, indomitable, terrible in anger and pursuing every expedient—sometimes brilliant, sometimes, for he was prepared to try almost everything, fantastic—that could bring about victory." Winston Churchill has spoken movingly about the debt that is owed to the few, and of that the Royal Air Force is proud. But what of our debt to him? What yardstick can we possibly use in trying to assess that?

THROUGHOUT THE SPRING and the early summer of 1942, Fighter Command conducted a continuous and strenuous air offensive out over France and Belgium, with fighters escorting the bombers on circuses, and the fighters alone going out in great sweeps. With the Russians having to face another German onslaught after the bitter winter, we were left in no doubt by them that they expected us to help in every way that we could to relieve the pressure on their front in the east. That we made the effort from Britain alone, quite apart from the Middle East, is revealed in our air losses. Over a period of about four months during that spring and early summer we lost 314 fighters and bombers, with the Germans losing only 90 aircraft. The new German fighters exacted a serious toll for our intrusion over their air space; but the pressure had to be maintained.

In all the efforts that were made during that time to try and find some way of helping the Russians there was planned one operation which has since been the source of seemingly endless controversy and heartache, not to mention inflamed tempers. As early as May, Alan Brooke was writing in his diary: "Little did I ever think in the old days of my regular journeys from Newhaven to Dieppe that I should have been planning as I was this morning." He was referring to the plan that had been put up by the Combined Operations Headquarters, under Admiral Lord Louis Mountbatten, for the raid on Dieppe.

I wonder how many there are now of those who in even greater numbers follow that well-traveled route from Newhaven to Dieppe who ever pause to think about what happened at Dieppe during seven hours in the morning of August 19, 1942? Such was the nature of the event that, in the words of one sober critic, it "must be counted among the most tragic and costly disasters in the annals of war." Irrational pressures were brought to bear—from the Americans as well as the Russians—for a landing on the French coast, and it was decided to make at least some sort of show by

527

capturing Dieppe, by holding it for a while in the face of an
expected opposition from the Germans, and by then bringing off
what would be considered a successful withdrawal.

In an operation as important as this my own command was
called upon to supply a massive fighter cover, and I had at my
disposal for it, limited though it was in its scope, a much larger
force of fighters than had fought even in the Battle of Britain.
Fighter Command looked forward with eagerness to a large-scale
encounter with the Luftwaffe, and I was familiar with all the
planning for the raid. The actual operations were to be handled by
No. 11 Group, under Trafford Leigh-Mallory.

At the start, the fighter side of the operation was planned by my
headquarters staff, and after that had been worked out, the details
and the execution of the show were in the hands of the group staff.
After the way in which the Royal Air Force had been operating in
the skies out over France, I thought that the whole operation, quite
apart from the air engagements, might be a good means of stirring
up the Germans on the ground and of keeping them on the hop.
From the Combined Operations point of view, we were inclined to
look upon it as possibly the first of a number of raids which would
help to train our own people, both on the ground and in the air, for
things to come.

What we got in stirring things up was far more than we had
bargained for, and ever since that day a great deal has been said
and written about the ill-fated Dieppe raid. It was difficult at the
time to see what was achieved because our casualties were so
heavy; and in the light of all that we now know it would appear
that there were many blunders Five thousand Canadian soliders
made the landing that morning, supported by detachments of
British commandos and the Royal Navy. By nightfall only just
over two thousand Canadians had managed to get back to England. It has been described by one historian, Eric Maguire, as "the
blackest day in Canadian military history" with the Canadian
Army losing "more men as prisoners of war than they did in all the
rest of the European campaign."

But heavy as the Canadian losses were—and that must never be
forgotten—there was much more to it than that. Lessons were
learned, admittedly at a very high price, so that it is not altogether
correct to say that the Dieppe raid was not worthwhile. For the
R.A.F. it was a hard-won success, and it provided us with an
enormous amount of experience through actual participation in an
amphibious operation. We learned in a short time a great deal
about methods of giving air support to a seaborne landing on the

ground, and it was that experience which was of the greatest value in the gigantic operations of this nature that lay ahead.

In the planning, the Canadians, who were never shy of a fight, were understandably keen enough about the whole idea of the raid, which is perhaps the reason why, in reaction, there was so much dissatisfaction over the result. Their keenness led them to expect a big success. They attacked with the utmost vigor, but they were repulsed from the outset with a surprising and overwhelming ferocity. There was a lot of chatter immediately afterward which bruited about the idea that the Germans had been alerted about our intentions, and that allegation has since gone on being repeated, but there is no very conclusive proof of it. In any case, the Germans had their own plans for the defense of Dieppe, just as they had for every other place along the French coast which they thought we might be likely to attack. They would have been a pretty stupid lot if they had not worked out by then comprehensive plans for defense.

What appealed to my imagination about the proposed operation was that it was a splendid opportunity to gain experience, and, at the same time, to catch the Luftwaffe, which was already extended through its commitments on the Russian front as well as in the Mediterranean, at a disadvantage and wholly on the defensive. In our offensive sweeps over France the Germans were becoming more and more difficult to provoke into accepting a strong challenge, and I felt that in this operation they would have to come up.

On the day itself the German Air Force accepted the challenge, and we were not as successful in actual scores as I had hoped for, or even as I had thought we were by the end of the day. With everything in our favor, we employed a force of over 600 fighters —56 of our fighter squadrons—and we went looking for a big air battle. "They had one of a size and ferocity sufficient to satisfy even the most bloodthirsty," Peter Wykeham has commented. The R.A.F. lost 106 aircraft, 88 of which were fighters. Forty-eight enemy aircraft were destroyed, and 24 were damaged.

But as was so often the case, bare statistics do not reveal the whole story. My fighters succeeded in every way in keeping the Luftwaffe away from the battle area, and our troops on the ground were at least not harassed or molested by opposing enemy air attacks. The naval and military commanders in the operation credited our cooperation in the air with being "faultless"; and the later report from Combined Operations Headquarters stated: "The most striking achievement was the success of the Royal Air Force in providing cover . . ." With that assurance we could at least feel that so far as the air was concerned we had contributed a fair share to the Dieppe operation, even if the overall picture of that day's work was such a sorry one.

Even before the raid on Dieppe, we had come to realize that we were not destroying as many enemy aircraft as we had hoped that we would be able to in our operations out over France and Belgium. In speaking of the results of the Dieppe raid, Sir Arthur Bryant has said: "This bloody affair, though productive of many valuable lessons, ended the summer's attempt to draw off planes from Russia by trailing Fighter Command's coat over northern France—a gesture that had cost Britain nearly a thousand pilots and aircraft."

That gesture had indeed been a costly one, and while I was not at all happy about having to curtail our activities, we had to ease off with our fighter offensive. Other theaters of the war were making their demands for aircraft and air crews, and these demands had to be met. So far as home defense was concerned, we were more than strong enough, and with the Anglo-American landings in northwest Africa early in November, 1942, the attacks on this country from the Luftwaffe dwindled away even more as the Germans went about the occupation that they then made of the rest of France, and the movement of many of their aircraft down to the Mediterranean.

By the end of 1942 the strength and power of Fighter Command had reached what were to be the greatest of its entire existence. I had then been its Commander-in-Chief for two years, and during that time events had occurred on the various fronts of the war—which had become a world-wide conflagration—that were of the utmost significance. Not the least of these was the increasing activity in the battles along the North African coast, which were being waged at the same time that the Russian counteroffensive at Stalingrad became the key to what was to happen on the Eastern Front.

Some weeks after the Dieppe raid, I was sent for by Sir Archibald Sinclair. He told me that I was to be appointed Air Officer Commanding-in-Chief, Middle East, in place of Arthur Tedder. Sinclair also told me that a big attack was about to be launched in the desert at Alamein, but, he said, it was thought only fair not to move Tedder—who was to return to the United Kingdom to become Vice-Chief of the Air Staff—until that battle had been fought. Tedder had been in the Middle East since December, 1940, first as deputy Commander-in-Chief, and then as Commander-in-

Chief, with his headquarters in Cairo since June 1, 1941. He had
worked hard on the plans for this forthcoming campaign, and it
was obviously only right that he should be allowed to see the job
through. His concern had been to bring the Desert Air Force up
to the highest possible state of efficiency, with special training for
the support that it was to give to the Eighth Army.

From what I heard through other sources, my posting to the
Middle East was not exactly welcomed by everybody. The Prime
Minister, for one, was opposed to it, being of the opinion that I
should stay where I was at Fighter Command; and apparently
Arthur Tedder himself did not like the idea of being replaced. He
felt, as any operational commander would have, that he was being
rather shunted into a back room, important though that back room
might be, in his appointment to the Air Ministry as V.-C.A.S.

I agreed with those at the Air Ministry who thought that it
would be fairer to let Arthur Tedder fight at least the start of the
air side of the launching of the offensive by the Eighth Army at
Alamein. At the same time this news of a move for me caused in
my own mind rather mixed feelings. I was particularly attached to
Fighter Command, where I felt that I was doing reasonably well;
and I was also finding extremely interesting the work that I was
doing in the long-term planning for the air side of the future
invasion of France, if that should ever come off.

On the other hand, I knew the Middle East through having
served there. I had liked it, and, in a way, I had come under the
odd spell that it can exert, so that I had no personal objection to
going back there. The appointment itself was a senior and important one, and it also promised to be of great interest because I
realized that the projected operations along the whole of the North
African coast might well lead to important successes in the war.
There was, in fact, a far more definite promise of immediate action
out there than there was in any of the planning that was being
done for what might take place from Great Britain.

By the end of the year, and after some weeks of an unsatisfactory state of indecision, it was finally decided that the time had
come for me to be on my way, and for Arthur Tedder to come
back to London; and at the end of November I handed over
Fighter Command to Trafford Leigh-Mallory. But even then,
problems arose about how I was to get out to Egypt. The Air
Ministry had decided on selecting the safest possible routes for
their senior officers on journeys to the Middle East, and I had to

accept the plan that I should follow what was called the Horse-shoe Route.

For the start this roundabout journey meant flying out to Freetown, in west Africa, by B.O.A.C. flyingboat, with one stop at Lisbon. But no sooner had we arrived in Lisbon—my personal assistant, Ronnie Edwards, was going out with me—than the flyingboat became unserviceable. Our Ambassador in Lisbon invited me to stay at the Embassy, but that meant that I was almost in a state of confinement. Portugal was neutral, and Lisbon was crawling with spies. I had to wear civilian clothes all the time that I spent there—which was a curious enough experience after having been for so long in uniform—and I was advised not to venture outside the precincts of the Embassy. But I did manage to make a quiet and unobtrusive visit to the airport at Lisbon, where I watched some German transport aircraft as they arrived and departed. I could not help wondering about the nature of their business, and what was going on behind the scenes at the other end of their flights.

When the whole story was revealed after the war of the way in which the Nazi leaders brought such ruin to their own country, I learned that it was at this time, at the beginning of 1943, when the future of my own fortunes was being shaped in a way which I would never have thought possible, that Hermann Goering began his decline. His old flying comrade Karl Bodenschatz eventually came to reveal that decline, which was accompanied by a mounting antipathy on Hitler's part toward the Luftwaffe. By then Goering, in his drug addiction and megalomania, had lost all sense of reality, and he appeared to spend most of his time acquiring vast collections of works of art. There was precious little time left for him to attend to affairs of state, or to those of the Luftwaffe for which he was still responsible.

The refusal by Hermann Goering, or his inability, to face the facts has been described by Adolf Galland, who was then the youngest major-general in the German Air Force, as "an irresponsibility of such magnitude that it can only be measured by the consequences it had for the Reich and for all the people entrusted to his care and protection." No one could ever question the willingness of the men of the Luftwaffe such as Adolf Galland to fight for their own country, and as a young commander he had with Goering "clashes which went far beyond what can be judged as permissible between the C.-in-C. and his subordinate even in the most liberal army." We had our own problems in the clashes of temperaments and opinions that occurred between junior and senior commanders, but they were nothing compared to the sheer insanity of the treatment of the German Air Force by the Nazi leaders.

From Lisbon I flew by flyingboat on to Freetown, across central Africa in a Hudson to Khartoum, and from there by the B.O.A.C. flyingboat that had come up from South Africa, following the Nile down to Cairo. It was a great relief to complete the tedious journey, which had only served to make me particularly anxious to get back to work. But from the moment that I arrived at our headquarters in Cairo I realized that it was not going to be quite as simple as all that. I had known Arthur Tedder, who was by then also an air chief marshal, for many years, and I had come to think that we understood each other; and for all that I had heard about his reluctance to give up what was a very important and active operational command, I did not anticipate any difficulties.

But it was impossible for me to avoid the unhappy impression that I got as soon as I arrived in Cairo that I was not welcome there, though why that should have been I could not quite understand. Arthur Tedder tried in several different ways (including arrangements for me to make a tour of inspection of R.A.F. units in Palestine, Syria, Iraq and Persia as an introduction to my new command) to delay as long as possible having to hand over to me. I gathered from what he said that he definitely did not want to be Vice-Chief of the Air Staff. But I had a feeling that there was something more to it than that, and a couple of weeks later there was provided the answer.

A full-scale conference was held in Casablanca, in Morocco, in the middle of January, 1943, at which President Roosevelt and our Prime Minister and their staffs met to decide upon important and far-reaching plans for the future of the war. One of the decisions reached was to establish immediately a new structure so far as the air was concerned which was to be known as Mediterranean Air Command. Subordinate to it were to be the Middle East, my own command; Malta, under Keith Park; and the North-West African Air Forces which were commanded by Tooey Spaatz. Arthur Tedder was appointed Air Commander-in-Chief of the new structure, with headquarters alongside Eisenhower's in Algiers.

I had heard some vague talk that Arthur Tedder had been urging upon the High Command in Algiers and on the Air Ministry the need for a single, overall command of the air in the Mediterranean, but for some reason that I did not understand I was never fully informed about it. The plan called for a unification which would embrace all the British and American air forces all the way from Algeria to the Middle East, and including the whole of the latter so far as operations were concerned. It sounded like a reasonable enough idea, and Tedder, with all his recent experience, was naturally just the man for the job.

But there was one aspect of it which was to provide the seeds for future snags, and it is to be found in the statement made by the official historians which reads: "The Air Commander-in-Chief would be responsible to Eisenhower for operations in connection with Tunisia, but to the British Chiefs of Staff for operations in the Middle East."

For a few weeks after taking over the command in the Middle East from Arthur Tedder, I had the superb experience of being the Commander-in-Chief of the Royal Air Force which was supporting the Eighth Army under General Sir Bernard Montgomery, as he had recently become, in their great drive along the coast of North Africa. But then the battle ran away from me, and I found myself more or less left at the wrong end of the Mediterranean without any great amount of operational activity.

The Middle East Command of the Royal Air Force was a well established one, dating back to its origin in the First World War with the formation in 1916 of the Middle East Brigade of the Royal Flying Corps, whose task was "to establish a central command in Egypt for the administration, organisation, and maintenance of all Royal Flying Corps detachments in Egypt, Mesopotamia, East Africa, and, in due course, Salonika." That "in due course, Salonika" was to have a curiously apt connotation in what we were to endeavor to achieve twenty-seven years later.

The "ample boundaries" of the Middle East, as Philip Guedalla once described them, had come to include a vast and complicated organization. I had under my command the Desert Air Force, which had been working with the victorious Eighth Army on its great fight through Cyrenaica and Tripoli, as well as all the many Air Force units located in Egypt itself; and I was also responsible for the air side of our military affairs in Palestine, Lebanon, Syria, Iraq, Iran, the Persian Gulf, Aden, the Sudan and East Africa. That called for vast administrative problems alone, all of which were handled by my headquarters in Cairo, and they were quite apart from our more active role as a fully operational command.

To all of us it was the work of the Desert Air Force and the bomber groups in the Western Desert that claimed our closest attention. The battle had been moving rapidly to the west, and the Eighth Army was just east of Tripoli itself when I took over the Air Force in the Middle East. The western limit of my command was the boundary between Tripoli and Tunisia, and the matter of greatest interest to me was the planning that was being done for the capture of Tripoli. With that in mind, I made it one of my first tasks to pay a visit to the headquarters up in the desert, and there I had discussions with Mary Coningham, who was doing very well as the Air Officer Commanding the Desert Air Force with the rank of air vice-marshal.

"Army and Air Force worked on one plan, closely knitted together, and the two headquarters were side by side," Montgomery has said of the campaign in the desert. On my first visit to their headquarters I stayed with Mary Coningham in one of his caravans, and together we had dinner with Monty in a tent in the desert not very far from Tripoli. Enemy bombers droned low overhead throughout dinner, apparently looking for a chink of light on which to lob some bombs. It reminded me of the nights at Bertangles, on the Western Front, in 1918, when the German bombers used to come over in just the same way, and how one night they caught us out with disastrous results.

It was so immensely interesting being able to see Monty in action. He had made a great success of the job that he had been more or less pitchforked into, and from the discussions that I had with him and with Mary Coningham about their immediate plans it was apparent that the spirit of cooperation between the Army and the Air Force was exceedingly good. It was then that I came to form the strong admiration for Montgomery that I have found no reason to alter, for all the quirks of his character and the outbursts to which he is so addicted. I have always liked and respected him, and out there in the desert I saw in full bloom his perspicacity, his quickness in being able to grasp the significance of every situation, and his energy and enthusiasm.

After all the years during which we in the Air Force had had to fight so hard in order to explain the air to the generals and the admirals, it was so encouraging to find in Montgomery a senior British general who was prepared to treat the R.A.F. as we wished to be treated: as an equal Service with problems that were uniquely ours. Many senior Army commanders just went their way in ignorance of the air and ignoring us or, at best, looking upon us as a subordinate command to which orders should be given as to what they should do and how they should do it.

When I first arrived out in the Middle East, the air headquarters at Malta were still under my command. Keith Park had been there since July, 1942, and he had conducted the air battles over Malta with the same dexterity that he had shown at No. 11 Group during the Battle of Britain. But with the formation of Mediterranean Air Command at the beginning of 1943, Malta was taken away from the Middle East. It was absorbed into the new structure, and so became responsible to Arthur Tedder in Algiers.

In the talks that I had with Arthur Tedder on my visits to his headquarters I learned that the plans were already well along for the invasion of Sicily. In casting our thoughts further ahead we discussed the possibilities of making use of my command in attacks on Greece and in the Aegean; but I found that the Americans were not at all interested in anything more than Sicily. They were already showing what was to become such a marked antipathy toward any action in the eastern Mediterranean.

But this antipathy really went back even earlier than that. While he was still the Australian Minister in Washington, and long before he became Minister of State in Cairo, Richard Casey (now Lord Casey, the Governor-General of Australia) had found this strong American disinclination to become involved in the Middle East. In his diary for October 26, 1941, before the United States was even in the war, he wrote: "In particular, the U.S. Army tend to cry down the Middle East campaign, to find fault continually with the British conduct of that campaign, and even to maintain that it is a hopeless cause."

The great success of the Eighth Army in storming along the coast of North Africa had given ample proof that ours was far from being a "hopeless cause." With the Anglo-American landings in North Africa there was a joint effort between our combined forces to push to the east and join up with the Eighth Army as it made its advance to the west. It was then that Dwight D. Eisenhower was called upon to exercise what was probably his greatest attribute: his unequaled ability to keep under control the somewhat unexpected frictions which came about when the Americans and the British were called upon to work so closely together.

These frictions came about largely through petty international jealousies, and Eisenhower, as the Supreme Commander, made it known that he had the strongest aversion to any expressions or demonstrations of such jealousies. It was a situation that was only aggravated when our vastly experienced and battle-hardened Eighth Army made such a fast and victorious advance into Tunisia while the Americans, who were so new to battle, had to face serious setbacks as they came in from Algeria. There were faults on both sides, and if we, the British, flushed with victory, were perhaps inclined to be arrogant about what we had achieved, the Americans showed what was at times all too clearly a marked disinclination to learn from our bitter experience.

But for all this undercurrent of such a regrettable friction, which, although sternly suppressed, went on developing, in my own contacts with the senior American commanders I experienced moments that were both amusing and enlightening. Just before the invasion of Sicily I encountered—any meeting with such a great character cannot be described in any other way—the colorful and likeable General George Patton. It came about through Patton, then already a prominent figure in the American Army, being sent to make a show of himself in Cairo. That, for Patton, was all too easy.

It was believed that the Germans were becoming anxious and uncertain about just what the Anglo-American forces in North Africa were going to do next. They could not very well avoid knowing that we were up to something, but whether it was going to be Sicily or Greece that we were going to invade was what they had to try and find out. We wanted to lead them as far astray as possible, and, if possible, into thinking that we were going for Greece. Part of the plan was to have Patton, who was so well known as one of Eisenhower's generals in the western part of the Mediterranean, stay in Cairo for a week or so with the hope that his presence there might lead the enemy into thinking that the main strike was going to be launched in the eastern Mediterranean.

While it would have been in keeping for George Patton to be taken care of by our Army, for some reason or other it fell to me to look after him while he was in Cairo. My instructions were to take Patton around and show him off so that there could be no doubt in the minds of any of those who might be interested that he was in Cairo. There was no difficulty in putting on the show because Patton himself was a sight to behold, and all too easily identifiable. A man of a commanding figure and presence, he was invariably well turned out, quite often in cavalry breeches and brightly polished field boots.

We enjoyed the company of George Patton during his short stay with us in a way that is still a delight to think about, and at night we took him around on a more or less public display, hoping that any enemy agents lurking around would pay due heed to what they were seeing. Whether we achieved anything in this particular piece of deceptive strategy I do not know, but we were at least provided with a particularly amusing experience which was far divorced from the sterner realities of war. But above all else George Patton was a fighting soldier, and at the end of his little act he went off back to the western Mediterranean. There he took part in the invasion of Sicily, which was much more to his liking than being on display in Cairo; and I did not hear much more about him until he became involved in an unhappy incident in his misguided attempt to discipline a soldier in a hospital, for which he went temporarily into what he himself once described to me as the doghouse.

In addition to the Desert Air Force, we had also had under our control up until the time of reaching the western boundary of Middle East Command fairly strong forces of squadrons of medium and heavy bombers, principally Wellingtons. But when that boundary was reached, they also passed out of our hands and into those of the North-West African Air Forces, and under the control of the Strategic Air Force under the command of Major General James Doolittle, of the United States Army Air Forces. "The exploits of Doolittle in leading the first raid on Tokyo . . . provide a pleasing contradiction to his name," our official historians have said. While there were no problems over the change of command so far as our fighters were concerned—they became part of the Tactical Air Force under Mary Coningham—some of our bomber squadrons were not at first happy about coming under the command of an American general.

When I heard about that I did my best to reassure them, and I pointed out that Jimmy Doolittle was a man of exceptional experience and ability, and that he had already won the Congressional Medal of Honor for the sensational raid that he had led on Tokyo. His record was such that one could not but have for him the greatest admiration and respect. But it was Doolittle himself who most effectively dispelled any doubts that our air crews had about serving under an American. On the very first night on which they were to operate under his command, he appeared at one of our squadrons, and he asked to be allowed to fly with them. The favorable impression that that made on the R.A.F. squadrons which were now serving under him was just what was needed, and we heard nothing more than the occasional grouse about not wanting to serve under an American general.

With so much of our operational force removed from my command, and the bigger war pushing up into Tunisia, I was able to settle down in Cairo and devote more of my time to what was going on in the eastern Mediterranean. I was well satisfied with my relations with the Commanders-in-Chief of the Royal Navy and the Army. When I first got to Cairo, the C.-in-C. of the Army was General Sir Harold Alexander. I found him, as always, a man of great charm and tact, and he was also a skillful and experienced soldier. The Royal Navy was under the command of Admiral Sir Andrew Cunningham, the forthright and able "A.B.C." who was one of the foremost sailors of the second war.

So long as the German and the Italian armies had remained on the threshold of Egypt, the post of the Army Commander-in-Chief in the Middle East was, in the words of Sir Arthur Bryant, "after the post of C.I.G.S. the most important in the Army." Before Harold Alexander had come to fill that appointment—as recently as August of the year before—Middle East had been under the command of General Sir Claude Auchinleck, whom I had known well from the time when he and I had been students together, along with Alan Brooke, on the first course of the Imperial Defence College in 1927.

Despite all that had happened during the time when Auchinleck was in command in the Middle East, with reverses that caused a great deal of mud to be slung at him, I have always believed that he did well in the Middle East, and that his achievements have been unhappily belittled. He was there in a very difficult time, and he had to work with far less resources than were available later, and that was perhaps the biggest factor that contributed to the bad patch in his career, and to what Alan Brooke described as the "intensely distasteful decision" to relieve him of his command.

One could not help but feel some sympathy for the Army out in the Middle East over the rapidity of the changes in their high command. Harold Alexander was C.-in-C. in Cairo for only a few months when he was moved, along with Arthur Tedder, to Algiers, where he became Eisenhower's deputy and commander of all the Allied armies in North Africa. His place in Cairo was then taken by General Sir Maitland Wilson, who was known, because of his massive stature, as "Jumbo." Wilson was altogether different from Alexander. I came to value highly his very good judgment, and over the period of practically the whole of 1943 we worked closely together.

I found Jumbo Wilson particularly helpful in the new sphere of international diplomacy into which I was plunged, and in which I was quite inexperienced. This was coming to play an increasingly important, and so far as I was concerned not very welcome, part in all our work in the Middle East, and we had to maintain close contact with our Ambassador in Cairo, who was Sir Miles Lampson, later to become Lord Killearn. He was a very able and experienced diplomat, but we were never able to see exactly eye to eye, and I was to have several brushes with him which were irritating to me and, I believe, not exactly helpful in certain interests which could have been handled with more discretion.

The Royal Air Force was more fortunate in having at headquarters in Cairo a less hectic switching around of senior officers than that to which the Army was subjected. Quite a few of those on my staff had been there for some time, and there were some whom I had known well for many years. My air officer-in-charge of administration, Air Vice-Marshal G. C. (now Air Chief Marshal Sir George) Pirie, had been a fellow student with me at the Imperial Defence College in 1927. He was a sound, capable administrator, and such was the quality of his mind that it led him, on his retirement from the Royal Air Force, to further his interest in and start practicing law.

It was always of a distinct advantage to a Commander-in-Chief to have on his staff officers whom he could trust either through having served with them through the course of his Service career or through a firsthand experience of their abilities under the more pressing conditions of war. I knew the men upon whom I could rely, and we all understood each other in our work. But in the new sphere of international relations that were more of a diplomatic than a service nature that I encountered in Cairo, I anticipated standing rather in the position of an outsider. It was obvious at the outset that I was going to have to play some part in the tangled scheme of things which has always prevailed in the Middle East. To what extent, and just how I was to play that role, was unknown to me, and it was an experience about which, I felt, I was going to have to be very much on my guard.

But such is the curiously long arm of coincidence that a good deal of guidance in this new field came to me from the least expected but most important quarter. When I arrived in Cairo I resumed a friendship that had started on the Western Front in 1918. I had not seen him since that time, but Dick Casey had already been in Cairo since May, 1942, filling the responsible post, as a member of the War Cabinet, of Minister of State. His advice to me was invaluable. In describing his own work, he has said, "my task in the Middle East was 'to represent the War Cabinet in the area and to act in its name,' to co-ordinate our war effort, endeavouring, with the three Commanders-in-Chief, to ensure that we held Malta and Egypt and as far west as possible, and later to ensure that we drove the enemy out of all the southern coast of the Mediterranean."

That Dick Casey was successful in his work was indicated clearly enough in the great confidence that was placed in him by both the Prime Minister and the President of the United States, as well as all the Service chiefs; and in some ways he had come to represent for Australia, but in an admittedly lesser degree, the unique position in international affairs that was filled by the older South African diplomat Jan Christian Smuts. Of his position by the time that I arrived in Cairo, Casey has said: "In 1943, my task as Minister of State became one of large-scale housekeeping in the Middle East." It was that housekeeping which was to worry nearly all of us.

The last time that I had seen Dick Casey was at Bertangles, near Amiens, in 1918: twenty-five years before. Then he was a major on the headquarters staff of the Australian Corps in France, which was located in the chateau alongside our airfield from which I was flying with my fighter squadron. Casey and I met frequently during that time, and he was interested even then in aviation, and he had taken every opportunity that was offered to fly as an observer. He actually saw Richthofen crash from only half a mile away when the great German fighter pilot was shot down near Bertangles in 1918. After the war, Casey and his wife Maie both became pilots, and they continued to do a great deal of flying together, even to the extent of having their own aircraft in the United States during the time that he was there as the Australian Minister.

There was much more to Winston Churchill's appointment of Richard Casey to the Middle East than many people suspected. Before going on to France in the First World War, Casey had served with the Australian Army at Gallipoli. During the interwar years he had made a name for himself as a statesman with an international reputation, and early in 1940 he became the Australian Minister in Washington, the first such Australian post to be established in a foreign country. He was to serve there for the next two years, and it was an experience which provided him with good reason to say: "Although I am an Australian of the third generation, and have lived the greater part of my life in Australia, I have in addition lived and worked in England and in the United States for many years, and I like to believe that I have some reasonable idea of the attributes and characteristics of each of these remarkable peoples in some degree of perspective."

For all the sharp criticism that he had noted while he was in Washington of the British efforts in the Middle East, when the time came for Dick Casey to say good-bye to President Roosevelt on his appointment to the Middle East in May, 1942, the President had said to him: "This is grand; it will give me a direct and personal link with the Middle East I have never had before. The Middle East is supremely important . . ."

With that background, there was no man better suited than Dick Casey for the work that had to be done in the diplomatic field in the Middle East, for the Americans had started to pour supplies and support into that area. Only a month after his arrival there they had ordered, in their own words, the "activation of the United States Army Middle East Air Force," which undertook at first the task of providing "heavies over the Mediterranean and mediums and fighters in support of the British Eighth Army's push across North Africa."

This strong force of Americans became the U.S. Ninth Air Force, and they can be rightly proud of their own statement: "The record of the Ninth is inseparable from that of the British Eighth Army and all air units which supported its east to west drive against the Axis Afrika Korps. The operational bond, closer at the outset, widened as experience was accumulated and the medium bombers and fighters of the Ninth were able to operate more on their own initiative." They were to suffer in that as heavily as any air force has ever had to suffer, and they performed with great gallantry during the "supremely important" time that they served with us in the Middle East.

As far back as the spring of 1939, months before the war broke out, there had been reached an agreement with Turkey, our old enemy in the first war, about what Winston Churchill called "mutually protecting vital interests." Ever since that time there had been a great deal of thought on our part about how we might induce Turkey to come into the war on our side. There had been for some time a steady flow of equipment and technicians to Turkey, and by the early months of 1943 the volume of both had greatly increased. During the first five months of that year alone "some £16,000,000 worth of equipment, other than petrol, was carried to Turkey from the Middle East," the official history has stated.

Late in January of 1943 the Prime Minister, Alan Brooke and Jumbo Wilson visited Turkey. At a conference at Adana, at which they appeared looking, in Brooke's words, "more like a third-rate theatrical travelling company than anything else" because of the civilian clothes that they had had to borrow in Cairo at the last moment for use in place of uniforms, they tried to get the Turks to come into the war. "It has been a most satisfactory trip, and I never thought that we should make such headway with the Turks," Brooke said on his return to Cairo. "Some of my wild dreams of bringing Turkey along with us no longer look quite so wild."

A few weeks after that I received instructions from London that the Prime Minister wanted me to go up to Ankara and discuss with the Turks the air side of our efforts to get them to come into the war. For all the many and prolonged overtures that had already been made to them, the Turks were still stalling, giving as one reason their fear that if they did come in, the Germans would immediately bomb Istanbul. Being an old city constructed very largely of wood, it would burn like tinder, and the Turks were afraid that this, their largest and wealthiest city, could very easily be destroyed in one night. The Germans had already given proof enough in the Balkans of what they could achieve in the way of destruction.

My brief was to try and convince the Turkish Government that what we needed was a certain amount of freedom in the early movement of our aircraft and personnel into Turkey. If they would allow us that, we would be in a good position to give them a fully effective air defense right from the beginning, and Istanbul would be safe from destruction. It was not an easy matter to argue, but plans for the air defense of Turkey had been under consideration at our headquarters in Cairo for quite a long time, and they had been worked out in very great detail.

By this time there were quite a number of our people at work in Turkey on airfield projects and the preparation of antiaircraft gun sites. They were there as civilians, all of them dressed in sports coats and flannel trousers that were as much of a pattern as to be a uniform. I do not know if we ever fooled anybody about what we were up to because there were some shrewd enough Germans roaming around the country in one guise or another, and the usual host of spies.

With my briefcase bulging with the plan for the air defense of

Turkey, and suitably dressed in civilian clothes, I flew up to Adana with some of the officers of my staff also disguised as civilians. From there we went on by train through the magnificent Taurus Mountains to the Turkish capital at Ankara. I was met at the station by Vice-Marshal R. A. (later Sir Robert) George, our knowledgeable air attaché to Greece as well as Turkey, who had been in Ankara since before the war. Bobbie George was an old friend of mine from the First World War: we had first met in 1916 while he had been serving in the Gordon Highlanders at Stirling at the time when I was forming there the first squadron that I commanded in the Royal Flying Corps. George was a man with a vigorous Scottish charm and a lively sense of humor, and he was a particularly good mixer, all of which enabled him over the years that lay ahead to become in various important appointments our air attaché par excellence.

With Bobbie George to meet me at the station was General Sefik Cakmak, the Chief of Staff of the Turkish Air Force, with whom I was to have discussions about these problems of air defense. From the station I was driven straight to our Embassy, where I was to stay, and I was welcomed there by our Ambassador, Sir Hughe Knatchbull-Hugessen.

One of the first remarks made by my host was to ask: "Have you any secret papers in that briefcase you're carrying?"

"I have," I replied. "I've got the plan for the air defense of Turkey in the event of their coming into the war on our side."

"You'd better let me have it to lock away in my safe for the night," Knatchbull-Hugessen replied. "Too many of our servants seem to be spies."

"Why don't you get rid of them?" I asked.

The Ambassador's reply was made with all the aplomb that we think of as typical of the Foreign Office. "But they are such good servants," he said, "and in any case any others we might get would also probably be spies."

I did not think anything more about what Knatchbull-Hugessen had said until some years after the end of the war. It was then revealed that late in that year of 1943 and early in the following year his own valet had been the spy who became so well known as Cicero: the man who had fed the Germans with top-secret information which had been kept locked away in the Ambassador's safe.

During the week that we spent in Ankara we met the Turkish general staff in daily conferences, and we described and developed for them the plan that we had worked out for the air defense of their country. I thought at the time that on the whole the discussions went quite well, and that I had won over most of the Turks, including even Field-Marshal Fevzi Cakmak, the chief of the Turkish general staff, to the view that we could look after them.

The Field Marshal was the father-in-law of Sefik Cakmak, the head of their Air Force, and in appearance and manner old Fevzi Cakmak was charming and courteous, but at first I felt, as Alan Brooke had reported, that he did not seem to be able to understand much of what we were talking about. Bobbie George had had a great deal of experience of working with the Turks, and he quickly corrected this wrong impression. He assured me that the old man was very well aware of all that was going on.

But not all of them were convinced. The deputy chief of the general staff, General Azim Gunduz, was firmly against us. He even took the trouble to invite me into his office where there was on the wall a huge map of Europe, and there he proceeded to deliver a lecture to me in which he thought that he was proving conclusively to me that the Germans must inevitably win the war. I was not surprised when I heard that he had been trained in the German Army, and that he had fought with them against us during the First World War.

I also had talks during that week in Ankara with the President of Turkey, Ismet Inonu, the Prime Minister, Surru Saracoglu, and the Foreign Minister, Numan Menemencioglu. They all seemed to be quite favorably disposed to our cause. After the discussions were over, we all returned to Cairo feeling, as Alan Brooke had, rather pleased with what we thought we had been able to accomplish, and I sent in a report for submission to the Prime Minister which presented the position in a reasonably favorable light.

In a letter that I wrote to my mother after I got back to Cairo, I was able to give her a more personal picture of what had happened. "I had a very strenuous time in Ankara, as, apart from numerous conferences and interviews with everyone from the President downward, I had to endure an unending succession of banquets, luncheons, cocktail parties, etc.," I wrote. "You have to eat and drink a certain amount for fear of offending one's hosts. So I went about feeling very bloated, airing my very indifferent French to the best advantage. All very wearing. Anyway I seem to have been something of a success, and I got a personal cable of congratulations from Winston."

With the final expulsion of the Germans and the Italians from North Africa, and the successful Allied landings in Sicily, I felt

546 COMBAT AND COMMAND

that we were at last about to see daylight in the winning of the war. "The news is good just now, what with our victory in Tunisia and this successful attack on the two dams in Germany," I wrote to my mother. "I am hopeful that the war in Europe will be over next year—autumn, 1944. Then we shall have to clean up the Japs. That should take another year, I suppose."

There was no particular reason why I should have made that reference to the war in the Far East. My concern with what was going on in the Mediterranean was all consuming, and I was left with no time to think about the state of the war elsewhere. In fact, that reference was the only occasion for a long time when what was going on in the Far East had come into my mind. But only shortly after the launching of the assault on Sicily, I was given cause to think more seriously about it.

Sir Archibald Sinclair had arrived in Tripoli from England, and I flew there to meet him for the start of a quick tour that he was to make out in the Middle East, and from there I took him back with me to Cairo. I have always had the greatest affection for Archie Sinclair, and I was glad that he was able to stay with us for a few days. He spent most of his time visiting various units stationed in the Nile delta, and the appearance of the Secretary of State for Air did a lot to make us feel that we were not altogether in a backwater of the war. At night Sinclair and I talked quietly together, and it was then that he told me, in confidence, that I was to be appointed to a new command which was in the process of being created in southeast Asia.

This was the first that I heard of anything about what was later to become the well-known South-East Asia Command—S.E.A.C. —and the news that I was to be the supreme commander rather stunned me, for such an appointment had never entered my mind. My first reaction was one of relief, for it meant that I would at least have the chance of getting back into a more fully operational command. But it did not take a great deal of thought after that for me to change my feelings.

It was apparently to be a new command of all three Services, and I saw that there would inevitably be in that a lot of teething troubles. And since I had had no previous experience at all of conditions in the Far East, or of any of the countries in which I would have to work, there would be a great deal that I would have to learn before I could ever begin to think in terms of operations. But I said nothing about these doubts to Archie Sinclair, and I merely indicated to him that I was prepared to do whatever the Air Ministry, or the Government, decided upon, and we left it at that.

In writing to my mother I commented: "I gather there is a possibility that I may be changing my job for something bigger. Can't say more yet. You may hear of it first from the papers."

Shortly after that visit from Archie Sinclair, we received a visit in the Middle East from Boom Trenchard, and while we were all delighted to see him, and he was worth his weight in gold in the way in which he visited the squadrons and talked to the air and ground crews, I knew that his heart was heavy, for he was suffering severely from personal family losses in the war. His son Hugh had died in action with the Guards Brigade in North Africa; and both his stepsons were also to die on active service: one with the Royal Scots Fusiliers, his old regiment as well as that of Winston Churchill and Archie Sinclair, in Italy, and the other in a flying accident. "Yet grief was not allowed to interrupt the strict routine which he laid down and religiously followed," Andrew Boyle has commented. Sad though that knowledge was, the manner in which Trenchard conducted himself when he came to see us made us feel all the more strongly the warmth of the admiration that we had for the man who had done so much for all of us.

29 / A World Apart

HE IS AN UNWISE MAN who thinks there is any certain way of winning this war, or indeed any other war between equals in strength," Winston Churchill once said. "The only plan is to persevere."

In all my thinking about what happened in the Middle East once the main war effort in the Mediterranean had passed out of our hands and into those who were running it to the west of us, it was perseverance that seemed to be the dominant quality that was demanded of us: perseverance in the face of not a great deal of action, and a very great amount of what Richard Casey had called "housekeeping." In floor space alone our house covered such a vast area, and in many ways it seemed to belong to a world that was quite apart from what I had known up to that time.

But the movement of the brisker war from Africa to Sicily, and so on into Italy, did not mean that the Air Force in the Middle East exactly dwindled away or languished. I still had quite sizeable forces under my control, and they were forces of a wide variety all the way from single-engined fighter squadrons on through bombers to the largest transport group in the entire Royal Air Force; and they were dispersed throughout the eastern Mediterranean, including the Western Desert, Egypt, the Levant and on to Iraq and Persia, Aden and East Africa. I had also inherited from Arthur Tedder as part of my command a remarkably efficient maintenance organization which had to keep supplies of aircraft and parts flowing throughout the Mediterranean as well as my own command. In many ways I now had under my command an almost self-contained air force.

While I could not help feeling that, for all this activity, my own work in the Middle East appeared to be heading for less and less of a fully operational nature, there was nevertheless no lack of work. Through my command being so self-contained, the aspects of administration alone carried with them heavy responsibilities. Even after the Germans were finally flung out of North Africa and

548

our Army crossed into Sicily and then on to Italy, we still had on our hands a vast amount of organization for the part that we were to play in keeping up for the R.A.F. a supply of aircraft.

To help with supplies there had been built up in Cairo an outstandingly efficient maintenance and repair organization. The credit for this great achievement was due entirely to Air Vice-marshal Graham Dawson, the chief maintenance and supply officer of Middle East Command, and later of the Mediterranean Air Command. A smallish, alert man of quite extraordinary ability, Dawson had served under Lord Beaverbrook at the Ministry of Aircraft Production, and he was in the Beaverbrook mold: a live wire with an intense dislike of red tape. He was a fully qualified engineer, and wisely urged on by Arthur Tedder, the ingenuity and energy that were so marked in Dawson's character had led to the building up of a first-class and complex organization which worked marvels in salvaging and repairing engines and aircraft.

In the Mokattam Hills, on the edge of the valley of the Nile some miles outside Cairo, there are the large and extensive Tura caves from which the stone had been hewn thousands of years before for the building of the Pyramids. They were enormous, and they were well protected from any possibility of bombing by enemy aircraft. In these huge caverns, which, because of their dryness, were admirably suited for the work, Graham Dawson had set up a vast engine repair depot which was staffed largely by Egyptian mechanics working under the supervision of British officers and N.C.O.'s.

At first the Egyptians had not been particularly skilled, but Dawson had broken down all the work that was to be done into a sort of mass production technique, and with these detailed and simplified operations each Egyptian was taught how to carry out one small job and no more, and just go on doing that. The skilled British mechanics were then left free for the important work of assembling all the finished bits and pieces into complete engines.

Another of Graham Dawson's enterprises came unexpectedly to life in the rough and disorderly area of Cairo known as the Bulak District, which was a vast rabbit warren of small native workshops of almost every description. Here a great number of highly skilled coppersmiths, tinsmiths and blacksmiths and similar craftsmen worked each in his own little shop and almost entirely by hand. Dawson had allocated to many of these tradesmen some particular job or other having to do with repairs. Tinsmiths were put on to beating out engine cowlings and other metal surfaces, and others were given the work of repairing propellers, which is a highly skilled job in the first place, but which these Egyptians managed to master surprisingly well. Since it was all hand work it would sometimes take them forty-eight hours to get a propeller blade straightened to the extent where it could go through the template; but since there were available plenty of these workers it was a simple and effective way of getting propellers repaired, and of meeting the demands created by a great shortage of supplies.

There seemed to be no limit to Graham Dawson's ingenuity, and he drove himself and everybody else without giving a thought to how many corns he might be treading on. In the words of Philip Guedalla: "Engines that Bristol and California had made and the Desert spoilt renewed their youth under the busy fingers of the East." Dawson's name must rank with that of Frank Whittle's, although in a lesser degree, in the history of the engineering achievements of the Royal Air Force, and his death in an air crash later in the war was a grave loss to the Service.

At the time when it had become generally known that I was leaving Fighter Command to go to the Middle East there had occurred some quiet expressions of a personal allegiance to me which I found unexpectedly touching. Several of my fully operational flying officers of squadron leader and wing commander rank started exerting pressure all the way from their own various subterranean channels of influence to outright personal requests to me to be allowed to go out with me to the Middle East. All of them had a great deal of experience of operational flying, particularly in the Battle of Britain, and I was distinctly moved by these signs of loyalty to me. I had come to feel a warm affection for these young men who were all so typical of the best that I had known among my contemporaries when I was myself a young pilot in the First World War.

Before I left London we had a small farewell party together which was organized by Ronnie Edwards, and in the usual light-hearted fashion there were bandied about ways in which they might fly out to the Middle East. Under pressure from Max Aitken and Johnny Kent, these enterprising young fighter pilots of mine began toying with the bright idea that it would be a good thing if they saved themselves a lot of time and, as a crew, flew a bomber out to Cairo.

It was while this idea was being toyed with that Bob Wright, who was in town on leave from the night fighter squadron in which he was serving, and who was at the party, nearly had the wits scared out of him. The suggestion was made that he should join the crew and act as their navigator. He knew that Johnny Kent and Max Aitken had had plenty of experience in twin-engined aircraft, but the reputation that they all enjoyed as day fighter pilots appeared to be too much for Wright to be able to contemplate with much enthusiasm the prospect of flying out to Egypt with them. Muttering to himself about a lot of harum-scarum day fighter boys, he beat a hasty retreat back to his night fighter pilots. In any case, he had already made his own plans to be with his squadron in the invasion of North Africa.

After as pretty a piece of wire-pulling as I did not at the time want to hear about, Johnny Kent and Ian Gleed and Barry Heath, all wing commanders, did eventually fly a Wellington out to the Middle East. Max Aitken and John Simpson, also both wing commanders, made their way out by different means, as did John Grandy, who, a regular officer, was one of the youngest group captains that I had in Fighter Command. He is now, as Air Chief Marshal Sir John Grandy, a distinguished Commander-in-Chief in the Royal Air Force. In getting out to the Mediterranean they showed toward me a loyalty that I greatly appreciated, and they all came to fill important posts in my command in the Middle East.

At the time when I had first started discussing with the Air Ministry my own plans for the Middle East, I called in one day to see Wilfrid Freeman, who was then still Vice-Chief of the Air Staff. We talked about the various senior officers whom I would have under my command, and he told me about the new transport group that was being formed out there. It was to be a large and important group, covering a wide area and range of operations, and although it was to be part of Transport Command it would be under my command for operations.

"Why not have Whitney Straight out there to run it?" Freeman suggested.

I had heard that Whitney Straight was just back from the tiresome year that he had been forced to spend interned in France, and I agreed that he was just the man to have as Air Officer Commanding this new group. Freeman told me that he was in touch with Arthur Tedder about it, and that the immediate decision would be up to him. So far as I was concerned, I made it clear that I would be well pleased with having Straight in the command after I took over from Tedder.

While Wilfrid Freeman and I were talking about this, Whitney Straight was on leave, and he and his wife Daphne were cycling together through the West Country. They had been on the road

and far from the war for about four days when they were stopped
by an Automobile Association patrol man, who asked their names.
After a long search he had at last found his quarry: Whitney
Straight was to report back to the Air Ministry immediately.

When he got to the Air Ministry, Whitney Straight was told that
there was a choice for him of three different jobs. The first was to
take command of the fighter station at Hawkinge, in Kent; the
second was to command the Spitfires in Malta; and the third,
which was what he was really wanted for, was to go out to the
Middle East to take command of the new No. 216 (transport)
Group. Common sense told Straight that the transport job was the
one for which he was most suited, and he agreed to that.

By the time that I arrived in Cairo, Whitney Straight was
already well in the saddle in command of the group with his own
headquarters there, and with promotion to the rank of air commodore. The activities of No. 216 Group ranged along the entire
southern coast of the Mediterranean from Morocco to the Persian
Gulf, and from the west coast of Africa up through the center of
the continent and on to Syria. Later it also came to serve the south
of France, Italy, Yugoslavia, Greece and on out to India. Its work
included ferrying aircraft of all descriptions from west Africa,
where they were assembled after being sent out from England by
sea, to North Africa and the Middle East; the creation of airdromes throughout the whole of Middle East Command and on up
into Italy, many of which were the forerunners of well-known civil
airdromes of today; the administration of a far-flung system of
staging posts; and the maintenance of scheduled air services for
Transport Command of the R.A.F.; and support for all the air
operations of the R.A.F., including the flying in of supplies to the
Partisans in Yugoslavia, and the delivery of aircraft to the Russians.

While the task of the Air Officer Commanding this group called
for a firm seat behind a desk at his headquarters, Whitney Straight
by no means anchored himself there, and during the time that he
was in command he also flew a great deal, including fifteen
hundred hours alone as a pilot of a Dakota. And he led his group
in the air in the important work that it did in the invasion of
Sicily.

For a long time Whitney Straight was loath to talk about his
experiences in the hands of the Vichy French. On one occasion
when I had Noel Coward visiting me in Cairo he did open up a
little under pressure. He told us something of what had happened,
and in a way which Coward later described as "movingly and with

understatement." Coward added: "The experience has changed him too. I don't know whether or not he realises this but it is true. He was always attractive and pleasant to meet and he still is but he has gained something extra now."

There were so many brilliant escapes made by our air crews of the R.A.F. during the war after they were shot down and captured, and many of them make exciting reading. Whitney Straight's story is not one of excitement, but it is unusual. Because he has said so little about it himself, and because of what has been said about his eventual escape by other people who have more often than not given false impressions, it deserves to be presented in its true light.

In his logbook of the flying that he did during the war, there is an entry that was made later by Whitney Straight about his being shot down in July, 1941, that he "failed to return (sez you)." A whole year was to pass before Straight got back to the United Kingdom, and I think that his actions during that year reflect great credit upon him for his perseverance in the face of the dreariest problems.

After being hit by cannon fire in his attack on the flak ship in the Channel, Straight had to make for the French coast, where, with a dead engine, he made a forced landing in a field. He was rather knocked about in that landing, but he got away from the wreckage of his aircraft as quickly as possible. All our pilots had been well briefed about what they should do, and Straight was prepared for any emergencies. He was equipped with passport photographs, and he had French money, and his uniform was quickly convertible into something approaching civilian clothes. He spoke fluent French, and he knew the country, and he promptly started off in the direction of Paris.

The only way out of France was far to the south: over the Pyrenees and into neutral Spain. France was divided between that part which was completely occupied by the Germans and that which was still under the control of the Vichy Government, even though it was pro-German in its inclinations. When Straight got to Paris he made for the American Embassy, where he was personally well known. But the Embassy was officially closed, and the caretaker wanted to have nothing at all to do with him. The B.B.C. had made the mistake of broadcasting that Straight had been shot down, and apparently everybody knew about it; and that meant that he was going to have to be particularly cautious.

Heading for unoccupied France, Whitney Straight made his way by train and bus to the south, and twenty-four hours later he was in Toulouse. From there he boarded the train that went to Biarritz, on the Atlantic coast, and he got off at Pau, just beyond Lourdes. There he caught yet another train which took him farther south to the Pyrenees; but at Bedous, within only a few miles of the Spanish frontier, a gendarme asked to see his papers. Bluffing about having left them in Pau, Straight was turned off the train, and he continued the last stage of his journey toward the Pyrenees on foot. He put up for the night in a small village, planning to get some rest before making his final escape the next day from Vichy France and over the Pyrenees into Spain. But an alert gendarme became suspicious, and he was arrested just over a week after crashing in northern France.

Realizing that if he revealed his true identity it might be made additionally difficult for him, Whitney Straight gave his name as John Willard, the surname being his first Christian name, and he described himself as a captain in the Royal Army Service Corps. He was taken away and placed in an internment camp for other British escapees at St-Hippolyte, some miles to the northwest of Nîmes. There he found a curious assortment made up largely from men who had failed to get away at the time of the evacuation at Dunkirk. One of the other men interned there has since described the bulk of these three hundred occupants of the camp as the dregs of the Army. In that atmosphere of sour defeat Straight decided to rest for a while and regain his strength, but even then he and two other officers made one attempt at escape, only to be quickly picked up.

The French commandant of the camp became aware of Whitney Straight's true identity, but he advised Straight to go on using his name of Willard. Under that name he became the senior officer of the camp, and he then discovered that there was an arrangement whereby prisoners declared by the French medical authorities as unfit for any further active service could be repatriated. There was a small but steady flow into the camp of air crews of the R.A.F. who had been shot down and then captured, as he had been, and they were nearly all well worth getting back to England for further service.

So far as Straight was concerned, the organization of this must be his objective, and he went about rallying the men while at the same time inducing in them, and in any others who were interested, a state of health which would give them this adverse medical category. He did not have to do much to shake up his own system. He was able to irritate the wounds that he had received in Norway and the knocking about when he had force-landed in France, and overdoses of aspirin just before medical examination caused his heart to act up, and he was passed as quite unfit. Forty-two others, some faked and some real, were also placed in this category.

After seven months spent in this miserable atmosphere of internment, the papers arrived from the Vichy Government for their release, and on March 5, 1942, the party of forty-three set out for Spain under the care of their French custodians. Whitney Straight and his more alert companions had been busy collecting information of any and every character which they thought might be of value to our intelligence people. Part of this information, for instance, was even hidden in the turban of an officer of the Indian Army who was among those being repatriated. But when the party got down to Perpignan, the last stop before crossing into Spain, they were turned back on orders from the French Government at Vichy, and they were all returned to St-Hippolyte.

This bitter pill was forced down their throats as a reprisal for the raid in which the R.A.F. had heavily bombed the Renault works near Paris only two nights before, and in which, it was reported, there had been heavy casualties among the French. Whitney Straight was not to know that there had been only five casualties out of the three thousand workers at the factory, which was a perfectly legitimate military target. In his despair he sent an indignant telegram to Anthony Eden in which he deplored the way innocent people were being killed.

By then Whitney Straight's true identity had become well known to the American Consular officials in Marseilles, who were acting on behalf of British interests, and also those at the American Embassy in Vichy. Immediately after his return to the internment camp, Straight wrote to them. He clearly stated his position, explaining that he regarded it as his duty "firstly, to take all possible steps to secure the return to active service of all valuable personnel, particularly R.A.F., and secondly, to make the situation of these men who cannot return home as bearable as possible, and thirdly, to gather as much information as possible which may be of value having regard to future military operations." He saw no point in making ineffectual solitary breaks for freedom, and he rightly felt that it was his duty, as the commanding officer, to organize a mass evacuation of his fellow internees.

Two weeks after the collapse of the plan for their repatriation through Spain, the internees were moved from St-Hippolyte—from which, the authorities now considered, it was too easy for them to escape—to a new camp at Fort de la Revere, in the mountains just

behind Nice. It was a much tougher place to attempt to break out
of, and the regulations were enforced with a rigor that showed a
callous lack of consideration for their position as internees. "I
have commanded Detachment W for nine months," Whitney
Straight reported in a letter to the American Consul in Nice. "This
Command has been difficult and exhausting." To the French
general commanding the Department des Alpes-Maritimes he
wrote an official protest, stating, "We are not being treated as
internees, nor even as prisoners of war, but as criminals."

It had been made clear to Whitney Straight that any effort on his
part to escape would wreck the discussions about the repatriation
of the group, but it was becoming even clearer to him that the
authorities now had no intention of living up to their promises. By
this time Straight was in fact a sick man, and he was moved to the
military hospital in Nice. That left him with only one step that he
could take, and in company with another Englishman and a Pole
he managed to escape. He joined up with the French Resistance
people, who helped him to make his way along the coast of the
south of France which he had known well before the war to a spot
near the Spanish border. There he boarded a trawler, which was
manned by, as he put it, "a crew of enthusiastic R.N.V.R.
characters," and he was taken to Gibraltar; and shortly after that
he was on his way back to England.

For anyone possessed of the temperament of an Aitken it was
impossible for young Max to think of being solely on the defensive. When he first arrived out in the Middle East a few months
after Whitney Straight had got there, I had had him posted to the
Air Headquarters, Eastern Mediterranean, which were also in
Cairo, where he was placed in charge of operational training.
Almost immediately the agitation started for a more active job, but
I insisted that Aitken should have a rest from the long time that he
had spent commanding a night fighter squadron in England.

It was our task in the eastern Mediterranean to harry the
Germans who were occupying the Balkans and Greece, and we still
had left with us in the Middle East fairly reasonable forces of
heavy, medium and light bombers as well as fighters. With these
we attacked targets in Greece and the Balkans in an effort to try
and keep the Germans pinned down while the more spectacular
war was waged to the west of us; and offensive sweeps were
maintained all the time against enemy shipping trying to supply the
islands which the Germans and the Italians were occupying in the
Aegean.

By July I could hold out no longer against Max Aitken's persistent efforts to get back to a more operational job—he was typical of those who had to get themselves mixed up in a shooting war—and I gave him command of No. 219 Group. With this came promotion to the rank of group captain, and he had his headquarters in Alexandria. He was responsible for the defense of the North African coast from Tripoli in the west to the delta of the Nile—and in particular the cities of Cairo and Alexandria—and for that job he had a mixed bag of day and night fighters, and strike torpedo and photographic reconnaissance aircraft.

Almost immediately after taking over this group, Max Aitken organized an operation against German-occupied Crete. We sent over a strong force of over one hundred fighters escorting medium bombers made up of Baltimores and strike Beaufighters. It was intended more as an effort to show the flag than anything, but unfortunately we had some rather severe losses: thirteen fighters and five bombers. But that only served to whet Aitken's appetite for further bites into the Aegean, with which I could not help but be in agreement. And that was soon to lead us to more ambitious action.

With the establishment of the Mediterranean Air Command, it had become necessary for me to travel even further afield than the confines of my own command. Early in the year I flew on one occasion from Cairo to Algiers for conferences with Arthur Tedder and Eisenhower. The fighting was then still taking place to the west of Tripoli, so I had had to fly in a big detour to the south. When we landed fairly early in the morning at Maison Blanche, the airfield just outside Algiers, the first people I saw there as I got out of my aircraft were George McLannahan, who was later to become one of my senior pilots in British European Airways, and his navigator, Bob Wright. They were with the night fighter squadron stationed there, and they were both decked out in Mae Wests and flying boots, and they were looking very hostile, with revolvers strapped to their hips. The night fighters were being kept at readiness with their Beaufighters because all the day fighters were up at the front in Tunisia, and it was the turn of McLannahan and Wright to be on the job at just the time that I arrived at their airfield.

"Do you mean to say you've been responsible for protecting us from any interference?" I demanded.

"Playing day fighter boys," Wright replied. "And it's not my idea of fun."

"What're you doing with that bloody great revolver?" I asked.

It was the one that had been issued to him, Wright explained, during the Battle of Britain, when he was Stuffy Dowding's personal assistant at Fighter Command and part of his bodyguard, and as he was also later to serve under me. In Algeria they were under orders to go armed at all times. "But for the fact that George is such a good pilot I suppose it could be said that I use it to keep him on course," he added.

Both McLannahan and Wright were by then at the end of their first tour of operational flying, and they were due for a rest. Shortly afterward they both came to the Middle East, where McLannahan went on to Whitney Straight's staff, and Wright joined my staff in Cairo, which led to nothing but squawks from him about getting back to operational flying. When I discovered that through his defective eyesight he had by then been passed permanently unfit for flying, I put him to work in my public relations branch, and I had to silence his squawks with a definite order to do as he was told and stay at his desk.

Through my own experience I knew that once a man had become a member of an air crew—and it did not matter much in which category—it was difficult for him to be anything but on the alert for some sort of attacking enterprise. By the time that Johnny Kent, who was a pilot of exceptional experience, arrived out in the Middle East I felt that he would make a suitable commander of a fighter sector, and I sent him up to Benghazi. But he also could not resist replacing the chair at his desk with the seat of a fighter wherever he saw the opportunity. On one of his unofficial forays he added to his score by shooting down an enemy aircraft off the coast of Cyrenaica.

When Max Aitken went on to command the group at Alexandria, I brought Johnny Kent down to take his place on the planning staff. Some time later, shortly after I had left the Middle East, I heard that Aitken had also made for himself a fine night out in search of action. He had set off from Egypt in a Beaufighter, and on a lone patrol over Crete that could only be described as a purely personal affair he shot down three Ju. 52's and damaged a fourth.

One of the more difficult aspects of life in Cairo was the way in which I found myself becoming inevitably and deeply involved in the social life. It was quite different from my time at Fighter Command, and there was no way out of it because the Egyptian capital seemed to have become a crossroads between the east and the west, and some sort of general meeting point. We were constantly on the go, and for all his care in warding off the intruders, Ronnie Edwards seemed to have lined up for me a formidable and endless list of social engagements which occupied altogether too much of my time, and which meant that Alma Williams, my secretary, who was a captain in the South African Air Force, was always having to chase me to keep up with the paper work.

In its way the social round was amusing enough, but there were many times when I would find myself looking at the whole thing with rather a wondering eye. All said and done we were at war, but one would scarcely have thought it from the way in which the rounds of social affairs and entertainment were conducted. I did not have my wife with me—a privilege which some of the other senior officers had enjoyed—and that left me feeling at times rather at a loose end; and as the war continued to recede from our part of the Mediterranean there began to creep over my mind a feeling of irritation and frustration.

In his book *Middle East Diary* which Noel Coward published the following year, he spoke of this not altogether happy impression that Cairo had also made upon him at this time, and there is one brief picture that he gives which has in it the essence of what it was like. "Uniforms indicated that perhaps somewhere in the vague outside world there might be a war of some sort going on," he stated. "This place is the last refuge of the soi-disant 'International Set.' All the fripperies of pre-war luxury living are still in existence here; rich people, idle people, cocktail-parties, dinner parties, jewels and evening dress."

Noel Coward was an old friend of mine from long before the war, and he gives an amusing account of his experiences during the extensive tour that he made of the North African and Mediterranean areas and on into Persia between July and October, 1943. The object of the tour was to entertain the troops, and no performer whom I saw giving this service during the war did better than Coward. He went everywhere and never spared himself, and it was small wonder that he was in a state of exhaustion by the time that he got back to England.

On one occasion I had to ask Noel Coward at very short notice if he would fill in for one of the American stars who had been taken ill, and he did it in a way for which I shall always be grateful. It was a big show that had been organized for British and American airmen, and since it was known that I knew Coward personally I was asked if I would approach him about acting as a substitute for the American star. I knew how temperamental some leading actors could be, but I phoned Coward and put it up to him. He agreed without the slightest hesitation to do the show, and he gave a splendid performance.

In addition to the extraordinary conglomeration of people, civilians as well as Service, who were then living, working, playing, and so many of them wasting away in Cairo, there was also in Egypt at this time what could be well-nigh described as a plethora of kings. The principal one was naturally King Farouk. It was his country, and by the rules of protocol none of them was more important than he was, despite his unpopularity with some of our people. It has been recorded by Dick Casey that when there were any discussions in his office about these kings then resident in Egypt they used to refer to Farouk as "the local king." In our relationships with these kings, local or otherwise, there were stresses which could have become serious but which, treated with an appropriate sense of humor, ironed themselves out and became quite simple and human affairs.

One of the reasons for the diplomatic stresses that occurred from time to time was due to a situation that Dick Casey has called "unique in history." We and the Germans and the Italians were fighting each other in some countries that were technically neutral. The governments of the countries in the whole of that part of the world—the Balkans and the Middle East—have always been notoriously prickly, and, as we now know to our cost, none was more so than that of Egypt, where we were so solidly based.

It was not long after I arrived in Cairo that I came to realize that there was in existence there a state of tension between King Farouk and the British, which, so far as I could see, was both dangerous and unnecessary. It was none of my business to interfere because that sphere of activity was strictly the province of the Foreign Office. In the normal course of events, I would never have been drawn into it, other than with a mere formal and official recognition of my position as one of the British commanders; and I was not left in any doubt that, in the minds of those who did not know the whole story of what happened, I was stepping out of place in allowing myself to become involved. How little they all knew of what took place, and how, much against my wish, it led me into quite a deep involvement.

The unfortunate clash that had developed into an open breach between King Farouk and our official representatives in Egypt had occurred some time before I arrived there, and our Ambassador and the King seemed to loathe the sight and sound of each other.

The Germans and the Italians had already made their bid with the Egyptian King to try and gain some shape or form of control over him, and in doing it they had shrewdly treated him as an adult.

From the moment that I arrived in Cairo I found our people talking about and treating King Farouk as if he were nothing but a naughty and rather silly boy. So far as I could make out he was indeed naughty, and he was still very young, being only in his early twenties; but to my way of thinking, and taking a hard-headed view, he was also the King of Egypt. It seemed to me that it would be much wiser, no matter how one felt personally, to have him as a friend and an ally rather than play into the hands of our enemies by antagonizing him and giving him cause to work against our vital interests, which, in his anger over the way in which we were treating him, he was quite capable of doing.

We were in King Farouk's country, and no matter how much we might consider that we had every right to be there, and even to dominate the country, Farouk's people at that time were devoted to him. He had enormous power, stemming largely from his great wealth, and he was in a position to be able to do a very great deal to help us from our base which was implanted in Egypt. But Farouk was clearly at odds with us and not inclined to help, and in certain quarters of our Foreign Office there was precious little being done about correcting that.

As a Commander-in-Chief it was my duty to do more than merely sit behind a desk and pass judgment on how such and such an air battle was or was not to be fought. There was a very wide range of subjects that called for my consideration, including many decisions about administration; and in a place which was as eruptive as the Middle East I had to know as much as possible about what was going on. The better the work of my staff, the more detail I was spared, and the more time and thought I was able to give to making decisions; but the range of those decisions became wider out in the Middle East than I had ever known before. One of the very minor ones that came up to me early in 1943 was about what action we should take over the requests from London that we should try and raise some money in Egypt for the R.A.F. Benevolent Fund. That may sound far enough removed from the prosecution of a war that a C.-in-C. would be expected to make on active service; but it was to have surprising results.

My deputy in the Middle East for a short time before he returned to England to become the Member of the Air Council in charge of training was Air Marshal Sir Peter Drummond. He was well known in the Middle East, having served there during the First

World War, and for a long time since before the outbreak of the second war. Drummond was an Australian by birth, and he had transferred from the Australian Imperial Forces to the Royal Flying Corps in the first war. As early as the autumn of 1916 he was flying over the Turco-Egyptian frontier—which today is roughly the border between Egypt and Israel—where the German Air Force was then operating. His record as a pilot was a particularly distinguished one, and after the war he was given a permanent commission in the Royal Air Force, and he had been a fellow student with me in 1922 on the first course of the R.A.F. Staff College.

Never lacking in initiative, Peter Drummond put up to me a scheme for prying money for the R.A.F. Benevolent Fund from the Egyptians, many of whom were making fortunes out of us in the war. We had just received one of the first copies of a film entitled *Desert Victory,* which told the story of the advance that the Eighth Army was making after its great initial success at Alamein. Peter Drummond suggested that we should have a public showing of the film in Cairo, and that the premiere should be done in a big way with an appeal to those Egyptians who were ready to spend money. And for that no better magnet could be provided, he added, than the presence of King Farouk. If we could get him to come, the Egyptians would all want to buy tickets.

"Put him in a box and all the millionaires in Cairo will be there," Drummond said.

He was quite right. I invited King Farouk to be present as my guest, and we dressed the show well with a guard of honor and all the trimmings that we could think of. The Egyptians paid handsomely for the opportunity to be there in the presence of their King. In all we raised around £10,000 for the Benevolent Fund in that one evening alone. But important though that was we also succeeded in something which we had not expected, and which from that time on was to occupy a great deal of my attention.

It was not at all to our credit that up to that time King Farouk had been cold-shouldered by our people in a way which had not helped at all in our relationship with him. He had certainly never been accorded such a smart turnout as the respect paid to him by our guard of honor at that film premiere. The poor man even admitted to me at that time that he felt that at last the British were taking some notice of him. His pleasure over this was both evident and sincere, and I came to feel that it might do some good if we went on making a bit of a fuss of him. I asked him to dine with us

at Air House, and in a very short time he was making the house a
port of call whenever he was at a loose end—which seemed to be
all too often—dropping in unannounced whenever he felt like it.

To my surprise I found that King Farouk appeared to like me,
and it became easy to get on to quite close and even intimate
terms with him. In return for my hospitality he decided that he
would take me around the nightclubs of Cairo. I was not particularly averse to that, except that I found that he used to keep me up
much too late; and staying up doing the rounds of the nightclubs
until four or five o'clock in the morning was rather a burden when
one had to spend strenuous days in an office trying to help fight a
war.

There were times when this informal approach of King Farouk's
in dropping in at Air House rather threw my staff into a state of
confusion because we had to do a great deal of official entertaining, and some of the dinners that were arranged were quite formal
affairs. On one occasion he arrived without any warning just as
we were about to go in to dinner at which I was entertaining the
King of Greece. Protocol has never meant much to me, but that
evening it was of necessity in full bloom, and all the arrangements
had been carefully settled, but then, with the appearance of the
local king, protocol became very severely strained.

With two kings unexpectedly present for dinner, the question
immediately arose about which one should take precedence over
the other. While I did some astute entertaining and cast an amused
eye over the whole situation, my staff went into a rapid conference.
It was quickly decided that Air House was on the same level as an
Embassy, and that it was therefore British territory, and that since
the Greek King was an official guest and the Egyptian King was an
unofficial one, the King of Greece came first. King Farouk seemed
to be as little worried about it as I was, and so far as he was
concerned it was just another party.

But for all the ease of that occasion, we were seldom left in
doubt about the way in which Farouk could be relied upon to put
his foot in it; and the fact that he was trying to be merely facetious
and act and speak in a way which he thought was English only led
to the embarrassing situations that had to develop. We had an
informal party one night at Air House to which I had invited him.
Dick and Maie Casey also came, bringing with them Noel Coward,
who was staying with them. In his book, Coward published an
account of that party, and he finished with the statement: "At one-
thirty a.m. I was told that the king was anxious to hear me sing,
which proved in him a supreme capacity for taking punishment,

and so I seated myself dismally at an upright and very upstanding piano and churned out three or four songs. I don't think I have ever performed so vilely in my life but I was far too weary to care. After this Dick and Maie and I shot off home."

I do not doubt that Noel Coward was weary. He had been working hard and traveling great distances in his earnest desire to entertain the troops. But what had caused him to perform so badly at our party—and it was indeed an embarrassingly poor show— was a comment that King Farouk made when I asked Coward if he would be so good as to play for us. In his high-pitched voice, which rang out so that nobody could escape hearing it, Farouk exclaimed: "Yes . . . come and sing for your supper." If looks could have killed, the one shot at Farouk by Coward would have resulted in his losing his throne far quicker than he did.

It was the hour of the morning at which Noel Coward records that this occurred that was so typical of what Farouk would do to us in his delight at finding one British home at which he could feel that he was welcome. So long as the King was there, no one could leave, and all too often he used to keep us up until the most ungodly hours of the morning.

After a time, and much to the annoyance and indignation of quite a few of our people in Cairo, I began genuinely to like Farouk. There was no indication then, so far as I could see, that there was anything that was at all vicious about him, although he could at times become very annoying through his flippancy. Another failing that he had was that he appeared to be almost fanatically keen on acquiring great wealth. He told me on one occasion that he thought that his personal fortune must be around six million pounds, and he revealed all too clearly his shortsightedness in stating openly that one of his main interests in life was to increase that fortune. This led him into currying favor with the rich people in Egypt—as they did with him—at the expense of the common people, in whom he had little or no interest.

But for all his flippancy there were times when I did manage to get Farouk to talk quite seriously, and then he would reveal that he was an intelligent young man. He was well informed and well read, and he was by no means the fool that he appeared to be through the stupid way in which he quite often behaved in public. He would mix our talks with seriousness and joking, which was what probably mystified the people who saw us together quite often in the nightclubs of Cairo. He was also, strange as it may sound, particularly interested in religion, about which I have always held decided views of my own.

"Look here," I said to him once. "I simply cannot understand why you are a Mohammedan. It's such a lousy religion."

Farouk laughed, not taking any offense, and he replied: "And I don't understand why you are a Communist."

That I was definitely not a Communist was completely beyond his understanding when he tried to cope with what I explained to him about my political views. For all his intelligence, he was very right wing in his own outlook, and feudal enough not to be able to understand what I meant when I talked about my own belief in socialism. Whenever we started a political discussion I was almost forced to move much further to the left than I was, in fact, in my views and opinions. It was perhaps that reactionary attitude of his which led Farouk to do the silly things that he did, and which were so much against his own long-term interests as well as ours.

I tried once to explain to Farouk that the great contrast that existed in Egypt between wealth and poverty, between the few who were so very rich and the vast hordes of the poverty stricken fellaheen, illustrated the unsound state of affairs that existed in his country. I pointed out that, unless he did something about it, sooner or later there would be a revolution, with the masses of the grossly underprivileged rising against the overopulent. At that time Farouk was unquestionably very popular with his people, and I told him that after the war he would find himself in a strong position if he took the right stand and tried to better things, but all that would be lost if he did not do something to alleviate the poverty and the misery of the masses of Egypt. Farouk listened carefully to me, and he expressed his interest in what I was saying, and even a certain sympathy; but there was some unbridgeable gap in our understanding of each other's views.

"King Farouk had a magnificent opportunity to do good for his country, but he apparently did not have the background, or the will to do it," Dick Casey has since commented. "The social abuses in Egypt were evident, but he chose the role of playboy, and avoided giving the guidance that would have put Egypt on the way to very necessary social and economic reforms, and might, at the same time, have saved his throne."

Years afterward, in talking with Bob Wright about the time when we were all together out in Egypt in 1943, Dick Casey said that he felt that there had been a great deal of misunderstanding about what I had been able to achieve in the course of my short association with King Farouk. Casey himself had advised the

Government to give Farouk one of our more distinguished decorations and a Rolls-Royce, gold-plated if necessary, to help offset the presents which were lavished upon him by the Italians and the Germans; but in their stiff-necked fashion certain sections of the Foreign Office would not consider any such proposals.

From what was said to me later in the year by the Prime Minister, I knew that both he and the Foreign Secretary, Anthony Eden, understood and appreciated what I was doing in trying to establish a better liaison with the King of Egypt. But for all that, it has not been easy to tolerate the criticism that has been made of me by the ill-informed, including some of the senior officers in my own Service, particularly when it meant that I came very near to sacrificing my own career. How far, I have been compelled to ask myself a little wistfully, is a serving officer expected to go in the performance of his duty?

30 / The Mounting Fury

WHILE MY CONCERN with my own command in the Middle East was absorbing enough in the complexity of its operations and administration, I was still able to note with a keen interest all that was happening in the growth of our own Bomber Command in England. The great four-engined bombers which we had planned for while I was still at the Air Ministry were now in full flow from the aircraft factories, and by the summer of 1943 the Lancaster—which was the most successful of our heavy bombers during the Second World War—was to the forefront in the attacks that were made by Bomber Command from bases in England. Ten Victoria Crosses came to be awarded to the men who flew in the Lancasters.

Decorations for feats of derring-do in time of war can be, and are, looked upon in a variety of ways, all the way from the skepticism and even derision of those who do not receive them to the often silent reticence of those who, in the heat of action, win them and then wonder why. But for all that there should be no doubt in anybody's mind about the merit of and the respect which we should all have for our Victoria Cross, and its American equivalent, the Congressional Medal of Honor. These are awards of the highest order that are sparingly given and, rightly, very highly treasured. In the course of my Service career I was to have quite a little contact with the winners of both, and I never ceased to be amazed at the extraordinarily wide diversity of the characters of the men who won them.

One of the Americans who won a Congressional Medal of Honor for his exploits as a fighter pilot in the First World War was that famous, if not fabulous, character Eddie Rickenbacker, who was to become a good friend of mine after the Second World War when we were both deeply concerned with civil aviation: he as the head of Eastern Airlines, one of the foremost in the United States, and I as chairman of British European Airways.

After the first war Eddie Rickenbacker went into the motor car

567

business, and then he became a civil airline operator, and from that a general man of affairs with a finger in a great many pies in public life. I have always thought of him as the most colorful character that has ever been known in American aviation. By the time of the outbreak of the Second World War, he was one of the foremost executives in American civil aviation, and a man known for his pronounced and highly individualistic views on almost everything.

I had met Rickenbacker once during those days on the Western Front of the first war, and he had struck me then as being a rather brash character who was nevertheless a man of parts, and that he had his head screwed on in the right way. I did not meet him again until his sudden arrival in Cairo in the summer of 1943, although I had heard all about his progress during the years between the wars. He came breezing into my office one day without any warning, and he greeted me with a warmth that I found rather touching. It was almost as if I were a long-lost friend.

We had all heard about the extraordinary experience that Eddie Rickenbacker had had in the Pacific only the year before. The aircraft in which he was a passenger had run out of fuel and had crashed, and he had floated around in a raft north of Samoa for twenty-three days. At our meeting in Cairo he told me the whole story, and it was without any understatement or restraint. He had been on his way from the United States to the Far East, and they had had to ditch, and after a while they had been given up for lost. A U.S. Navy flyingboat eventually found them, and the news of the dramatic rescue after their harrowing experience rang around the world.

"My hat made a big difference," Rickenbacker told me. "I was the only one who had a hat."

Through that hat they had been able to catch a little rain water; and on one occasion, Rickenbacker told me, he had caught a seagull that had actually perched on his head. He had watched the eyes of one of the other men in the raft who kept his gaze fixed on the seagull, and at just the right moment he suddenly reached up and grabbed the bird. They tore it to pieces and devoured it raw. The story of this exploit of Rickenbacker's is an epic one in the history of flying, and it had served to endear him even more in the hearts of the American people who already cherished him as one of their heroes.

While I was pleased enough to see Rickenbacker again, I was rather at a loss to understand why he was a civilian and not in one of the Services, and I never did learn the reason for that.

"What are you doing out here?" I asked.

"I've been sent out personally by the President to report on the war and, if possible, to bring Turkey into it," he announced.

Since he had no written orders to substantiate this claim, I had to take Rickenbacker's word, and that of the American authorities in Cairo, that what he was saying was true. Knowing the man for what he was I saw no reason to doubt it. And such a purpose was of immediate appeal to me because of my own interest in it.

"What's the first thing you want to do?" I asked.

"Send me up to Turkey, to Ankara, straight away," he replied. "I'll see what I can do to get them into the war."

The R.A.F. was running a regular service into Turkey, and passage for Rickenbacker was easy enough to arrange; but it was not without some vague feeling of misgiving that I put him on board one of our aircraft and sent him off. There was peace for about forty-eight hours, and then suddenly all hell broke loose. Urgent signals started arriving from our people in Ankara demanding that they and the other Allied diplomats should be informed immediately about what authority Rickenbacker had for being there, and for behaving in the way that he appeared to be conducting himself.

So far as I could make out, Rickenbacker had been to see the President of Turkey, the Prime Minister, and Field-Marshal Cakmak, the chief of the Turkish General Staff, and, from the reports that we were receiving, he had told them all in no uncertain terms that Turkey had got to get into the war, and get into it quickly. This blunt statement from the man who, it was reported, was claiming to be there as the personal representative of the President, was apparently creating a great deal of alarm. After several days of some quite dramatic exchanges of signals flashing backwards and forwards, Eddie Rickenbacker reappeared in Cairo. When he came to see me he was a little crestfallen, and he told me that he was disappointed with the behavior of the Turks.

"What're you going to do now?" I asked, rather overawed by his marked assurance in his own ability to achieve anything upon which he set his mind.

"I want to go to wherever the Russian Government has moved to," Rickenbacker replied. "I must see Stalin."

Another of our regular services was a weekly flight from Cairo to Kuibyshev, to which the Russian Government had moved from Moscow, and we were using for these flights the big four-engined American Liberators. I arranged for a passage for Rickenbacker, and sent him off; and then held my breath, waiting for another explosion. For about six weeks all was peace and quiet, and then Rickenbacker reappeared in Cairo. He seemed to be quite happy and contented, and he reported that he had had interviews with many of the important men in the Russian Government, and even with Stalin, who had apparently treated him with great courtesy and had discussed with him a number of important issues having to do with the war.

After telling me all about that, Rickenbacker went on his way, and I did not see him again until some years after the war, by which time we were both heads of our different civil airlines. He has never failed to be a man of the most intriguing character, with a mind filled with a great wealth of original ideas on every subject under the sun, all the way from aviation to politics to religion. I disagree strongly with many of Eddie Rickenbacker's ideas, but I have always found him well worth listening to; and at the same time I have continued to enjoy a great liking for him as a man.

In the massive Allied air assault that was made upon Germany during the Second World War, the Americans and the British worked with one object in mind, and if the views about the ways in which that object was to be achieved were not always in unison, our two air forces nevertheless worked well together. There were disagreements which we felt came about at times through a surprising unwillingness on the part of some American air commanders to consider fully the wealth of hard experience that we had already gained before they came into the war; but it is possible that a contributing factor to that was our own inability to explain what we were talking about in terms that the Americans could understand and evaluate in their own way.

I was to be associated with the Americans in one of their most gallant efforts in the air in the second war, and it made upon me an unforgettable impression. Through such contacts with them, and in other ways as well, I came to feel strongly about the need on our part to make a firm contribution in helping toward a mutual understanding about the use that was to be made of the air. We had the experience, and they were rapidly producing additional power of formidable proportions. Between us, I felt, we were bound to make a very big impact on the course of the war.

The start of the American air attack was made when there were staged some low-level attacks on targets in Holland early in July, 1942, by some American air crews flying American aircraft which belonged to the R.A.F. On August 17, just over a month later, and two days before we made our ill-fated raid on Dieppe, the United

States Army Air Forces made their first bombing raid from England with their own aircraft. Escorted by strong wings of our Spitfires, twelve Flying Fortresses made a daylight raid on the railway marshaling yards at Rouen. In the words of one of their historians: "The strike, in itself, was a trivial one."

But on June 12, two months before that, there had been an American operation that has been rather overlooked. On that date they had made their first heavy bombing raid on German-occupied Europe, and it came from a totally unexpected source. In a round trip of some two thousand miles, thirteen Liberators flew from Egypt and attacked one of the most important targets held by the Germans: the oil refineries at Ploesti, in Romania.

By that time our own Bomber Command attacks at night were being mounted with an increasing fury. For a variety of reasons, some of which were in conflict with our own views, the Americans had elected to conduct their bombing operations in daylight; and between us we began giving Germany a round-the-clock pounding. But the American daylight operations proved immensely costly in aircraft and crews. From the outset the Americans were convinced that their bombers could operate without fighter escort, and that they were quite capable of fighting their own way to and from the targets which they were to bomb. We tried to warn them against this, basing our warning on our own bitter experiences. But the Americans were so sure about their own theories, and they would not listen to us, which was sad because we had learned our lessons in a very hard school.

"In June of 1943 I was instructed to give first priority to centres of German aircraft production, because of the growing strength of the German air force, which threatened both the bomber offensive itself and the projected invasion of Europe," Bert Harris has commented. At this time when our aircraft were carrying out these raids at night, the American bombers were detailed, in their daylight attacks, to go for the specialized aircraft factories themselves.

In the middle of August, 1943, the Americans, still slow to listen to our advice about the need for more adequate fighter escort for their heavy bombers, conducted the first of their famous daylight mass raids on Regensburg and Schweinfurt, both deep in Germany. Three hundred and fifteen Flying Fortresses took part in the raids, and sixty of them were lost. One can but acknowledge with wonder the gallantry of those American air crews on those daylight raids, particularly when, as Bert Harris put it, "the target experts went completely mad." He has also said: "If I were asked

what were the relations between Bomber Command and the
American bomber force I should say that we had no relations. The
word is inapplicable to what actually happened; we and they were
one force. As for the American bomber crews, they were the
bravest of the brave, and I know that I am speaking for my own
bomber crews when I pay this tribute."

In my own case I have a particular reason for agreeing with
what has been said by Bert Harris. One of the features of the
American participation in the war at this time which was a never-
ending source of astonishment to us out in the Middle East—as it
was to those in the United Kingdom—was the rapidity and the
vast scale of the way in which they poured supplies in aircraft and
parts as well as air crews into the war effort. The U.S. Ninth Army
Air Force in the Western Desert became very powerful in its own
right.

This strong force was directly commanded by Major General
Lewis H. Brereton. He was an eager and combat-minded commander who had started life as a U.S. naval officer, but who had
changed over to the Army and had become one of the first of the
American squadron commanders on the Western Front in the First
World War. When America came into the war, he was commanding their Air Force in the Philippines. From the Far East he came
to the Mediterranean, arriving there six months before I took over
from Arthur Tedder. During the next year he built up his forces
with speed and an admirable efficiency, and by August 1, 1943, he
had assembled on the desert airfields around Benghazi very nearly
two hundred great four-engined Liberators.

The American bombers were kept at Benghazi after the battle
had moved to the west for one definite purpose: another bombing,
and this time a very heavy one, of the important oil refineries at
Ploesti. It was to be a massive operation which called for this great
armada to fly a round trip of some 2,700 miles. These refineries at
Ploesti were producing a third of all the high-octane petrol and the
fuel and the oil being used by the German Air Force and Army,
and in the eyes of the Joint Chiefs of Staff it had become necessary
that they should be eliminated; and the fact that these vast
installations were strongly defended was not to be allowed to
interfere with any plans for the attack.

Right from the time of my first meeting with him—the Americans also had their headquarters in Cairo—my relationship with
Lewis Brereton was good and as sound as I had hoped for all
along in my work with the U.S.A.A.F. Of his understanding of

what had been happening out in the Middle East he was later to write: "No account of the British stand which stopped Rommel can fail to record the fine part played by the R.A.F. and the New Zealand division under General Freyberg. These two undoubtedly saved the Eighth Army from complete defeat." And from the time of the advance of the Eighth Army after the battle at Alamein along the coast of North Africa he gave us every support.

But while the U.S. Ninth Air Force was supporting the advance of our Eighth Army, these other plans were being hatched for them, and although Lewis Brereton was always quite open in discussing them with me I felt the need to be cautious about appearing to play too heavy a hand even if they were a part of my overall command. Brereton was as keen as I was about keeping our joint forces together for attacks against what we considered were the main objectives: the support of the Army in Tunisia and the invasion of Sicily. While I felt that I was getting along well with the Americans, and there had been no reason whatsoever for me to believe that I was not in the closest of harmony with them, they were nevertheless inclined to be a little touchy about anything that they might consider bordered on criticism.

Among the matters discussed at the important meetings held at Casablanca early in that year there had been the possibility of further bombing of these rich oil refineries at Ploesti. That was more than enough to give the planners in Washington a chance to start concocting schemes for their bombers to make a long-range attack from the North African bases. In his diary for April 9 of that year, Lewis Brereton stated: "Discuss with A.C.M. Douglas the detailed plans for the Rumanian operation. I told him that we were prepared to put it on but repeated that I was strongly opposed at this time. He agreed and is sending a message to Whitehall."

I certainly did agree with Brereton, and the signal that I sent to the Air Ministry read: "Although I agree it is most important to destroy as many of the Ploesti refineries as soon as we can, I do not think that much will be accomplished in a single stunt attack at extreme range." I submitted that I thought that it was a mistake to carry out such an operation at that time, and that our whole effort should be directed against the enemy in softening up Sicily, and I finished up with the request: "Let us keep our eye on the ball."

The reply that I received to this expression of my views from the Air Ministry was that they agreed with me in principal, but Brereton and I got no further than that. In Cairo two months later there was, in his words, a "joint conference with the R.A.F. at which A.C.M. Douglas presided, for further discussions of Operations Husky and Soapsuds . . ." Husky was the code name for the Allied invasion of Sicily; and Soapsuds was the name first selected, and later changed to Tidal Wave, for the raid on Ploesti. At that meeting there was a Colonel of the U.S.A.A.F. who had just arrived from Washington via London with the plans for the Ploesti attack. To our astonishment it was to be made at the lowest possible level.

From that time on, I felt the deepest sympathy for Lewis Brereton and those under his command who were going to have to make the raid. He had not been consulted in full as he might have been, or should have been, about the nature of the way in which this big attack was to be made, and all he could do was to implement the plans that were handed to him by the brains at work in Washington. Peter Portal had expressed his doubts about the value of the attack; Bert Harris was known to be opposed to it; Arthur Tedder was not at all keen about it; and Eisenhower was, in the words of one historian, "anything but enthusiastic." But the plan came from those who thought that they knew best, and there was nothing that we could do—or, perhaps I should say, the Americans could do, because it was their show—but get on with it. And in any case, Winston Churchill was all for it because of what was to his imagination such an element of surprise.

Ten days later Lewis Brereton records that he "presented my plan of employment for Operation Tidal Wave to the Mediterranean Air Command which was accepted without any alteration." At the same time he was writing in his diary: "I knew that the Liberator was definitely not suited for a low-level attack, but I felt that the surprise element would weigh heavily in our favor."

There was never any doubt in any of our minds that the Liberator—known to the Americans as the B-24—was a first-rate heavy bomber, and one of the finest aircraft designed by the Americans in the Second World War. Built by the Consolidated Vultee Aircraft people in California, it was a huge machine designed for work on operations at heights up to and even just over thirty thousand feet, and it had exceptional range. It also carried a large number of heavy machine guns for defense. In all, the R.A.F. received just short of seventeen hundred Liberators from the American manufacturers, and we had forty-four of our own squadrons equipped with them. The United States Army Air Forces must have had many thousands of them in use.

A vast amount of hard work went into preparing for this raid on Ploesti, and the American Liberator squadrons which were sta-

tioned on the desert airfields around Benghazi devoted a great deal
of time to training for it. One of those who felt most bitterly about
the way in which the experts had their way in the use of the air
forces in attacking what he has called "panacea" targets such as
Ploesti was Bert Harris. "Many squadrons of American bombers
had to be taken off the main offensive against German industry for
long periods, sent to bases in the Mediterranean, and specially
trained to make a spectacular, low level attack on the oil refineries," he has complained, not, I think, without justification.
"The loss of these squadrons for many months materially reduced
the American build-up for the main offensive against Germany
itself."

There is some truth in that, but we who were out there and
involved in the operation were much more concerned in our own
minds about the way in which it was to be conducted. And in any
case, one has to bear in mind Harris's freely admitted dislike in
this, as in other operations, of the influence of the economic
experts, whose predictions, he has stated, he "had learnt from
bitter experience to regard . . . with the greatest suspicion and
largely to discount . . . in advance."

Through the conferences that were held over a period of two
months in Cairo and in Benghazi, I came to meet all the senior
officers of the United States Army Air Forces who were to take
part in the hazardous Ploesti operation, and I was greatly impressed by the caliber of the men who were to be the leaders. They
are now almost legendary figures in American Air Force history,
but the names of men such as Brigadier General Uzal G. Ent,
Colonel John R. ("Killer") Kane, Colonel Leon W. Johnson, and
Colonel Keith K. Compton became almost equally well known in
the Royal Air Force out in the Middle East as in their own service.

As the date planned for the Ploesti operation approached, the
increasing intensity of the preparations was matched with our
anxiety about the way in which it was to be performed. For all the
fact that it was an American and not a British show, I could not
help taking the keenest interest. Lewis Brereton was keeping me
fully informed, and once the die was cast and the decision was
accepted that the raid would be made at the lowest possible
height—literally at nought feet—I sensed in all the air crews who
were to be involved in it a spirit that was truly one of dedication.

Some miles out in the desert to the south of Benghazi there had
been constructed something that was in the nature of a full-scale
replica of the Ploesti installations, with oil drums and tons of white

wash and even some dummy plant, all of which would give the air crews some idea of what the place was going to look like from the air. The first practice runs were made using dummy bombs, and at heights of less than one hundred feet and more or less in formation. For heavy bombers to operate in this way, even in training, was a nerve-racking business, and for a period of two weeks nearly two hundred Liberators thundered over that dummy target laid out in the desert.

As I watched those lumbering great Liberators—elephantine, they have been called—I could not help feeling with a sinking heart that low down they were such vulnerable targets for fire from the ground. They were heavily enough armed to fight back, as we knew from our own use of them in the R.A.F., and perhaps I was wrong in feeling that way. But it did seem to me that any heavy bomber instructed to carry out an operation of this nature was bound to be in for very heavy punishment.

On the two days just before the raid was due to take place, there were made the last of the practice runs, with the entire force using live bombs. This full dress rehearsal over the desert, which I watched from the air in my own aircraft, was an impressive affair. But it drew from the American commanders only the stern admonition that the pilots had to get even lower down and bomb with even greater precision. Since they had already been told that Ploesti was one of the most heavily defended targets in Europe, and it was generally known among them that, for all the security precautions, the enemy knew all about what was going to happen, those air crews faced a grim enough prospect.

At seven o'clock on Sunday morning, August 1, the first of the 178 great Liberators detailed for the raid took off from the North African desert, followed for the next hour by the rest of the force as they circled their airfields getting into formations at two thousand feet. And then the force set off on the long flight which was to take them across the Mediterranean to Corfu, and then across Albania, Yugoslavia, Bulgaria and on into Romania to their target at Ploesti, some miles to the north of Bucharest. Manning that fleet of heavy bombers were 1,763 American airmen. There was also one Englishman, an R.A.F. gunnery expert named Squadron Leader George C. Barwell.

For sheer guts in the face of a staggering defense, the attacks made by the Liberators that did get to the refineries at Ploesti were delivered with an astonishing courage. Mishaps occurred and mistakes were made, but the attack was completed right down at nought feet, and then those who survived set off, many of them badly crippled, for the long flight home. So low down was the attack made that even Adolf Galland, who has been rather ungenerous in his comments about the courage of the Americans, had to admit: "The success of the defence in this instance went mainly to the flak."

By the end of that day we knew that Ploesti had been hit, and hit hard, but already it was clear that it was at a fearful cost. In the words of the historian Leon Wolff: "It was the worst catastrophe in the history of the U.S. Army Air Forces." We did not know until long afterward that the enemy had been on the alert from the time when the Liberators had started taking off from Benghazi, and that they had shrewdly plotted them on the whole of the long flight to Ploesti. They were ready and waiting for the arrival of the Americans.

Reports came in to our headquarters in Cairo of badly damaged Liberators being forced to land, it seemed, all over the eastern Mediterranean, including Turkey. How true it is I do not know, but Leon Wolff records that the girl who was so well known to our people in the desert for her singing of "Lili Marlene" on the German radio made the comment: "Fine job on Ploesti, Brereton, but you lost too many."

It was a long time before the actual figures of those losses were known, but now it appears that out of the 1,763 airmen who set out on the raid, 446 were killed or missing, and 130 were wounded. Later we heard that 108 were prisoners of war in Romania, and 76 were interned in Turkey, where 8 of the Liberators had been forced to land. Three had crashed into the sea, 23 had managed to stagger as far as our airfields in Cyprus, Sicily and Malta. Over 50 had been shot down over Ploesti, and of the 178 great Liberators that had set off from Benghazi, only 88 got back there, of which 55 were damaged.

Such was the extraordinary spirit shown by these American air crews that I sent a signal immediately to Lewis Brereton up in the desert in which I said: "Please congratulate Brigadier-General Ent and the Ninth U.S. Bomber Command on the successful raid on the Roumanian oil refineries yesterday. The gallantry and dash displayed by your air crews in carrying out the attack at such a low altitude in the face of very strong defences is beyond praise."

A few days later there arrived in Richard Casey's office a copy of a signal that had been sent by our Ambassador in Ankara to the Foreign Office in London. Casey passed it on to me, and in it I thought I detected the fine hand of Bobbie George, our air attaché in Turkey. It was a very complete report on the extensive damage that had been inflicted on the Ploesti installations, and it came from the Turkish Minister of Foreign Affairs who, in turn, had received it from the Turkish Ambassador in Bucharest. In its way that alleviated a little the effects of the appalling losses that had been suffered by the American Ninth Air Force, which in a few hours had become so depleted.

But in the words of Leon Wolff, who was himself an officer during the war in the American Air Force: "Blunders of execution had nullified the original hope, perhaps euphoric, that the refineries could be put out of commission for a long period of time . . . the raid had not been executed successfully. The percentage of casualties set an A.A.F. record. The raid now appears in retrospect to have been perhaps ill-advised in its original conception." It is true that the raid was not nearly as successful as we had at first thought; and only a few weeks afterward the refineries were again in full operation.

A month later, on September 4, there was a ceremony in Cairo at the club at Gezira which, with its golf course, polo field, swimming pool and tennis courts, we all used for relaxation. But this ceremony was not a moment for any frivolity, and we all accepted it as a solemn and serious affair. Lewis Brereton distributed decorations to those who had taken part in the Ploesti raid. It was his last official act in the Middle East before going to a new appointment with the U.S. Army Air Forces in England.

It is now a matter of record that for that raid five Congressional Medals of Honor alone eventually came to be awarded: the greatest number ever awarded for any one single action in American military history. But for all that recognition, in the hearts of all of those of us who were out in the Middle East at that time, whether we were actively associated with the actual raid or not, there was a heavy ache of regret; and we who were the commanders were very conscious of that.

The savage losses that were being suffered in the air, particularly by the bombers of the U.S. Army Air Forces, were, to my mind, attributable largely to the persistence with which our own people as well as the Americans would insist that the heavily armed bombers could fight their way through, by day and by night, without fighter escorts. For years there were those in the Royal Air Force who simply would not accept the need for fighter escorts; and I used to have very strenuous battles in trying to prove my point that such escorts were necessary.

With the Americans it seemed that they were even more sure of the invulnerability of their heavy bombers. It took the terrible losses that they suffered in their massed daylight raids on Regensburg, Schweinfurt and Ploesti, to name only three objectives, to convince them that fighter operations would have to be planned in such a way that long-range fighters could be included to provide the necessary escorts to ward off the German fighters. For the Americans and their daylight raids the answer was provided mainly with the Mustang; and for the R.A.F. at night we started using our own highly developed Mosquito night fighters.

One of those greatly concerned about the heavy losses which the Americans were suffering was Larry Callahan, and while I was still at Fighter Command he had been making his inquiries into ways and means of giving adequate fighter protection to the American bombers. He became particularly intrigued with the special service that we had for listening in to and keeping track of the dispositions and, whenever possible, the plans of the German fighter forces. Being at heart a fighter pilot, and having actually flown in the First World War with Mick Mannock, one of the first of the great fighter tacticians, he started examining more closely our thoughts about bomber protection, and to those he added his own through the practical experience that he had had in the earlier war. He then went off to his own people at the United States Air Forces Headquarters with an idea which, he has stated, "involved close collaboration with British intelligence . . . and an entirely new deployment in the air of our fighters . . . the idea for which I got from Mannock. We had many operational and intelligence people, both British and American, involved in this study and came out with a plan which worked."

In a further exchange of views about this, Larry Callahan wrote again, saying: "Our basic idea was that if we were to achieve ultimate air supremacy we had to abandon the impossible task of close escort and substitute the plan, as carried out very successfully, of locating the swarms of enemy fighters and destroying and breaking them up before they could reach the bombers."

Not the least of the contributions to the success of that plan— "which was based on the conclusion that we could not physically escort the bombers, but must attack the Hun before he hit the bombers"—came about through Larry Callahan's outstanding ability as a liaison officer. Although not a regular officer, he had evolved from the rather typical young harum-scarum fighter pilot of the First World War into a staff officer—albeit only a wartime one—of exceptional vision. "The application of the theory of aerial warfare that Mannock had was absolutely right," Callahan

once told Bob Wright when, a few years ago, they talked about
this problem. "We used it just straight down the line." And with
the ear of Tooey Spaatz, who was the one who had brought
Callahan back into the United States Army Air Forces, Callahan
could, in his own words, "get places and do things and look at
operations critically." Tooey Spaatz had returned to England by
then from North Africa, and was in command of all the American
strategic bombing forces operating from England.

31 / "One of the sharpest pangs"

URING THE COURSE of the whole of the Second World War, I was constantly involved, first as a senior member of the Air Staff, and then as a Commander-in-Chief, in implementing the decisions arrived at by the high authority in matters of grand strategy. There were times when I did not altogether agree with what I was told to do, and there were times when I accepted with eagerness the directives that came my way; but in either case I did what I was told, knowing, as a professional airman, that it was my duty to obey orders, provided that those orders were legitimate. There were only two occasions during the war—there was to be a third after the end of the war—when I felt so strongly about the way in which events in which I was involved were being allowed to shape themselves that I had to protest. The first was over an actual military operation; the second was in the more personal matter of the use that was to be made of my services.

It was over the operation in the islands of the Dodecanese, in the Aegean, during the months of September, October and November of 1943, that I came to feel the very real need to rebel against the way in which we were left out on a limb. In this I was probably more deeply involved in affairs of grand strategy than at any other point in my career. But I was not alone in that. "I remained—and remain—in my heart unconvinced that the capture of Rhodes could not have been fitted in," Winston Churchill stated of his own views. And of his having to agree not to wrest control of Rhodes from the Germans, he added that it caused him "one of the sharpest pangs I suffered in the war." With that I wholeheartedly agree.

"Immediately after the surrender of Italy in early September there arose a situation in the eastern Mediterranean that not only caused us great concern but which will be argued pro and con for a long time to come," General Eisenhower commented even before Churchill had made his statement.

I have no way of knowing if Eisenhower was then beginning to feel that the attitude taken toward the affairs of the eastern Mediterranean by his government and his staff in the latter part of 1943 was possibly open to question; but in that statement he did at least open the door for an airing of opinions. And in view of all that has arisen since in the discussions that have taken place on both sides of the Atlantic about whether the policy of the Allies in the planning of our attack upon the enemy during the last two years of the war was too inflexible, it is of importance to examine in some detail what happened in the Aegean.

Even after all these years I still feel keenly about what Eisenhower called the "situation," and the main point in his statement, and in his whole attitude, is that there will be continued argument. The key to my disagreement with his views is contained in the summary that he made about the relative merits of a projected operation in the Dodecanese and the war that was going on in Italy. "Those islands, in my judgment," he stated, "while of considerable strategic importance, did not compare in military value to success in the Italian battle." Therein lies what was to be such a bone of contention.

It has always been my belief that had we been given the opportunity to exploit to the full the start that we made in the summer of 1943 to penetrate the islands of the Aegean then occupied by the Germans and the Italians, we could have achieved very far-reaching results. Not the least of these could possibly have been not only an earlier crippling of Germany but also the halting of the advance of the Russians in their sweep across the Balkans and on into the countries over which they today exercise such a tight control. I am not alone in that thought, the foremost advocate of it being Winston Churchill; but it has long been the subject of unhappy disagreement, starting back in 1943, between us and the Americans.

Since I was one of the three Commanders-in-Chief actually involved in the operation, I can speak with some authority at least about the way in which the actual operation was conducted; and I should like to be able to present the facts in such a fashion that I shall not leave myself open to charges of trying to excuse our failure. Excuses are not necessary. We did fail; but it was not for want of trying. The reason for the failure is to be found in the record, which, in the long run, was more political than military.

With the unconditional surrender of Italy on September 8, 1943, our thoughts turned to the best possible way of continuing to chase the Germans back from the eastern Mediterranean. The collapse of the Italians by no means meant that the Germans in Italy were giving up, and they continued to offer a savage resistance to our armies which were fighting their way up Italy from the south, the Americans on the left and the British on the right. And with that a question began to be asked. Was that slugging match in Italy the only way of crushing the Germans? The Americans were thinking about and planning wholeheartedly for a second front in the form of a massive invasion of France across the English Channel. They were unquestionably right in that thinking, and we were giving them our full support in the planning; but was their singlemindedness the only answer?

As was to be expected, the more flexible mind of Winston Churchill, coupled with his vast experience, was seeing additional possibilities opening up for attacks upon the Germans. It was not that he wanted in any way to detract from the cross-Channel invasion; but he did want to take full advantage of all the opportunities that were being offered to hit the enemy from every quarter. With the Italian collapse he saw such an opportunity offered in the Aegean, and the more he thought about it the keener he became on "gaining important prizes in the Aegean at very small cost and effort."

In elaborating on that, Churchill stated: "It seemed to me a rebuff to fortune not to pick up these treasures. The command of the Aegean by air and by sea was within our reach. The effect of this might be decisive upon Turkey, at that time deeply moved by the Italian collapse." And then he summed up a further great advantage. "If we could use the Aegean and the Dardanelles the naval short cut to Russia was established," he added.

At the bare mention of the Dardanelles there were many who started up the cry that Churchill was harking back to the First World War and the ill-fated operation there in 1915, and that he was trying in some way to erase the defeat that he had suffered then. Such accusations are ridiculous. The campaign at Gallipoli had been sound enough in its conception: it was in its execution that it went wrong. And one of the reasons for Churchill's pangs over the operation in the Aegean in 1943 must be because, again, it was in its execution that it went wrong.

Sensing what was going to happen, Winston Churchill instructed the Chiefs of Staff Committee a month before the Italian surrender to give thought to having the Middle East commanders make plans for action in the Aegean. "This is no time for conventional establishments, but rather for using whatever fighting elements there are," he stated. "I hope the Staffs will be able to stimulate action, which may gain immense prizes at little cost, though not at little risk."

Out in Cairo we had been working for months on plans for a penetration of the islands of the Dodecanese, off the southwest coast of Turkey; but in the realms of grand strategy that appeared to have been relegated to a position of only minor importance. Even before the collapse of the Italians the shipping that we had earmarked for such an expedition had been taken away from us. "To our chagrin," Jumbo Wilson recorded, "orders were received from the combined Chiefs of Staff to send all the shipping and assault craft to India for an operation against Arakan, which in the end never came off." The Army also found that the troops which they had planned on using for the Aegean, and which had even gone through practice exercises for the landings on the islands, were under orders to go to the central Mediterranean for use there.

In all that happened from then on there was a strong clash of opinions at the highest levels, and it is important to understand the reasons for that clash. Winston Churchill became increasingly anxious to press forward with the operation in the Aegean. The Army commander in the Middle East, Jumbo Wilson, and I were entirely in agreement with him. The naval commander, Admiral Sir Andrew Cunningham, was, in his own words, "well aware of the situation," and eager to cooperate. A.B.C. had particular reason to feel somewhat strongly about the islands of the Aegean because he had spent a long time during the First World War as a young officer in command of a destroyer in the Mediterranean, and he was present throughout the Gallipoli campaign. The "multitude of lovely islands in the Aegean were old friends," he has said; and through firsthand experience during those years of the earlier war he knew all about Leros, which was being used by the enemy as a naval base, now that he was Commander-in-Chief in the Mediterranean in the second war.

But we who were in command in the eastern Mediterranean were left standing strangely alone. To my disappointment I found that my old friend Alan Brooke, the C.I.G.S. and head of the Chiefs of Staff Committee, by no means felt as enthusiastic as the Prime Minister about the possibilities in the Aegean. "Unfortunately, for the past month the Prime Minister had been pressing on the Americans a course of action in the Mediterranean calculated to make them even more suspicious than usual of British intentions in that sea," Sir Arthur Bryant has recorded of the attitude of Brooke toward our problems.

While I understand the use that Bryant makes of the word

"unfortunately," I think that it would have been better if he had said either "unfortunately for Alan Brooke" or had omitted it altogether. In the official history, *Grand Strategy*, John Ehrman offered a well-balanced appreciation of the whole situation. "As an element in the immediate strategy, the capture of the Dodecanese had much to commend it," he stated. "But it had another, and potentially greater, significance. It might bring Turkey into the war." We had had our discussions about this with the Turks earlier in the year, including the possibility of capturing the islands of the Dodecanese; and they had expressed to us quite early that they were, as Ehrman put it, "afraid of an undisputed Russian domination of the Balkans." It is of value to remember that that apprehension on the part of the Turks was expressed to us well over twenty years ago.

Out in the eastern Mediterranean we became very conscious of the way in which we were being urged by the Prime Minister to press on with our plans for the Dodecanese operation. "Good. This is the time to play high. Improvise and dare," he signaled us on September 9 in reply to a statement that we, the Commanders-in-Chief on the spot, had sent to London three days earlier about our intentions. "The Chiefs of Staff agree that the prize was worth the risk," Ehrman recorded.

We knew that right from the outset we would be handicapped through shortage of suitable aircraft and landing craft, but we hoped, even though Eisenhower, to whom a copy of our signal had gone, could not see his way clear to give us unqualified support, that by exercising the boldness called for by the Prime Minister we would pull it off. But Hitler felt the same way that we did about the Aegean, and, while we were left to struggle along as best we could, he saw to it that his garrisons received full support.

The detailed story of all that happened in the operations so far as the air was concerned has been described admirably enough by Denis Richards and Hilary St. George Saunders in their official history; but I find it hard to accept their findings that "this rash experiment . . . ill-judged from the beginning, had been the result of over-confidence, an unconscious flouting of a cardinal principle of modern warfare." Such a dismissal is much too cavalier in fashion of the whole complicated story of those weeks of the late summer and the autumn of 1943, and in such an assessment one cannot help recalling all that was said about Gallipoli in 1915. Even the words themselves have a sadly familar ring.

This opinion also conflicts so much with Winston Churchill's description of "Wilson's well-conceived plans for rapid action in the Dodecanese," as well as with the views expressed by the Chief of the Air Staff. At one period Peter Portal sent a signal to Arthur Tedder, my immediate superior in the Mediterranean, telling him that he considered that Leros was "more important than strategic objectives in southern France and north Italy."

In the eastern Mediterranean we were admittedly attempting to launch our operation with the severest of handicaps through lack of men and ships and aircraft, and Winston Churchill in London was struggling mightily for more support for us. Relying on the decision already reached by the Combined British and American Chiefs of Staff in Washington, in which they approved an effort "in respect of Rhodes and other islands in the Dodecanese," Churchill urged us on to be bold in our actions. And on the British Chiefs of Staff he urged that they should think of it as "a business of great consequence to be thrust forward by every means."

The immediate concern of the Air Force in our plan to pry open the islands of the Aegean was to secure fighter airfields, and the immediate objective for that was the island of Rhodes. On September 11 we were able to advise London that the small island of Castelrosso, just off the southern coast of Turkey, had been successfully occupied, and that Major Earl Jellicoe—the son of the famous admiral of the First World War—had been dropped by parachute in Rhodes, where he was in touch with the Italian commander.

On the same day I sent a signal to Arthur Tedder stating that we had received from our mission in Rhodes a request from the Italian governor that we should bomb two airfields on the island which were in German hands. I asked for permission to use the bombers of the American Ninth Air Force—the veterans of Ploesti—for this purpose. They were still at the airfield at Benghazi, waiting to move forward to Tunisia for operations in the Italian campaign.

But the very next day I had to advise Tedder that things were not going as well as we had thought in Rhodes. In spite of the Italian governor's request, Jellicoe had received a refusal from the Italian commander to cooperate with us. The Italian garrison had gone over to the Germans, who had seized control of the whole island. We had sent in Beaufighters and Wellingtons from our Middle East bases in the Nile delta and Cyprus to bomb the airfields during the evening of the day before, and during the next day, and the American Liberators had made similar attacks. I thanked Tedder for his assistance, but I had to tell him that we considered that "no further military action can be usefully taken against Rhodes at present." This information was also sent on to London.

How close we came to taking Rhodes is revealed by our official naval historian. He quotes the War Diary of the German Naval Group Command, South, of September 12 as recording: "If the enemy had made full use of the moment of weakness [following on the Italian armistice] he could easily have taken Rhodes." He further quotes A. B. Cunningham as reporting to the First Sea Lord on September 19 that "if they had left us 'Accolade' [i.e. the forces earmarked for the capture of Rhodes] for just a few days longer we could not have failed to take Rhodes, and the situation would then have been simple."

We had then had to think of bypassing Rhodes, and two days after my last report I sent a personal signal to the Chief of the Air Staff in which I stated that it had become evident that without Allied military and air reinforcement Italian resistance to the Germans in the islands would be negligible. It was clear, I told him, that the Germans were taking energetic action to obtain possession of all the important islands in the Aegean. We had pressed on beyond Rhodes and I was able to tell him that the Italian commander on the island of Cos, some sixty miles to the northwest of Rhodes, was cooperating with us, and that for work with the Army and the Royal Navy, who had joined us in the combined assault on the island, we had six Spitfires on the airfield there, which was the only island other than Rhodes with a suitable airdrome. We were maintaining them with Dakotas flying to Cos from Cyprus, routed over Turkey.

"It is a bit risky putting in this flight," I added, "but I think this is the time to take risks," and I concluded with the comment: "It was a great pity that we were ordered to send on to India the ships which we had asked to be allowed to hold for an assault loaded brigade. If we could have pushed this brigade into Rhodes on the day after the Armistice was signed, I think we could have seized and held the island."

Nine days after we had signaled the Chiefs of Staff an outline of our plans—which had drawn from Churchill such a prompt and stirring response—they sent us a reply stating: "We agree that with the resources at present at your disposal action you are taking in Aegean Islands to exploit Italy's capitulation is best possible." They urged us "on political grounds" to include Greek troops in those occupying the islands, which was one way of needlessly reminding us of the work that we had been doing for some time in encouraging from our bases in the Middle East the resistance in German-occupied Greece and the rest of the Balkans. But nothing was said about helping us with more ships and aircraft.

The forces that we had available for the air side of the operation consisted of four Beaufighter squadrons—two for day and two for night work—a squadron of torpedo-bomber Wellingtons, four general reconnaissance squadrons—made up of Baltimores and Hudsons—five fighter squadrons of Spitfires and Hurricanes, a number of Spitfires for photographic reconnaissance, and the invaluable Dakotas of the transport group.

In bypassing Rhodes we occupied, in addition to Cos, the important islands of Leros—which had an Italian naval base—and Samos, which were yet another sixty miles further into the Aegean. The Army also got small parties ashore on the islands of Lipsos, Patmos, Phoúrnoi and Icaria, alongside Samos. But all this further extended the distances by air, and we were by then nearly four hundred miles from our base on the island of Cyprus.

On September 17 I sent a personal signal to Peter Portal in which I reported that the Dodecanese operations were "going well so far," and that we had flown in a detachment of the R.A.F. regiment for antiaircraft defense of the airfield on Cos as well as radar warning sets and operators. The Army was also with us in Cos and Leros, and "at present" our shipping, with escorting destroyers, was moving freely between the islands. "Wish we had a bomber striking force here to attack Rhodes aerodromes, but realise this is asking a lot until situation in Italy improves," I commented. I had repeated the signal to Arthur Tedder, and I added a last word saying: "Would Tedder bear this in mind however for the future."

Immediately after my last signal to Peter Portal, I flew to Cyprus to see for myself how things were going in the work of maintaining contact with the islands. I stayed for the weekend at a pleasant hotel in Kyrenia, on the north coast of the island. It was an almost idyllic place for a rest, and one afternoon we made our way up to the old Crusader castle of St. Hilarion. During the war Cyprus was a haven—in such sad contrast to what it has since become—and it was popular with all those who were serving in the eastern Mediterranean as a reliable place for a few days' leave.

The people of Cyprus appeared to be contented enough, and they always treated us with the greatest friendliness. But Dick Casey, being more politically minded, had made more penetrating inquiries on his visits to the island, and only a few months before he had noticed that there were occasions when the Cypriots would call out the word *Enosis* as he passed by, even though it was always expressed in the most polite fashion, and with no apparent dislike of us whatsoever. But it was apparently known well enough to those concerned that "the biggest political problem in Cyprus in 1943 was the local demand for *Enosis* (Union with Greece)," as Casey has put it. He records stopping when he heard the cry, and asking who had told the simple people to cry out *"Enosis";* and in view of all that has happened in Cyprus since then, the reply that he always got is, to say the least, illuminating. "The priest," they said.

Among the more active of my senior officers who was also doing a great deal to keep us informed about what was going on in the islands of the Dodecanese was Max Aitken, who was in command of all fighter operations in the Aegean. He was flying both twin-engined Beaufighters as well as Spitfires up to Cos, on one occasion taking in the air officer commanding, Eastern Mediterranean, Air Vice-Marshal R. E. Saul, who had been one of my group commanders in Fighter Command. Aitken has always felt that with more support we could have pulled off our thrust into the Aegean. Whitney Straight's transport aircraft were parachuting our troops into Cos, as well as keeping the island supplied with all that was necessary for maintaining the garrison there. Our soldiers found that, as with Rhodes, the Italians there were wavering, but in the case of Cos they were able to provide them with a sufficient degree of stiffening to their morale to bring them over to our side.

But on the very day of my signal to Peter Portal in which I had said that things were "going well so far," the Germans launched the start of their counterattack. Ju. 88's with escorts of Me. 109's gave Cos a beating, putting the airfield out of service, and damaging some of the transport aircraft on it. These attacks continued for two more days. A second landing strip was brought into use by our people, and that provided some help for our aircraft. By then the Germans were pouring bombers and fighters into the Aegean; and not having to make the long flights with which our pilots were faced before even getting to Cos, they were able to operate much more effectively. Our garrison on the ground dug in as best they could and prepared for what looked like an onslaught.

In response to our appeal for help, Tedder's headquarters had the heavy bombers make night attacks on enemy-occupied airfields near Athens as well as those on Crete and Rhodes; but that did not seem to deter the Germans, although there came a few days after that when we were left in peace. We sent more Spitfires up to Cos, but they were, in the words of Richards and Saunders, "too few to prevent or drive away an enemy smarting under recent reverses and determined to use to the full the local air superiority he had created by moving squadrons so swiftly from bases as far distant as the south of France." We did not know that we were going through the lull before the storm.

"Once Rhodes was denied to us our gains throughout the Aegean became precarious," Winston Churchill wrote. "Only a powerful use of air forces could give us what we needed." And then he stated clearly what I feel was the reason why the operation was allowed to go awry. "General Eisenhower and his staff seemed unaware of what lay at our finger-tips," he commented, "although we had voluntarily placed all our considerable resources entirely in their hands."

We knew that Eisenhower was having difficulties with the stiff German resistance in Italy, but I felt, as others probably did, that the slugging match there showed dangerous signs of developing into a repetition of all that had happened in the First World War. What I felt "lay at our finger-tips" was the great opportunity to avoid this head-on clash by hitting the Germans hard from our vantage point in the Aegean, on his flank. They were more exposed there, and vulnerable, and that was the place to attack.

On my return from Cyprus I had sent a signal to Arthur Tedder reporting that the "buildup in Cos" was going satisfactorily, and that "we are making a useful catch of enemy aircraft." I was able to report that we had in fact shot down six Ju. 88's, two Me. 109's, two He. 111's and "various 52's and Arados," with a loss to us of three Spitfires and their pilots, although we had had some aircraft destroyed and damaged on the ground through enemy bombing.

After a brief respite of four days, I was able to report to the C.A.S. that the "situation in Dodecanese quiet, with no enemy air attacks on Cos." We had the second landing strip on the island in use by then, and we were proceeding with the construction of a third, although our equipment for this work was as primitive as one could imagine. "Whole position is beginning to look pretty secure," I was able to conclude in that signal of September 25.

But almost immediately my intelligence people reported to me that the Germans were about to hit back, and on September 29 they did it with a heavy raid on Cos. I was becoming alarmed at both the speed and the scale of the reinforcements that the Germans were rushing into the Aegean. I warned Tedder that the loss of Cos "would jeopardize not only our present holding in the Dodecanese but also any projected operations against Rhodes," and that "the possession of workable aerodromes in Cos is fundamental to the latter operation."

Later the same day I had to signal Tedder again telling him that two of the three landing strips on Cos were now so badly cratered through enemy bombing that they were likely to be out of action for several days. By then the Germans were bombing with Ju. 88's which were accompanied by strong escorts of Me. 109's. Tedder replied the same day agreeing that the "situation in Aegean has developed so as to call for increased air support on our part, particularly against enemy bomber and fighter bases in the Balkans." He agreed to allow me to use for a while a wing of two squadrons of bombers which was under orders to go to the central Mediterranean; but he refused my request that the American heavy bombers should be allowed to come to our aid, giving as his reason attacks on Germany that had already been planned for them.

To my surprise Arthur Tedder then made the comment that he was "very concerned at the way in which the Aegean operations have developed and involved commitments of which I have had no prior opportunity of assessing," and he went on to say that "procedure by which Commanders-in-Chief, Middle East, launch operations without full consultation with me and Eisenhower is I feel most dangerous." My surprise turned to somewhat breathless astonishment—particularly when I noticed that Tedder had also sent a copy of the signal to the C.A.S. in London—when I read his concluding comment. In this he made the perplexing rebuke: "Events have shown what I feel ought to have been evident before, that Balkan operations particularly from an air point of view are part of those in the rest of the Mediterranean and must be considered as part of that one problem. I do not wish to waste time by criticising the past and will do my best to help but I must insist on being kept fully informed as to plans for future operations so that the possible commitments and consequent moves of and employment of air forces can be properly arranged."

A further reason for my astonishment was that at the time that I received this rebuke from Arthur Tedder I also received a copy of a signal which the Chief of the Air Staff had just sent to him. Marked "Private and personal for Tedder repeat Douglas from C.A.S," it was of the same date as Tedder's signal to me, and it commenced with the statement: "I am very pleased with the forward policy adopted at Cos and am strongly in favour of doing everything possible to build up defensive strength of fighters and A.A. Its value for attack on Rhodes is obvious."

It struck me that, in some curious way, Tedder appeared to be the only one who was not fully acquainted with what was going on. Even London knew and approved. It confirmed for me my opinion that the time was more than ripe for a fundamental change in the structure of the overall command in the Mediterranean. I naturally agreed with Tedder that we could not expect to continue to operate at all satisfactorily if the air commander in the Mediterranean was not always in the picture. It was my responsibility to support Jumbo Wilson and his Army in the Middle East while I was still under the operational control of the air commander at Eisenhower's headquarters. But Wilson was not under Eisenhower's control, being directly responsible to London.

At the same time, I was being urged on by London to give Wilson all the support I could, and that seemed to be regardless of what might come from Eisenhower's headquarters. "We should fight the German Air Force wherever it goes," Portal's signal continued. "We can better afford a diversion to the Aegean than they can, and wastage inflicted in Greece and the Aegean is just as desirable as anywhere else. Moreover, the German diversion to the Eastern area is a clear indication of the importance he attaches to denying us our object there and thus of the value to us of meeting and defeating him."

While agreeing that we should not "deny our forces in Italy their legitimate air requirements for successful progress," Portal pointed out that we must not neglect the insurgents in the Balkans. "Nevertheless I believe that the Air Forces in the Mediterranean are ample to enable us to afford . . . support for maintaining our position in the Aegean and defeating the German attempt to dislodge us by air action," he stated, and he finished with the "hope that the Malta spirit exists among the defenders of Cos."

The German invasion of Cos came at dawn four days later. The Navy had been very active in trying to keep track of the ships from Greece and Crete which were bearing the German assault, and their destroyers and submarines were instructed to intercept them following a sighting at sea by our aircraft. But no interception was made, and the Germans effected their landings, supported by heavy air attacks and the dropping of parachute troops. Our long-range Beaufighters from Cyprus went into the attack, but despite the great effort that they made—and their losses were severe—we were overwhelmed; and after holding the island for only about three weeks we were flung out. It was a bitter disappointment.

It was also a hard pill for Winston Churchill to swallow. He had been keeping a particularly watchful eye on all that had been happening, and he was becoming distinctly apprehensive. "Found P.M. in a great flutter owing to the attack on Cos island," Alan Brooke recorded in his diary on October 4; and two days later he was recalling an opinion that was, one must assume, somewhat different from that held by Peter Portal. "It is quite clear in my mind that with the commitments we have in Italy we should not undertake serious operations in the Aegean," he wrote in his diary.

From the outset I was far from happy about the way in which our efforts in the eastern Mediterranean were considered by Eisenhower's headquarters. The answers they were giving us to our signals to them could never be considered as properly thought out, and I could not understand Arthur Tedder's position in all this. He had appeared to approve of our plans to start with, and it was not until some three weeks after we had stated our intentions, and we had actually put them into operation, that he lodged his disturbing complaint about not being consulted.

One of our difficulties lay in that fact that whereas Jumbo Wilson was an independent commander—with the Army in the Middle East being his sole responsibility and for which he was answerable only to London—the Air Force in the Middle East under my command was under the general operational control of Arthur Tedder, at Eisenhower's headquarters. I had no compunction in giving Wilson right from the outset assurance of my fullest support. But in the face of the little that Tedder appeared to be prepared to do to help us, I began to feel that we were letting Wilson down.

In order to try and help clarify the position, Jumbo Wilson agreed that it might help if I made a trip to London, and I had flown there, and I was present with Andrew Cunningham, who had also returned to London, at a Chiefs of Staff conference on October 6 at which the Prime Minister presided, and of which Alan Brooke recorded in his diary: "P.M. by now determined to go for Rhodes without looking at the effects on Italy, or at any rate refusing to look the implications square in the face. I had a heated argument with him . . ."

In his briefing to me, Jumbo Wilson had urged me to try and get the Prime Minister and the Chiefs of Staff to produce the urgently needed landing craft which would be of help to him to get his troops ashore in the Dodecanese. Churchill was unquestionably on our side, and most sympathetic in the hearing that he gave me; but I did not know then about the difficulties that he was having through the objections from the American Chiefs of Staff, and the President himself, to the appeals that he was making for support for our efforts in the Aegean.

It was an unexpected and unhappy experience for me to find that Alan Brooke was so opposed to our way of thinking; and it has been made even unhappier since then in reading the published extracts from his diaries, if only because the remarks that he made in those diaries reveal to me a state of mind that was not typical of the man I had known so well.

Should those highly personal remarks of Alan Brooke's, which were made in such a manner that they acted as safety valves, be held against him? There are those who think that they should, but I cannot subscribe to that view. For the sake of the record they are well worth examining, particularly since we also have on record the story of the events of those times by the Prime Minister himself, as well as the stories of many of the other protagonists. Such records are the raw material from which there can be determined, for the writing of history, just what happened in the events that came to have such great effects on all our lives.

"Another one-and-a-half hours battle with P.M. to hold on to what I think is right," Alan Brooke recorded the next day; and the day after that he wrote: "I can now control him no more. He has worked himself into a frenzy of excitement about the Rhodes attack, has magnified its importance so that he can no longer see anything else and has set his heart on capturing this one island even at the expense of endangering his relations with the President and the Americans and the future of the Italian campaign."

How divided our counsels were at this time is revealed in that one passage alone. No one could deny that Alan Brooke had the full right to hold on to his views, but even he seems to have been guilty at that very time of the excessive fervor of which he rather unjustly accused the Prime Minister. Nearly three weeks before, Churchill—"greatly troubled at our inability to support the Aegean operations"—had signaled Eisenhower pointing out that "the requirements which the Middle East ask for are small." He appealed for what he later described as "the landing-craft for a single division, a few days' assistance from the main Allied Air Force, and Rhodes would be ours."

While Alan Brooke was expressing his regret at having lost "control" of Churchill, the Prime Minister had already "laid the issue before the President in its full scope" in a long and, to my way of thinking, admirable appreciation of the whole situation. Cos had already fallen, and the threat to Leros was imminent. "I believe it will be found that the Italian and Balkan peninsulars are militarily and politically united," he stated, "and that really it is one theatre with which we have to deal." Calling attention to the importance that the Germans attach to "this Eastern sphere," Churchill continued: "They have to apprehend desertion by Hungary and Roumania and a violent schism in Bulgaria. At any moment Turkey may lean her weight against them." The recurring secondary theme of the whole problem was sounded again by Churchill with his statement: "This air-power is all one, and the more continually it can be fought the better."

But for all the eloquence of his pleading, Churchill was "pained to receive from the President" a reply "which practically amounted to the refusal of all help and left me, already committed, with his and the American Chiefs of Staffs approval, to face the impending blow." In summarizing the situation as it then stood, he stated: "The negative forces which hitherto had been so narrowly overcome had indeed resumed their control."

"I am opposed to any diversion which will in Eisenhower's opinion jeopardize the security of his current situation in Italy," the President stated in his reply the next day, adding that nothing should be allowed to "prejudice 'Overlord' as planned."

How strongly that smacked of the bludgeoning tactics of the First World War, with its refusal to permit of any elasticity of strategy, is reflected in Churchill's comment that such an attitude "was to reject all sense of proportion"; and I believe that there is to be found in that the great fault in the thinking at that time. Our own thinking as well as that of the Americans shared that fault.

His eagerness to achieve something in the Aegean prompted Churchill to make another appeal to the President of the United States. He defined the ignoring of the eastern Mediterranean as "a cardinal error in strategy." Roosevelt's reply to that was to ask what would happen if, in "a Balkan campaign," we did get the Aegean islands. He said that he preferred leaving the whole matter to be worked out by the Chiefs of Staff. That was a situation which Churchill found "quenched my last hopes," since it had by then been arranged that Eisenhower should hold a conference the next day in Tunisia. But he was still able to signal Jumbo Wilson in

Cairo and tell him that "you should press most strongly at the conference for further support for 'Accolade' [Rhodes] . . . demand what is necessary . . . I am doing all I can."

In all fairness to the stand taken by President Roosevelt, it must be recorded that he signaled Eisenhower, telling him that, in response to Churchill's request, the conference "is free to examine the whole question in all its bearings." But how prejudiced that freedom was is revealed in the comment that Alan Brooke made in his diary for that day about what Churchill was trying to accomplish. "He is placing himself, quite unnecessarily, in a false position," he stated. "The Americans are already desperately suspicious of him, and this will make matters worse."

There, it would appear, was to be found the kernel of the problem: the American suspicions. Even Jumbo Wilson was all too well aware of that, and of his doubts before setting off from Cairo for Tunisia he has stated: "I was not too sanguine . . . as the U. S. policy had hitherto been constant in avoiding any commitments in the Balkans . . ."

Of the conference held at Eisenhower's headquarters at La Marsa, in Tunisia, it has been stated a little sweepingly that all the commanders in the Mediterranean were present. I, for one, was still in London, and my deputy took my place. Eisenhower has stated that "it was the simplest, most unargumentative of any similar conference I attended during the war"; and immediately after that: "I outlined the entire situation as we saw it and announced the decision I had reached, which was to be final unless overridden by the Combined Chiefs of Staff. Its purport was . . . that we could and would do nothing about the islands."

Some effort must be made, in all fairness to all those concerned, to put the story of what happened in a better perspective. Even though I was not there, I know that Jumbo Wilson tried hard to advance our case. Eisenhower has admitted that "those islands, in my judgment, while of considerable strategic importance, did not compare in military value to success in the Italian battle." It was the state of the latter that was really the deciding factor, for within the last forty-eight hours it had become clear that the Germans were going to offer a much stiffer resistance than had been expected to our advance on Rome. So far as I was concerned, that provided yet another threat of a possibility of all that we had been trying so hard to avoid: a static slugging match between opposing armies which were well bogged down.

The scales had been tipped in favor of the operations in Italy by the report of the past few hours of the stiffening there of the German resistance. Eisenhower's statement in his signal to Churchill that "it is personally distressing to me to have to advise against a project in which you believe so earnestly," was followed by a signal to the Prime Minister in which Jumbo Wilson stated that while the Middle East commanders "could but agree" that the sudden change in conditions meant that the operation in Italy "ought to have the whole of the available resources," they were nevertheless working "on the assumption that Rhodes would not take place till a later date," and that in the meantime "we came to the conclusion that the holding of Leros and Samos is not impossible."

As Eisenhower had anticipated, Winston Churchill was bitterly disappointed over the outcome of the La Marsa conference, and in answer to Wilson's signal he replied: "Cling on if you possibly can. If after everything has been done you are forced to quit I will support you, but victory is the prize." And later, when he came to write his own story of all that happened, Churchill stated: "If one has to submit it is wasteful not to do so with the best grace possible. When so many grave issues were pending I could not risk any jar in my personal relations with the President." In agreeing to what had been decided at La Marsa, he added: "I will not waste words in explaining how painful this decision is to me."

On October 23 the Middle East commanders sent to the Chiefs of Staff in London, repeating it to Eisenhower, an appreciation of the situation in the Aegean, pointing out that without "adequate air reinforcements which would have to be considerable" our "hold on Leros will continue to be precarious." We received no reply. Three days later, and re-emphasizing it again two days after that, we asked Arthur Tedder's headquarters for heavy bombers to be sent to help in our operations. That drew a firm refusal; but there was a promise that a heavy force would be put on to the Greek airfields "when targets offer." On November 1 we again sent an appreciation to the Chiefs of Staff in London, repeating it to Eisenhower, stating our "specific requirement" for American heavy bombers and American long-range fighters. There was no reply. And so our requests went on, with either refusals of help or no replies.

In criticizing Eisenhower's headquarters for not giving us greater help in the Aegean I am not saying that they gave us no help at all. Shortly after the fall of Cos on October 3 they agreed to our continuing with the use of some heavy bombers, and they provided us for a short time with some long-range fighters and some Mitchells armed with heavy cannon. The Royal Navy was more definite in their action, and they sent stronger reinforcement to the Aegean.

But the Royal Navy was operating, as we were, under one great handicap. "By the beginning of November it was apparent that, quite apart from the serious trouble encountered in the Aegean, the system of command was unsuitable to the task in hand," the official Naval historian has stated. "We had in fact embarked on a combined operation without an integrated command organisation . . ." That handicap left us all faced with the great superiority that the enemy had in the air. The situation was made still more acute through the withdrawal of the long-range fighters which had been allotted to us for a few days, a move which, in Churchill's words, "sealed the fate of Leros."

Our intelligence left us in no doubt about the preparations that were being made by the Germans for an invasion of Leros, and on November 12 the enemy made a landing from the sea, and then dropped between six and eight hundred parachutists on a part of the island which, we had been told, could not be touched in this way. Our troops fought for four days to resist the enemy invasion, but they were overwhelmed; and in his report to the Prime Minister on what had happened, Jumbo Wilson had rightly to refer to the "overwhelming air attack" made by the Germans. Winston Churchill was then on his way from England to Cairo by sea, and in his reply to Wilson he stated that "like you I feel I have been fighting with my hands tied behind my back."

The whole situation in the Aegean was by then not much more than chaotic, and it was causing concern enough in London. It was on that day of November 12 that Peter Portal sent his signal to Arthur Tedder urging the view that Leros was now "more important at the moment than strategic objectives in southern France or north Italy." But it was then too late for any help, even if Eisenhower had been prepared to give it.

By that time A. B. Cunningham had become the First Sea Lord, and as such the third member of the Chiefs of Staff Committee. "It is easy to be wise after the event," he wrote in his autobiography some years after the war, "but I am still strongly of the opinion that Leros might have been held." And in his dispatch he rightly places the reason for the collapse of our effort in the Aegean on "the enemy's command of the air."

In all these operations it was the Royal Navy which took the worst beating. In that inimitable way of theirs, they had done their utmost to help hold things together, and they had never flinched, even when their losses were quite appalling. During the time of our attempt to occupy and hold the islands of the Dodecanese we suffered many severe losses, and I do not think I can do better, in offering an illustration of what I mean by that, than to quote Captain S. W. Roskill, the naval historian. "The British and Greek navies had four cruisers damaged (one, the *Carlisle,* beyond repair), six destroyers sunk and four others damaged," he has recorded. "Two submarines and ten coastal craft and mine sweepers were also lost; and many warship crews had been subjected to ordeals which can reasonably be compared with those undergone off Norway and Crete several years earlier."

Our Beaufighters did their best to provide air strikes against the enemy ships which carried the invading forces, but, as the naval historian himself records, they "were by no means ideally suited for such work." He also refers to the naval Commander-in-Chief's report on the "overwhelming air superiority" of the enemy. That forced us finally to evacuate as best we could the garrison that we still had on the other islands.

Our Army had suffered bad losses in men in the whole operation—nearly five thousand, including those taken as prisoners—but so had the Germans in their all-out effort to gain full control of the islands. My chief intelligence officer gave the German Air Force losses in his first report on the entire operation as 86 aircraft destroyed in the air, and 54 destroyed on the ground and 148 damaged in the air and on the ground, against a loss to us of 48 aircraft of all types either known destroyed or reported as missing. Our losses had later to be adjusted to 115 aircraft lost. "Even today it is difficult to assess the price exacted from the enemy for his success," Captain Roskill commented many years later.

With the ending of our efforts to gain a foothold in the Aegean, I prepared a paper in which I summarized all that had happened in the last days of the operation. I was in no mood to pull any punches, and I started off with the blunt statement: "I am very dissatisfied with the assistance that I received during the Leros operation." I pointed out that when the deterioration of the weather in Italy had bogged down the battle there—right at the period during which Leros was being attacked—"a wider view should have been taken of the dispositions of heavy and medium bombers and of long-range fighters." I further pointed out that we had asked "not once but many times" for Liberators and Lightnings to be located in Cyrenaica, and that "all we got were a few B. 25's, at first with disgruntled and later with untrained pilots and armed with semi-experimental 75 mm. guns." That left us with no day striking force; and our own long-range fighter force of Beaufighter squadrons was quite inadequate, and they could give no cover for the Navy in daylight operations.

For a long period between October 27 and November 14, I protested, no attack had been made by our heavy bombers from the central Mediterranean on the Greek airfields from which the Germans were operating against us, again stating that "I am not satisfied that . . . every opportunity was taken. . . ." For example, I pointed out, on November 14 ninety-one B–25's with forty-nine Lightnings as escort had bombed Sofia, in Bulgaria. "This effort put on the Greek airfields," I stated, "might have made a considerable difference to the scale of enemy air attack on Leros at a very critical moment."

I concluded my report with the strong protest: "It appears to me that sufficient air effort could have been spared from the central Mediterranean to give us a reasonable chance of saving Leros without detriment, as it turns out, to operations in Italy or elsewhere." This paper, dated November 20, was sent off immediately to Arthur Tedder.

"Mediterranean Air Command had not remained indifferent to the situation in the Middle East Command," Richards and Saunders recorded in their history. Much as I admire their work, in this statement I feel that they are entirely wrong. I believed at the time, and I believe now, that it was the disregard by the Americans in general and the indifference of Mediterranean Air Command in particular which left us in the difficult position in which we found ourselves. The situation in Italy by the middle of October had become serious, and in his diary for the twenty-fifth of that month Alan Brooke wrote: "We shall have to have an almighty row with the Americans who have put us in this position with their insistence to abandon the Mediterranean operations . . . it is quite heart-breaking when we see what we might have done this year if our strategy had not been distorted by the Americans."

While I know that Alan Brooke was not then including the Aegean in that assessment, I add now that it was also "quite heart-breaking" for us in the eastern Mediterranean; and if Brooke found that "the attitude of Ike's H.Q. was not encouraging," our reactions out in Egypt were even more depressed. But in his diary for November 1, Alan Brooke wrote:

When I look at the Mediterranean I realise only too well how far I have failed. If only I had had sufficient force of character to swing those American Chiefs of Staff and make them see daylight, how different the war might be. We should have had the whole Balkans ablaze by now, and the war might have been finished in 1943. I blame myself, yet doubt whether it was humanly possible to alter the American point of view more than I succeeded in doing.

Fifteen years later Alan Brooke was to add the comment: "At very little cost Crete and Rhodes could have been rendered possible operations without affecting Italy. Success in Crete and Rhodes might have had the happiest repercussions in Turkey and the Balkans without even committing a single man in the Balkans."

"My own recommendation, then as always, was that no operation should be undertaken in the Mediterranean except as a directly supporting move for the Channel attack," Eisenhower later stated, "and that our planned re-deployment to England should proceed with all possible speed." That is a clear enough expression of the rigidity of the American thinking and planning in that time of late 1943 in the Mediterranean.

While I am fully aware of, and am to a large extent in agreement with, the more or less academic reasons for our failure in the Aegean, I feel that the cozy explanations that have so far been given are not sufficient to excuse the ineptitude of some of our planning, and that one needs to be a little more explicit, even explosive, in trying to reach conclusions. The dependence of my Middle East Command on the higher command in the central Mediterranean, with the resultant failure of effective and compact operational control of the air in the eastern Mediterranean, was a major flaw. Our continued efforts to operate in the Aegean after our failure to capture Rhodes admittedly left us without what has been described as "the key to control" the area.

As late as November 11 our own Chiefs of Staff Committee were still recommending that "we should bring Turkey into the war this year," and that "we should aim to open the Dardanelles as soon as possible," even if such operations necessitated "putting back the date upon which the forces agreed to be necessary for 'Overlord' will be available." The Prime Minister "cordially"

agreed to this; and it was part of the official British plan put
forward to the Combined Chiefs of Staff.

But our pleas still made no impression on the Americans. They
adhered rigidly to their singleminded interest in the planned invasion of the Continent across the English Channel, and they even
clung to their suspicions about our desire to participate in that, let
alone our intention. It became for me sad and discouraging that no
matter what we said or what we did to try and convince them that
we were not against their plans for the invasion, the Americans
seemed to be so resolutely opposed to our efforts to exploit every,
not just one, opportunity to hit the Germans, and that they never
seemed to be able to understand what we were getting at.

If (and how largely that word looms over this whole affair), if
we had only received adequate support from the Combined Chiefs
of Staff in Washington in providing us with a few landing craft and
some additional troops and aircraft, and a more proper support
from Eisenhower's headquarters in the Mediterranean, we could
have captured Rhodes without much difficulty; and after that we
would have been able to hold on to Cos, Leros, Samos and the
other islands. But the obtuseness of the American planners and the
stiffness of the German resistance led to the inevitable collapse of
a plan which had so much to commend it.

"If we are never going to proceed on anything but certainties we
must certainly face the prospect of a prolonged war," Winston
Churchill stated at that time; and later he referred to the clash of
opinions over the operations in the Dodecanese as "the most acute
difference I ever had with General Eisenhower." Perhaps it is
because of the closeness of my own participation in this operation,
and the intensity of my own personal feelings about it, that I still
feel so strongly about the way in which, I believe, we were let
down; and for that reason I always felt for Winston Churchill the
strongest sympathy in his statement: "I was grieved that the small
request I had made for strategic purposes almost as high as those
already achieved should have been so obdurately resisted and
rejected."

32 / At Low Ebb

I<small>F THERE WAS EVER</small> a time in my whole career when, through influences over which I appeared to have no control, it seemed that I was in grave danger of coming to a dead stop, it was during the last three months of 1943. It so happened that the situation was quite closely associated with the vitally important events that took place out in the Middle East at that time, and although my own personal problems were of but little consequence in the general scheme of things they were nevertheless of considerable importance to me. At the time I was distinctly upset, and even angry, over some of the events that occurred; but time has helped to assuage my feelings over what then seemed to be so strangely at odds with all that was both just and sane.

That strong hand of chance which had played such a large part in my life seemed to go, for a change, altogether too persistently against my interests, and that had a depressing effect on my personal outlook. After a time I began to feel that there was one of two things that I could do: either sit back and just let the slide proceed downhill, or fasten my safety belt and start answering back. It was not likely that I should sit back and let things slide.

I had heard nothing more about what Archie Sinclair had told me some time before that I might be appointed to the new command in southeast Asia until Bob Wright came to my office with a slip of paper that he had just torn off the wire-service machine in our public relations department. It was a press communiqué announcing the appointment of Lord Louis Mountbatten as the Supreme Commander of southeast Asia. That could hardly be described as the pleasantest way of hearing that I was not getting the job.

In writing to my mother about my not getting the appointment to S.E.A.C. I said: "I gather that I was definitely selected at one time by Winston, but someone changed their minds. However I am not disappointed—it would be a difficult and tiresome job for at least a year, as obviously we have got to devote the major

603

proportion of our resources to knocking out the Hun, and there
won't be much left over for the Far East. I don't know what will
happen to me now. I don't see how they can leave me here much
longer—in fact I shall refuse to stay."

Right on top of that there came to my ears another rumor that
in the new year the rank of the Air Officer Commanding-in-Chief,
Middle East, was to be downgraded to that of air marshal, which
meant that I would certainly be too senior for it, and that I would
have to return to England. But to what? There was vague talk
about my possibly going to an Air Ministry appointment, but that
was an utterly dreary prospect. So far as another operational
command was concerned, and that was what I wanted, the outlook
was bleak, although there were some hints, again only very vague,
about the possibility of my being given Transport Command. The
whole position left me facing a blank wall just as there were to
take place, right on our own doorstep, the important Cairo and
Teheran conferences.

I would be guilty of evading an issue that has since become of
an ever-increasing importance in Anglo-American relations if I
were to gloss over my personal reactions to the allegations that
were made at this time about my not getting along with the Americans. I was definitely disturbed about this because I felt that they
were quite untrue. But there was at stake by then a much graver
issue than my personal feelings.

While I know that there were too many faults on our side which
brought about the strain in our relationships with the Americans, I
cannot feel that we were entirely to blame. Dick Casey has
recorded that earlier in the year he had been told by one American
general who was visiting the Middle East as the personal representative of the President that he had been warned by his own
State Department in Washington to be on his guard against what,
it was considered, was happening to too many of their people:
falling for the British. It seemed to me—and that small item more
or less confirmed it—that the Americans were allowing themselves
to become so unnecessarily suspicious of us that they were prepared to believe almost anything of us, and that was only building
up a distressingly unhealthy atmosphere.

In the increasing divergence of views between the Americans
and the British about the way in which the war should be fought so
far as Europe was concerned, it was perhaps the speed with which
conditions were changing that, more than anything, caused this

clash of opinions. We were more accustomed than they were to having to make rapid changes in our stance, and they appeared to find it difficult to make quick readjustments in their thinking and their planning. The effect of this on grand strategy was such that, in the words of John Ehrman, "the British chafed increasingly at the limitations to which they were subjected."

"My dear friend, this is much the greatest thing we have ever attempted," Winston Churchill stated in the course of a long signal to President Roosevelt about the planning for the cross-Channel invasion that he sent on October 23, 1943, "and I am not satisfied that we have yet taken the measures necessary to give it the best chance of success."

In the eagerness of that probing mind of his, Winston Churchill was ever anxious to explore every opportunity of getting at the enemy, and through the long periods of working with him which we who were his Commanders-in-Chief in the Services had by now experienced, we knew that we must think of every possibility for offensive action. I was not surprised, therefore, when I heard that there was to be yet another top-level conference between the Prime Minister and the President and their staffs. That year of 1943 was to see more of these high-flying conferences than any of the other years of the war: Casablanca, Washington, Quebec, Cairo and Teheran. I was pleased when I heard that this one was to be held in our domain in Egypt because it would give me the only opportunity I had had up to that time of at least being on the spot at one of these great meetings.

By the third week in November, President Roosevelt and Winston Churchill and all the members of the Chiefs of Staff committees of both America and Britain had arrived in Cairo, and they were ready to talk. But the plans for discussion, and our own rather lofty tolerance of the lapses in security, were all thrown into confusion by the arrival of and the attendance at the meetings of General Chiang Kai-shek and his wife, and a full Chinese delegation. To the distress of the British contingent this called for far too much futile discussion between the Americans and the Chinese about the position of China in the war, and a corresponding waste of time.

"Why the Americans attached such importance to Chiang I have never discovered," Alan Brooke later commented. "All he did for them was to lead them down a garden path to a Communist China." Our discouragement over this is further reflected in

Brooke's description of the way in which we all seemed so ready
"to pander sufficiently to Chiang to affect possible operations in
the Aegean against our own primary enemy."

The main object of the conference so far as the British were
concerned was to try and arrive at some agreement with the
Americans about future operations in Europe. That was necessary
for the discussions with Stalin and his staff that were planned for
the meeting which, it had been arranged, was to take place at
Teheran, the Persian capital, in the following week. Of what
happened in Cario there has been a great deal put on record,
including accounts by nearly all the principal participants, and
there are accounts of the incidents that occurred that run all the
way from something in the nature of a barroom brawl to the sillier
aspects of musical comedy.

The first aspect was sharply described by the American General
Joseph W. Stilwell—there was apparently reason enough for his
nickname of "Vinegar Joe"—in his book *The Stilwell Papers*. His
sphere of operations was out in the Far East, but he was present at
the Cairo Conference, and in referring to a meeting of the Combined Chiefs of Staff on November 23 he spoke about a clash that
occurred between Admiral King, the American Naval Chief of Staff,
and Alan Brooke. In a somewhat startling fashion he stated:
"Christ. Brooke got nasty and King got good and sore. King
almost climbed over the table at Brooke. God, he was mad. I wish
he had socked him." It was an unedifying wish, and indicative of
the mood of some of the participants.

In his own diary, Alan Brooke spoke of this meeting as being
"somewhat heated," but he added that when they dined together
that night "King was as nice as could be and quite transformed
from his morning's attitude." And on the lighter side, there is
Brooke's comment on a display of Madame Chiang's shapely legs
at a critical moment during one of the meetings: "This caused a
rustle amongst some of those attending the conference, and I even
thought I heard a suppressed neigh come from a group of the
younger members!" Having just met Madame Chiang myself, I
understood what he meant, and I hope that although my age might
just include me in the younger category, my seniority in rank at
least precluded me from being included in the neighing chorus.

Right from the outset it was obvious that there was unquestionably the strongest suspicion in the minds of the Americans about
our intentions in the Aegean. "Our persistent British friends strove
mightily to create diversions in the Mediterranean area," Admiral

Leahy, Roosevelt's Chief of Staff, later recorded. There is only too much evidence on record to prove just how suspicious the Americans were of our intentions.

Perhaps the most succinct comment on that was made by Robert E. Sherwood. In *The White House Papers of Harry L. Hopkins* he stated: "The U.S. Chiefs of Staff had no doubt in their own minds as to just what all this signified. They felt certain that whenever the persistent Prime Minister started talking about Rhodes, or veering toward the 'right' from Northern Italy, he was resuming the advocacy of strategic diversions into South-Eastern Europe and away from North France. They prepared themselves for battles at Teheran in which the Americans and the Russians would form a united front."

Such was the predetermined attitude on the part of the Americans as they sat down with us in Cairo to discuss the future that there was bound to be a clash. Eisenhower even went so far as to say, in speaking of the views of his own staff, that this was "including its British members," which leaves one to infer that they must have been the only British officers by then not following the pace set by their own Prime Minister. In referring to what the Americans had brought themselves to believe as a British reluctance to embark on a cross-Channel invasion, Eisenhower once said of the Prime Minister: "How often I heard him say, in speaking of 'Overlord' prospects: 'We must take care that the tides do not run red with the blood of American and British youth, or the beaches be choked with their bodies.' "

The reference made in that way to Churchill's comment gives, in its own curious way, an interesting slant on the whole of the American attitude, which was one that was so different, for very good reasons, from our own. I grant that in the Civil War in the United States the Americans had a taste of the tragedy of casualties; but they did not have the terrible repugnance of such casualties that was instilled into us, and which filled our minds through the horror that was peculiar to the First World War. That was understandable enough. The Americans were informed about our terrifying losses, but they had not been involved deeply enough or long enough in that war to know, as we had, what, to use one of their own expressions, a traumatic experience it was for us.

Eisenhower had some idea of what we felt, and he referred to our fears of "a repetition of the trench warfare of World War I." He spoke understandingly of our "vivid and bitter memories of

Passchendaele and Vimy Ridge," and he said that "none of us wanted any repetition of those experiences." One could never question at any time the readiness of the Americans to fight; but I believe that they were not able to understand us in our more cautious and seasoned approach toward the sheer brutality of war. I could well appreciate and understand that the Americans were a peace-loving people; but they could never begin to hate war as much as we did, if only because of our greater experience of it.

There persists to this day among the Americans this firm and at times almost angry belief that they fully understood what the British were planning, whereas they had, in fact, induced in themselves a state of mind that showed what was, for us, such a sad lack of understanding. Nearly two weeks before the start of the Cairo Conference, our Chiefs of Staff prepared a paper, with which Churchill "cordially" agreed, in which it was stated that "for some time past it has been clear to us, and doubtless also to the U.S. Chiefs of Staff, that disagreement exists between us as to what we should do now in the Mediterranean, with particular reference to the effect of future action on 'Overlord' . . . the issue is clouding the whole of our future strategic outlook, and must be resolved . . ."

The resolving that had to be done was called for at the forthcoming conference, and this paper stated clearly in its breadth and depth that "we emphasize that we do not in any way recoil from, or wish to sidetrack, our agreed intention to attack the Germans across the Channel in the late Spring or early Summer of 1944." We even stated that, under certain conditions, such an attack might possibly be mounted even earlier than the spring or summer. This paper was passed on to the Americans as an official statement of our views on future strategy.

"It is important to be clear on this," John Ehrman has stated. "Much was said at the time, and has since been written, on British, and particularly on Churchillian, strategy in the Mediterranean during this period, which is misleading not only for the period but for the same problem in later periods." I have since come to feel strongly about that misleading confusion that has developed, and I would even suggest that the reasons for the way in which the Americans appeared to adopt such a rigid refusal to accept any explanation on our part of our views—and, as the evidence proves, we tried hard enough to explain—might well prove worthy of more detailed examination.

So far as the British were concerned, we were left with a strange feeling almost from the outset of those meetings in Cairo that our American associates, so many of whom we looked upon as close friends, had all worked themselves up into some mystical state that bordered on self-deception, and in that state they seemed to want to present a united and determined front that simply would not listen to any further discussion of our ideas. So far as grand strategy was concerned, it is of some value to present the views expressed by our official historian. He has stated: "It has often been asserted—and despite the evidence to the contrary, seems still to be widely believed—that the British, either under Churchill's influence or through him as their spokesman, wished in the second half of 1943 to develop a campaign in the Balkans towards the north, if necessary at the expense of 'Overlord,' for strategic or diplomatic reasons, or for a combination of both. Whatever may have been the case later, this was not so at that time."

The value of such a campaign "towards the north" would, in the long run, certainly have been immense. If we had been able to conduct such a campaign, and if we had carried the Americans with us, the map of Europe today would look very different from what it has become.

In January, 1943, there had been the first of the year's conferences, held at Casablanca, and I had heard that it had become apparent even then that serious difficulties were appearing in the way of Anglo-American cooperation. The only point on which the Americans appeared to be able to reach anything approaching agreement among themselves was that there should be this cross-Channel invasion. Jack Slessor was at this conference, and he has spoken of the "apparently wide divergence of opinion on basic strategy," and of discussions that "at times became uncomfortably warm." The only concrete result that appeared to have been achieved at the Casablanca Conference was agreement that a demand should be made for the "unconditional surrender" of Germany, Italy and Japan; and that demand has been the subject of controversy ever since. There cannot be much doubt that all it did was to strengthen the German resistance rather than to intimidate it.

No sooner were the members of the staffs of both countries assembled at the famous hotel which stands at the foot of the Pyramids, just outside Cairo, for this very important conference at the end of the year than that divergence of views again became only too obvious. At the meetings which I was called upon to attend I was able to watch and to listen with one advantage. While being a senior operational commander, I was not as deeply surrounded by the trees as the Chiefs of Staff themselves.

From this somewhat detached position, and for all my deep, personal involvement in the plans for the Aegean, I came to form an impression that the whole business was more a negative, automatic rejection of the views of the British by the Americans than any positive approach to a consideration of any new ideas. In the discussions that we had among ourselves at the more informal gatherings there was this recurring note, almost of wonderment, over the blank refusal on the part of the Americans to listen to what we had to say. And in deciding to conduct discussions with the Chinese about the war in the Far East before getting down to the much more important matter of the strategy to be adopted for future operations in Europe, we faced, in the words of Pug Ismay, "the necessity of putting the cart before the horse."

In his own account of the Cairo Conference, Winston Churchill revealed that on the way to it he "had prepared what was in effect an indictment of our mismanagement of operations in the Mediterranean," and this long paper was passed on to the British Chiefs of Staff. In its final form there appeared a sound comment on the structure of the command in the Mediterranean. "One command has the forces but not the responsibilities," it stated, "the other the responsibilities but not the forces. This can hardly be considered an ideal arrangement." In this I had the greatest interest, and I was impressed with the summary that was made of the reasons for our failure in the Dodecanese and the Aegean. "All this of course is outside the parish of the High North African Command . . . ," the report stated.

At the conference, Churchill spoke about the need to settle these unsatisfactory "Command arrangements," and "to open the Aegean"; and Pug Ismay has recorded that "the Prime Minister also pleaded that Wilson should be given the very, very little that he needed to capture Rhodes, within the next two months." Jumbo Wilson, Algernon Willis—who had taken over as Naval C.-in-C. in the eastern Mediterranean—and I were deeply concerned with all this, and we continued with our work at a British Chiefs of Staff meeting one morning to give final shape to all the views that we had been exchanging about possible future operations in the Aegean. In the afternoon the three of us, representing the eastern Mediterranean, attended a full meeting of the Combined Chiefs of Staff, along with Eisenhower, John Cunningham and Arthur Tedder representing the central Mediterranean.

When Winston Churchill brought up the matter of the Aegean, the Americans, in Pug Ismay's words, "were up in arms at once." It was at that afternoon meeting of the Combined Chiefs of Staff that I had the unhappy—though perversely stimulating—experience of hearing Alan Brooke and the great American General George Marshall, Brooke's opposite number, have what Brooke himself described as "the father and mother of a row." Even the contained Admiral Leahy later admitted: "The discussion became almost acrimonious at times." All that we were able to get the Americans to agree to was that further consideration might be given to operations in the Aegean if they could be arranged for without disturbing in any way at all the plans for Overlord.

With this unhappy conclusion there came the end of the first stage of the conference. The principals went off to Teheran to meet Stalin to explain to him what they had decided. Since no decisions of any import had been reached, I could not help wondering rather dismally what the next round had in store for us.

During the conferences that were held in Cairo I had the opportunity to meet and to talk quite freely with President Roosevelt. It was the only time that I had such an opportunity, and it was of immense interest to me when I received one day a message saying that he wanted to meet me. I had already seen him in action at some of the meetings which were being held, but I knew nothing more about him than the impression that he had made upon me in public and what I had been told by those who knew him. I had met Mrs. Roosevelt when she had visited my headquarters while I was at Fighter Command, and I had been impressed then by the forcefulness and alertness of her mind; and I had been told that she and her husband shared a great strength of character.

I went out to the villa near the Pyramids in which President Roosevelt was staying, and I was ushered into the sittingroom, and a few minutes later the President was carried in in his chair by a bodyguard of United States Marines. He was accompanied by several staff officers. After the chair had been put down, Roosevelt sent the bodyguard and all the others out of the room, and I was thus able to have a heart-to-heart talk entirely alone with him. Even at that late stage in his life Roosevelt was, for all the paralysis of his legs, a handsome and impressive figure of a man. And I could not help feeling that it was that impression which he seemed to want to create first of all. His opening remarks were more in the nature of a harangue than a talk.

"Sholto Douglas, one of the most famous names in Scottish history," he stated; and from that he proceeded to give me a lecture on Scottish history and the achievements of the Douglases which went on for several minutes. He added that one of the features of the history of his own family of which he was proudest was that he had had a Scottish grandmother.

It was all very flattering, and I could not help feeling most touched by all that the President was saying, so much so, in fact, that I found that tears were coming to my eyes. But at the same time there was some indefinable flaw in his manner, and it was that which turned what he was saying into something approaching a performance. I could not escape from the feeling that there was something about it that was very nearly an act. I did not doubt that there was a strong feeling of sincerity in his opening remarks; but it was obvious to me that Roosevelt was in some ways a skillful actor. I could also appreciate that he had been very well briefed for our meeting.

With that first impression that he made on me, Roosevelt very nearly had me eating out of his hand. We went on to talk about the war, and I ventured the opinion that it was a pity that the Dodecanese operation had been so starved, and that we had not been given the chance to bring it to a more satisfactory conclusion. He brushed what I had to say to one side, and he gave me the impression that he looked upon it as a minor skirmish of no importance. I could not very well accept that, and I tried to assure him that so far as the commanders in the Middle East were concerned it was an operation of deadly seriousness and importance. But I made no impression upon him. I know now what little impression even Winston Churchill was able to make in this particular issue, so it was not likely that I, for all the earnestness of my approach, should be able to get anywhere.

But that made no difference to the pleasantness of the President's manner, and we parted on good terms, and I hoped that I had, perhaps, helped to correct any of the false ideas about me which, it was alleged, had been presented to him. My memory of him as a man is of a vivid and vital personality. I have the same memory of Eleanor Roosevelt, who, many years later, during one of my visits to the United States, invited me to appear on one of her television shows.

Any study of the ways in which the great men of one's time, and with whom one has worked, conducted the routine of their own work has always been of interest to me. In great contrast to the voluminous and detailed records left by Winston Churchill, with their mass of notes and appreciations, all carefully recorded at the actual time of the happening of the events, President Roosevelt apparently left little in the way of actual notes of his various talks with other people or, as Herbert Feis, the American author, has put it, "expositions of his ideas and calculations." It is from Feis, incidentally, that there has come the interesting suggestion that "governments should favor the efforts of private historians from whose revelations and treatments of the disturbing truth they can dissociate themselves."

With that in mind, the comparison drawn between Churchill and Roosevelt by Dick Casey, who had a great deal of firsthand experience in working with both men, is of particular value. "Churchill . . . had a more far-reaching, wide-ranging and penetrating mind," he has said. "He never let up; and he took a great deal of convincing that his own ideas were wrong or that other competing ideas were right. I had the impression that Roosevelt was more dependent on his advisers than Churchill, also that Roosevelt did not much concern himself with affairs until they 'ripened' and came up for decision, whereas Churchill seemed to be always reaching out for new initiatives in advance, sometimes to the distress of his immediate senior advisers."

That particular "distress" was known well enough to us, and I was very soon to have administered to me the strongest dose of it that I knew during the entire course of the war.

Only a week before they attended the Cairo Conference, the Americans held a meeting which produced results that led our own official historian, John Ehrman, to quote the American official history as saying that "the prospects of mounting 'Overlord' as planned could not have seemed very bright to the Joint Chiefs of Staff as they travelled to Cairo for the first conversations with the British . . ." Those prospects in the American mind after the Cairo meetings appeared, for all that we had done to try and foster them, to have shriveled, and, as Ehrman has said, "misunderstanding, as is not unusual, brought a certain resentment." It was in that mood that the delegations departed from Cairo for Teheran.

"Strategy, like politics, is the art of the possible," John Ehrman commented in summing up the issue over our hopes for a thrust into the Aegean. The plans that we had made as a result of those hopes were far more realistic than the Americans have ever given us credit for, and he calls attention to Churchill's reply to Smuts, who was pressing for a campaign in Italy and the Balkans in preference to the cross-Channel invasion. "There can be no question whatever of breaking arrangements we have made with United States for 'Overlord,' " Churchill signaled Smuts. "British loyalty to 'Overlord' is keystone of arch of Anglo-American co-operation. Personally I think enough forces exist for both hands to be played and I believe this to be the right strategy." Could any firmer answer have been made to those who contended that the British were trying to get out of their commitment to the American wish for the cross-Channel operation?

In all these accounts of the welter of personal conflicts and clashes of national interests that occurred it has been rather overlooked that for all the scrapping and arguing there were, through the blowing-off of something in the nature of a safety valve, some very valuable exchanges. I have rather stressed the personal aspect of what happened in Cairo because of my own personal involvement; but I must point out that not all the time was spent in these brusque personal exchanges between the leading participants. There were sessions of long and serious and hard work that were of the utmost importance during this difficult period in Anglo-American relations.

Our people soon found in their meetings with the Russians in Teheran that Stalin had no interest whatsoever in opening up the Dardanelles. It was the first time that Churchill, Roosevelt and Stalin had met together around the same table. Stalin "had by then pretty definite ideas as to how he wanted the Balkans run after the war," Alan Brooke wrote. "British and American assistance was therefore no longer desirable in the Eastern Mediterranean." It was then that Stalin's long-term political aims began to emerge, and it was the inability on the part of most of us to realize what those aims were that has since cost us so dearly.

In its historical context it is of interest that the major shaping of Russian policy so far as Europe was concerned should coincide with the great change that came about in American thinking in foreign affairs. This was the time when the Americans moved out of the shroud of isolationism, and they took their rightful place as one of the great powers in the world. That, in turn, meant an irrevocable American commitment in Europe. There can be no question about the difficulties facing Americans in this emergence; and the urgent need for a rapid maturing on their part, particularly in their military minds, was probably the reason for much of what appeared to us, the British, as such tangled thinking.

Arthur Bryant has described the work done at Teheran as "probably the most important achievement of Brooke's career," and that together Churchill and Brooke "averted what might well have led to the worst disaster in British—and American—military history." That story of Churchill's struggle against what appeared to be a betrayal by Roosevelt, and Brooke's hammering away at trying to convince the Russians and the Americans that they should face the facts of life, has been well recorded. It was what effect the struggle was to have on the policy for the eastern Mediterranean that was of concern to me.

During the time that everybody was in Teheran, Jumbo Wilson and I were able to examine what had come out of the "five hectic days of coming and going" in Cairo, as Wilson has described them, so far as they affected us, and there was not much that was of any comfort. In the course of the next four days, decisions were made at Teheran that were to determine the policy for operations in Europe for months to come. Again it was of little comfort to us. It was agreed that in addition to the planning for Overlord, which was fair enough, the campaign in Italy should be continued. We could understand and agree with that. The plans evolved for the invasion of the south of France sounded to those of us who would have preferred to have seen a drive into the Aegean very much like a waste of a lot of good effort and time. But the Americans wanted to go into the south of France, and Stalin backed them in that, although he did agree with Churchill to his face that an effort should be made to get Turkey into the war.

"Stalin's interest in an attack on southern France took the Western delegates by surprise," John Ehrman has commented. But it is now obvious that it was scarcely surprising in view of the only too apparent differences of opinion that existed between the British and the Americans about operations in the eastern Mediterranean. The Russians shrewdly seized on that difference, agreed with both sides, and so strengthened their own insistence on the importance of the cross-Channel invasion: the Second Front, as Overlord was more popularly, if incorrectly, named.

It must be placed squarely on the shoulders of President Roosevelt that there had been no agreement at Teheran about further plans for the Aegean. In Robert E. Sherwood's *White House Papers* there is an illuminating, if unintentional, revelation of the way in which Roosevelt was taken in by Stalin. Sherwood wrote of Roosevelt's heartfelt belief that he had achieved a great deal, and then he stated: "Roosevelt now felt sure that, to use his own term,

Stalin was 'getatable,' despite his bludgeoning tactics and his attitude of cynicism towards such matters as the rights of small nations, and that when Russia could be convinced that her legitimate claims and requirements—such as the right of access to warm-water ports—were to be given full recognition, she would prove tractable and co-operative in maintaining the peace of the postwar world."

What we know now is that for all the avowed interest that Stalin had shown in getting Turkey into the war—and for quite some time before the meeting in Teheran he had shown a reasonably firm interest—he was actually thinking along quite different lines. In *The Struggle for Europe,* Chester Wilmot commented: "It was apparent—to Churchill at any rate—that Stalin did not want any Anglo-American forces in the Balkan countries which he was bent upon 'liberating.' There was a long-term political strategy behind the Russian desire for the Allies to concentrate on Western Europe and the Western Mediterranean." In a further telling comment, Wilmot points out: "Pushed by the Russians and pulled by the Americans, the overall strategy of the Western Powers had been diverted away from the area of Soviet aspirations." How effective that Russian strategy was to become is a crucial part of any understanding that one may try to reach of what happened during that critical time.

The position of the Turks throughout our efforts to secure a foothold in the Dodecanese was an extremely difficult one, but there was never any doubt about the direction in which their sympathies lay. "It was perhaps at this period that we received a greater degree of material assistance from the Turks and at a greater risk to themselves than at any other time," Sir Hughe Knatchbull-Hugessen wrote of his experiences as our Ambassador in Turkey at that time. "Without the slightest hesitation the Turkish Government came to our aid and supplies were shipped regularly from the Turkish mainland and communication facilitated with our forces in the Islands. The Turks gave us every help when the moment came for evacuation."

But they were having demonstrated right on their doorstep a warning that they could not possibly disregard. "The Germans had had an opportunity for showing what they could do by way of air attack within a few miles of the Turkish mainland," Knatchbull-Hugessen further recorded. With that staring him in the face, our Ambassador was called upon to make an effort to get Turkey into the war that could not help but be against some pretty stiff odds.

But they did go so far as to give him a statement in which there was announced "clearly Turkey's decision in principle to enter the war." But attached to that was the condition that Turkey should receive adequate support for defense against German attack. That, in turn, was sufficient reason for yet further urgent consideration of our whole policy in the Balkans and the Aegean.

It was of the utmost importance to the Turks that they should have defense against attacks from the German Air Force. They asked us for an astonishing number of R.A.F. squadrons which, even though we had long had plans for going to their aid, we could never have supplied. We had already sent to Turkey large detachments, and we assembled what squadrons and antiaircraft batteries we had available, and we got them all ready to move in. And then we waited for our orders.

On December 2 the Prime Minister and the President of the United States and the British and American Chiefs of Staff arrived back in Cairo from Teheran. Among the subjects in the discussions that then took place there were the matters of getting Turkey into the war and of reopening operations in the Aegean. The Prime Minister was "queering our pitch," as Alan Brooke put it, by talking rather wildly about ways of forcing the Germans in Rhodes to surrender; but three days later it was agreed by the Combined Chiefs of Staff that "operations in the Aegean, including in particular the capture of Rhodes, are desirable . . ." But it was with the proviso that they should be executed "without detriment" to the invasions across the Channel and of the south of France.

During this last round of the Cairo conferences, the President of Turkey and a Turkish delegation were in Cairo for further discussions with the Prime Minister and the President about the suggestions that they should come into the war on our side. One can scarcely blame the Turks, after all that had happened in the Aegean, for not showing any particularly keen interest. Talks went on for several days. The Turks wanted the seventeen R.A.F. squadrons that were to be supplied from my command—which was much less than the total that they were asking for—to be moved into Turkey ahead of our technicians and supplies because they were afraid that if the technicians and supplies went in first the Germans might attack. Reports were coming in of German troop movements in Bulgaria which were disturbing to the Turks. We felt that the men and supplies must be on the spot before we could send in the squadrons.

It struck me that we might be able to make a little impression on the Turkish President and his colleagues if they were to meet face to face some of the more outstandingly successful young Royal Air Force commanders who had been doing the actual fighting in the air. We arranged for some of them to come to Cairo, and they attended a dinner which was given at our Embassy, at which Winston Churchill was able to present them to the Turks. The young wing commanders and group captains whom I produced—there were about twenty-five of them—seemed to enjoy themselves with their customary gusto, and many years later Max Aitken—who was one of those at the dinner—spoke about two incidents which, at the time, caused no little amusement. Aitken had the additional responsibility, through his group, of providing the special air protection for Cairo during the course of the whole of the important conferences.

In the course of the general discussion that Winston Churchill had with the Turkish President during dinner, Ismet Inonu refused to be nailed down to any hard facts. He indulged in the usual pleasantries, and he then started talking about his keen interest in game shooting as a sport. It was with his own infectious delight that Aitken reported to me the response that this caused to erupt from Winston Churchill.

"That's not the sort of shooting I want to talk about!" our Prime Minister exclaimed.

When the time came at the dinner for the speeches to be made, Winston Churchill launched forth in that brand of French that was so peculiarly his own. The President of Turkey could not speak English, and Churchill could not speak Turkish, and French was the language that provided the link between them. Anthony Eden was sitting, as our Foreign Secretary, beside Numan Menemencioglu, the Turkish Foreign Secretary, and as Churchill made his speech, Eden gave his Turkish opposite number a more understandable version, in French, of what our Prime Minister was saying. Churchill could hear what Eden was doing, and it was upon this occasion that he made another of his famous remarks. Looking sharply at Eden, and speaking in English, he exclaimed: "Anthony . . . will you please stop translating my French into French!"

That was just the kind of situation that appealed most to the uninhibited Air Force, and if there was any embarrassment felt by anybody there it was completely smothered by the guffaws of delight that came from us.

But all that emerged from those last meetings with the Turks was that there should be a further examination of the position by British military experts, who should proceed immediately to Turkey. The Turkish officials returned to their own country still uncommitted; and for all our efforts they remained in that state until late in February, 1945, when, only a few weeks before the end of the war in Europe, they came in on our side.

33 / A Test of Patience

THAT THE HEALTH of Winston Churchill was not good was only too apparent to all of us as soon as we saw him on his arrival for the start of the Cairo Conference. I was told that on the way out from England by sea he had been suffering from a cold. He could not, and being Churchill he did not, spare himself during the first days in Cairo, and by the time that he got to Teheran he was obviously feeling the strain. "P.M. has a throat and has practically lost his voice," Alan Brooke wrote in his diary on their second day there. "He is not fit and consequently not in the best of moods."

The pressure of work was even greater in Teheran than it had been in Cairo, and again there could not be any relaxation. By the time that they got back to Cairo, the Prime Minister was obviously very tired, and Brooke was finding it difficult to "get him to absorb" all that was calling for his personal attention. During this second stage of the Cairo Conference his old friend Smuts had been in attendance, and he spoke to Alan Brooke about his concern over the state of the Prime Minister's health, going so far as to express doubts about "whether he would stay the course," and saying that "he was noticing changes in him."

I had dinner with Alan Brooke and Jumbo Wilson that night, and we discussed the possibility of future operations in the eastern Mediterranean, and also the reorganization of the structure of the overall command in the Mediterranean. After that, Brooke went to the Embassy to collect the Prime Minister, and from there we all drove out to the airdrome just beyond the Pyramids, from which they took off for Tunisia at one o'clock in the morning.

Out of the decisions that were reached during those discussions in Cairo at the end of 1943 there had come plans for the future employment of quite a few of those who were to be in positions of high command in the forthcoming invasion of Europe. We all aspired to play a part in it, and since I had spent some months right at the beginning, while I was still at Fighter Command, in

620

starting the planning of the air side of this great operation, I naturally hoped that I would be given an opportunity to play a positive part in these future operations.

One of the most important decisions reached was that General Eisenhower should be the Supreme Commander for Overlord; and shortly after the end of the conference, a revised structure of the command in the Mediterranean that had been argreed upon was brought into effect. With the decision that an American should command the cross-Channel invasion, it was agreed that the Mediterranean should be under the overall command of a British officer, and Jumbo Wilson was selected to take Eisenhower's place.

Of immediate concern to me in this new structure was the way in which the air was to be handled, as well as the matter of my own position. During the time that he had been with the British delegation at the conferences in Cairo I had had several good talks with Peter Portal, and he had mentioned to me that there was to be something new for me. There were several alternatives, he stated, and I was to be given some choice in the matter. On December 10 what had previously been the Mediterranean Air Command became the Mediterranean Allied Air Forces, and it covered, under the supreme command of Jumbo Wilson, control of all air operations throughout the Mediterranean.

The new command structure, which spread over a vast area, was much too complex in character, and after giving it a great deal of thought I sent Arthur Tedder and the Air Ministry a long paper in which I developed my views that placing control of the Middle East for all purposes, both operational and administrative, entirely under the control of the Mediterranean Allied Air Forces Headquarters "is unworkable, and will lead to inefficiency and friction." I agreed that the Air Commander-in-Chief, Mediterranean Allied Air Forces, should control operations in the whole Mediterranean area, including operational control of Middle East Command; but I urged that in the administrative sphere my command "should be permitted to exercise the greatest degree of autonomy that it is possible to allow."

The appreciation that I prepared was a very thorough one, and I was greatly concerned about what was in store for my own command, as well as for me. Arthur Tedder's reaction was to reply that he did not think that we were "very far apart regarding the degree of administration," but to my surprise he said that "in the circumstances I feel it is far better if I do not intervene." Perhaps, in view of what was about to happen to him, that was understandable. He was to become Eisenhower's deputy for Overlord, and there was no particular reason why he should now worry himself about something that was not going to be of any further concern to him.

All these moves and changes were of the greatest interest to everybody, and by that Christmas of 1943 the rumors were buzzing around our headquarters in Cairo about a number of other senior appointments that were to be made in the Mediterranean. I still had no official word, even after what Peter Portal had told me before he left Cairo, about just what was going to happen to me; but on December 23, the day of my fiftieth birthday, I received from the Air Ministry a signal stating that Keith Park was to be appointed in my place as Air Officer Commanding-in-Chief, Middle East.

Although I was naturally pleased, after our long association, that Keith Park should be taking over from me, there was still no official indication at all about what I was going to do. In his diary Bob Wright recorded that we had a party that night for my birthday, and that I "was not in good form at all." About midnight he found me standing alone staring out of the window, and when he joined me there and commented that I did not seem to be enjoying myself I apparently replied in disgust: "Hell . . . I'm fifty!"

But that was not the reason for my feeling of something approaching dejection. He had not heard the rumor that had just been brought to my attention. The news had come to me in the most roundabout way, and it was quite unofficial, but from what was being said I gathered that I was to be appointed Deputy Commander-in-Chief of the Mediterranean Allied Air Forces, which was to be under Ira Eaker in place of Arthur Tedder.

This information, and the casual way in which I came to hear about it, caused in me feelings of some sort of bewilderment. I had come to know Ira Eaker quite well from the time when, about eighteen months before, and as a colonel in the American Army Air Forces, he had first come to see me at Bentley Priory. That was after I had been C.-in-C. of Fighter Command for quite some time. I liked Eaker personally, and I respected him for his undoubted ability; but I could not help feeling that it was a strange state of affairs which could cause an officer with all my experience of high command, not to mention seniority, to be appointed as a deputy to an American officer so much junior to me in rank and experience.

The day after I received the information about Keith Park taking over from me I received a copy of a signal sent by Peter

Portal to Arthur Tedder in which he said: "I much regret that Douglas has been kept in the dark about his future." He pointed out to Tedder that while in Tunis on his way home from Cairo he had received definite instructions from the Prime Minister that he was not to discuss the matter with me, and because of that he had assumed that Churchill intended to do so himself. He suggested to Tedder that he might put it up to Churchill "that he should either send for Douglas or else allow me to tell him what is proposed."

The impression that I had formed by then was that Peter Portal and Arthur Tedder were not at all happy about what somebody was going to have to tell me. My patience was being somewhat tried, and my feeling was strengthened when, three days later, I received a signal from Tedder which was repeated to the Air Ministry, saying that the Prime Minister had left Tunisia—he had gone to Morocco to convalesce from the serious illness which set in right after leaving Cairo—before the signal from the C.A.S. had arrived. Tedder referred to Portal's signal and told me that he had raised the question with Churchill before he left, and that he had emphasized the need for clarifying the situation regarding senior appointments. "I understood from him that they would all be announced tomorrow," he stated. "If announcement is not made I hope C.A.S. will take up question."

As soon as I saw this reference to the Prime Minister's having left Tunisia I felt that there were difficulties ahead because we all knew by then that Winston Churchill was very ill. Almost immediately after his arrival in Tunisia from Cairo it had been found that the decline in the state of his health was such that, as he put it himself, it "has ripened into pneumonia." We had received signals in Cairo calling for equipment and medical people to be flown to Tunisia. "I did not at any time relinquish my part in the direction of affairs, and there was not the slightest delay in giving the decisions which were required from me," Churchill said later, and there is evidence enough that he did continue "bearing my burdens," as he put it, in the most extraordinary manner.

It was a lot to expect of those concerned—Portal in London, Tedder in Tunisia, Churchill in Morocco, and myself in Egypt—that there should be an easy exchange of views even under the best of circumstances. Distance alone, not to mention the involved communications under conditions of war, were against that. But, feeling as I did, I could not merely accept these handicaps and acquiesce to something which everybody seemed to know about, but which was being withheld from me, without making some protest. Immediately after receiving Tedder's signal I sent one to

Portal saying that I "must insist that no (R) no announcement is made about any appointment for me without my being consulted." I stated that I considered that the "whole procedure seems extraordinary to me and I feel that I am being jockeyed into a false position."

The next day I signaled Portal again, pointing out that when he and I had talked together in Cairo only a short time before he had told me that there were several alternatives for my next appointment, and that I would be given some choice in the matter. Now I felt that I was "about to be presented with a *fait accompli* and, if I read the signs aright, it is a *fait accompli* which I may be unable to accept." I stated that I "would be most grateful if you could give me some definite information so that I can have an opportunity of saying what I think."

The firm stand that I was trying to take brought an immediate and sympathetic reply from Peter Portal. He said that he was sorry that I should feel that I had been put in a false position, and he quite understood that I had been left in the dark. At the same time, Portal stated, both he and the Secretary of State "are in urgent communication with the P.M. about future appointments." He said that they both thought that in time of war "it is seemly for Senior Officers to accept posts in which their services are required," but he did soften that a little by saying that they were both "equally desirous of obtaining for you a post which will give full scope for your exceptional qualities and qualifications." He said that he hoped to be able to let me know something shortly, and that he would certainly endeavor "to do so before anything is published."

Through the long years of my association with Peter Portal, I knew him well enough to be able to see in that signal an indication of his genuine distress that I should have been placed in such an awkward position. I had no wish whatsoever to be difficult, but now was the time, I felt, to lodge any effective protest. I sent a further signal to Portal, and it was a long one, in which I voiced fully my objections to almost everything that was happening to me and to my command.

"I cannot understand why I cannot be told what is provisionally in the wind," I stated. I pointed out that if the indications that I was to be appointed as Ira Eaker's deputy were true, he should bear in mind that he was putting me under the command of an officer of rank lower than my own. I was already a Commander-in-Chief—not a deputy—"in a semi-independent position." I stated that as Eaker's deputy I would have no operational functions or responsibilities, and that I would become little more than a glorified administration officer of the British Air Forces in the Mediterranean.

In addition to these personal considerations, I told the C.A.S., there were many things about the new air command with which I was not in sympathy, and that I had already put up my views about that to both Arthur Tedder and the Air Ministry. I pointed out to him that because of that it looked as if I was going to be "asked to operate an organization of which in many ways I disapprove." So far as obeying orders was concerned, I stated: "Generally speaking I agree with the sentiment . . . that officers should not as a rule argue about their appointments, but go where the good of the Service requires. In this case, however, I feel that it is not so much the good of the Service or even of the war effort as political considerations to which I am being sacrificed."

There was a valid reason for that last observation. I had already heard that my appointment under Ira Eaker was the outcome of a discussion between the Prime Minister and the President of the United States. When Churchill had managed to persuade Roosevelt that the overall command in the Mediterranean should be given to a British general—Jumbo Wilson—and the naval command to a British admiral—John Cunningham—Roosevelt had replied that the British would at least have to give the senior Air Force command to an American.

It was inevitable that Arthur Tedder should know how strongly I was feeling about the appointment that was being proposed for me as Ira Eaker's deputy. He was involved in it in the first place. He also had the long report that I had put up to him about my views on the structure of the new Mediterranean Allied Air Forces command. "I cannot but sympathise very strongly with you," he wrote to me. "The great chess players do not, I think, have much regard for pawns like you and me . . . I suppose the only thing to do is to take it!"

I was saddened by Tedder's comments; but I have never been able to consider myself as a pawn, and I had no intention of allowing myself to be pushed around. From then on, I began to feel increasingly angry about the way in which things were going, and one morning I expressed myself fully to Max Aitken, to whom it was always easy to talk, about my dislike of the position in which I found myself. He was on a visit to headquarters in Cairo and he had come in, as he always did on these visits, to see me.

"I've half a mind to resign," I told him.

Aitken looked at me in astonishment for a moment, and then, with the broad and cheerful grin with which he received almost everything, he exclaimed: "But you can't do that . . . not in time of war."

"Oh yes, I can," I replied.

"You'll find yourself a corporal in the Home Guard if you do," Aitken commented.

The objection made by Aitken that I could not resign in time of war was quite understandable; but I was not the only one who felt that he was so out of sympathy with the way in which things were going that he must take that drastic step. It was quite permissible, if not always acceptable, under our system. I was called upon to give a great deal of thought to it under the Nazi system at the time of the findings of the Nuremberg Trials in 1946. At times Alan Brooke contemplated the step during his arduous service as C.I.G.S.; Wavell apparently thought about it while serving as the viceroy of India; and at one stage the patient and loyal Pug Ismay had even handed in his resignation, only to have it ignored.

My long signal of protest drew from the highest levels immediate answers that were not lacking in a sense urgency. The very next day a reply from Peter Portal informed me that both he and the Secretary of State for Air had taken up with the Prime Minister—who was still in Morocco—my reluctance to accept the post under Ira Eaker. He said that they had "suggested to him a possible alternative post." But, Portal continued, it was the Prime Minister who had put my name up to the President for this job, and Churchill "now informed us that in his opinion this is the best post for you." And then came the order: "He does not consider it is for you to say where you will be employed."

"As I have often told you before, I sympathise very much with your feeling of partial frustration since you left Fighter Command," Portal stated, and I knew that he meant that. He pointed out that I would be the leader of the R.A.F. throughout the Mediterranean and Middle East, and "be able to exercise an immense effect on their morale, fighting value and tactical efficiency"; and that, through my experience and "your intrinsic qualities which I know he respects highly," I would be rendering good service to Ira Eaker.

There was no denying the strong appeal that Portal made to my sense of loyalty. About any disparaging conclusions that might be arrived at over my serving under an American officer of junior rank, he stated: "If there is any criticism it will be directed against me and the Government and not against you." I could appreciate the good sense of that view, even if I did not altogether agree with it. "The Secretary of State and I therefore both hope very much that if the appointment is offered to you you will accept it," he concluded.

At the same time a personal signal for me arrived from Archie Sinclair. "My opinion, which Portal shares, about the importance of giving you the greatest possible scope in fighting this war is clear and strong," he stated; and so well had I come to know him by then that I could almost hear him declaiming it. The Secretary of State repeated some of Peter Portal's arguments, and he then produced one that I could not help chuckling over, particularly when I recalled that only a few months before he had told me that I was going to be the Supreme Commander in S.E.A.C. There was such a vast difference between that and the latest proposal.

"We should indeed be glad if it were possible for your role and Eaker's to be reversed, but no exact comparison can be drawn between British and American ranks," he stated; and then, at full throttle, he continued: "Remember too that our military affairs are going to be mixed up with those of the Americans for some time, perhaps for many years to come. It is therefore important that they should have an opportunity of working closely with you and getting to know you better than they now do."

While I was still not convinced that this was anything more than a political move, and that I was being compelled to act as a pawn, I could not refuse to listen to those who were my superiors in the Service and who were men for whom I had the greatest respect. For the next two days I thought as carefully and as sanely as I could about the whole business.

On the first day of the new year I replied with a personal signal to the Secretary of State in which I said: "In view of what you say I will of course accept the appointment. You can rely on me to bury any feeling of disappointment and give Eaker full and loyal support." At the same time I signaled Peter Portal, and I told him that I felt that what I had heard about Eaker's intention to set up our headquarters in Algiers struck me as being the correct one, and that I was prepared to hand Middle East Command over to Keith Park immediately and to report to Algiers within a week's time. But in the privacy of my own thoughts the prospect of being stuck in Algiers filled me with gloom.

In his account of all that happened at that time, Winston Churchill quoted the signal that he sent to President Roosevelt some days before my exchange of views with Peter Portal. In it he stated: "Sholto Douglas will be Deputy Air Officer Commanding-in-Chief" in the new structure in the Mediterranean. This statement is another of those which he placed on record—as he did with the alleged statement by Stuffy Dowding—and left as a fact achieved, and there has never been any effort made to correct it. Whether Churchill was to blame for that, or whether it is the fault of whoever did the research for the air side of the material for the books, I do not know. But that statement is not the whole story.

Only twenty-four hours after accepting the appeal made by Archie Sinclair, I received from him another signal in which he stated that he was "grateful" for what I had decided to do. But just before receiving it, he explained, he had "obtained Prime Minister's agreement (which he had previously withheld on incomplete information about American appointments in Mediterranean) to making you the offer of Coastal Command." In a brief moment, it seemed, my whole position had changed, and I was being offered something which I felt was an honor, and which genuinely delighted me. "Portal has now confirmed that your appointment would be welcome to the Admiralty," Sinclair continued. "I shall be glad and confident of your success if you accept either," he concluded, leaving to me the choice between Coastal Command and the Mediterranean.

"Would certainly prefer Coastal Command," I signaled in reply; and Archie Sinclair then informed me that "my offer of Coastal Command is confirmed." He also told me that Jack Slessor, who was then C.-in-C. of Coastal Command, and whose place I would be taking, would become Ira Eaker's deputy, but for the present I was to keep that "strictly to yourself." I could not help feeling a pang over that, for it appeared that Slessor was now going to be subjected to all that I had just been through.

Many years later I heard that Jack Slessor was rushed out to the Mediterranean at only a few hours' notice, all of which he accepted then, as he does now, in the spirit, albeit "sadly," which has always made of him one of the most cooperative and understanding of all the senior officers we have ever had in the Royal Air Force. I have always hoped that he considered that the circumstances of my case were exceptional. My own response to the new situation was to send a signal to Archie Sinclair stating briefly: "I am very grateful."

When I had finally agreed to accept the appointment as Ira Eaker's deputy I wrote personally to Winston Churchill, and I placed before him the position in which I felt that I had been placed. Then came the change in the plans, and my appointment to Coastal Command. In reply to my letter I received from "Colonel Warden" a personal signal in which he stated: "Thank you so much for your letter. Am watching over your affairs carefully." I felt grateful to Churchill for that statement because it indicated to me that the way in which I had dug my heels in over something about which I had felt so strongly was not being held against me.

During the First World War the military leaders had had too much of the political skirmishings to contend with, and in all my reading and study I had come to know, with feelings of the strongest revulsion, all about that. The relationship between the politicians and the military leaders in the second war were so much more forthright and honest, due mainly to the influence of Winston Churchill, who, above all others, saw to it that on the political side—and he was the greatest and most agile and experienced politician of them all—there should be only one object: to win the war. Even when he was at his most irritating and difficult—as Alan Brooke was to know more than anybody else—he was always absolutely honest and straightforward with his Commanders-in-Chief.

I doubt if there was anybody who knew what a great relief it was for me to be released from all the conflict and the extraneous influences that I had known during the year that I had spent in Cairo. The prospect of returning to England with a fully operational and integrated command was almost like awakening from a bad dream; and when I realized that I was awake I could not complete quickly enough handing over to Keith Park the affairs of Middle East Command. But even then I was not to get away from Egypt without one final unpleasantness which, trivial though it was, made me only too glad to be on my way out of the political and diplomatic ring.

When Winston Churchill had left Cairo at the end of the conferences, and I had paid my respects to him in saying good-bye, he had told me that Anthony Eden himself had intimated to him that the Foreign Office thought that it would be a good idea to leave me where I was in Cairo because I was persona grata with King Farouk. "It is useful from the Foreign Secretary's point of view," he said; and I knew from that remark that, for all the gossip, the official view was that my time spent in Farouk's company had not been wasted. I must have looked rather taken aback, because Churchill had quickly added: "But don't worry about that."

As soon as it was settled about what I was going to do, I told King Farouk that I was leaving Egypt immediately and returning to England. His response to that was to indicate that he would like to present me with the Order of Ismael, which was one of the higher official Egyptian decorations. Our own King's Regulations made it necessary for me to ask for permission before I could accept any foreign decoration, and I went through the normal procedure of setting the machinery in motion. The outcome was the information that the Foreign Office had ruled that I could not accept any such Egyptian decoration. That all sounded trivial enough, and it was of no importance to me. But the repercussions were heated, embarrassing, and, I felt, quite unnecessary; and in what happened I found myself involved in yet another round of hostilities between the King of Egypt and our Ambassador.

Such was his anger over my not being allowed to accept the decoration that he wanted to give me that King Farouk demanded point-blank to be told why, as he saw the situation, I was refusing it. I had to tell him that the decision was not mine, and that it had been made by our own Foreign Office in London. Farouk immediately said that he detected in all that the hand of our Ambassador. I was inclined to think, to myself, that he might be right; but I told Farouk that it was nothing to do with the Ambassador, and that it was an official decision arrived at in London. Farouk then stated that he took it as a personal insult to him that I had refused this high decoration.

By then I was feeling more than a little irritation myself over being drawn into such an unseemly squabble, particularly after what I had been told only a short time before by our own Prime Minister about the Foreign Office asking that I should be retained in Egypt to help keep on the right side of Farouk. It was a thoroughly stupid state of affairs, and I then told our Ambassador, Sir Miles Lampson—who later became Lord Killearn—that, while the decoration meant nothing at all to me, my not being allowed to accept it was causing King Farouk to become unnecessarily annoyed, with an increasing feeling of grievance against the British. But Lampson was adamant about the Foreign Office ruling, and it was even left to me to perform the unpleasant task of having to write formally to King Farouk about not being able to accept the decoration. It was a small enough matter in our eyes; but so far as the Egyptians were concerned it was made quite clear to me that they regarded it as yet another rebuff to add to the list that was already far too long.

The firm stand that I made in objecting to the appointment that I had been very nearly jockeyed into out in the Mediterranean at the beginning of 1944 was to play a vitally important part for me in the years that lay ahead. Instead of being sidetracked into something which could so easily have led to a dead end, I found myself instead in what was to be, in so many ways, the most absorbing of all the appointments that I held as a Commander-in-Chief; and through that I was able to enjoy, quite unexpectedly, what I now look back upon as the happiest period of my service during the Second World War.

In the middle of January, 1944, I finally relinquished command of the Middle East and returned to England, and a week later I took over as Commander-in-Chief of Coastal Command. The fighter pilots and the bomber crews of the Royal Air Force have received full and well-justified acclaim for all that they did in the Second World War; but not nearly enough has been said about the work done by the crews of Coastal Command, and the splendid achievements of those who served in it. Much too often there was recorded, when it came to the routine reporting of the work of Coastal Command, nothing more than that they had flown such and such a number of sorties, and such cold statistics cannot even begin to tell the story. But it could not very well be otherwise, for so much of the work of the Coastal crews was of a nature that it was not at all advisable to let the enemy know too much about it.

For all the way in which fortune had led to my becoming one of the first of the fighter pilots, and since then more of an authority in the use of fighters than of any other aircraft, I had always been intensely interested in the work of Coastal Command because of my high regard for the Royal Navy. In saying that, the eyebrows of some will shoot up in surprise, but many of my best friends in the R.A.F. had formerly been naval officers; and at one time, while I was still at school at Tonbridge, I had thought about trying to get into the Royal Navy, but I was by then too old.

Through all my Staff College work, and my Staff appointments at the Air Ministry, I was thoroughly familiar with the operations of Coastal Command, even if I had never served in it; and while I was Deputy Chief of the Air Staff at the Air Ministry during part of the first year of the war the Directorate of Naval Co-operation was under my control. That had brought me into close contact with the Admiralty, and in addition to the bomb versus battleship controversy, in which I had been so directly involved, I knew well the way of thought in the Royal Navy. Up to that time I also knew that, so far as strategy was concerned, the Navy was very sadly behind in understanding how important air power was becoming at sea.

The controversy over whether the Royal Navy or the Royal Air Force should have control of Coastal Command was an old one, and there are those who will argue about it even to this day. Coastal came into being as a separate R.A.F. command in 1936, along with Fighter and Bomber commands; but even that did not altogether settle the controversy. The function of the new command was defined clearly enough, and it has since been well described by Denis Richards in his statement: "Coastal Command, in the new element of air, was to help the navy in the old, traditional tasks at sea—the maintenance of our communications, the severance of the enemy's."

But that seemed to mean little in certain quarters in both Services, and the argument over which of the two—the R.A.F. or the Royal Navy—should exercise the operational control of Coastal Command continued on its way, as it had from long before the start of the war. The Admiralty had always argued that any phase of a war at sea was their responsibility, and that they should have operational control of all aircraft as well as ships. The Air Ministry, on the other hand, argued that the air is one and that it did not matter whether the aircraft were operating over the sea or the land: they should still be under the control of the one authority, the Air Ministry.

Before and during the early years of the war the arguments became at times particularly bitter. In 1940 there was a demand—this time from political sources—that the Admiralty should be responsible for all maritime aircraft; but even the Sea Lords themselves were not at all keen about that idea, and it was rightly turned down. The Commander-in-Chief of Coastal Command then was Air Chief Marshal Sir Frederick Bowhill. One of those who had been a sailor before becoming an airman, "Ginger" Bowhill was at Coastal from August, 1937, until June, 1941, and his struggle for aircraft for his command was a continuous one, with a background of a state that bordered on starvation. He was short of flyingboats; he had no up-to-date aircraft for reconnaissance; and he had to put up with endless delays in being provided with even medium-range torpedo-bombers.

Two of the new aircraft with which Bowhill was provided, and from which great things were expected in Coastal Command—the

Lerwick flyingboat and the Botha—were both failures. Bowhill had to endure a great deal of unfair criticism, and just hang on as best he could until he did begin to receive adequate aircraft for Coastal's purposes. Handicapped as the Command was during the early part of the war, they did good work, and after making do with aircraft which were both outdated and insufficient in numbers, they eventually began to receive American Catalinas and Hudsons in sufficient numbers to be able to operate more effectively.

But it was when Bomber Command decided that the Liberator—the American B-24—was not suitable for their night operations that Coastal's near starvation came to an end. The bomber barons' decision resulted in these aircraft going to Coastal; and it was unquestionably the addition of large numbers of these fine aircraft that helped to bring about what Jack Slessor has described as "the enormous advance in the lethal efficiency of Coastal Command." By the time that I became C.-in-C. of Coastal we were using twelve squadrons of them.

The unsatisfactory situation over the operational control of escort operations in the North Atlantic had been raised often enough by the Commanders-in-Chief of Coastal Command and by the Chief of the Air Staff, and the discussions, not to mention arguments, still went on, with the Americans also becoming deeply involved when they came into the war. In fact, their inter-Service controversies were even harsher than ours. To some of our people it seemed that, as it was put to me, "their Navy Air was literally not on speaking terms with their Army Air." The feeling between them was so strong that they had to be allocated to different airfields when they were serving in Coastal Command. But by the time that I arrived on the scene, the storm so far as the differences between the Royal Navy and the Royal Air Force were concerned had blown itself out.

The early compromise that had been arranged was that Coastal Command should come under the Admiralty for operational control, which was to be exercised through the Air Officer Commanding-in-Chief. Of this, Jack Slessor has made the comment, "the actual outcome of this was precisely nothing, except a legacy of ill-feeling in the Command of which the last traces had hardly disappeared" when he took over in February, 1943. But such was his success that, by the time that I, in turn, took over the Command from him a year later, I found little or no traces of any ill-feeling left, and the issue had become scarcely more than an academic one. On the other hand, I cannot agree with the generalization made by Denis

Richards: "Contrary to popular legend, liaison with the naval authorities was from the very beginning close and effective." Cooperation at squadron and ship level was good; but the same thing could not be said of what had gone on at higher levels.

The staff that I inherited from Jack Slessor at the headquarters of Coastal Command was a sound and able one: they would have had to be under the command of a man of Slessor's ability and drive. Although in theory I had a fair knowledge of the background of the functions of the command, I fully realized that my practical knowledge of the work that was being done—particularly in the war against the German submarines: the U-boats which were constantly trying to get at our all-important convoys of merchant shipping—was all too sketchy. I had to bring myself very quickly up to date by hard and concentrated studying, and with probing talks with my staff and frequent visits to the squadrons. My new command ranged from Gibraltar to Iceland, and to the Azores far out into the Atlantic, and, almost as with the Middle East, it covered a tremendous area.

Whenever I think now of the work that was done by the air crews of the Royal Air Force during the Second World War, I still feel warm and deep sympathy for those who flew in Coastal Command. On the one hand they had a hard-slogging and, except for brief moments, a rather unspectacular job on their very long-range escort duties, especially in view of the cautious restriction by the Admiralty on any references to the sinking of U-boats. Quite often some months passed before any descriptions of these actions were released, and then they seldom contained any of the color that there was to be found in the stories of those actions. At the other extreme there was the work of the strike wings, and strikes they were, hitting hard and at speed against enemy surface vessels. In both, the risk of casualties was very high.

But it was possibly the tedium of the long-range escorts that was most trying for those Coastal air crews. The strike wings did at least know when they would be going into action, and they struck and returned to their bases in much the same way employed by the fighters against surface craft, except that I think they ran even greater risks than those faced by the fighters. Their tour of duty on operational flying was very much longer than in any of the other commands. The anti-U-boat crews normally did eighteen months of operational flying, compared with about four months for the bomber crews and about six months for fighter pilots. An anti–U-boat crew might fly for a whole year without sighting a single enemy submarine. When they did get a sighting, their chances of

making an attack were only about one in three and their chances
of actually sinking the U-boat were much less. And there was
always a good fifty-fifty chance of either being shot down or
crashing in making the attack.

There was never any lack of activity in Coastal Command. I
would even go so far as to say that my command was more
constantly on the go than any other command in the R.A.F.; but
the whole atmosphere and tempo—which seemed to be more of
endurance than anything—were more relaxed and less hectic than
in the other two commands that I had held. By its nature, Fighter
Command was inclined to be hectic, but that was inevitable. And
the Middle East, with all its assorted jobs and wide variety of
interest—not all of them Service—called for a bewildering variety
in the attention that one had to give to it. But in Coastal Command
I found for the first time—after four years of war—steadier and
quieter, though by no means less important, work to be done. It
meant that I had more time to think and to plan, and in an
atmosphere that was relatively tranquil, compared to what I had
known before, I could consider more carefully the decisions that
had to be taken.

Of all those who were so helpful in my immediate study and
examination of the structure and operation of my new command,
two men were outstanding in the support that they gave me. The
first was my righthand man, then Air Vice-Marshal Aubrey Ellwood, who was my senior air staff officer. He had been a Coastal
group commander before coming to the command headquarters at
Northwood, and he knew intimately the operational side of the
work. His particular pigeon as a group commander had been paying attention to the quite large amount of shipping devoted to
enemy interests which passed along the Norwegian coast and the
area around the Frisian Islands. Ellwood was a fine staff officer,
possessed of sound common sense, and he was never easily ruffled.
He went out of his way to give me the most loyal support, particularly during the time when, in the beginning, I was finding my feet.

The other man upon whom I came to rely very heavily, and
who probably contributed over a long period of time more than
any other single man to the smooth running of Coastal Command,
was the senior naval staff officer, Captain D. V. Peyton-Ward,
R.N. No account of Coastal Command's activities could ever be
complete without mention of "P.-W.," as he was known to
everybody. To quote Jack Slessor's opinion: "Though always loyal
to his parent Service, he became in all but uniform and rank an

officer of the Royal Air Force." Quite recently P.-W. revealed the
essential nature of his own attitude in a remark that he made to me
when he spoke about "the vital importance of all branches of the
Air in any form of Maritime War."

Captain Peyton-Ward had served in submarines in the First
World War. After reading the story of my own experiences as a
fighter pilot in that first war in *Years of Combat* (the first of the
two volumes of the English edition of this book), he wrote to me
and said: "We are almost exactly the same age, but while you
really were fighting the war I was either a First Lieutenant or
Captain of a submarine whose only idea was to get up to London
between our periods at sea so as to view the latest edition of Chu
Chin Chow or the current review at the Alhambra." My interests
in the shows in London at that time were identically the same as
his, but I must say that I consider that his work in submarines then
was much more dangerous and unpleasant than mine was in tearing
round the skies over the Western Front in a fighter.

In having the mind of a submariner, Peyton-Ward could sense
just what action would be likely to be taken by the U-boat
commanders against whom we were waging such a constant battle.
He had been invalided out of the Royal Navy through arthritis, but
on the outbreak of the second war he had rejoined the Service, and
he spent the entire war at Coastal Command. Quite often P.-W.
was obviously in pain, but he never allowed that to interfere with
his work. It was as if he was permanently on duty, and one could
always count on him to be in the operations room when he was
needed. The main link between Coastal Command and the Admiralty was provided by Peyton-Ward and his staff, and to those
whose names which I have already suggested are outstanding in
the work of liaison—Spears for the Army, George for the R.A.F.
and Casey in the diplomatic field—I would add that, in my own
experience, Peyton-Ward was the outstanding naval liaison officer.

Our operations rooms at Coastal Command headquarters as
well as the headquarters of our groups all the way from Gibraltar
and the Azores to Iceland, as well as those in the United Kingdom,
were constantly manned by combined staffs from the Royal Navy
and R.A.F. The Admiralty and my staff at Northwood and I were
always able to see eye to eye because we were always looking at
the same operational picture of what was happening. Out in the
groups, the Admirals and the Air Officers Commanding, or their
chief staff officers, worked literally sitting side by side, and they
were able to discuss instantly any action that might be called for;
and with these practical commanders working together on the spot,

and able to exchange views face to face, there was rarely any disagreement about the appropriate action that should be taken.

With the sea and the air involved so intimately together in fighting their phase of the war, it was a fact, even if it does sound a little incongruous, that the operational control of Coastal Command became largely a question of an admiral and an air vice-marshal sitting down together more often than not in a glorified dugout looking at the same picture and discussing the action that should be taken. And all that was possible because of the excellent liaison that had come to be developed between Coastal Command and the Admiralty.

"Disagreements in high places," Jack Slessor has commented, "must be put in their proper perspective and it should not be imagined that they diverted more than a small percentage of our energies from the real business of fighting the war at sea." After my experiences in the Middle East it was an immense relief to find at Coastal Command that the percentage was almost nonexistent.

34 / On Guard

OF ALL THE ERRORS of judgment that were indulged in by the belligerents during the First World War, one of the most curious was the way in which the Germans saw fit to conduct their submarine warfare. That such a war at sea should come to be fought was natural enough because we were trying then to maintain a blockade of Germany, and the Germans had to hit back at that with the use of submarines. But in hitting back they went about a ruthless, unrestricted submarine warfare that was to cause them untold trouble.

In the second war we were to know much the same gigantic struggle on the part of the Germans to carry the war out to and under the sea by the use of submarines, and they did it with great skill and ingenuity and daring. When the passenger ship *Athenia* was sunk through being torpedoed by a German submarine off the northwest coast of Ireland within hours of the outbreak of war in September, 1939, many of us wondered if we were in for more German frightfulness at sea. From a coldly professional point of view, the German Navy fought a long hard war both on and below the oceans and with great dexterity; but it was not done without a repetition of that frightfulness.

In my work at Coastal Command I was called upon to exercise a more singleminded concentration than I had known previously in any of my work. The operations were fought with all the intensity of that indulged in by the other commands of the Royal Air Force but, because of the restrictions imposed by security, with no allowance for public information. I do not say that that was wrong, but it did mean that we worked more alone, standing on guard, and doing it quietly and without any fanfares. Even to this day there is still very little known by the public about the important part that was played by Coastal Command in the course of the war, and if ever there were unsung heroes, they were to be found among the air crews of that command.

By 1943 the losses through the attacks of the German U-boats against convoys, which were crossing the Atlantic and bringing to us urgently needed supplies of every nature, had reached such serious proportions that the Royal Navy and the Royal Air Force—the two Services concerned with the protection of those convoys—as well as the Americans came to feel about the situation the gravest concern. But during May and again during October and November of 1943, the German U-boat attacks on our great and small convoys crossing the oceans suffered severe reverses. These were inflicted by the joint action planned and executed by the Royal Navy at sea, and by the Royal Air Force, mainly through the use of the very long-range heavy aircraft of Coastal Command, over the sea.

So successful were these operations of ours during that year that by the end of November the German U-boat commander—Admiral Doenitz—had had to abandon his extensive submarine operations against the convoys crossing the Atlantic. So effective were our patrols that even at night the U-boats found themselves denied the necessary time to surface for recharging of their batteries. This winning of what has come to be called the Battle of the Atlantic was, to quote Captain S. W. Roskill, "in its own way as decisive as the Battle of Britain in the summer of 1940; for never again was the German Navy able seriously to threaten our lifeline—let alone come within measurable distance of severing it."

This was the time of the fiercest part of the Battle of the Atlantic; and it had seen, in the words of Captain Peyton-Ward, "the scenes of fierce duels between aircraft and U-boats on the surface." By the latter part of the summer, the heavy casualties suffered by the Germans had forced them to make their passages submerged, spending the least possible time on the surface at night for the recharging of their batteries.

At the same time that these actions were taking place out in the Atlantic, air action by Coastal Command against the German shipping proceeding along the Norwegian coast down into the southern North Sea, heading for the German and Dutch ports, had increased during the latter part of 1943 with the introduction of strike wings of Beaufighters carrying torpedoes, rockets and cannon. These strike wings, which were almost continuously in action, were to become particularly effective in their sweeps along the Norwegian coast; and in the southern North Sea, mines laid by aircraft of Bomber Command, as well as action by the light craft of the Royal Navy, eventually closed the great port of Rotterdam to any further use by the Germans.

But these services at sea were not the only ones being rendered by Coastal Command. Other operations which were our responsibility included high-flying photographic reconnaissance missions, lonely ones performed mostly in unarmed Spitfires. Bomber Command relied on the photographs obtained on these flights for assessments of the results of their raids. Through those reconnaissance flights there were also maintained constant checks on the movements of the warships and the merchant ships of the enemy, the extent to which shipbuilding was proceeding in the enemy yards, right on down to the dispositions of the Luftwaffe, the enemy antiaircraft, and Army encampments and the states of the railways and marshaling yards.

From the work done by our aircraft flying from the airfield at Benson, near Oxford, the Photographic Reconnaissance Unit produced hundreds of thousands of prints. These were put to every conceivable use by the interpretation units of all the Services. As many as five squadrons alone were maintained at Benson by Coastal Command, all of them devoting their time to this work which could be, on occasions, as uncomfortable as any other type of flying.

It was also part of Coastal Command's duties to maintain with a fleet of high-powered and fast motorboats, as well as two squadrons of aircraft, the service for the rescuing of American and British air crews who were forced down in the sea, dashing out at any time and in all sorts of weather to their rescue. Furthermore, it was Coastal's job to keep going some fifty aircraft for the meteorological service which, in their probing for information beyond the friendly home shores, was the sole source of information for all the weather forecasting used for operations by the Royal Air Force, the Royal Navy and the other Services.

When I took over Coastal Command from Jack Slessor, a great victory had already been won by him and by Admiral Sir Max Horton in the battle against the U-boats in the Atlantic. The German submarines were never completely beaten, and I was to continue to experience activity enough against them during the period that I was to spend as C.-in-C. of the Command; but the main battle had been in the decisive campaign that had been fought against the U-boat and won before I appeared on the scene.

So far as the air was concerned, in administering that defeat Jack Slessor had also had to struggle hard to get the appropriate aircraft and air crews in sufficient numbers for the work. Much has been said and written about the clashes that occurred over the provision of aircraft for Bomber and Coastal commands. Sir

Charles Webster and Noble Frankland, the official historians, have said: "Sir Arthur Harris was fired with a burning conviction that the strategic air offensive was the only means by which the war could be won in reasonable time and at bearable cost." Just before that statement they also record that Bert Harris had, at one time in 1942, expressed the view that Coastal Command was "merely an obstacle to victory." He was clamoring for the return to his command of all the heavy aircraft which he felt that he must have in order to build up what he described as the "only offensive weapon against Germany."

It was always the view taken by Bert Harris that the way to hit the U-boat menace was to bomb it at its sources: in German ports, bases and yards. That was the task for Bomber Command. But Sir Dudley Pound, who was the First Sea Lord in 1942, had made the statement: "If we lose the war at sea, we lose the war." And Winston Churchill later commented: "The Battle of the Atlantic was the dominating factor all through the war." The Prime Minister did not share Harris's view that a bombing offensive alone would win the war, and although he did suggest late in 1942 that two squadrons should be transferred from Coastal to Bomber Command to help build up the strength of the latter, he never lost sight of the value of Coastal Command.

Into this atmosphere of controversy over priorities there were introduced, as aways, the opinions of many advisers and experts. Of the views held by Professor Lindemann, the Earl of Birkenhead has said: "His desire to bomb Germany led him to constant efforts to prevent the Army, Navy, Coastal and Fighter Commands from claiming what he regarded as an excessive share of the national resources, and to increase the effectiveness of bombing." To that he added that Lindemann "indulged in a long and embittered complaint about Coastal Command demands for aircraft and radar equipment."

We who were responsible for the active operation of the Navy, the Army and the Air Force could not help but be aware of the astonishing arguments indulged in by those in whose hands there rested so much that could assist or impair our ability to wage the war. It had always been so, and it persisted throughout the second war, although the wrangling was less virulent than it was in the first war. Lindemann made no secret of how he felt and what he believed in; and all the other pundits also indulged in their arguments; but, in the end, Coastal Command still got what it wanted as a fighting command. What is more, the Command had the young men with the skill and the guts to use those aircraft and that equipment in action. Sitting around tables in rooms in White-hall indulging in personal feuds meant nothing to them. Having known over a long period of time what it was like to be out on a limb both as a young pilot and as a senior commander, I came to feel very strongly about the ways of some of the Whitehall warriors.

The types of aircraft that were being used in Coastal Command by the time that it became my responsibility were of an almost staggering variety, and it was noticeable how successful we were with American aircraft. We had the antiquated Swordfish of the Fleet Air Arm, the Spitfires of the photographic reconnaissance units, the twin-engined Hudsons, Warwicks, Mosquitos, Beau-fighters, Wellingtons and Catalinas, and the great four-engined Fortresses, Liberators, Halifaxes and Sunderland flyingboats. And for the flying of this very wide range of aircraft we had to have air crews whose training alone presented us with an extraordinary complexity of problems.

With the Battle of the Atlantic going in our favor, the German submarines started operating in looser groups than the methods that they had earlier employed of hunting in packs. They worked to the westward of Scotland and Ireland, on the lookout for convoys coming up from or going down to west Africa, as well as across the Atlantic. As soon as I felt that I had a firmer under-standing of what was going on, I decided to cut down the number of aircraft patrols penetrating down into the Bay of Biscay, and to increase our anti–U-boat activity nearer home, in the seas to the west.

The close cooperation provided by the Royal Navy enabled both of us to sink quite a fair number of U-boats, and that forced Admiral Doenitz to abandon his attacks on our ocean convoys. He drew his submarines in closer to the bases that he had on the French coast of the Bay of Biscay. In all this work I had the opportunity to come into contact a great deal with Admiral Sir Max Horton. A distinguished sailor, he was a man who always knew his own mind: decisive, efficient, and, so far as the R.A.F. was concerned, as cooperative as he was well liked.

Shortly after the escape of the *Scharnhorst* and *Gneisenau* through the English Channel, Max Horton had prepared a paper on the affair which he later turned into what his biographer has described as "a general appreciation of the war situation"; and it was extraordinarily revealing how soundly Horton understood what we in the Air Force were trying to preach about air power.

"Recent events have proved that fleets cannot operate without the close co-operation of air power," he stated. "If we are to hold our own during this vital year, and wear down the enemy before we ourselves are exhausted, it is essential that the whole of our naval and air force strength should be concentrated and employed in the battle for sea power."

Although I had never met him, I had heard a lot about Max Horton long before I ever got to Coastal Command. He was the naval Commander-in-Chief of the Western Approaches from November, 1942, until August, 1945, and he had his headquarters in Liverpool. One of my groups, at that time commanded by Air Vice-Marshal L. H. Slatter, also had its headquarters there, and they shared an underground combined operations room in the Liverpool docks. The way in which the two services were able to cooperate was remarkably good, with not the slightest sign of any friction, and the admiral was always able to consider his operations against the U-boats with the Air Officer Commanding right alongside him.

In all the work that was done by the Royal Navy and Coastal Command, the operations that were of longer range were usually taken care of by the Royal Air Force, while the Navy worked more closely inshore. Two of the features about Max Horton's attitude toward fighting the war made a strong appeal to me: his insistence upon training, and the need for the utmost patience. He saw to it that the crews of his frigates and corvettes were hard at their training all the time. There were periods on operations during which all appeared to be quiet, and it was inevitable that they should then become bored; but Horton kept them at it for days and weeks on end, insisting that they should stay at sea and continue with their training.

Whenever a U-boat that was being attacked disappeared below the surface of the sea with no trace of what might have happened to it, there was a great temptation to both the air and naval crews to give up the hunt after a reasonable time had been spent searching for it. But with the stern training that Max Horton insisted upon, and the great need for patience that was in itself one of the outstanding traits in his own character, his crews went on hunting for days and days on end, knowing that that submarine had to come up somewhere, and that they would then be ready to make another attack. That they were successful is revealed clearly enough in their achievements. As a young officer Max Horton had been a submarine commander during the First World War, and he knew the ways of the fish that he was after during the time when he was the chief angler of Western Approaches.

"The dangers of inshore navigation in all weathers put a heavy strain on the commanding officers of the hunting craft," Admiral W. S. Chalmers, Max Horton's biographer, has stated. "They had the additional anxiety of keeping their ships off the rocks while seeking out dormant U-boats. An Asdic contact every half-hour over a period of three weeks was not uncommon."

It was the intensity of this work which imposed such strains on the naval crews, just as it did on my air crews, and I frequently discussed this with Max Horton. I always found him particularly sensible in his concern for those serving under him at sea. Admiral Chalmers has spoken of that, saying: "Nobody could be harder if he suspected negligence or even stupidity, but an error of judgment in a difficult situation or a frank confession of fault usually won his sympathy. On the other hand his post mortems and cross-examinations were often more disturbing to the victim than the incident itself."

Just as we had in the R.A.F. those who were very successful, through some sort of dedication and outstanding ability, so the Royal Navy—as well as the Army—had young commanders who excelled in their work. Under Max Horton's command there was one man who did extremely well: Captain F. J. Walker, R.N., who commanded one of the escort groups. He had made a great name for himself as a U-boat killer long before I took over Coastal Command, and he continued to track down the enemy in the most relentless and effective way. He was the Royal Navy's outstandingly successful U-boat hunter, until July, 1944, when he died from a stroke brought on through what has been described by the official naval historian as "the immense strain he had borne during nearly five years of almost continuous anti-submarine operations."

In January, 1944, there began to gather in England all those who were to make the final plans for, and to lead, the mighty invasion that was to be launched against German-occupied Europe. That the Germans knew that it was in the wind is beyond doubt. They would have been an extremely stupid lot—which, for all their shortcomings, and although they were greatly misled, they were not—if they had failed to note through their intelligence sources the arrival back in the United Kingdom of quite a number of admirals and generals and air marshals of the most senior ranks in the Allied Services. From that time onward the one objective was the opening up of the second front for which the Russians had been clamoring for so long. It was to be, in fact, a third or even fourth front: for the Anglo-American air forces had been fighting from our own island for a long time; our joint forces had not been exactly lounging around in the Mediterranean; and in Burma and on out into the reaches of the Far East there had been strenuous British and American assaults on the partners of the German effort to gain control of the entire world.

That I was not to have command of the air side of the invasion was naturally a little disappointing for me. Again the hand of chance had intervened, and while I was still out in the Mediterranean the cards had fallen in such a way that Trafford Leigh-Mallory, who had taken my place as C.-in-C., Fighter Command, had been appointed the Air Commander-in-Chief of the Allied Expeditionary Air Force.

Almost all of those who came to fill the senior posts in the Services for the organization of the invasion were known to me, many of them through long years of personal experience. Trafford Leigh-Mallory had done well as Commander-in-Chief of Fighter Command; but his somewhat uncompromising, and at times even aggressive, manner seemed to rub the Americans the wrong way. I began to hear rumors that he was not getting along as well as we would have liked with, among others, Eisenhower and his chief of staff, Bedell Smith, and Lewis Brereton. Long afterward Lewis Brereton published in his diaries some firm views about the differences between the British and the Americans during the last stages of the working up for the invasion, and he spoke of clashes with Leigh-Mallory. Knowing both men as I did, I could understand how Leigh-Mallory, who could be rather tactless at times, could give Brereton cause to feel at odds with him.

I saw a lot of Leigh-Mallory at the various conferences that were held, but I was never sure how much his differences with the Americans over the way in which the invasion of Europe should be conducted had to do with his being given that change to a higher command. But he played his part in the invasion, and toward the end of 1944 he was posted to the Far East to take up the appointment of Commander-in-Chief of the Allied Air Forces in southeast Asia, under Louis Mountbatten. He asked me to select for him a suitable crew for his aircraft, a York, believing, rightly, I think, that the Coastal Command crews were the most experienced in the R.A.F. in generally being able to find their way around. I had my staff carefully select a reliable and seasoned pilot, and an equally good and experienced navigator. They were from among the best in Coastal Command.

On November 14, 1944, Leigh-Mallory, his wife, and his personal staff officer took off in the York from Northolt on the first leg of their flight out to the Far East. The aircraft crashed in the mountains on the border between France and Switzerland, south of Grenoble, and everybody on board was killed. I was deeply shocked when I heard about it. They had apparently started off in the face of a bad weather report, and I have often wondered why such an experienced pilot had not advised against the starting of the flight. Perhaps he had, because it was the practice of all senior officers, and one which I strictly adhered to, not to allow rank to interfere with the decisions that can be made only by the captain of the aircraft in which one happened to be flying. I have wondered if the answer does not perhaps lie in the final words of Hilary St. G. Saunders when he said of the death of Leigh-Mallory: "Not brooking opposition easily, he had persevered with the tenacity which had earned him a high reputation over the battlefields of France in 1916, 1917, and 1918, and his loss was one which the Royal Air Force could ill afford."

All the clashes and differences of opinion that found expression over the planning of the invasion in 1944, and even in its execution, were rather outside the sphere of my own work as Air Officer Commanding-in-Chief of Coastal Command, although I was deeply involved in it. I was glad of that because it left me free to get on with my work with a minimum of interference. I was more closely in contact with the Royal Navy and the United States Navy than I was with my own Service or the United States Army Air Forces, although I used to meet the other air commanders frequently enough at all the conferences.

One of the most interesting to me of all the appointments that were made to senior posts for the invasion was that of Bertie Ramsay as the commander of the Allied Naval Expeditionary Force. During the months of the planning for it and immediately after it took place, I was in frequent contact with him, and again I had known what a delight it was to be able to work with him. But after a while our work took us along divergent paths, and I saw less of him.

On January 2, 1945, there came the shocking news that Bertie Ramsay had been killed. He had been in a light transport aircraft, and on taking off from an airfield in France in bad weather and snow for a trip back to England the aircraft had stalled and crashed, killing all five people on board. Within a few weeks, of the three men who had commanded the invasion forces under Eisenhower—Ramsay the naval side, Montgomery the Army, and Leigh-Mallory the air—two were dead as the result of aircraft crashes.

During those early months of 1944 all our efforts were given to the launching of the invasion about which there had been for so long so much discussion and argument. Of all the colorful characters among the many different British and American commanders who were involved none was more vivid than Bernard Montgomery. He was to command the U.S. First Army and the British Second Army in the actual Overlord attack—representing the entire Allied Army—and it is no exaggeration to say that he went about his work with a gusto that was so typical of the man. He has told in his own story how he felt about "the need to get experienced fighting commanders 'in on' future operational plans early"; and one of the first things that Monty did when he was presented by the Prime Minister with the plan for Overlord which had been agreed to by the Chiefs of Staff was to rewrite certain parts of it. And if not on paper at least in execution he went on rewriting it in a way which I think, for all the controversy that has swirled around his name, was entirely right.

But Montgomery was not alone in wanting right at the beginning changes in the actual plans that had been made for the invasion. As early as December, 1943, the Prime Minister had informed the Chiefs of Staff that "both Eisenhower and Montgomery have expressed themselves entirely dissatisfied with what they have heard of the present plan . . ." In all the conferences and discussions that were held after we had all returned to England in January, I was again brought into contact with Eisenhower, and it was encouraging to me to find that he had a genuine appreciation of the important role that my command was to play in the forthcoming invasion. In all our meetings and conferences at which Eisenhower was present, I was deeply impressed by the honesty and the sincerity of this man who had emerged so quickly from nowhere, and who now, as Supreme Commander of the Allied invasion, carried on his shoulders such an enormous load of responsibility.

There were many of us who had had a great deal more experience than Eisenhower had been able to acquire of actual war, and who were both better equipped and better trained in military affairs to take positions of high command; but none of us could match the strength of his ability to induce the greatest possible cooperation between those appointed to serve under him. There were the clashes of temperament and personalities—he had some pretty high-powered prima donnas to contend with—and there were at times the strains of international jealousies; but these were aspects of the high command about which Eisenhower was particularly firm. Even when we disagreed with him, as it was inevitable that all of us did at some time or other, for he was not infallible and he never pretended that he was, we knew that he had given the problem his most careful thought, and that to the very best of his considerable ability he was giving an honest answer. Eisenhower's great ability was the way in which he could pour oil on troubled waters and reduce in severity the thoroughly honest clashes of opinions that threatened at times to disrupt our planning.

In the differences of opinion that occurred between Montgomery and Eisenhower I have always been inclined to support Montgomery, although I would have been happier if Monty had been less dogmatic in the attacks into which he has since allowed himself to be provoked. Eisenhower's restraint in the face of some of these attacks redounds greatly to his credit, for, as we now know, great pressures were brought to bear upon him from Washington. The Americans had those faceless pacers of the corridors of power just as much as we did, and it must not be forgotten that, in addition to being Supreme Commander of Overlord, Eisenhower had to contend with them as well.

Nor was Eisenhower exactly spared in the restlessness of the energy and drive of the commanders that he had under him. If we, the British, caused him headaches, there were also those among his own commanders who caused him at times to wonder just what was going on; and one of them was George Patton, one of his closest friends and his most successful fighting general. Just before the invasion I met Patton again for the first time since his visit to us in Cairo. It was right at the moment when he had managed to get himself under yet another cloud.

As the time for the invasion approached, the various Army, Navy and Air Force Commanders-in-Chief met nearly every day for consultations. These meetings were often held in what, only eighteen months before, had been my large underground operations room at Fighter Command at Bentley Priory. It was at one of these meetings that George Patton appeared. Noticing that he was much quieter than was usual for him, I asked him how he was feeling.

"Oh . . . hell . . . I'm in the dog house again," he replied.

I had heard that after the unhappy incident in Sicily, which was followed by a period out in the cold, Patton had been reinstated by Eisenhower in the forces for the invasion and that he was about to be given command of the American Third Army. There was no questioning Patton's very great ability as a fighting general, and nobody knew that better than Eisenhower. Patton was, to use an American expression, "one of the greatest ground gainers" they had; and their most popular sobriquet for him was "Old Blood and Guts."

"What's the trouble now?" I asked.

In putting the question to Patton I was fully prepared for one of those outrageous remarks of his of which Eisenhower once commented: "He had a genius for explosive statements that rarely failed to startle his hearers."

"I've just had two bastards shot," Patton replied.

The penalty for rape in most armies, and the American Army as well as ours, was the death sentence, but it was usual for the Commander-in-Chief who had to deal with such cases to commute the death sentence to one of a term of imprisonment. Two soldiers under George Patton's command had been found guilty of rape, and when the sentences had come up to him for confirmation his anger had got the better of him. He had refused to commute the death penalties, and in telling me about that he said, in his own fashion, that he had snapped the order: "Shoot the bastards."

"Well . . . what happened then?" I asked.

Mournfully Patton explained that Mrs. Eleanor Roosevelt, the wife of the President, had got after him about these executions, and was protesting so vigorously that there were political repercussions. There was no comfort that I could give him because it was not for me to tell him that I thought that Mrs. Roosevelt was right, and that he had been wrong not to commute the sentences.

After only a few months at Northwood, and as we became more and more deeply involved in our plans for the invasion, I began to feel that I had recovered from the curiously deadening effect that the frustrations out in the Middle East had had upon my mind. My relationship with the members of my staff became a distinct pleasure to me; and in speaking of my method of working Roy Faville, who had been on the staff under Slessor and is now a retired air vice marshal, once told Bob Wright: "Sholto was so thorough. He used his staff, and they had confidence because they knew that they would receive clear, lucid decisions on the points they brought up. His concept of the relationship between a commander and his staff was quite exemplary." Rather shrewdly, Faville added: "He sometimes overcalled his hand, but it was to him an eminently sensible tactic, and he knew what he was doing."

With all my experience of and belief in the value of training, and, in Fighter Command in particular, the use of airborne radar, I felt that we would be well advised to step up the intensity of our own training in Coastal Command in the use of both radar and the Leigh Light working together in the closest cooperation. The urgent need for Leigh Light aircraft over the previous two years had meant that air crews were manning these aircraft which had not had sufficient training in techniques which were involved and very exacting.

As far back as 1940, Squadron Leader H. de V. Leigh, one of the personnel staff officers on the headquarters at Northwood, had suggested fitting a searchlight to certain Coastal aircraft so that it could be used at night to illuminate any radar contact that might be established with a U-boat. Leigh was by no means an expert or of any authority in this work, and it was merely an idea that he had worked out in his own mind. But he pressed on with his idea with a great deal of persuasion. We had had much the same idea with our Turbinlite aircraft in Fighter Command for night fighting, but whereas that was a failure, the Leigh Light, working in a fundamentally different way, became a great success, and far more effective than the primitive business of dropping flares for purposes of illumination.

By the time of the invasion we had in Coastal Command eight Liberator and Wellington squadrons equipped with radar and the Leigh Light, and we had devoted a great deal of attention to the training of the crews of these squadrons. The technique of getting a radar contact on a submarine on the surface at night, and of then using the light to illuminate it in making an attack with depth charges, was undoubtedly one of the most dangerous tasks that any air crews had to undertake. In training alone we were losing crews through the aircraft flying slap into the sea.

Selection of better than average pilots at instrument flying was one of the answers, and after that had been done there came the training of the crews as teams in the handling of such large aircraft as the Wellington and the huge Liberator very low down over the sea at night. This problem of training was the experience that I had had with night fighter crews in Fighter Command all over again, except that it was on a wider scale. Launching an attack on an enemy submarine was at any time a tricky business that called for a great deal of skill as well as courage, and by night it called into play a highly involved technique.

While on patrol, and already warned by intelligence to be on the lookout for U-boats in the patrol area, the radar operator would be searching through the use of his equipment the surface of the sea. In daylight, and in rough seas, it was hard enough for the pilot to be able to see anything as small as a submarine, if it happened to be on the surface, no matter how accurate his radar operator's reports might be. At night, the crew would have to wait for exactly the right moment before switching on their Leigh Light to illuminate the object being seen by the radar operator.

From then on, by day or by night, the pilot had to contend with the hazards of the sea as well as the return fire from the enemy submarine. His radar operator would guide him in, and he would then have to bring his aircraft down to a height that at times was only fifty to a hundred feet above the sea, maintaining a steady course straight for his objective in order to straddle it with his depth charges.

It was not likely that the enemy would accept these attacks without answering back, and all the time that our aircraft were making their careful approach the Germans would be firing back with the normal heavy armament carried by the U-boats. After dropping the depth charges, our aircraft were still sitting ducks because there was no chance with those large, cumbersome aircraft of making any quick climbing turns and rushing away while still so low down over the sea. They had to get away as fast and as best they could, hoping that they would not be hit by enemy fire or clutched at and torn down as they skimmed over what were quite often turbulent seas.

The extent to which Coastal Command was to operate as a uniquely independent force in the invasion is indicated in the statement that was made by General Eisenhower in his book *Crusade in Europe*. In discussing the last stages of the planning for Overlord he wrote: "All air forces in Britain, excepting only the Coastal Command, should come under my control. This would include the Strategic Air Forces, comprising the British Bomber Command under Air Chief Marshal Sir Arthur Harris, and the U.S. Eighth Air Force under General Doolittle."

That definite freedom to get on with our work as we saw fit had in it for me an attractive independence. But after all that I had heard about the difficulties that had existed, earlier in the war, in the relationship between the Air Ministry and the Admiralty over the control of Coastal Command, I nevertheless conducted myself as C.-in-C. of Coastal with a certain caution. The work done by my predecessors had solved all the major problems, and rather to my surprise I found that I rarely received any direct operational instructions from the Admiralty. That led me to take a step shortly before the invasion which, in its result, revealed more than anything else how well we had come to work together.

There was a constant state of discussion between the officers of my headquarters and those of the Admiralty over the way in which our operations should be conducted; and I myself talked frequently with the Deputy Chief of the Naval Staff, or with the First Sea Lord, who was then Admiral of the Fleet Sir Andrew Cunningham. Since all of us, from Whitehall to command headquarters and on down to group headquarters, were, in the Navy and the Air Force alike, all the time looking at the same picture, we all knew very well what was in each other's minds. And with a stormy petrel like Max Horton vitally concerned with all our plans—he was just as prepared to have stand-up rows with his fellow admirals as with anybody else—we were all kept on our toes.

In April, a couple of months before the invasion was due to take place, I issued to all my group commanders a directive which set out in full detail the tasks which each of the groups would be expected to perform. From the information that I had received through our good liaison with the Royal Navy, I outlined what I thought the Admiralty anticipated might be done by the enemy. The main part of the action that we expected would come from the U-boats trying to force their way up the St. George's, the Bristol and the English Channels.

It was obviously our duty to bring the main force of our anti–U-boat aircraft into operation in the southwestern approaches. We made plans for the whole area to be saturated with air patrols in depth, or, perhaps I should say, in width. With aircraft in the vicinity, if not actually overhead, every thirty minutes, that would compel the U-boats to exercise extreme caution in trying to get at our fleets of ships being used in the invasion.

After a great deal of discussion it was agreed by all concerned that the main battle zone, if one should develop, would be between a line from Portland to Jersey in the west, and from North Foreland to Calais in the east. With that in mind, it was the primary task of Coastal Command aircraft to operate on the flanks of this area, and to keep any operations within it down to a minimum.

About three weeks before the invasion was due to take place, it dawned on me that, much as I was enjoying the freedom that had been mine from any harassment from the Admiralty, there had arisen a situation that appeared to me to be rather ridiculous. In the course of the discussions about our planning for the invasion, we at Coastal Command had made all our arrangements for the dispositions of our squadrons, their patrol areas and their duties. My detailed instructions had already been issued to my group commanders about the parts that they were to play in the overall plan. But, I suddenly realized, I had had no formal or definite directive from the Admiralty about what was expected of us.

Since we were nominally under the operational control of the Admiralty, this seemed to be rather an odd state of affairs. I rang up the Deputy Chief of the Naval Staff and discussed the situation with him. "Here I am supposed to be under your operational control," I told him, "and yet I haven't received a line from the Admiralty on the duty of Coastal Command in the invasion."

In the pleasantest fashion, the D.C.N.S. tried to assure me that there was nothing to worry about; but I told him that I would have to insist upon having a proper directive. I pointed out that if something were to go wrong through some blunder on the part of Coastal Command, I would be the one who would be held responsible. "What happens then if the real reason turns out to be through my not having had proper instructions or directions from you?" I asked.

There was a somewhat amused note in the voice of the D.C.N.S. as he replied: "I see your point. You'll get a directive."

But no directive arrived, even though I rang up the D.C.N.S. again and reminded him about it. By then I was becoming a little annoyed. It was only a formality, I knew, but it was a formality that I felt should be observed in an operation that was as important as the one we were about to embark upon. About ten days or so before the date of the invasion I went to the Admiralty, and I made my way to the First Sea Lord's office. There I told A. B. Cunningham that I felt that it was all wrong that I should not have been issued with one single word on what the Admiralty expected of me and my command.

"You know perfectly well what you've got to do, Sholto," Cunningham replied, laughing as he said it. "Get on with it."

What Cunningham was saying was perfectly true. "But surely, as I am under your operational control," I objected, "I should have some written instructions for what is going to be our part in the greatest operation in history?"

Perhaps I was being too cautious, or too correct in my attitude. On the other hand, perhaps I should have been more grateful for

the very obvious reliance that the Royal Navy was placing upon
my ability to do what was expected of me. Knowing A. B. Cunningham as I did, I also knew that, if trouble did arise, he would
never let me down. Whatever it may have been, and for all my
concern, I could not seem to make any more of an impression on
the First Sea Lord than one of amusement. He merely laughed
again and said:

"All right, if you insist upon it. I'll see that you get a directive."

When it did arrive the directive consisted of about six lines of
generalizations; and in effect it left to me everything having to do
with the operation of my command. When I read it the vagueness
of its contents was enough to indicate to me that the Admiralty
had no doubts in their own minds about my fitness to carry out my
job. I could not help feeling that, after all the arguments and
quarrels that had gone on over such a long period of time about
the operational control of Coastal Command, the question turned
out, in the face of the final and crucial test, to be largely an
academic one.

But while I was happy that all the fuss and heat had gone out of
the arguments, and that there was now such an excellent state in
the liaison between the Admiralty and Coastal Command, I was
nevertheless well aware of the debt that I owed to my predecessors
in my office for all that they had done in paving the way to this
sounder understanding and mutual trust. The results of that trust
were later summed up by A. B. Cunningham in his autobiography.
In writing about the crossings made by the great armadas of ships
between this country and Normandy, he stated: "Our comparative
immunity to submarine attack was principally due to the enthusiastic efficiency of Coastal Command."

35 / Constant Endeavor

I N ONE OF THE communiqués issued by Coastal Command, after consultation with the Admiralty, about the work that was done by my command with the start of the invasion there is the statement: "The land battle was spectacular, the sea battle was not." I am not so sure that that statement is correct. I do not deny that the forcing of the landings over the beaches and up the cliffs of Normandy, and the fighting that followed inland, was spectacular; but the work done by our air and naval craft over the seas on the flanks of the invasion area provided action that was spectacular enough.

There was also an added reason for the determination of the way in which we went about our work. So far as the Royal Air Force was concerned, it was an anger that affected us in much the same way as the Royal Navy had been affected (and which has been described by Captain S. W. Roskill) over atrocities committed by the enemy. In the case of the Air Force it was through what happened in what is known generally as the Stalag Luft III, or Sagan, case.

"Sagan is an historic place," Aidan Crawley has written of the position of the prisoner-of-war camp which was located at this site well to the southeast of Berlin. Crawley has reason to know all about Sagan because he was himself a prisoner there after being shot down while commanding a fighter squadron in the desert of North Africa. "The surrounding country is dead flat, the horizon broken only by pinewoods," he has added. "It is perhaps the ugliest part of the North German Plain." Out of an effort made by a gallant band of Allied airmen to regain their freedom in a fashion that was perfectly justified, there came the ugliest business in the whole of the relationship between the Royal Air Force and the Nazis.

On May 19, 1944, the Allies were deeply shocked by a statement that was made in the House of Commons by Anthony Eden, the Foreign Secretary. He told the House that on March 22 forty-seven officers of the R.A.F. and Dominion and Allied air forces had been shot by the Germans after a mass escape by seventy-six officers from Stalag Luft III, the prisoner-of-war camp for captured air crews which was maintained at Sagan. The Germans gave as an explanation for these shootings the excuse that the officers concerned had resisted recapture. There was an immediate outcry demanding to know why there had been so many killings with not one being reported wounded.

Reports of acts of barbarism on the part of the Nazis were not new to us. They had piled up over the years a list of outrages such as no other nation of modern times could have ever thought possible. But this latest act by the Nazis struck me with a personal force, and it aroused in me, as it did in everybody else, feelings of the deepest indignation. Under international law, all prisoners-of-war were protected from such violence in their legitimate attempts to escape. It was clearly understood in the Services that it was one's duty to try and escape, and the Royal Air Force had not been backward in carrying that out. But this slaughter, and the way in which it was done, left us with feelings of the deepest outrage and repugnance.

Just over a month later the Foreign Secretary revealed that it had since been learned that the number of officers shot on this occasion was actually fifty. Describing these deeds as acts of cold-blooded butchery, Anthony Eden stated that every effort would be made to collect the evidence which would identify those responsible and bring them to justice. In due course that evidence came to be revealed at the major war crimes trials at Nuremberg during 1946.

Of the fifty airmen who were murdered, thirty-two had been in the Royal Air Force, including six Poles, one Lithuanian, one Belgian and one Czech; six in the Royal Canadian Air Force; three in the Royal Australian Air Force; two in the Royal New Zealand Air Force; three in the South African Air Force; two in the Royal Norwegian Air Force; one in the Free French Air Force; and one in the Royal Hellenic Air Force.

Among those who were shot who had been in the R.A.F. were Squadron Leader Roger Bushell and Flight Lieutenant D. O. Street, who was the son of Sir Arthur Street. I did not know Bushell personally, but I had heard quite a lot about him because he had been, with Max Aitken and Whitney Straight, one of the colorful characters in No. 601 Squadron. In the case of the death of Arthur Street's son, I felt the deepest sympathy for a very good friend.

I had come to know Arthur Street well in the course of the great service that he rendered as the Permanent Under-Secretary of State for Air, and one could not but think of him as one of the great stalwarts at the Air Ministry. By the time that we heard the terrible news of the death of his son he had already grossly overworked himself in his efforts to further the Air Force to which he was devoted. We all knew him for the way he would sit at his desk in his office night after night working away at a great mass of paper. And yet he was always cheerful and always, for all the pressure of the work, so charming and even-tempered. Arthur Street was a great human being, and whenever I had the opportunity I would call in to have a talk with him, and I never hesitated to discuss with him anything that I was worried about or had pressing on my mind. Of all the people in the top echelon at the Air Ministry, and indeed in the Royal Air Force, it was so monstrous that he should have been made to suffer as he did over the hideous way in which his son was murdered.

The enthusiasm and efficiency with which Coastal Command was credited by A. B. Cunningham was not by any means a sudden blooming. The work had been going on for a long time in the fashion indicated in the motto of the Command: "Constant Endeavor." That endeavor had been exercised for a long time, and because of the grueling nature of the work there was no question about its constancy. One of the features about the work of the Command which struck me most forcibly right at the outset was the nonstop nature of its operations.

Out of the complex system of our intelligence and reporting of enemy activity we knew the positions of all the enemy U-boats which were at sea, and moreover we knew those positions within fairly narrow limits. In the first place they were detected when they left their bases. Most of them came from the Baltic. Many times they were also detected somewhere along the Norwegian coast before they finally set out for the vast reaches of the Atlantic Ocean. The German U-boat crews were great chatterers, and that led them to make a pretty free use of their wireless, and from that we were able to add to our information about their positions. They had been the same in the First World War, and they never seemed to learn the value of radio silence, or caution or discipline in the use of it.

With all this information, naval intelligence always had a very shrewd idea about the movements of the U-boats on their way out into the Atlantic. The submarines would have to go around the north of Scotland and to the north of Ireland, or even between Iceland and Greenland. Their choice of routes was fairly wide, but our people became wise to their ways, and from the reports of the last sightings and the interceptions of wireless messages, and their knowledge of the thinking of the commanders of the U-boats, our staff were able to work out quite accurately the areas in which the submarines could be expected to operate. Even as late as 1944, the U-boat commanders were still all too free in reporting their positions by wireless to the headquarters of Admiral Doenitz. It was madness, but to our gratification they went on doing it, even giving what sometimes turned out to be quite valuable weather reports.

Our radio direction finding system was always on the alert, and even if a U-boat came up with only a short signal our operators would swoop on it and quickly establish the exact position of its origin, and, more often than not, just which U-boat it came from. Toward the end of the war the Germans thought up the idea of trying to beat us by putting their messages on tapes, and of then transmitting them at very high speed. But our people soon cottoned on to that, and we had no trouble at all in breaking them down, and the Germans never seemed to realize that that was presenting for us no problem at all.

In the final analysis, Max Horton and I had at our fingertips up-to-the-minute information about all the U-boats and their positions, and that could be relied upon to within limits of twenty or thirty miles; and on that information we were able to base our plans to search for them. At the time when I took over Coastal Command they used to come to the surface once in every twenty-four hours to recharge their batteries. We would try and anticipate that and plan ahead, and we would wait hopefully for those periods during which we thought that they might be forced to surface.

With the naval escort groups—from which came ninety per cent of the contacts on the U-boats—it was a case of searching, constantly searching, and most of the contacts were made by the Navy's own asdic detection equipment on U-boats that were diving, or already on the bottom. But even with their motors stopped, and lying on the bottom, there was no escaping from asdic because it gave a response to the hull of a submarine irrespective of its motion.

In the air, the crews of Coastal Command had the same spirit of endurance and patience, which was a feature about them that I always found so impressive on the tours that I made visiting the squadrons. Being so much of a stranger in the Command, and always aware of the critical, if not downright cynical, eye with which the air crews looked upon anybody above their own squadron or station commanders, I wondered at times, because of the warmth of the way in which I came to feel about them, what impression I was making on them.

Part of the answer to that came many years later. A Canadian navigator named J. E. Griffith who was with one of the very long-range Liberator squadrons, wrote to Bob Wright about it. "The new C.–in–C. (Sholto) was the biggest shot in the arm that the flying crews ever got during the time that I was in contact with them," Griffith said, and he stressed that he was not criticizing my predecessors. "The fact that squadrons were being re-equipped with more modern aircraft may have been purely coincidental, and the result of long term planning; but the result of that first visit of Sholto's was to quicken the pulses in a lot of men who had been slogging away for a long time on one of the least spectacular and perhaps the most soul-destroying jobs of flying that the war produced."

At the same time that Joe Griffith said that, Peyton-Ward, from the point of view of a senior officer on my headquarters staff, also commented in a letter to Wright on my approach toward the Coastal air crews. In it he stated: "His humanness of contact with those under him led him to take the trouble to visit all the widely scattered squadrons of his Command thereby instilling a high morale and sense of mattering."

While it was unquestionably pleasant to learn, so long afterward, that I was able to achieve that—and I was touched by these comments—there nevertheless remains the fact that any Commander-in-Chief who was worth his salt knew that what always mattered most was the state of mind of the men who were doing the actual operational flying.

By March we knew from our own intelligence that the Germans were obviously aware that something was brewing because they began to concentrate their U-boats in the French ports along the Bay of Biscay. Our problem was to work out the best use that we could make of the 430-odd aircraft that we would have available for the protection of the great armadas of ships which would be involved in the invasion of D Day and afterward. So far as we could see, the main threats to our cross-Channel shipping would be from U-boats coming from these bases in the Biscay ports, from destroyers and torpedo boats from Brest and Cherbourg, from more destroyers and torpedo and E-boats coming down from Dutch ports, as well as from Le Havre and Boulogne. From Admiralty reports we knew that the Germans had reduced the number of their submarines at sea during March and April, so we concluded that they must be preparing for any attacks that might be necessary against our shipping in the English Channel.

As a guard against the possibility of these submarine attacks we began to concentrate our anti–U-boat patrols in the western end of the Channel, allowing for a flexibility which would enable us to intensify or vary them to meet any change that might occur in the anticipated attacks. These became known generally as the "cork" patrols: the bottle being the Channel itself. At the other end of the Channel—to the east—we built up, for work over the southern North Sea and down into the Channel, a strike force which could take action against all forms of enemy surface craft. They were also detailed to keep up day and night sweeps and patrols, on the lookout for enemy surface craft of all kinds in the invasion and adjoining areas.

The area of my responsibility covered the Atlantic from the west coast of Europe to a position about halfway across it to the west, where we linked up with the American and Canadian anti–U-boat patrols operating from North American bases. The U-boats were based primarily in German waters in the Baltic, from which they could proceed up to the west coast of Norway, where they would stop at ports such as Bergen and Trondheim to complete fitting out and making their final preparations for their journeys out into the Atlantic. During those passages they were likely to be attacked by our patrols at any moment, for we were operating from bases as far north as Iceland. Once safely out into the vast reaches of the Atlantic, the U-boats would attack anything that they happened to run across.

But the success that we had had in the Battle of the Atlantic had forced the Germans to give up shadowing our convoys. Our escorts both on the sea and in the air were too much on the alert for their liking, and they had become too skilled in their work for the Germans to expect anything but very expensive casualties from the tactics which they had formerly been using. As they prowled around more loosely in the Atlantic, always having to be on the alert themselves, most of the U-boats would work their way south into the Bay of Biscay; and they would complete their own long patrols at sea by making for their bases in the French ports of Bordeaux, St-Nazaire, Lorient, La Pallice and Brest.

In standing on guard, Coastal Command had more to cope with

than merely the U-boat menace. In the strongest contrast to the work that was done by our long-range heavy aircraft—the Liberators, the Sunderlands and the Catalinas and, to a lesser degree, the Wellingtons—we also continued with, and increased, the activities of our strike wings. These wings of twin-engined aircraft for, as the name implied, rapid strike action, had been slowly evolving from plans made quite some time before, and from their bases between East Anglia and Scotland they were able to hit out at enemy surface craft all the way from the Dutch coast to as far north as Trondheim. The strike squadrons from the wings which were based at North Coates, in Norfolk, and at Wick and Leuchars in the north, had already achieved a record for action that was as audacious as any in the Service.

At first, Beaufighters had been used in these strike wings, but later we were able to add Mosquitos; and while Bomber Command and Fighter Command were blasting away at the enemy inland on the Continent, and our anti–U-boat aircraft were prowling around looking for submarines, the squadrons of the strike wings came to play an ever-increasingly important role in hitting constantly at enemy surface shipping.

Apart from delivering attacks from the air—supplementing the attacks being made at sea by the Royal Navy—against the enemy E-boats and other surface craft of the German Navy and Merchant Marine, and preparing to guard the flanks for the forthcoming invasion, these strike squadrons sought out and delivered attacks upon the German convoys which, sneaking along the coasts of Norway, Holland and France, were carrying men and supplies urgently needed by the German garrisons occupying those countries.

One of the intriguing features of the mighty invasion of Europe that was launched from this country in June, 1944, was the failure of the German intelligence services to take more careful note of the preparations which had been going on in the south of England. It did not seem possible, so gigantic was the buildup for this operation, that our own security, good though it was, could have shielded so well from the Germans most of our intentions.

But the Germans were fooled; and many were the sighs of relief when we discovered that. The main reason was that they were denied any chance of air reconnaissance over the Channel and the south of England. What with the obliteration of their airfields by Bomber Command and the powerful forces of fighters that we had available, the German Air Force had no opportunity to make any reconnaissance flights, and they could not see what we were building up along the south coast of England. The official German historians have admitted that "the outstanding factor both before and during the invasion was the overwhelming air superiority of the enemy."

It was my good fortune, as Commander-in-Chief of Coastal Command, to be given the chance to play a fair part in the planning for the invasion, for which, in the words of Cyril Falls, "the preparations were the most elaborate in the history of warfare." And then I had the further good luck of being able to execute to the full the use of my Command in that great venture.

Operation Overlord took place over twenty years ago, and it is already becoming scarcely more than an event in history; but to those who participated in it, all the way from the men who did the actual fighting on the ground and at sea and in the air to those of us who were in overall command, it was an event of such magnitude that it cannot but remain a very vivid memory. In some ways I think of it as the Second World War equivalent, on a very much larger scale, of the launching of the offensive on the Western Front in August, 1918, in which I had participated as a young fighter pilot, and which had led to the ending of the First World War.

My own command in June, 1944, was charged with the vitally important task of working with the Royal Navy in clearing the seas of enemy ships and submarines, and of seeing to it that the massive armada which left these shores proceeded on its way unmolested. Coastal Command had twenty-one anti–U-boat squadrons, two anti-shipping squadrons, and four Fleet Air Arm squadrons operating in the area of the southwestern approaches; and five anti-shipping squadrons operating to the east of what we regarded as the main battle area.

In the early hours of that fateful June day in 1944, the cork patrols of Coastal Command were in place. During the night, reports had come in that upward of fifty U-boats had set out from the Bay ports heading for the Channel, which, in itself, was a worrying enough threat, but of gleeful prospect to the air crews. We also had anti-ship sweeps patrolling down the French coast of the Bay of Biscay. Some U-boats were sighted close inshore, heading northward; and three destroyers which were sighted were attacked and, damaged, had to put in to Brest.

During the first four days of the invasion, thirty-six U-boats were sighted by our Coastal aircraft off the Brest peninsula and in the mouth of the English Channel. Twenty-three were attacked, and six were destroyed and three were seriously damaged. Sixteen of these attacks were made at night. In almost every case the Germans fought back desperately with their antiaircraft guns. It was too important that they should get at our invasion shipping in a hurry for them to make the passage submerged; and from prisoners-of-war whom we captured from the stricken U-boats we learned that the Germans considered the penetration of the Channel was a nightmare. Two of their U-boats were actually sunk one night within twenty minutes of each other by the same aircraft, a Liberator, which was enough to send a Coastal Command pilot into deliriums of joy.

Five days after the launching of the invasion, Admiral Doenitz gave orders that only those submarines which were fitted with the schnorkel device were to operate in the area of the Channel. Bolder handling of the German submarines could have achieved successes which would have been serious for us, and we clearly saw in the tactics of employing the U-boats constantly submerged, and using their breathing tubes, a very serious threat; but the morale of the German submarine crews was by then sinking to a pretty low level. It was not until June 15—nine days after the launching of the invasion—that the first U-boat got up the Channel as far as the direct route between the Isle of Wight and Normandy. A few others later managed to break through, but they were allowed no opportunity to interfere with the heavy cross-Channel traffic; and from then on there was no interference with it at all.

At the other end of the Channel, in the southern North Sea, no attempts were made by U-boats to break through. But they continued their patrols along the coast of Norway and on to the north to try and attack our convoys bound for Russia, and, since this was in the area where there was no darkness, there were fought some very savage actions.

As we had expected, now that the U-boats were equipped with the schnorkel breathing tubes, our crews had their eyes and their patience strained to the utmost, and in the approaches to the Channel all that they could ever see were the periscopes and the tops of the tubes, which they attacked vigorously enough. In the three weeks following the start of the invasion, fifty-seven sightings were made, with the launching of thirty-three attacks. But up in the far reaches of the North Sea it was quite a different matter. The German U-boats were in too much of a hurry to get out into the Atlantic to proceed submerged, and their crews seemed to be confident in the efficiency of their antiaircraft defenses. They stayed on the surface, where they could make better speed, and they fought it out; and by the end of July our anti–U-boat aircraft were fighting them well up in Arctic waters, at times more than eight hundred miles from our own bases.

"Invading Europe was bound to be a bloody business, but few realised that the far Northern phase of the invasion operations was in its way as hard as the assault on the Norman beaches," a joint Coastal Command-Admiralty communiqué stated quite fairly at this time, adding: "One Canadian squadron—a unit smaller than a company of infantry—sank four U-boats and lost three Catalinas in June alone."

Within three weeks during June and July, two of our Coastal Command pilots won Victoria Crosses. Flight Lieutenant D. E. Horwell, of No. 162 Squadron of the Royal Canadian Air Force, found and attacked a U-boat in the northern waters, and the Catalina that he was commanding was badly hit and set on fire by return fire from the enemy submarine. The U-boat was sunk, but Horwell had to bring his crippled Catalina down on the surface of the sea. After twenty-four hours either in a dinghy or clinging to it—there was not enough room in the only one left for all of the crew of the aircraft—they were rescued; but Horwell and two members of his crew died of exposure. He was awarded the Victoria Cross posthumously.

One of the fiercest of the actions that were taking place occurred when another Catalina, of No. 210 Squadron, commanded by Flying Officer J. A. Cruickshank, made an attack on a German submarine on the surface off the Norwegian Coast. It attracted a withering return fire from the German gunners, but when the time came to drop his depth charges Cruickshank found that they were hung up. He turned and made another attack, with the U-boat gunners still blazing back. The Catalina was torn to shreds, but it was still flying. The navigator was killed, the second pilot and two members of the crew were wounded, but Cruickshank made another attack, got his depth charges away, and destroyed the U-boat. It was later found that he had been hit seventy-two times; but he stayed alive, refusing even to have morphine injections to kill the pain in case it might dull his senses for the landing, and between them he and his second pilot managed to get their shattered aircraft back to their base, where it took them an hour to get it up on to the beach. Cruickshank lived to receive his Victoria Cross, and later he came to work on my headquarters staff.

Those whose interests lie in statistics might find some little understanding of the battle fought by Coastal Command in some of the cold figures. Although productive enough in the number of submarines sunk and damaged, it cost us dearly, and in speaking of the period between mid-May and the end of August in my official report on the operations of Coastal Command, I stated: "In these operations, where skill counted as much as courage, and where both were indispensable, we lost thirty-eight anti U-boat aircraft by enemy action and another twenty-two through the hazards of maintaining our patrols in fair weather and in foul. A high proportion of these aircraft were four-engined heavies with large crews."

For quite some time the Germans had been working feverishly with the further development of this device of the schnorkel for their U-boats which, in the words of Peyton-Ward, eventually "resolved the U-boat war into almost a stalemate." The schnorkel was simple enough in theory: it was the way in which the Germans managed to solve its mechanical effectiveness which was to their credit. It was nothing more than a mere breathing tube which stuck up just above water level and which enabled the submarine to recharge its batteries while it still remained submerged. With only the tops of these tubes sticking up out of the water the effectiveness of our watch, both visual and by radar, was greatly reduced. But it was a measure which, so far as the U-boats were concerned, and as Peyton-Ward put it, "led to very slow passages, immobility on patrol, and relative incapacity to harm our shipping."

On the other hand, from the German point of view, the introduction of the schnorkel was successful in cutting down the number of their submarines being sunk, and our score declined from the time when they brought it into general use.

By August, 1944, the Allied armies in northwest France had broken through the German resistance inland to such an extent that Admiral Doenitz was compelled to give the order for all his submarines to give up their bases in the French ports on the Bay of Biscay. They could not very well make their way back through the English Channel—we had that well corked up at each end—and they had to make their way out into the Atlantic, and on the long return journey around to the north to try and reach some of their bases in Norway. Both the Royal Air Force and the Royal Navy were then given a chance to get at them, and there were further actions which were fought at sea with a notable fury.

The German Navy was by no means ready to give in, and after a short time spent in gathering together their U-boat forces in the Norwegian bases, and readjusting their plans, the enemy submarines were sent out to carry on with the fight, futile though it must have seemed to many of them. Their new plan was to set up a system of inshore diving patrols around our coasts, and in the second week of September we had to reorganize yet again all our plans, and turn on air patrols off Cape Wrath, off the northernmost tip of Scotland, and off northern Ireland, as well as provide aircraft for patrols further to the south, over the St. George's and Bristol Channels. On land, our Army and Air Force were striking into the Continent; but there was still plenty of guarding to do at sea around our own coasts.

But from that time until the end of the war, it was the strike wings of Coastal Command which were to take the heaviest punishment. The Beaufighter and Mosquito squadrons, with their torpedoes, rockets and cannon, employed tactics which meant that there was never any respite for the enemy. They kept up pulverizing attacks on the German convoys, particularly along the Norwegian coast. In one particular attack on an enemy convoy, which was made up of forty vessels, hits were registered on every one of the ships.

The attacks made by the strike wings in searching out the enemy surface craft were also carried into the fjords of the Norwegian coast, and they were made against murderous odds. After the long flight across the North Sea, our aircraft would have to face the heavy enemy flak from the ground as well as from the ships which were sheltering in the fjords. The shipping was also very difficult to attack because quite often the aircraft had to fly right into the fjords, diving down on to the ships and having to pull up very sharply to avoid hitting the steep cliffs. The work done by the strike wings was outstandingly successful; but their casualties in carrying it out were heavier than in any other flying done by the Royal Air Force during the last six months of the war.

About three months after I had taken over Coastal Command, I arranged for Max Aitken to come back from the Middle East. For the third time he had asked to serve directly under my command, and I was anxious to have with me a man of his ability who could make such a loyal effort. It would have been very easy for him, with his fine record, to have accepted any one of a number of attractive appointments which could have been so easily looked upon as plums; but Aitken deliberately chose to go for one of the difficult ones.

I knew from the experience that I now had of Aitken's ability both as a pilot and as a commander that he was one of those upon whom I could rely to produce results, and I arranged for him to form a new strike wing that was to operate from Banff, in Scot-

land. In time this wing came to consist of six squadrons of
Mosquitos, and, as with the other strike wings, its job was to
attack all enemy shipping plying along the coast of Norway.

Setting about his task with his usual enthusiasm and good
humor, Aitken soon had under his control what he has described
as "an amazing gang." At one time, he has recalled, his six
squadron commanders, all wing commanders, were an Englishman, an Australian, a New Zealander, a Norwegian, a Frenchman
and an Irishman. Such was the severity of their casualties that four
of these commanding officers alone were killed on operations.

Early in the new year of 1945—as the events of the last year of
the war rushed to what was now an obvious conclusion—we found
through air reconnaissance that the Germans were still operating
more shipping than we had expected all the way from Oslo Fjord,
in the south, to about nearly halfway up the west coast of Norway;
and the Fleet Air Arm, and motor torpedo boats and submarines
of the Royal Navy, and our own strike wings kept up nonstop
operations against all this shipping. The Germans still had operating from Norway their fighters of the Luftwaffe, and they added to
the hazards of the work done by the strike wings, but we got help
for them in the form of escorts of Mustangs from Fighter Command. With that help our strike wings were operating out as far as
the Skagerrack, but in doing that they continued to take a severe
thrashing.

On the other hand, our anti–U-boat squadrons, working closely
with the Royal Navy, were causing heavy losses among the enemy
submarines. But early in that new year of 1945 we were warned by
the Admiralty, in what Peyton-Ward described as a grave forecast,
that the Germans were about to bring into use new types of
submarines—the XXI and the XXIII—and that there was a
possibility of a new offensive from them. It was also known that
the Germans were launching new submarines faster, for all our
successes against them, than we were sinking them.

"There were grounds for believing that, unless we could reverse
the unfavourable trends, the enemy might regain the initiative
sufficiently to renew the campaign against our North Atlantic
convoys in strength," S. W. Roskill has stated; "and heavy losses
in that theatre might, so the Admiralty considered, jeopardise the
whole land campaign in western Europe."

But Bomber Command were delivering shattering blows to the
shipbuilding yards, as they were to everywhere else in Germany,
and shortly afterward production of the new types of U-boats was
ruined. But that did not prevent the fertile mind of Captain Peyton-

Ward from putting up to me the idea that we should intrude over the area of the western Baltic around the island of Bornholm, which was known to be a training ground for new U-boat crews, and frighten the lives out of these crews right at the outset. Some special sweeps were organized for this, in which we proposed using at night the Leigh Light aircraft. In addition to administering some nasty shocks, we hoped that there might also be a chance of bagging a few U-boats.

A great deal of work was done on this planning, and careful arrangements were made for photographing any results that we might be able to achieve. And then P.-W. came up with the idea that he should be allowed to go along in one of the aircraft. I knew how keen he was, and how loyally he had stuck to his post in the operations room; but I had to give him a firm refusal because he was far too valuable at our headquarters. The sweeps were staged, but we were never sure of what we actually achieved because, to my intense disgust, there was an almost complete breakdown in the photographic side of the venture.

When I had given up Fighter Command at the end of 1942 to go to the Middle East, the Command had reached the peak of the strength that it has known at any time in its history. By February, 1945, I was to have the same experience with Coastal Command, when its maximum strength was reached: 793 aircraft, of which over 500 were at work against the U-boats.

While it was of immense and consuming interest to have under my control such a formidable air power, and the operations of the command were absorbing, there were other events that, from time to time, were of such note that they forced themselves on the attention of all of us. One such event was the Yalta Conference. "The Allied leaders and their train of several hundred experts and clerks had arrived at Yalta at a moment when Russian military prestige stood at its highest," Sir Arthur Bryant has recorded of the start of the conference. It ended with Winston Churchill fighting, to quote Bryant further, "his losing battle for Europe's future against the cynical chauvinism of his Russian partner and the credulity and growing weariness of his American one."

From all that we know now about the conference held at Yalta, in the Crimea, at the beginning of February, 1945, at which President Roosevelt, Winston Churchill, and Joseph Stalin and their staffs sat down and talked, one can only wonder at the agony that it must have imposed on the mind of our Prime Minister.

Promises were recorded and fine speeches were made; but the first sprouting from the seeds that had been sown at Teheran late in 1943 could be seen even by then. Again British and American liaison seemed to fall apart in the presence of the granite-like attitude of the Russians as dictated by Stalin.

"The decisions of the Three Powers at Yalta to persist in their demand for 'Unconditional Surrender' made it certain that the war against Germany would not end until the Western and Eastern armies met in the heart of Europe," Chester Wilmot has stated. They also brought about the impasse in which we find ourselves today. At Yalta it was agreed, Churchill recorded, that "Berlin, Prague and Vienna could be taken by whoever got there first." That the Russians got there first through tactics that were countenanced by the Americans and the British will be a never-ending source of wonder and controversy.

"The whole relationship of Russia with the Western Allies was in flux," Churchill wrote about the situation as it developed during the closing stages of the war. "Every question about the future was unsettled between us. The agreements and understandings of Yalta, such as they were, had already been broken and brushed aside by the triumphant Kremlin. New perils, perhaps as terrible as those we had surmounted, loomed and glared upon the torn and harassed world."

How right Winston Churchill was to feel as he did about the future I was to learn to my cost not long afterward; but at that time I was far more concerned with the practical problems with which I was faced in my work with my active command. Admiral Doenitz had promised Hitler only a few weeks before the Yalta meeting was held that the new U-boats, of an advanced design and performance, would bring about a "revolution at sea." That was to remain nothing more than a promise.

If there is one thing that must be said for the German U-boat service during those last weeks of the war it is that they fought it out right to the bitter end. Throughout that time Coastal and Bomber and Fighter commands were called upon to give almost constant attention to the route followed by the U-boats as they made their way out of the Baltic through the Kattegat and the Skagerrack. "It was a continuous onslaught on the U-boats which the Germans were starting to move in large numbers to Norway," Peyton-Ward has stated in his appreciation of the situation at that time.

That air onslaught on German shipping and U-boats extending

over the whole area of the sea between the Skagerrack and the western Baltic was conducted by Coastal aircraft joined by aircraft from our Second Tactical Air Force, which was based on the Continent. In the "general exodus," as the official historians call it, of the U-boats from Germany to Norway, the Banff wing, under Max Aitken, had particularly good innings, and on April 9 alone their Mosquitos sank with rocket fire three enemy submarines. From then on there was a heavy toll of U-boat killings, with the Beaufighters of two of my squadrons from their base in Norfolk sinking five of them in two days.

The fighting that had developed by then between aircraft and submarines in the final stages of the war came to resemble all too often what had happened out in the Bay of Biscay during 1943. So far as the Royal Navy was concerned, they were, for obvious reasons, even more eager to get at the U-boats. "We British are notoriously slow to give vent to the passion of hatred," S. W. Roskill has stated; "but there is no doubt that the ruthlessness and cunning of the U-boats ultimately aroused feelings of intense loathing in the minds of our seamen."

The outcome of the war at sea in the Atlantic and in the seas around the United Kingdom "was mainly a struggle between the U-boats and the British Navy and Air Force," Captain Roskill has recorded; "and those two services actually shared as equally in the successes achieved as they had shared the burden of the long struggle."

With the war in Europe apparently at an end, and the Germans surrendering in droves, there was a sense of relief. In certain quarters it was even of jubilation. That was understandable enough, but I was not quite prepared to accept it as fully as that. A long time afterward Max Aitken commented on that in talking with Bob Wright about those last hours of the war. He produced from his logbook a copy of a signal that I had sent from Coastal Command headquarters to all groups and stations. It was dated May 5, the day after Montgomery had reported to Supreme Headquarters that the unconditional surrender of the Germans was to become effective at eight o'clock that morning. Marked immediate and personal from the A.O.C.-in-C., it read:

In spite of surrender of German forces on the Continent there is as yet no indication that they contemplate surrender in Norway. We may, therefore, expect the continuance of intense U-boat operations from Norwegian bases. All ranks must realize that for Coastal Command the war goes on as before. We started first we finish last. I call upon all squadrons for a great final effort against our old enemy. It falls to Coastal Command to strike the final blow against the enemy's one remaining weapon.

One of those who took particularly to heart my comment about starting first and finishing last and striking a final blow was Max Aitken himself. Having flown on the very first day of the war, he saw to it that he also flew on the last day. The instrument of surrender was signed by the Germans in the small hours of the morning of May 7, with all operations to cease by midnight of the next day, May 8, which became known as VE Day. On that day the German forces surrendered in the Dodecanese, in the Aegean; and from Banff, in Scotland, flying in a Mosquito, Max Aitken flew a last patrol out across the North Sea as far as Aalborg, in northern Denmark.

In the final analysis made after the war we learned that the Germans had built 1,162 U-boats, of which 785 were lost through various causes. The Royal Air Force, by which I mean Coastal Command, is credited by the historians with having accounted unaided during the course of the war for 245 of these, and with a share in the sinking of a further 50; and with sinking nearly 350 enemy ships. "For this a high price was paid," H. St. G. Saunders has commented. We lost 5,866 pilots and other members of air crews in Coastal Command, and 1,777 aircraft either did not return to their bases, or crashed on landing back at them.

That gentle little man, Hilary St. G. Saunders, was quite well known to me, and just as Sir Walter Raleigh and H. A. Jones between them had memorable things to say about the Air Force in the First World War, so Saunders, with Denis Richards, has told with warmth our story in the second war. In speaking of Coastal Command's activities during the war, Saunders has said: "Figures, save to the impassioned mathematician, are cold symbols, but when they are used to express in concentrated form the gallantry, fortitude and steadfastness displayed by men in the prime of life, who, unhesitating and unflinching, gave the last service of all, they ring out like the crash of cymbals. An island people who, for more than a thousand years, have known the sea and grown great by reason of that acquaintance, must for ever mourn, though it cannot begrudge, so great a sacrifice."

With the war in Europe at an end, and my own time with Coastal Command coming to a close, I had come to feel, rather unexpectedly, that there had been more than mere interest in my work of the past seventeen months. I had been fully aware of the importance of the Command at the time when I had taken it over from Jack Slessor, but during my time with the Coastal boys I had come to know an unexpected contentment, if I may use that word, for that was what the satisfaction in doing the work induced in me. I came to feel quite strongly that, for all the pride that I had had in my other commands, it was a signal honor for me to have had the command which had lived up so well to the spirit of "Constant Endeavor."

On the day after VE Day I received from Peter Portal, the Chief of the Air Staff, a personal letter which, because of our long association, I have always valued very highly. He showed a touching understanding of my position, and it was written in his own hand. In it he stated:

This is just a personal note, written in haste and quite inadequate, to try to express to you a little of the deep gratitude which I feel towards you for your tremendous personal contribution to the achievement of the Service in the war. From my point of view no one in the whole of the R.A.F. has given in fuller measure, personally or officially, the support and loyal co-operation without which I could not have carried on. I am very conscious of the fact that your great talents might have been used more fully, but it is rarely possible to arrange all things for the best. As it is, you have done magnificently every job entrusted to you, and I do most sincerely thank you.

About three weeks later Archie Sinclair gave up the office of Secretary of State for Air, an office which he had filled with vigor and great ability and success for five wearing years. I wrote to him at the time, and he replied:

Many charming letters softened the blow of my departure from the Air Ministry but none which I shall treasure more than the one which you sent me. You were my first friend at the Air Ministry—I had met you with Oliver and Maureen [Stanley]—the only officer on the Air Staff I knew—apart from an acquaintance with Newall. You helped me enormously in those early days—in particular, when we had to take risks in order to speed up the production of pilots. I felt as though I had won a battle when I got Fighter Command into your hands—and, looking back, how right I was! Cairo was a sad mis-carriage; but Northwood, which I thought was a pis-aller, you made into a triumph to which history will do justice in spite of the Admiralty. Now, good luck to you in Berlin. Never have I had better friends and comrades to work with than I found in the Air Ministry and the R.A.F. and I shall always be deeply grateful for your help, counsel and friendship.

36 / Realignments

THOSE FEW DAYS at the end of April and the beginning of May, 1945, provided a sudden rush of momentous events, and there was brought to a finish the Second World War so far as Europe was concerned. There was still the massive war in the Pacific to be dealt with, and that had to be borne firmly in mind; but it was hard to comprehend that so much could have happened so quickly. The ending of the war in Europe was something in the nature of a blind, mad rush. Within forty-eight hours, as if to mark the end in its own weird way, there came the butchering of Benito Mussolini in northern Italy, and the suicide of Adolf Hitler in a hole in the ground in Berlin. That the deaths of the two dictators should have happened within hours of each other was additionally telling in the impact on one's mind because neither of these violent deaths was in any way related, other than in marking the macabre ends of two tyrants.

At the back of my mind there was the personal hope that there would be some relief for me from the heavy pressure that I had been under throughout the war. But it was not to end there, and even before the end I began to hear rumors that I was to be appointed to yet another command. Moreover, it was to be to one that I was not at all keen about accepting. But just as the course that I had followed after the First World War had led to an unexpected career in the Royal Air Force, so the course that I was to follow immediately after the end of the second war was to lead to an ending of that career which was at least unique.

When it came to making decisions about the officials who were to govern the different zones into which conquered Germany had been split, it was natural that the selection should be made of those military commanders who had led the successful armies. In the British Zone, Field-Marshal Montgomery became Commander-in-Chief and Military Governor; General Eisenhower filled a similar office in the American Zone; Marshal Zhukov, a redoubtable warrior, and the captor of Berlin, was in control of the Russian

673

Zone; and the French Zone was under General de Lattre de Tassigny.

"I have always considered this to have been a major error on the part of the Western Allies," Montgomery has stated. "The whole of eastern Germany was one zone controlled by one man [Zhukov]; we split western Germany into three separate zones, each controlled by a separate Military Governor. I hold the view that Eisenhower should have been left in overall control of the western half of Germany; we would then have confronted the Russians with a united front. We were to pay the penalty for this nationalistic self-importance."

With complete control of the British Zone of Germany through the Army, the Navy and the Air Force on the military side and the newly-created Control Commission on the civil side, Montgomery was faced with formidable problems, for Germany was in a state of devastation. Our Army became known as the British Army of the Rhine, and the Air Force as the British Air Forces of Occupation; and for the latter an officer of the most senior rank was needed to take command.

This new Air Force command, which was formed out in Germany from the Second Tactical Air Force, had been in existence, under the vigorous command of Mary Coningham, since the landings in Normandy over a year before. But there had developed a distinct strain during those last months of the war in the relationship between Mary Coningham and Montgomery. It was generally known that I had always worked well with Montgomery, and being of senior rank it was decided by Archie Sinclair and Peter Portal that I should become the Air Commander-in-Chief of the British Air Forces of Occupation.

It was a great pity that Montgomery and Coningham were not seeing eye to eye, particularly after the fine way in which they had worked together in North Africa. I imagined that it was yet another case of a clash of personalities after each had achieved distinct success and fame. Montgomery refers to the difficulties in his *Memoirs* as being due to the chain of command; but I feel that there was something more personal in it than that, for both Montgomery and Coningham were noted for the forcefulness of their temperaments. Montgomery had done so well, and he and his Twenty-first Army Group were getting a great deal of the limelight; and it is possible that, rather like Bert Harris and Bomber Command, Mary Coningham had come to feel that his Second Tactical Air Force, which had provided such good air support for Montgomery, was not getting a fair share of the credit.

When Peter Portal discussed the position with me, and we decided that my title should be that of Air Commander-in-Chief, we also decided that my command should be known as the British Air Forces of Occupation—known more familiarly in the years that lay ahead as B.A.F.O.—in place of the battle-scarred Second Tactical Air Force. There had been some talk that the job might be offered to Bert Harris, the Commander-in-Chief of Bomber Command. That was apparently before my name came to be considered, and whoever thought of such an idea must have been completely lacking in an understanding of personalities. To have placed Harris and Montgomery together in such a structure would have been courting disaster. And after all that Bomber Command had done to Germany, it was scarcely the place for Harris to relax in any way from what would have to be a constant vigilance.

After all that had happened in the two world wars in which I had participated, I felt less like going to Germany than to anywhere else. There was also in my mind a feeling of regret that was perhaps only natural, since I was a professional airman, about the fate of the German Air Force. That it had been thoroughly defeated in the air was fair enough; but the Luftwaffe had been so badly smashed from within. The man who was responsible for that defeat from the inside was Hermann Goering, and the way in which he had treated his own Air Force, of which, in the earlier war, he had been a proud member, was a thoroughly wretched story.

In the early days of the war, Tooey Spaatz had made the comment: "Long before America entered the war the soldiers everywhere were agreed . . . it was the German Air Force which dominated world diplomacy and won for Hitler the bloodless political victories of the late thirties." By the last days of the war, during April and May, 1945, the German Air Force had ceased to exist as an effective service. The Anglo-American-Russian air forces were too great and too powerful for it. But even then it can never be said of it that the Luftwaffe was reduced to a state of collapse in its morale. The great problem which it had to face was that it simply ran out of the lifeblood necessary to keep it in action: there were no supplies of the fuel and oil to keep the many aircraft that the Germans still had—including the first of the jet fighters—in the air. It had been starved of enough new types of aircraft during the war through Hitler's misguided decisions; but in the end the German Air Force died through lack of the essential nourishment that would keep its engines running.

Hitler was dead, Goebbels was dead, Himmler was dead, all by suicide, and Germany had surrendered unconditionally, but whether Hermann Goering, the drug addict, knew that he was now no more than a museum piece must forever remain unknown. He established contact with the advancing Americans—his entourage caught in a traffic jam near Salzburg—on May 8, a week after Hitler's death; and what happened after that, in the reports that were broadcast to the world, left me, as it did many other people, with feelings of astonishment, and which apparently caused in Eisenhower reactions of a most understandable distate.

It was reported that immediately after his capture Hermann Goering was seen in the company of the cheerful American officers to whom he had surrendered with a champagne glass in hand, laughing and joking with them, and that he was photographed standing with them beside the flag of the division of the American Army to which his captors belonged. There was a public outcry against such treatment of this man whose name was so notorious.

But Eisenhower was standing for no nonsense, and he was even quicker in his reaction. He refused to see Goering, and he gave orders that such ridiculous behavior as that indulged in by some of his officers was to cease immediately, and that Goering was to be treated as nothing more than just another prisoner-of-war. My own reaction to what had happened was to wonder at the difference there was between the defiant fighter pilot that Goering had been in 1918 and the debased sycophant that he had apparently become by 1945.

After handing over Coastal Command to Air Marshal Sir Leonard Slatter at the end of June—he had done well as my group commander working in Liverpool with Max Horton—I spent ten days on leave in Cornwall; and on July 14, just over two months after the war in Europe had come to an end, I flew out to Germany to take command of the British Air Forces of Occupation.

As was only to be expected after the long years that we had spent working together in the Service, Mary Coningham made the handing over to me of what had been his Second Tactical Air Force an easy and understanding task. Coningham was always an attractive character, and a gallant one as well, and his disappearance on a flight over the Atlantic two and a half years later was yet another serious loss to the R.A.F. in officers of senior rank and great experience.

The headquarters of the British Air Forces of Occupation were in the hotel of the spa at Bad Eilsen, which was located in an attractive part of the hills just to the east of Minden, and not far from Hanover. Some of the members of the staff were men whom I had known for many years, and in whom I knew that I could place my full trust. That applied particularly to Charles Steele, who was to be my senior air staff officer. He was then an air vice-marshal, and he is now retired as Air Marshal Sir Charles Steele. Another was my air officer-in-charge of administration, Air Vice-Marshal F. L. Hopps, who had been one of my group commanders in Coastal Command.

After having had to get out of France in a hurry in 1940—he had made his escape in a coal boat from La Rochelle—Charles Steele had spent a couple of years in Rhodesia working on our training scheme which was in operation there. On his return to England he came to me in Fighter Command. He was Air Officer Commanding No. 10 Group, down in the West Country, and after that he became A.O.C. of No. 85 Group in the Second Tactical Air Force and as such he took part in the advance across Europe.

With the surrender of Germany, Charles Steele was posted to take command of the R.A.F. in Berlin; but even before he could take up that appointment he was to have a strange and unpleasant personal experience in another of the weirder aspects of the collapse of Germany. After all the years that I had known him I had come to understand that Steele was, by nature, a man of a pronounced sincerity, and of a decidedly retiring disposition. I knew his worth as a pilot from our having flown together during and after the first war, and out in the Sudan, and also as a capable staff officer; but I knew that he detested fuss and demonstrations, and that he much preferred to be left to work steadily in the background rather than to have to be any sort of showpiece commander.

Early in May, Arthur Tedder had sent Charles Steele, as the British representative of an Anglo-American team headed by Major General Robert W. Harper, of the United States Army Air Forces, to Berchtesgaden and Salzburg to try and find what was left of the German Air Ministry, which, it was reported, had been moved from Berlin down to a retreat somewhere in the mountains to the south. Only a few days before that there had been enacted in Berlin the closing scenes of Hitler's tumultuous life. At a final meeting in the bunker he had given what was to be one of his last orders. He had instructed Field-Marshal Ritter von Greim to get out of Berlin and to take command of the Luftwaffe in place of the discredited Hermann Goering.

Ritter von Greim had been a distinguished fighter pilot in the

First World War who had risen to high rank in the German Air Force, and his son had been shot down and taken prisoner while flying with the Luftwaffe in Tunisia. Severely wounded in the leg, Von Greim had made his way out of the bunker in which Hitler and Goebbels and their families and staffs were hiding. In an exploit that can only be described as fantastic he was flown out of Berlin at night, taking off in a light airplane from one of the main thoroughfares in the center of the city, and under heavy Russian gunfire. The flying was done by Hanna Reitsch, a remarkable woman who was an exceptionally good pilot.

But Von Greim was too ill to be able to carry out effectively any orders, and in any case it was all too late. He was firm in his loyalty to Hitler, and strongly opposed to the way in which Goering had been conducting himself; but Germany had surrendered, and Von Greim was admitted to a civilian hospital near Salzburg. Steele and Harper and their special unit found remnants of the German Air Ministry, and they also captured Von Greim, who was then taken to another hospital in Salzburg, all this happening at about the same time that, not far away, Goering was gladly surrendering to the Americans.

Arrangements were made for one of our aircraft to fly to Salzburg to pick up Von Greim and to take him to England, and the Anglo-American party took him to the airfield. But the aircraft did not arrive as expected, and in the evening they returned Von Greim to the hospital. The next morning he was called and told to get ready for the flight to England.

"He asked to be left alone while he dressed," Steele has recalled. "It was then that he swallowed poison."

And so died, by his own hand, and in the fashion typical of them, yet another of Germany's war leaders, and the last Commander-in-Chief of its wartime Luftwaffe. But Steele and Harper did not return empty handed. "Von Greim's second-in-command was very helpful and communicative," Steele has said. "He wrote up a tremendously long report for us which we were able to forward to S.H.A.E.F."

It was having Charles Steele with me in Germany that eased the burden of being out there. Steele and Hopps lived in the same house with me and my personal staff. I had selected Roy Faville to go out to Germany with me as my personal staff officer. After serving on my staff at Coastal Command for some time, he had attended the Staff College course; he was a regular officer in the Royal Air Force—which he had joined when he came to England from New Zealand in the early thirties after taking his degree in engineering at a university in his home country—and I felt that I could rely on an experienced and full-trained officer to watch over the affairs of my office. Ronnie Edwards also went out to Germany with us, but it was more in the capacity of handing over—or back—to Bob Wright as my personal assistant. Edwards had been with me from the time when he took over from Wright at Fighter Command, and he had given me invaluable service; but with the ending of the war in Europe he felt that he had to get back to his civilian life in the City.

When Bob Wright rejoined my staff he was not exactly a sadder man, but he was definitely a wiser one, and what had happened to give him that added wisdom was, as he put it, "an experience in itself to be avoided if possible but to be made the most of if it did happen." For all the orders that I had given him in Cairo about staying behind a desk at a staff job, he had gone to work on Keith Park—for whom he was acting as personal assistant—the moment I left Cairo to return to England. In some way known only to himself he had had his medical category reversed. Keith Park then arranged for him to return to England for a second tour of flying in night fighters. At first I felt a little cross when I heard about that; but I could not help being more sympathetic when he told me that he had arranged to join No. 85 Squadron, in Fighter Command. Under the command of John Cunningham, most of his friends from No. 604 Squadron had found their way to No. 85 for their second tour of flying; but to me and to Wright it also meant that he was joining the squadron of the "War Birds" of the First World War.

After chasing flying bombs for a while, No. 85 Squadron had been transferred to Bomber Command for work as long-range night fighter escort for our bombers on their raids over Germany. The next thing that I heard was that, halfway through his second tour of flying, Wright was in hospital, burned as the result of a bad crash. After several months spent there being patched up he was due to come and stay with me at our house in Northwood; but he arrived rather sooner than any of us expected. Only twelve hours after starting his sick leave, a V.2 had landed fifty yards away from his parents' home in Kent, and Wright had been carted off to the local hospital. I sent my car to pick him up, and had him brought to Northwood. He was a sorry enough sight, but I could not resist reminding him that, while he had my deepest sympathy, he really had stuck his neck out and asked for trouble. By the time that I was ready to go out to Germany, Wright was quite fit again, even if, in appearance, he was a little the worse for wear.

In addition to maintaining the effective tactical air force that was under my command in the British Zone of Germany, I also had under my control a large and separate Air Force contingent, under the command of Air Marshal Sir Philip Wigglesworth, whose work was to disband and in fact demolish the German Air Force. On the one hand I had to see to it that the R.A.F. was in full operational shape, and on the other I had to make sure that the Luftwaffe ceased to exist; and for these such violently opposed tasks I was responsible to Field-Marshal Montgomery, our Military Governor.

Toward the end of June there had been signed in San Francisco, in an atmosphere of such high hope, the Charter for what was to become the organization known as the United Nations. Three weeks later, and three days after I had arrived in Germany, the last of the great conferences was held, when the heads of the governments of the victorious Allies met to discuss the future. This was the conference at which Truman, the new President of the United States, Stalin, and Winston Churchill sat down around a table at Potsdam, a few miles to the southwest of Berlin. It was a continuation of the struggle that had started at Teheran, and had been going on ever since then to try and find some way of reconciling their differences. That those differences were irreconcilable was a thought that was by that time lurking in the backs of the minds of many of those involved; but there was at least a sincere effort on the part of the Western Powers to come to terms with the Russians, who were completely dominated by Stalin.

It is almost an historical curiosity now that at the end of the Second World War in Europe, at the time of the Potsdam Conference in July, 1945, it was we, the British, guided by Winston Churchill's apprehension about Stalin's motives, who were sounding the warnings about what the Communists were planning. The Americans were merely continuing the policy laid down by Roosevelt, which was to believe that they, for all Churchill's misgivings, could work out with the Russians solutions to all the problems facing us. It was not so very long before the roles came to be reversed, and it was then we who were saying that some way must be found to get along with the Russians, until finally we were watching with the gravest apprehension the antagonism that had developed between America and Russia, an antagonism which grew to such bewildering proportions.

For the concluding volume of his massive history of the Second World War, Winston Churchill chose the title *Triumph and Tragedy*. In doing that he was not referring to his own personal position, when, as a result of our general election in the middle of the Potsdam Conference, he found himself deposed as Prime Minister and replaced by Clement Attlee, with the Labour Party in office. To the surprise of the Russians they found that a change in government could be effected through the will of the people and without civil strife and bloodshed; and that, moreover, the foreign policy of our country could continue, for all the change in the nature of the government, along much the same lines as before. But our change in government did not in any way alter the course which Stalin was so determined to follow. He looked upon his attendance at the Potsdam Conference as that of one of the supreme architects for the future, but so far as he was concerned the reconstruction was to go all his way.

The change that came about in our government at the end of the war in Europe brought to the attention of the world a group of British politicians which was composed of some already well known, and quite a few who were almost entirely unknown. As a serving officer I was precluded from making known publicly my own political beliefs; but it was known to my friends and closer associates that the change was to my liking, although, through some oversight or other, I had not been able to register my vote in the general election.

But my interest in seeing what the Labour Party would be able to do did not mean that I had ever harbored any doubts about the way in which the wartime coalition government had conducted our affairs. During the second war we were almost entirely free, for all the clashes of temperament and opinions that occurred, from the constant and sickening intrigues that went on among the politicians and the senior commanders in the First World War. Most of the credit for seeing to it that such disruptive influences were avoided must go to Winston Churchill. He knew better, from his own wealth of past experience, than to let squabbling cause things to get out of control. He could be provocative, and he was an astute and worldly politician, and he knew well all the tricks of his trade; but one always felt, with good reason, that in one's dealings with him one could expect complete honesty, and that he had at heart only the good of the country and the winning of the war.

My first visit to Berlin came a couple of days before the start of the Potsdam Conference, and during that visit I was taken on a tour of the city. I had only just arrived out in Germany for the first time, and my headquarters at Bad Eilsen and the house that was provided for me out in the country a few miles away from the spa had been quite untouched by the war. They were in attractive, hilly, well-wooded country; and they were in the greatest possible contrast with the sights that I saw in Berlin. The vast scale of the destruction there horrified me, as it did everybody else. What with our bombing—by the R.A.F. and the United States Army Air Forces—and the street fighting in the Russian capture of the German capital, the city was in a state of devastation that one had to see in order to understand.

The destruction in Berlin was far worse than anything that I had ever seen before, and even the inspired provision of accommodation for me in an undamaged house in a street bearing the name of Douglasstrasse—it was the actual name of the street—did little to lift the depression that I could not help feeling over what I saw amidst the ruins of what had once been one of the world's great cities. The task of rehabilitating a people who had been reduced to such a low level was obviously going to be a formidable one. I did not envy Montgomery what he was having to face, and I was thankful that my responsibilities were confined to those of being the Air Force commander.

While the Potsdam Conference was still in progress, and after I got back from Berlin, I went to see Montgomery for the first time at the Schloss that he used as his headquarters at Ostenvalde, in the British Zone. It was in a quiet, secluded spot some miles to the west of Minden. We talked about what was going on in Berlin, and in his memoirs Monty later referred to the way in which Clement Attlee and Ernest Bevin went about their work when they took over from Winston Churchill and Anthony Eden, saying: "These two grasped the problems with both hands and created a very good impression on everyone."

During lunch that day Monty spoke feelingly about the manner in which Ernie Bevin had been handling Molotov, his opposite number, who was notorious for being the most troublesome of all the Russians. At one particular session, Monty told us, when it was the British turn to be in the chair, Molotov was disagreeing, as usual, about everything. Being the hardheaded realist that he was, Bevin saw that there was not much point in getting into any senseless arguments.

"So, Mr. Molotov, you disagree," he said as soon as an argument showed signs of looming up. "Very well . . . we'll move on to the next question."

And so the meeting went on, and instead of interminable arguments with nothing accomplished there was, still with nothing being accomplished, no argument. That seemed to give the Russians a severe shaking, for at the very next meeting they apparently permitted a much saner atmosphere for discussion and negotiation.

During the years since the end of the war there have been some curious expressions of views—some of which are of value, and some that can only be called downright stupid—about the value and the nature of the man whom we all know as Monty. A great deal of criticism has been leveled at him, and he has himself hurled not a little at other people. But for all the fire and brimstone, and for all my disagreement with the way in which he has come to express some of his views in more recent years, I have always greatly liked and admired him. Monty is essentially courageous and straightforward: characteristics which are not, apparently, to everybody's liking. What is important about him, which should never be forgotten, is that as an Army commander he had the unmistakable touch of genius. Some of the battles that he fought will come in time to be regarded as classics in military history. He had always made an intense study of his profession, and he was very well read in military history, and as a result of all that he had a deep understanding of strategy and tactics. Out of all the many contacts that I had with him, I always appreciated that Montgomery was a thoroughgoing professional.

From time to time ever since the end of the Second World War there have also been expressions of opinions and, on occasions, outbursts from various military leaders on both sides of the Atlantic. While righteously bemoaning this, and even openly denying Service chiefs their own right to speak as they see fit, many critics have inevitably endeavored in their own fashion to stoke up the fires of controversy and to keep boiling the hot pot of dispute. A great deal of so-called interpretation has been printed about quite simple and valid remarks; but in all the arguments that have raged there is one important aspect of the High Command at the end of the war in Europe that appears to have been largely overlooked.

At the root of nearly all the misunderstandings that have arisen through the expressions of their views by the British and the American commanders, and the reason why some pretty harsh things are still being said on both sides of the Atlantic, there lies the difference of the way in which the British and the Americans handled and implemented at the end of the war what is known as

grand strategy. In so many ways it was the story of what happened
out in the Mediterranean at the end of 1943, and the misunderstandings, all over again, were rooted in the same problems.

In the case of the British, we had, through long experience,
evolved a system whereby all our Service commanders were under
the very firm control of the Chiefs of Staff and the Minister of
Defence, who was the Prime Minister, Winston Churchill. But
while the Americans also had their own Chiefs of Staff Committee,
with their President as the Commander-in-Chief of their armed
forces, they did not exercise such a strict control over their own
commanders in matters of grand strategy. There was the Combined Chiefs of Staff, made up, as the name implies, of the chiefs
of the Services of both countries; but the American system permitted the Supreme Commanders more freedom to get on with the
actual fighting of the war, even if it meant shooting first and asking
questions afterward.

This freedom led, as the battle on the Western Front was waged
in the winter of 1944–45, to what John Ehrman has called "the
apparent disappearance of a master plan," and British opinion,
and Montgomery's in particular, became disturbed over the apparent American reliance upon the Supreme Commander, Eisenhower, to run the show with the object of winning the battles and
leaving the political considerations to be dealt with later. To
British minds this failed in the control that should be exercised
over military operations so that they should conform with what
was seen in terms of grand strategy and long-term plannning.
When there was added to that the strong opposition that was felt
by our people, and by Montgomery in particular, to the way in
which Eisenhower conducted, with the freedom which he enjoyed
as the Supreme Commander, his planning during the last stages of
the war, there was bound to be a sowing of the seeds of discontent.

Since the war Montgomery has stated quite clearly his views
about what he considered were the mistakes that were made in the
campaigns in the west during the last year of the war. Quite
recently he referred to what he described as "a simple lesson" that
should be borne in mind by all Service chiefs, which is that "the
higher direction of war must remain in political hands." I have
always believed that Monty was right and that Eisenhower was
wrong in the views that they held on the way in which the final
campaigns should have been waged; but Eisenhower was the
Supreme Commander, and he had what appeared at the time, and
to many people, good reasons for his planning. Not all the
Americans have agreed with him, but he did what he thought was

right, and Montgomery, right or wrong, had to accept that.

When these matters of disagreement over military affairs were referred to Winston Churchill there were intense efforts on his part to arrive at well-thought-out conclusions. In the case of President Roosevelt, however, he was more inclined to leave strictly military affairs to those directly concerned. "He seemed to most of his associates to be a haphazard administrator," John Ehrman has commented, "although his methods may in fact have formed a skilful adaptation of his personality to the complex political world which he understood so well. In military affairs, he was well content to leave detail—and detail was all-important—to the professionals. Compared with Churchill, therefore, he kept a loose hand on the reins."

For that reason it has always seemed to me that Montgomery, with his knowledge and background, was compelled to keep his sights fixed on objectives that were of much more importance, in the long-term view, than those aimed at by Eisenhower. Montgomery was compelled to think more in terms of, and to reach a greater understanding of, the meaning of grand strategy. It was the system of control which led to one leader enjoying a more far-seeing appreciation of the situation than the other; and it was this "loose hand on the reins" which has since caused the exchanges of views to become rather too personal, and to be unnecessarily reduced, by some commentators, to the level of what would appear to be a lot of bickering.

A short time ago, Robert Murphy, the distinguished American diplomat who was Eisenhower's political adviser during the time when we were all out in Germany together, made a statement that reveals this unhappy lack of control on the part of the Americans. In his book *Diplomat Among Warriors*—which is an apt title for what Murphy was to experience in the Mediterranean, in Europe and in Japan—he comments:

Despite Eisenhower's conviction that military commanders should not usurp civilian functions, he and his staff were required during the final months of the war to make a number of political decisions which have had lasting international consequences. These decisions were imposed upon the Supreme Commander because the civilians responsible for American foreign policy—the President and the Secretary of State— did not choose to assert their authority. The most important example was the decision not to try to capture Berlin, a decision of such international significance that no Army chief should have been required to make it. When the time came to decide about Berlin, the entire responsibility was placed upon General Marshall, as Chief of Staff, and

General Eisenhower, as Theatre Commander. Both of these Army officers accepted this responsibility without complaint, then or afterwards, but it was inevitable that they would regard Berlin from the military point of view.

The repercussions from that so far as Montgomery was concerned were understandable. He was irked, and he has gone on feeling that way, and while he is possibly given to expressing himself in too vivid a manner about politics—his knowledge and understanding of which are not nearly as good as his appreciation of military affairs—no one can deny that he has not opened the door and let in a splendid blast of fresh air. Perhaps his outlook, in an intellectual sense, is inclined to be rather narrow: I doubt, for instance, if he ever, from choice, reads a novel or listens to any music. He also has a sense of humor that is inclined to be a little too waspish. But the overall effect is that Monty has always had, for me, an indefinable and humane sort of charm that is all his own. No matter what may be thought or said about him, our country can be very thankful that we had him, and grateful to him for all that he achieved as a fighting commander of men.

In his *Memoirs,* Montgomery dealt in some detail with the period of the first year after the war during which he was Military Governor of the British Zone of Germany. My immediate concern during most of that time was my responsibility to him as the Air Commander-in-Chief. But there was one aspect of the Allied occupation of Germany which became effective with the surrender of the enemy which perplexed me; and even after examining, since that time, the way in which it had evolved, I still find it difficult to understand how we, the Allies, could have permitted it to come about.

The effects at the time of the plans that were made were curious enough, to say the least; but they are felt to this day, and so far as one can see they will go on being felt. It all had to do with the way in which we were to control Germany after the war, and I could not help feeling that Monty was right when he criticized, at the outset, the way in which we went about dividing up the country. And the particular aspect of that which was most perplexing was the vital matter of our access to Berlin from the west.

Even before the ending of the war in Europe there had come into operation the plans that had been agreed upon by the Allies at the Yalta Conference in February, 1945. There was to be a combined military and civil control of Germany, with the country being divided for the purposes of that control into four zones: British, American, French and Russian. Berlin itself was to be deep in what became the Russian Zone, and one of the features of the boundaries that had been established which puzzled me even at the time, and which has since been such a source of trouble, was that there was no provision for any clearly defined international land corridor from the west into the German capital.

With Berlin isolated deep in the heart of the Russian Zone, the boundary between the part of Germany which Russia was to control and those parts of the country which were to be under British and American and French control were well over one hundred miles to the west of it. Berlin itself was to be under the joint control of the four powers, with, again, definite divisions into sectors. But it was isolated, and the Western Powers could only get to it by land with the permission of the Russians to travel through the territory which was under their control. There was provision for freedom of travel by air along certain restricted corridors, and it all worked simply enough at first; but later, when the bickering started, there was to develop a great deal of friction.

It has since been said that the arrangement between the Allies for access to Berlin from the west was as bad, from the Western point of view, as it could have been, and many times it has been asked how such an arrangement—or a lack of one—could have come about. It has been thought of as a mystery, but why it should be regarded as a mystery I cannot quite understand. There is documentary proof enough of how there came to be allowed to develop such an unhappy and, at times, near catastrophic state of affairs.

In addition to the examination made by Montgomery in his *Memoirs,* the whole matter is dealt with at some length by General Lucius D. Clay in his book *Decision in Germany.* He was deeply concerned for a long period of time with affairs in Germany, first as Eisenhower's deputy in the American Zone of Occupation, and later when he himself became the American Military Governor of that zone. Robert Murphy has also dealt, from the American viewpoint, with this thorn which grew out of the deliberations of a body known as the European Advisory Commission, which sat in London during 1944 working out the details of the agreement which was announced at Yalta about the administration of Germany after that country had finally been defeated. The British delegate on the European Advisory Commission was Sir William (later Lord) Strang, and the United States of America was represented by their Ambassador to this country, John Winant. There was also, of course, a Russian delegate. Murphy is very critical of the lack of decision on the part of his own people during those deliberations, mainly, it would appear, "because President Roosevelt had not made known his own view, and three departments of the government were wrangling among themselves about post-war Germany."

In November, 1944, the European Advisory Commission finally managed to reach some sort of agreements, and of the papers relating to the discussions Lucius Clay commented: "It is interesting to note that all of these documents accepted a common occupation of Berlin and yet no one of them contained any guarantee of access or specific provision for truck, rail and air right of way. This omission was not accidental and had been discussed with our representative on the European Advisory Commission by Mr. Murphy. Ambassador Winant believed that the right to be in Berlin carried with it right of access and that it would only confuse the issue to raise it in connection with the agreement. He felt strongly that it would arouse Soviet suspicion and make mutual understanding more difficult to attain. He believed it possible to develop a mutual friendly understanding in which differences would disappear."

It is perhaps scarcely to be wondered at that the American Ambassador should feel as he did. Quite apart from the essential honesty and integrity of the man, John Winant was following the lead set by President Roosevelt. That lead has been described by Robert Murphy in his account of a talk that he had with Roosevelt in September, 1944, just before he took up his post as Eisenhower's political adviser on German affairs. "He was confident that a permanent Soviet-American understanding could be reached," Murphy stated. "He urged me to bear in mind that our primary post-war objective was Soviet-American co-operation—without which world peace would be impossible—and that Germany would be the proving ground for such co-operation."

When in the autumn of 1944 Robert Murphy came to study the agreements reached by the European Advisory Commission, he "observed that Berlin was more than a hundred miles inside the Russian Zone and no provision had been made for the Anglo-American powers to reach the city." He commented on that to one of his associates in the American State Department, who replied that he had "had a head-on clash" with Winant, and had been accused "of not having any faith in Soviet intentions."

John Winant was an old acquaintance of mine, and he had made on me, as he did on everybody else, a singularly strong impression as a man of great strength of character. Strang described him as "a self-tortured soul, noble and passionate, inarticulate, deceptively simple, the pattern of honour"; and in a letter which Richard Casey wrote to me long afterward he spoke of Winant, saying: "I was very fond of him . . . a man without the gift of speech."

There is a great deal of revealing information to be gained from Lord Strang's book on the vital matter of these communications with Berlin, and in it he revealed that "it was not our expectation that the zones would be sealed from one another. (This was a Soviet conception which only became apparent in the late summer of 1945, when the occupation was an accomplished fact.)" To that Strang added: "It is fair to say that this was not the fault of Winant and of his civilian advisers," and he records that "in May, 1944, Winant advocated in Washington the preparation of detailed provisions safeguarding access to Berlin by road, rail and air." Winant pursued that idea, Strang recorded, with further recommendations in May and June, 1945; but he stated, "the duty of reaching allied agreement which would provide for adequate access to Berlin was, by decision of the American military staff, left for direct negotiation among the allied military commanders in Berlin."

On the other hand, Robert Murphy has stated that "Winant never consulted the State Department on the subject of access to Berlin," and he wrote with feeling about "Winant's grave responsibility for the personal diplomacy which he exercised in the Advisory Commission negotiations."

Attention was also called by Lord Strang to Lucius Clay's own published record of what happened in his negotiations when he became one of the "military commanders" involved. "He did not want an agreement in writing which established anything less than the right of unrestricted access," Strang pointed out, "and hoped that as a good understanding developed among the four powers, many problems would be solved."

From a consideration of what Lord Strang and Lucius Clay and Robert Murphy have said in their books alone there emerges a very good reason why no formal agreement was reached that would have been more helpful to us, and why, as Murphy put it, "the matter of a defined right of access to Berlin was left hanging —and is still hanging today." There is no mystery about it. The Western representatives were handicapped by two things: first, through the simple fact that they were men of good will; and second, by the extraordinary naïveté on the part of certain elements of the American Government which led them to believe that they alone were the ones who would be able to arrive at satisfactory arrangements with the Russian Government of that time.

"There can be no doubt that the deliberate decision not to seek a specific understanding on the Berlin access question had a disastrous aftermath," Robert Murphy has written, so many years later. "Winant's idealistic notions about Soviet-American relations were matched by Roosevelt's confidence, frequently expressed in his phrase, 'I can handle Stalin.' "

"Many things were fuzzy in the basic documents," General Eisenhower commented, also many years later, on the decisions reached by the European Advisory Commission in 1944—"especially the absence of specified routes of access—and of course the Russians would never allow any revision or official interpretation that might give the Allies any expanded or better-defined rights."

When I had taken over Fighter Command after the Battle of Britain, I found that the headquarters attracted a great many rather curious visitors. My headquarters of the British Air Forces in Germany seemed to become, with the ending of the war in Europe, an even greater magnet; but this time it was not the Air Force that the curious wanted to see. Such was the disrupted state of road and rail transport that by far the easiest way of getting to Germany was to fly out, and since the R.A.F. was the only service that was available—if official permission to use it could be obtained—the destination had to be my headquarters. We became inundated with visitors, many of whom immediately went off swanning around Germany and satisfying their own personal curiosity about what had happened to the country.

But not all of these visitors were in that category. There were those who had plenty of work to do, and there were distinguished members of our own and foreign governments. Early in August the Regent of Iraq and General Nuri as-Said, his closest associate in the running of Iraq, both of whom were so well disposed toward Britain, came out and stayed a night with me, and the next day I showed them the effects of the bombing in the city of Hanover. They were both men of charm and wisdom; but for all that they were both to die in the most violent way in the revolution in Baghdad thirteen years later.

Shortly after I arrived out in Germany, Prince Bernhard of the Netherlands began to fly over from Holland, and on several occasions he stayed with me. His mother and other members of his family lived not far away from my headquarters. By then he had become a very competent pilot of many different types of aircraft, and he genuinely enjoyed flying. I had always liked him and admired him for the way in which he conducted himself during the war, and he became a good friend of mine. Prince Bernhard has a lively mind, and is of a cheerful and attractive nature; and I gladly accepted his invitations to visit Holland. On one of these visits I was to receive from him the Dutch decoration of the Order of Orange Nassau; and in order to get to the palace where the royal family was living, I landed at the nearest airfield that we could find. It turned out to be the airdrome at Soesterberg, which I had not seen since the time when, piloting a Handley Page V/1500 bomber, I had landed there in 1919.

For all the rush of visitors, and our own quite extensive journeys—we were constantly on the go with visits to Berlin and London, and to Paris, Oslo and Copenhagen—we tried at my headquarters at B.A.F.O. to keep our weekends free from work. That was at least for me some small relief after the way in which I had worked during the war years, when weekends had meant nothing at all and one grasped at the opportunity for a few hours of time off only when it presented itself. My wife was not in Germany with me at that time, and I tried to get back as often as I could to London. But it did not take any of us long to discover that if the weather was not suitable for flying, it was better not to try to make any journeys at all. Early in August I learned a sharp lesson about that. After having been in London for the weekend, I started off by air to return to Germany, but through a rapid deterioration in the weather we could not get any farther than Ghent, in Belgium. Since the weather reports for the next few days were most unfavorable, I had to start out on the rest of the long journey, from Ghent to Bad Eilsen, in Germany, by car; and it took us twelve hours of the most miserable motoring that I have ever known to get back to my headquarters. The wretchedness of the weather that week continued, and on the following Sunday it caused an incident that led to my experiencing at firsthand the closing stages of what I consider was one of the saddest stories of the war.

We were all enjoying a lazy Sunday at the house in which I lived with my staff, and I had gone for a walk through the wooded hills with Roy Faville. When I got back to the house I was told that Bob Wright had suddenly rushed off in response to an urgent phone call from our nearest airfield, which was at Bückeburg. It appeared that the Czechoslovakian squadrons which had been serving with the Royal Air Force had started off that day on their way back from England on a triumphal return to their own country; but they had all been forced by the wretchedness of the weather to land on some of our airfields in Germany. Wright returned fairly soon, and he had arranged for Air Vice-Marshal Karel Janousek, the gallant Czech leader who was going back with his squardrons, to come and stay with me.

I had known Karel Janousek from the time when he had first arrived in England. He often came to see me at both Fighter and Coastal commands, and I greatly admired him for the spirit that he had shown in fighting for his country while in exile. He was known as a staunch Czech patriot, and I had been told that in the first war he had been one of that gallant band which, known as the Czech Legion, had fought its way to freedom from the Austrians and the Bolsheviks. With the German occupation of Czechoslovakia, and the later outbreak of war, he had come to Britain, and he was tireless in organizing squadrons of his fellow-countrymen who had also found their way to us. That was done by him in time for some Czechs to fight with us both before and during the Battle of Britain.

When Janousek arrived at the house, he was in a very agitated state, and he kept repeating that somehow or other his squadrons had to get back to Prague on time. A great national welcome had been arranged for them, he explained, and he did not want to let his people down. But so far as we could make out, the airfields where they had landed were all badly waterlogged. After dinner I asked Janousek what news he had of his family, which he had been forced to leave behind in Czechoslovakia. I was horrified when he told me, quietly and with a sternly controlled resignation, that so far as he had been able to ascertain all of them, including his wife and children, had been killed in one way or another.

We spent the next morning doing all that we could to help the Czechs. With a fortunate break in the weather, they managed to get off from our airfields after lunch, and start on their way back to Prague. A week later, in company with Strath Evill, who had been Vice-Chief of the Air Staff since March, 1943, and several other senior officers of the R.A.F., I paid an official visit to Prague where we were decorated with their Order of the White Lion; and again I was able to meet Karel Janousek, the Chief of their Air Force, and I had talks with him and with some of his senior officers, as well as some of the younger pilots who had flown under my command.

During that visit to Prague I also had a long talk with Dr. Eduard Beneš, the President of Czechoslovakia. He told me that he felt that the tide of Communism was receding, and that he was quite optimistic about his country not falling under its control. They had experienced enough when the Russians had been allowed to liberate Prague, and they were fully aware of what it meant to be under Communist domination. All said and done, they had only just been freed from the grip of the Nazi control.

How sadly the whole political position of Czechoslovakia was misjudged was revealed less than a year later, when the Communists gained complete control of the country. One of those who felt that he could not endure life under a totalitarian regime was Karel Janousek. But in endeavoring to escape to freedom from the country to which he was devoted, and for which he had done so much, he was captured on the border and flung into prison. We heard nothing more about this gallant little man until May, 1952, when it was reported that he had died while still in prison in Pilsen.

It was not until only very recently that I learned that Karel Janousek was, in fact, still alive. After years spent in so many different prisons that all trace of him appeared to have been lost, and he was believed to be dead, he was released. Since then he has apparently been living, still in his own country, in the humblest of circumstances, able to do nothing more than barely support himself as a storekeeper in a warehouse.

37 / The Shapes to Come

WHILE THE Potsdam Conference was in progress in Germany, the world's first atomic bomb was successfully exploded for test purposes in the United States. When President Truman revealed to Stalin, in a personal conversation with him in Berlin, the result of this successful experiment, it is said that the Russian leader showed no signs of any great surprise or even particular interest. It has since come to be understood that, for all our rigid security precautions, Stalin knew about the work on atomic research and development that had been going on in the United States.

Three weeks after that test explosion the first atomic bomb was dropped, on August 6, on Hiroshima, with results that were to change, with no improvement, the whole course of the world's thinking. The information about the existence of such a weapon may have found its way to Stalin, but the whole project was nevertheless one of the most successfully guarded secrets of the Second World War. There were a few of our own people who knew about it, and naturally the Chiefs of Staff were well informed, but Robert Murphy has stated that "scarcely a dozen men at Potsdam had heard about this new weapon."

Alan Brooke has recorded that he "had some nasty moments wondering whether the Boche would forestall us with the Atomic Bomb and snatch victory from under our noses." When he discussed the news of the first test explosion with Winston Churchill, he "tried to crush his over-optimism" which the Prime Minister felt about the value of having the bomb. Later Brooke was to comment: "Winston's appreciation of its value in the future international balance of power was far more accurate than mine."

In common with most other commanders in the field, I knew nothing whatsoever about the existence of such a weapon until the news was released to the public that the first atomic bomb had been dropped on Hiroshima. I heard that news in my flat in London, where I was spending the weekend after touring around some of the R.A.F. units in Germany. As with everybody else, the release of the news of this mighty secret caused in me a feeling that was, as Robert Murphy put it, "literally earth-shaking."

In all the arguments and the discussions that have raged since that first use of the atomic bomb, it has become an issue about which most people appear to feel that they must take a stand on one side or the other. When the news first came, and we heard of the devastating power of the new weapon, I was as startled and as overawed as anybody, and there were questions about its use that I felt one was going to have to resolve in one's own mind about certain almost indefinable responsibilities.

It was not until some time after the two bombs had been dropped on Japan that I learned about any part that we, the British, had played in the decision that the bomb should be used. "The decision to drop an atomic bomb on Japan . . . was taken in the United States, on evidence available in its entirety to the Americans alone," John Ehrman has recorded. To that he has added the comment: "The balance of power, both in the atomic project and in the Pacific, lay too heavily with the United States for the British to be able, or to wish, to participate in this decision."

The British nevertheless did formally agree that it should be used, and Alan Brooke, in speaking about Winston Churchill's enthusiasm, summed up the Prime Minister's views with the statement: "The secret of this explosive and the power to use it would completely alter the diplomatic equilibrium which was adrift since the defeat of Germany." Churchill at that moment, before the bomb had actually been used against Japan, had in mind more the way in which it might be used as a means to curb the threat that he saw looming up in our relationships with the Russians.

There was never any doubt in my own mind about how I felt over the use that was made of the bomb. The passage of time should have enabled all of us to gain more objective views on that; but instead the controversy has become one of the most heated of our times. The arguments that have been produced have only served to confirm the conclusion that I came to in the first place, and I am still very firmly of the opinion that the decision to use the bomb was, at the time, the right one. President Truman showed a great moral courage in making the decision to use it, and in giving the order that was necessary to implement that grave decision.

There has developed the strong argument, which was all too easy to start on its way after the war was over, that it would have been better if the atomic bomb had not been used. But one should put oneself in the place of the men—and particularly in the place of President Truman—who had to make the decision at the time. Much has been made of the nearness of a Japanese surrender; but so far as could be seen at the time, and in a realistic light, the Japanese were still fighting very strongly, and apparently intended to go on fighting. This presented the American and British leaders with the prospect of having to launch an amphibious operation and invasion of Japan on a scale similar to that mounted for the invasion of Normandy, but from a much less convenient and spacious base.

There was a proposal that a demonstration might have been staged beforehand as a warning to the Japanese; but any such demonstration would not have been effective. The Japanese would have regarded it as a trick. Being the fanatics that they were, it is much more likely that it would have moved them to even more vigorous opposition. The unconditional surrender that was being demanded of them would have imperiled the whole position of their godlike Emperor, and it was the guiding principle of the army clique politically in control of Japan to refuse any form of surrender.

The code of behavior of the Japanese under almost any conditions was beyond the comprehension of most Western minds, and all that our leaders could be sure of was that any attempt to conquer Japan by invasion would present appalling problems. They were left with no choice but to use the atomic bombs; and the effects of that decision, for all its wisdom, were such that, in themselves, they have become appalling, and far more tormenting in the minds of men than was ever imagined possible. The bombs compelled the Japanese to make a quick surrender. They also greatly overshadowed in the minds of most people the more important fact of the moment, which was that, with the Japanese surrender, the Second World War was over.

During the year that I had spent in Cairo in 1943, I had had more than enough of trying to play a part, small though it was, in the tortuous game that can take place in the diplomatic sphere. When I went out to Germany in July, 1945, I expected to have to cope with no more than matters having to do with the Air Force. But even then I was not able to escape from becoming involved in some of the problems in the international bickering that came crowding in on us with the ending of the war.

The part that the Polish Air Force had taken in working with the Royal Air Force during the years between 1939 and 1945 is an honorable part of our own history as a Service. After the war in Europe was over, I had Polish squadrons out in Germany under my command as part of the air forces of occupation. They were poised and understandably eager to make their return to their own country, and I was being constantly reminded of that. Only a few days after I arrived in Germany, their Commander-in-Chief, Air Vice-Marshal Izycki, had come out from England to see what could be done, and his eagerness to get his air force back to Poland was just as keen as that displayed by the Czech leader, Karel Janousek, to get back to his country. But we were faced with many complex problems in getting the Poles back to their own country—a matter about which they felt so intensely.

Toward the end of October the Air Ministry made arrangements for an exhibition to be staged in Warsaw in which the Poles could be shown something of the work done by the R.A.F., with particular emphasis on the splendid contributions that were made by the Polish squadrons stationed in Britain. I was asked by the Air Ministry to go to Warsaw to open the exhibition, and I flew there, taking with me Air Commodore Lord Willoughby de Broke, who was then director of public relations at the Air Ministry, and Group Captain Sir Louis Greig, who was on the personal staff of the Secretary of State for Air. They were both old friends of mine.

There was quite a strong opposition from the Russian-dominated Polish officials in Warsaw both to the exhibition and to my going there; but feeling as I did about the Poles, who had served us so gallantly and who were still in exile, I was in no mood for any stalling. I insisted that we should make the trip to Warsaw, and we set off to fly there from Berlin.

The mood of those who were with me on board my Dakota was sounded when we arrived over the battered airfield of Oketsie on the outskirts of the Polish capital. During the last part of the flight from Berlin eastward, over Poland, Bob Wright had been up in the cockpit with the pilot, and when we got to Warsaw he came back into the cabin to tell us what was happening. Around his neck he had slung the pair of binoculars that he had been using. Willoughby de Broke and Louis Greig and Roy Faville and I had been reading and talking. We all looked up when Wright came into the cabin and told us that we were safely on the circuit of the airdrome for Warsaw.

"Any flak coming up, Bob?" Willoughby de Broke asked with the humor typical of the Auxiliary Air Force of which he had long been a member.

"You know, John," Louis Greig remarked, "as a peer of the realm you're not a bad type."

After we had landed and we got out of the Dakota, we were welcomed by the British Ambassador in Warsaw, Victor Cavendish-Bentinck, and several members of his staff; but there was no sign of any official welcome from the Polish Government or their armed forces. From what I had been told beforehand I was not surprised, and the Ambassador warned me as we drove together into Warsaw that the situation was a decidedly tricky one. But the exhibition was ready, I was assured, and it was now a matter of formally opening it.

What I began to see as we approached the heart of Warsaw was even worse than what I had seen in Berlin. The city was in almost complete ruins. Despite the German bombing in 1939, Warsaw had apparently remained in fair shape, or as fair as could be expected, until the time of the uprising of the Polish underground movement in 1944, except, that is, for the ghetto. There, in the spring of 1943, over fifty thousand Jews, all that were left of the four hundred thousand who had been concentrated in the small area of the ghetto by the Germans in 1940, rebelled against their tormenters, who had systematically starved and then exterminated them in what, to the Germans, was to become known as the "resettlement" program. The Germans answered that rebellion with tanks, artillery, flame-throwers and dynamite squads. For a month the fight went on, and at the end of it the German general in command of the operation reported "a total of 56,065 Jews whose extermination can be proved." The ghetto was in ruins. But at that time the rest of the city was still habitable, even if badly scarred.

By the end of July of the next year, 1944, the Russians had driven the Germans so far back that they had reached the suburbs of Warsaw on the eastern side of the Vistula, the river that divides the city in two. The Poles were confident that the Russians would immediately launch their attack upon the city itself, and so relieve it of the German occupation.

In broadcasts from Moscow at the end of July, appeals were made to the great Polish underground movement to start their uprising. With the Russians on the outskirts of Warsaw, the Poles felt, perhaps ill-advisedly, that their time had at last come, and on August 1 they rose and started fighting the Germans; and it was then, in Warsaw, that there was enacted one of the most savage tragedies of the war. While the Poles fought their hated enemies with whatever weapons they could lay their hands on, the Russians ceased all operations and sat on the other side of the river, and merely watched and waited. Stalin promised the Poles help, but only under conditions which would have meant the almost complete extinction of the Polish Government that had been in exile in London, and the establishment in its place of a puppet government under Communist domination.

At first the Polish uprising in Warsaw had been a success; but with the greater power of the German Army in the city—and no help whatsoever from the Russians who sat looking on—their fortunes began to change. All Polish appeals to the Russians were either ignored or answered with the accusation that the uprising had been ordered by the Polish Government in London, that it had been ill-advised and ill-timed, and that no effort had been made to coordinate it with the Soviet High Command.

For sixty-three days the Poles fought the Germans, and by the end the Nazis had killed some two hundred thousand men, women and children; and after ferociously destroying the city they retreated. Early in the new year of 1945, the Russians then liberated what was left of the Polish capital, and they established there the Communist government of their choosing. With that the legitimate Polish government in exile in London became a thing of the past.

In the ruins of Warsaw when we arrived in the city in October, 1945, there was one fairly big hotel, the Polonia, which was in a sufficiently reasonable shape for it to be made habitable. The American Embassy was on the second floor, and on the fourth floor there was the British Embassy; and the staffs of both were working under the most difficult and cramped conditions. After being shown around the appalling devastation of the city—the ghetto was literally nothing more than one vast mound of rubble—I was taken to meet the Polish Minister of Defense. He was a Polish general, but nothing more than a Communist puppet, and he started off by demanding rather truculently to know why we saw fit to stage our exhibition in Warsaw. But in the end he was amenable enough, and we were even able to have a good, if inconclusive, talk. I did at least manage to induce him to come with me and open the exhibition.

On the morning of our third day in Warsaw we gladly left the hotel for our return to Germany; but when we got to the airfield we found that our departure was to be in marked contrast to our arrival. There was lined up a large guard of honor, and some rather villainous-looking Polish generals were in attendance; and a band was playing our national anthem in a way that had to be heard to be believed.

On all the various trips that I made we saw to it that my Dakota was well stocked with necessary supplies—we never knew what was likely to happen—and since the Polish generals all looked so miserable, and even sour, I invited them on board. That led to "a whisky drinking session in the aircraft at a quarter to ten in the morning!" Bob Wright recorded in his diary. When we left, the generals were in a much friendlier mood, but it was little wonder that Wright added the comment: "We all dozed on the way back to Berlin, feeling foul."

One of the first questions that was put to me when we got back to my headquarters in the British Zone came from my Polish Air Force officers. They naturally wanted to know when they would be going back to Poland. They were all determined to return there with their flags flying and the bands playing, and was there ever a band of men who had a greater right to return with honor to their home country? But I could only tell them the truth, and I would have been shirking a stern duty to them if I had tried to fob them off in any way. I had to tell them that, for all that they had done and all that they had achieved, the only way in which they could go back would be by an undercover route. The situation was now an entirely political one, and they were, unhappily, on the wrong side of the fence.

It was a terrible thing to have to tell these gallant men, and although one of the agreements reached at the Potsdam Conference only a few weeks before had been about "facilitating the return to Poland as soon as practicable of all Poles abroad who wished to go, including members of the Polish armed forces," I knew that they would never be able to return in the way which they so ardently desired. They were understandably bitter and desperate about what I had to tell them.

Two weeks later Air Vice-Marshal Izycki and his chief of staff flew out from London to see me, and they stayed the night, and in his diary Bob Wright recorded: "A terrific political discussion blew up before dinner with Izycki laying down the law about freedom and not going back to Poland until they were free, and the Chief telling him that the only way to get freedom was to go back to Poland and fight for it."

These political issues were beginning to overshadow, in all our minds, almost everything else, and because I felt that I was strictly an Air Force commander, I rather resented the way in which they were intruding in all our thinking. But there was no avoiding them, and already there had begun to sprout from the seeds that had been planted the first indications of what we might expect in the way of a harvest.

The day after I got back from Warsaw, I drove over to see Montgomery at his headquarters at Ostenvalde, and I reported to him on what I had learned from my visit to Poland. In turn, Monty told me about his concern over the way in which the French Government was acting, and about their refusal to cooperate as we were hoping for in the negotiations of the four-power Control Council in Berlin. Earlier in the month there had been a meeting of the Allied foreign ministers in London that had ended in a way which later led Montgomery to comment: "It was now fairly clear that we were heading for trouble in a big way." That trouble, Montgomery explained to me, was right on our own doorstep, and he had a host of serious problems on his mind.

A couple of weeks later, Bob Wright came to me one evening as I was getting ready for yet another dinner which we were having to give for some visitors. Montgomery's military assistant was on the phone with a message for me from Monty asking if I would represent him officially at the opening of the Major War Crimes Trials in Nuremberg. I promptly put a flea in Wright's ear—his writer's curiosity had gained the upper hand—and I told him that under no conditions whatsoever would I consider going to or having anything to do with what was about to take place in Nuremberg. He received with rather a long face my firm instructions to tell Monty's M.A. that I could not possibly do what was being asked of me.

It is already a long time since Chester Wilmot made a comment in 1952 in his book *The Struggle for Europe* that, at the time, caused quite a stir, but which is now accepted with resignation as such a sad truth. "The two most serious miscalculations of the Second World War both concerned the Soviet Union," he wrote: "Hitler's miscalculation of Russia's military strength, and Roosevelt's miscalculation of Russia's political ambition. It was these two errors of judgement which gave Stalin the opportunity of establishing the Soviet Union as the dominant power in Europe." The first effects of the latter of these two miscalculations began to dawn on some Western minds, including American, even before the end of the war; and then there began the definite moves by Stalin, moves which were in the nature of probes, in what was to develop into the complex and highly controversial cold war that has existed ever since the end of the Second World War.

My own experience of the first of these probes made by the Russians was an incident that occurred in November, 1945. Not a great deal of public attention appears to have been paid to it at the time, but Montgomery later dealt with the broader aspects of the incident in his *Memoirs*. It came, as he has put it, "just when I was thinking we were beginning to get our affairs in the British Zone into good working order." It took the form of an official complaint from the Russian Military Governor, Marshal Zhukov, which was lodged with the Control Commission in Berlin, and it accused us, the British, of unnecessarily keeping in existence in our zone quite large units of the German armed forces.

It still seems difficult to believe that this utterly senseless complaint was made so soon after the end of years of a terrible war in which we and the Russians had thought of ourselves as allies. There had been indications before then, and even before the war came to an end, that, for all the fine speeches, the partnership was far from being the close and cordial one that we were wishing for on our part. Out in Germany, suspicion was all too clearly in the air, and no matter how we tried to dispel it through endeavoring to be helpful and cordial in our relationships with the Russians, it still lurked in every corner.

Then there came this calculated Russian move which I have since thought of as one of the first in the beginning of the cold war. It was such a stupid one that it would have been laughable had we not been forced to become aware of that suspicion. Even ten years after the Russians had made the accusation, which was thoroughly discredited, they were still harping on it, with Zhukov, by then their Deputy Minister of Defense, stating: "The history of international relations and military history know few examples of such treachery to obligations under an alliance, or of the bad faith Mr. Churchill and Field-Marshal Montgomery displayed at the end of the Second World War." My part in that alleged "treachery" had to do with the air, and Zhukov had not spared us.

The first indication to me that something had happened came when I got down to breakfast one morning toward the end of November. I could not help noticing that Bob Wright, who was sitting alone at the table, was looking rather grim-faced. He knew better than to start discussing anything with me at that time of the day. But no sooner were we in the car and on our way to my headquarters than he produced a copy of a signal that had come in during the night from Berlin, and which had caused Roy Faville to depart for the headquarters very much earlier than usual. It was a memorandum that had been sent by Marshal Zhukov to Montgomery, with copies for information to the American and French Military Governors.

At first I felt inclined to dismiss the whole thing as being too absurd for serious consideration. "It's a lot of tripe," I commented. "They're trying something on."

"If . . . just if . . . the Russians should move," Wright said, "how long would it take them to get to Cap Griz Nez?"

"Three weeks," I replied.

"And you?"

"Twenty-four hours."

But any flippancy that we felt that morning was only the mood of the moment, and as soon as I got to my office I went over in detail the memorandum which had been sent, and all the information that Roy Faville had been gathering together from various sources about the air side of the Russian allegations. In his memorandum, Zhukov had referred to the decisions reached at the Potsdam Conference "in order for all times to eliminate the rebirth or reorganization of German militarism and Nazism." A specific allegation was then made by him that we were keeping the German Air Force in existence to the extent that, he stated: "The Air Components and authority in the British Occupied Zone of Germany are represented in the form of II Air District which includes the antiaircraft components [detachments of the 18th Antiaircraft Division], bomber squadrons, fighter squadrons, attack squadrons and close-reconnaissance groups. The II Air District has a staff similar to the staff of the Air Force in wartime."

This matter of the disbandment of the German Air Force was in the hands of my deputy, Air Marshal Sir Philip Wigglesworth, and he immediately consulted me about the allegations that were being made, and we carefully examined the whole position. The next day I had to fly to London for conferences, and in my name Wigglesworth sent a report on the air side of the Zhukov memorandum to Montgomery's headquarters stating: "The Air C.-in-C. considers the allegations in the Russian Memorandum as unjustified and basically untrue."

In dealing with the details, we made the clear statement: "There exists in the British Zone no Luftwaffe Headquarters or any other constituted German Air Force Authority or Staff similar in any way to a German Air Force in wartime. Emphatically there are no German bomber squadrons, fighter squadrons, attack squadrons or close-reconnaissance groups in the British Zone." After giving in full the numbers of Luftwaffe personnel disbanded and "discharged to civilian life," we pointed out that "the majority of the remainder comprise Luftwaffe personnel who are resident normally in the Russian Occupied Zone of Germany, and who are awaiting transfer to the Russian Zone."

So far as the 18th Antiaircraft Division was concerned, to which the Russians had made particular reference, we reported that we had disarmed the formations of this division which had been found in Schleswig-Holstein, and we further pointed out that "the remainder of the 18th Antiaircraft Division . . . was captured by the Russians . . ."

On the same day, Philip Wigglesworth sent a signal to the Air Ministry in London repeating all that had been said in the report to Montgomery. When I got back to Germany a few days later, I found among the papers on my desk a confidential report from the Air Ministry on the state of the Russian Air Force. It was stronger than we had expected, and it looked as if it was particularly good on the army support side. On the day after that there arrived for my information a draft of the reply that Montgomery proposed to make to Zhukov's allegations at the Control Council meeting that was to be held in two days' time.

In his *Memoirs,* Montgomery refers to this meeting, and to the statement that he made "expressing my astonishment." He called attention to the fact that it was "the first occasion on which one Ally had criticised the conduct of another in the Control Council." He has stated that "I decided that a heavy counterattack must be launched against the Soviet delegation"; and that, with his customary vigor, was just what Monty proceeded to do, and the balloon that had gone up was quickly deflated.

By this time it was an inescapable fact that we all had to face that the Russians were trying, for some reason that was not altogether clear, to rock us back on our heels and generally to embarrass us. But why, I asked myself, were they trying to bluff us in such a blatantly ham-fisted way? It was so easy for us to prove how wrong they were in the statements that they were making; and we could even, if we wished, make capital out of that. The Russian delegation had obviously launched this attack on orders from Moscow. But was it part of any plan? In trying to find the answer to that, I wondered if a very slight incident that had occurred earlier in the month could have had anything to do with it.

This was a silly enough little affair that had occurred in Berlin. After one of the Control Council meetings, which were held every ten days, Montgomery had invited the Allied Commanders to dine with him. Marshal Zhukov, with some of his staff, was there, along with Lucius Clay representing the Americans, and General Koeltz the French; and Admiral Sir Harold Burrough, the British Naval C.-in-C. for Germany, and I were also at the dinner.

As normally happened, Monty kept things going at a lively pace during dinner by indulging in that waspish brand of humor of his which seemed to enjoy so much the sillier expressions of inter-Service banter. For a while it was all quite innocuous and light-hearted, and then suddenly Zhukov made a remark to Harold Burrough that I thought was a little harsh. He had already referred to what he considered was a habit of the Royal Navy of helping itself whenever it wanted anything.

"You are an anarchist," Zhukov declared, "you want every-thing, but you'll give nothing."

"No, he isn't," I exclaimed, trying to inject a light note into what was becoming too serious a discussion, "he's a flag officer of the Royal Navy."

There was a good-natured protest from Harold Burrough—who was an old and valued friend of mine—and since my remark was exactly the sort of inter-Service ribbing that appealed to Monty, and he was thoroughly enjoying it, he laughed in the quick, rather sharp way that was his. But before we could continue any further, we found, to our astonishment, that the Russians had all become stony-faced, and no explanations on our part could dispel the frigid attitude that they had suddenly come to adopt toward us. And then I realized what must have happened. What was mere banter with us was being entirely misunderstood or misinterpreted by the Russians, and it was to them dissension among the British; and they were carefully watching and listening to us, and taking it all in for their own future reference.

It has never been an inclination of mine to indulge myself in the "if only" way of looking at my life and times, but in both there must be, as there has to be in the lives of all thinking people, questions about the wisdom, or the lack of it, in certain aspects of the work in which one has been involved. By the latter part of 1945 I began to feel that somewhere or other there was something that was definitely wrong; but I could not be sure what it was, even when I tried to define it. Was it in my own life, or was it in the times in which we were living? At the back of my mind there was the thought that it might be that, while I was strictly an Air Force commander, I was finding myself being drawn again into the web of international political turmoil.

Because I could not be sure of the root of the trouble, there was little that I could do about it. Much more understandable, through hard experience, was the inevitable reaction that I knew I was feeling from the years of tension under which we had all been living. I had been through these aftereffects of war in a full measure while I was still a young man after the First World War, and I was able to recognize in myself the symptoms of the same state of mind developing again now that the second war was over. I was becoming restless and unnecessarily depressed. And working and living in a country for which I had no liking, and never being able for a moment to be off duty, meant that my position as the Commander-in-Chief of my own Service was, by circumstance, a particularly lonely one.

In many ways I found my life becoming too austere and monotonous. I had the companionship of the officers who were living with me, and they were men whom I liked and who had all become personal friends of mine; but all the time, even when we were off duty, we were in a strictly Service atmosphere. They were in no position, through Service discipline alone, to be able to talk to me as equals, much, at times, as I would have liked it. It was also difficult for them, I knew, working together as they did all day at the headquarters and sitting around in the house together at night still talking about the things that we had all been discussing all day. I do not doubt that they wished, as much as I did, for some variety of company other than the stream of official visitors. But they could at least argue with each other: nobody, unfortunately, could argue with me. On one occasion, Bob Wright recorded, I exploded at dinner and told them all that I was sick and tired of being a Commander-in-Chief with everybody so completely dependent upon what I decided to do about everything. It was petulant of me to be like that, but it was nevertheless the truth.

It was then, I think, that I possibly came closer to my father, in sympathy and understanding, than at any other time in my life. By then he had been living in the United States for some years, and he had created for himself yet another career in his work. We began to exchange longer and more intimate letters than was usual for us. He had written to me asking about my plans and prospects for the future, and I told him exactly how I felt about the way in which my life seemed to be taking shape, and it was in a way that was beyond my control and liking, which was why I had come to feel so depressed about it.

After my father died, Jean, his widow, sent me one letter of mine of this time that he had kept. It is dated December 13, 1945, just ten days before my fifty-second birthday, and in it there is a good summary of my feelings. It bears recording if only for its expression of my personal thoughts after having been a Commander-in-Chief for an unbroken period of five years: "Longer in fact than any other commander in this war."

"I think I bear my responsibilities lightly on the whole, but I have been under a continuous strain of responsibility for a long time," I wrote. "The result is that I am tired—tired out." Stressing my need for a rest—I had had only four weeks' leave in the past six years—I explained that I definitely wanted a change of occupation. And then I spoke of the life that I was leading and the work that I was doing. "I don't think you appreciate what an unpleasant life we lead in Germany at the present time," I said. "I won't enlarge on this, but I loathe"—I underlined the word—"being here. We live in an atmosphere of misery and starvation . . ."

That there were times when one was forced to accept unpleasant conditions in order to advance one's prospects, I knew well enough, and I told my father that I knew what it was to endure something unpleasant in the present in order to gain something better in the future. "But there is now no such incentive in my case," I wrote. "I have reached the top of the tree; I have earned my maximum pension; and all I have to look forward to in the Service is another two, three or at the outside four years doing just what I am doing now, either here or elsewhere . . . just marking time and hanging on till they throw you out as being too old!"

From the financial point of view, I explained, it was just as frustrating. He knew that I had always lived and supported myself and my wife on my Service pay, with no other source of income. But now "the whole of my income and more is used up in maintaining a 'state' which I don't enjoy," I pointed out, putting in the right perspective just what many another C.-in-C. has known, "and in entertaining a crowd of people, visitors for the most part, many of whom bore me stiff and some of whom I actively dislike. At the worst, if I retire, I can live quietly but quite happily on my pension. Anything that I can earn over and above that will provide the luxuries." The feeling that I had about getting work in civilian life I summed up with the comment: "I have something to sell now—a name and a reputation. But the public memory is short, particularly where Service chiefs are concerned. I shall be forgotten in three or four years' time."

In answer to his question about the political situation at home, I told my father that I thought that the Labour Government would "win through all right" and that I was sure that "their policy of nationalisation is right so far as they propose to go at present.

There is of course always a danger that the hotheads will want to drag the Government too fast and too far. But I don't think that there is really much danger of that."

At the end of my letter I mentioned one further point that had to be considered. It was, by custom, a course followed by many Service chiefs to accept on retirement appointments to some governorship or other. My own views on this were quite firm. "I have asked not to be considered for this," I wrote. "It would be as bad as being a Commander-in-Chief—worse! To be on one's best behaviour all the time! I couldn't stand it." I finished that particular letter with the comment: "I simply must have rest (for a time) and a change of occupation."

What I had not told my father in our exchange of views was something which had been told to me in confidence by Louis Greig on one of his visits to us in Germany, and which I found unexpectedly disturbing. Toward the end of August I had told Charles Steele that what I really wanted to do was to resign and get out of the Service and make a fresh start. Steele then told me that he had heard that Montgomery was going back to England to become Chief of the Imperial General Staff, and that there was talk about Arthur Tedder coming out to take his place. A month later Louis Greig told me in a quiet talk that we had together that I was in the running with Arthur Tedder to become Chief of the Air Staff in place of Peter Portal. On a visit to London toward the end of October I learned that Arthur Tedder was to become C.A.S. in the New Year.

A week later, in Berlin the night before we flew to Warsaw, I was having a drink with Roy Faville and Bob Wright in the small cottage on the banks of the Wannsee where we used to stay. I listened to them, and I could not help being amused over the way in which they were expressing themselves about my not having become C.A.S. I appreciated the loyalty that was prompting them to air their views, but I had to tell them: "You are both taking it much more to heart than I am."

That remark led to further discussion about the future because, I told them, I was determined to retire. Of that talk, Bob Wright recorded in his diary: "That the Chief would have liked to have become C.A.S. he did not deny; but he is not sorry that he did not get it. He felt that it would be too exhausting a job for the next three years, and that he would be in no state after it to start making another career for himself, whereas now he could go out and start in with something before it's too late."

Shortly after that I started the wheels in motion to bring about my retirement, but before anything could be settled it was announced in the honors list for the New Year of 1946 that Bert Harris and I were among those created Knights Grand Cross of the Order of the Bath. Also, we were both promoted to the rank of Marshal of the Royal Air Force, the highest rank that there is in the R.A.F., and the equivalent of that of field marshal in the Army and admiral of the fleet in the Royal Navy. We thus became the only two officers in the Air Force who have ever attained that rank without having served as Chief of the Air Staff. I had told my father that I had reached the top of the tree: I had not thought of the one final step that was possible above even that.

One of the pleasantest letters that I received at this time was from Archie Sinclair. "A Happy New Year—and most delighted congratulations on your G.C.B. and your promotion to Marshal of the Royal Air Force," he wrote. "High as these honours are, when the full story is told of your work as D.C.A.S. in the highest war councils, as Commander-in-Chief, Fighter Command (and the defeat of the German bombing offensive), and as C.-in-C. Coastal Command, history will add to them. Some reputations, especially after a war, fade and wither, but the more that is told of the war in the air (down with the Admiralty censors, now!) the better for yours."

Early in the new year I went through a severe bout of influenza, and the aftereffects of that left me feeling particularly washed out. What with that and finding that my mood generally was in much the same state as that which I had known after the First World War—"nervy," we used to call it then—I began to feel very much at a loose end. And since Arthur Tedder had become Chief of the Air Staff in place of Peter Portal, there was now definitely nothing more that the Service could offer me.

Of all the senior officers who have ever served in the Royal Air Force, Peter Portal has come to be the one above all others for whom there is unqualified admiration and the highest respect. The service that he rendered to the R.A.F. and to the country as Chief of the Air Staff during most of the Second World War places him in the position of being, in my estimation, the outstanding man in the whole history of our Service. In that I rank him even ahead of Boom Trenchard. Portal was a great Chief of the Air Staff; but he was also the backbone of the Chiefs of Staff Committee, in which he exerted an immensely sensible and steadying influence. In addition to his great experience as a pilot, he proved himself to be a highly intelligent leader in senior staff appointments; and it was these two features which most helped him to do so well when he got to the top. By the time that the war was over, Portal was an extremely tired man; but at no time did he ever show the slightest sign of losing control of either himself or his tremendous responsibilities.

The more I thought about my own position—I was only just fifty-two years of age—the more anxious I became to make a fresh start with some work in civilian life. It took a little time for the wheels at the Air Ministry to go through their motions, but eventually I was informed that permission had been granted for me to relinquish my last command; and it was with a relief that was quite heartfelt that, in the early weeks of 1946, I went about winding up my connection with the R.A.F. in Germany. How short-lived that relief was to be came in a fashion that had in it both humor and, for me, a feeling that was akin to despair.

I might have known that, what with Arthur Tedder being appointed C.A.S. instead of to Montgomery's job as Military Governor, and with Montgomery himself going back to England as C.I.G.S., there was something in the air; but I suppose I was too jaded and too anxious to get out of the Service to be able to think very clearly about what lay ahead. As Commander-in-Chief and Military Governor of the British Zone, Montgomery was my boss, and since I had always liked him and got along well with him I went over to his headquarters in the first week in January to tell him about my leaving the Service, and to say good-bye. As usual, Monty came very smartly to the point.

"Sholto . . . I'm very glad to see you," he said. "I've made all my plans for you to be back here on the 1st of April."

"What are you talking about?" I demanded. "I've just resigned from the R.A.F., and I'm going to be a civilian."

With that short, sharp laugh of his, which verges on being a snort, Montgomery exclaimed: "Oh, no, you're not! Hasn't anyone told you? You're taking over from me."

That caught me completely off balance. "Like hell I am!" I snapped. "I'm not coming back to Germany."

"You can't say that," Montgomery replied.

"Why not?" I demanded.

And then Montgomery played what must have appeared to him to be his trump card. "Because I recommended you for the job," he said; and he then proceeded to read me a lecture on my duty to my King, to my country, to the Royal Air Force, and, by no means of least importance, to him.

The more that Montgomery went on about the multifarious

duties that he considered were mine, the more determined I became that I would never consider returning to Germany. I had had enough, I told him, and I wanted to cut free and to start a new life while I was still young enough to be able to do it. But Montgomery could not, or would not, see the validity of my argument, even though I persisted with it; and although, when we parted, we were friendly enough, there was a certain coolness in our relationship.

At the same time that this happened I was approached by Arthur Tedder, who asked in a somewhat different fashion from Montgomery's if I would consider taking on the job. And with that, the pressure from other sources to try and induce me to take over from Montgomery began to build up. A week later I wrote to Montgomery and to Tedder, and I told them that, with what I admitted was not much grace, I would take on the job, but that first of all I must have a couple of months' leave. A few days later the press got hold of the story and promptly released it, which caused my wife in London, who knew nothing about what was brewing, to send urgent messages asking what it was all about and what she was to reply to the questions that were being put to her. She was not at all in favor of the proposal, and there was still nothing official about what was going to happen; and I began to find the news reports and questions more of an embarrassment than anything. I gave instructions to all those on my staff that there were to be made no comments of any nature.

I finally relinquished command of the British Air Forces of Occupation in Germany at the end of January, handing over to Philip Wigglesworth. When I got downstairs on the last morning, I found the whole staff assembled outside the headquarters, and the send-off that they gave me as I drove away was of a warmth that I found unexpectedly touching. I was moved in a way that I had not experienced before in my entire Service career. Perhaps it was that which acted as some sort of a releasing agent of the emotions that I had been trying hard to keep under control; but as we drove from Bad Eilsen to the airfield at Bückeburg, I felt that it must be the end to my experience of Germany. It was a pleasant note to finish on, and to remember; and Bob Wright later recalled that I turned to him and said:

"Really, you know . . . I simply cannot come back to Germany."

Why I should have felt such a strong reluctance about accepting what many of my friends did not hesitate to tell me that they considered was a most important, and even glittering, appointment, I am still not altogether sure. I was very tired, and I could not relish in any way at all the prospect of the strife that, for all the ending of the war, seemed to be tormenting the way in which we, the former Allies, were conducting our running of Occupied Germany. It might have been some sort of premonition that I was headed for difficulties, but I have never given much credence to that sort of thing. Whatever it was, I made it known at the Air Ministry when I got back to London that I was not at all happy about having said that I would take over from Montgomery. I spoke to Arthur Tedder about that, and he agreed to try and stall off any decision until March. But only the day after that, the newspapers again came out with the statement that I would be taking over from Monty.

I had been back in London only a couple of weeks when I received a telephone call from No. 10 Downing Street asking me if I would go and see the Prime Minister, Clement Attlee, whom I knew fairly well. I had a pretty shrewd idea about what was going to happen, and I was not looking forward to the interview. When I got there I was ushered into the long Cabinet Room, and my mood was still one of trying to resist as strongly as I could any firm decision about my going back to Germany. The only person in the room was the Prime Minister, who was sitting at the middle of the long table, hunched over it, and sucking away at his curved pipe. After greeting me affably enough, he asked me to sit down.

"I am told, Sholto, that you do not want to go back to Germany," he said. "But the Cabinet discussed the matter this morning, and you were unanimously elected to the job. I think you ought to go."

It was all said in that quiet way in which Clement Attlee always spoke, almost as an aside; and when it was put to me in that way it caused a wilting of my determination. His sincerity and seriousness were so obvious, and from further comments that he made I knew that he clearly considered that it was my duty, if the Government wanted me there, to return to Germany. If he had tried to force me, or to bully me, that would have hardened my determination to refuse the job; but he did not behave in that way because he was not like that.

"How long shall I have to stay?" I asked.

"About eighteen months or two years," he replied.

I asked the Prime Minister if he would allow me to write to him when that time was up to remind him of what he had said, and if he would then see to it that I was relieved of the appointment.

"Of course," he said. "I will do that."

There was nothing more that I could say, and, much as I disliked the prospect, I agreed to do what was being asked of me. It was further agreed that I should take over from Montgomery on May 1; and I then had to start revising all my plans for the immediate future. My bridges were finally burned the next day when it was announced officially that I was to become the Commander-in-Chief of the Armed Forces and Military Governor of the British Zone of Occupied Germany and the British member of the four-power Control Council in Berlin.

Shortly after that, there came the first and, as it turned out, the last meeting that I was to have with Montgomery about his actually handing over to me. Somewhat characteristically, but nevertheless to my astonishment, he had announced that he would come and have breakfast with me at my flat—which was a time of the day that I have never recognized as human—and my wife made preparations for that; but when Monty arrived he had already had breakfast, and he wanted to get down without further delay to a serious discussion.

For an hour and a half Montgomery lectured me in his high-spirited way about what I should do in the work that lay ahead for me. One of the biggest problems, he stressed, was still that of food, for the Germans were then receiving only one third of what we were having in Britain under our own rationing scheme, which itself was not exactly plentiful. There were innumerable problems, and as Monty went on talking about them I was forced to realize that the prospect was a grim one.

By the time that Montgomery left, I knew full well that the task that I was about to undertake was going to be formidable not so much through the bleakness of the outlook, which was bad enough, as the great range of affairs for which I was going to be responsible. It was clearly going to be a heavier and more difficult load of responsibility than I had ever had to carry before, and unique for an officer of the Royal Air Force. I would not have been human if I had not considered that with feelings of some apprehension.

38 / The Changing World

WITH STILL over a month to go before I was due to take over from Montgomery, I was free to have whatever rest or change I saw fit; and while I was thinking about what to do there came up, quite by chance, an opportunity to enjoy a light-hearted and pleasant interlude which provided just the necessary relaxation. It started in a casual and amusing fashion, and it continued in that strain for three weeks, and it provided me with a welcome relief from the thoughts that I had about the future.

Even before it was finally and officially decided that I should take Montgomery's place, I had asked Bob Wright if he would continue to serve on my staff, and when he agreed to do it I had him made my personal staff officer. As such he had been shuttling backward and forward between Germany and England making preliminary arrangements; and then, in London on a quick trip back one day, he sprang on me what sounded at first like a rather crazy idea for a spree.

While up in Berlin the day before, Wright had been to see Major General Robert W. Harper, of the United States Army Air Forces, who was by then on the staff of the American Military Governor. Wright and I had both come to know Bob Harper quite well, and we liked him for his cheerfulness and his understanding attitude in Anglo-American relations. Harper had suggested to Wright that he might like to go to the United States with him for two or three weeks. He had to go to Washington for consultations, and he thought that it would be a good chance for Wright to renew his contacts with his American friends. So far as I could see, there was no reason why Wright should not go—there was plenty of time to spare before I was due to go back to Germany, and all the arrangements for that were well under control—so I gave my permission. It was then that I suddenly realized that the idea was not such a crazy one.

"Why can't I go too?" I asked.

I was told that the tone in my voice was a little plaintive, and

714

Wright thought for a moment; and then he said: "I don't know. Would you like to?"

"Of course I would," I replied. "I've never been to America, and you know my father lives there."

With that Wright went straight off back to Berlin. He had a talk with Bob Harper, and within forty-eight hours an official letter arrived from the War Department in Washington inviting me to pay an unofficial and informal visit to the United States.

Two weeks later, I flew to Paris, and early the next morning we took off for the flight to the United States. We were to travel in the comfortably appointed B-17—known to us as the Fortress—which was the four-engined aircraft converted from a bomber and used by Bob Harper. My wife's final instructions to me had been to be sure to have a good time; and what happened after that Bob Wright and I have always referred to as "the lost three weeks." That B-17 of Bob Harper's was to take us as far as California and back to London.

After staying the night at the U.S. Army Air Forces airfield at Santa Maria, in the Azores, and for a few hours at Stephenville, in Newfoundland, we arrived over New York. Crossing the Atlantic by air was then still a long journey. We landed at Mitchell Field, the Army Air Forces airfield on the outskirts of New York, where I was welcomed by Lewis Brereton, who had become the general commanding the New York area.

There were two aspects of that visit to the United States in April, 1946, which I have viewed with a slight air of wonder. In the first place, even as an informal guest of the U.S. War Department I enjoyed meeting new people about whom I had heard a great deal, and of renewing contacts with old friends in the Services, and all that was on a perfectly normal level. On another level which, although perhaps not quite normal, was both pleasant and amusing, Bob Wright and I found ourselves almost immersed in seemingly nonstop rounds of entertainment which were provided by the Americans in that hospitable way of theirs which can only be fully appreciated through an actual visit to the United States.

The point of particular personal interest for me which came with our arrival in New York was in being able to spend a little time with my father and his third wife, Jean, in their apartment there. Six years had passed since I had last seen them when they had uprooted and left London with their young family to start a new life in the United States. My father was eighty-two years of age when I saw him in New York, and during the time that he had been in America he had been as active as ever in his work, and he

had established himself as a lecturer at Harvard, Princeton and
New York universities, as well as in the museums of New York
and Boston. He had also continued writing about his special
subject, which was still Italian art, and he had had published more
books and many articles.

Age was showing, in that physically my father was frailer than
when I had seen him last, but his mind was as alert as ever; and
several times we were able to indulge in our favorite pastime
whenever we were together. People used to wonder about the way
in which we argued with each other, for our exchanges of views
were made with a vehemence that never failed to perplex those
who heard us and who did not understand us.

One afternoon I spent a little time walking idly down Park
Avenue with my half-sister, Claire. She was then about thirteen
years of age, and I was looking for a place to buy her a present.
She had no idea then how much she and her mother were to
become so firmly rooted in the new world. Two years later my
father became a naturalized American citizen; and not long after
that, following a serious illness, he felt a yearning to return to
Italy. He and his wife went there, and in 1951, at the age of eighty-
seven, he died in Florence. He had expressed the wish to be buried
in the ancient city of Siena, the city of which he was so fond and to
the history of which he had devoted so much of his time. He had
been made an honorary citizen of Siena, and the authorities gave
him an official funeral. My mother had continued to live in
Tonbridge, in Kent, ever since my days at school there, and she
died there a few years after the death of my father in Italy.

For some years my father's widow, Jean, lived in Rome. Claire
was by then grown up, and she had married the American writer J.
D. Salinger, and she had settled in New York. A few years ago,
Jean married one of my father's oldest and staunchest friends,
Edward Fowles, the former owner of the famous Duveen Galleries,
and with that she returned to live in the United States.

From New York we were flown by the Americans to Washington,
where they handed us over for a short time to the R.A.F. delegation which was well established there and under the command of
Robin Willock, an old Service friend. Our Ambassador to the
United States at that time was Lord Halifax, and during a brief
talk that I had with him at the British Embassy, before being taken
by him to the White House, he saw fit to warn me that I would not
be particularly impressed by President Truman. When we got to
the White House, Halifax took me into the President's office,

where he made the formal introduction; and then he left me alone with Mr. Truman, and we were able to talk freely about affairs in Germany.

President Truman knew that I would shortly be taking over from Montgomery as the Military Governor of the British Zone, and he did not hesitate to express his own views on the German problems that we were going to have to face. In a sensible, trenchant style, he outlined the policy which he thought that the British and the Americans should follow. As I listened to what the President had to say, I realized that in the views which Halifax had expressed to me about Mr. Truman he was quite wrong in his appreciation, or understanding, of the American President, and of the problems with which we were faced in Germany.

It was obvious to me that President Truman was the type of man who would never make any pretentions about being an intellectual; but he did impress me as being a man who was fully capable of making his own decisions, and that those decisions would be based on a sound and exceptionally shrewd common sense. The proof of that came in the way in which, practically unaided, he got himself re-elected as President two years later. His ability to make hard decisions was demonstrated in his orders for the use of the atomic bombs against Japan the year before; and later, in the war in Korea which started in 1951, he showed it again in the way in which he handled his differences with the redoubtable General Douglas MacArthur. In the latter event he was both correct and to the point.

In my discussion with President Truman in his office in the White House, I found him of a decided and firm frame of mind in the presence of what Churchill had described to him, over a year before, as "this enormous Muscovite advance into the centre of Europe." I was left in no doubt that the Americans were definitely hardening in their thoughts about the intentions of our former ally; but I never for a moment thought, at that time, that it would all develop in the way that it has. But I was not alone in that.

After seeing President Truman I was taken by Bob Harper to the Pentagon, where I had a talk with Eisenhower, who had relinquished his post of American Military Governor in Germany some six months before, and had become Chief of Staff of the United States Army. Ike made me welcome in that genial way of his, and although we talked about Germany it struck me that he was burdened down with more immediate problems at home, one of which was obviously the pressing need for the demobilization of

the vast United States Army. He and Montgomery in London were
to share that same unpalatable dish.

For a few days after the talks that I was able to have with the
American leaders in Washington, thoughts about the future were
banished by an expedition that we made to California. We flew out
there, still with Bob Harper in his aircraft, and we stayed in
Hollywood as the guests of Robert Montgomery, whom we had
not seen since the time when he was with us at my headquarters at
Fighter Command in 1941. Since then Montgomery had known
plenty of action at sea as an officer in the United States Navy,
particularly in the war in the Pacific. He had left the Service with
the rank of commander, and he was back at work in films.

California was a world that was entirely new to me, although I
have come to know it well since then during my time as chairman
of a civil airline; but for Bob Wright it was to be a return to
something that, nearly five and half years before, he had known
very well. While I greatly appreciated all that Bob Montgomery
was doing for us, and it was amusing and interesting, I could only
feel that this world that he and Wright knew was so far away from
everything that I had ever known. It seemed more like life on
another planet. It was not so much that it was a world untouched
by the war, except for the vast production of certain war materials,
as it was that it seemed to have so little interest in what the war
had done to the rest of the world.

After a while I found, in talking with him, that Bob Montgomery had also come to look at Hollywood in a way that was
apparently quite different from what he had known before the war.
Service at sea over a fairly long period of time in the United States
Navy had given him an entirely different perspective on life from
that which one might consider as being typical of a world-famous
film actor. Montgomery took us around the film studios, and we
met many people in the film industry, and there were gay and
amusing parties; but all the time he would steer our talk, without
possibly even realizing it, back to Service life. It struck me that, for
all his success as a film actor, his experiences during the war had
rather led to his becoming something of a fish out of water.

The same reaction began to show itself in Bob Wright's attitude.
Whenever he and Montgomery talked together it was not about
California, as one might have expected, but about life in the
Services; and, by the last day of our stay in Hollywood, Wright
was showing definite symptoms of being a sadder as well as a wiser
man. He had been seeing some of his old prewar friends, and as we

were having breakfast together in the morning a telegram arrived
for him which caused him, after he had glanced at it, to go to the
window and stand there for a moment staring out of it.

"Anything wrong?" I asked.

"No," he said. "No . . . nothing wrong. It's only that I've
made up my mind that it would be wiser for me not to come back
here when I do become a civilian again."

I knew that Wright had a great liking for, and strong ties with,
California, and that all along he had thought that he would go
back there after the war; but now something personal had happened to make him change his mind. I asked myself then if there is
a man or a woman alive who has not in his or her mind those
strictly personal recesses where there lurk the regrets, perhaps even
some remorse, over the course that that hand of chance decides for
us. One was not always lucky. I know that those regrets have
existed in my own mind over some of the events in my life; but I
have always tried to banish any conscious worry about them in a
more or less total absorption in the work, and the play, of the
moment.

There was play enough that last night in Hollywood. Bob
Montgomery had taken over Mike Romanoff's popular restaurant
for the evening, and the small farewell party that he said that he
had arranged for us turned out to be a lavish dinner party with
some fifty or sixty friends of his. They were all people well known
in the film world. From that it developed into an all-night party;
and in the small hours of the morning I found myself in a
nightclub with Charles Bennett, an English screenwriter whom I
had known well for many years, and who had gone out to
Hollywood with Alfred Hitchcock during the thirties. I was sitting
talking with a quite attractive girl when there suddenly loomed
over us a biggish man who, I gathered from his manner, was the
girl's possessive friend. In a somewhat truculent way he demanded
to know my name.

"Douglas," I replied. "What's yours?"

I had always been a keen reader of the Erle Stanley Gardner
mystery stories—reading thrillers, and playing bridge and tennis
whenever I could, provided me with any relaxation that I felt I
needed—and I knew well the characters that Gardner had created
in his stories, and which have since become known in every
household through television.

"I'm from the office of the district attorney of Los Angeles," the
man announced.

There was only one answer that I could possibly make to that, and I made it. "Do you happen to know Perry Mason?" I asked.

It was the right note on which to end that visit to a world which was such a curious mixture of harsh reality and wistful make-believe.

In the small hours of the morning a few days later we were well out over the Atlantic in Bob Harper's aircraft, flying at about twelve thousand feet on our way back from Newfoundland to England. Not being able to sleep, I had gone up to the roomy and comfortable cockpit, and I had offered to take over the controls for a while. The pilot agreed readily enough because we were in for a long, nonstop flight back across the Atlantic which was to take thirteen and a half hours. I had settled down to flying the B-17 on instruments while, it seemed, all the members of the American crew on board were asleep; and we droned on through the night.

After a while there was a shaft of light behind me as the cabin door opened and closed. Bob Wright appeared out of the darkness, and he slipped into the second pilot's seat.

"How long have you been doing this?" he asked.

"About a couple of hours," I replied.

"I wouldn't mind betting that it's the only time a Marshal of the Royal Air Force has piloted an American bomber across the Atlantic at night," he commented. "And it's a far cry from 1919 and those V/1500's."

"It's a damn sight more comfortable," I said.

We sat there in silence as I flew on through the night, and I thought back to the time when, twenty-seven years before, I used to fly our big Handley Page V/1500 bombers. Then we had had open cockpits, and the instruments for the four engines were out on the engine mountings between the main-planes, and were far from easy to see. The V/1500 was an even larger aircraft than the B-17, and we had almost the same range and endurance; but the speed and the power of our engines had been only one third of those of this famous American bomber of the second war. The flight that I made that night in the B-17 across the Atlantic was the last one of any sustained length of time that I was to make on instruments.

From the moment that we got back to London, late in the afternoon, I was caught up again in what was almost a continuous mass of detailed work. It was what I had become accustomed to during the years of the war, except that now it was all so much more far-reaching than a concern with purely military affairs; and

I was having to acquaint myself more fully with the wishes of and the ways of the Labour Government, which had by then been in power for some eight months.

One of those who was at first greatly disturbed by the change of the government that had taken place as a result of the general election was Alan Brooke; but he was later to admit that he came to view the new Prime Minister, for all that he already knew of him, in quite a different light. Brooke learned to feel about Clement Attlee's way of going about his work as I did, and later he wrote: "I remember being very impressed by the efficiency with which Attlee ran his Cabinet. There was not the same touch of genius as with Winston, but there were more business-like methods. We kept to the agenda and he maintained complete order with a somewhat difficult crowd. Our work was quickly and efficiently completed."

Alan Brooke also commented in his diary on another member of the Labour Cabinet for whom I had the greatest admiration: the Foreign Secretary, Ernest Bevin. I have always thought of Bevin as one of the staunchest Englishmen of our times, and I was to come to work closely under him while I was out in Germany; and I learned to agree with Alan Brooke's comment: "He is a most wonderful helpful individual always full of ideas. It is astonishing the ease with which he absorbs international situations and the soundness of his judgment." In writing much later on the position of our country in the reconstruction that was necessary after the war, Winston Churchill also paid a handsome tribute to Bevin with the comment: "The British Government, much inspired by the stout-hearted and wise Mr. Ernest Bevin, took the lead in rebuilding something of the concert of Europe, at least in what was left of Europe."

It was upon my share in the rebuilding of something which we all knew was in such perilous shape in Europe that I embarked three days after getting back to London from the United States. I returned to Germany charged with my own part to play as Commander-in-Chief and Military Governor of the British Zone. I tried hard to avoid giving any indications about how I felt about that personally: I had accepted what I realized was an important and difficult assignment, and it was up to me to get on with it. But I know now that it did not escape everyone's attention that I was not liking at all the prospect of what lay ahead for us.

Accompanied by my personal staff, I flew to Berlin on May 1, 1946. For most of the journey out from England I had an odd feeling of being more alone, or, perhaps I should say, on my own, as a commander than I had ever experienced before. When we arrived over the airfield at Gatow, on the western outskirts of Berlin, I saw, when I looked down, that a full-scale ceremonial parade had been lined up with units from all three Services. That, for a start, was disturbing enough because throughout my Service life I had always had a strong aversion to such pomp and ceremony.

Among those who were at the airfield was Charles Steele, and it was a comfort to see the rather boyish grin on his face that I had known for so many years. I beckoned to him to join me in my car when, after the inspection of the guard of honor, the time came for me to leave for the drive into Berlin. The car was surrounded by a gleaming escort of motorcyclists of the Military Police which had been provided by the Army, and the roar of engines and the screaming of sirens deafened us, and Steele and I turned and almost gaped at each other in astonishment.

Many people have spoken to me about what a wonderful experience it must have been to have had the power and authority of a Military Governor. There was provided every creature comfort that one could ask for: a fine big Schloss in which to live in the British Zone; a very pleasant house on the banks of the Wannsee for the visits to Berlin; innumerable servants and motor cars; and an airplane, a Dakota, with an experienced crew, for my own personal use. Life under these conditions, everybody seemed to think, must have been a splendid affair; but at heart I was much too simple in my tastes for all that, and I never at any time saw it in that light.

Being part of an army of occupation was a difficult position to be in if only because one obviously could not expect to be liked— particularly when one was in the position of being the actual Governor—by those whom one was governing. So far as my own attitude toward the Germans was concerned, I suppose I was suffering, in a way, from a sort of schizophrenia. On the one hand I had spent ten years of my life most vigorously fighting them in two world wars, and I could scarcely be expected all of a sudden to start loving them; but, on the other hand, I now had a definite duty to perform in taking care of them.

I am a tolerably kindhearted man, and I have a distinct dislike of seeing physical injury or suffering. But now I was going to have to see both in the midst of all the misery of starvation and the living conditions of what had become something approaching a wilderness. The well-being of these people was in my hands. In all the work that I had done before, I had known only a responsibility for the men and women of a fighting service; but now I was going to have to think of the welfare of a civilian population as well, and in the British Zone alone it numbered over twenty-two million men, women and children.

With that on my mind I felt that this was no time for pomp and ceremony, and those wailing sirens of the escort of Military Police seemed to me to sound the exact note that I did not want in the role that I was to play. In the car on the way into Berlin I gave a firm order to Bob Wright to see to it that there was to be no more of that sort of nonsense. He was looking as pained over all the noise as Charles Steele and I were, but, as three Air Force officers in the hands of the Army, we were obliged, at least for the moment, to bear it with a good grace.

When Wright reported to me later that he had been asked by some senior Army officers at the official reception that we went to in Berlin—at which I was able to meet the Service chiefs and all the heads of the various divisions of the Control Commission—if I had been pleased with the escort provided, I could not help noticing that there was a gleam in his eye. It appeared that the Army had not been at all happy about the order that I had given, and that Wright had had to exercise a quick and adroit maneuver in order to avoid giving offense. I always felt during my time in Germany that the Army, for all their good intentions, never did come to understand that I had this genuine dislike of pomp and ceremony.

All the arrangements for my arrival in Germany had been in the hands of the officials out there, and I at least expected that Montgomery, from whom I was taking over, would be on hand to meet me and to give me his views on the lastest state of affairs. There was a great deal that I wanted to discuss with him, and the only time that we had had together had been the hour or so that he had spent with me when he had visited me in my flat in London early one morning some weeks before. I was a little disappointed when I was told that he was not in Berlin, and it rather aggravated my own personal feeling of being so much on my own.

In Montgomery's place on my arrival there was General Sir Brian (now Lord) Robertson, who was in charge of the Control Commission, which was also my responsibility, and who was to serve as my deputy as Military Governor; and I knew from the outset that I was going to have to lean very heavily on him. Brian

Robertson was the son of the famous Field-Marshal Sir William Robertson—who had played such a prominent part as one of our leaders in the First World War—and he had made a name for himself as a sound administrator during the time that he served under Montgomery from the days of the Eighth Army in North Africa.

It was not until many years later, in 1958, that I learned, from reading his *Memoirs,* that Montgomery was still in Germany at the time of my arrival. He was in the Schloss which I was to take over from him, and he was at work on a long and detailed report of which, in his book, he said: "After prolonged thought I decided it was my duty to prepare a memorandum for the British Government on the situation in Germany as I believed it to be." On his return to London the next day—still without my knowing that he was in Germany—Montgomery handed this memorandum "personally to the Prime Minister."

In his book this long and important document is quoted by Montgomery in full. Strange as it may sound, I knew nothing whatsoever about it until I saw it published in that book twelve years later. When I read it then, I found that it would have been of the greatest value to me if I had been shown a copy of it at the time when it was produced, and that it would have provided an excellent basis for a fuller briefing on the work that was expected of me.

When I asked Brian Robertson about it late in 1960 he told me that he knew of no reason why it had not been shown to me. "It is evident that it was very much in the nature of a personal memorandum," he stated after making some inquiries, "and I do not think that it was given any circulation within the Control Commission." At the same time that I asked Brian Robertson about the memorandum I also approached Clement Attlee about it, explaining to him that up until the time of the appearance of the Montgomery *Memoirs* I had not even known of its existence. Attlee had inquiries made in the Cabinet office, and he then wrote to me, early in 1961, saying: "It was handed to me personally and copies were sent to members of the Cabinet and Chiefs of Staff."

It does seem to me—and I make this observation, after the lapse of so many years, much more in sorrow than in anger—that it was an extraordinary state of affairs that such a vitally important document should have been handed around in London while the man who was most intimately concerned—the man who was literally on the spot in taking over from Montgomery—should have been left so much in the dark. It is yet another example of the way in which there can occur such serious lapses in liaison.

In addition to being Commander-in-Chief of all our armed forces in Germany, I was also, as Military Governor, to have control over the lives of those twenty-two million Germans living in the British Zone. There was also going to be a great need for the closest work and, if possible, cooperation with the Americans, the French and the Russians. Ever since the end of the war in Europe there had been conflicts enough between us about how, and even if, we were to get the Germans back on their feet.

In a comment that Captain Peyton-Ward made many years later to Bob Wright about my time as Commander-in-Chief of Coastal Command, he said of my methods of working: "He used his Staff the right way in that they were expected to devil out detailed and accurate briefs on which he acted with ruthless efficiency, and with a wonderful power of accurate, quick decision." Flattering though that may sound, I had learned the lesson of working in that way from some past masters in my own Service; and I soon came to realize that, if the detail of the work as Military Governor out in Germany was not to get on top of me, I was going to have to bring into play everything that I had ever learned about using my staff.

So far as the armed forces were concerned, they ran themselves. I had no problems there other than that, in the face of a massive Russian Army, they were being very greatly reduced in strength, and routine ones which could be dealt with quite satisfactorily by those who were in command. Under Brian Robertson our Control Commission had much more difficult problems to cope with, and I had to spend most of my time working with him and the heads of the various divisions. By far the most difficult problem of the lot, however, was unquestionably the deterioration of the relationship which had set in between the East and the West, and in that I had to rely greatly on the advice of Sir William Strang, who was my political adviser, with the status of an ambassador.

In this realm of international politics and diplomacy into which I had been pitchforked it was essential that I should have the best possible guidance. As a result of my experience in the Middle East I was not altogether unfamiliar with the way in which this other world thought and operated; but it was the first time that I had taken the tiller in steering a course about which, it seemed, there was so little decision over its direction. The guidance that I had a right to expect from London was not, at least at first, all that it might have been; but the Americans were having the same difficulties. Robert Murphy, who was Strang's opposite number, has referred to the way in which they were "shackled by . . . inflexible directive from Washington . . ."

I was fortunate in having William Strang beside me, for he had had a great deal of experience in dealing with the Russians, including extensive negotiations with them on their home ground in Moscow. And apart from that purely technical aspect of our work, I always rather enjoyed listening to what he had to say. Highly strung, and very experienced, he was inclined at times to advise caution; but that was only natural. His was the diplomatic approach, whereas mine was the military, which he has described as "very natural in any profession of arms . . . an urge to take an immediate decision: act first and think afterwards." That urge, I well knew, had to be curbed because, as Strang puts it, "in politics . . . this is not usually the best course."

In writing about what had happened at the time of Munich, Strang referred to "the professional diplomatists accustomed to the decencies of international life." By the time that he was with me in Germany, some eight years later, all such decencies appeared to be a thing of the past. In the postwar world the realities of "international life" were harsh and unrelenting; and I was prepared for that when I attended as the British member my first Allied Control Council meeting a few days after I arrived back in Germany.

The representatives of the other countries which were members of the Control Council were men of substance for whom one could not but have the highest respect. When Eisenhower had returned to the United States, in November of 1945, his place as the Military Governor of the American Zone had been taken by General Joseph T. McNarney, an airman who had seen service as a pilot on the Western Front in the First World War. He had had a great deal of experience of working with the British, and he was acknowledged as a good, sound administrator. Toward the end of the war he had become Deputy Supreme Allied Commander in the Mediterranean. Of him, Robert Murphy, who was his political adviser, said: "McNarney's combat record was impressive, and his handling of the American garrison was unexceptionable, but he lacked the flair for politics which distinguished both Eisenhower and Clay."

At about the same time that there had been a change in the American command, the Russians had replaced Marshal Zhukov —who then disappeared, or was banished, into obscurity, and did not reappear on the public scene until quite recently—with his deputy as their Military Governor. He was a younger but equally impressive soldier, and he later became well known as Marshal Vassily Sokolovsky. An outstandingly handsome man, always immaculately turned out, generally imperturbable, and courteous or tough in manner just as the situation demanded, Sokolovsky had a mind that worked like lightning. I soon learned that it paid to watch him with an eye constantly on the alert. "He was in any circle a man of competence," Lucius Clay has said, using the very word that I applied to Clay.

The French were represented on the Control Council by General Joseph Pierre Koenig, who was one of their foremost fighting generals. He had joined the Free French forces after his country was occupied by the Germans; and he had made his name in history for the way in which the soldiers under his command had withstood, in 1942, Rommel's attacks at Bir Hacheim in the North African desert. But his position was made difficult by his government's disbelief that it would be possible to create any sort of real democracy in Germany, and that, as well as their suspicions about Russian motives, led to his making only infrequent visits to Berlin. The French were electing to follow a course of their own choosing, and, at times, of only their own understanding.

With the departure of Montgomery, Eisenhower and Zhukov from the Control Council, and the arrival of their replacements, "the glamour had been replaced by the daily grind," as Lucius Clay put it; and we were grinding to something that none of us could escape from seeing was showing signs of becoming some sort of a stop in our endeavors to bring about cooperation between the East and the West. With every meeting that we had, negotiations became more and more difficult, although on the personal level we—the Military Governors and our deputies—were still quite friendly enough in our relationships.

When I had first taken over as Military Governor, I had as my adviser on economic affairs Sir Percy (now Lord) Mills. He had been serving in that capacity under Montgomery, but some months later he returned to England, and his place was taken by Sir Cecil Weir. There was an amusing similarity between William Strang and Cecil Weir in that they were both small, very alert men, and they were both great enthusiasts.

Some years later Weir made a comment in a book that he wrote that was similar to the one made by Peyton-Ward on my methods of working. He went so far as to describe me as "a man of shrewd judgement, quick in decision, giving subordinates he trusts a full delegation of authority and supporting them in the exercise of it."

When I had the support of men of the caliber of Robertson, Strang and Weir, to name only three of those who served the Control Commission so well, I would have been very foolish if I had not given them full authority.

In addition to spending three days out of every ten in Berlin, I had to make frequent journeys back to London for various conferences, and the rest of my time—or what there was left of it—I spent at the Schloss at Ostenvalde, and at work in the zonal headquarters of the Control Commission which were in the small town of Lubbecke, a few miles to the east, on the way to Minden. I have never been able to work in the house in which I live, and I had offices and a staff in Lubbecke where I was able to get on more or less undisturbed with the great mass of detail that called for attention, particularly in digesting documents and reports that came in from the Services and all the various divisions of the Control Commission.

There was always this endless stream of problems: the handling of our international affairs, the supply of food, the health of the people of the country, a host of economic affairs, education, intelligence and information, local administration and politics, denazification, disarmament and reparations and refugees, and legal affairs. There was never a shortage of paper work; and on my visits to Berlin my time was fully taken up with meetings and conferences.

And all the time there was the flood of visitors. One of those who came to stay with us a couple of weeks after I settled down in the Schloss, and who was particularly welcome, was Jan Christian Smuts. He was then seventy-six years of age, and Prime Minister of South Africa; but I welcomed him as, next to Winston Churchill, the greatest man of our times. Talking with Smuts and listening to him express his views was of the utmost interest. He had just been up to see Berlin, which he had known before the war, and when he saw what had happened there he had made the embracing comment: "What a different world it is now."

In the talks that I was able to have with Smuts I sensed in that wonderful man that, for all his world-weariness, there was an understanding that was as profound as ever. It was rooted, as it was with Churchill, deep in a simplicity that could never be clouded by minor issues. I listened carefully to the expression of his views; and it was only a few days after his stay with us that he repeated in a public speech in London much of what he had said to me in Germany.

"It seems to me that the world is shaping on these lines today,"

Smuts said: "a vast, powerful, almost impregnable group in the East, and another vast, almost impregnable Power in the far West. In between you have ourselves—you have this British group, not so powerful, not so concentrated, but with immense imponderable assets. We have the experience of human outlook, the knowledge of affairs, of things you learn only by generations of experience."

Only a few days after talking with Smuts, I had reason to ponder over what he had said. I attended a routine Control Council meeting in Berlin which we expected would last only a few minutes. Instead it went on for an hour and a half. For some reason known only to themselves, the Russians did not seem to want to understand what the rest of us were talking about. The difficulties were developing, and it was a relief to get away from Berlin. I flew back to the Zone, and from there on to Paris for talks with Duff Cooper, who was then our Ambassador in France, and Bobbie George, who was further enhancing his career as our air attaché and head of the R.A.F. delegation in Paris.

From what I learned during our discussions in Paris the feeling there showed an even stronger awareness of the cancer that was beginning to spread through the whole of the relationship between the East and the West. The French were very deeply concerned about the military strength that was being maintained by the Russians in their zone of occupied Germany, and the French defenses were, to put it mildly, in a parlous state. They were looking to us for help. And since the first protection would have to be in the air, and they had no air force, it fell on Bobbie George's shoulders to advise that the Royal Air Force would have to help the French to build up their air defenses.

Our Ambassador in Paris was well aware of the situation, and he was making strenuous efforts to bring about an Anglo-French agreement on matters of mutual defense. Later he was to place on record a letter that he wrote to the Foreign Office about his great concern in this matter. "After the former war Great Britain and France were, in 1919, the strongest and best armed Powers in Europe," Duff Cooper stated. "If they had then maintained their strength and concluded an alliance, they could have preserved the peace of the world. But they threw away their weapons and drifted apart, and by their criminal folly permitted the second catastrophe to occur. For God's sake, and for the sake of humanity, don't let that happen again."

The concern of the French about their own air defenses became so pressing that eventually Duff Cooper advised Bobbie George to go ahead and complete, within the structure of the R.A.F., the plans that he and his staff had been making for the supplying to the French of aircraft and a radar warning system. That meant bypassing our Foreign Office; and as a Service matter the French Air Force was rebuilt by the R.A.F. Out of that collaboration there was to develop the military side of the North Atlantic Treaty Organization. "In those days we called it the club," George has said. But all that lay in the future, and at that time my discussions with Duff Cooper and Bobbie George were limited, by the circumstances, to examinations of what was developing in the relations between the East and the West out in Germany.

In his autobiography Duff Cooper wrote feelingly about the difficulties that he had, as our Ambassador in France, in getting London to appreciate what he described as "those many small matters upon the settlement of which depends the fate of great nations." At that time I was having the same difficulty out in Germany. Our affairs in Germany were then the direct responsibility of the Chancellor of the Duchy of Lancaster, and the Permanent Secretary for a while was my old and trusted friend Sir Arthur Street. I could at least speak freely to him.

Toward the end of June, and at the start of the time when I began to feel that my difficulties in getting firm decisions from London were becoming unnecessarily trying, Arthur Street arrived in Berlin. He was just about to reliquish his office, and he stayed the night with me, and of our discussion Bob Wright recorded in his diary: "The Chief laying down the law to Arthur Street about the strait-jacket he is having to wear out here. They were at it for hours."

There was indeed a strait jacket imposed upon me over far too many points of detail. But in the meetings of the Control Council I felt that the other delegates were in much the same position. We would indulge in long discussions about various problems, and the Russians would always manage to prolong them, even if they did come eventually to agree with us on some of the items.

All our proceedings at the Control Council meetings were made additionally slow through having to use interpreters. There were times without number when, even with the interpreters at their best, it became obvious that, while we might arrive at some agreement with the Russians about the literal interpretation of critical words in our debates, there was nevertheless a basic difference in our thinking about what was meant by them. The outstanding example of that was our respective understandings of what was meant by the simple word "democracy." To the Russians it appeared to be something quite different from what was understood by our Western way of thought.

Most of the hard slogging of the work in the affairs of the Control Commission was done in what was known as the Coordinating Committee, which was the meeting ground for the Deputy Military Governors. In their deliberations they handled the detail, and then passed up to us, the Allied Control Council, the major points requiring final decisions. As Eisenhower's deputy, Lucius Clay was one of the original members of this committee, and Sokolovsky had also served his apprenticeship in it from its inception. Later Brian Robertson came to serve on this committee. "We had the form and, we thought, the substance for the exercise of four-power government," Clay said of that time. "We did not foresee the long hours of wrangling ending in deadlock which would characterize the work of the committees and directorates."

While the tensions in our relationships with the Russians were developing so inexorably on the one hand, we had to cope at the same time with the very difficult internal problem of the denazification of the Germans. While I personally had no particular liking for the Germans as a people, I felt that it was imperative, in the position in which I was placed, that I should approach this problem with as broad and as fair a frame of mind as possible. There was more than enough vindictiveness in the air, and I felt that there was a very great need for caution over what could all too easily become vengeance. What we had suffered at the hands of the Germans during the war, and what we had discovered when we occupied Germany, were enough to encourage the cries for vengeance; but they had to be stilled if we were to achieve at least the relief of the very great burden on the shoulders of our own people of propping up the Germans.

It was reported by Sir Arthur Street that just before Montgomery handed over to me Monty had said that three quarters of the population of Germany were "hard-bitten Nazis." In his *Memoirs,* Montgomery later stated that "my information was that a large percentage, probably 60 per cent, were out-and-out Nazis."

I have never known how Montgomery arrived at these figures which he quoted, and they do not in any way tally with those given in the actual files of the Nazi Party, which were one of the early finds made in Germany in the seizing of vital German documents. In the summer of 1945, very soon after the war, and to quote Michael Balfour in his work for the Royal Institute of International Affairs, "the complete index of members of the Nazi

Party and its auxiliaries was found in a Munich paper mill on the point of being reduced to pulp (the Germans having presumably decided that its destruction by burning would be unjustifiable waste)."

A year later the Chancellor of the Duchy of Lancaster stated in the House of Commons that the Nazi Party had numbered—for the whole of Germany—some eight million, with possibly another four million in what have been described as "dependent organisations." That made the actual overall Party membership number about twenty per cent of the population of the country. But was even every single one of that fifth of the total population a dyed-in-the-wool Nazi? What we had to decide upon was some way of differentiating between the many shades that existed all the way from the "hard-bitten" Nazi on the one hand and the merely loyal German on the other.

"The period between May 1945 and December 1946 . . . was probably one of the most difficult and unhappy periods in the whole of German history, when, as the result of Nazi ambition, the country was overwhelmed by great problems and great misery," the chairman of the Royal Institute of International Affairs stated in his introduction to the work published by Michael Balfour for that body in 1956. It was quite by chance that that chairman happened to be my old friend Bill Elliot, who was by then a retired air chief marshal. In what Elliot said he was speaking objectively about a scholarly study that had been made of the conditions out in Germany, and without any thought to my having been Military Governor at the time.

Under the rules that were laid down for denazification it was our duty to examine the records of all those who had ever had any connection with the Nazi Party. The Americans were insisting upon much stricter rules than we, the British, were prepared to accept, and it was required that we should prohibit all those with the slightest connection with the Party from any form of work in administering the country. It was understandable enough that we should hold for trial all those who were suspected of any criminal offenses; but where was the line to be drawn when it came to those who, for quite inoffensive reasons, and perhaps even under coercion, had joined the Party, and who were urgently needed for work to help us in the running of the country?

That there should still be Nazi influences at work, even though they were undercover, was understandable enough, and in my own thinking I felt that such resistance was only to be expected. It was surprising that it was not stronger. The Germans had had instilled into them during the past twelve years, in a way that was unique in history, a creed in which a great many of them had admittedly come to believe, and which a great many more had been compelled, of necessity, at least to acknowledge as being in existence. The problem, as I saw it, was just how far that "hard core" had come to affect the Germans, and how we were to cope with the infection. Prosecution of those Nazis who were found to be suspect of criminal acts was almost an automatic procedure, and we knew that many must have escaped our screening and gone into hiding. But even then we were holding under arrest in the British Zone alone by the end of 1946 nearly seventy thousand Party members.

For some time we had as the education adviser to the Control Commission the humanist Robert Birley, who was later to become headmaster of Eton. His views on the course that some Germans must have been forced to follow in order to avoid "loss of employment, poverty, torture, and possibly death for themselves and their families" was quoted by our official historian. Speaking of the two and a half years that he spent in Germany, Birley stated:

I was left with one very strong impression, that thousands of men and women in that country during the period of Nazi rule had found themselves faced with what seemed to be an impossible dilemma. They did not approve of the regime; many felt utterly ashamed of it. But what were they to do? Resistance seemed quite futile, and what would happen to their wives or husbands, their parents or children, if they made their protest? Most men and women are not strong enough to solve such a dilemma, and certainly someone who has not had to live in a totalitarian country has no right to condemn them.

There was no doubt in the minds of those of us who were governing Germany that although we had managed to struggle through that first winter after the war without, as might well have been expected, any general breakdown in the country which we were occupying, the prospects for the future were not good. We have been given to referring to the way in which we, the occupying powers, won the battle of that first winter. "Though fair enough as a dramatization of the difficult and dangerous situation facing the forces of occupation," our own official historian was to write quite a few years later, "this must nevertheless have caused a certain lifting of the eye-brows among Germans, dazed and war-weary though they might be. For indeed it was their resilience and industry, their ability to survive on a ration that the experts had pronounced insufficient to sustain life and make work possible for more than a few months, that enabled the battle to be won."

But with the prospects for the future so uncertain, and with the Germans eying us very narrowly, we desperately needed supplies of food and fuel, principally coal, if we were to get them back on their feet; and so far as we were concerned our major task was to help them to do just that. We had won a war that had been forced upon us, but we had no wish to talk about or think in terms of conquest; and in getting the people whom we had so soundly beaten back on the right path, we had to clear their minds of the poison of that evil creed with which they had become infected.

With the help that was given to the Germans by the Americans and the British they were able to survive without any widespread epidemics or starvation, although bare existence was grim enough for them. In a way it was the very nature of the people which came to help them. As a race the Germans have always been only too ready and even eager to follow a leader, and now that they were down and out and physically and emotionally exhausted they were even more ready to do as they were told, almost regardless of the origin of the orders.

The Germans had been bitten, but I felt that it was not quite in the way that Montgomery had meant; and the torments and the furies of the twelve years of Nazi tyranny to which they had been subjected was even more than they, a race with a liking for being told what to do, could stomach. On top of that they had been smashed by five and a half years of the merciless pounding of war. The vast majority of the German people were emotionaly exhausted, physically debilitated, and thoroughly apathetic and disillusioned.

But our problem in helping them was to guide them to help themselves. We could not go on forever supplying them with the large quantities of supplies of every nature that were needed to supplement their daily needs. Nor could we go on forever governing them. We had to find among the Germans themselves those who could and would lead their people back on to a path of sanity and reconstruction. At the same time we had to make sure that any of those who did come forward as prospective leaders were not in the category of dyed-in-the-wool Nazis, or of the older Prussian Junker mold, merely biding their time before they could again seize power. That was the task which we faced after the administration of the first aid.

In our dealings with the German people we also had to be cautious about the way in which we referred to the nature of their guilt for the war, for that could not help but cause in the people themselves certain feelings of resentment. That those responsible for the war and the atrocities that were committed during it—the men who were to become known as the war criminals—had to be tracked down and dealt with was a responsibility that was distinctly ours. And in that, in the midst of all our worries about the feeding and the welfare of the German people, there suddenly came down on my shoulders an added and totally unexpected responsibility: a share in the decision about what was to happen to the worst of all those found guilty of being war criminals.

39 / A Matter of Conscience

WHEN I HAD TAKEN on the task of being Commander-in-Chief and Military Governor of the British Zone of Germany and the head of the British element of the four-power Allied Control Council, I had no inkling that the final court of appeal against the sentences passed after the findings of the trials of the German major war criminals before the International Military Tribunal at Nuremberg would be the Control Council. It was not until the last moment that I learned, to my distress, that in company with General McNarney for America, General Koenig for France and Marshal Sokolovsky for Russia I was to have the distasteful duty of sitting in judgment on these appeals after the trials at Nuremberg.

At the time when I had been asked by Montgomery to represent him at the opening of the Nuremberg Trials some ten months before, I had had some doubts about their legality, and, since I had deliberately avoided paying much attention to what was going on at Nuremberg, there was no particular reason why I should have changed my mind. But when I found that, as the head of the British element of the Control Commission and a member of the Control Council, I was going to be one of the four men who were going to have to participate in this final judgment, I realized that it was of the utmost importance that I should, first of all, be quite clear about my own feelings on the subject. That meant that I would have to make inquiries into those aspects of the trials about which I was most troubled.

In my own mind I felt that there were three points that I would have to understand as clearly as possible, and when I came to face the task of making sure that I was thinking along the right lines I was glad that I had not been to Nuremberg. It would have been wrong for me to have had any actual contact with the trials, and attending them, even as an onlooker, could only too easily have affected my outlook. I had that brought home quite forcibly by what I was told by Bob Wright. With my permission, but against

736

my advice, he had gone to Nuremberg for a few days in August, and when he got back he was clearly disturbed by what he had seen and heard.

The sight of Hermann Goering in what Wright described as a close-up—coming face to face with him at close range—had made a particularly harsh impression on him, and he told me that he wished that he had listened to my advice because he found the experience of his visits to the trials one of the most distressing that he had ever known.

First of all in what I wanted to know was the need to understand the question of the actual legality of the trials. That this legality must have been established I felt was reasonably certain, but I wanted to assure myself about it. Second, there was the matter that was one of the most controversial raised at the trials: the obeying of orders by those in the positions of the highest command. And third, just what had been proved in the matter of the ill treatment and the killing of prisoners-of-war.

For my guidance I had available a wealth of material, none of which was more important than the actual proceedings of the trials, and to these I could refer for opinions expressed by the finest legal minds. But so far as I was concerned, there was much more to the whole issue than just the matter of legality. That can scarcely be wondered at because of the inescapable interest that I had always had in all that Hermann Goering had been doing, and which was almost of personal concern to me.

During the years that have passed since late 1946, I have thought a great deal about the task that I had to face then in Berlin, and for quite a long time there still lurked in my mind some indefinable doubt about the legality of the trials. At the time I did not entertain any particularly strong views on this matter, and when called upon to review the appeals I certainly had no compunction about making any decisions. Because of his close association with me as my personal staff officer at that time, and his own doubts then about the legality of the trials, Bob Wright had also continued to think about what had happened. Eventually we both came to feel so strongly about the need to clear our own minds on the subject that we made quite exhaustive studies. It now seems to me that the confusion in the minds of so many people over the trials at Nuremberg could have been avoided if a little more care had been taken and thought given at the time to the way in which information about them was presented to the public.

The charter that had brought into being the machinery for the International Military Tribunal for the trials at Nuremberg was a fairly short document that was signed in London on August 8, 1945, on behalf of Great Britain, the United States, France and Russia "for the prosecution and punishment of the major war criminals of the European Axis." Of particular importance in this charter is Article 6, which called for the trial and the punishment of those who committed any of the crimes in the categories listed as:

(a) Crimes against peace: namely, planning, preparation, initiation or waging of a war of aggression, or a war in violation of international treaties, agreements or assurances, or participation in a common plan or conspiracy for the accomplishment of any of the foregoing;
(b) War crimes: namely, violations of the laws or customs of war. Such violations shall include, but not be limited to, murder, ill-treatment or deportation to slave labour or for any other purpose of civilian population of or in occupied territory, murder or ill-treatment of prisoners of war or persons on the seas, killing of hostages, plunder of public or private property, wanton destruction of cities, towns or villages, or devastation not justified by military necessity;
(c) Crimes against humanity: namely, murder, extermination, enslavement, deportation, and other inhumane acts committed against any civilian population, before or during the war, or persecutions on political, racial or religious grounds in execution of or in connection with any crime within the jurisdiction of the Tribunal, whether or not in violation of the domestic law of the country where perpetrated.

This article concluded with the statement: "Leaders, organisers, instigators and accomplices participating in the formulation or execution of a common plan or conspiracy to commit any of the foregoing crimes are responsible for all acts performed by any persons in execution of such plan."

In this important matter of responsibility, which was to play such a vital part in the trials, Article 7 stated: "The official position of defendants, whether as Heads of State or responsible officials in Government Departments, shall not be considered as freeing them from responsibility or mitigating punishment." Article 8 went one step further. It stated: "The fact that the Defendant acted pursuant to order of his Government or of a superior shall not free him from responsibility, but may be considered in mitigation of punishment if the Tribunal determines that justice so requires." This was to be the source of a great deal of argument and debate, and at Nuremberg the Germans never seemed to grasp the meaning of what was so clearly defined.

The first paragraph of Article 26 of the charter, which came under the heading of "Judgement and Sentence," stated: "The judgement of the Tribunal as to the guilt or the innocence of any Defendant shall give the reasons on which it is based, and shall be final and not subject to review." This relieved the Allied Control Council of having to make any decisions about the findings of actual guilt; and in Article 29 there was defined the extent of the duties that we, the members of the Control Council, were to perform. "In case of guilt," it was stated, "sentences shall be carried out in accordance with the orders of the Control Council for Germany, which may at any time reduce or otherwise alter the sentences, but may not increase the severity thereof."

It is no exaggeration to say that the documents and various records and other papers produced at Nuremberg came to be weighed literally in many hundreds of tons. "It has often and very fairly been said that there has never been such a wealth of material for cross-examination as at Nuremberg," the Earl of Kilmuir has stated. He was then Sir David Maxwell-Fyfe, and responsible for conducting the British cross-examination.

It was with some apprehension that, with so little warning, I had to face the formidable task of finding my way through and digesting all the paper work put up to me. I did that away from Berlin and in the comparative quiet of my office in the zonal headquarters of the Control Commission at Lubbecke. I gave Bob Wright firm instructions that he was to see to it that I was left entirely free from any other work so that I could concentrate on this onerous task, and that no one was to get past him, and that, until the whole business was settled, he was to give me only the papers having to do with Nuremberg. I had little enough time in which to make up my mind about the decisions that would be called for.

With their characteristic thoroughness, the Germans had kept the official records of the years of the Nazi regime in a manner that was complete in almost every way, and to the astonishment of the investigators—and the later gratification of the historians—these records were found almost intact except for those of the German Air Force. The latter went up in one great bonfire.

Times without number the prosecution was able to produce as evidence at Nuremberg documents of an almost bewildering variety, and of a compelling authority. In speaking of this in the judgment at the end of the trials, Lord Justice Lawrence, the president of the tribunal, commented: "Much of the evidence presented to the Tribunal on behalf of the prosecution was documentary evidence, captured by the Allied armies in German Army headquarters, Government buildings, and elsewhere. Some of the documents were found in salt mines, buried in the ground, hidden behind false walls and in other places thought to be secure from discovery. The case, therefore, against the defendants rests in a large measure on documents of their own making, the authority of which has not been challenged except in one or two cases."

In his opening address, Lord Justice Lawrence described the trials that were to take place as "unique in the history of jurisprudence of the world." The steps that had been taken before the creation of the actual charter gave good support to that. As early as January, 1942, a conference was held in London that was attended by representatives of all the Allies, and they discussed the punishment "through the channel of organized justice" of war crimes. Later in that same year President Roosevelt issued a warning to all those who indulged in war crimes "that the time will come when they shall have to stand in the courts of law in the very countries which they are now oppressing and answer for their acts." This was followed a few weeks later in 1942 by declarations by the governments of Britain and of the United States that they intended "to apprehend and punish war criminals, as well as to create an agency to investigate war crimes."

Late in 1943 there was brought into being in London a body which was given the title of the United Nations War Crimes Commission. This was a fact-finding organization, and sixteen of the Allied countries were represented by some of their most prominent lawyers. The Soviet Union was not a member of this commission because it had set up one of its own. On August 8, 1945, agreement was reached in London by Great Britain, the United States, France and Russia which led to the creation of the International Military Tribunal, the purpose of which, as stated by Lord Justice Lawrence, was "to be the just and prompt trial and punishment of the Major War Criminals of the European Axis."

In the reading of the indictment at Nuremberg on November 20, 1945, Sir David Maxwell-Fyfe named in detail the "international treaties, agreements and assurances" which, it was alleged, were violated. These various pacts agreed to by Germany started with "The Convention for the Pacific Settlement of International Disputes" signed at The Hague in 1899, and proceeded through other agreements signed in 1907, the Versailles Treaty of 1919, the Locarno Treaties and Conventions of 1925, the Kellogg-Briand Pact of 1928, other international treaties of 1929, 1934, 1935,

being brought to bear at that time which could in any way impinge upon my conscience. I stated that I thought that it was neither necessary nor proper for us to examine the legality of the proceedings at Nuremberg, and I urged that we should determine on humanitarian grounds whether we should exercise our power of clemency in the reduction of any sentences.

"The Council should consider these pleas of clemency not as legal experts but as men of the world," I stated.

I took that firm stand because I could not see that there was any other that one could take. The finest legal brains in the world had been at work for a long time on the problems raised at Nuremberg, and our own legal advisers could scarcely be expected to add anything to that work. McNarney and Noiret came around to my way of thinking, and stated that they were then prepared to agree with what I had suggested.

But even after this, there were further repercussions from London, this time to our directive of September 7. It was reported that Justice Robert H. Jackson, the chief of counsel for the United States, was objecting to the directive on the ground that it contemplated a review of the judgment and the sentences that were to come from Nuremberg, and that it was his view that petitions for clemency should be dealt with as a matter of policy, and that there should be no review on legal grounds. It was pointed out to me that this was the same line that our people at home were adopting, and that they hoped that we in Berlin would follow it.

The next meeting of the Control Council was held in Berlin on September 30. This was to be the last occasion for that month on which I would be acting as chairman; and in Nuremberg that morning the tribunal had resumed its sittings, with Lord Justice Lawrence starting a reading of the long judgment that had resulted from the deliberations of the judges during the past month. We had as a guest at our Council meeting that day General Eisenhower, who was on a visit to Germany.

The main topic of discussion at our meeting was again the way in which we should handle the appeals that we expected would be coming from Nuremberg. General Koenig repeated the French suggestion for a commission to consider pleas for clemency; and McNarney suggested yet again that the matter should be referred first of all to the coordinating committee. Sokolovsky was against such proposals; and again I agreed with him. I stuck out for the agreement that we had reached only ten days before about settling everything ourselves, and I managed to bring McNarney and

Koenig around once again to my way of thinking, although Koenig did record his regret at having to abandon the French proposal. But that did at least settle the procedure that we were to follow.

The handing down of the judgment by the Military Tribunal at Nuremberg, and the sentences that were passed on those found guilty, occupied the days of September 30 and October 1. Two days later I received in my office in Lubbecke the first of the papers—the judgment and the sentences—from Nuremberg, and I was then able to go about informing myself more fully about what had happened. The next day I received from the last quarter that I ever expected an instruction that involved me deeply in what I considered was a matter of conscience, and which was very disturbing in its implications.

It came in the form of a personal signal to me from London marked top secret, and it stated that Ernest Bevin, the Secretary of State for Foreign Affairs, held strong views about the way in which the results of the Nuremberg Trials should be handled. I was asked to consult him before the Control Council reached any decision about confirmation of the Nuremberg sentences, and it was stressed that Bevin was particularly concerned about any measures of clemency which might be decided upon.

In all the dealings that I ever had with Ernie Bevin, of whom I was very fond and whom I greatly admired, this was the only occasion upon which I had to take exception to anything that he ever said or did. This time I had to take the strongest exception. I regarded myself as being in a judicial position, and I did not think that the Foreign Secretary or anybody else had any right whatso-ever to tell me what I should do, and that it was up to me to give my verdicts according to my conscience and my conscience alone. It was the old question all over again of how far the executive is entitled to interfere with the judiciary; and in this case I felt that Bevin was entirely wrong in interfering and in trying to tell me what I should do. It was also the unhappy situation of political interference with a serving officer in the execution of his duty.

After writing a personal letter to Bevin in which I stated my case, I replied officially to the signal that I had received, making it clear that I regarded my function in the Nuremberg business as being judicial rather than political, and that it was also a question involving my own conscience. I further stated that I considered that it would be quite improper for me to hold up the proceedings of the Control Council while I consulted the Secretary of State about each and all of our decisions, and I felt that the other members would resent such an action. I suggested that the Secretary of State should let me have immediately his views on the commutation or reduction of the sentences, and that I would take these views into account when it came to making up my own mind. The petitions for clemency had not yet been received, and I stated that I would let the Secretary of State know what I intended to recommend before the Control Council met, although that did not mean to say that I could forecast what would be finally decided.

This drew from London, as a result of a Cabinet meeting, further instructions to me in a long, personal signal which I received in Berlin on the morning of October 8, after flying up from the British Zone. I was told that it was considered that there was some misapprehension on my part as to my exact position in this matter, and that it was not considered that I was in the position of a Commander-in-Chief reviewing a court-martial sentence, or filling the role of a Colonial Governor or the Home Secretary.

When I read that signal I did have to stop myself dead in my tracks and ask myself if my official title was not "Military Governor and Commander-in-Chief." It was further stressed to me that it was not for the representatives on the Control Council to decide about the reduction or mitigation of sentences, and that it was the view of His Majesty's Government that from a political point of view it would be an advantage if there were no alterations in the sentences.

It was at the mention of political points of view that I began to feel developing in my mind a sense of outrage at the way in which these orders were being given to me. The officials in London had not yet even seen the petitions for clemency, and yet they were already making up their minds, from political points of view, about what I was to do. Finally, I was told that if there was any disposition among my colleagues on the Control Council to make any alterations in the sentences I was to refer to London for further instructions.

One of the main issues that I was going to have to consider in the appeals for clemency was the matter of the way in which the orders given to the German military leaders by the political heads of the Nazi state had been observed. What part must conscience play in the obeying of such orders? I believed that, in any considerations whatsoever, it must play a vitally important part. Now I was being told that my beliefs and feelings in the matter, my conscience, did not count: I was to accept orders.

No reply came from Ernie Bevin to the personal letter that I had written to him. Under the circumstances, there was not much that he could say. I have always felt that, being the very sensible and conscientious man that he was, he agreed in his heart with the point of view that I had placed before him, even if he did have to place political considerations before any personal feelings. I nevertheless experienced a mounting objection to being treated merely as a mouthpiece for the Government in a matter that was of the deepest personal concern to me; and I came to feel that there was the danger that I might be placed in very much the same position as that occupied by Sokolovsky in his relationship with the Russian Government.

It was of little wonder that Bob Wright recorded in his diary for that day: "The Chief in the most filthy temper and barking at everyone. All afternoon in the office snowed under with Nuremberg business. By late afternoon he was at a new low—or high— and he had sharp words with Charles Steele on the 'phone." I must have been in a very difficult mood to have taken things out on Steele, who was one of my oldest and closest friends.

That evening, Wright recorded, I "opened up a little as we had a drink, and . . . talked about what [I] proposed doing at the Control Council meetings starting tomorrow." The action that I planned to take over the instructions that I had received that morning from London was that I would do as I was told unless— as Wright recorded of our talk—"the issue was very clear cut, in which case he would make decisions off his own bat and to the devil with H.M.G."

That might sound as if I was in a reckless state of rebellion, but such was not the case. I was in a rebellious mood, but there was nothing reckless about it. The Government's having approved the stand that I had taken, acting on my own initiative, at the Control Council meeting of September 20—nearly three weeks before— when I had won my point about considering the pleas for clemency "not as legal experts but as men of the world" (and that exact statement was on record for all to read in the minutes of that meeting), I felt that it was asking too much to expect me to fill now a role that would be nothing more than that of a puppet.

The indictment presented to the tribunal at the opening of the Nuremberg Trials is a record of the horrors committed by the Nazis in the west and the east—in fact, in particular on their eastern front—that is long and detailed enough to make anyone's flesh creep. I have found that a rereading of certain parts of it even today, so many years later, leaves in no way dimmed the sense of outrage that assaults one. And yet so much was made by the defendants during the trial, right up to the very end, of what they claimed was the inescapable demand for their blind obedience in following out orders that led to those atrocities.

"Political loyalty, military obedience, are excellent things, but they neither require nor do they justify the commission of patently wicked acts," Sir Hartley Shawcross, chief prosecutor for Britain, and our Attorney General, had stated in his opening address before the tribunal. "There comes a point when a man must refuse to answer to his leader if he is also to answer to his conscience."

Many months later, M. Auguste Champetier de Ribes, the chief prosecutor for France, made his closing speech, in the course of which he said: "Hitler might have governed their bodies but not their souls. By disobeying him they might perhaps have lost their liberty or even their lives, but they would at least have saved their honour."

In the final judgment it was clearly ruled that anyone who had committed criminal acts could not hide behind the excuse that he was only obeying orders. Nor could he claim that his crimes were acts of state. Therefore, no one could plead that he was merely obeying the orders of his superiors; and the superiors could not plead that their orders were acts of state. "The true test, which is found in varying degrees in the criminal law of most nations," the judgment stated, "is not the existence of the order, but whether moral choice was in fact possible."

On the matter of the involvement of the military leaders, which was of particular concern to me personally, Lord Kilmuir has since stated: "There has been and will always be considerable discussion as to the correctness of placing military commanders on trial. It is a point from which we must not flinch that henceforward, if a General is conscious that the plans are the actual, practical, and proximate plans for aggressive war, he becomes criminally liable if he takes part. This point must not be obscured by the further fact that in the case of the Nazi commanders, owing to the evil methods adopted, they were all guilty of war crimes and crimes against humanity as well. These men were found guilty, on very good evidence of what was nothing less than murder. It is still murder although you hire someone else to fire the gun."

Just before I left my office in Berlin to go to the first of the meetings at which we were to consider the appeals, a telegram arrived addressed to me by a group of retired German Army officers saying that we must let off the Army commanders—Keitel and Jodl—in order that they might take their stand for the future beside the German people. For an indication of the strength of my views on this there is an entry made in his diary by Bob Wright which reveals that I wrote across the bottom of the form: "Rot—will these people never learn."

Twenty-one men had been tried as major war criminals at Nuremberg. They were the survivors of those who had ruled the Nazi Party and Germany. Adolf Hitler, Joseph Goebbels, Heinrich Himmler and Robert Ley had all committed suicide, and Martin Bormann had disappeared. Of those of the Nazi leaders who were captured and arraigned before the Military Tribunal at Nuremberg, three were found not guilty of the charges made and were acquitted. They were Hjalmar Schacht, one of Germany's masterminds in economics and banking, Franz von Papen, the German diplomat and politician who had an astonishing record of intrigue, and Hans Fritzsche, an assistant to Goebbels in the Nazi Propaganda Ministry.

Of the remaining eighteen who had been found guilty of one or more of the crimes alleged, Ernst Kaltenbrunner, notorious as Himmler's deputy and chief of the Security Police, who was condemned to death, Baldur von Schirach, the leader of the Hitler Youth, who received a sentence of twenty years' imprisonment, and Albert Speer, the brilliant planner in armaments and war production, who was also sentenced to twenty years' imprisonment, seemed to realize that the game was up. They made no appeals against the sentences.

The Allied Control Council was thus left to deal with fifteen petitions for clemency. At one time the names of these men whose appeals we had on our hands were known with terrifying familiarity throughout the world. It is now twenty years since the determination of their guilt, and there are many who were too young then to know anything about them and who even as adults today know only vaguely what it was that these men represented and about the monstrous wickedness of the crimes that they perpetrated. But their names should never be forgotten, and history itself amply records the extraordinary evil that existed in all of them. They were:

Hermann Wilhelm Goering. Next to Hitler, he was the most prominent figure in the Nazi Party. Utterly corrupt in every way, he had equipped himself with a glittering array of vain titles, of which the most important were such that, until the very end, they would have enabled him to become Hitler's successor. He was the supreme head of the German Air Force, which he neglected to the point of wrecking it as a Service. Aged fifty-two, he was condemned to death.

Rudolf Hess. One of Hitler's earliest and closest supporters. Up until the time of his flight to England in 1941, he was Deputy Fuehrer of the Nazi Party. He was a man apparently broken in health and in mind. Aged fifty-two, he was sentenced to life imprisonment, which he is still serving at the prison in Berlin.

Joachim von Ribbentrop. Foreign Minister during the war, he had at one time been the German Ambassador to this country. A conniving and utterly ruthless opportunist, aged fifty-three, he was sentenced to death.

Wilhelm Keitel. A field marshal and Chief of Staff of the High Command and directly responsible to Hitler, he was well known as a political general. Although an old soldier, and claiming to be an honorable one, he countenanced appalling atrocities. Aged sixty-three, he was sentenced to death.

Alfred Rosenberg. A muddle-headed thinker, he was described as the principal philosopher of the Nazis. He was later German Minister for the Eastern Occupied Territories, and was responsible for much of the brutality and terror that occurred there. Aged fifty-three, he was sentenced to death.

Hans Frank. Spoken of as Hitler's lawyer, he was later to gain for himself an appalling notoriety as the Governor-General of Occupied Poland, introducing there concentration camps and a reign of terror. Aged forty-six, he was sentenced to death.

Wilhelm Frick. A politician and one of the old guard of the Nazi Party. Described as "the first Nazi bureaucrat," he was for a time the Minister of the Interior. Aged sixty-nine, he was rabidly anti-Semitic, and along with others he signed the documents which led to the mass destruction of the Jews. He was sentenced to death.

Julius Streicher. Another of the old guard of the Nazi Party, he early acquired an evil notoriety for the violence and the lewdness of his anti-Semitism. He conducted what the Nuremberg judgment described as a "propaganda of death"; and his general repulsiveness had led to his being ostracized even within the Nazi Party. Aged sixty-one, he was sentenced to death.

Walter Funk. Another of the economic experts, he succeeded Schacht as Minister of Economics. But he was also an official in the Ministry of Propaganda and the Chamber of Culture. He worked closely with Himmler, and he was one of those concerned with the exploitation of forced slave labor. Aged fifty-six, he was sentenced to life imprisonment.

Karl Doenitz. A grand admiral and a Commander-in-Chief of the German Navy, he was Hitler's successor after Goering's fall from grace. Aged fifty-five, he was found guilty of crimes against peace and war crimes, which included ruthless submarine warfare. He received a sentence of ten years' imprisonment.

Erich Raeder. Also a grand admiral, and Commander-in-Chief of the German Navy until 1943, when his place was taken by Doenitz. Aged seventy, he was found guilty of the planning and waging of aggressive war, and sentenced to life imprisonment. Stress was laid on the way in which he "carried out unrestricted submarine warfare."

Fritz Sauckel. In charge of all manpower problems, he was responsible for the vast slave labor program brought into effect by the Nazis, a program described in the Nuremberg judgment as involving "deportation for slave labour of more than 5,000,000 human beings, many of them under terrible conditions of cruelty and suffering." Forty-eight years of age, he was sentenced to death.

Alfred Jodl. Another of the political generals, he was Chief of Operations of the High Command, working directly under Keitel and completely subservient to Hitler. Aged fifty-six, he was found guilty on all counts, and he was sentenced to death.

Artur Seyss-Inquart. An Austrian politician, he later became Reich Commissioner for the Netherlands, and he imposed the Nazi rules that led to hundreds of thousands of Dutchmen being sent to Germany as slave labor, and the deportation of over one hundred thousand Jews from Holland to German concentration camps. Aged fifty-four, he was sentenced to death.

Konstantin von Neurath. A foreign minister in the early years of the Nazi regime, he later became Protector of Bohemia and Moravia. It was found that he knew that "war crimes and crimes against humanity were being committed under his authority" in Czechoslovakia. Aged seventy-two, he was sentenced to fifteen years' imprisonment.

For two days we sat in Berlin in sessions of the Allied Control Council discussing the appeals for clemency, and I can still feel the perplexity that I experienced then over the manner in which the other delegates conducted themselves. It was the turn of the French to be in charge of the meetings, and General Koenig was in the chair. The British delegation occupied the position to the left of the chairman along the side of the square around which we all sat. This meant that, after introducing the name of the man whose appeal we were to consider, Koenig turned first to me, and I had to start the ball rolling. I gave in each case, and in some detail, the views that I held and the reasons for my decision. When Koenig asked McNarney and Sokolovsky for their views they merely said that they agreed, and he, in turn, then agreed. We then passed on to the next appeal.

It went on like that for some time, and it seemed to me that I was doing all the talking with nothing more than formal assent from the others. After a while I asked Koenig if we could, for a change, reverse the order. He agreed amiably enough. Sokolovsky and McNarney merely announced their decisions, and again I was left to give my reasons and detailed opinions and findings. And on I went, left to present my review of each of the cases, just as I had been doing before, the only one to do that in such detail. Eventually we rejected all the appeals, and all the sentences were confirmed.

It is not likely that I shall ever forget the moment when I came to the end of the summary of my views on the appeal lodged in the name of Hermann Goering. It should be recorded that he did not himself appeal: it was made by his lawyer without his direct order. Goering had petitioned that he might "be spared the ignominy of hanging and be allowed to die as a soldier before a firing squad"; but that had been rejected. The sentence was death by hanging. When I stated at the Control Council meeting that for the reasons that I had given I was rejecting that particular appeal I felt that in my own life I was saying the last word in what had been a long and intensely personal experience, and that it was something which could not be understood, even if they knew about it, by the other delegates.

One of the points that I had examined with particular care was the question of Goering's involvement in the shooting of our airmen after their mass escape from Stalag Luft III in March, 1944. In Lord Kilmuir's cross-examination, Goering—"the most formidable witness I have ever cross-examined," Kilmuir said of him—had tried to absolve himself by claiming that it had happened while he was on leave. But the evidence proved that while he did not finish his leave until March 29—some six days after the escapes—the shootings were still going on until as late as April 13.

It had been established that Goering's second in command—Field Marshal Milch—knew what was happening; and commenting later on that, Lord Kilmuir has said: "It then became a question whether it was humanly conceivable that on so vital a matter, with Hitler ordering the shooting and that the urns containing the ashes of the bodies—ashes that did not show the cause of death—should be exhibited in the camp, the head of the Air Force should not have been told."

Twenty-eight years before, Goering and I, as young fighter pilots, had fought each other in the cleaner atmosphere of the air. As I spoke the words that meant for Goering an irrevocable death sentence I could not help feeling, for all my loathing of what he had become, the strongest revulsion that I should have to be one of those so directly concerned with it.

The only point of disagreement that arose during these deliberations of the Allied Control Council was over the sentence that had been passed on General Jodl, who had been Hitler's chief of staff. He had received the death sentence, which meant that he was due to be hanged. Koenig and McNarney were of the opinion that, being a general, he should at least be given the privilege of being shot. Sokolovsky spoke out very strongly against that. He said that Jodl deserved to be hanged just as much as any of the other criminals, and that, because he wore a uniform and had the rank of a general, there was no reason why he should be exempted in any way from the penalty that had been decided upon by the tribunal at Nuremberg.

While I agreed with Sokolovsky in this matter of the manner in which Jodl should die, it was for a different reason. I believed that these German generals had betrayed themselves. What had happened after the mass escape from Stalag Luft III, and the way in which fifty of our airmen were shot after they were recaptured, was proof enough of that for me.

In his book on the Nuremberg Trials, R. W. Cooper has said: "There are no doubt many soldiers all over the world who looked on the arraignment of Keitel and Jodl with serious misgivings, who would subscribe, perhaps, to the cynical bon mot that the ultimate crime in war is to lose it." I was emphatically not one of those. It became all too clear to me as I studied the evidence that these two high-ranking German officers were being tried, as Cooper has pointed out, for "their responsibility in abominable crimes," and not for being soldiers.

One of the more telling points made by Lord Kilmuir in his cross-examination of Keitel, and to which Keitel could give no answer, was to emphasize that it was just as true of the code of the Germans as it was of ours that no soldier was forced to obey an order which was a crime and which, knowing it to be a crime, he obeyed against his conscience. "I want you to understand this," he said to Keitel. "As far as I know, in the German military code, as in every military code, there is no obligation on the part of a soldier to obey an order which he knows is wrong, which he knows is contrary to the laws of war and criminal law. It is the same in your Army and our Army and I think in every Army, isn't that so?"

Keitel gave no direct answer, so Kilmuir then flung at him: "I want to make this point perfectly clear. You were a Field Marshal, Kesselring was a Field Marshal, Milch was a Field Marshal, all, I gather, with military training behind them and all having their influence, if not their command, amongst the Armed Forces of Germany. How was it that there was not one man of your rank, of your military tradition, with the courage to stand up and oppose cold-blooded murder? That is what I want to know."

There was only evasion in the answer given by Keitel. In his questions to Keitel about the exact responsibility for the shootings after the escapes from Stalag Luft III, Kilmuir asked:

"So that it comes to this, defendant, doesn't it: That you will go as far as this: You were present at the meeting with Hitler and Himmler. That is what you say. At that meeting Hitler said that the prisoners who were caught by the police were to remain in the hands of the police. You had a strong belief that these prisoners would be shot and with that you used this incident as a deterrent to try and prevent other prisoners of war escaping. All that you admit, as I understand your answers this morning, don't you?"

"Yes, I do admit that," Keitel admitted; but he went on to state that the warning "was on the instruction of Hitler . . ."

So strongly did I feel about this that I made a somewhat impassioned outburst at the Control Council meeting, aiming it at the American Military Governor, who was also an airman. I asked McNarney if he believed that if, for the sake of argument, President Roosevelt had suddenly gone out of his mind and told General Eisenhower to shoot fifty German prisoners-of-war, Eisenhower would have obeyed that order. I pointed out with some vigor that Eisenhower would have resigned, even if it had meant that his own life was at stake, rather than countenance an order that would have been so much against the dictates of his conscience.

At the end of the second day of the meetings in Berlin, there was a discussion about the way in which the bodies should be cremated after the hangings, and how to dispose of the ashes. Of that final nauseating discussion at the Control Council meeting, which he attended with me, Bob Wright made the comment in his diary: "All very depressing." While I am prepared to agree with what Wright has said about my bad temper during these sessions—the whole business did get on my nerves in the most unpleasant way—his appreciation of the effect on me at the end when he said that I was "very low" is a distinct understatement. I have seldom, if ever, known a feeling of such acute distaste as that which I experienced when I found myself having to participate in this last macabre discussion.

It had been arranged that the executions should take place in the prison at Nuremberg in the small hours of the morning of October 16. Only two hours before he was due to be hanged, Hermann Goering committed suicide by swallowing poison. When the news was brought to me that he had managed to dodge the hangman, I must admit that I felt a slight relief. As might be expected, there was an awful commotion about this suicide, and an inquiry was held to try and find out how it had happened. I could not help feeling that it could not have mattered less, and that an inquiry was merely recording the facts, if they were needed, for the benefit of history.

The post-mortem that was held led to another discussion at the meeting of the Allied Control Council on October 30. On this occasion, because of what we were going to discuss, it was decided to restrict the number of those present to the members of each delegation who were most directly concerned. The merely curious had to leave. Only just before the meeting I had received my copy of the report on the way in which Goering had committed suicide, along with copies of the last letter that he wrote to his wife and a statement that could be regarded as his final testament.

It was agreed at our meeting that all the copies of these documents which were in existence should be gathered up, and that all of them except one—which should be preserved in the archives of the Control Commission—should be destroyed. It was further agreed that no information should ever be made public about the contents of any of these documents, that nothing more need be said by any of us, and that we should forever remain silent about what had already been said that day. "The Chief very sullen and in a bad temper," Bob Wright recorded in his diary, and he described the proceedings at the Control Council meeting as "very disturbing."

I knew well enough that I was being sullen, and I also knew that I had been bad-tempered; and because I am of a temperament that, under normal circumstances, does not countenance either sullenness or bad temper I was only too glad to be finished with the whole sordid business.

40 / Impasse

WITH GERMAN militarism flattened, and the rabid nationalism of the people of that country quiescent, it had been hoped that the ending of a state of war would enable the four occupying powers to govern at least in peace. So far as we of the West were concerned, we had set ourselves the task of bringing to the Germans a liberal settlement of their condition; but the East had other ideas. Stalin was not interested in a liberal reorientation of the German pepole, or of helping them to get back on their feet. The cold war began to develop still further, with Berlin as its focal point; and what happened in 1946 and 1947, during my time there, is all too clearly reflected in the situation as it is today.

Before we even got there, the Russians had already stripped Berlin, including the sectors allotted to the West, of everything that they thought might be of use to them, and their continuing demand was for impossible reparations. The Americans and the British were trying to help the Germans, and as we went about that the Russians were just as busily at work extracting all that they could from the country. From the economic point of view alone it was becoming a thoroughly impossible situation: a drain down which we saw prospects of pouring aid which would benefit the Russians more than the Germans. And in Berlin it had become even more than that. There was by then a struggle for the minds of the people.

Split in two, with the Russians occupying the eastern half, the French the northwestern, the British the central western, and the Americans the southwestern part, Berlin was nevertheless at that time still one city. In addition to being the capital, it had long been the largest and most important industrial city in Germany. At the time there were no restrictions whatsoever about movement between the eastern and the western parts, although the signs which indicated which sector of the city one was in were ominous, and the Russian guards were always on view on their boundary. But in those days they did nothing more than look at us as we looked at them.

The first battle that was to take place between the East and the West went on behind the scenes; and it was the Berliners them-selves who made the decision about the outcome. They were given the opportunity to achieve what they did through the arguments that we, the Allies, had around the conference table during the sessions of the Control Council. The Communists clumsily over-played their hand, and they got a shock that led first to the sulks, then attempts at strangulation.

Berlin had a long history and reputation for being robustly socialist-minded. With a totally false reasoning, the Russians persuaded themselves that such views must mean that they were ripe for Communism, and that if a Communist regime could be grafted on Berlin, we of the West would very soon be kicked out. All that was needed, the Russians seemed to believe, was a massive propaganda campaign, and then, naïve as it may sound, the free elections that we were insisting upon would turn in their favor. The Berliners got both: Communist propaganda that was blatant throughout all of the four sectors of Berlin; and through the work of the Western Allies in the Control Council the right to vote as they saw fit.

But although the Communists went to work in their usual way and made every effort to gain control, when the final results of the elections became known it was clearly revealed that the Berliners in the western part of the city wanted no part of them. It was a sharp and unexpected rebuff for the Russians, but they had to accept it. In doing that they closed their ranks, and the Iron Curtain was lowered with a horrible clang.

At the time of the conferences in Cairo in December, 1943, Eisenhower had private talks, he later recorded, with President Roosevelt about how Germany should be handled in a postwar occupation, and he stated that the President "listened sympa-thetically to my contention that occupation should become a responsibility of civil agencies of government as soon as the exigencies of war might permit."

After the business of the Nuremberg Trials, and with the arguments that began to develop around the conference table of the Allied Control Council after the reverses suffered by the Russians in the elections in Berlin, I began to feel as Eisenhower had much earlier about the advisability of civil agencies being responsible for governing the country we were occupying. The arguments and stalling tactics that the Russians started indulging in were tiresome and so obviously dominated by political issues.

What with the negative atmosphere that began to hover over our quadripartite meetings at the highest level, and the continuing struggle to cope with the economic and other crises which we had to face during that winter of 1946–47, I found myself wondering quite often why I, an Air Force officer, should be trying to solve problems which should have been in the hands of the politicians. It seemed to be such an interminable period of largely standing still, and although there was more than enough detail in the day-to-day work to deal with, and the problems associated with that work were real enough, I could not help wondering if we were making any real progress.

But progress was made, and in a remarkably short time the British and the Americans came to realize that there was no point at all in standing separately against the massive Russian threat that was lining up to the east. And with that, the United States Government did a complete about-face in their whole attitude toward Russia. By the end of July, 1946, our two governments had already agreed to an economic fusion of their two zones.

As the heads of the administrative side of our control of the West, Brian Robertson and Lucius Clay, the British and American Deputy Military Governors, had worked hard for this fusion, and as soldiers in what was more a civilian enterprise than a military one they achieved a great deal. For one thing, it meant that the more highly industrialized British Zone had some access to the greater agricultural resources of the American Zone. It was also a firm step forward toward the freedom and establishment of what is today the western Federal Republic of Germany, made up of the former American, British and French zones. But it caused the Communists to become even more rigid in their attitude toward us, with their eventual changing of the name of their eastern zone into what is now called the German Democratic Republic.

In March, 1947, Lucius Clay succeeded General McNarney as the American Military Governor, and of the meetings of the Allied Control Council that continued to be held in Berlin, and which we attended together, he has said: "They seemed to have lost substance and I, for one, felt that we were merely going through meaningless motions." That I was in agreement with him about that Clay well understood, and there is proof of that in a statement which I made at one meeting in the course of an argument that we got into with Sokolovsky. Clay had given an answer which he discusses in his book *Decision in Germany* to a matter raised by

Sokolovsky; and he then quotes my comment: "My conception of the solution is the same as General Clay's."

The British and the Americans were by then in agreement on all major issues, which led Sokolovsky to make the accusation later in the year that "the United States and British military administrations have taken the road of a complete breaking away from the decisions of the Potsdam Conference." It suited the Russians to talk in that way, even if agreements reached at the Potsdam Conference had been violated by them times without number.

During that time of the Stalinist era it was a curious and depressing experience to watch and listen to men who, one knew, were intelligent and sane behaving like so many puppets, zigzagging this way and that, at times doubling back on their own tracks, and generally talking and behaving in a way which made one wonder if, after all, they were as sane as one believed them to be. I had come to know Sokolovsky quite well, and I liked him; but I could never pretend that I knew which way he was likely to jump next. Most of the time I doubt if he knew himself, and his telephone link with Moscow must have been a decidedly hot one.

With Lucius Clay it was altogether different, and I found him one of the most able and forthright and clear-thinking of all the American commanders whom I came to know. He was immensely experienced and shrewd, and he was not afraid of having to stand on his own feet, and he was the most active of all the Military Governors who worked in Germany. Descended from a well-known political family, he was a professional soldier and an engineer and administrator of unusually wide experience. His father had been a Senator, and from the days of his boyhood he had lived in the heady political atmosphere of Washington. Clay knew his way around in any circles.

At the same time that Lucius Clay became the Military Governor of the American Zone of Germany, there were changes in some of the departments in our own government in London. Frank Pakenham, who was then Lord Pakenham and is now the Earl of Longford, became the Chancellor of the Duchy of Lancaster. Of his approach to his responsibility for our affairs in Germany he said: "There is no aspect of British policy which has lain so close to my heart these last few years as our policy towards Germany."

Such a statement could have led the cynics—and out in Germany we were not short of them—to sneer at what might have been regarded as yet another speech by yet another politician. If anybody did feel that way, they could not have made a greater mistake. And when Pakenham added the comment: "I was already imbued with an almost fanatical interest in the fate of the stricken Germans," he meant every word of it. He had the background for such an interest: as a don at Oxford his subject had been international history between the years of 1871 and 1914.

But it was not as a don or as a politician that Frank Pakenham came to make the great impression on me that he did after we got to know each other. His great heart and integrity and enthusiasm were the qualities about him that appealed to me and which, in turn, provided a fillip to my own flagging spirit. And in addition to his deep compassion for the Germans, he was always so fair in trying his utmost to help those of us who were serving out in Germany during that very difficult time.

The exceptionally harsh winter of 1946–47 caused acute suffering in Germany through lack of food and coal and proper shelter, and we who had to control and administer the country were all too conscious of that, as well as being only too well aware of the criticism that was being expressed at home of us and our administration. Of his understanding of my personal feelings at that time, Pakenham has written with the perception which I soon came to admire so much in him. "Sholto, in Germany, by the time I met him, was not happy and was indeed staying on as Commander-in-Chief and Military Governor for reasons of duty," he stated. "After seven years as Commander-in-Chief he longed to cast off official harness for a time; as he put it himself, to ride a bicycle down the street in grey flannels without anybody looking at him. And in every good sense of the word he is so completely human that many features of the occupation caused him distress: the semi-starvation, the bitterness it generated and, to mention only one other thing, the number of death warrants he had to sign."

From the time of my very first talks with Frank Pakenham I had to stress—not that he did not understand and appreciate the situation—the dire necessity of food for the Germans. "Food—food—food," he wrote later. "Everything came back to food. The education of the young and the spiritual recovery of the whole people were the subjects closest to my heart, but in a mental and moral sense you could not expect much progress while the mind of the whole people was dominated by hunger."

That winter of 1946–47 was recorded in Germany as the worst that they had known for fifty years, and that alone, quite apart from the aftermath of the war and conditions as they were, made it all the more brutal for the Germans. But in trying to find for us answers to the problems which, in addition to our shortage of food, we were facing at that time, Pakenham also had to take into account the views and plans of the Foreign Secretary. Neither Pakenham nor Ernest Bevin, both of them great humanitarians, was as free to act as he would have liked. Bevin had to think about international relations and the agreements that had been arrived at with the other Allies by his predecessors; and being the man that he was he found himself compelled to act with a sincerity that at times led to some tension and even friction.

That the decisions reached at Potsdam had broken down the Foreign Secretary knew just as well as everybody else, and in the House of Commons as early as June 4, 1946—only a year after the conference—Ernie Bevin said of the Potsdam agreement that it "envisaged Germany being treated as a whole, which meant that the surplus food supplies of the East would feed the West, and the goods of the West would go to the East, and so on; and sufficient earnings would be produced, so that Germany would not be a charge on any of the allies. That was the basis."

It sounded all very fine and proper, but events did not work out that way. The basis had already become quite different; but even then the fears of the French and the opposition of the Russians could not stop the progress that had to be made, somehow or other, at least in the West. What the Russians were planning for in their part of Germany, the East, became an ever-increasing mystery as they clamped down on all information about their intentions. All that we were offered by them was their objection to what we were doing, from which we had to grope our way as best we could toward some understanding of what they were up to.

The British and the American administrations were both faced with gigantic problems of reconstruction, and solving them called for a close and sympathetic liaison between us. On our side, the one man who did most to help develop this good relationship was my deputy, Brian Robertson, through his work with the Control Commission. It is easy to talk about Robertson as being a tower of strength; but there was much more to it than that. He proved himself to be a man of infinite patience and quiet strength, and with a very clear view of what was required of him. In handling the exacting task of correlating our efforts with those of the Americans to bring about the fusion of our zones he worked with great skill, and in that alone he commanded our admiration, and at the same time won the great respect of the Americans.

During all this time I also came to know well and to respect a man whom I have always thought of as more of a man of peace than anyone I have ever known. He was Count Folke Bernadotte, the member of the Swedish royal family who played an intriguing and dangerous part in the closing stages of the war in the effort that he made as an intermediary to bring about a truce between the Germans, represented by Heinrich Himmler, and the Allies. Bernadotte was a great humanitarian, and having known him personally—he used to come and stay with us at my Schloss during his time in Germany—as well as having had close dealings with him officially in the work that he was doing, I came to appreciate the exceptional and genuine quality of compassion in the character of this man, and the fairness of his mind.

It is sad that in the story of those times the work done by Folke Bernadotte should have become shadowed by a controversy that, I believe, is entirely unnecessary. As the head of the Swedish Red Cross, he rendered a very great service, particularly in the British Zone of Germany, in helping in his own way, and, as much as his organization could, to care for and feed those who were in such dire straits. I knew well his side of the story in trying to act as an intermediary in the closing stages of the war, and it has been distressing to me that an historian as well known and as respected as Professor H. R. Trevor-Roper should see fit to write as he has about Bernadotte and his work.

In speaking to Bernadotte's widow—who is an American by birth—about this matter many years later, she expressed to me the opinion that it might all have been quite different if the two men had been able to meet and to exchange views. I gathered from what she said that there had never been any meeting between them, although I know that Folke Bernadotte wrote to Professor Trevor-Roper and tried, in a very sensible way, to straighten out the record.

It is a comment on our times that needs no elaboration when one has to record that, while serving as the United Nations mediator in Palestine over the hostilities that were being waged there between the Arabs and the Jews, Folke Bernadotte was murdered by terrorists in Jerusalem in September, 1948. One of their men thrust a sten gun through the window of the car in which Bernadotte, in Red Cross uniform, was driving, and which had been stopped. He fired a burst into Bernadotte's chest at a range of only a few inches. Although the identity of the assassin must have been known, he has never been brought to book.

"The food crisis was appalling," Frank Pakenham has said of the situation in Germany when he first came out to visit me in the spring of 1947.

We who had to live with that crisis were ever conscious of its severity. One of the constant reminders was the sight of the hordes of people, mostly women and children, on the verge of starvation and wandering aimlessly about, all so obviously suffering from the diseases that accompany starvation. The summer that followed the harsh winter turned out to be one of the driest that had been known for years, and that only further limited the production of a possible rich harvest upon which we were all pinning our hopes.

The German local authorities themselves did not hesitate to appeal to what one had to accept both as a sense of duty and a responsibility. Their anxiety about the basic welfare of their own people was natural enough, and time after time on my tours of inspection the local burgomasters would come out to meet me, and I would have to listen to them as they pointed to the only too obvious distress of their people and reminded me of the threat that starvation carried as it loomed over the entire country.

"What are you going to do about it?" they would ask. "You are the government, and it is your responsibility."

It was unquestionably our responsibility, and I was acutely aware of that; but in all our considerations there was always one question to which there never seemed to be an answer. What was the exact nature of the help that I was receiving from home? The Government itself did not seem to be able to make up its mind, and when I say that I am not speaking in terms of any party political issues. There was a broad division of public opinion at that time throughout our own country, as well as a general and sad lack of an understanding of what was causing the trouble, for it to be any issue of that nature. And to add to our difficulties it seemed that, no matter what we who were on the spot said or did, we were under an almost constant fire of criticism from the press, most of which was astonishingly thoughtless and ill-advised.

In my thoughts about how we should handle the German people, I had known all along that we were having to cope with more than just a defeated nation. As a people they had been fed, and a great many of them nurtured, on the Nazi ideology; and that had been done to the rabid exclusion of all other ways and ideas of life. At first I had thought, in common with a great many other people, that the Germans must have become so completely indoctrinated that it would be very difficult for us to get through to them with any new way of thinking. But we were wrong in that, and it did not take long for us to understand that the disasters which had befallen them as a result of the Nazi domination, and the monstrous failure on the part of Adolf Hitler to provide for them anything more than utter disaster, had gone a long way in purging

the minds of most of those who had been inclined to accept the
Nazi promises.

But even with this cleansing of a corrupted thinking, it was in
the older Germans, in those of a generation that was mature at the
time of the first war, that we found the men who were to lead their
own people. That was perhaps understandable because, apart from
the terrible losses during the war of their younger men, the more
mature minds of the older men had not been led so far astray. I
was not alone in this realization that there was a genuine willingness on the part of the Germans to try and help themselves. "In
their own misery they found means to help the needy and to
organise relief work effectively," Lucius Clay has stated. "I think
that the realisation of Nazi brutality elsewhere had rekindled in
many German hearts a feeling for the suffering of others, which all
but died out under Hitler."

In writing about the feeling in England about Germany at that
time, Frank Pakenham has referred to "the intense public disquiet." But that disquiet had been whipped up about the wrong
things. "The German 'show' was regarded as a shambles reflecting
no credit, to put it mildly, on the Englishmen concerned in it,
whether on the Governmental or administrative level," Pakenham
has written of that feeling. To that he added the comment: "The
personnel of the Control Commission in Germany were tarred with
every sort of cruel innuendo, justified in relation to an occasional
scallywag, but otherwise wickedly untrue."

So grotesque did the tarring become that by the summer of 1947
there were appearing in certain sections of our national press in
London vindictive suggestions and personal allegations about loot-
ing leveled against even those of us who were in the most senior
appointments. We all knew that, no matter how stringent the
regulations might be, irregularities did occur, and when the
offenders were caught in anything that might be only the mildest of
lapses they were dealt with in the firmest fashion.

I became greatly concerned about these attacks published in the
press. They achieved nothing, and they had a demoralizing effect on
the men and women of unquestionable integrity who were serving
in the Control Commission. I asked for an impartial examination
of the allegations to be made by Scotland Yard, and Inspector
Hayward was sent out to Germany and attached to the Control
Commission staff. I gave instructions that he should be assisted in
every way possible, and eventually a copy of his report was passed
on to me.

This report proved conclusively the falsity of the newspaper attacks, and I purposely went out of my way to invite publication of its findings in the press. But my offer was not accepted, and the tumbrils continued on their merciless way. There was something so inexcusable about the shameful criticism that was expressed of us by our own people at home at that time, and I can still feel the anger that it caused in my own mind. It was all so cheap and shabby, and it only confused the minds of the British public about the great issues that we were striving to settle in that important year of 1947.

As a result of all the constructive work that was done by our experts in their joint efforts to bring about a fusion of the American and British zones, and their constant drive to raise the level of industry in Bizonia, as that fusion was called, Lucius Clay and I were able to place before the Allied Control Council in Berlin in the summer of 1947 our revised plan for industry in our zones. It was this that drew from Sokolovsky his sharp accusation that we had "taken the road of a complete breaking away from the decisions of the Potsdam Conference."

But by then there was no coping with the refusal of the Communists to pay any attention at all to any record, other than as their leader chose to look at it. Our meetings of the Control Council became scarcely more than formal occasions which provided the Soviet members with a launching pad for wild and at times vicious propaganda. But we went on with our reconstruction, at times groping almost desperately for some means of making the Germans self-supporting and self-reliant.

The war of nerves was inexorably gathering momentum, but if we of the West were worried about the shape the future was taking there must have been some desperate thinking going on in the Kremlin. We will never know exactly whether it was Stalin who was doing it, or those who were closest to him; but out in Berlin we came to realize from our close contacts with the Russians that, no matter what they might say, they were under orders to bring about a calculated deterioration in the state of Germany.

All that stood between Stalin and his effort to dominate Europe was the stand that was made at that time by the Americans and the British. That stand demonstrated clearly enough that we were not prepared to yield any further. At that early stage, however, it was mainly one of arguments, and our rejection in those arguments of the vicious and invariably untrue accusations which were coldly and deliberately hurled at us by the Russians. As Lucius Clay was to comment: "Sokolovsky really 'threw the book' at us."

Britain and America together had taken, by then, two vastly important steps: first, the establishment of a free political life among the Germans in our zones; and second, the fusion of our zones into one. The way ahead was opened up for what was to become the creation of a government of Western Germany by the Germans themselves. But although we managed to make progress toward that, it was still in the future; and the Communists were always ready to try and strangle any such effort on our part.

In the long course of my service as a commander-in-chief in the Royal Air Force and finally as a Military Governor, I naturally came to know a great deal about what happened during and after the war that was highly confidential, or secret, at the time; and much of it must remain so even now. There is quite a lot that one would like to speak about, but for the sake of discretion, quite apart from other considerations, one is compelled to remain silent. "We are apt to feel submerged by the cascade of writing about World War II," the American historian Herbert Feis commented some years ago; and to that he added: "Actually, many sources have not been tapped, and there is still much to be learned about what happened, and how and why."

Of all the questions that have come to be asked, there is one in the minds of everybody which begs so urgently for an answer. Why was the international situation allowed to develop as it did during those years immediately after the war? It is a question that has bedeviled so much of my own thinking. To say that, at the time, it was not for me, one of the military leaders, to question why is only a part of the answer that I try to make to myself. I was faced with a difficult granting of authority with one hand and a snatching away of it with the other. I had a duty to perform in a very high office, but it was not likely that I would merely sit back and obey orders and not think and worry about what was going on. There was my dilemma.

By the end of the summer of 1947, I found all too often that the questions that came to my mind about what we were doing appeared to be insoluble. One of the reasons for that was my belief that we had passed beyond the stage where the situation could be handled by a Military Governor, and that the work entailed should by then have passed out of the hands of the military and into those of more highly qualified civilian administrators. Eisenhower had believed that right from the beginning, and I knew that Lucius Clay felt the same way.

In the work that he was doing with such enthusiasm and

devotion even Frank Pakenham was finding that his relationship with the Foreign Secretary was not altogether free from what we both felt was too much restraint. Of his own attitude, Pakenham has taken it upon himself to say that because he "concentrated so single-mindedly on my task and mission, I found it difficult to make the proper allowances." Much as we both admired Ernie Bevin, we felt that there was between him on one side and us on the other what Pakenham has described as "a cleavage of policy."

Rather overgenerously, Pakenham has added to that view the comment that of his own differences with Bevin it was perhaps "a case of a steady far-seeing statesman on the one hand, and a young man in a hurry on the other." But in saying that I do not think that he is being quite fair to himself. He and I were having to face harsher and more intimate realities than those which were placed before the Foreign Secretary.

The differences that occurred were due to the nature of the approaches that each of us had to make to our problems. For all his humanity—and that Ernie Bevin was a man with a very great heart can never be denied—the Foreign Secretary had a wide variety of problems with which to cope, and Germany was only one of them. His view was of necessity more detached, and even impersonal, than that which compelled both Pakenham and me to look at our problems.

"My own conflict of mind was very intense during those days," Pakenham has said. We were sharing that unrest through the views that we held and the duties that we had to perform; but there was one duty which even he could not share with me, although he was well aware of its nature. It was by far the most distressing part of my work while I was in Germany and it rested in the many death sentences with which I had to deal. As Military Governor I was called upon to make the final decisions about all the death sentences which were passed by the courts in our Zone, either confirming or commuting them as I saw fit; and there is in my memory a deep scar from that odious experience of having to deal with hundreds of these cases.

The range of the nature of the crimes which had led to these sentences ran all the way from more of the war criminals condemned to death to unfortunate displaced persons—among whom there were many Poles who had found ways of disposing of their hated German oppressors—to a Briton in the forces who had committed a murder such as strangling his German girl friend. Up to that time I had not given a great deal of thought to the problems of capital punishment, although I did have a definite antipathy toward it; but my personal experiences during my time in Germany changed that antipathy into a strong conviction that the death penalty should be abolished.

Week after week the files on these cases used to appear on my desk. They were all thick files in which there were recorded the details of all the evidence, and the findings that had been arrived at in the trials. Attached to each of these files there would be a brief summary of the case prepared by my legal adviser, with a certificate stating that, from the legal point of view, the sentence was a correct one. Added to that there would be the appeals—often enough quite piteous ones—for clemency made by various relatives or friends. On top of the whole file there would be a buff-colored form to which I had to sign my name if I confirmed the sentence, and which would lead to the convicted person being hanged within a fairly brief space of time. It was such a distasteful and cold-blooded business, and one which I found repugnant.

There were some sentences, I must admit, that I did not mind confirming: ones such as those passed on the wardens at some of the concentration camps and other officials who were responsible for the killing of so many hundreds of thousands of Jews. There could be no hesitation about those; but most of the cases that I had to deal with were far more difficult to assess. For instance, what was one to do about some unfortunate dim-witted German peasant who, while serving as a private in the Army, had been told by his officer to shoot one of our parachutists? Had the poor devil refused to do it he would more likely than not have been shot for not obeying orders. How was he to know that in international law the order given by his officer was illegal? Was his lack of knowledge sufficient reason to commute the sentence?

Whenever there was in my mind the slightest doubt about out and out guilt I did not hesitate to commute the sentence to one of a term of imprisonment, and because of that I commuted most of the cases that came before me. I am, I believe, a reasonably humane man, although, when the occasion demands it, I can become hard-hearted enough. It is one thing to kill a fellow human being in the heat of battle; but these cold judicial executions were, so far as I was concerned, an entirely different matter.

While I was still a serving officer in the Royal Air Force I had become by this time far divorced from my work as an airman. I had had no wish in the first place for the post that I was filling; and I certainly had no expectation, when I agreed to do as I was asked, that I would have an experience as trying as this matter of the death sentences. The Nuremberg Trials and appeals had been bad enough; but once they were disposed of they became something that belonged to the past, and I did my best to forget them.

But the steady stream of files from the legal division on the continuing death sentences became an added irritant that only aggravated the unhappy state of mind that I was in about other aspects of our affairs in Germany. In his position as the American Military Governor, Lucius Clay was in the same position as I was about death sentences, and of his feelings about them he has said: "My responsibility as reviewing officer [there was no court of appeal] and as clemency officer was great, and there was no other which weighed more heavily on me."

In August of that year I had a talk with Ernie Bevin about the position that I found myself in, and I told him frankly how I felt about it. I pointed out to him that it was my sincere wish to make a clean break, and to get away from all official and Service life. In my personal dealings with Bevin I always found that he did his best to be considerate and understanding. He had a forthright warmness all of his own, and after listening to me he expressed his sympathy. He spoke to the Prime Minister about my request, who then intimated that he was prepared to grant it. As a result of that I then wrote to Clement Attlee reminding him that, when I had agreed to take on the appointment of Military Governor, he had said that it would be for about eighteen months or two years.

"The eighteen months are up on 1st November," I wrote. "By that time I shall have completed seven consecutive years as a Commander-in-Chief. (You may remember that I took over Fighter Command at the beginning of November, 1940.) I know of no other officer, either British or Allied, who has done seven years on end as a C.-in-C.—indeed I believe it is a world record for our generation! During those seven years I have had very little leave, and consequently am feeling a bit stale and tired. I feel I need a few months rest, and then a change of occupation."

A few days later I received from the Prime Minister, written in his own hand, a letter in which he expressed his full understanding of my position. "We are all indebted to you for the way you have carried out a most difficult and exacting task," he stated. "You have had a very long spell of highly responsible work and have fully earned a good holiday." About the future, he volunteered, to my sight apprehension, the comment: "I should very much like to have a talk with you when you are in London in September. I am sure there is work for you to do."

This was followed a couple of days later by a letter from Ernie

Bevin, in the course of which he said: "We have agreed that the best arrangement will be that when your tour of duty ends on November 1st you will be succeeded as Commander-in-Chief by Robertson. I am writing to him separately to this effect." He concluded with a comment that, coming from Bevin, I found both understanding and touching. "I should like to take this opportunity of telling you in a letter how much we appreciate all that you have done in Germany in the series of difficulties with which you have had to grapple ever since you assumed your post there," he stated. "Your firm and energetic leadership has contributed greatly to maintaining calm and order and in ensuring that the best possible use was made of the limited resources which have been at our disposal."

In those expressions I had the views that were held by my masters of my work at that time. It was not until many years later that I was to learn what my personal staff, who lived in the same houses with me, and through that were constantly with me, thought about the way in which I handled myself in this trying situation. In some ways it was a revelation. Bob Wright had found the life in Germany too difficult, and he had returned to England earlier in the year. His place as my personal staff officer was taken by an old friend, Johnny Kent. As a regular officer in the R.A.F., Kent was conditioned by Service discipline, even if he was a fighter pilot after my own heart, to the performance of his duties without comment. What Wright thought about it all is amply shown in the work that we have since done together in the writing of the story of my experiences.

They both knew, as by that time did quite a few other people, that it was with a very great relief that I was able finally to give up all the reins of office. Brian Robertson became Military Governor and Commander-in-Chief in my place, and it was on his shoulders that there fell in the following year the more aggressive moves by the Soviet Union, including the collapse of the Allied Control Council and the blockade of Berlin which was defeated by the massive Anglo-American airlift. But Robertson's shoulders were broad, and between them he and Clay made a team that was fully capable, both through experience and by temperament, of standing up to anything that might be tried on by Stalin.

It is still impossible for me to think of the time that I spent as Military Governor and Commander-in-Chief in Germany as anything but the unhappiest period of my entire official life. There were too many difficulties that came to be placed in our way, and many of them were quite unnecessary and only served to confuse the efforts that we were making to overcome the greater problems of that time. I also know that I was much too simple in my tastes for the trappings of such an office; and since I was essentially an R.A.F. officer there was so much about it that, having nothing to do with the Service, I found far from congenial.

In the honors that were conferred in the New Year of 1948 it was announced that I had been elevated to the peerage. I was just a few days over fifty-four years of age, and for my title I selected a name with a Scottish flavor. In the southern part of Scotland— which for centuries has known so well the name of Douglas, and which has provided me with many pleasant memories—there is a small river which bears the name of Kirtle. It flows into the Solway Firth, and it struck me that it would be appropriate, since my ancestors originally hailed from this corner of Scotland, if I associated my name with that river.

With the freedom to live in any reasonable manner that I cared to choose, it seemed that at last my wish would be granted for a quiet life of retirement in the country. I went about making plans for that; and I also made known my political views. It seemed to me that, upon being created a peer, the only honorable thing to do would be to declare where I stood, and how I had felt all my life. I joined the Labour Party, and I took my seat on the Labour benches in the House of Lords. I did not believe in merely sitting on the cross-benches and thereby avoiding having to declare one's political convictions. That way out has always seemed to me to be a rather cowardly one. While I have always been a convinced Socialist, I am not by any means a fanatical one, and my associates in the Labour Party have always known that; and the hustings have never held any attraction for me.

Shortly after I returned home to England, Frank Pakenham became Minister of Civil Aviation. Since we had come to know and to understand each other well during the time that we had spent working together over the problems with which we were faced in Germany, we continued to meet, and we discussed the problems that he was having to deal with in his new appointment. I was just about to complete my plans for settling down to a life in the country that I had never had the opportunity of knowing, but for which I had a definite hankering, when once again that curious hand of chance intervened and altered the whole course of my life.

As the Minister of Civil Aviation, and with a rapidly expanding industry on his hands, Frank Pakenham developed some ideas which led to Clement Attlee's comment to me about "work for you to do" coming all too true. In the spring of 1949, after a period on the board of B.O.A.C., I was appointed chairman of British European Airways. This caused, in Pakenham's words, "a discreditable cry of 'jobs for the boys' " which both he and I felt was as distasteful as it was untrue. I was a professional airman of some standing, and I was being appointed to yet another command. "His leadership, technical knowledge and humanity soon killed that nonsense," Pakenham commented about the bleating of the sheep.

Thirty years had passed since I had made a brief foray in 1919 as one of this country's first airline captains in the entirely new world of civil aviation. In returning to it after a lifetime spent in the Royal Air Force I was back where I belonged: in the world of aviation. Moreover, it was again to fill the role of what amounted to being a commander-in-chief; and for the next fifteen years I was to be in charge of one of the world's foremost airlines.

Index

773